A Guide to Jewish Religious Practice

Volume VI in the **Moreshet Series,** Studies in Jewish History, Literature and Thought

A Guide to Jewish Religious Practice

by ISAAC KLEIN

THE JEWISH THEOLOGICAL SEMINARY OF AMERICA
NEW YORK 1979

Library of Congress Cataloging in Publication Data

Klein, Isaac.
A guide to Jewish religious practice.

(The Moreshet series ; 6)
Bibliography: p.
Includes index.
1. Jews—Rites and ceremonies. 2. Jews. Liturgy and ritual. 3. Jews—Dietary laws. 4. Jewish law. 5. Conservative Judaism. I. Title. II. Series: Moreshet (New York) ; 6.
BM700.K54 296.4 78-12159
ISBN 0-87334-004-3

Distributed by KTAV Publishing House, Inc.
Manufactured in the United States of America

Table of Contents

Abbreviations

Arak.	*'Arakhin* (talmudic tractate)
Avot	*'Avot* (talmudic tractate)
A.Z.	*'Avodah Zarah* (talmudic tractate)
b.	born; *ben, bar*
B.	Babylonian Talmud (=*Talmud Babli*)
B.B.	*Bava Batra* (talmudic tractate)
B.C.E.	Before Common Era (= B.C.)
Bek.	*Bekhorot* (talmudic tractate)
Ber.	*Berakhot* (talmudic tractate)
B.H.	*Ba'er Heitev* (commentaries on *Shulḥan 'Arukh* by R. Judah Ashkenazi [*O.H.* and *E.H.*] and R. Zechariah Mendel of Belz [*Y.D.* and *H.M.*])
Bik.	*Bikkurim* (talmudic tractate)
B.M.	*Bava Meẓia* (talmudic tractate)
B.Q.	*Bava Qamma* (talmudic tractate)
C.E.	Common Era (= A.D.)
cf.	compare
chap., chaps.	chapter, chapters
I (or II) Chron.	Chronicles, Book I or II (Bible)
d.	died
Dan.	Daniel (Bible)
Dem.	*Demai* (talmudic tractate)
Deut.	Deuteronomy (Bible)
D.M.	*Darkhei Moshe* (codification by R. Moses Isserles)
Eccles.	Ecclesiastes (Bible)
Eccles. Rabbah	*Ecclesiastes Rabbah*
ed.	editor, edited
Eduy.	*'Eduyyot* (mishnaic tractate)
E.H.	*Even Ha-'ezer* (section of *'Arba'ah Ṭurim* and *Shulḥan 'Arukh*)
'Eruv.	*'Eruvin* (talmudic tractate)
Exod.	Exodus (Bible)
Ezek.	Ezekiel (Bible)
f., ff.	and following page(s)

Gen.	Genesis (Bible)
Giṭ.	*Giṭṭin* (talmudic tractate)
Hab.	Habakkuk (Bible)
Ḥag.	*Ḥagigah* (talmudic tractate)
Ḥal.	*Ḥallah* (talmudic tractate)
H.M.	*Ḥoshen Mishpat* (section of *'Arba'ah Ṭurim* and *Shulḥan 'Arukh*)
Hor.	*Horayot* (talmudic tractate)
Hos.	Hosea (Bible)
Ḥul.	*Ḥullin* (talmudic tractate)
Isa.	Isaiah (Bible)
J.	Jerusalem Talmud (= *Talmud Yerushalmi*)
Jer.	Jeremiah (Bible)
Josh.	Joshua (Bible)
Judg.	Judges (Bible)
Kelim	*Kelim* (mishnaic tractate)
Ker.	*Keritot* (talmudic tractate)
Ket.	*Ketubbot* (talmudic tractate)
Kil.	*Kilayim* (talmudic tractate)
Kin.	*Kinnim* (mishnaic tractate)
Lam.	Lamentations (Bible)
Lev.	Leviticus (Bible)
lit.	literally
loc. cit.	in the place cited
M.	Mishnah
M.A.	*Magen Avraham* (commentary on *Shulḥan 'Arukh* by R. Abraham Abele Gombiner)
I (or II) Macc.	Maccabees, Book I or II (Apocrypha)
Maharil	R. Jacob b. Moses Moellin
Mak.	*Makkot* (talmudic tractate)
Mal.	Malachi (Bible)
M.D.	*Magen David* (commentary on *Shulḥan 'Arukh* by R. David B. Samuel Halevi [Ṭaz])
Meg.	*Megillah* (talmudic tractate)
Men.	*Menaḥot* (talmudic tractate)
Mid.	*Middot* (mishnaic tractate)
Mik.	*Mikva'ot* (mishnaic tractate)
M.Q.	*Moe'ed Qatan* (talmudic tractate)
Nah.	Nahum (Bible)
Naz.	*Nazir* (talmudic tractate)

Ned.	*Nedarim* (talmudic tractate)
Neg.	*Nega'im* (mishnaic tractate)
Neh.	Nehemiah (Bible)
Nid.	*Niddah* (talmudic tractate)
no., nos.	number(s)
Num.	Numbers (Bible)
Obad.	Obadiah (Bible)
O.H.	*'Oraḥ Ḥayyim* (section of *'Arba'ah Ṭurim and Shulḥan 'Arukh*)
Pes.	*Pesaḥim* (talmudic tractate)
Prov.	Proverbs (Bible)
Ps.	Psalms (Bible)
Qid.	*Qiddushin* (talmudic tractate)
R.	Rabbi or Rav (before names)
Rama	R. Moses b. Israel Isserles (commentator on *Shulḥan 'Arukh*)
Rashi	R. Solomon b. Isaac (commentator on Bible and Talmud)
R.H.	*Rosh Hashanah* (talmudic tractate)
I and II Sam.	Samuel, Books I and II (Bible)
San.	*Sanhedrin* (talmudic tractate)
Shab.	*Shabbat* (talmudic tractate)
Shakh	*Siftei Kohen* (commentary on *Shulḥan 'Arukh* by R. Shabbetai b. Meir Hakohen)
Shek.	*Shekalim* (talmudic tractate)
Song	Song of Songs (Bible)
Soṭ.	*Soṭah* (talmudic tractate)
Suk.	*Sukkah* (talmudic tractate)
Ta'an.	*Ta'anit* (talmudic tractate)
Tam.	*Tamid* (Mishnaic tractate)
Tanh.	*Tanḥuma*
Ṭaz	*Ṭurei Zahav* (commentary on *Shulḥan 'Arukh* by R. David b. Samuel Halevi)
Tem.	*Temurah* (talmudic tractate)
Ter.	*Terumot* (mishnaic tractate)
Toh.	*Tohorot* (mishnaic tractate)
Ṭur	*'Arba'ah Turim* (legal code of R. Jacob b. Asher)
Yad.	*Yadayim* (mishnaic tractate)
Yev.	*Yevamot* (talmudic tractate)
Y.D.	*Yoreh De'ah* (section of *'Arba'ah Ṭurim* and *Shulḥan 'Arukh*)

Zav.	*Zavim* (mishnaic tractate)
Zech.	Zechariah (Bible)
Zeph.	Zephaniah (Bible)
Zev.	*Zevaḥim* (talmudic tractate)

Table of Transliterations[1]

ʼ	א		ts	צ
b	בּ		q	ק
v	ב		r	ר
g	ג		s	שׂ
d	ד		sh	שׁ
h	ה		t	ת
w	ו		a	◌ָ
z	ז		o	◌ָ (*qaṭan*)
ḥ	ח		o	◌ֳ
ṭ	ט		a	◌ַ
y	י		a	◌ֲ
k	כּ		ei	◌ֵ
kh	כ		e	◌ֶ
l	ל		e	◌ֱ
m	מ		o	וֹ
n	נ		o	◌ֹ
s	ס		u	וּ
ʻ	ע		u	◌ֻ
p	פּ		i	◌ִ
f	פ		e	◌ְ (*naʻ*)

[1]Council of National Library Associations, *American National Standard Romanization of Hebrew* (New York: American National Standards Institute, 1975), p. 11, table 2 ("More Exact Romanization Style").

ISAAC KLEIN
January 23, 1979
24 Tevet 5739

Rabbi Klein did not live to see a bound copy of this work. As the Rabbis understood the Song of Songs 7:10, his lips move from the place of his eternal rest and speak to us through this book.

תנצב״ה

And as for Me, this is my covenant with them, saith the Lord. My spirit that is upon thee, and my words which I have put in thy mouth, shall not depart out of thy mouth, nor out of the mouth of thy seed, nor out of the mouth of thy seed's seed, saith the Lord from henceforth and for ever (Is. 59:21)

דברי אשר שמתי בפיך לא ימושו מפיך ומפי זרעך ומפי זרע זרעך מעתה ועד עולם (ישע. נט:כא)

Dedicated to my daughters:
Hannah and her husband Rabbi Paul Katz
Miriam and her husband Dr. Saul Shapiro
Rivke and her husband Dr. Gerald Berkowitz

מוקדש לבנותי
חנה ובעלה הרב פרץ כ״ץ
מרים ובעלה דר. שלמה שפירא
רבקה ובעלה דר. יעקב ברקביץ

And To My Grandchildren:
Michael Samuel
Moshe David
Ron Uri
Ethan Joel
Katz

ולנכדי
מיכאל שמואל
משה דוד
רון אורי
איתן יואל
לבית כ״ץ

Ephraim Avraham
Sara Faith
Rachel Ellen
Simchah Reuven
Rivka Dinah
Shapiro

אפרים אברהם
שרה פרומע
רחל חיה עלקע
שמחה ראובן
רבקה דינה
לבית שפירא

Talia Hadas
Ya-el Ge-ulah
Leora Michal
Boaz Nechemyah
Berkowitz

טליה הדס
יעל גאולה
ליאורה מיכל
בעז נחמיה
לבית ברקביץ

In Gratefulness to the Good Lord that all these consider this volume as their guide to Jewish Life.

ואני תודה שבכולם יתקיים הפסוק אשרי תמימי דרך ההולכים בתורת ד׳. (תהילים קי״ט:א)

Foreword

Classical Judaism has no word for "religion." The closest counterpart in classical Jewish vocabulary and, hence, *in the Jewish mind,* is Torah. Torah, however, includes far more than what we moderns understand by "religion." Torah encompasses and seeks to regulate every moment of life, including even its termination in death. Nothing human is beyond the scope of its concern and, accordingly, of its scale of judgment and its program of prescription.

It is for this reason that Torah is often called a way of life, for its purpose is to teach Jews how to act, think and even feel. The premise on which Torah is based is that all aspects of life—leisure no less than business, worship or rites of passage (birth, *bar mitzvah,* marriage, divorce, death)—are part of the covenant and mandate under which every Jew is to serve God in everything he does. In the eyes of Torah there is, strictly speaking, no such thing as the purely private domain, for even in solitude—be it the privacy of the bath or the unconsciousness of sleep—one has the capacity and the duty to serve God.

This comprehensive outlook on life and its regulation is basically alien to most modern systems of value—even to religious ones. To most moderns, religion is one domain among several. This division is most poignantly reflected in "the separation of church and state." In other words, each domain of life is considered to be fundamentally autonomous and governed by its own "legitimate" scale of values. To be sure, certain values extend from one domain to another. The standards of honesty and decency are conceded to be operative on the beach as well as in the house of worship. But *au fond* we moderns begin with an assumption that certain areas and forms of activity are "my own and no other's business."

There is no question but that this posture, the consequence of a revolt against totalist authoritarianism, has brought much blessing to humanity. But it has already curtailed the influence and undermined the stability of whole patterns of life and of many hallowed institutions and organizations—most notably the family and the house of worship. Above all, it has broken the continuum from cradle and home to playground, school, place of business, political organization and burial ground that is the hallmark of

Judaism. This continuum is precisely what Torah prescribes and promulgates. The consequence of its interruption has been a vacuum, or vacuums, in the lives of many. Since many are now seeking to reconquer some structured and orchestrated way of life that bespeaks Jewish commitment and value, it is important to understand how Torah—particularly its normative and prescriptive teachings of *halakha*—coordinates all realms of human existence, and how those loyal to it should conduct their lives.

By setting forth afresh the prescriptive or legal aspects of Torah as they are currently applicable, the present work represents an historic achievement. Ever since the emancipation of European Jewry, the role of Jewish law, or *halakha*, in the life of the modern Jew has been at best, seriously misunderstood or, at worst, dispensed with entirely. Particularly in the context of modern democracy, the need for a concise guide to Jewish practice has long been urgent. To begin with, the collapse of the Jewish judicial autonomy, which has been part of the ancient and medieval framework of all Jewish life, made the *halakha*, from the point of view of human enforcement, voluntaristic, i.e., a matter of personal choice. Little leverage is left today in the hands of the rabbinate for dealing with violators of Jewish ritual law. The stability of a legal system—and that is what the Torah or *halakha* is—for which modes of enforcement are conspicuously lacking is, to say the least, precarious.

Moreover, the temper of modernity itself has been extremely potent in promoting a hasty verdict of "anachronistic" or "irrelevant" on a body of law whose roots lie in antiquity. Many American Jews have, accordingly, become more concerned with the universal ethical values inherent in the Jewish tradition than with those particularistic laws which define the Jewish culture and way of life. But however prevalent, this tendency to divide the corpus of Jewish law into ethics versus ritual is foreign to the Jewish tradition, for the ethical precepts of the Torah are embodied and reflected in the ritual. The two are inseparably intertwined into a system that bears the imprint of the covenant between God and Israel. Thus, the *Mishna* of Rabbi Judah the Prince was as clear in its instructions for proper separation of tithes as it was in its exhortations to be charitable toward the needy.

It follows, then, that no one area of Jewish law is less important than another because, in the classical rabbinic view, every area of life is under the mandate of God; is in need of, and capable of, sanctification; and is part of the covenant. *Halakha* provides a framework, in form and content, for that sanctification. In a very real sense, the recent corporate non-enforceability of the provisions of Jewish law serves to underscore its voluntaristic character and its covenantal nature. Rather than a haphazardly compiled set of laws, it is a thoroughly pervasive religious program for the Jew's service to God.

Since the legal literature of Judaism is vast and complex, the need has always been felt for a concise digest and summary which would obviate the necessity to scan an overwhelming collection of legal works. It was this need that motivated Maimonides to compose a code "so that a man can read Scripture and in conjunction with this compendium have access to all of the tradition without need of consulting another book."

Given the consequences of constant change in the form and content of life—technologically, politically, economically, and even changes in the perception of human dignity—each generation requires a code or guide which responds to its geographical, social and temporal peculiarities. Each era of Jewish history has produced such condensed codes, from the Mishna, redacted *circa* 200 C.E., to Maimonides' *Mishneh Torah* of ca. 1180, to the famous *Shulhan Arukh* of Rabbi Joseph Karo, published in the sixteenth century. Needless to say, every one of these codes has reflected the social, political and scientific milieu of its time. But until now, the Jews of America, especially those who hold a developmental view of Jewish law, have not produced a digest of their own, reflecting both the realities of twentieth century America and a commitment to tradition.

Rabbi Isaac Klein has now filled that gap in the Jewish legal tradition. His *A Guide to Jewish Religious Practice* is the product of, and is intended for, the vibrant Jewish community which continues to flourish in the United States. Compiled and written in the authentic spirit of the Conservative Movement, it continues in the millennia-old tradition of normative Jewish practice. Part and parcel of that tradition is the recognition that changes in the laws have taken place and must take place within the general *halakhic* parameters hallowed by past generations. Thus, this *Guide* speaks to the Jews of twentieth-century America: it incorporates decisions reached by the Rabbinical Assembly Committee on Jewish Law and Standards; it deals with such contemporary issues as artificial insemination and corneal transplants, which reflect some of the most recent scientific advances of our day; and, it bespeaks a commitment to a life guided by law which is indispensable for the health and vitality of Judaism.

The attitude of Conservative Judaism toward *halakha* was eloquently expressed forty years ago by Professor Louis Finkelstein:

> There are those who would think that we have but two alternatives, to reject or to accept the law, but in either case to treat it as a dead letter. Both of these alternatives are repugnant to the whole tradition of Judaism, and it is to combat them that the (Jewish Theological) Seminary was brought into being. . . . Jewish law must be preserved but . . . it is subject to interpretation by those who have mastered it, and . . . the interpretation placed upon it by duly authorized masters in every generation must be accepted with as much reverence as those which were given in previous generations.

Throughout the ninety years of its existence, this Seminary has been dedicated to that philosophy as the surest means of nourishing Jewish life in modern day America. For over forty of those years, Rabbi Klein has served the American Jewish community as a dedicated rabbi, eminent Jewish scholar, and revered teacher. Indeed, the present volume originated as lectures delivered by Rabbi Klein to students in the Seminary's Rabbinical School. The Seminary is, therefore, proud to present, as part of its Moreshet Series, this *A Guide to Jewish Religious Practice.* We present it not as an official credo or guide to Conservative Jewish practice, nor even as the position of the Seminary, but rather as a traditional yet modern interpretation of *halakha* by one of the truly competent Jewish legal masters of our time. It is one legitimate synthesis which does not preclude others. Rabbi Klein has set forth before his readers a compendium of decisions which, while they apply to the modern situation, are born out of the timeless dictates to which our ancestors have adhered through the generations and are close in spirit to the traditional reading of *halakha* we have known to date.

A legend preserved in the Babylonian Talmud (Aboda Zarah 5a) states, "The Holy One, Blessed be He, showed the first man each generation with its exegetes, each generation with its sages." With the publication of this *A Guide to Jewish Religious Practice,* Rabbi Isaac Klein truly establishes himself as an exegete and sage of our generation, and his work as a further link in the endless chain of Jewish tradition.

Gerson D. Cohen

Preface

In the year 1959, Dr. Louis Finkelstein, then Chancellor of the Jewish Theological Seminary, invited me to lecture to the students of the Rabbinical School on the subject of "Laws and Standards for Religious Observance."

This course of lectures formed the basis for the present volume. Its purpose was to give the students a *halakhah lema'aseh,* a guide for their personal observance, as well as a source for the instruction they would subsequently provide to their congregants. Hence the lectures, and the present volume as well, included all the rules and regulations that observant Jews regard as norms, and on which they usually seek guidance from their rabbis—in other words, the same matters that are covered in the *Shulḥan 'Arukh,* except for the rules of civil law treated in the *Ḥoshen Mishpaṭ,* since nowadays the guidance of an attorney rather than a rabbi is usually sought in this area. While the subject of ethical conduct is also not included, since it has greater affinity to the matters covered in *Ḥoshen Mishpaṭ* than to those treated in the other parts of the *Shulḥan 'Arukh,* ethical questions arising in connection with the ritual law are treated as an integral part of the subjects to which they pertain.

In discussing the standard codes that had acquired great authority in the Jewish community, Professor Solomon Schechter said: "But however great the literary value of a code may be, it does not invest it with the attribute of infallibility, nor does it exempt the student from the duty of examining each paragraph on its own merits, and subjecting it to the same rules of interpretation that were always applied to tradition" (*Studies in Judaism,* 1:211). If this attitude was necessary vis-à-vis the classical works revered by Klal Yisra'el, how much the more does it apply to this modest effort.

Obviously, my treatment of the law did not start *de novo.* Rather, my code is in line with an ample body of literature that has a long and illustrious history. What is new in my code, however, is the point of view from which it was written, as will be explained below. Nonetheless, in compiling this work I was guided by the great codes that have attained authority in the Jewish community, particularly the *Mishneh Torah* of Maimonides (1135–1204), the *Ṭur* of Rabbi Jacob ben Asher (1280–1340), and the *Shulḥan 'Arukh* of Rabbi Joseph Caro (1488–1578). The code of Rabbi Jacob ben Asher widened its base by including the authorities and practices of the Jews of France and Germany. The code of Rabbi Joseph Caro, originally acceptable only in the Sefardic Jewish communities, achieved universal acceptance by Klal Yisra'el after Rabbi Moses Isserles (1510–1572), better known as the Rama, added glosses which gave the practices of the Jewish communities of Eastern Europe and the decisions of their rabbinic authorities.

Each of these codes had its own special virtue which enabled it to achieve wide acceptance. As has often been noted, the code of Maimonides begins with a philosophical treatise, whereas Caro's *Shulḥan 'Arukh* begins with an exhortation to start eachday in zealous service of the Lord. It has been suggested that Maimonides, who lived in a highly sophisticated age of reason, was obliged not only to state the law but also to explain "why"; Caro, who lived in an age of faith, needed only to explain "how."

Obviously, our era is more like that of Maimonides than that of Caro, and therefore I have provided philosophical and moralistic introductions to my discussions wherever the subject warrants it. In addition, I have followed the method pursued by Rabbi Mordecai Yaffe (1530–1612) in his *Levush*—a code which deserves wider study—giving the sources, development, and reasons for each law wherever possible. This is very much in conformity with the modern temper, which seeks relevance in the laws we abide by.

Another important feaure of the present work is the inclusion of the decisions of the Committee on Law and Standards of the Rabbinical Assembly wherever these have modified, deviated from, or added to the traditional norms.

All through my preparation of this code, I was conscious of the underlying philosophy of the Conservative Movement and its unique approach to Jewish law, which takes into consideration the historical and sociological factors, both past and present, operating in the development of the Halakhah.

When Rabbi Moses Isserles wrote his glosses on the *Shulḥan 'Arukh,* he insisted on the authority of the scholars of Eastern Europe and on the validity of the practices (*minhagim*) that obtained in the East European communities, even when these were at variance with the laws laid down by Rabbi Joseph Caro.

In like manner, in preparing this work I have insisted on the authority of our Conservative scholars and on the validity of the practices of our Conservative congregations. Similarly, just as the Rama followed the *aḥaronim* (later authorities), on the principle of *halakhah kevatrai* ("the law is decided according to the decision of the later authorities"), so I have maintained that our *aḥaronim* are within the tradition of halakhic development and should be accorded the same consideration. Moreover, again like the Rama, I have taken into consideration the customs, conditions, and new factors that are operative in our time and place. Isserles added the practices that obtained in the Eastern Europe of his era, and I have added the practices that obtain in the present-day Conservative synagogue. The code I have prepared, therefore, will serve as a guide for those congregations that are affiliated with the United Synagogue and the World Council of Synagogues, as well as for individuals in accord with their principles.

I am indebted to the many people who have been helpful to me in the preparation of this work.

First, thanks are due to Dr. Louis Finkelstein, who conceived the idea of these lectures, invited me to deliver them before the students of the Seminary, and showed a keen interest in my work throughout the time of its preparation.

To Dr. Gerson Cohen I am indebted for putting his imprimatur on this work by having it published under the seal of the Seminary, a distinct honor, for reading the manuscript, and for authoring the foreword to the book.

Dr. Neil Gillman, Dean of Academic Affairs of the Rabbinical School, drew up the initial syllabus for the lectures, carefully read and edited each chapter as it appeared, suggested additions and deletions, and supervised the preparation of these discourses from the beginning to the very end. He was a constant source of encouragement throughout the years of my work on this project. How can I thank him for all this?

I am grateful to Rabbi Gillman as well for choosing two excellent students, both at the Rabbinical School, Wayne Allen and Lionel Moses, who went through the manuscript with a fine comb, checking the references, correcting errors, and making many suggestions for the improvement of the work. I am also grateful to Mrs. Florence Green, Dr. Gillman's secretary, for typing the manuscript, supervising its preparation and distribution, and cheerfully cooperating at all times. To Dr. David Lieber, President of the University of Judaism in Los Angeles, I am grateful for reading the manuscript with a sharp critical eye and for his valuable suggestions for the improvement of the book.

In preparing this work I utilized the expert knowledge of scientists and scholars in many areas where I needed their competence. Dr. Sheldon Moline, a most expert food chemist, advised me on the chemical composition of many food products, and this helped me to determine whether they were kosher. Dr. Sol Narotsky, a veterinarian, helped me with the study of the anatomy of kosher animals and fowl. Dr. Theodore Shulman, an obstetrician, gave me the necessary books and guided me in the study of the human reproductive organs, both male and female, and read the sections of this work that are relevant to the subject. Mr. Paul Birzon, a scholarly attorney, was my source of information on family law in America and supplied me with the relevant material. Mr. Moe Frey was also helpful in regard to many of the legal questions I dealt with. Dr. Carl Gans, Chairman of the Department of Zoology of the University of Michigan, was my source of information on fish, and Drs. Richard Rosenblatt and Carl Hubbs of the Scripps Institute of Oceanography, La Jolla, California, provided their expert knowledge of ichthyology and in addition enabled me to see live specimens of the species of fish about which I had questions. Professor Jeffrey Linsky, Department of Astrophysics, University of Colorado (and also an astrophysicist for the National Bureau of Standards), applied his astronomical expertise in helping me to determine the length of the Sabbath and Festivals, i.e., the duration of the twilight period (*ben hashemashot*). My sons-in-law were also very helpful: Rabbi Paul Katz read the manuscript and made some valuable suggestions; Dr. Saul Shapiro aided me with the chapter on the Jewish calendar, a subject in which he is an expert, and with the proper assignment of Torah readings for occasions where there is some doubt; and Professor Gerald Berkowitz was of great help, both through his knowledge of chemistry, and also by reading the manuscript, making the text more readable by smoothing out many stylistic rough spots.

My teachers not only taught me and imparted knowledge to me but also implanted in me a love of Torah and its study. To them I owe the "enjoyment" of learning and the pursuit thereof, even when under the pressure of an active rabbinate and when serving in the Armed Forces of the United States. I must begin with my teachers in *cheder* in the little village of Palanka, at the foot of the Carpathian Mountains in pre–Versailles Treaty Hungary. My first teacher was Reb Sholem (Hennik), who started me at the age of four, and at the ripe age of seven introduced me to the Talmud. I then transferred to Reb Elyeh (Seif) of Stry, with whom I stayed eight years, and during the last three was able to handle a *blatt Gemara* with all the commentaries, as well as the standard codes and their commentaries. Coming to America, I studied at the Rabbi Isaac Elhanan Yeshivah under the fiery and sharp Reb Shloimeh Levine, and the saintly, profound, and lucid scholar, the Maicheter Illui, Reb Shloimeh Palatchic, who introduced me to the inductive-analytic method of study that prevailed in the great Yeshivot of Eastern Europe. Above all, I am indebted to my teachers at the Jewish

Theological Seminary, especially to the great talmudic master of his age, a giant among scholars, Professor Louis Ginzberg, who combined the *lamdanut* of the East European scholars with the critical-historical approach characteristic of the Western universities. They all taught me, guided me, and inspired me—and their memory remains an inspiration to me to this day.

I am also grateful to Mr. Bernard Scharfstein for the deep interest he has taken in the publication of this book, and for the attention he has given to it far beyond the call of business and professional competence. I owe thanks as well to Mrs. Harriet Catlin for seeing the volume through the press.

To my wife, Henriette, I owe more than I can express, for her moral support, her constant encouragement of my scholarly pursuits, and her unfailing inspiration for all my endeavors.

UNIT I

INTRODUCTION

Upon Arising in the Morning: The Tsitsit
Tefilin

I. Introduction

Judaism rises and falls in accordance with the degree to which Halakhah permeates and penetrates the life of the Jewish people. Despite the occasional successes scored by secular Judaism, and the apparent growth in some branches of Judaism that do not maintain Halakhah, the lasting quality of Judaism and the Jewish people is intimately tied up with the observance of Mitswot Ma'asiyot, the religious practices that characterize Jewish life and give it the dimension of holiness.

Contrary to the conception current in certain groups, Conservative Judaism has continued in this tradition and has emphasized the validity and necessity of normative Judaism, the Halakhah which regulates our conduct.

Says Dr. Louis Finkelstein: "Judaism is a way of life that endeavors to transform virtually every human action into a means of communion with God. Through this communion with God, the Jew is enabled to make his contribution to the establishment of the Kingdom of God and the brotherhood of man on earth" (*The Jews,* p. 1739).

This corresponds to the talmudic statement: "Which is a short passage in Scripture upon which all the principles of the Torah depend? It is: 'In all thy ways acknowledge God, and He will direct thy paths' [Prov. 3:6]" (B. *Ber.* 63a).

Halakhah, or normative Judaism, is the primary expression of the Jew's relation to God, and the one authentic path to Jewish existence. Normative Judaism expressed itself not in a creed but in a program of conduct. While we no longer deny that Judaism has a theology, we still maintain that the unique character of Jewish life, the factor responsible for the endurance of the Jewish people, the ingredient that gave holiness to its existence, is the mitswot, the performance of the religious commandments. Without these, beliefs and opinions are abstract and hollow, and touch life very tenuously.

The soul of the Jewish people revealed itself in its religious way of life; it found its expression in a life lived according to Halakhah.

Jewish life will find its *tiqqun,* its salvation, when it continues to live in this tradition. When Jewish life was at its best, fullest, and profoundest (see Heschel, *The Earth Is the Lord's*), its life was *sustained* by the norms enshrined in its codes of religious law, and these codes were more effective than any other force in uniting the Jewish people.

Today we must reaffirm that these norms have an important place in Jewish life, and must stress that while Conservative Judaism has its own approach to the development of Halakhah, it stands firmly on the ground of normative Judaism, patterned on accepted laws and standards.

1. Upon Arising in the Morning: The Tsitsit

The Midrash tells: Once when Hillel took leave of his disciples, they accompanied him part of the way and asked him whither he was going. He answered that he was going to do a mitswah, to wash himself. When they asked what kind of mitswah that was, he gave an instructive answer. The statues of kings are washed regularly, he said, and this is considered a noble responsibility. Man is the image of God, and as such he should certainly receive the same care; this care should also be considered a noble and important function (*Wayiqra Rabbah* 34:3).

1. We have a regular routine of morning hygiene that is followed for reasons of health. Long before we became aware of the hygienic value of these practices, they were prescribed by Jewish law for religious reasons. ("Religion is not a special function of man's spiritual life, but it is the dimension of depth in all of its functions"—Paul Tillich.) The purpose was to pay proper respect to the body, which was created in the image of God and is the abode of the spirit.

Hence, when a person arises in the morning he should first recite the short prayer מוֹדֶה אֲנִי לְפָנֶיךָ מֶלֶךְ חַי וְקַיָּם שֶׁהֶחֱזַרְתָּ בִּי נִשְׁמָתִי בְּחֶמְלָה, רַבָּה אֱמוּנָתֶךָ and immediately thereafter wash his hands and face. He may recite this short prayer even before he washes his hands because it does not mention the name of God. Then he may proceed to all the other practices that have to do with morning hygiene (*B.H.* 5 on *O.H.* 1:1).

2. After dressing, one should proceed immediately to morning prayers. This means that one should not eat before the morning prayers (B. *Ber.* 10b; Ṭur, *O.H.* 89; *O.H.* 89:3). It is permitted, however, to drink liquids before the morning prayers (*O.H.* 89:3). When the prayer service is long, as on the Sabbath or on festivals, people in poor health who find it difficult to wait until the conclusion of the service are permitted to have a light breakfast before the morning prayers (*O.H.* 89:3; *M.A.* 12, 13).

3. When dressing one should add to his garments the Ṭalit Qatan (little

ṭalit), better known as 'Arba' Kanfot (four corners), which should be worn all day. The Ṭalit Qatan consists of an oblong piece of cloth with a hole cut in the middle large enough for the head to go through. It should be large enough to fold over the upper body in front and back, and should have Tsitsit on its four corners (*O.H.* 8:3–11, 24:1).

4. In ancient times all garments with four corners that were worn during the day had Tsitsit on the four corners. The Tsitsit, as the Torah prescribes, serve as a reminder of God's commandments: "And ye shall look at it and remember all the commandments of the Lord" (Num. 15:39). Since the use of a fringed outer garment has been limited to the Ṭalit worn during morning prayers, only the Ṭalit Qatan, which one wears the whole day, now serves as the prescribed reminder. Upon donning the Ṭalit Qatan, one should recite the blessing עַל מִצְוַת צִיצִת (Rama, *O.H.* 8:6).*

5. Rabbi Yoḥanan suggests (B. *Ber.* 14b f.) that one who wishes to accept the yoke of the Kingdom of Heaven should perform his hygienic needs, don the Tefilin, and recite the שְׁמַע. Hence, one should proceed to the morning prayers as soon as possible after rising.

6. Before one begins the morning service he should put on the Ṭalit and the Tefilin. There are variations in custom regarding the age at which one starts to wear a Ṭalit. In some places all male worshippers, regardless of age, wear a Ṭalit (*O.H.* 17:3); some start at the age of thirteen (ibid. in *B.H.* 4); and some only after marriage (ibid. in *B.H.* 4, quoting the Maharil). In most American synagogues the first practice has been adopted.

7. The Ṭalit is usually made of wool, silk, or rayon. The Tsitsit must be made of the same material, except that woolen Tsitsit can be used on every Ṭalit regardless of the material of the Ṭalit itself. Other materials can be used only when the Ṭalit is made of the same kind of cloth (*O.H.* 9:2–3).

8. The Tsitsit are attached in the following manner: At the corner of the Ṭalit there is a hole (or two) an inch or two from the hem. Four threads, three of equal length and the fourth longer, are brought through the hole and folded over, now making eight threads. These are folded so that seven are of equal length and the eighth, designated as the Shamash, is longer. A double knot is made with the two sets of four threads. After the double knot the Shamash is wound seven times around the other seven. Another double knot is made and the Shamash is now wound eight times around the seven threads. Again a double knot, and the Shamash is wound around another

*There are two basic formulae for introductory benedictions. Consult a daily prayer book for the precise formulation in each case.

eleven times. The process is repeated with thirteen rings, and then a fifth and final double knot is made (*O.H.* 11:14; *M.A.* 22).

9. The length of the Tsitsit after this process should be about eighteen finger-breadths, with the part containing the knots making up one-third of the total length (*O.H.* 11:4; *M.D.*, ad loc. 3).

10. When putting on the Ṭalit, one should hold it with both hands, recite the blessing לְהִתְעַטֵּף בְּצִיצִת, then put it over the head, wrap it around, and recite the verses מַה יָּקָר חַסְדְּךָ (Idelsohn, *Jewish Liturgy*, p. 80).

11. We have mentioned that the Torah says: "You shall look at the Tsitsit and you will be reminded of all the commandments of the Lord." The method of making the Tsitsit helps in achieving this purpose. Thus, according to Rashi, the eight threads correspond to the eight days that elapsed between the day that the children of Israel began their journey from Egypt and the day they sang the Song of the Red Sea. The five knots correspond to the five books of Moses (Ṭur, *O.H.* 24). The number of rings wound around the Tsitsit equals thirty-nine, corresponding to the numerical value of the letters in יְהֹוָה אֶחָד. The four corners insure that one will see this reminder in whatever direction one looks (*O.H.* 8:4).

12. In addition to wearing the Ṭalit while reciting the morning prayers, one should take the Tsitsit in one's hands and kiss them during certain parts of the service. According to the rabbis, this is done to show devotion and love for the mitswah (Rama, *O.H.* 24:4). The Tsitsit are kissed at the end of בָּרוּךְ שֶׁאָמַר, during the recital of the third passage of the שְׁמַע whenever the word Tsitsit is mentioned, at the conclusion of this passage with the word אֱמֶת, and in the succeeding prayer with the words קַיֶּמֶת and וּלְעוֹלְמֵי עוֹלָמִים (*O.H.* 24:4).

13. If one removes the Ṭalit temporarily during the services with the intention of putting it on again, one does not have to repeat the blessing לְהִתְעַטֵּף בְּצִיצִת (Rama, *O.H.* 8:14).

14. If one of the threads is missing, the Ṭalit should not be used (*O.H.* 12:1).

Today the Tsitsit come ready-made, attached properly to the Ṭalit and Ṭalit Qatan. One may move the Tsitsit from one Ṭalit to another. One may remove the Tsitsit from a Ṭalit and put on better ones in their stead, or replace a thread that has been severed. The discarded Tsitsit, however, should be treated with the consideration due to holy objects (*O.H.* 15:1, 21:1).

15. Each person should own his own Ṭalit. There is no objection, however, to the use of someone else's Ṭalit, since it is assumed that the

owner is pleased when a mitswah is performed with one of his possessions, especially when no material loss is suffered (*O.H.* 14:4).

2. Tefilin

1. We have quoted the statement of Rabbi Yoḥanan to the effect that one who wants to accept the sovereignty of God should perform his hygienic needs, then put on his Tefilin and recite the שְׁמַע (see above, p. 4).

The purpose of the Tefilin is best expressed in the prayer that is said before putting them on. God has commanded us to wear the Tefilin on the arm in memory of His outstretched arm; opposite the heart to intimate that we ought to subject our hearts' desires and designs to the service of God, blessed be He; and on the head, opposite the brain, to intimate that the mind, and all senses and faculties, ought to be subjected to His service, blessed be He (*O.H.* 25:5).

2. The Tefilin consist of two black leather boxes. Each of these contains four passages of the Torah which mention the mitswah of Tefilin: i.e., the first two sections of the שְׁמַע (Deut. 6:4–9 and 11:13–21) and Exodus 13:1–10, 11–16, each paragraph of which is interpreted as containing a reference to the Tefilin (vv. 9 and 16).

3. The Shel Rosh, or headpiece, has the four passages in four separate compartments, whereas in the Shel Yad, or handpiece, they are all written on one parchment in one compartment (*O.H.* 32:2).

This has been interpreted as meaning that while we should encourage honest differences of opinion, we should nevertheless strive to achieve a uniformity of practice.

4. The Tefilin are put on before beginning the daily morning prayers (*O.H.* 25:4). On the ninth of Av, however, they are worn at Minḥah.

The Tefilin are not worn on the Sabbath or on the major festivals (the High Holy Days, Sukkot, Shemini 'Atseret, Pesaḥ, and Shavu'ot). This is because Tefilin are a "sign upon thy hand." Since Sabbaths and festivals themselves serve as such signs, Tefilin are not necessary on these occasions (B. *Erub.* 96a; *O.H.* 31:1).

5. The practices of the Sefardim and the Ashkenazim differ during the intermediate days of Pesaḥ and Sukkot. The Sefardim do not put on Tefilin during the intermediate days, but the Ashkenazim do (*O.H.* 31:2). The Hassidim follow the practice of the Sefardim. In Israel, too, the general custom is not to put on Tefilin (Tucatzinsky, *Qitsur Shulḥan 'Arukh,* supp., 11:4; also Gelis, *Minhagei Erets Yisrael,* p. 135, sec. 62).

6. The accepted practice today is that one starts to put on Tefilin at the age of thirteen, when he becomes a Bar Mitswah. According to the Talmud, when a child becomes mature enough to observe the rules concerning the Tefilin, his father should buy him a pair and teach him to use and care for them properly. While the precise time of attaining such maturity may vary with the mental capacity of each child, the practice has become uniform, on the assumption that maturity has always been achieved by the age of thirteen (*O.H.* 37:3; Rama, ad loc.).

7. The procedure of putting on the Tefilin is as follows: They should be put on immediately after the Ṭalit. The Shel Yad is taken first and put over the muscle of the left arm, with the *ma'abarta* (the protruding part of the base of the Shel Yad, which has the *retsu'ah,* or leather strap, threaded through it) toward the shoulder, the *tétura* (or *qetsitsah*—the protruding part of the base on the opposite side) toward the hand, and the *yod* (the knot, which looks like the letter *yod*) toward the heart. Before tightening the *retsu'ah* one should recite the blessing לְהָנִיחַ תְּפִלִּין. Then the *retsu'ah* is tightened so that the *bayit* (the boxlike part of Tefilin) holds fast to the arm and the *yod* touches the *bayit.* Then the *retsu'ah* is wound seven times over the arm between the elbow and the wrist (*O.H.* 27:1–3, 8; 25:5). The method of winding varies according to custom—some winding clockwise; others winding counterclockwise.

Next the Shel Rosh is placed over the head so that the *bayit* is over the hair, with the outer edge not extending below where the hair begins to grow. The *qesher* (the knot making the loop that surrounds the head) should rest on the base of the skull above the nape of the neck. The blessing עַל מִצְוַת תְּפִלִּין is then recited, followed by the verse בָּרוּךְ שֵׁם כְּבוֹד מַלְכוּתוֹ לְעוֹלָם וָעֶד (*O.H.* 27:9–10, 25:5; Rama, ad loc.).

בָּרוּךְ שֵׁם is said because there is some doubt whether a second benediction is necessary, since the first benediction may be meant for both the Shel Yad and the Shel Rosh. In such cases we add בָּרוּךְ שֵׁם to avoid taking the name of God in vain.

After the blessing on the Shel Rosh, the rest of the *retsu'ah* of the Shel Yad is wound around the middle finger, twice on the lower joint and once on the middle joint. The remainder is then wound around the palm. When this is properly done, the three letters spelling the name שַׁדַּי will be seen on the hand (*O.H.* 27:8; *B.H.* ad loc., 13).

8. The Tefilin should rest directly on the arm and the head with nothing coming between them and the body (*O.H.* 27:4).

9. When the Tefilin are taken off, the order of putting them on is re-

versed. Thus, first the *retsu'ah* around the hand and finger is unwound; then the Shel Rosh is removed and returned to the Tefilin bag; finally the rest of the *retsu'ah* of the Shel Yad is unwound, and the Shel Yad is removed and returned to the Tefilin bag (*O.H.* 28:2).

When the Tefilin are returned to the bag, the Shel Rosh should be placed on the right side and the Shel Yad on the left. This is to insure that we will know where to reach for the Shel Yad, which has to be taken out first, when we use the Tefilin again (*O.H.* 28:2).

10. A left-handed person should put the Tefilin Shel Yad on his right arm. The determining factor in deciding who is left-handed is writing. If one writes with his right hand, even though he does everything else with his left hand, he is considered right-handed. An ambidextrous person wears the Tefilin on his left arm (*O.H.* 27:6).

11. Because of the sacredness of the Tefilin, we observe certain practices and precautions that indicate care and reverence.

One should stand while putting on the Tefilin (*O.H.* 25:1 f. in Rama and *B.H.* ad loc.)

A person with an illness that makes it difficult to keep the body clean (e.g., diarrhea, dysentery) should not put on Tefilin, nor should a person who suffers from severe pain, because he will not be able to give the necessary attention (*O.H.* 38:1, 9).

One should kiss the Tefilin while putting them on and taking them off, and at several points in the service (*O.H.* 28:3). These are the customary ones:

אוֹזֵר יִשְׂרָאֵל בִּגְבוּרָה
עוֹטֵר יִשְׂרָאֵל בְּתִפְאָרָה
יִשְׂמְחוּ הַשָּׁמַיִם וְתָגֵל הָאָרֶץ
פּוֹתֵחַ אֶת יָדֶךָ
וּקְשַׁרְתָּם לְאוֹת . . . (twice)

One should not eat or sleep while wearing the Tefilin (*O.H.* 40:8, 44:1).

12. Since the script on the parchment inside the Tefilin boxes must be clear, it should be examined by a competent scribe where possible twice in seven years. If there is reason to believe that the script may have deteriorated, as when the Tefilin have fallen into water, or were in a damp place for a long period of time, the parchments should be checked immediately (*B.H.* on *O.H.* 39:9).

13. The Tefilin are removed after the conclusion of the service, but not before the Qaddish Titqabel, which is said after וּבָא לְצִיּוֹן. On Rosh Ḥodesh

they are removed after the Torah is returned to the ark, immediately before the Musaf 'Amidah. In localities where Tefilin are worn on the intermediate days of festivals, they are removed before Hallel (*O.H.* 25:13).

14. As with the Ṭalit, a person may borrow Tefilin belonging to someone else even without his knowledge, on the assumption that a person is pleased when a mitswah is performed with his belongings (*O.H.* 14:4).

15. The effect the Tefilin should have upon the worshipper is best expressed in the rabbinic interpretation of the commandment, "Thou shalt not take the name of the Lord thy God in vain." According to the rabbis, this means that one should not wrap himself in a Ṭalit and don Tefilin, and then defraud people, because in so doing he bears the name of God fraudulently (*Pesiqta Rabbati* 22; ed. Meir Ish Shalom, 111b).

16. *Tefilin d'Rabbeinu Tam.* A small number of scrupulously pious people still maintain the practice of putting on two pairs of Tefilin, wearing one from the beginning of the morning service until after the 'Amidah, and the second for the rest of the Shaḥarit prayers.

The reason for this practice is as follows. The Tefilin contain pieces of parchment on which four *parashiyot* of the Torah that mention Tefilin are written. There is a difference of opinion about the order in which these *parashiyot* ought to be arranged. According to Rashi, we should follow the sequence in which they appear in the Torah: (1) קַדֶּשׁ, (2) וְהָיָה כִּי יְבִיאֲךָ, (3) שְׁמַע, (4) וְהָיָה אִם שָׁמֹעַ. According to Rabbeinu Tam, שְׁמַע should come last. The general practice follows Rashi's ruling. The scrupulously pious, however, wishing to satisfy both rulings, take off their regular (Rashi) Tefilin immediately after the 'Amidah, and then, without reciting a blessing, put on the *Tefilin d'Rabbeinu Tam*, after which they say שְׁמַע, וְהָיָה אִם שָׁמֹעַ, and the rest of the Shaḥarit prayers which follow the 'Amidah (*O.H.* 34:1).

UNIT II

DAILY PRAYER

Source
Preparations
Time
The Minyan
Shaḥarit
Birkhot Hashaḥar
Pesuqei Dezimrah
The Shema'
The 'Amidah
Taḥanun
Qeri'at HaTorah
Concluding Prayers
Minḥah
Ma'ariv
The Qaddish

II. Daily Prayer

Rabbi Yoḥanan said: "Would that man would pray all day" (B. *Ber.* 21a). The implication is that man, when and as moved by the spirit, can commune with God and confront Him.

This thought is further emphasized by the following statement in the *Ethics of the Fathers:* "When you pray, do not make your prayers a set routine, but offer them as a plea for mercy and grace before God" (2:13).

Despite the preceding admonition, experience has shown prayer to be so central to the religious life that it cannot be left dependent upon uncertainties of mood and spirit. As a result, Judaism has established statutory prayers—a schedule of times, seasons, and occasions when one should come before God; in other words, a tradition of formal prayer. This tradition of formal prayer, of course, does not preclude spontaneous prayer, which is always welcome and beneficial to the life of the spirit. The rules, regulations, and prescribed standards set forth below, however, apply mainly to formal and statutory prayers.

1. Source

The Jewish tradition prescribes three daily services: Shaḥarit, the morning prayer; Minḥah, the afternoon prayer; and Ma'ariv, the evening prayer.

The Talmud offers three explanations for this practice:

a. It corresponds to the three natural changes in the day: sunrise, approaching sunset, and night.
b. The precedent of the Patriarchs: according to rabbinic interpretation, Abraham prayed in the morning, Isaac, in the afternoon, and Jacob, at night.
c. It corresponds to the daily sacrificial offerings in the Temple in Jerusalem: in the morning, at twilight, and at the burning of the remains of the sacrifices at night (Y. *Ber.* 4:1; B. *Ber.* 26b).

2. Preparations

Since prayer is a sacred act, a person praying should be properly prepared for worship, and the place where he prays should be suitable.

Thus a person should be properly dressed at prayer, whether he prays alone in the privacy of his home, or in the synagogue (*O.H.* 91).

The person who is praying and the place of prayer should both be clean. Therefore one should not pray where there are offensive odors, sharp or pungent smells, or indecent objects. These distract the mind and make it difficult to attain a reverent mood (*O.H.* 85; *Qitsur Shulḥan 'Arukh* 5).

Some synagogues provide facilities for washing the hands immediately before prayer (*O.H.* 92:4).

One should choose a place of worship where one will pray regularly. One should occupy a set place in the synagogue where one worships. These are psychological factors that aid in creating a prayerful mood (*O.H.* 90:19).

Many synagogues have a charity box in which every worshipper deposits a contribution. This is not a means of raising funds—though the proceeds are used for a charitable cause—but rather an opportunity for us to show concern for our fellow man before we offer prayer for ourselves (*O.H.* 92:10). Psalms 17:15 is often quoted in regard to this custom (*Y.D.* 294:14; Shakh, ad loc.).

3. Time

The period during which the morning prayer may be recited begins at sunrise and continues for one-third of the day (M. *Ber.* 4:1).

The rabbis in the Talmud speak of a time span of four hours, because, for the sake of uniformity, they speak in terms of days and nights of equal duration, i.e., twelve hours each. Four hours, then, constitute one-third of the day. When the days are longer, the time is proportionately longer; when the days are shorter, it is proportionately shorter.

When necessary, one may begin his prayer at dawn. Thus, people who go to work early may recite the morning prayer even before sunrise (*'Arukh Hashulḥan, O.H.* 58:1 f., 89:11; Felder, *Yesodei Yeshurun,* 1:362).

If, by error, one has recited his prayers later than the prescribed time, the prayers are valid, though the optimum is to recite them on time. One should not, in any event, recite the morning prayer after noon (*'Arukh Hashulḥan, O.H.* 89:13 f.).

Daniel, the Bible tells us, prayed facing Jerusalem (Dan. 6:11). We follow the custom of facing east toward the land of Israel when we pray (B. *Ber.* 30a). Those who live in Israel face toward Jerusalem, and those who are in Jerusalem face toward the site of the Temple.

4. The Minyan

A minyan is required for the recitation of קַדִּישׁ, בָּרְכוּ, and קְדֻשָּׁה. The public reading of the Torah also requires a minyan (*O.H.* 55:1, 3 and Rama).

Traditionally, a minyan consists of ten Jewish male adults—i.e., males thirteen years of age or older. The Rabbinical Assembly Committee on Law and Standards, at its meeting on August 29, 1973, ruled by a majority vote to allow women to be counted for a minyan, but left it to each rabbi and congregation to decide whether to abide by the traditional rule or adopt the new ruling.

In an emergency, nine adults and a minor over six years old holding a Ḥumash may constitute a minyan. This practice should not be encouraged (*O.H.* 55:4; B. *Ber.* 48a; Tosafot, and Rosh, ad loc.).

Praying with a minyan is called תְּפִלָּה בְּצִבּוּר, or public prayer. The rabbis clearly preferred public to private prayer and praised it very highly. They urged, therefore, that a person should always seek to pray in a synagogue together with a congregation (*O.H.* 90:9).

Dr. Elie Munk has written: "The idea is frequently encountered in Biblical and Rabbinical literature, that the Divine Presence dwells in the midst of the community, and that the larger the congregation the more resplendent the revelation of the Shekhina will be. . . . It [the community] does not suffer deficiencies. What is lacking in one individual is made up by the other. The individual, then, can only discharge his duties completely when he collaborates with the community. The rabbis, therefore, placed the strongest emphasis on *tefilah betsibur,* prayer in the midst of the community" (*World of Prayer,* 1:89).

Today we can add psychological reasons. Public prayer is conducive to greater solemnity and exaltation. Only participation in the community can effectively guarantee the individual's progress toward achieving the highest ideals. For this reason the Torah was entrusted to the "community of Jacob" (מוֹרָשָׁה קְהִלַּת יַעֲקֹב). Hence also, a דָּבָר שֶׁבִּקְדֻשָּׁה may be recited only in the assembly of the community, or in the presence of ten, the smallest number that may legitimately represent the community.

According to the late Chief Rabbi Kook, the basis of prayer, established by divine wisdom for the fulfillment of man's needs, lies in its impelling the moral improvement of man, exalting and stabilizing his mind by strengthening his spiritual powers. The compelling force of this moral training does not come about when man is in seclusion, but rather when he joins with his fellow men in communal life. Therefore, the main point and purpose of prayer lies in the coming together of men. Man's intellectual self-perfection can be accomplished by study alone, but the morality necessary for communal life is established through prayer. Hence, public prayer is the main form of prayer, and even private prayer will more readily produce the desired results when it is recited within a congregation. Further, the עֵת רָצוֹן, or acceptable time, even for private prayer, is the time when the congregation prays (paraphrased from *'Olat Re'iyah,* p. 261).

5. Shaḥarit

The morning service consists of the following sections:

1. Birkhot Hashaḥar
2. Pesuqei Dezimrah
3. The Shema'
4. The 'Amidah
5. Taḥanun
6. Qeri'at HaTorah (on Mondays and Thursdays)
7. Concluding prayers

6. Birkhot Hashaḥar

Dr. Louis Finkelstein has written: "The fundamental concept of the Jewish ceremonial system is that God continually reveals Himself in nature, in history, and in man's daily life. Each ceremony seeks to emphasize some aspect of this Divine revelation, and thus becomes a special means for communion between man and God. . . .

"Jewish tradition has evolved the system of ritual blessings as an effective means for achieving continual realization of God's manifestation in the world" ("The Jewish Religion," in *The Jews,* p. 1764).

Accordingly, it became customary to recite a benediction for each act one performs during the morning routine at the time of performance: a benediction when the hands are washed, a benediction when one dresses, a benediction after answering to one's natural needs, etc. Maimonides, following the Talmud, prescribed such a procedure. The practice we follow, however, is that of the later codes: we include all the benedictions at the beginning of the morning service (*O.H.* 46:1). Thus, in current practice, at a public service with a minyan, the reader begins with the benediction אֲשֶׁר נָתַן לַשֶּׂכְוִי בִינָה. This introduces the בִּרְכוֹת הַשַּׁחַר, the preliminary prayers. Preceding this benediction are prayers and benedictions that the worshipper recites by himself.

At the conclusion of the בִּרְכוֹת הַשַּׁחַר Psalm 30 is read, after which the mourner's Qaddish is recited.

7. Pesuqei Dezimrah

The Talmud records that pious Jews used to come to the synagogue well before the service and spend some time in meditation before beginning to pray (M. *Ber.* 5:1). This period of meditation was an attempt to attain a mood appropriate for authentic prayer.

The rabbis also suggested that we should begin our worship service praising God (B. *Ber.* 32a). Rabbi Meir of Rothenburg (1220–1293) formalized this early custom by introducing a series of passages from the Bible which are read before the beginning of the formal service (which commences with the Barekhu). We call these passages פְּסוּקֵי דְזִמְרָא, or passages of song, because their central theme is the praise of God.

The Pesuqei Dezimrah portion of the service, in its present form, is the result of an evolution which took place over many centuries, with different passages added at different times. Even today the Ashkenazic and Sefardic minhagim differ as to the passages recited and the order in which they are said. All agree, however, that the central portion of the Pesuqei Dezimrah is the אַשְׁרֵי, Psalm 145 and the two preceding verses, Psalms 84:5 and 144:15. The rabbis (B. *Ber.* 4b) suggest that Ashrei should be said three times daily: once during the Pesuqei Dezimrah, once as part of the concluding prayers of Shaḥarit, and once during the Minḥah service.

On Sabbaths and festivals, additional psalms are added to the Pesuqei Dezimrah.

The Pesuqei Dezimrah part of the service begins with בָּרוּךְ שֶׁאָמַר and ends with יִשְׁתַּבַּח, following the established practice of beginning and ending each section of the service with a benediction (*O.H.* 51:4; *M.A.*).

When reciting בָּרוּךְ שֶׁאָמַר, the worshipper should stand, taking two of the Tsitsit of his Ṭalit in his hand. On concluding he should kiss the Tsitsit and release them, and then sit down (*O.H.* 51:1; *M.A.*).

Customs vary regarding standing during different parts of the service. As far as the Pesuqei Dezimrah is concerned, there is a consensus on the following: the worshipper should stand during בָּרוּךְ שֶׁאָמַר, when reciting Psalm 100 (מִזְמוֹר לְתוֹדָה), and from וַיְבָרֶךְ to the end of the Song of the Red Sea (Rama, *O.H.* 51:7).

Psalm 100 is omitted on Sabbaths and festivals, on the morning before Pesaḥ, and on the morning before Yom Kippur. Since it is a psalm of thanksgiving, recited in place of the ancient קָרְבַּן תּוֹדָה, or thanksgiving sacrifice, it is omitted on all occasions when such a sacrifice could not be brought (Rama,*O.H.* 51:9).

The Pesuqei Dezimrah close with יִשְׁתַּבַּח. The reader follows this with the half-Qaddish, which is usually said after the conclusion of a part of a service.

One should not interrupt the Pesuqei Dezimrah with conversation (*O.H.* 51:4) except to respond Amein to a benediction or to join the congregation when it recites the first paragraph of the Shema' or Barekhu or Qedushah (*O.H.* 66:1 in *B.H.* and *M.A.*).

If one enters the synagogue when the congregation is ready to begin Pesuqei Dezimrah and does not have a Ṭalit and Tefilin as yet but expects to obtain them later, he may join the congregation in the service and put on the Ṭalit and Tefilin after יִשְׁתַּבַּח, before the benediction Yotseir 'Or (*Qitsur Shulḥan 'Arukh* 14:8).

If one enters the synagogue while the congregation is reciting Pesuqei Dezimrah, he should aim to join the congregation for the 'Amidah. Therefore he should recite בָּרוּךְ שֶׁאָמַר, אַשְׁרֵי, and as many other passages from the Pesuqei Dezimrah as he may have time for, then conclude with יִשְׁתַּבַּח and recite the Shema' with its blessings. If, however, the congregation has already begun the recitation of the Shema' and there is no time for reciting even the shortest form of Pesuqei Dezimrah, he should join the congregation in reciting the Shema' and continue to the 'Amidah (*O.H.* 52:1). If there is clearly no time to recite the Shema' and join the congregation for the 'Amidah, he should proceed through the service at his own pace (*O.H.* 111:3).

8. The Shema‘

The Shema‘ is the proclamation of the unity of God, the central affirmation of Judaism and its greatest contribution to the religious thought of mankind. It constitutes a basic confession of faith, declaring that the God worshipped and proclaimed by Israel is One; and that He alone is God who was, is, and will be.

The Shema‘ is among the first prayers taught to children and the last prayer said by the dying. The watchword of Israel throughout the ages, it has been the traditional final utterance of Jewish martyrs.

The opening sentence of the Shema‘ embodies the most fundamental ideas of our faith, and because of this it rightly occupies the central place in Jewish religious thought and in the liturgy.

The Shema‘ section begins with בָּרְכוּ, the call to worship by the reader (*ḥazzan*). The congregation responds with בָּרוּךְ יְיָ הַמְבוֹרָךְ לְעוֹלָם וָעֶד, and the reader, inasmuch as he not only leads the congregation in prayer but prays himself as well, repeats the congregation's response (*O.H.* 57:1). A person called up to the Torah follows the same procedure (*O.H.* 139:6–7).

The Mishnah prescribes that the Shema‘ should be preceded and followed by benedictions at both the morning and evening services (M. *Ber.* 1:4). The morning service has two benedictions before the Shema‘ and one after. The first benediction begins with יוֹצֵר אוֹר. Since the Shema‘ proclaims the unity of God, this benediction forms an appropriate opening. Based on Isaiah 45:7, it offers thanks to God for creating the light of day, and for renewing His creation each morning. The second benediction praises Him as the giver of the Torah, and the third, as the redeemer of Israel.

The Shema‘ itself consists of three biblical passages: שְׁמַע (Deut. 6:4–9), וְהָיָה (Deut. 11:13–21), and וַיֹּאמֶר (Num. 15:37–41). By reciting the first paragraph, one accepts the yoke of the Kingdom of Heaven; by reciting the second, the yoke of the commandments (M. *Ber.* 2:2). The third paragraph contains a remembrance of the exodus from Egypt and mentions the Tsitsit, which recall all the commandments (B. *Ber.* 12b).

When one prays alone without a minyan, the Shema‘ is preceded by the three words אֵל מֶלֶךְ נֶאֱמָן, "God is a faithful King." The source of this addition is Kabbalistic. The Shema‘ has 245 words. According to tradition, the body has 248 parts. In order to make the number of words in the Shema‘ correspond to the number of parts, these three words are added, as if to say that man should worship God with all the parts of his body.

When one prays with a minyan, the reader repeats the last three words,

יְיָ אֱלֹהֵיכֶם אֱמֶת, making the number of words equal to 248 without the addition of אֵל מֶלֶךְ נֶאֱמָן (*O.H.* 61:3).

After the first verse of the Shema' is said aloud, it is followed by בָּרוּךְ שֵׁם כְּבוֹד מַלְכוּתוֹ לְעוֹלָם וָעֶד in a subdued voice (*O.H.* 61:13). This verse is not from the Bible; it is, rather, a response to the mention of the name of God in the preceding verse, similar to the response בָּרוּךְ הוּא וּבָרוּךְ שְׁמוֹ.

Scholars believe that this insertion dates from the period of Roman rule, when emperor worship was practiced. The insertion was intended to emphasize that only God, who is eternal, is to be praised. As a matter of prudence it was said quietly.

Dr. Max Arzt suggests that the verse is recited in an undertone because it is a nonbiblical passage interpolated into a section of biblical verses, which as such have a higher degree of sanctity (*Justice and Mercy,* pp. 72 f.).

At the end of the Shema', the word אֱמֶת, the first word of the last benediction, is joined with the concluding words of the Shema' to make יְיָ אֱלֹהֵיכֶם אֱמֶת. Thus, no hiatus is introduced between God and Truth (*O.H.* 61; *M.A.* 1).

There should be no interruption during this entire portion of the service, except to answer Amein to a benediction, to respond to *Barekhu,* or to join the congregation in reciting the Qedushah (*O.H.* 66:3 and in Rama; *Qitsur Shulḥan 'Arukh* 16:2).

When the worshipper reaches the words וַהֲבִיאֵנוּ toward the end of the second benediction, he takes the four Tsitsit in his hand.

The first verse of the Shema' is recited aloud. Some people follow the practice of Rabbi Judah Hanasi (third century C.E.) (B. *Ber.* 13b) and place their hand over their eyes when saying this verse in order to prevent distractions (*O.H.* 61:4, 5).

At the end of the first passage of the Shema' there is a reference to the commandment of Tefilin. To show our awareness of the commandment, and also to show חִבּוּב מִצְוָה, love for the mitswah, we touch the Shel Yad with the fingers of the other hand when we say וּקְשַׁרְתָּם and repeat the gesture with the Shel Rosh when we say וְהָיוּ לְטוֹטָפֹת (*O.H.* 28:1).

For the same reason, we repeat the two gestures at the end of the second paragraph, where this commandment is reiterated.

The mitswah of Tsitsit is the subject of the third passage of the Shema'. We kiss the Tsitsit of the Ṭalit each time the word *tsitsit* occurs, and also at the end of the passage when we say יְיָ אֱלֹהֵיכֶם אֱמֶת, and finally when we say נֶאֱמָנִים וְנֶחֱמָדִים לָעַד (*Qitsur Shulḥan 'Arukh* 17:7; *O.H.* 24 in *M.A.* sec. 1).

At תְּהִלּוֹת לְאֵל עֶלְיוֹן, toward the end of the blessing after the Shema', the worshipper begins to prepare himself for the 'Amidah. He rises and takes three steps backward, then continues to the end of the benediction and takes three steps forward, returning to his original position, as one would approach an important dignitary (*O.H.* 95:1 and Rama; *'Arukh Hashulḥan* 95:3; *Qitsur Shulḥan 'Arukh* 18:2).

The Shema' is concluded with the benediction גָּאַל יִשְׂרָאֵל. There should be no interruption between *ge'ulah* and *tefilah,* i.e., between the prayer for the redemption of Israel and the 'Amidah (*O.H.* 66:8).

It has become customary for the reader to say the concluding words of the benediction quietly lest the congregation have to respond with Amein and thereby interrupt the sequence of prayer (Felder, *Yesodei Yeshurun,* 1:84; Arzt, *Justice and Mercy,* pp. 80 f.; *O.H.* 66:7; *M.A.* 11).

9. The 'Amidah

When the Mishnah speaks simply of תְּפִלָּה, "prayer," it always refers to the 'Amidah, which was considered the prayer par excellence. In its religious spirit, the 'Amidah resembles the great devotional utterances of Scripture, and through it the voice of Judaism speaks with the classical accent of the Prophets and the Psalmist.

The 'Amidah is not a mere collection of short independent prayers loosely strung together without inner sequence. There is a logical order to the benedictions (B. *Meg.* 17b). They may be divided into three groups:

a. Praise: the three opening blessings
b. Petitions: the thirteen intermediate blessings
c. Thanksgiving: the three concluding blessings

This, too, has its logic: we begin with praise, express our petitions, and conclude with thanksgiving.

The first three benedictions and the last three are the same at every service—on weekdays as well as on Sabbaths and festivals. The intermediate ones are different on Sabbaths and festivals because petitions would detract from the joy of such occasions. In their place, prayers suitable to the significance of the day are recited.

The Talmud designates each benediction by a name. These are listed below in order to facilitate reference.

1. *Avot*—God of our fathers
2. *Gevurot*—the mighty God

3. *Qedushat Hashem*—the sanctification of God
4. *Binah*—for understanding
5. *Teshuvah*—for repentance
6. *Seliḥah*—for forgiveness
7. *Ge'ulah*—for redemption
8. *Refu'ah*—for healing
9. *Hashanim*—for natural abundance
10. *Qibbuts Galuyot*—for the ingathering of the Exile
11. *Mishpaṭ*—for the establishment of justice
12. *Haminim*—for the destruction of oppression
13. *Tsadiqim*—for the righteous
14. *Yerushalayim*—for the rebuilding of Jerusalem
15. *Dawid*—for the advent of the Messiah
16. *Tefilah*—that our prayer be heard
17. *'Avodah*—for the restoration of the Temple
18. *Hoda'ah*—our expression of gratitude
19. *Kohanim*—the prayer for peace

During the repetition of the 'Amidah, the Qedushah, which speaks of the holiness of God, is recited before the third benediction. It is recited in the most solemn manner, as a responsive chant between the reader and the congregation.

The Qedushah begins with a call: "We will (or, "Let us") sanctify thy name." We are asked to fashion our sanctification of the name of God in consonance with that of the higher beings, for the two verses that form the heart of the Qedushah (Isa. 6:3—קָדוֹשׁ קָדוֹשׁ קָדוֹשׁ and Ezek. 3:12—בָּרוּךְ כְּבוֹד) were recited by the celestial hosts. Man is called to praise God in the same manner.

The Qedushah is truly the climax of the service. Hence it is recited standing, with feet together, and in the presence of a minyan (B. *Ber.* 21b; *O.H.* 125:1, 2; 55:1, 3).

Variations and Insertions in the 'Amidah

Though the text of the 'Amidah is fixed, there are occasions when special prayers are inserted or wordings changed.

1. During Ma'ariv, at the conclusion of Sabbaths and festivals (also at the conclusion of the first two days of Pesaḥ and Sukkot), the prayer אַתָּה חוֹנַנְתָּנוּ is inserted into the middle of *Binah*. It speaks of the distinction between light and darkness, the holy and the profane, etc.

The fourth benediction was chosen for this insertion because it is our prayer for understanding and knowledge (B. *Ber.* 33a), and one must first have knowledge and understanding if he is to make analyses and distinctions. Furthermore, since this prayer marks the conclusion of the Sabbath and the transition to the working day, it should be recited at the very beginning of the passages that are specifically intended for weekday worship.

2. The Talmud prescribes that a prayer with special reference to a particular day be inserted into the *'Avodah* benediction—מֵעֵין הַמְּאוֹרָע בַּעֲבוֹדָה (B. *Shab.* 24a). This prayer in our liturgy is יַעֲלֶה וְיָבֹא. It was included in the *'Avodah* because the latter is our prayer for the rebuilding of the Temple in Jerusalem, and יַעֲלֶה וְיָבֹא has a similar reference (Tosafot ad loc., s.v. בְּבוֹנֵה).

3. On a public fast day the prayer עֲנֵנוּ is inserted in *Tefilah* by the worshipper when he recites the Minḥah 'Amidah silently; the reader inserts it between *Ge'ulah* and *Refu'ah* when he repeats the 'Amidah aloud at both Shaḥarit and Minḥah services. Since a fast day is considered to be an עֵת רָצוֹן (propitious time), we pray that our prayers be answered on this day in particular.

4. On the ninth day of Av, at Minḥah, the prayer נַחֵם is added before the closing verse of *Birkat Yerushalayim.* It is a prayer for the rebuilding of Zion and Jerusalem.

5. On Ḥanukkah and Purim, עַל הַנִּסִּים is added to the middle of *Birkat Hoda'ah.* In the new *Weekday Prayer Book* of the Rabbinical Assembly, there is another עַל הַנִּסִּים to be said on Yom Ha'atsma'ut, Israel Independence Day (see *Weekday Prayer Book,* p. 64). This prayer introduces appropriate historical references into our liturgy on these occasions.

6. During the Ten Days of Penitence, עֲשֶׂרֶת יְמֵי תְשׁוּבָה, we make the following additions and changes which reflect the main themes of the High Holy Day liturgy.

a. Between the first and second paragraphs of *Avot,* זָכְרֵנוּ is added.
b. Between the first and second paragraphs of *Gevurot,* מִי כָמוֹךָ is added.
c. The last words in the third benediction (הָאֵל הַקָּדוֹשׁ) are changed to הַמֶּלֶךְ הַקָּדוֹשׁ, and the last words in the *Birkat Mishpaṭ* (מֶלֶךְ אוֹהֵב צְדָקָה וּמִשְׁפָּט) are changed to הַמֶּלֶךְ הַמִּשְׁפָּט.
d. Before the last paragraph of *Hoda'ah,* וּכְתוֹב לְחַיִּים טוֹבִים is inserted.
e. Before the closing verse of *Birkat Kohanim,* בְּסֵפֶר חַיִּים is added.

7. When the reader repeats the 'Amidah and reaches the words מוֹדִים אֲנַחְנוּ לָךְ, the congregation recites the מוֹדִים דְּרַבָּנָן—so called because it is com-

posed of various versions of this prayer adopted by different rabbis (B. *Soṭah* 40a). We do so in order to express thanks ourselves rather than through an agent (the reader) (*Abudraham Hashalem,* p. 115).

8. Certain miscellaneous variations:

   a. *Qedushat Hashem* has a different text, לְדוֹר וָדוֹר, for the reader repeating the ʻAmidah.
   b. *Birkat Kohanim* has the text שָׁלוֹם רָב for Minḥah and Maʻariv in place of the שִׂים שָׁלוֹם of Shaḥarit. Sefardim, however, recite שָׁלוֹם רָב only at Maʻariv. (שִׂים שָׁלוֹם is retained at Minḥah of fast days.) Because שִׂים שָׁלוֹם has a direct reference to the priestly blessing, it is recited only when it is preceded by the priestly blessing. When the priestly blessing is omitted, as at Minḥah and Maʻariv, שָׁלוֹם רָב is used. The priestly blessing is not said by the individual worshipper when he prays silently; it is said only by the reader when he repeats the ʻAmidah aloud (*O.H.* 121:3).
   c. Between the first and second paragraphs of *Gevurot*, מַשִּׁיב הָרוּחַ וּמוֹרִיד הַגָּשֶׁם is added during the winter months, beginning with the Musaf of Shemini ʻAtseret and ending with the Musaf of the first day of Pesaḥ. The Sefardim add מוֹרִיד הַטָּל when מַשִּׁיב הָרוּחַ is not said.
   d. A variation exists in the middle of *Birkat Hashanim.* From Pesaḥ to December 5 or 6, sixty days after the fall equinox as computed by the rabbis, וְתֵן בְּרָכָה is said; from the Maʻariv of December 5 (if February of that year had 28 days) or December 6 (if February of that year had 29 days) to Pesaḥ, וְתֵן טַל וּמָטָר לִבְרָכָה is said. This blessing expresses the concern of the inhabitants of the Holy Land for adequate rainfall during the rainy season.

The prayer אֱלֹהַי נְצוֹר has been added at the conclusion of the ʻAmidah. The Talmud gives a number of personal prayers that some rabbis were accustomed to add to the formal prayer, following the suggestion that one should not let his prayer become mere routine (B. *Ber.* 29b). One of these was selected for use by all worshippers. When the reader repeats the ʻAmidah, he omits this prayer. While reciting the last sentence, עוֹשֶׂה שָׁלוֹם, the worshipper takes three steps back, and bows to the left, then to the right, and then forward. As the reader begins to repeat the service, the worshipper returns to his original position, taking three steps forward, just as he did before starting the ʻAmidah (*O.H.* 123:1, 2).

During the recitation of the ʻAmidah there are four places where one should bow: at the beginning and end of the first benediction, and at the beginning and end of the eighteenth benediction (at the words מוֹדִים אֲנַחְנוּ לָךְ

and at the end of the paragraph וְכֹל הַחַיִּים) (B. *Ber.* 34a; *O.H.* 113:1). The procedure is to bend the knee at בָּרוּךְ, bow down while saying אַתָּה, and return to the erect position before uttering the name of God (*O.H.* 113:7).

Throughout the recitation of the ʻAmidah one should stand with his feet together as the angels stood in worshipping God (Ezek. 1:7; *O.H.* 95:1). The same posture should be assumed when saying the Qedushah (*O.H.* 95:4). The ʻAmidah is recited silently and should be said with complete devotion. While this applies to all prayers, there should be an added measure of reverence during the ʻAmidah (*O.H.* 98).

The silent devotion should not be interrupted, even to respond to Qaddish or for the Qedushah. Rather, one should keep silent and concentrate on what the reader is saying; this is tantamount to a response. One does not interrupt the ʻAmidah even to be called up to the Torah for an ʻAliyah (*O.H.* 104:7 in Rama).

After completing the benedictions, however, even though one has not said the closing prayer, אֱלֹהַי נְצוֹר, he may respond to all of the above (ibid. 8).

Ḥazarat Hashats

The Talmud deems the recital of the ʻAmidah to be obligatory for everyone in the congregation. Hence each person recites the ʻAmidah privately in silent devotion.

The practice of repeating the ʻAmidah was initiated because without the aid of prayer books, which did not come into use until the eighth century C.E., many people did not know the text of the ʻAmidah and the order of the blessings.

The repetition of the ʻAmidah is designated חֲזָרַת הַשַּׁ״ץ ("the repetition by the reader"), *shats* being the abbreviation for שְׁלִיחַ צִבּוּר, "emissary of the congregation." By listening attentively to the repetition of the ʻAmidah as it is rendered by the "emissary of the congregation," and saying Amein to each blessing, persons unfamiliar with the prayer can fulfill their obligation (*O.H.* 124:1, 4, 6).

Even if everyone in the congregation is familiar with the prayer, we still repeat the ʻAmidah because doing so has become an established custom (*O.H.* 124:3). However, we omit *Ḥazarat Hashats* when the time prescribed for prayer will pass if both ʻAmidahs are recited. In such cases, the reader says the first two benedictions aloud and the congregation recites them silently along with him. The remaining benedictions are said silently. In some present-day synagogues, this procedure is followed more frequently in order to keep the service reasonably short.

At Minḥah, among the Sefardim, the reader and the congregation recite the first three benedictions aloud, the intermediate benedictions are recited silently, and the last three benedictions are recited aloud by the reader only (ibid. in *B.H.* 4).

10. Taḥanun

תַּחֲנוּן, which we translate as "supplication," is the general name for the prayers between the 'Amidah and the concluding prayers. The recital of the 'Amidah concludes the statutory congregational prayer. In past centuries each person was now free to pour out the burden of his heart in silent devotion. Gradually, however, these devotions became formalized.

They now appear in two forms, one brief and the other longer. The longer one, known as "the long וְהוּא רַחוּם," is said on Mondays and Thursdays; the shorter one is said on the other weekdays.

The Briefer Form of Taḥanun

The briefer form consists of the following:

1. וַיֹּאמֶר דָּוִד—a verse from II Samuel 24:14 which forms a fitting introduction to the short confession that follows.
2. רַחוּם וְחַנּוּן—a short confession.
3. יְיָ אַל בְּאַפְּךָ—Psalm 6, without the introductory phrase. In it David pleads with God for mercy, and then feels confident of God's compassion and forgiveness.
4. שׁוֹמֵר יִשְׂרָאֵל—a hymn that continues the plea for compassion. The protection of He who watches over Israel is invoked for the remnant of Israel that faithfully sustains God's unity and glory.
5. וַאֲנַחְנוּ לֹא נֵדַע—a collection of biblical verses. The first is from the prayer of King Jehoshaphat in II Chronicles 20:12; the remaining verses, following in the same vein, are from the Book of Psalms. The first verse expresses our complete dependence upon God. We have already exhausted every form of posture in prayer—sitting, standing, and prostrating (this last, in the part of the Taḥanun before שׁוֹמֵר יִשְׂרָאֵל—see below). Now we can only rely on the mercy of the Lord.

Rules Regarding Taḥanun

There must be no interruption between the 'Amidah and the Taḥanun (*O.H.* 131:1). Hence, the customary half-Qaddish that should have followed the 'Amidah is deferred to after Taḥanun (Munk, *World of Prayer,* 1:167).

When one recites וַיֹּאמֶר דָּוִד and the following confession and psalm, he should rest his brow on his arm (*O.H.* 131:1). This is known as נְפִילַת אַפַּיִם. Originally the worshipper prostrated his whole body, thus symbolically indicating his complete humility before God and committing his destiny entirely into His hands (Hertz, *Daily Prayer Book,* p. 180).

The נְפִילַת אַפַּיִם should be performed while sitting. We use the left arm when not wearing Tefilin, as at the Minḥah service, and the right arm when Tefilin are worn (*O.H.* 131:1, 2).The procedure is reversed by left-handed people.

The נְפִילַת אַפַּיִם is performed only in a place where there is an ark with a Sefer Torah in it (*O.H.* 131:2 in Rama).

The Longer Taḥanun

On Mondays and Thursdays, which are considered יְמֵי רָצוֹן, days of grace on which prayer, as it were, is more readily accepted, the longer supplications are recited (*O.H.* 134:1 in Rama). The special merit of these days is ascribed to the tradition that Moses ascended Mt. Sinai for the second tablets on a Thursday and returned forty days later, on a Monday (*O.H.* 134:1 in *M.D.*).

The longer Taḥanun has seven prayers that form a group of somber, deeply moving elegies and penitential prayers. They are said silently and standing (*O.H.* 134:1).

These are followed by the shorter Taḥanun, except that immediately before שׁוֹמֵר יִשְׂרָאֵל there is another penitential hymn, יְיָ אֱלֹהֵי יִשְׂרָאֵל, speaking of the horrors of persecution and of our need for mercy and help.

The Taḥanun concludes with the half-Qaddish, as do all sections of the service. On Mondays and Thursdays אֶל אֶרֶךְ אַפַּיִם is added after the Qaddish. This too is said standing (*O.H.* 134:1 in *M.A.* 1).

Days on Which Taḥanun Is Not said

Taḥanun is omitted on days of joy and sorrow. On days of joy, these doleful prayers would detract from the joy; on days of sorrow, there is no need to add to sorrow.

Hence we omit Taḥanun on Rosh Ḥodesh, during the whole month of Nisan, on Lag Be'omer, from Rosh Ḥodesh Sivan until and including the day after Shavu'ot, on Tish'ah Be'Av, on the fifteenth of Av (M. *Ta'anit* 4:9; B. *Ta'anit* 30b), on the morning before Rosh Hashanah, from the morning before Yom Kippur until and including the day after Sukkot, on the fourteenth and fifteenth of Adar (in a leap year, on these dates in both Adars), and on the fifteenth of Shevat.

It is also omitted in a house of mourning during the days of Shiv'ah, on a wedding day if the groom is present at services (in some places this also applies to שִׁבְעַת יְמֵי הַמִּשְׁתֶּה, the seven days of festivity that begin with the wedding day), and on the occasion of a Berit if the father, the Sandek, or the Mohel is present (*O.H.* 131:4, 6, 7).

In the Rabbinical Assembly *Weekday Prayer Book,* Yom Ha'atsma'ut (Israel Independence Day—the fifth of Iyar) is also included as an occasion on which Taḥanun is not said.

Avinu Malkeinu

On fast days and during the Ten Days of Penitence, *Avinu Malkeinu* is recited before Taḥanun, every morning and every afternoon, except on Friday afternoons and on the day before Yom Kippur. If Yom Kippur is on a Shabbat, it is said on Friday morning (*O.H.* 102:1; Singer, *Ziv Haminhagim,* pp. 181–82). It is said standing and the ark is opened.

There are textual differences between the *Avinu Malkeinu* said during the Ten Days of Penitence, and the one said on fast days. During the Ten Days of Penitence, the words used are חַדֵּשׁ עָלֵינוּ שָׁנָה טוֹבָה. On fast days בָּרֵךְ עָלֵינוּ שָׁנָה טוֹבָה is substituted. Also, whenever the word כָּתְבֵנוּ is used during the Ten Days of Penitence, the word זָכְרֵנוּ is substituted on fast days.

11. Qeri'at HaTorah

The value and meaning of the Torah to the Jewish people, and, in this case, the relevance of our reading from the Torah in the synagogue, is beautifully expressed in an aggadic interpretation of the verse "and they traveled three days in the wilderness and found no water" (Exod. 15:22). Water, according to the interpreters, is a metaphor for Torah. When the children of Israel went for three days without Torah, they became demoralized. It was decided, therefore, that three days would never be allowed to pass without a Torah reading; hence, its public reading on Mondays, Thursdays, and Saturdays (B. *B.Q.* 82a).

Procedure

On the Sabbath a preliminary prayer is recited as an introduction to the Torah service (see *Soferim* 14:8). אֵין כָּמוֹךָ praises the Lord, who is incomparable, and asks that He deal kindly with Zion. This prayer is omitted on weekdays.

Two prayers are recited at the opening of the ark.

1. וַיְהִי בִּנְסֹעַ is composed of appropriate verses from the Bible.
   a. The verse Moses used to recite when the children of Israel broke camp and the ark of the covenant was carried forward by the Levites (Num. 10:35).
   b. The vision of Isaiah that Torah, i.e., moral instruction, shall go forth out of Zion to the whole world (Isa. 2:3).
   c. A praise to God who has given the Torah to Israel.
2. בְּרִיךְ שְׁמֵהּ is a beautiful prayer taken from the *Zohar* (Parashat vayakhel); it is prefaced in the original with the following explanation: "When the congregation removes the Torah from the ark, the Gates of Mercy are opened and love is awakened on High. At that point this prayer should be recited." (In many prayer books this passage is omitted from the weekday prayers [*O.H.* 282:1 *M.A.*]. In some congregations, it is never said.)

The Torah is then removed, the ark is closed, and the reader and those standing with him face the worshippers. On Sabbaths the reader recites the first verse of the Shema' and the line אֶחָד אֱלֹהֵינוּ, and the congregation responds (*Soferim* 14:9, 10). On weekdays the reader begins with גַּדְּלוּ לַיְיָ while facing the ark, and the worshippers respond with לְךָ יְיָ הַגְּדֻלָּה, while the reader carries the Torah from the ark to the reading table. As he faces the congregation, he leaves by the right side and returns by the left (*O.H.* 134:2). The Torah should always be carried in the right arm (ibid. in Rama).

After the Torah is placed on the reading table and prepared for the reading by removing its wraps and opening it to the proper place, the reader recites an introductory prayer—on weekdays וְתִגָּלֶה, and on Sabbaths and festivals, וְיַעֲזוֹר. He then calls a member of the congregation by his Hebrew name, also mentioning his father's name. This is an עֲלִיָּה, the honor of being called to the reading of the Torah (*O.H.* 139:3 in Rama).

In many present-day synagogues, in order not to prolong the service, or to avoid embarrassing anyone who does not know his Hebrew name, congregants are not called by name. Instead they are given a card with the name of the ʻaliyah for which they will be called. The reader then announces the portion to be read and the designated person steps forward.

In some synagogues, for the same reason, names are called out immediately before the reading of the Torah, not individually but collectively. This custom has the additional merit of making use of the congregant's Hebrew name.

The person called for an ʻaliyah should wear a Ṭalit (*O.H.* 14:3 in M.A. 6).

When the congregant comes up to the bimah (the rostrum where the Torah is read), the reader shows him the place in the scroll where the reading will begin. The congregant touches the place with his Ṭalit, then kisses the portion of the Ṭalit that touched the Torah. Then, taking hold of the two עֲצֵי חַיִּים (*O.H.* 139:11), the rollers of the scroll, and with the scroll open, he recites the first blessing (B. *Meg.* 32a; *O.H.* 139:4 in *B.H.* 2): בָּרְכוּ, the call to worship. The congregation responds with בָּרוּךְ יְיָ הַמְבֹרָךְ. He repeats the congregational response, then recites the *Birkat HaTorah,* or benediction for the Torah (*O.H.* 139:6, 7, 8, 10). The reader then reads the prescribed portion. At the end of the reading, the person called to the Torah kisses the Torah again, closes the scroll, and recites the second benediction. Out of respect to the Torah he does not leave immediately but stays on the bimah until the person following him with the next ʻaliyah has completed his second benediction (*O.H.* 141:7 in *B.H.*).

One who is given an ʻaliyah should always approach the Torah by the shorter way and leave by the longer to indicate his eagerness for the Torah and his reluctance to leave it. If the approach and the descent are of equal distance, he should ascend on the right and descend on the left (*O.H.* 141:7).

Between two ʻaliyot—בֵּין גַּבְרָא לְגַבְרָא—the scroll is kept rolled together and covered with a mantle (*O.H.* 139:5).

Originally, the person who was called read his portion. If he could not chant it properly he was not called (*O.H.* 139:1, 2). Today there is a special reader known as the בַּעַל קְרִיאָה. Some Sefardic communities still maintain the original custom.

It is customary to call a Kohen for the first ʻaliyah, a Levite for the second, and an Israelite for the third and succeeding prescribed ʻaliyot (*O.H.* 135:3). The Talmud comments that this order is מִפְּנֵי דַרְכֵי שָׁלוֹם, "for the sake of peace" (B. *Git.* 59a).

If there is no Kohen present, a person who is not a Kohen may be called. In such cases the reader adds the words בִּמְקוֹם כֹּהֵן to indicate that this congregant was called in place of a Kohen and that no Levite should succeed him (*O.H.* 135:6). If there is no Levite present, the Kohen takes the second 'aliyah as well (*O.H.* 135:8).

On the Sabbath, when more than the prescribed seven 'aliyot may be given, a Kohen or a Levite may be called up after the prescribed seven as אַחֲרוֹן or "last" עֲלִיָּה (*O.H.* 135:10 in Rama).

The Number of People to be Called

Only three 'aliyot are called on Mondays and Thursdays, because these are working days and therefore we should not lengthen the service (*O.H.* 135:1 and *M.A.* 1).

On Sabbath afternoons there are also only three 'aliyot because it is close to the conclusion of the Sabbath (ibid.).

On fast days, Purim, and Ḥanukkah, three 'aliyot are called as well.

On days other than festivals when there is a Musaf service, such as Rosh Ḥodesh and the intermediate days of Pesaḥ and Sukkot, there are four 'aliyot (*O.H.* 135:1 in *M.A.* 1).

On the three pilgrimage festivals—Pesaḥ, Shavu'ot, and Sukkot—and on Rosh Hashanah, there are five 'aliyot.

On Yom Kippur there are six 'aliyot.

On the Sabbath there are seven 'aliyot. These do not include the Mafṭir (the person called to chant the Hafṭarah).

The number of 'aliyot is fixed on all occasions except the Sabbath, when the number may be increased (*O.H.* 135:1, 282:1). Today this is discouraged in many synagogues lest we prolong the service.

On days when there are only three 'aliyot, a minimum of ten verses must be read (*O.H.* 137:1). These must be divided so that at least three verses are read for each 'aliyah (ibid. 2). On Purim, however, only nine verses are read.

Prescribed Readings

The Torah is divided into fifty-four portions. One of these (or sometimes two, depending on a variety of factors) is read each Sabbath.

The Talmud mentions that in Palestine it was customary to complete the reading of the Torah in three years rather than one (B. *Meg.* 29b; Maimonides, *Hil. Tefilah* 13:1; Tigay, "Triennial Confusion"). The use of a triennial cycle has been revived in many Conservative synagogues.

On Sabbath afternoons, at Minḥah, the reader begins where he left off that morning, i.e., the beginning of next week's Sidrah. The same portion is read on the following Monday and Thursday (*O.H.* 135:2).

On fast days, at Shaḥarit and Minḥah, we read וַיְחַל (Exod. 32:11–14, 34:1–10). Three people are called up, and the third at Minḥah chants the Hafṭarah from Isaiah 55:6–56:8.

The only exception to this rule is the morning service of Tish'ah Be'Av, when the Torah reading is Deuteronomy 4:25–40 and the Hafṭarah, also chanted by the person called for the third 'aliyah, is Jeremiah 8:13–9:23.

Each festival and Rosh Ḥodesh has a Torah reading in the morning (except if it falls on a Sabbath, when there is also a Torah reading at Minḥah as usual, and on Simḥat Torah, when there is a Torah reading at Ma'ariv); the reading is always relevant to the day (M. *Meg.* 3:4–6).

When the Torah reading is completed, the half-Qaddish is said (*O.H.* 282:4), except at the Minḥah service, since a half-Qaddish will be said immediately before the 'Amidah (*O.H.* 29:2 in *B.H.* 2).

After the half-Qaddish is recited, the person who will chant the Hafṭarah (the *ba'al mafṭir*) is called. He recites the prescribed blessings before and after the reader's chanting of the concluding verses of the Torah portion. This is done as a sign of respect for the Torah, which enjoys a sanctity higher than that of the prophetic books (*O.H.* 282:4 and *M.D.* 2).

Because the Mafṭir is called to the Torah after the prescribed weekly portion has been completed, the half-Qaddish is recited before the brief Torah portion is read in order to mark the official end of the prescribed Torah reading.

Immediately after the Torah reading is completed, two people are called up, one to lift up the Torah, הַגְבָּהַת הַתּוֹרָה, and the other to roll it together, bind it, and cover it with the mantle, גְּלִילַת הַתּוֹרָה.

The מַגְבִּיהַּ raises the Torah with the scroll open and shows the writing to the congregation. Thereupon the congregation says וְזֹאת הַתּוֹרָה (*O.H.* 134:2 and in Rama). He then sits down while the גּוֹלֵל readies the Torah for its return to the ark.

The Sefardim raise the Torah in similar fashion before the reading of the Torah (ibid.).

Only after the Torah is covered does the Mafṭir chant the Hafṭarah (*O.H.* 147:7). It is preceded by two benedictions and followed by four. When a Hafṭarah is chanted on a weekday, the last benediction is omitted.

On weekdays when Taḥanun is said, the reader says a series of short prayers, יְהִי רָצוֹן, while the Torah is being prepared for its return to the ark. These are prayers for the protection of all Jewish communities, for scholars, and for captives and travelers on land and sea (*Qitsur Shulḥan 'Arukh* 23:27; *Seder Rav 'Amram Ga'on*, ed. Goldschmidt).

If there is no one present who can read the Torah with the proper pronunciation and cantillation, one of the congregants follows quietly in a printed Pentateuch and prompts the reader (*O.H.* 143:2 in Rama and in *B.H.* 3).

The reader should be over thirteen years old (*O.H.* 282:3 in B.H.).

If, due to circumstances beyond control, the Torah reading was omitted on a Monday, it may be included on Tuesday (*O.H.* 135 in *B.H.* 2).

If there is no Torah available, the portion is read aloud from a printed Pentateuch so that the institution of the reading of the Torah will not be forgotten. In such a case no benedictions are recited (*O.H.* 143:2 in *M.A.* 2).

If there is an error in the Torah, it should not be used at the services (*O.H.* 143:4). An error is defined as a missing word, an extra word, or a misspelling that changes the meaning of the word (*O.H.* 143:4 in Rama).

If a vowel letter, such as a *waw* or a *yod*, is missing or is written when not necessary, this does not disqualify the Torah (*M.D.* 2).

When there is a doubt about the identity of a letter, an average child who can read Hebrew is asked to read the verse. If he identifies the letter properly, the Torah may continue in use (*O.H.* 32:11; *Qitsur Shulḥan 'Arukh* 24:5).

If the error is discovered during the Torah reading, another Torah must be taken from the ark, and used for completing the prescribed reading. In such a case, if the error is discovered when at least three verses have already been read, and there are at least three more verses left before the end of the section, the person with the 'aliyah recites the second benediction before the first scroll is put away. The first benediction is then recited again before the reading is started in the second Sefer Torah and the number of 'aliyot is completed in it. Otherwise, we recite the second benediction only after the section is completed in the second scroll (*O.H.* 143:4 in Rama).

If there is no other Torah available, the reading is completed in the first scroll and the required number of people are still called up (*O.H.* 143:4). There is a difference of opinion as to whether benedictions should be recited in such a case (*Qitsur Shulḥan 'Arukh* 24:9).

Return of the Torah to the Ark

After the Torah has been rolled together and covered with its mantle and ornaments, the reader takes it in his right arm, faces the worshippers, and says יְהַלְלוּ. The people respond with הוֹדוֹ, a continuation of the same passage (Ps. 148:13–14). These verses emphasize that the ritual, pomp, and ceremony surrounding the reading of the Torah are not directed to the Torah, but to the glory, the power, and the majesty of the Lord, "for His name alone is exalted" (quoted from Roqeaḥ in *Otsar Hatefilot*).

Before being returned to the ark, the Torah is carried in procession around the bimah. The reader uses the opposite direction than when the Torah was taken out. The congregation chants Psalm 24 on weekdays and Sabbath afternoons and Psalm 29 on Sabbath and holiday mornings. Psalm 24 tells of the opening of the gates so that the King of Glory may enter (B. *Shab.* 30a). Psalm 29 speaks of the voice of God in nature, which is identified with the voice that speaks through the Torah, for, according to a rabbinic interpretation, the word *qol* occurs seven times in this psalm and seven times in the account of the revelation at Sinai (*Yalquṭ Shim'oni, Tehillim* 709; see also Ṭur, *O.H.*, at the end of chap. 284).

Just as when the Torah was taken out, we recited the verse that Moses recited when the ark was carried forward, we now say the verse that Moses spoke when the ark came to rest (Num. 10:36). Now, however, we add verses that mention the ark and the grandeur of the Torah.

The last verse, הֲשִׁיבֵנוּ, is also from the Bible (Lam. 5:21). It is a plea for the future, when a penitent and regenerated people will be restored to its former glory. The ark is then closed.

12. Concluding Prayers

The conclusion of the service begins with אַשְׁרֵי, Psalm 145, with introductory verses (84:5 and 144:15). Because Ashrei sums up the Jewish doctrine of God, the Talmud urges that it be said three times daily (B. *Ber.* 4b). Hence it is said twice at the morning service and once at the afternoon service.

Ashrei is followed by Psalm 20, which forms a fitting transition between the preceding Ashrei and וּבָא לְצִיּוֹן, which follows it. Like Ashrei, it speaks of God, who answers us when we are in distress, and like וּבָא לְצִיּוֹן, it speaks of the redeemer or the anointed: "Now know I that the Lord delivers the anointed" (v. 7). Because it speaks of "the day of trouble," Psalm 20 is generally omitted when Taḥanun is omitted (*O.H.* 131:1 in Rama; see *Peri Megadim* 131:5).

The prayer וּבָא לְצִיּוֹן is woven around the קְדֻשָּׁה and its Aramaic translation (and interpretation) as found in *Targum Jonathan*. This is the third

Qedushah in the morning service (the other two are the Qedushah in the first benediction of the Shema' and the Qedushah in the 'Amidah). According to some opinions, וּבָא לְצִיּוֹן is read in order to fulfill the duty to study the Torah daily (Rashi in B. *Sotah* 49a); hence its Aramaic translation and also its postponement to the Minḥah service on Sabbaths and festivals, when the extended Torah readings satisfy this requirement.

This being the conclusion of the service, the complete Qaddish is said. This Qaddish is appropriate here because it contains the prayer תִּתְקַבַּל, expressing the hope that God will accept our prayers.

This is followed by עָלֵינוּ. Originally, 'Aleinu was said only on Rosh Hashanah. Around the beginning of the fourteenth century it was added to the daily service because its sublime sentiments about the future unity of mankind made it a fitting finale. 'Aleinu should be said while standing. At the words וַאֲנַחְנוּ כּוֹרְעִים, one should bend the knee and bow down (*O.H.* 132:2 in Rama). 'Aleinu is followed by the mourner's Qaddish, קַדִּישׁ יָתוֹם (ibid.).

The Mishnah states that in the Temple a special psalm for each day of the week was recited at the time of the daily morning sacrifice (קָרְבַּן תָּמִיד) (M. *Tamid* 7:4). According to the Talmud, these psalms were chosen because each recalled the events of that day in the week of creation (B. *R.H.* 31a). Some prayer books print the psalm for the day at the end of the service; others, at the beginning, before Pesuqei Dezimrah.

13. Minḥah

The afternoon service, Minḥah, is associated with the daily sacrifice that was offered in the afternoon. The name מִנְחָה is associated with the prayer of Elijah when he challenged the priests of Baal (I Kings 18:29 and 36). There, the afternoon offering was called Minḥah.

The order of the afternoon service on an ordinary weekday is the following:

1. Ashrei followed by half-Qaddish.
2. The silent 'Amidah by the congregation or the individual.
3. The repetition by the reader, חֲזָרַת הַשַּׁ״ץ, with Qedushah by the congregation.
4. The short Taḥanun followed by the complete Qaddish.
5. 'Aleinu followed by the mourner's Qaddish.

The Minḥah service is essentially the 'Amidah, for (except 'Ashrei) there are no other prayers preceding the 'Amidah as in the Shaḥarit and Ma'ariv services, and the reading of the Shema' is restricted to the morning and the night (Deut. 6:7). 'Ashrei is said before the 'Amidah in conformity with the talmudic suggestion that it is proper to praise the Lord before we utter our petitions (B. *Ber.* 32a). At the same time we fulfill the suggestion of the Talmud that we say Ashrei three times a day.

The time for Minḥah, according to the present practice, is between 12:30 P.M. and sunset. The optimum time prescribed was from 3:30 P.M. until an hour and a quarter before nightfall, or 4:45 P.M., assuming the days and nights to be equal in length. (An adjustment of one hour must be made when daylight saving is in effect.)The period between 12:30 and sunset is called מִנְחָה גְּדוֹלָה, "the great Minḥah," while the period between 3:30 and sunset is called מִנְחָה קְטַנָּה, "the small Minḥah" (B. *Ber.* 25b in Rashi). When the pressure of time makes it necessary, one may start at one half-hour past noon and continue until nightfall (*O.H.* 233:1).

We have adopted the latter procedure, but even this practice suggests that Minḥah is unusually significant. We recite the morning prayer before we set out on our daily tasks. Ma'ariv comes at the end of the day, when we have completed these tasks. Minḥah, however, comes during broad daylight while we are taken up with the work of the day. We are asked to lay this aside and pray. Rabbenu Ya'aqov Ba'al Haturim, who lived in the fifteenth century, offered the preceding explanation of the importance of Minhah (Ṭur, *O.H.* 232).

It is customary to recite Minḥah close to nightfall, followed immediately by Ma'ariv, so as not to necessitate coming together again (*O.H.* 233:1).

If the Minḥah service is begun close to nightfall, we follow the practice of reciting the Minḥah 'Amidah without repetition; the reader recites the first two benedictions aloud and the congregation responds at the Qedushah. The reader then says the third benediction aloud and completes the rest silently. The congregation then recites the entire 'Amidah silently from the beginning (*O.H.* 124:2 and 232:1). (This procedure differs from that followed in Shaḥarit. There, no interruption is permitted between *Ge'ulah* and *Tefilah;* the congregation therefore recites the first two benedictions with the reader and continues silently after Qedushah.) In this case *Taḥanun*, too, is omitted (*O.H.* 131 in *M.A.* 9).

Taḥanun is also generally omitted when it is to be omitted the following morning at Shạharit.

The variations that are made in the 'Amidah at certain times and occasions were mentioned above.

On fast days and during the Ten Days of Penitence, אָבִינוּ מַלְכֵּנוּ is recited after the reader has repeated the 'Amidah.

On the Sabbath, and on all fast days, including Yom Kippur, the Torah is read at Minḥah before the 'Amidah. On Yom Kippur and fast days, a Hafṭarah is chanted after the Torah reading.

Only the reader wears a Ṭalit at Minḥah, but he should not make the prescribed benediction when he puts it on (Eisenstein, *'Otsar Dinim Uminhagim,* s.v. Minḥah, p. 238).

If one enters the synagogue and finds the congregation already reciting the 'Amidah, he should join them and say Ashrei after the 'Amidah. If he cannot finish the 'Amidah before Qedushah, he should wait for Qedushah, and then recite the 'Amidah. If this would result in his reciting Minḥah after the prescribed time, he should join the reader and follow him silently through the 'Amidah (*O.H.* 109:1, 2).

14. Ma'ariv

The Ma'ariv service runs parallel to Shaḥarit in that it consists mainly of the Shema', with its accompanying benedictions, and the 'Amidah. It does not, however, have the extensive preliminary and concluding prayers of the morning service.

Ma'ariv is prefaced by two verses (Ps. 78:38 and 20:10) appealing for divine pardon (Maimonides, *Hil. Tefilah* 9:9).

As in the morning, the service begins with a call to prayer, to which the congregation responds. Again, as in the morning, the Shema' is preceded by two benedictions, but unlike the morning, it is followed by two benedictions (B. *Ber.* 11b; *O.H.* 236:1).

The two preceding benedictions correspond in thought and sentiment to the benedictions of Shaḥarit. The first speaks of God as revealed in the recurrent phenomena of nature. The second praises God for revealing Himself to Israel through the Torah. The third again praises God as the redeemer of Israel and for the signs and wonders of the exodus from Egypt.

The rule of linking *Ge'ulah* to *Tefilah* without any interruption also applies to the Ma'ariv service. Yet we have a number of prayers between the third benediction and the 'Amidah. The Talmud explains that these are not an interruption but an extension of the third benediction, גְּאֻלָּה אֲרִיכְתָּא, or "prolonged [benediction of] redemption" (B. *Ber.* 4b). The fourth benediction, which is thus considered an extension of the third, is a prayer for peace and security during the night. A rabbinic comment poetically explains the addition of this prayer.

The Ṭalit, which symbolizes a protecting canopy, is not worn at night. Hence we pray that God spread His protecting tent of peace over us (*Midrash Tehilim* 6:1). It is also explained that this benediction is added to make a total of seven benedictions recited during the daily services, corresponding to the practice of the Psalmist, who said: "Seven times a day do I praise Thee" (Ps. 119:164; *O.H.* 236:1 in *M.D.* 1).

Another benediction, בָּרוּךְ יְיָ לְעוֹלָם, has been inserted beyond the four benedictions prescribed in the Mishnah. It was originally a substitute for the Ma'ariv service and was instituted at a time when synagogues were built in the fields and people were afraid to stay after dark in order to recite the Ma'ariv service at the proper time. This prayer mentions the name of God eighteen times, corresponding to the original number of benedictions in the 'Amidah, and was recited before dark. Later, when Ma'ariv was recited in the synagogue at the prescribed time, the custom of reciting this benediction continued. It is omitted on Sabbaths and festivals, since on these occasions the 'Amidah does not have eighteen benedictions.

After this benediction the reader recites half-Qaddish and the congregation, including the reader, recites the 'Amidah silently. Since Ma'ariv was originally considered to be רְשׁוּת, or optional, there is no repetition of the 'Amidah at this service (B. *Ber.* 27b; Maimonides, *Hil. Tefilah* 1:6).

Taḥanun is not recited at night (*O.H.* 237:1 in Rama); the reader says the whole Qaddish immediately after the conclusion of the 'Amidah. (See below for additions on Saturday night, Purim and the Ninth of Av.)

The concluding prayer is 'Aleinu, which is followed by the mourner's Qaddish as at the other two services.

The time prescribed for the Ma'ariv service is when three stars appear in the sky (*O.H.* 235:1). Today we use sunset as our guide.

Since it has become the established custom to recite the Ma'ariv service immediately after Minḥah, it was permitted even before nightfall lest we burden the congregation with having to gather again for prayer (*O.H.* 233:1). However, it should not be recited too early, i.e., more than an hour and a quarter before sundown, assuming the day and night to be of equal length. This is about one-eighth of the day. The actual time span should be adjusted proportionately when the days are longer or shorter.

In case one does recite the Ma'ariv service before nightfall, he should repeat the Shema' without its accompanying benedictions at the proper time after sunset (*O.H.* 235:1). According to Rashi, one performs that obligation with the Shema‘ recited before retiring (ibid. in *M.A.* 2). Since this concession is made in order to make it possible for one to pray with a minyan, one who prays alone must adhere to the rule that Ma‘ariv be recited only after sunset (*O.H.* 233 in *M.A.* 7).

While it is preferable to recite Ma‘ariv before midnight, one is actually permitted to recite it until dawn (B. *Ber.* 2a; *O.H.* 235:3).

If one enters the synagogue and finds that the congregation has already recited the Shema‘, he should join the congregation with the ‘Amidah and recite the Shema‘ after the ‘Amidah (*O.H.* 236:3).

15. The Qaddish

There are five forms of the Qaddish:

1. קַדִּישׁ דְּרַבָּנָן, the scholars' Qaddish, which was recited after the completion of a study session at the academy (B. *Ber.* 49a; *Soferim* 19:12). This was the original use of the Qaddish; it formed a doxology at the conclusion of the religious discourse of the teacher or preacher, who would in this way dismiss his hearers with a glorification of God and with the Messianic hope for the speedy establishment of His Kingdom. The doxology was in Aramaic because the discourse was in Aramaic, the language spoken by the Jews after the Babylonian exile (see Levi, *Yesodot Hatefilah,* pp. 173 ff., for further study).

   Today Qaddish Derabbanan is still said after parts of the service that have passages from rabbinic literature and after sessions of study in the synagogue.
2. קַדִּישׁ שָׁלֵם, the complete Qaddish, recited by the reader at the end of a service. While the Qaddish was first said mainly in the house of study, it soon passed from the school to the synagogue, where it marked the end of a service.
3. חֲצִי קַדִּישׁ, the half-Qaddish, recited by the reader at the end of a section of the service.
4. קַדִּישׁ יָתוֹם, the mourner's Qaddish (literally "Qaddish of the orphan"), recited by the mourner at the end of the service after ‘Aleinu, and after the recitation of certain psalms, such as the psalm for the day.

5. קַדִּישׁ לְאִתְחַדָּתָא, an expanded form of the mourner's Qaddish recited by some at the cemetery after a burial. With the addition of a paragraph from the Qaddish Derabbanan it is also recited at the conclusion of a talmudic tractate.

The Qaddish, when recited by the reader at the conclusion of a religious service, is a prayer for the establishment of God's Kingdom, when His sovereignty will be acknowledged throughout the earth.

When recited by the mourner, Qaddish is a glorification of God even in times of sorrow. There is no reference to the dead in the mourner's Qaddish. Rather, it mitigates the grief of bereavement by a vision of the Kingdom of God triumphant. The highest test of a person's faith is his ability to praise God at the moment of grief.

The mourner recites the Qaddish for eleven months minus a day (*Y.D.* 376:4 in Rama) so that a full thirty days will pass before the end of the year (Greenwald, *Kol Bo 'al Aveilut,* pp. 369 f.). The eleven-month rule also applies to a leap year, when there are thirteen months (Deutsch, *Duda'ei Hasadeh,* no. 28).

An adopted child has the same status as one born into the family, and therefore is obliged to say Qaddish after the death of his adoptive parent (see below unit 26).

If one does not know the date of the death of the person after whom Qaddish is to be recited, he should choose a day arbitrarily and keep it as the Yahrzeit henceforth (*O.H.* 568 in *M.A.* 20).

The Yahrzeit is always reckoned from the day of death rather than the day of burial (*O.H.* 568:8; *Y.D.* 402:12). If three days or more elapsed between death and burial, according to one opinion, the Yahrzeit is reckoned from the day of burial—but only for the first year. After the first year the Yahrzeit is observed on the day of death (*Y.D.* 402 in Shakh 10; Greenwald, *Kol Bo 'al Aveilut,* p. 371, sec. 13).

It has become customary for people who find it difficult to come to the synagogue regularly to hire another person to recite the Qaddish. While this is permitted (*Y.D.* 376:4), it should be discouraged unless there is no alternative (Greenwald, *Kol Bo 'al Aveilut,* p. 376, sec. 23).

UNIT III

BLESSINGS FOR VARIOUS OCCASIONS

Blessings Before Food
Grace After Meals
Birkhot Hanehenin
Benedictions of Thanksgiving
Washing the Hands Before Meals
The Laws of Mezuzah

Covering the Head

III. Blessings for Various Occasions

The Psalmist said: "The earth is the Lord's and the fullness thereof" (Ps. 24:1). Taking this statement literally, and deeming it appropriate to acknowledge the fruits of the earth as a gift from the Lord, the rabbis instituted the practice of reciting a benediction when partaking of any of them.

Hence, Judaism prescribes blessings to be said before and after eating, as well as before enjoying fragrant aromas, or upon seeing pleasing and awe-inspiring sights. In this way, the satisfaction of a physical craving is raised into the realm of the spirit. Eating becomes a religious act (Hertz, *Daily Prayer Book,* p. 961).

Rabbi Abraham Isaac Kook elaborates this concept, explaining that physical enjoyment fulfills its purpose only if it serves at the same time as a vehicle for moral satisfaction, i.e., the acknowledgment of God in the world. A person who partakes of things without saying a blessing first, and uses them only for the satisfaction of physical needs, reduces the value of the thing enjoyed by not fulfilling its higher purpose in the world (Kook, *'Olat Re'iyah,* 1:345).

He further stresses that holiness rests in man's seeking moral fulfillment even in physical pleasures. When man acknowledges God with a benediction, and thus recognizes God's creation in whatever he enjoys, he will experience a heightened appreciation of God's grace, lovingkindness, and wisdom which are present in all creation (ibid., p. 347).

1. Blessings Before Food

Benedictions are said before eating any food or drinking any beverage. Each benediction begins with the words: בָּרוּךְ אַתָּה יְיָ אֱלֹהֵינוּ מֶלֶךְ הָעוֹלָם. The ending depends on what is to be eaten or drunk.

For all fruit that grows on a tree the benediction is בּוֹרֵא פְּרִי הָעֵץ (*O.H.* 202:1). A tree is defined as a plant whose branches do not perish in the winter, and whose leaves grow from the trunk and from the branches but not from the roots (*O.H.* 203:2). This would exclude the banana tree, whose branches grow anew every year. Dried fruit has the status of ordinary fruit (*O.H.* 202:9 in *B.H.* 19).

For things that grow in or near the earth, such as vegetables, beans, potatoes, or turnips, the benediction is בּוֹרֵא פְּרִי הָאֲדָמָה (*O.H.* 203:1).

For foods which are not the product of the soil, such as meat, fish, milk, and cheese, and for all beverages except wine, the benediction is שֶׁהַכֹּל נִהְיָה בִּדְבָרוֹ (*O.H.* 204:1).

For pastry, the talmudic פַּת הַבָּאָה בְּכִיסְנִין, or "food made from the dough" of any of the five species of grain, kneaded mainly with fat, oil, honey, milk, eggs, or fruit juice, but not with water exclusively, or for dough filled with fruit, meat, cheese, or the like, the benediction is בּוֹרֵא מִינֵי מְזוֹנוֹת (*O.H.* 168:6, 208:2).

For bread, because it is the staff of life, there is a specific individual blessing: הַמּוֹצִיא לֶחֶם מִן הָאָרֶץ (*O.H.* 167:2). Bread is the product of a baking process. If it is then boiled, or boiled before and then baked (as the modern bagel), it still has the status of bread (*O.H.* 168:13–14).

Wine, too, because of its distinction as a beverage, has a special benediction: בּוֹרֵא פְּרִי הַגָּפֶן (*O.H.* 202:1).

Vegetables and fruits that are eaten both raw and cooked have the same benediction in both states (*O.H.* 202:12, 205:1). But for any vegetable that is usually eaten cooked, the benediction when eaten raw is שֶׁהַכֹּל (ibid.). When eaten cooked, the blessing is בּוֹרֵא פְּרִי הָעֵץ for fruit (*O.H.* 202:12) and בּוֹרֵא פְּרִי הָאֲדָמָה for vegetables (*O.H.* 205:1).

When one eats several foods that have different blessings, the more significant food determines the benediction to be recited (*O.H.* 204:12).

At a meal, the benediction for bread at the beginning is sufficient for all the food and beverages that will be served except for the wine, which always commands a benediction for itself (*O.H.* 177:1, 174:1).

If one eats or drinks for medicinal purposes, a benediction should be recited even over forbidden food, which becomes permissible when taken as a medicine (*O.H.* 204:8). If, however, the medicine is bitter and unpalatable, no benediction is necessary (Rama, *O.H.* 208:8).

Once the benediction has been recited, one should eat immediately without conversation or too long a pause (*O.H.* 167:6).

2. Grace After Meals

The Torah, followed by the Talmud, prescribes a benediction after eating as well (Deut. 8:10; B. *Ber.* 35a). There are three forms of the Grace after meals:

a. בּוֹרֵא נְפָשׁוֹת (B. *Ber.* 37a).
b. בְּרָכָה אַחַת מֵעֵין שָׁלשׁ (M. *Ber.* 6:8; B. *Ber.* 37a)
c. בִּרְכַּת הַמָּזוֹן (ibid.)

a. The first and simplest is בָּרוּךְ אַתָּה יְיָ אֱלֹהֵינוּ מֶלֶךְ הָעוֹלָם בּוֹרֵא נְפָשׁוֹת רַבּוֹת וְחֶסְרוֹנָן עַל כָּל מַה שֶׁבָּרָאתָ לְהַחֲיוֹת בָּהֶם נֶפֶשׁ כָּל חָי, בָּרוּךְ חֵי הָעוֹלָמִים.

This benediction is recited over foods which are preceded by the benedictions בּוֹרֵא פְּרִי הָעֵץ, בּוֹרֵא פְּרִי הָאֲדָמָה, or שֶׁהַכֹּל (*O.H.* 207:1).

b. The rabbis gave special consideration to seven species with which the Bible says the Land of Israel was blessed: "For the Lord thy God bringeth thee into a good land . . . a land of wheat and barley, and vines and fig trees and pomegranates; a land of olive trees and honey" (Deut. 8:7–8).

Hence after eating these we recite the בְּרָכָה אַחַת מֵעֵין שָׁלשׁ, "one benediction which has the form of three," i.e., a shortened form of the longer Grace after meals (*O.H.* 208). It is recited after foods which are preceded by the benedictions בּוֹרֵא מִינֵי מְזוֹנוֹת or בּוֹרֵא פְּרִי הַגָּפֶן, and for the fruits enumerated among the seven species: figs, pomegranates, olives, and dates (the honey referred to in this verse is not of bees but of dates).

The shortened form, also known as עַל הַמִּחְיָה, begins with the usual formula and then varies according to what was eaten: after wine, עַל הַגֶּפֶן וְעַל פְּרִי הַגֶּפֶן , after fruit, עַל הָעֵץ וְעַל פְּרִי הָעֵץ, after pastry, עַל הַמִּחְיָה וְעַל הַכַּלְכָּלָה. When two varieties have been eaten, a combination of the above is recited. Then follows a summary of the benedictions in the longer Grace after meals. Before the closing formula, there is an insertion for Sabbaths, Rosh Ḥodesh, or festivals. The closing sentence again indicates what food was eaten.

c. The full *Birkat Hamazon* is recited whenever the meal was preceded by הַמּוֹצִיא לֶחֶם מִן הָאָרֶץ.

Like the benediction before the meal, the Grace afterwards raises the satisfaction of a physical craving into the realm of the spirit. Through the Grace, the family table becomes the family altar. The prayer not only expresses gratefulness for the food, but also binds the participants to their people by expressing gratitude to God for past favors to the people as a whole and hope for its blessed future.

Before the actual Grace is recited an introductory psalm is said. On weekdays we recite Psalm 137, עַל נַהֲרוֹת בָּבֶל, to express our mourning for the destruction of Zion, an event which should not be forgotten even during our meals. On Sabbaths and festivals we recite Psalm 126. In place of the sorrowful remembrance of past tragedies, it is an optimistic vision of the future rebuilding of Zion.

When three or more adults have eaten together and each one has to recite the Grace after meals, a formal invitation to say Grace is said (M. *Ber.* 7:1; *O.H.* 192:1), on the principle that before a sacred function is performed there should be an invitation to the participants to join. This helps establish the proper mood for the ritual. כָּל מִילֵּי דִקְדוּשָּׁה בָּעֵי הַזְמָנָה (*Zohar,* quoted in *M.A.* 1 on *O.H.* 192:1).

This quorum of three is called a *mezuman* from the name of the prayer, *Birkat Zimun* (from the verb זמן, "to invite"). The honor of leading the *mezuman* is accorded by the host to the most distinguished person present (B. *Ber.* 47a). If a Kohen is present he should be given the honor (*O.H.* 201:2); otherwise it is given to a *talmid ḥakham,* a learned person, or to a guest (*O.H.* 201:1–2).

The leader calls the people together with רַבּוֹתַי נְבָרֵךְ, and they respond with יְהִי שֵׁם יְיָ מְבֹרָךְ מֵעַתָּה וְעַד עוֹלָם. The leader responds with בִּרְשׁוּת מָרָנָן וְרַבָּנָן וְרַבּוֹתַי נְבָרֵךְ שֶׁאָכַלְנוּ מִשֶּׁלּוֹ asking the permission of those present to praise God. If ten or more adults are present the word אֱלֹהֵינוּ is added after נְבָרֵךְ. The people respond with בָּרוּךְ שֶׁאָכַלְנוּ מִשֶּׁלּוֹ וּבְטוּבוֹ חָיִינוּ. Again if there are ten or more adults present the word אֱלֹהֵינוּ is added after *barukh.*

Grace itself then follows. It has four benedictions, designated in the Talmud by specific names (B. *Ber.* 48b):

1. *Birkat Hazan* praises God for providing food for all. It represents a public thanksgiving for God's goodness to all humanity.
2. *Birkat Ha'arets.* This benediction has two paragraphs:
   a. נוֹדֶה לְּךָ offers thanks to God for all past favors granted to our people.
   b. וְעַל הַכֹּל summarizes the preceding enumeration of blessings and concludes with a benediction. On Ḥanukkah and Purim the special prayer עַל הַנִּסִּים assigned for these holidays is recited between the two paragraphs.The Rabbinical Assembly *Weekly Prayer Book* contains an עַל הַנִּסִּים for Yom Ha'atsma'ut as well.
3. בּוֹנֵה יְרוּשָׁלָיִם. While the previous benedictions were expressions of gratitude for past favors, this is a prayer for the future flowering

of Zion and Jerusalem and for the continued blessing of God. It concludes with וּבְנֵה יְרוּשָׁלַיִם, a prayer for the rebuilding of Jerusalem.

On the Sabbath a special prayer, רְצֵה, is inserted before וּבְנֵה. On Rosh Ḥodesh and on festivals יַעֲלֶה וְיָבֹא is inserted before וּבְנֵה, making appropriate reference to the day.

4. הַטּוֹב וְהַמֵּטִיב. This benediction was added around 137 C.E. after the revolt of Bar Kokhba. According to the Talmud, it was instituted when the Roman authorities relented and granted permission to bury the "slain of Betar," the last Jewish stronghold, whose inhabitants were put to the sword (B. *Ber.* 48b).

The conclusion of this benediction, לְעוֹלָם אַל יְחַסְּרֵנוּ, marks the end of the statutory Grace after meals. However, as with the other services, other prayers were added in time, such as the series of short prayers beginning with הָרַחֲמָן. The texts of these vary, but all versions contain a prayer for the host and for those present, a prayer for the coming of Elijah the prophet, and a prayer that we may be worthy to see the days of the Messiah.

This passage includes the words מַגְדִּל יְשׁוּעוֹת מַלְכּוֹ. On Sabbaths, festivals, and Rosh Ḥodesh, the word מַגְדִּל is changed to מִגְדּוֹל. Various explanations for this have been given (*O.H.* 189 in *M.A.* 1). The verse in question comes from Psalm 18:51, where מַגְדִּל is used. However, in II Samuel 22:51, where Psalm 18 is repeated, the word מִגְדּוֹל is read. It has been suggested that the original text of the Grace had מַגְדִּל, but that someone added the parenthetical phrase ובש״ב מגדול indicating that the reading is מִגְדּוֹל in II Samuel. This was later misread as an abbreviation for וּבְשַׁבָּת, and it was assumed that we are to say מִגְדּוֹל on the Sabbath. Whatever the reason, this has become the established custom, and as usual in such cases, it is easier to reinterpret than to abolish.

The passage ends with עֹשֶׂה שָׁלוֹם, the prayer for peace, which has special significance in the *Birkat Hamazon.* On the verse "And I will give peace in the land" (Lev. 26:6), Rashi comments: "And if you shall say, So there is food and drink; but without peace what good are they? Therefore, with the expression of thanks for food we also pray for peace, which will make it possible for us to enjoy these blessings" (*Maṭeh Mosheh,* quoted in Landau, *Tselota d'Avraham,* 2:556).

The final passage, יְראוּ אֶת יְיָ, is a collection of biblical verses. These are said silently out of consideration for any poor people who may be present at the table. The passage states: "They who fear the Lord know not want" (Ps.

34:10) and "I have been young and now I am old, yet have I not seen a righteous man forsaken, nor his seed begging for food" (Ps. 37:25). Since this is an ideal and a hope rather than a fact, it is better said in a hushed voice.

Since it was felt that the full Grace after meals was a bit too long, many prayer books have a shortened form alongside the full text. One of them is quoted in *O.H.* 192 in B.H. 1, and it contains all the essential elements required by the Talmud. The shortened Grace may be used when brevity is desired. The United Synagogue has adopted one, with additions in English, for general use in Conservative synagogues.

3. Birkhot Hanehenin

It is quite obvious that within the ambit of the enjoyment of God's blessings, we must include enjoyments that issue via all the senses. In the Siddur edited by Rabbi de Sola Pool for the Sefardic communities, the benedictions are therefore arranged according to the senses used, i.e., taste, smell, sight, hearing, and touch (see also Landau, *Tselota d'Avraham,* p. 596). We have already enumerated the blessings which are enjoyed by means of the sense of taste. We shall now proceed to the others.

Professor Heschel distinguishes between the approach to nature of the practical secularist and that of the religiously oriented person. Today the prevalent approach is to look at nature as presenting a challenge to us; we seek to discover its secrets, and we use this knowledge in order to exploit it. The religious person looks at nature with a wonder born of awe. His reaction is that of worship and gratitude. This sense of wonder is often expressed with benedictions. These involve mainly the senses of sight and hearing (see Heschel, *God in Search of Man,* pp. 95–99).

Thus, on seeing a rainbow one says the benediction זוֹכֵר הַבְּרִית וְנֶאֱמָן בִּבְרִיתוֹ וְקַיָּם בְּמַאֲמָרוֹ, "who remembers the covenant, is faithful to His covenant, and keeps His promise"; on seeing the wonders of nature, such as lightning or high mountains, עוֹשֶׂה מַעֲשֵׂה בְרֵאשִׁית, "who has made the creation"; on seeing the ocean (for one who does not see it frequently), שֶׁעָשָׂה אֶת הַיָּם הַגָּדוֹל, "who has made the great sea"; on seeing beautiful trees or animals, שֶׁכָּכָה לוֹ בְּעוֹלָמוֹ, "who has such as these in His world"; on seeing a man learned in the Torah, שֶׁחָלַק מֵחָכְמָתוֹ לִירֵאָיו, "who has imparted of His wisdom to them that fear Him"; on seeing a man of great intellectual distinction, שֶׁנָּתַן מֵחָכְמָתוֹ לְבָשָׂר וָדָם, "who has imparted of His wisdom to flesh and blood"; on seeing an exalted ruler, שֶׁנָּתַן מִכְּבוֹדוֹ לְבָשָׂר וָדָם, "who has given of His glory to flesh and blood."

For the sense of hearing we have the following benedictions: on hearing thunder, שֶׁכֹּחוֹ וּגְבוּרָתוֹ מָלֵא עוֹלָם, "whose strength and might fill the world"; on hearing bad tidings, דַּיַּן הָאֱמֶת, "the true judge"; on hearing good tidings, הַטּוֹב וְהַמֵּטִיב, "who is good and dispenses good."

For the sense of smell we have the following: on smelling fragrant spices, בּוֹרֵא מִינֵי בְשָׂמִים, "who creates divers kinds of spices"; on smelling fragrant herbs or flowers, בּוֹרֵא עִשְׂבֵּי בְשָׂמִים, "who creates odorous plants"; on smelling fragrant trees or aromatic bark, בּוֹרֵא עֲצֵי בְשָׂמִים, "who creates fragrant wood"; on smelling fruits, הַנּוֹתֵן רֵיחַ טוֹב בַּפֵּרוֹת "who gives a goodly scent to fruit" (see Dvorkes, *Siddur Minḥat Yerushalayim,* pp. 321–31).

In addition to the above benedictions, there are also benedictions of thanksgiving and benedictions recited before the performance of a mitswah. We shall discuss these benedictions when we treat the respective subjects. At this point, we shall mention only those most frequently recited.

4. Benedictions of Thanksgiving

Whenever we experience something new, such as eating fruit for the first time in its season, the advent of a holiday, or a joyous occasion in the family, we recite שֶׁהֶחֱיָנוּ וְקִיְּמָנוּ וְהִגִּיעָנוּ לַזְּמַן הַזֶּה. This benediction is either added to the benediction already required, as before eating a fruit, or is recited by itself.

Another benediction which is a prayer of thanksgiving is the בִּרְכַּת הַגּוֹמֵל, which expresses gratitude to God after having come through danger unharmed. According to the Talmud there are four who should recite this benediction: one who has made a sea journey, one who has traveled through a desert, one who was seriously ill and recovered, and one who was imprisoned and released (B. *Ber.* 54b; *O.H.* 219:1).

The common denominator of the four is that the life of a person was endangered. We therefore generalize and say that anyone who has passed through a harrowing experience that has endangered his life should recite this benediction (*O.H.* 219:9). We extend this today, for example, to one who has survived an automobile accident, or has traveled across the ocean by air.

It has become the custom to recite this benediction after the second Torah blessing when one is called up for an 'aliyah (*O.H.* 219:3). The person reciting the benediction says: הַגּוֹמֵל לְחַיָּבִים טוֹבוֹת שֶׁגְּמָלַנִי כָּל טוֹב, "who grants favors to the undeserving, that He has shown me kindness"; and the congregation responds: מִי שֶׁגְּמָלְךָ כָּל טוֹב הוּא יִגְמָלְךָ כָּל טוֹב סֶלָה, "He who has shown you kindness, may He deal kindly with you forever" (*O.H.* 219:2).

In the category of benedictions recited before the performance of a ritual, we shall mention here only two: the benediction recited at the washing of the hands before meals, and the one recited before affixing a Mezuzah to the doorpost of one's home.

5. Washing the Hands before Meals

We have already mentioned that a religious ritual lifts a biological act from the realm of the physical and raises it to the realm of the spiritual. Hence, the benedictions before eating.

The rabbis made a distinction between casual eating, אֲכִילַת עַרְאַי, and a regular meal, סְעוּדַת קֶבַע (B. *Yoma* 79b). Lest the distinction become arbitrary, they based it on the eating of bread and the recital of הַמּוֹצִיא. Bread is the staff of life, and therefore the eating of bread determines whether the meal is considered casual or regular. A meal at which bread is eaten must be preceded by the washing of the hands.

Since this washing of the hands is not a hygienic measure (because one has to wash even if his hands are clean), but rather a religious ritual, it must be done in a specified way.

The washing should be performed with a vessel, כְּלִי, and it should result from human effort, כֹּחַ גַּבְרָא. Hence, holding one's hands under an open faucet with the water already running is to be avoided (*O.H.* 159:7). One should fill a vessel with the water, hold it in one hand, and pour it over the other, and then do the same with the second hand.

The vessel should not be chipped or broken (*O.H.* 159:1 in *M.D.* ad loc.).

After both hands are washed, one should recite the benediction אֲשֶׁר קִדְּשָׁנוּ בְּמִצְוֹתָיו וְצִוָּנוּ עַל נְטִילַת יָדָיִם as he proceeds to dry them.

6. The Laws of Mezuzah

The biblical commandment "And ye shall write them upon the doorposts of thy house and upon thy gates" (Deut. 6:9) is the source for the practice of affixing a Mezuzah to the doorposts of houses.

The Mezuzah is a piece of parchment on which the two first paragraphs of the Shema' (Deut. 6:4–9, 11:13–21) are written. The parchment is rolled, put into a small case, and affixed to the right-hand doorpost. A small opening is left in the case where the word Shadai on the back of the scroll is visible. Some have interpreted שדי to be the initials of the words שׁוֹמֵר דַּלְתוֹת יִשְׂרָאֵל, "guardian of the doors of Israel" (Ṭur, *Y.D.* 288, in *D.M.* 3).

The Mezuzah (literally: "doorpost") is therefore one of the mitswot that serve as reminders. Thus the Talmud says: "He who has Tefilin on his head and arm, Tsitsit on his garment, and a Mezuzah on his door will surely not sin" (B. *Men.* 43b). Maimonides also emphasizes that one should diligently perform the mitswah of Mezuzah because each time one enters or leaves his house, he will encounter the name of God, be reminded of His love, and turn from the vanities of this world to choose the righteous path (Maimonides, *Hil. Mezuzah* 6:13).

The Mezuzah should be affixed to every door (except that of the bathroom), even if there be many rooms in the house, even if the room has more than one door, and even if only one of these doors is normally used. As long as the door can be used as an entrance and an exit, a Mezuzah should be affixed to the doorpost (*Y.D.* 286).

It should be affixed to the doorpost on the right-hand side of a person entering the room (*Y.D.* 289:2).

Before affixing the Mezuzah the following benediction is recited: אֲשֶׁר קִדְּשָׁנוּ בְּמִצְוֹתָיו וְצִוָּנוּ לִקְבּוֹעַ מְזוּזָה.

Even if one affixes more than one Mezuzah at the same time, one benediction is sufficient (*Y.D.* 289:1).

Only an entrance that has two doorposts and a lintel over them needs a Mezuzah (*Y.D.* 287:1 in Rama).

The doors of a synagogue do not need a Mezuzah because it is not used as a permanent dwelling (*Y.D.* 286:10). If there is an apartment in the synagogue, however, the main doors do require a Mezuzah (*Y.D.* 286:3).

The Mezuzah should be affixed within the upper third of the doorpost, and should be attached diagonally, with the upper end tilted toward the house or inside the room (*Y.D.* 289:6). If the doorpost is not wide enough to hold the Mezuzah in a diagonal position, it may be affixed in a vertical position (*Y.D.* 289 in Eisenstadt, *Pitḥei Teshuvah* 9).

The obligation of affixing a Mezuzah rests not on the owner but on the tenant. Hence, if one rents an apartment he must affix the Mezuzot to the doors (*Y.D.* 286:22, 23).

Only a permanent resident has to affix a Mezuzah. If one lives in a house thirty days, he is considered a permanent resident (*Y.D.* 286:22).

In our day the Mezuzah has become a means of Jewish identification and a symbol of Jewish unity and solidarity all over the world (see Landau, *Tselota d'Avraham,* p. 632).

7. Covering the Head

The theoretical approach to the regulations regarding the covering of the head will lead us into a controversial field. There are sources that make covering the head by a Jewish male a special practice of the pious, מִדַּת חֲסִידוּת, and there are sources indicating that it is mandatory for all. There are also differing opinions regarding when the custom started and how widespread it was. Proof is brought that in some countries the custom was unknown, while in others it was limited to the times when one was occupied with the performance of sacred acts, such as prayer, the study of sacred literature, or the performance of a religious ritual (see Krauss, "Covering the Head"; Lauterbach, "Worshipping with Covered Heads," in Schwartz, *Responsa of the CCAR,* pp. 208–218, reprinted in Lauterbach, *Studies in Jewish Law, Custom, and Folklore,* pp. 225 ff.; Eisenstein, *Otsar Dinim Uminhagim,* s.v. *Gilui Rosh; Encyclopedia Talmudit,* s.v. *Gilui Rosh*).

Of one thing we can be sure, however; in the generations preceding ours, the general practice among traditional Jews was to have the head covered at all times.

The reasons given were twofold. First, it was the Jewish way of showing reverence and respect (B. *Qid.* 31a; Maimonides, *Hil. De'ot* 5:6). Secondly, uncovering the head was the custom of the Gentiles; hence, it must be avoided by Jews (see *Encyclopedia Talmudit,* 6:117). Covering the head thus served as a means of identification and a barrier against assimilation.

While the practice was uniform in the generations preceding ours, it now runs the gamut from those Orthodox who retain the old practice of having the head covered at all times to those Reform who discard the custom entirely.

Our practice should be—

a. To cover the head when in the sanctuary of a synagogue (see *O.H.* 91 in *M.A.* 3 and *Peri Megadim,* and in *Eishel Avraham,* ibid., n. 3).
b. To cover the head when praying and when studying or reading from our sacred literature (*O.H.* 282:3).

c. To cover the head when performing a ritual.
d. To cover the head when eating, since eating is preceded and followed by a benediction. (Some follow the custom of certain Jewish communities in Germany and cover their heads during the benedictions before and after the meal but not during the meal itself.)

UNIT IV

THE SABBATH (I): LITURGY

Preparation for the Sabbath
Lighting the Sabbath Candles
Evening Services
Friday Night at Home
Late Friday Night Services
Sabbath Morning
The Musaf Service
The Sabbath Noon Meal
Sabbath Afternoon
Minḥah
Se'udah Shelishit
Evening Service
Havdalah Service

IV.
The Sabbath (I)

One of the great tragedies of Jewish life in America is the loss of the Sabbath. Jewish life will not be restored to good health unless the Sabbath regains its sanctity and its central place.

The decline of the Sabbath, at least in America, began through force of circumstance; our parents and grandparents had to work on the Sabbath because of the economic pressures of the Western world. In order to hold a job they had to work on the Sabbath. What was first done בְּאוֹנֶס (by necessity) later was done בְּרָצוֹן (voluntarily). Today people neglect the Sabbath not because economic conditions force them to do so, but by habit and because of the increasing secularization of life.

The secular world also recognizes the value of a day of rest, but it has changed the Sabbath into a weekend. The Sabbath and a weekend are quite different, however (see Pieper, *Leisure: The Basis of Culture*). What the High Holy Days are for us today the Sabbath used to be for all Israel, because it was observed as meticulously as we observe Yom Kippur. The records show that secular holidays and weekends are marked by the greatest amount of crime, drunkenness, lewdness, and accidental deaths. When a holiday loses its religious connotation, it can become a source of evil.

At best the purpose of a weekend is rest and change. In the case of the Sabbath, however, the Bible enjoins: "Remember the Sabbath day to keep it holy" (Exod. 20:8); and our liturgy repeats: "a day of rest and holiness hast thou given unto thy people." The day of rest must also become a day of holiness.

Holiness is not a flight from the world into fasting and contemplation. The prophet wrote: "And thou shalt call the Sabbath a delight" (Isa. 58:13). This is not attained simply by the cessation of our weekday routine. The prophet continues: "and shalt honor it, not doing thy wonted ways nor pursuing thy business nor speaking thereof." The rabbis interpret this to mean: "that thy speech on the Sabbath shall not be as thy speech on the weekdays (B. *Shab.* 113a).

To experience the Sabbath properly, there must be a transfiguration. Professor Heschel's words are an elaboration of this thought. "He who wants to enter the holiness of the day must first lay down the profanity of clattering commerce, of being yoked to toil. . . . Six days a week we seek to dominate the world, on the seventh we try to dominate the self" (Heschel, *The Sabbath,* p. 13).

Professor Morris Levine, of blessed memory, once compared the traditional Sabbath to the perfect harmony of a work of art. Any erasure would mar the harmony. All parts of the Sabbath must be preserved if it is to retain its unity as a work of art.

1. Preparation for the Sabbath

Psychologically, it is necessary to prepare for a moment of heightened experience if it is to be fully appreciated. Hence, the approach of the Sabbath should be anticipated with acts of preparation. We are told in the Talmud how many of the sages personally prepared for the Sabbath.

The sage Shammai began his preparations on the first day of the week. If he saw a choice article of food, he immediately set it aside for the Sabbath. If, subsequently, he found one that was even finer, he set the latter aside for the Sabbath and used the other one beforehand (B. *Beṭ.* 16a).

Some sages even went so far as to help with the preparation of the food or with the cutting of the wood (B. *Shab.* 119a). Hence the ruling that even persons of affluence, who have many servants to do their bidding, should reserve some act of Sabbath preparation for themselves (*O.H.* 250:1).

The more obvious preparatory steps, such as washing and dressing in a special way, should certainly be taken before the Sabbath (B. *Shab.* 113a). Even today, when people are normally well groomed and well dressed, special attention should be given to this in honor of the Sabbath (*O.H.* 260:1).

Before the approach of the Sabbath, one should make sure that his pockets are emptied so that he will not carry things that should not be carried on the Sabbath.

2. Lighting the Sabbath Candles

"When all work is brought to a standstill, the candles are lit. Just as creation began with the word, 'Let there be light!' so does the celebration of creation begin with the kindling of lights. It is the woman who ushers in the joy and sets up the most exquisite symbol, light, to dominate the atmosphere of the home" (Heschel, *The Sabbath*, p. 66).

It is a mitswah to light candles on the eve of the Sabbath, before sunset, at home in the room where the meal is taken.

The commandment applies to men as well as to women, but it devolves more upon women because women are more associated with the home (B. *Shab*. 31b; Maimonides, *Hil. Shabbat* 5:3; *O.H*. 263:2, 3). The candles should be lit no later than eighteen minutes before sunset.

Customs vary as to the number of candles to be lit. Some light two candles, one for זָכוֹר and one for שָׁמוֹר, the words with which the fourth commandment begins in the two versions of the Decalogue (Exod. 20:8, Deut. 5:12). Some light seven, a favorite number in religious symbolism; some start with two and add one each time there is an addition to the family. The prevalent custom is to light two at all times (*O.H*. 263:1).

Upon lighting the candles the woman covers her eyes with her hands and recites the benediction אֲשֶׁר קִדְּשָׁנוּ בְּמִצְוֹתָיו וְצִוָּנוּ לְהַדְלִיק נֵר שֶׁל שַׁבָּת. It is customary to add a silent prayer for the health and welfare of the family (*O.H*. 263:5 in *B.H.*).

Covering the eyes is a gesture of prayer which helps in the attainment of Kawwanah, concentration. The reason for it here, however, is slightly more complicated. Normally a benediction is recited before the act is performed. This benediction marks the beginning of the Sabbath, and during the Sabbath we are forbidden to create light. Hence the woman lights the candles first, but in order to satisfy the requirement that the benediction be recited before the act, she covers her eyes so as not to see the light. When she removes her hands and sees the light, the benediction is considered to have preceded the act (Rama on *O.H*. 263:5). Though the lighting of candles is permitted on festivals, the same procedure is followed to avoid differentiation.

The candlesticks used in the kindling of the Sabbath candles should not be removed from the table or touched during the Sabbath (*O.H*. 263:14).

With the lighting of the candles, even if done earlier than required, the Sabbath has begun for the woman who lit them, and she must observe the Sabbath rules from then on (*O.H*. 263:10). The other members of the family are not subject to this restriction, and may do work until the official beginning of the Sabbath (*O.H*. 263:14). There are those who maintain that the woman may make a reservation that the lighting of the candles does not prevent her from doing certain work until the Sabbath has officially begun (*O.H*. 263:10).

The problem of attempting to specify the precise time at which the Sabbath begins and ends is complex. One of the causes of this complexity is the varying definitions of בֵּין הַשְּׁמָשׁוֹת. This term is usually taken to designate the period between the astronomical sunset and the appearance of stars.

There are differences of opinion about the length of this period, but in any case before בֵּין הַשְּׁמָשׁוֹת it is day and after בֵּין הַשְּׁמָשׁוֹת it is night. As far as the period itself is concerned, however, since it may be either day or night, we follow the principle of סְפֵיקָא דְאוֹרַיְיתָא לְחוּמְרָא (in a doubt concerning a biblical law we follow the stricter measure), and בֵּין הַשְּׁמָשׁוֹת is always considered as part of the Sabbath, both on Friday and on Saturday. Therefore, the Sabbath begins with the astronomical sunset on Friday and ends with the appearance of the stars on Saturday night.

There is, however, the additional complication of a תּוֹסֶפֶת שַׁבָּת (addition to the Sabbath) and of מוֹסִיפִין מֵחוֹל עַל הַקּוֹדֶשׁ (we add from the profane to the holy) (B. *R.H.* 9a). We are commanded to add to the Sabbath by beginning before the astronomical sunset and ending later than the end of בֵּין הַשְּׁמָשׁוֹת. There is an opinion that this תּוֹסֶפֶת is optional (*O.H.* 261:2), but the prevalent view holds that it is obligatory. However, the duration of this period is in dispute, and opinions range from a כָּל שֶׁהוּא (minimum) to a full hour, hence the variety of practices in regard to the termination of the Sabbath.

But the core of the problem lies in the attempt to determine the exact duration of בֵּין הַשְּׁמָשׁוֹת. The most accepted determination is the time it takes to walk three-quarters of a mile (1,500 cubits)—or about eighteen minutes (*O.H.* 261:2; B. *Shab.* 34b). By this reckoning, the sign of night is the appearance of three stars in the sky. The Talmud suggests that they must be of medium size (B. *Shab.* 35b), and the *Shulḥan 'Arukh* stipulates that they must be together and not scattered about the sky (*O.H.* 293:2). These signs are quite vague, however. Leo Levi, a physicist and also a talmudic scholar, drew up a chart which shows the times at which stars appear after sunset. He suggests that there are actually three separate times at which stars can be said to appear, depending on whether the observer is a trained astronomer, an ordinary person, or someone between these two (Levi, "Twilight in Halakha," in *Breuer Jubilee Volume,* p. 260; and also *"Zeman ben Hashemashot," Noam* V:213). It is Levi's opinion that the maximum time which can elapse between the astronomical sunset and the appearance of the third star is twenty-five minutes (on the day of the summer solstice and for the Temperate Zone).

From these considerations, it would seem, then, that the minimum period one should wait after the astronomical sunset before terminating the Sabbath, on the longest Sabbath of the year, is twenty-five minutes (i.e., forty-three minutes after the time the candles were lit on Friday).

The time given here is local time, and the hour is שָׁעָה זְמַנִּית, i.e., a proportional hour. A proportional hour is one-twelfth of the daytime period: e.g., where there are sixteen hours of daytime between sunrise and sunset, a proportional hour equals one and one-third hours, or eighty minutes, and a minute is eighty seconds. Thus, when we say that the Sabbath ends eighteen minutes after sunset (which, according to Levi's calculation, could be a maximum of twenty-five sixty-second minutes), it will depend on the length of the day. The length of the day depends on the time of year and the longitude of the area. To find out when twilight ends, take the area's sunrise and sunset times from the local newspaper. Determine the length of the day from these figures, and divide that by twelve to find the length of a proportional hour. For example, if sunrise is at 5:00 A.M. and sunset is at 8:00 P.M., the day is fifteen hours long. Fifteen hours divided by twelve is one and one-quarter hours, or seventy-five minutes, and a minute equals seventy-five seconds. To put it in formulaic form: a proportional hour = $x/12$, x = the length of the day.

For those who wish to wait longer, we can add כָּל הַמַּרְבֶּה הֲרֵי זֶה מְשֻׁבָּח "Whoever increases, is to be praised," or כָּל הַמַּחְמִיר תָּבוֹא עָלָיו בְּרָכָה "Whoever is strict, may blessing come to him."

3. Evening Services

While the woman ushers in the Sabbath with the lighting of the Sabbath candles, the man does so with the evening prayer.

We begin with the Minḥah service, which is still a weekday prayer and hence is the same as on every other day of the week; no Taḥanun is recited, however.

The Sabbath evening service itself begins with Ma'ariv. It is customary on Friday night to start the Ma'ariv service earlier than on weekday evenings (*O.H.* 267:2).

During the sixteenth century, the Kabbalists in Safed initiated the practice of Kabbalat Shabbat, inaugurating the Sabbath with prayer before the Ma'ariv service. This custom spread and is now the established procedure for the Friday night service.

The incentive for the Kabbalists came from an old personification of the

Sabbath as a bride. Solomon Schechter has written: "The Sabbath was a living reality, to be welcomed after six days absence with that expectant joy and impatient love with which the groom meets the bride" (Schechter, *Studies in Judaism II*, p. 228). This is based on what the Talmud tells about Rabbis Ḥanina and Yannai. Rabbi Ḥanina wrapped himself in a robe on the eve of the Sabbath and said: בּוֹאוּ וְנֵצֵא לִקְרַאת שַׁבָּת הַמַּלְכָּה "Come let us go out to greet the Sabbath queen." Rabbi Yannai attired himself on the eve of the Sabbath and said: בּוֹאִי כַלָּה בּוֹאִי כַלָּה (B. *Shab*, 119a; B. *B.Q.* 32a).

This personification found its formal expression among the Safed Kabbalists, who chose Psalms 95–99 and Psalm 29 to express it. These psalms speak of creation rejoicing before the Lord. They thus remind us of the six days of creation, culminating in the Sabbath.

The hymn לְכָה דוֹדִי, which follows, is from the same period. It was written by the mystic Shlomo Halevi Alkabetz and incorporates the phraseology of the Talmud. It is the climax of the liturgical personification of the Sabbath.

When the last stanza of לְכָה דוֹדִי is reached, the congregation turns and faces the entrance to the place of worship. This is a gesture of welcome to the Sabbath reminiscent of the practice of actually going out to meet the Sabbath. It has also become a custom at this point in the service to welcome and comfort any mourners who have suffered bereavement during the preceding week. All mourning is suspended with the approach of the Sabbath, which officially begins when the congregation has completed לְכָה דוֹדִי. It is the custom for the mourners to wait in the anteroom and be ushered in after the conclusion of לְכָה דוֹדִי. When the mourners enter they meet a congregation facing them who offer the condolence: הַמָּקוֹם יְנַחֵם אֶתְכֶם בְּתוֹךְ שְׁאָר אֲבֵלֵי צִיּוֹן וִירוּשָׁלָיִם (May the Lord comfort you among the other mourners for Zion and Jerusalem).

Much older is the practice of reciting Psalm 92, which follows. It is the psalm that the Levites recited while the *tamid* offering was being brought on Saturday (B. *Tamid* 33b). When the Sabbath coincides with, or immediately follows, one of the festivals, the evening service begins with this psalm.

In some communities it is customary to recite בַּמֶּה מַדְלִיקִין, the second chapter of the Mishnah of Tractate *Shabbat*, immediately before בָּרְכוּ (*O.H.* 270:1). The origin of this practice is that it delayed the Ma'ariv service a bit so that latecomers would not have to stay alone in the synagogue to complete their prayers. Synagogues used to be located in the fields outside the city, and going home alone was fraught with danger (*O.H.* 270:1 and *Kol Bo* 37b in the name of the Geonim). This chapter was chosen because it contains laws dealing with the approach of the Sabbath (*O.H.* 270.1 in *M.A.*).

In other synagogues the passage is said after Qiddush; at this point it does not delay the beginning of the Sabbath.

The Qeri'at Shema' of the Ma'ariv service is identical with that of the weekdays with the following exceptions. The introductory וְהוּא רַחוּם is omitted because it is not in keeping with the spirit of the Sabbath (see *O.H.* 268:11 in *B.H.*). The conclusion of הַשְׁכִּיבֵנוּ is different; the weeknight version ends with the benediction שׁוֹמֵר עַמּוֹ יִשְׂרָאֵל לָעַד. Since the Sabbath itself is, in a deeply religious sense, Israel's guardian, the form of the benediction is altered to express the peace which falls upon the Jewish house with the evening of the seventh day. Hence we say: וּפְרוֹשׂ עָלֵינוּ סֻכַּת שְׁלוֹמֶךָ . . . הַפּוֹרֵשׂ סֻכַּת שָׁלוֹם עָלֵינוּ וְעַל כָּל עַמּוֹ יִשְׂרָאֵל וְעַל יְרוּשָׁלָיִם (*O.H.* 267:3 and ibid. in Ṭur). Since Gaonic times וְשָׁמְרוּ has also been added, as if to say that if we observe the Sabbath, the Sabbath will protect us (*'Arukh Hashulḥan, O.H.* 267:7). We also omit the passage בָּרוּךְ יְיָ לְעוֹלָם אָמֵן וְאָמֵן because this passage, with its eighteen sentences, was originally compiled as a substitute for the eighteen benedictions of the weekday 'Amidah. Since the Sabbath 'Amidah consists of seven and not eighteen benedictions, and since another substitution, מָגֵן אָבוֹת, is provided later in the service, the passage is properly omitted on Friday night.

The 'Amidah has the same opening and closing benedictions as on weekdays. The thirteen intermediate benedictions are omitted because they are prayers of supplication and induce sadness, which is not in consonance with the Sabbath. Instead we have a benediction that expresses the sanctity of the Sabbath (*O.H.* 268:11 in *B.H.* 1). We must note, though, that this benediction varies with each of the three Sabbath services, while on festivals the same benediction is recited at each of the services.

The Ṭur gives an interesting explanation for this variation. The three forms were established to correspond to three Sabbaths: אַתָּה קִדַּשְׁתָּ of Ma'ariv for the Sabbath of Creation, as the content of the prayer would indicate; יִשְׂמַח מֹשֶׁה of Shaḥarit for the Sabbath of the granting of the Torah (there is general agreement that the Torah was given on a Sabbath); and the אַתָּה אֶחָד of Minḥah, for the Sabbath of the future (Ṭur, *O.H.* 292). (This corresponds to the three basic categories of Franz Rosenzweig in his *Star of Redemption:* creation, revelation, and redemption.)

After the 'Amidah, וַיְכֻלּוּ is recited aloud by the congregation while standing (*O.H.* 268:6). This prayer was first added only on festivals that coincide with the Sabbath, when וַיְכֻלּוּ is omitted in the 'Amidah. In order not to create distinctions between one Sabbath and another, it became the uniform practice for all Sabbaths (B. *Pes.* 106a; Tosafot, s.v. זוכרהו).

The prayer that follows is an abbreviated form of the 'Amidah which contains the substance of the seven benedictions (*O.H.* 268:8). It was not, however, a substitute for the 'Amidah, but rather a chant by the reader which gave the latecomers a chance to finish their prayers with the rest of the congregation (B. *Shab.* 24b; Rashi and Mordecai).

The prayer is concluded with Qaddish and followed by the Qiddush. Although the Qiddush is recited at home before the meal, it became the custom to recite it in the synagogue as well for the sake of wayfarers, who lodged in the synagogue premises and had their meals there (B. *Pes.* 101a). This was in the days when every synagogue had a הֶקְדֵּשׁ (hostel) attached to it. The custom remained even after the reason for its establishment ceased (*O.H.* 269:1). Today, Qiddush in the synagogue serves as a reminder for those who do not say Qiddush at home.

The service is then concluded with 'Aleinu and Qaddish as on weekdays.

It has become the custom in most synagogues to chant אֲדוֹן עוֹלָם or יִגְדַּל as the concluding hymn of the service.

4. Friday Night at Home

It is customary for parents to bless their children either at the conclusion of the service in the synagogue or upon returning home. For boys the blessing is יְשִׂמְךָ אֱלֹהִים כְּאֶפְרַיִם וְכִמְנַשֶּׁה. For girls the blessing is יְשִׂמֵךְ אֱלֹהִים כְּשָׂרָה, רִבְקָה, רָחֵל, וְלֵאָה. For boys and girls both, יְבָרֶכְךָ יְיָ וְיִשְׁמְרֶךָ, יָאֵר יְיָ פָּנָיו אֵלֶיךָ וִיחֻנֶּךָּ, יִשָּׂא יְיָ פָּנָיו אֵלֶיךָ, וְיָשֵׂם לְךָ שָׁלוֹם.

Special hymns are recited at home before the recitation of the Qiddush. The first one is שָׁלוֹם עֲלֵיכֶם, based on the talmudic statement that two angels accompany every Jew when he returns home from Friday evening services (B. *Shab.* 119b).

Then the verses from the Book of Proverbs describing the ideal wife are recited (Prov. 31:10–31). Again the connection between the sacredness of the Sabbath and the blessedness of the home is highlighted. The woman is the mainstay of the home.

After these preliminaries the Qiddush follows. It should be recited where the meal will be eaten, and over wine (*O.H.* 273:1, 10). If there is no wine, the Qiddush is recited over the חַלּוֹת (*O.H.* 289:2; ibid. in *M.A.; Ḥayyei Adam* 6:9).

After Qiddush the hands are washed and the Motsi is recited. In some places the hands are washed before the Qiddush and the Qiddush is not considered an interruption (*O.H.* 271:12).

At the beginning of the Sabbath, the table should be covered with a tablecloth. Two Ḥallot are always used, corresponding to the לֶחֶם מִשְׁנֶה, the double portion of manna that the children of Israel gathered on Fridays when they were in the desert (Exod. 16:22).

The Ḥallot should be covered with an appropriate cloth during the recitation of the Qiddush (*O.H.* 271:9).

When reciting the Motsi, one should place both hands on the two Ḥallot, then lift them and slice one of them (*O.H.* 274:1).

The Talmud already mentions that it was the custom during the Sabbath meal to speak דִּבְרֵי תוֹרָה at the table and to sing songs of praise (B. *Meg.* 12b). It has become customary to sing זְמִירוֹת, special Sabbath hymns, and also to discuss sacred texts. We certainly should not allow any conversation that will mar the sacredness of the day (*O.H.* 306, 307).

At the conclusion of the meal בִּרְכַּת הַמָּזוֹן is recited with the variations for the Sabbath. The introductory psalm is not Psalm 137, which tells of the desolation of Zion, but Psalm 126, which speaks of the restoration of Zion and is, therefore, more appropriate for a day of joy.

Before וּבְנֵה יְרוּשָׁלַיִם a special prayer for the Sabbath, רְצֵה, is introduced (B. *Ber.* 49a). The prayer concludes with the hope for the restoration of Zion and thus וּבְנֵה יְרוּשָׁלַיִם makes a fitting sequel.

Before the final הָרַחֲמָן, a special הָרַחֲמָן for the Sabbath is added. In the last הָרַחֲמָן the word מִגְדּוֹל is substituted for מַגְדִּיל.

5. Late Friday Night Services

Because of economic conditions and other factors in American life, it became difficult for most Jews to attend the Friday evening services at the prescribed time (sundown). To salvage some sense of the sanctity of the Sabbath and some awareness of this service, it became customary to hold Sabbath services later in the evening.

The late Friday night service has many merits. The most important, obviously, is that a large number of people are enabled to attend who otherwise would not have any chance to participate in the Sabbath evening service. It also provides an opportunity for instruction through a discourse or a sermon. Many people have formed the habit of setting aside Friday nights for services at the synagogue.

While this measure was dictated by necessity, it has now become an institution with roots in our synagogue life. Of late, dissident voices have been raised suggesting that the institution is at best a mixed blessing. The standing objection that קַבָּלַת שַׁבָּת is at sundown, and not an arbitrary hour decided by the ritual committee of the synagogue, is still cogent. The late service mars the traditional concept of ushering in the day with a public service. Furthermore, we have always emphasized that the value of the Sabbath is enhanced by the family spending the evening together at home. This is curtailed by the services later in the evening.

At present the old economic reasons are not as urgent as they were in the past. With the shorter working day it may become possible to reinstate the service at its proper time.

6. Sabbath Morning

The Sabbath morning procedures are identical with those of a weekday morning as far as ablutions and the prayers said upon rising are concerned. Since the pressure of daily occupations is absent on the Sabbath, the morning service starts later and is longer than on weekdays (Ṭur, *O.H.* 281; Rama on *O.H.* 281:1). This adds to the solemnity of the day as well.

The first addition comes in the פְּסוּקֵי דְזִמְרָא, where a number of psalms are inserted between הודו and יְהִי כְבוֹד. The choice of psalms has been variously interpreted. A medieval commentator finds in them a reference to the ten words (*Avot* 5:1) with which the world was created (*Abudraham Hashalem*, p. 162). A modern commentator suggests that they recall the three fundamental themes of the Sabbath: the creation of the world, the exodus from Egypt, and the Sabbath to come (Munk, *World of Prayer*, 2:21 f.).

The Ashkenazic and Sefardic rites differ on the choice of psalms as well as on the position of בָּרוּךְ שֶׁאָמַר. The Ashkenazim begin פְּסוּקֵי דְזִמְרָא with בָּרוּךְ שֶׁאָמַר in order to conform to the pattern of beginning and ending with a *berakhah*. The Sefardim prefer to give latecomers a chance to hear the *berakhah* and also suggest that since these psalms were later additions, they should be placed before בָּרוּךְ שֶׁאָמַר (*Abudraham Hashalem*, p. 164).

On weekdays Pesuqei Dezimrah concludes with יִשְׁתַּבַּח. On the Sabbath the complete Birkat Hashir (B. *Pes.* 118a), as found in the Passover Haggadah, is included (Ṭur, *O.H.* 281). It follows logically after the Song of the Red Sea since it praises God for the redemption from Egypt.

It is customary for the cantor to begin with שׁוֹכֵן עַד on the Sabbath, with

הָאֵל on the pilgrimage festivals, and with הַמֶּלֶךְ on the High Holy Days. "On the Sabbath, as *Nishmat* is concluded, the reader begins with *Shokhen 'Ad*, celebrating God's eternity as the Creator. On Festivals he begins with *Hael*, acclaiming Him as the omnipotent Protector of His people; and on Rosh Hashannah and Yom Kippur he begins with *Hamelekh*, proclaiming Him as Sovereign and Judge" (Arzt, *Justice and Mercy*, p. 42).

The *Barekhu* is followed by an expanded form of the first benediction before the Shema'. הַמֵּאִיר לָאָרֶץ, which in the weekday service follows immediately after the opening benediction, is preceded by expansions upon the word הַכֹּל, with which that benediction concludes, and which form a proper introduction to הַמֵּאִיר.

הַמֵּאִיר does not conclude with the weekday acrostic but rather with a series of verses beginning with אֵין כְּעֶרְכְּךָ, referring to the world to come, the days of the Messiah, and the resurrection of the dead. Then follows the hymn אֵל אָדוֹן, which is an expanded form of the weekday acrostic אֵל בָּרוּךְ גְּדוֹל דֵּעָה, (*Zohar*, *Terumah* 132a). This is followed by לָאֵל אֲשֶׁר שָׁבַת, a meditation that belongs to a group of seven hymns, one for each day of the week, recounting the work of creation completed on that day. In these hymns, each day proclaimed the praises of God in the words of the psalm set aside for that day (Hertz, *Daily Prayer Book*, p. 431). From this point to the 'Amidah, the service is identical with that of the weekday.

The 'Amidah follows the pattern of the Ma'ariv 'Amidah. The first and last three benedictions are the same as on weekdays. For the intermediate thirteen benedictions, one, which is different in each service, is substituted (see above). The core of the benediction is a biblical quotation concerning the Sabbath. This is preceded by an introductory paragraph, יִשְׂמַח מֹשֶׁה. While Moses is related to every commandment in the Torah, the rabbis ascribed to him a closer affinity to the commandment of the Sabbath. According to the Talmud, God said to Moses: "I have a precious gift in my treasure house called the Sabbath, and I want to give it to Israel" (B. *Shab.* 10b). The biblical core is followed by וְלֹא נְתַתּוֹ, a commentary on it telling us that the Sabbath is a peculiarly Jewish institution (based on *Mekhilta*, ed. Lauterbach, 3:199).

The concluding part of this segment, from עַם מְקַדְּשֵׁי שְׁבִיעִי through זֵכֶר לְמַעֲשֵׂה בְרֵאשִׁית, is part of a prayer beginning with יִשְׂמְחוּ. The Sefardic rite includes יִשְׂמְחוּ in every 'Amidah except Minḥah. In the Ashkenazic rite it is absent also in the Ma'ariv 'Amidah, incomplete in Shaḥarit, but complete in Musaf.

The last paragraph is the same as in Ma'ariv. In some *siddurim*, a slight textual variation is found. The Ma'ariv text reads וְיָנוּחוּ בָהּ; the Shaḥarit וְיָנוּחוּ בוֹ; and the Minḥah וְיָנוּחוּ בָם. The grammatical rule demands בָהּ since *Shabbat* is the antecedent; all new prayer books have בָהּ. According to some commentators these variations were not accidental, and some unusual explanations are suggested (*O.H.* 268 in *M.A.* 3).

In the *Ḥazarat Hashats,* the Qedushah is enlarged with several additional passages, some of which are mentioned in the older sources as part of the weekday Qedushah. Again, the availability of more time led to the addition. אָז בְּקוֹל corresponds to the sentences in *Birkat Yotser* that begin with וְהָאוֹפַנִּים. The passage מִמְּקוֹמְךָ is peculiar to this Qedushah and is reserved for the Sabbath. The Levush explains it as follows. On the Sabbath men strive to reach God with much greater fervor than they do during the rest of the week. Moreover, it was on the Sabbath Day that the Lord, long ago, took His place on His sovereign throne. The abode of His holiness is unknown even to the angels, and they say: Regardless of where it may be, let it be blessed. Even so, we also pray that the glory of God, wherever its abode may be, may shine over us, and that God's Kingdom may speedily arrive so that at long last the greatness and glory of God, of which the Qedushah sings, will become a living reality on earth as well (quoted by Munk, *World of Prayer,* 2:39 f.).

For the reading of the Torah and the prayers before and after, see above in the discussion of the daily prayers (unit 2).

7. The Musaf Service

On Sabbaths, festivals, and Rosh Ḥodesh, sacrifices were offered in the Temple in addition to the regular daily sacrifices brought every morning and evening. These additional sacrifices, prescribed in the Bible (Num. 28 and 29), followed the regular morning sacrifice (B. *Yoma* 33b). Since our prayers correspond to the sacrificial services, this additional service (Musaf) was introduced on the above days to correspond to the additional sacrifices.

The Musaf service should follow immediately after Shaḥarit, and at any rate should not be delayed more than one hour after mid-day (*O.H.* 281:1; B. *Suk.* 53a). It should, therefore, follow immediately upon the return of the Torah to the ark. A number of prayers have been added, however, between the conclusion of the Hafṭarah and the return of the Torah to the ark.

The first יְקוּם פֻּרְקָן is a prayer for the scholars and students of the Palestinian and Babylonian academies. The second יְקוּם פֻּרְקָן is a prayer for the congregation as a whole. מִי שֶׁבֵּרַךְ is a prayer for the congregation with special mention for those who labor for the welfare of the community and its institutions. הַנּוֹתֵן תְּשׁוּעָה (or any other version) is a prayer for the government. It is based on Jeremiah's admonition that we seek the peace of the city to which God has caused us to be carried away and that we pray unto the Lord for it, for its welfare is our peace (Jer. 29:7), and upon the admonition of the Mishnah: "Pray for the welfare of the government, since but for it, men would swallow each other alive" (*Avot* 3:2). Originally, the prayer included such requests as, "Put compassion into the king's heart and into the heart of his counselors and nobles, that they may deal kindly with us and with all Israel," harking back to the days when the fate of the Jew depended on the whim of the king and his counselors. In some places these fears are still present. In the democracies, however, the wording has been changed to fit the situation.

בִּרְכַּת הַחֹדֶשׁ is a prayer for the new month. It is recited here if a new month of the Jewish calendar begins during the following week (*O.H.* 417:1 in *M.A.*), except before Tishre (for which see below).

When the new month was fixed by observation, its actual arrival was declared by the Sanhedrin, and this declaration was accompanied by blessings and praises (*Soferim* 19:9). When the calendar was fixed, it became customary to announce the date of the beginning of the new month in the synagogue on the preceding Sabbath, when a larger congregation was present.

As was the case with the Sanhedrin's declaration, ours is accompanied by prayer. We use the following:

יְהִי רָצוֹן. Rav, the Babylonian scholar, said this prayer every day after concluding his morning prayers. It was adopted for this occasion by adding the introductory sentence שֶׁתְּחַדֵּשׁ עָלֵינוּ אֶת הַחֹדֶשׁ הַזֶּה.

מִי שֶׁעָשָׂה נִסִּים. This is probably based on the prayers recited when the Sanhedrin proclaimed the new month. The connection between the new month and the Messianic hope expressed in the prayer is the feature of renewal. Just as the moon appears to herald a new month, so Israel hopes to behold the coming of the Messiah, heralding a new ingathering of all Israel united in fellowship (Abrahams, *Companion to the Authorised Daily Prayer Book*, p. 161).

The precise day of the beginning of the new month is then announced, followed by יְחַדְּשֵׁהוּ, a most appropriate closing prayer.

The entire prayer for the new month is said standing, as was the custom when the Sanhedrin announced the new month (*O.H.* 417:1 in *M.A.*). When

מִי שֶׁעָשָׂה נִסִּים is about to be recited, the reader takes the Torah in his arms and holds it until the end of *Birkat Haḥodesh.*

On the Sabbath before the month of Tishre the prayer for the new month is not said. The main purpose of these prayers is to remind the people of the arrival of a new month so that they may perform the observances associated with Rosh Ḥodesh, but such a reminder is unnecessary before Rosh Hashanah. It may be of interest to recall another reason, which must now be relegated to the realm of folklore but which was very much accepted in the past. The prayer was omitted "to confuse Satan." Since Satan would be eager to act as the accuser when the children of Israel were judged on Rosh Hashanah, it was preferable not to remind him of the date with *Birkat Haḥodesh.*

In some synagogues, it is the custom at this point to recite אֵל מָלֵא רַחֲמִים, a prayer for the dead with special reference to the deceased whose Yahrzeit occurs during the week (*O.H.* 284:7). The prevalent custom is to recite it only four times a year: on Yom Kippur, Shemini 'Atseret, the last day of Pesaḥ, and the second day of Shavu'ot.

אַב הָרַחֲמִים, a prayer for the martyrs of Israel, was composed soon after the First Crusade, during which many Jewish communities in Western Europe were annihilated. It is omitted on Sabbaths when *Birkat Ḥaḥodesh* is recited (except during the 'Omer period) and on occasions when, on a weekday, Taḥanun would not be recited.

Ashrei. See the discussion of the weekday prayers (unit 2).

After Ashrei the Torah is returned to the ark. For the accompanying prayers, see unit 2.

As in the 'Amidah for each of the Sabbath services, the first and last three benedictions of the Musaf 'Amidah are the same as on the weekdays. The middle benediction is constructed in the same pattern as in the Sabbath 'Amidah of Ma'ariv and Shaḥarit. The core is a biblical passage, וּבְיוֹם הַשַּׁבָּת (Num. 28:9), which describes the sacrifices brought in the Temple on the Sabbath in addition (*musaf*) to the regular daily sacrifices.

The Musaf 'Amidah is preceded by an introductory prayer, תִּכַּנְתָּ, and followed by two concluding prayers, יִשְׂמְחוּ and אֱלֹהֵינוּ.

תִּכַּנְתָּ is a *piyyuṭ* with an inverse alphabetical acrostic, תשר״ק. The first part speaks of the past; the second, יְהִי רָצוֹן, of the future.

In the *Ḥazarat Hashats*, the Qedushah of Musaf has its own variations; there is also a difference between the Ashkenazic and Sefardic rites. The Ashkenazim begin with נַעֲרִיצְךָ and the Sefardim with כֶּתֶר (see Ginzberg, *Geonica,* 2:49, for full discussion of various texts).

The Musaf Qedushah is unusual in that it includes the responses שְׁמַע (Deut. 6:4), לִהְיוֹת לָכֶם לֵאלֹהִים (Num. 15:41), and אֲנִי יְיָ אֱלֹהֵיכֶם (Num. 15:41)—the opening and concluding verses of the Shema'. It has been suggested that these were added sometime between 438 and 518 C.E., when the Persian rulers of Babylonia banned the recitation of the Shema' because its proclamation of monotheism contradicted the dualistic tenets of the Zoroastrian religion. Persian officials were stationed in the synagogues during the morning service to make sure the Shema' was omitted. After they left, it was recited as part of the Musaf Qedushah. The practice continued even after the persecution had ceased (*Abudraham Hashalem,* p. 176; Ginzberg, *Ginze Schechter* 2:524; Arzt, *Justice and Mercy,* p. 172).

After the *'Amidah* the concluding prayers are:

אֵין כֵּאלֹהֵינוּ. This hymn sounds like a nursery rhyme but has a sublime message. The original text started with מִי כֵּאלֹהֵינוּ, followed by the response אֵין כֵּאלֹהֵינוּ. Then came the call נוֹדֶה לֵאלֹהֵינוּ and the responses בָּרוּךְ אֱלֹהֵינוּ and אַתָּה הוּא אֱלֹהֵינוּ (*Seder Rav 'Amram Ga'on,* ed. Goldschmidt, p. 39; *Maḥzor Vitry,* ed. Hurwitz p. 176, par. 193). This is a much more logical arrangement than the present one, which was motivated by the desire to have the initial letters of the first three stanzas spell out the word אָמֵן, followed by the next two stanzas, the first words of which are בָּרוּךְ אַתָּה—the first two words of all benedictions. Ein Keloheinu thus forms an acrostic which serves as an aid to the memory so that none of the stanzas will be omitted (*Abudraham Hashalem,* p. 184).

Another explanation is based on the suggestion that one should recite a hundred benedictions a day. The Sabbath and festival 'Amidahs have only seven benedictions instead of the nineteen of the daily 'Amidah. The present arrangement of Ein Keloheinu helps fill in the lack (*Siddur Rashi,* ed. Buber, Ot Alef, p. 3; *Maḥzor Vitry,* ed. Hurwitz, p. 106, par. 134).

The last verse, אַתָּה הוּא שֶׁהִקְטִירוּ, is not part of the hymn but is rather an introduction to פִּטּוּם הַקְּטֹרֶת, which follows. The Sefardic rite does not have this conclusion, but substitutes the verse from Psalm 102:14, which, though it does not mention incense, is still an appropriate transition to the incense passage.

פִּטּוּם הַקְּטֹרֶת is a passage from the Talmud (B. *Ker.* 6a) listing the constituents of the incense that was burnt every morning and evening in the Temple (Exod. 30:7–9). In many synagogues today it is omitted.

הַשִּׁיר שֶׁהַלְוִיִּם is a quotation from the Mishnah (*Tamid* 7:4) telling of the psalms that were recited each day of the week in the Temple, culminating with the psalm for the Sabbath day, and ending with the noble comment that this is also the psalm and song for the hereafter, for the day which will be wholly a Sabbath, and will bring rest through life everlasting.

אָמַר רַבִּי אֶלְעָזָר is an aggadic passage from the end of the first tractate of the Talmud (B. *Ber.* 64a). It is recited so that the rabbinic Qaddish may follow (*O.H.* 54:3 in *M.A.* 3; for an explanation of the quote, see Eits Yosef in *Otsar Hatefilot,* ad loc.). In the Sefardic rite and in some Ashkenazic prayer books it is preceded by a short aggadic passage from the end of the last tractate of the Talmud (B. *Nid.* 73a). It cannot be a coincidence that these are the concluding remarks of the first and last tractates of the Babylonian Talmud.

These passages are followed by the rabbinic Qaddish, 'Aleinu, the mourner's Qaddish, and the psalm of the day, followed again by the mourner's Qaddish. In some synagogues the psalm for the day is said toward the conclusion of Birkhot Hashaḥar before Psalm 30. It is thus in the Rabbinical Assembly's *Sabbath Prayers.*

שִׁיר הַכָּבוֹד—The Hymn of Glory. In some congregations, it was customary to recite this hymn, attributed to Rabbi Judah of Regensburg (R. Yehudah Heḥasid; 12th–13th cent.), at the weekday morning service (Baer, *'Avodat Yisrael,* p. 250). Rabbinic authorities felt it was too lofty for weekdays and recommended that it be recited only on Sabbaths and festivals (*Levush* 133). Others (Solomon Luria, Jacob Emden, the Vilna Gaon) limited it to festivals only. This explains the variety of customs.

The mourner's Qaddish follows.

אֲדוֹן עוֹלָם concludes the service. In most synagogues today the services end with a benediction or a concluding prayer by the rabbi.

8. The Sabbath Noon Meal

On Sabbath mornings, as on every other day, one should not eat prior to the morning prayer. Liquids are permitted, however, or a light breakfast, if required for reasons of health.

The procedure at the Sabbath noon meal is the same as on Friday night. Qiddush is recited over wine before the meal. The text, though called *Qiddusha Rabba,* the Great Qiddush, is much shorter than the Qiddush recited on Friday night. Essentially, the Qiddush is the benediction over wine (B. *Pes.* 106a); appropriate biblical quotations were added later, and they are recited today before the benediction over the wine (*O.H.* 289:1). It is now customary to recite the Qiddush of the morning meal over other alcoholic beverages as well (*O.H.* 289:2 in *Sha'are Teshuvah*). In such cases, the blessing שֶׁהַכֹּל is substituted for בּוֹרֵא פְּרִי הַגָּפֶן.

This is followed by the washing of the hands, the Motsi over לֶחֶם מִשְׁנֶה as on Friday night, with Zemirot, *divrei Torah*, and *Birkat Hamazon* (*O.H.* 289:1).

9. Sabbath Afternoon

On Sabbath afternoons during the winter months, beginning with the first Sabbath after Sukkot and ending with the Sabbath before Pesaḥ, it is customary to recite Psalms 104 and 120–134, the fifteen psalms that begin with the words שִׁיר הַמַּעֲלוֹת and are therefore termed "Songs of Ascent." In the summer months, beginning with the Sabbath after Pesaḥ and ending with the Sabbath before Rosh Hashanah, we study *Pirqei Avot.*

The recitation of Psalm 104 starts on the Sabbath when, in the morning, we read the creation story. Since it is also a description of the מַעֲשֵׂה בְרֵאשִׁית (work of creation), it is most appropriate at this time. The fifteen psalms that follow also relate to creation according to rabbinic legend (B. *Suk.* 53a f.; *Levush*, *O.H.* 669).

Pirqei Avot begins with: "Moses received the Torah at Sinai." The only festival that comes during the summer months is Shavu'ot, which is זְמַן מַתַּן תּוֹרָתֵנוּ (the season of the giving of our Torah), hence the practice of studying this material during these months (Ṭur, *O.H.* 292).

10. Minḥah

Minḥah begins with Ashrei as on weekdays. It is followed by וּבָא לְצִיּוֹן, which was omitted in the morning service, and the half-Qaddish (*O.H.* 292:1).

Just before the Torah is taken out, the verse וַאֲנִי תְפִלָּתִי (Ps. 69:14) is recited. An unusual reason is given for this practice. The verse preceding it in Psalms is: "They that sit in the gate talk of me, and I am the song of the drunkards." The contrast between the song of the drunkard and the one who prays to the Lord calls attention to the way Jews celebrate the Sabbath. Whereas other peoples celebrate their festivals with vulgar hilarity and excessive drinking, we have come to the end of a day of celebration, sober, in a prayerful mood, and ready to listen to the teaching of the Torah (Ṭur, *O.H.* 292; *O.H.* 292:1 in *M.A.* 1).

The prayers at the taking out and the returning of the Torah are the same as on weekdays.

The portion read is from the Sidrah of the following week. This is the practice even on a Sabbath that comes during a festival. At Minḥah we never read from the portions reserved for the festival, as we do in the mornings (*O.H.* 292:1). Three people, and no more, are called to the reading.

The 'Amidah follows the pattern of the other services. The first and last three benedictions are the same as during the week. The middle benediction has two passages. The second is the same as in the 'Amidah of the other services. The first is specifically for Minḥah. It speaks of the unique relation between God, Israel, and the Sabbath, and is based on a Midrash which teaches that these three testify for each other: God and Israel testify that the Sabbath is a day of rest; Israel and the Sabbath testify that God is one; God and the Sabbath testify that Israel is unique (Ṭur, *O.H.* 292). The Qedushah is the same as the one recited on weekdays.

Immediately after the *Ḥazarat Hashats,* before the Qaddish, three verses beginning with צִדְקָתְךָ are said—all three from the Psalms (Pss. 119:142, 71:19, 36:7). These are in the nature of the צִדּוּק הַדִּין said at a funeral. According to legend, Joseph, Moses, and David died on the Sabbath (Ṭur, *O.H.* 292; *B.H.* ad loc., quoting *Zohar, parashat terumah*).

The order in which we say these verses is the reverse of the order in which they appear in the Book of Psalms. It is suggested that this order represents an ascending scale of justice and a corresponding increase in the praise of God (Ṭur, *O.H.* 292 in *Perishah*). Also, in this order the passage ends with the name of God, forming a proper introduction to the Qaddish that follows (Abrahams, *Companion to the Authorized Daily Prayer Book*, p. 171). The Sefardic rite follows the order found in the Psalms (Ṭur, *O.H.* 292). It is also suggested that these verses may have been introduced as a replacement for the Taḥanun that is said at this point on weekdays (Abrahams, ibid.), and they are omitted when, if it were a weekday, Taḥanun would not be said.

The Qaddish is then recited, followed by 'Aleinu and the mourner's Qaddish as in the weekday prayers.

11. Se'udah Shelishit

It is customary to have a light meal between Minḥah and Ma'ariv. The practice is based on the talmudic provision that one should eat three meals on the Sabbath (B. *Shab.* 117b). This meal is usually taken on the synagogue premises so that the worshippers need not go home and have to return for the Ma'ariv service (Ṭur, *O.H.* 291, quoting Maimonides).

No Qiddush is recited, but the Motsi is said over bread (*O.H.* 291:4). When this is inconvenient, any food will do for this meal.

As with the other meals, the Se'udah Shelishit is accompanied by Zemirot. Since it comes at the end of the Sabbath, special pensive tunes have developed, expressing sorrow at the imminent departure of the Sabbath. Among the Kabbalists and the Ḥassidim, the Se'udah Shelishit assumed great significance with elaborate *divrei Torah* and lengthy Zemirot. In many of our synagogues the practice has been revived and given a new significance. The meal is concluded with the appropriate *Birkat Hamazon.*

12. Evening Service

The time for the Ma'ariv service at the conclusion of the Sabbath has been discussed above. The service is the regular weekday Ma'ariv service, except that אַתָּה חוֹנַנְתָּנוּ is inserted in the middle of the fourth benediction of the 'Amidah (*O.H.* 294:1). It stresses the distinction between the holy and the profane, light and darkness, Israel and the heathen nations, the Sabbath and the workdays, and continues with a prayer that the coming week may bring peace, freedom from sin, and attachment to the fear of God.

In order to prolong the Sabbath and postpone the official beginning of the weekdays, it is the custom in some synagogues to recite psalms before the Ma'ariv service. Also, just as the Sabbath was welcomed with song, so is it sped on its way with psalmody. Psalms 144 and 67 have been accepted as particularly appropriate. The praise of God as the One "who teacheth my hands to war and my fingers to fight" is suitable to the imminent renewal of the weekday struggle; after the Sabbath calm comes the intrusion of the world, against which the psalm proceeds to invoke God's protecting hand; the joys of a full garner and overflowing sheepfold are attained by the labor which is once more man's lot.

Psalm 67, which follows, has the same theme. It, too, suggests the thought of a prosperous harvest: "The earth had yielded its increase." Here again, we stress the working week with its hopes of prosperity. But for the psalmist, prosperity lifts the eye from earth to heaven; hence this psalm is a prayer for salvation in the widest sense, not for Israel alone, but for the world. Note also the beginning of the psalm, "God be gracious unto us and bless us," taken from the priestly benediction (Abrahams, *Companion to the Authorized Daily Prayer Book,* p. 180)

After the 'Amidah וִיהִי נֹעַם and וְאַתָּה קָדוֹשׁ are recited. וִיהִי נֹעַם consists of the last verse of Psalm 90 and the whole of Psalm 91. The first verse is an invocation for blessings upon the work we are to resume. Psalm 91 is a plea for protection from the dangers of life, and therefore is appropriate to this moment. It is also suggested that this was the hymn with which Moses blessed the children of Israel when they had completed the construction of the Tabernacle (Ṭur, *O.H.* 295).

וְאַתָּה קָדוֹשׁ was a glorification that followed the reading of passages from the Prophets or Hagiographa (Ginzberg, *Geonica* 2:299), hence its use after the psalms on Saturday night. Some scholars suggest that there used to be a period of study in the evening after the recitation of these psalms. The sessions were concluded with וְאַתָּה קָדוֹשׁ. Now, even though the study session does not take place, the saying of וְאַתָּה קָדוֹשׁ has remained (Elbogen, *Der jüdische Gottesdienst,* p. 121). The first few sentences, beginning with וּבָא לְצִיּוֹן, are omitted on Saturday nights because גְּאֻלָּה (redemption) does not take place at night (Ṭur, *O.H.* 295).

When a festival on which work is forbidden occurs during the coming week, both וִיהִי נֹעַם and וְאַתָּה קָדוֹשׁ are omitted, because there are no שֵׁשֶׁת יְמֵי הַמַּעֲשֶׂה (the six working days) in such a case (*O.H.* 295, n. 2 in *M.D.*; Ṭur, *O.H.* 295).

After וְאַתָּה קָדוֹשׁ, קַדִּישׁ תִּתְקַבַּל is recited. In some congregations this is followed by וְיִתֶּן לְךָ, which consists of a scriptural text giving assurance of divine blessing, deliverance, consolation, and peace (Abraham b. Nathan of Lunel, *Sefer Hamanhig, Shabbat,* sec. 75). The passage before the last is a talmudic discourse on humility. The last passage, Psalm 128, speaks of the dignity of labor. The Talmud (B. *Ber.* 8a) quotes this psalm in praising the one who lives by the labor of his hands. These passages were selected for meditation at the conclusion of the Sabbath because of their appropriateness.

Havdalah is recited in the synagogue for those who do not have the wherewithal to do it at home (*O.H.* 295:1). The first paragraph, הִנֵּה אֵל יְשׁוּעָתִי, consisting of introductory verses, is omitted in the synagogue.

The service is concluded with 'Aleinu and the mourner's Qaddish.

13. Havdalah Service

Although work is permitted after the recitation of אַתָּה חוֹנַנְתָּנוּ in the Ma'ariv 'Amidah, the formal conclusion of the Sabbath is marked by the Havdalah service. This ceremony should be performed immediately after the Ma'ariv service, though it may be delayed in cases of emergency even until Tuesday. When recited later than Saturday night, however, the spices and the candle are omitted (Ṭur, *O.H.* 299; B. *Shab.* 150b in Rashi, s.v. ועבדינן).

Just as the Sabbath is ushered in with Qiddush, which begins with the benediction over wine, so it is ushered out with Havdalah, also beginning with the benediction over wine. In Havdalah we also recite benedictions over spices, בּוֹרֵא מִינֵי בְשָׂמִים, and over light, בּוֹרֵא מְאוֹרֵי הָאֵשׁ, and the benediction of Havdalah itself, הַמַּבְדִּיל בֵּין קוֹדֶשׁ לְחוֹל, which lists a series of distinctions that God has made: the sacred and the profane, light and darkness, Israel and the nations, the seventh day and the six days of work. A convenient mnemonic to remember the order of the benedictions is יבנ״ה for יַיִן, בְּשָׂמִים, נֵר, הַבְדָּלָה. If the spices and candle are not available, Havdalah may be recited over wine alone (*O.H.* 297:1, 298:1).

Havdalah is recited standing, with the cup of wine in the right hand, and the spices in the left hand. After the benediction over the wine, the spices are taken in the right hand and that benediction is recited. The spices are then smelled. Then both the wine and the spices are put down, and the benediction over the light is recited. When this blessing is recited one should raise his hands and look at his palms, thus enjoying the use of the light while reciting the benediction. This prevents the blessing from becoming a בְּרָכָה לְבַטָּלָה (benediction recited in vain). The wine is then taken in the right hand again and the last benediction is recited. After this benediction the reader drinks the wine.

It is customary to pour out some wine into another container and extinguish the candle therein. Various other customs, which we would relegate to the realm of folklore, have been added to this service. Some dip the fingers in the wine and touch the eyes to signify מִצְוַת יְיָ בָּרָה מְאִירַת עֵינָיִם ("The commandment of the Lord is pure, enlightening the eyes"—Ps. 19:9). Others touch the wine and put their hands in their pockets as if to pray for a week of prosperity.

Havdalah may be said over wine or over any other beverage except water (*O.H.* 296:2).When using other beverages, שֶׁהַכֹּל is substituted for בּוֹרֵא פְּרִי הַגָּפֶן.

For the light, a torch consisting of two or more wicks should be used (Rama on *O.H.* 298:2; B. *Pes.* 103b; according to Rava there, a torch is preferable—a torch is a candle with at least two wicks). Today we use a braided candle made specifically for the purpose and called a Havdalah candle.

There are two explanations of the origins of the Havdalah ceremony.

According to one, it started as a home ceremony at the end of the Saturday afternoon meal. The wine was used for the *Birkat Hamazon* and would be customarily drunk after *Birkat Hamazon*, preceded by the benediction for wine. The kindling of the light would naturally mark the conclusion of the Sabbath, during which such kindling is forbidden. It was also customary at the close of the meal to bring in spices placed on burning coals. Since this could not be done on the Sabbath, spices were brought in only after the end of the third meal. Havdalah thus became associated with the end of the Sabbath (Saadia, quoted by Abrahams, *Companion to the Authorised Daily Prayer Book*, p.182).

According to a second theory, Havdalah started as a synagogue ceremony (B. *Ber.* 33a). Here the light is associated with the story of creation. Light was created on the first day, and accordingly it was ordained that we bless the light on the eve of every recurrent first day of the week (B. *Pes.* 53b; *Genesis Rabbah* 12:6).

Folklore also steps in with this story. After Adam was created on the sixth day, the sun shone for him throughout the entire Sabbath. When the sun set at the end of the Sabbath and darkness came, he was struck with fear. Thereupon the Lord gave him knowledge and brought him two stones. Adam struck these against each other and brought forth light, then recited the benediction: בּוֹרֵא מְאוֹרֵי הָאֵשׁ. We therefore recite the benediction on fire at the end of the Sabbath because that was when light was first created (B. *Pes.* 54a).

The pleasures gained by perception and the sense of smell are the most spiritual of all. The spices, then, comfort the Jew's נְשָׁמָה יְתֵרָה—the "oversoul" which is given to man on the Sabbath and taken away again at its conclusion (*Jewish Encyclopedia*, 6:119; B. *Ta'an.* 27b).

According to this theory, the soul is saddened by the exit of the Sabbath, but is soothed by the fragrance of the spices (Maimonides, *Hil. Shabbat* 29:29).

UNIT V

THE SABBATH (II):

PROHIBITION AGAINST WORK

Carrying
Muqtseh
Shevut
Traveling
Fire, Electric Lights, and Automatic Devices
Preparation of Food
Treatment of the Sick
Sports and Amusements
A Gentile Working for a Jew
Sabbath Boundaries
Electrical Appliances
Miscellaneous
Conclusion

V.
The Sabbath (II)
Prohibition Against Work

The central theme of the Sabbath is the prohibition of work. The Bible says: "Six days shalt thou labor, and do all thy work; but the seventh day is a Sabbath unto the Lord your God, in it thou shalt not do any manner of work" (Exod. 20:9–10).

The definition of work has always been a source of difficulty. The biblical commandment does not specify what kinds of work are forbidden, though certain acts are explicitly forbidden or mentioned as constituting a violation of the Sabbath. These include kindling a flame (Exod. 35:3), plowing, harvesting, and reaping (Exod. 34:21), gathering wood (Num. 15:32–35), baking and cooking (according to the traditional interpretation of Exod. 16:22), carrying a burden or carrying something out of the house (Jer. 17:21, 22; Neh. 13:19), treading wine presses, bringing in the corn, loading it on asses and transporting it, and buying and selling (Neh. 13:15–17).

In the Talmud, a massive edifice—called by the sages כַּהֲרָרִים הַתְּלוּיִן בְּשַׂעֲרָה ("like mountains hanging by a hair") or מִקְרָא מְעַט וַהֲלָכוֹת מְרֻבּוֹת ("scant scriptural basis but many laws") (M. *Ḥag.* 1:8)—is built on the prohibition of work. The sages enumerated thirty-nine אֲבוֹת מְלָאכוֹת, or major categories of work, and innumerable תּוֹלָדוֹת, or secondary categories of work derived from them. In addition, there are many more categories that are to be avoided because they are not in the spirit of the Sabbath. The source of the thirty-nine major categories lies in the biblical juxtaposition of the laws of the Sabbath with the description of the construction of the Tabernacle (Exod. 31:12–17). The fact that the Sabbath laws immediately precede the account of the construction suggested to the rabbis that the term *work* covered all manner of work done in connection with the construction of the Tabernacle (M. *Shab.* 7:2). Inasmuch as the Torah mentions that the work on the Tabernacle was מְלֶאכֶת מַחֲשֶׁבֶת, "skilled workmanship" (Exod. 35:33), the rabbis also made this a specification for work forbidden on the Sabbath: מְלֶאכֶת מַחֲשֶׁבֶת אָסְרָה תּוֹרָה—"The Torah forbade skilled work" (B. *Bet.* 13b; B. *San.* 62b). Based on this they also ruled: כָּל הַמְקַלְקְלִין פְּטוּרִין—"Whoever performs an act of destruction is not liable" (B. *Shab.* 106a). A complete analysis of the thirty-nine categories, along with their derivatives, can be found in *The Sabbath* by I. Grunfeld (pp. 35–38).

Actually, the list of prohibited labors reflects the activities required by the economy of the day, such as work in the field (plowing, sowing, reaping, threshing, etc.), preparation of food (grinding, kneading, baking, slaughtering, hunting), and preparation of clothing (sheep-shearing, dyeing, spinning, sewing).

Professor Meyer Waxman tries to find an underlying principle behind the large number of Sabbath prohibitions. "It is quite evident that in enacting these ordinances the Rabbis had an eye rather to the spirit than to the letter of the law, for some of these quasi-labors, such as buying and selling, violate the very intention of the Sabbath, which is to rest from all occupation aiming at material benefit or pursuit or gain. In regard to riding or traveling, modern conditions undoubtedly invalidate the original reason for this prohibition, yet it is still observed and with justice, for once traveling is permitted on the Sabbath, it becomes difficult to draw the line between a journey for pure pleasure and one for the pursuit of gain. An institution like the Sabbath which aims at the elevation of human life cannot allow deviation based on subjective distinctions" (Waxman, *Handbook of Judaism*, p. 32).

A definition of work which would be appropriate to our day and provide a contemporary rationale for all the prohibitions has been attempted by many writers on the subject. Basically they all refer back to the one given by Samson Raphael Hirsch (*Horeb*, pp. 64 f.), whose explanation has been utilized by such extremely Orthodox thinkers as Rabbi Chayim (Eduard) Biberfeld (*Menuḥah Nekhonah*, p. 16) and Dayan Dr. Grunfeld of London (*The Sabbath*, pp. 16–17), and at the opposite pole by Professor Mordecai Kaplan (*Judaism as a Civilization*, p. 444).

Dayan Grunfeld paraphrases the passage from Samson Raphael Hirsch as follows: "In arriving at his interpretation of '*melakhah*,' Rabbi S. R. Hirsch starts with the basic idea that the Sabbath testifies to God as the supreme creator of heaven and earth and all they contain. Man, however, is engaged in a constant struggle to gain mastery over God's creation, to bring nature under his control. By the use of his God-given intelligence, skill and energy, he has in large measure succeeded in this. He is thus constantly in danger of forgetting his own creaturehood—his utter and complete dependence on the Lord for all things. He tends to forget that the very powers he uses in his conquest of nature are derived from his Creator, in whose service his life and work should be conducted. . . .

"We renounce on this day every exercise of intelligent, purposeful control of natural objects and forces, we cease from every act of human power in order to proclaim God as the source of all power. By refraining from human creating, the Jew pays silent homage to the Creator" (*The Sabbath,* pp. 16 ff.).

On this basis Dayan Grunfeld defines a *melakhah* as "an act that shows man's mastery over the world by the constructive exercise of his intelligence and skill" (ibid., p. 19).

Professor Kaplan summarizes the thought in this fashion: "In the light of those explanations, the function of the Sabbath is to prohibit man from engaging in work which in any way alters the environment, so that he should not delude himself into the belief that he is complete master of his destiny" (*Judaism as a Civilization,* p. 444).

Professor Heschel expresses the same thought. "He who wants to enter the holiness of the day must first lay down the profanity of clattering commerce, of being yoked to toil. He must go away from the screech of dissonant days, from the nervousness and fury of acquisitiveness and the betrayal in embezzling his own life. He must say farewell to manual work and learn to understand that the world has already been created and will survive without the help of man. Six days a week we wrestle with the world, wringing profit from the earth; on the Sabbath we especially care for the seed of eternity planted in the soul. The world has our hands, but our soul belongs to Someone Else. Six days a week we seek to dominate the world, on the seventh day we try to dominate the self" (*The Sabbath,* p. 13).

With this as a background we shall treat several areas of Sabbath rest, concentrating on those most relevant to contemporary life.

The most comprehensive statement regarding the prohibition of work on the Sabbath would be that one should not perform his usual range of weekday activities. Isaiah said:

> If thou turn away thy foot because of the Sabbath,
> From pursuing thy business on my holy day;
> And call the Sabbath a delight,
> And the holy of the Lord honorable;
> And shalt honor it, not doing thy wonted ways,
> Nor pursuing thy business, nor speaking thereof . . . [Isa. 58:13]

The obvious intent of this passage is that one should not pursue his chosen profession, trade, or daily occupation on the Sabbath; the merchant should not go to his store, the manufacturer to his plant, the laborer to his shop, or the professional to his office.

But this is not enough to make the Sabbath holy. There is also an elaborate discipline prescribing what work may or may not be done on the Sabbath even while one is at home.

1. Carrying

As indicated above, the Mishnah enumerated thirty-nine major categories of work forbidden on the Sabbath (*M. Shab.* 7:2). We shall begin with the last of these: הוֹצָאָה מֵרְשׁוּת לִרְשׁוּת—"removing an object from one domain to another," better known as "carrying on the Sabbath." We begin here because carrying is the most common of activities and also because the regulations on carrying are the most disregarded. (The Mishnah in the tractate *Shabbat* begins with this one as well; see Tosafot to B. *Shab.* 2a, s.v. יְצִיאוֹת, and in *Tosafot Yom Tov* on *Shab.* 7:4, s.v. המוציא, for the reason.)

The verse "Let no man go out of his domain on the seventh day" (Exod. 16:29) is interpreted by the rabbis to mean that one should not carry any object from one domain into another (B. *Hor.* 4a; see *Masoret Hashass*). A more explicit statement to this effect is found in the Book of Jeremiah: "Thus saith the Lord: Take heed for the sake of your souls and bear no burden on the Sabbath day, nor bring it in by the gates of Jerusalem: neither carry forth a burden out of your houses on the Sabbath day" (Jer. 17:21–22).

The definition of a "domain" is given in the Talmud (B. *Shab.* 6a). The rabbis speak of four types of domains: a public domain (רְשׁוּת הָרַבִּים), a private domain (רְשׁוּת הַיָּחִיד), a כַּרְמְלִית, and a "free place" (מְקוֹם פְּטוּר).

A "public domain" is a road or a square frequented by the public, unroofed, open at both ends, and having a width of not less than sixteen cubits, or approximately twenty-eight feet (*O.H.* 345:7).

A "private domain" is any enclosed space not less than four hand-breadths (approximately fifteen inches) square, bounded by walls not less than ten hand-breadths (approximately three feet) high. (The term also includes a depression or elevation of not less than the above dimensions in a public square [*O.H.* 345:2]. A movable object of this size in a public domain also constitutes a private domain.) For our purposes a private domain would be a house, a yard, or a garden.

According to Rashi (B. *Shab.* 3b), a *karmelit* is an unfrequented place (for the literal meaning, see Lieberman in *Tosefta Kifshutah, Shab.* 1:1, vol. 3, pp. 3–4). The Talmud places it in the same category as a public domain, and it is subject to the same regulations even though it does not have the characteristics of a public domain. A *karmelit* includes a street less than twenty-eight feet wide, or a street not open at both ends, an enclosed space more than fifty yards square which is not attached to a dwelling place, open country, seas and rivers (*O.H.* 345:14). The rabbis prohibited carrying into or in a *karmelit* because if this were permitted, one might err and also carry in a public domain.

A "free place" is an enclosed space less than fifteen inches square in a public domain (*O.H.* 345:19), and the air space of a public domain or a *karmelit* above three feet from the ground. A private domain, however, retains its status as a private domain *ad coelum,* "to the heavens" (*O.H.* 345:5).

We are primarily interested in the prohibition against removing an object from a home to the street or vice versa, and against carrying it on the street a distance of approximately seven feet (אַרְבַּע אַמּוֹת). The latter prohibition is commonly included in this general category (B. *Shab.* 6a; *O.H.* 346:2).

The rabbis suggested that one should search his clothing before the advent of the Sabbath so that he would not unwittingly carry an object (*O.H.* 232:7; B. *Shab.* 12a). The only objects a person may carry on the Sabbath are articles of clothing or ornaments which he is wearing (*O.H.* 301:7).

Unconditional permission to carry objects is given only within a house inhabited by one family and the courtyard adjacent to it if it is surrounded by a fence about three feet high. The halls and lobby of an apartment house are also considered to be a private domain (*O.H.* 370:2).

This poses a problem for people living in multiple dwellings, such as duplex apartments which share a common yard. To overcome such difficulties the *'eruv* (lit. "mixing" or "pooling rights") has been established. If two or more Jewish families live in adjoining houses in the same building or attached to the same yard, one may carry from one dwelling to the other if they arrange for an *'eruv.* For this the families pool their rights of possession so that their dwellings become the joint property of them all. The symbol of this joint ownership is the *'eruv.* The *'eruv* is usually a loaf of bread or a matzah deposited in the custody of one of the dwellers as their joint property.

This is called עֵרוּבֵי חֲצֵרוֹת, or an *'eruv* made by people sharing the same courtyard (*O.H.* 366:1).

To establish an *'eruv*, one of the dwellers takes a loaf or a matzah of his own on the eve of the Sabbath and, through the agency of a third party, transfers the ownership thereof to all the tenants of the yard, saying to the agent: "Take this loaf and acquire ownership thereto on behalf of all those who dwell in this yard." The agent takes it and raises it one hand-breadth (*O.H.* 366:9). The one making the *'eruv* takes it back and recites the appropriate legal formula, which can be found in most Siddurim.

This legal device was used by the rabbis to adjust the law to the new urban situation of the Jewish community.

2. Muqtseh

The admonition of Isaiah: "And thou shalt honor it, not doing thy wonted work, nor pursuing thy business, nor speaking thereof (Isa. 58:13) was understood by the rabbis as an indication that to honor the Sabbath, one must withdraw from the spirit of weekday activities and not simply cease to work. The mood of holiness is best promoted by a complete severance from the tenor of the weekday life (B. *Shab.* 113a). A number of legal forms were developed to promote this kind of severance. The concept of *muqtseh* is one of these.

Muqtseh means "set aside" or "excluded"; it is the prohibition against handling any object which, for one reason or another, was not intended by us for use during the Sabbath day.

Several kinds of objects fall into this category:

1. Objects which can never be brought into use on the Sabbath without transgressing the Sabbath law—מוּקְצֶה מֵחֲמַת אִסּוּר—such as money, candlesticks in which candles were burnt, pencils, pens, cigarette lighters.
2. Objects which were inaccessible when the Sabbath started; e.g., fruit which at the advent of the Sabbath was still attached to the tree.
3. Objects normally used for work prohibited on the Sabbath, but also usable for purposes permissible on the Sabbath, may not be handled unless they are to be used for permissible purposes, or to

be moved because their place is needed. For instance, a hammer may be handled if it is to be used for cracking nuts or if its place is needed for something else. Otherwise it is *muqtseh*.

4. Useless objects (bones, potsherds, broken objects).
5. Religious objects which cannot be used on the Sabbath, such as a Shofar (Rama on *O.H.* 308:4), Tefilin (ibid.), Lulav (Rama on *O.H.* 658:2), etc. This is מוּקְצֶה מֵחֲמַת מִצְוָה (*O.H.* 308:4, 18).
6. Objects which in themselves are permitted, but contain things that are *muqtseh* (e.g., a purse with money in it), are forbidden. If the container is not used exclusively for money or for other objects that are *muqtseh*, it may be handled even if it contains money (Felder, *Yesodei Yeshurun*, 4:340). These prohibitions are flexible and do not apply where there is undue hardship, possible financial loss, or some other difficulty (Rama on *O.H.* 279:2). Instances given are broken glass and objects with an offensive odor (Rama on *O.H.* 308:6).

3. Shevut

The term שְׁבוּת ("resting") covers a whole area of activities which are not strictly work but are to be avoided because they are not in the spirit of the Sabbath (מִשּׁוּם עוּבְדִין דְּחוֹל), or because doing them may lead to acts that constitute a major desecration of the Sabbath (מִשּׁוּם גְּזֵירָה) (Maimonides, *Hil. Shabbat* 21:1). These include discussing business matters, asking a Gentile to do what is forbidden for a Jew to do on the Sabbath, making preparations during the Sabbath for a forbidden act that will be done immediately upon the conclusion of the Sabbath (e.g., packing a suitcase for a journey, sweeping or washing an unpaved floor [a form of leveling], doing heavy work that is permitted but requires great effort, reading business correspondence, hiring laborers to work during the week). These prohibitions seem particularly burdensome today, but the truth is that there can be no real Sabbath without *shevut*. It is, in effect, a means of preserving the special character of the Sabbath.

Professor Albeck explains that most of the hedges and protective enactments concerning prohibited Sabbath work were not newly instituted creations in the talmudic period but had been part of the pattern of observance among the people from early times. Since there was no clear definition of what constituted biblically prohibited work, it was only natural to refrain from all manner of work carried on during the week. It was only later that the sages of the Halakhah gave a clear definition of work, establishing the framework of thirty-nine categories of biblically prohibited work (Albeck, *Shishah Sidrei Mishnah, Seder Mo'ed,* p. 10). Thus the regulations of *shevut* were systematic expressions of earlier practices developed by the people as a means of sanctifying the Sabbath.

Whenever a mitswah or a public need is involved, the prohibitions of *shevut* are waived (*O.H.* 306:1).

We should add that the whole area of *shevut* has to be mapped out anew because the reason for the *gezeirot* and the nature of *'uvdin deḥol* have changed. What was in the spirit of the Sabbath a generation ago may not be considered so today. For example, buying on credit, provided price was not discussed, was not considered a violation of the Sabbath (*O.H.* 232:4), but we would not be willing to consider it so today when credit buying is so common. Some *gezeirot* are no longer applicable. Thus the Mishnah forbids clapping and dancing on Sabbaths and festivals because of the possibility that one of the musical instruments might break and someone would repair it (M. *Bet.* 5:2), but Tosafot (B. *Bet.* 30a, s.v. תנן אין מטפחין) permit these activities since in their day people were not skilled in making musical instruments. The doctrine that a *gezeirah* still stands even if the reason for initiating it has ceased is untenable as a general principle. However, if a practice is deeply rooted and stable, we are usually able to find new meaning in it for our day.

4. Traveling

Traveling on the Sabbath is another of the most frequent violations of the Sabbath. Even comparatively observant people have found the ban on traveling hard to abide by. They therefore rationalize that inasmuch as the reason given in the Talmud—lest the traveler, in need of a switch to guide or prod his animal, cut a twig from a tree (B. *Bet.* 36b)—does not apply to modern conditions, the entire prohibition falls by the wayside. Actually, modern conditions present many more violations of the Sabbath than were possible in the era of horse-drawn vehicles.

Most modern travel is by car. It is often claimed that driving requires less effort than walking, but, in fact, it is easy to find halakhic reasons to avoid driving on the Sabbath. First, there is the prohibition against creating fire. Even according to the opinion that electricity is not fire, actual fire is created in the engine of a car. (The argument that combustion was not included in the prohibition is not convincing; see Adler et al., "Responsum on the Sabbath," pp. 130 f.) Furthermore, if the *gezeirah* of "lest one cut off a switch from a tree" sounded far-fetched in ancient times, there are very good reasons for such *gezeirot* today. When driving a car, there is always the possibility of needing to buy gas, and the chance of a flat tire or other necessary repairs. Traveling beyond the city limits also involves אִסּוּר תְּחוּמִים (see below).

The Law Committee of the Rabbinical Assembly, in its celebrated resolution on travel on the Sabbath, has made one exception to this rule. Under the conditions of our day, many congregants live far from the synagogue and cannot attend services unless they ride. For many of these people, attendance at services is their only contact with religious life and practically their only awareness of the sanctity of the Sabbath. Hence it was ruled: "As we have already indicated, participation in public service on the Sabbath is in the light of modern conditions to be regarded as a great *mitswah,* since it is indispensable to the preservation of the religious life of American Jewry. Therefore it is our considered opinion that the positive value involved in the participation in public worship on the Sabbath outweighs the negative value of refraining from riding in an automobile" (Waxman, *Tradition and Change,* p. 370; Adler et al., "Responsum on the Sabbath," p. 132).

This resolution was passed by a majority opinion of the Law Committee with a sizable minority opposed. But the decision must not be understood as outright permission to travel to the synagogue. The case presents a conflict between two values—not riding on the Sabbath and participating in public worship—and we must each opt for one or the other of them. Our fathers, and many of us today, would opt not to ride. We can understand the feelings of those who opt for public worship because of the changed conditions under which we live. Yet we must not construe this option as a general *heter,* but rather as applying to individual cases where a choice must be made. Every other alternative must be exhausted first. (See David Novak, *Law and Theology in Judaism,* pp. 21–30.)

In regard to traveling by ship, if the vessel departs on a weekday, even on Friday, and is definitely to be enroute on the Sabbath, it is permitted to go aboard and to travel. The ruling that such a trip is permitted only לִדְבַר מִצְוָה, "for the purpose of (fulfilling) a commandment," has been construed by Rabbeinu Tam to include practically all trips, even those for business and social purposes (Ṭur, *O.H.* 248; *O.H.* 248:1).

If the ship is to depart on the Sabbath, one should arrange to board and be settled (קוֹנֶה שְׁבִיתָה) before the advent of the Sabbath. Once this is done, one may leave the boat and re-enter on the Sabbath provided no other violation of the Sabbath is involved (*O.H.* 248:3, Rama ad loc.).

If the ship docks at a port on its journey, the passengers may disembark and visit within the *tehum shabbat* (see below, Sabbath Boundaries), again provided that no other violation is involved (*O.H.* 404:1).

5. Fire, Electric Lights, and Automatic Devices

The prohibition of kindling fire on the Sabbath (Exod. 35:3) is one of the thirty-nine categories of forbidden work. It affects any activity that involves the initiation, transferring, or prolongation of combustion.

The question has arisen today whether the use of electricity—specifically, the turning on of an electric light—is included in this general prohibition. A responsum of the Law Committee of the Rabbinical Assembly, approved by a majority opinion, concluded that electricity is not a form of fire (Adler et al., "Responsum on the Sabbath," p. 129; Neulander, "The Use of Electricity on the Sabbath," p. 167). The difficulties with this decision are not only halakhic. In common parlance we certainly associate electricity with fire because it is used for the same purposes as fire: illumination, heating, cooking, and burning. The empirical argument that the use of electric lights adds to the joy of the Sabbath is too subjective. The use of other forms of electricity will be discussed separately below.

This leads us to the subject of automation. People who refrain from switching on electric lights on the Sabbath have used electric timers that turn lights on and off automatically.

Forms of automation existed long before the introduction of electricity. Examples are an alarm clock that was set before the advent of the Sabbath (*O.H.* 338:3), a winepress that worked automatically (B. *Shab.* 18a), and the setting of traps or nets to capture animals or fish on the Sabbath (*O.H.* 252:1). The analogy is obvious. Any work that proceeds automatically is permitted, provided the machinery was set in motion before the Sabbath.

6. Preparation of Food

By the preparation of food we mean making raw food edible by the use of heat, i.e., by some form of cooking. This prohibition is independent of the prohibition against making fire. Thus, cooking on the Sabbath is prohibited even if the fire was lit and the food was put on the fire before the advent of the Sabbath. All food that is to be consumed on the Sabbath must be already cooked and water must be already boiled when the Sabbath begins, though these may remain on the fire throughout the Sabbath (*O.H.* 254:2–3). The term *cooked* in this context implies that the food should be minimally edible—מַאֲכָל בֶּן דְּרוֹסָאי—at the beginning of the Sabbath.

The rabbis were cautious about permitting us to warm food on the Sabbath because the dividing line between warming and cooking is not always recognizable. Further, there is the fear that warming will lead inadvertently to tampering with the fire. The following are the rules regarding the warming of food:

1. Solids may be warmed under all circumstances (*O.H.* 318:15).
2. Liquids which are not entirely cold may be warmed (Rama, ibid.).
3. Liquids which are entirely cold may be warmed over a low fire which will not make the liquid too hot or bring it once again to a boil (ibid.; see also *Sha'arei Teshuvah,* sec. 35).
4. In all these cases the fire itself must be covered to serve as a reminder lest we tamper with it (*Ḥayyei Adam, Klal* 20, sec. 12; *O.H.* 253:3 in *M.A.*, sec. 31).

   One should, therefore, cover the fire with a tin plate (*blech*) to prevent any tampering with the fire and to keep the flame low enough to prevent boiling. Modern appliances that regulate the heat so that it can be kept at a low temperature at all times are a great help in this respect.

7. Treatment of the Sick

Since the rabbis had a high regard for human life and happiness, they applied the words וָחַי בָּהֶם—"and live by them" (Lev. 18:5)—to many areas of religion. The greatest application was in the area of treating the sick on the Sabbath, where they established the principle of פִּקּוּחַ נֶפֶשׁ דּוֹחֶה אֶת הַשַּׁבָּת (B. *Yoma* 85a; *Shab.* 132a)—"the saving of life waives any restrictions due to the Sabbath." This applies not only to cases where the saving of a life is definitely involved, but also where there is only a suspicion that this may be the case—כָּל סְפֵק נְפָשׁוֹת דּוֹחֶה אֶת הַשַּׁבָּת (M. *Yoma* 8:6).

Thus, all medical treatment is permitted on the Sabbath. The old distinctions of סַכָּנַת נְפָשׁוֹת, danger to life, and סְפֵק נְפָשׁוֹת, possible danger to life, have been given a new meaning by medical science. What was once considered harmless is now often known to be potentially serious if not treated immediately (*O.H.* 328:47 in *Mishnah Berurah*, n. 47). Hence, we should follow the recommendation of the physician in all cases.

The rabbis warned that in the case of medical treatment one should not follow the suggestion כָּל הַמַּחֲמִיר תָּבוֹא עָלָיו בְּרָכָה ("whoever is more scrupulous, may blessing be upon him"), urging that in such a case it is a mitswah to violate the Sabbath, and the more zealous one is, the better (*O.H.* 328:2). They even stated that a sick person may be compelled to accept treatment, since unwillingness to accept treatment is a foolish kind of piety (ibid. in *B.H.* 1).

This obviously does not include a routine physical checkup which could be done on another day.

Giving birth has always been considered by the rabbis to be similar to a case of חוֹלֶה שֶׁיֵּשׁ בּוֹ סַכָּנָה, a dangerous illness, and they permitted everything that is necessary for the comfort of the mother (*O.H.* 330:1).

8. Sports and Amusements

We must distinguish between commercialized sports and amusements and activities one indulges in for personal enjoyment. Commercialized sports and amusements are obviously not recommended because of the many violations of the Sabbath that are involved.

Individual sports and amusements in themselves, where no other violation of the Sabbath is involved, are permissible. Thus ball-playing in a private domain, or anywhere that carrying is allowed, is permissible (Rama on *O.H.* 308:45). Gymnastics is also permitted (*O.H.* 301:2). Bathing in a pool in a private domain is permitted (*O.H.* 326:7; *Mishnah Berurah*, n. 24); in an open place it is also permitted but with some restrictions, i.e., one should dry oneself before fully leaving the water (*O.H.* 326:7). Swimming has been forbidden lest one be tempted to make an aid to swimming (כְּלִי שַׁיָּטִין). This concern is not relevant today.

The only caution here is that one should avoid participating in such activities to the point of overexertion and fatigue, which would make the act not in the spirit of the Sabbath.

In the case of social amusements that may take place at home or in the synagogue, we can only suggest the following as a guide: "The Sabbath is a sacred day and there are certain kinds of enjoyment which by their very nature, are out of harmony with its inherent holiness. Participation in them on the Sabbath is like a sudden intrusion of a shrill street organ on a beautiful melody sung by a lovely voice.

"It is difficult, almost impossible, to lay down a definite rule on this point to say, 'This sort of amusement is allowable, that sort, improper on the Sabbath.' The matter must be left to the individual conscience, to each person's sense of what is seemly" (Joseph, *Judaism as Creed and Life*, p. 208).

As an illustration, we would suggest that playing poker on the Sabbath, even without money, would be considered unseemly; playing chess would not. Attending a poetry reading would be permissible; going to a wrestling match would not.

9. A Gentile Working for a Jew

The law states explicitly as a general principle that we may not ask a non-Jew to do anything on the Sabbath that we may not do ourselves (Maimonides, *Hil. Shabbat* 24:4). Because of the exceptions to this rule, the institution of the "Shabbes-goy" came into being. The exceptions are in the following cases:

1. Illness or other emergencies
2. Lighting a fire in cold weather
3. To relieve an animal in pain
4. Where the act is done by a non-Jew for his own purpose even though a Jew may benefit (B. *Shab.* 122b)

These exceptions have been stretched to the point that some Sabbath observers have non-Jews to do every manner of work around the house that is usually forbidden. The general idea of a Shabbes-goy is repugnant, however, and in most cases it has become unnecessary because of modern automatic devices.

However, the problem still remains relevant in the field of business and industry. May a Jew use a suit made for him by a non-Jewish tailor on the Sabbath? May a non-Jewish partner of a business or industrial establishment work on the Sabbath? May a non-Jewish contractor doing a construction job for a Jew work on the Sabbath?

The rabbis laid down the general principle that if the non-Jew is independent, is paid for the job as a whole, and is not told specifically to work on the Sabbath, he may do his work (*O.H.* 244:5, 252:2). One may give his clothes to the laundry, ask a non-Jewish tailor to fix his garments, or ask a non-Jew to do any other similar type of work, even if he knows that it will be done on the Sabbath, as long as the non-Jew is free to decide when the work should be done. An employee of a house or synagogue who is assigned specific duties on the Sabbath as part of his total responsibilities would also come under this category. Such a person is not called a Shabbes-goy.

The only exception to this rule is when the work is done in the open and is obviously being done for a Jew (*O.H.* 244:1, 252:3). This includes the case of a non-Jewish contractor who has been engaged to build a synagogue. Theoretically, since he has the option to work whenever he wants, he should be permitted to work on the Sabbath, but because it would be obvious that the work is being done for Jews, it is not permitted. The same applies to work done on the premises of a synagogue (*O.H.* 244:5).

10. Sabbath Boundaries

"Abide ye every man in his place, let no man go out of his place on the seventh day" (Exod. 16:29).

The rabbis interpreted this passage to mean that a person should not go long distances away from his home, or place of residence, on the Sabbath (B. *Eruv.* 51a).

We refer here, of course, to travel by means which are normally permissible on the Sabbath. Part of Sabbath rest involves being close to home and near to the family circle. Modern means of communication have both helped and harmed this situation, but on the Sabbath a sense of community is important.

The following are the regulations regarding the distances one may travel:

1. Within a city, no matter how large, one is permitted to walk any distance (Maimonides, *Hil. Shabbat* 27:2).
2. City limits are defined as seventy and two-thirds cubits (about 150 ft.) beyond the last house. Thus, if there is another town beyond the last house, seventy and two-thirds cubits away, the two towns are counted as one (*O.H.* 398:5–8).

3. Beyond city limits one may walk two thousand cubits—about three quarters of a mile (*O.H.* 398:5). This is the *teḥum shabbat*, or Sabbath boundary.
4. Obviously, when it is a matter of פִּקּוּחַ נֶפֶשׁ one is permitted to go beyond the *teḥum shabbat*. A doctor, midwife, policeman, or fireman who is called for an emergency is in this category.

When, for the sake of a mitswah, one has to go beyond the *teḥum shabbat*, but not more than another *teḥum*, we have the device of the *'eruv*. Since we count the place where one eats as a dwelling place, one should put the minimum equivalent of two meals at the end of the *teḥum* before the advent of the Sabbath. Thereafter one is permitted to walk beyond this point another two thousand cubits on the Sabbath. The Talmud gives an example of the kind of mitswah for which one may make such an *'eruv:* A sage is to appear in some town beyond the *teḥum;* a person who wants to listen to his discourse may make an *'eruv* (B. *Eruv.* 37b).

11. Electrical Appliances

The question of using an elevator on the Sabbath has arisen in connection with modern multi-storied apartment houses. Two problems are involved, since pressing the button usually turns on a light and also sets machinery in motion. The latter problem exists even for those who have no objection to turning on lights. According to the responsum of Rabbi Neulander (but not according to the opinion of the other respondents on the question), the solution is to use the elevator only when it is already being used by a non-Jew (Ouziel, *Mishpeṭei 'Uzi'el,* 1:226–30).

An automatic clock may be set in advance to light a stove to warm food on the Sabbath if there is no other violation in regard to warming or cooking on the Sabbath (*Maharam Schick, O.H.* 157).

It is permissible to use a microphone on the Sabbath if it was turned on before the Sabbath, or if it is used in some other manner that does not involve a violation of the Sabbath (Grünfeld, Maharshag, 2:118, in the view of the questioner).

The question of appliances which use electricity generated by dry cells (batteries) requires further study.

12. Miscellaneous

It is permissible to make soup by pouring hot water over bouillon cubes or powder on the Sabbath (ibid., 1:51).

It is permissible to use an article that arrived by mail on the Sabbath (Maharsham, 328:8). Similarly, one may use a garment delivered by the cleaner on the Sabbath (*Qitsur Shulḥan 'Arukh* 73:9), though, of course, one should never instruct a tradesman to make a delivery on the Sabbath.

Milk deliveries on the Sabbath, where daily delivery is part of the contractual arrangement, are permitted in cases of hardship, e.g., where there is no refrigeration and where children who need milk daily are present (*Tashbets,* 4:13).

Cans and barrels may be opened on the Sabbath if their contents are to be used on that day (*O.H.* 314:6).

It is permissible to wash dishes on the Sabbath if the dishes are to be used on the Sabbath (*O.H.* 323:6). Detergents may be used (*O.H.* 323:9), but an abrasive substance that may scratch the surface should not be used.

Visits to the sick and condolence calls are permissible on the Sabbath, even though they may detract from the joy of the day (*O.H.* 287:1).

One may open the radiator valve to heat the house on the Sabbath (*She'eilot Uteshuvot MiYehudah, O.H.* 36).

Photography is not recommended on the Sabbath—neither to photograph nor to be photographed (Braun, *She'arim Metsuyanim Bahalahkhah* 2:125).

Weddings may not take place on the Sabbath even if the Ketubah is not written on the Sabbath (ibid. 2:137).

A number of practical questions dealing with Sabbath observance in our day have not been discussed here. For further study of the issues involved in each case, the following responsa may be consulted:

1. *Melamed Leho'il* by Rabbi David Hoffmann
2. *Mishpeṭei 'Uzi'el* by Rabbi Ben-Zion Ḥai Ouziel
3. *Seridei Eish* by Rabbi Yeḥi'el Ya'aqov Weinberg
4. *Tsits Eli'ezer* by Rabbi Eliezer Yehuda Waldenberg
5. *Igrot Mosheh* By Rabbi Moses Feinstein
6. *No'am,* an annual published in Israel
7. The archives of the Committee on Law and Standards of the Rabbinical Assembly of America

13. Conclusion

The importance of the Sabbath cannot be overestimated. It was Aḥad Ha'am who said that more than the Jew kept the Sabbath, the Sabbath kept the Jew. The change from the daily routine to that of the Sabbath is accomplished by refraining from the types of work that characterize our weekday activities. That alone, however, does not make the Sabbath, for one could comply with the prohibitions by sleeping through the Sabbath day; they simply provide the matrix for the activities that bring about the sacredness of the Sabbath.

The most important activities for the sanctification of the day are prayer and study. The uplift that the Sabbath gave the Jew even in the darkest days of persecution and oppression saved him from being brutalized. The Sabbath enabled the Jew to retain his dignity and his hope for a better world. This is why the millennium was called יוֹם שֶׁכֻּלּוֹ שַׁבָּת, for it is these spiritual activities that bring out the best in man. Without the fanfare of organization, the Sabbath also embodied a system of adult education and provided for the moral training of the community. It is a tested institution which modern man in search of his soul would be wise to adopt.

UNIT VI

THE FESTIVALS: INTRODUCTION

VI.
The Festivals
Introduction

1. Preface

Life must have a rhythm. Nature has provided us with the rhythm of day and night, summer and winter, cold and warmth, and many others. Without these life would be drab and monotonous. To these the body adds its own inner rhythms: rest and activity, hunger and satiety, health and illness.

But the world of the spirit must have its rhythms as well, such as sadness and joy, moments of uneventful living and moments of exultation. The moments of exultation represent the peaks in our lives, lifting our spirits and giving us a sense of eternity.

Franz Rosenzweig wrote: "The river of life . . . flows from birth towards death. Day follows day with wearisome monotony. Only the holidays twine themselves together to form the circle of the year. Only through the holidays does life experience the eternity of the river that returns to its source. Then life becomes eternal" (quoted in Karp, *The Jewish Way of Life*, p. 149).

The festivals are the moments of exultation that dot the Jewish year and elevate it from domination by the workaday world. Rabbi Abraham Karp has written: "The holidays are the jewels on the crown of Judaism. They add beauty to the life of a people whose vocation is to proclaim the sovereignty of God. . . . They elevate man above the rest of creation, liberating him from the chains of nature which bind him to unceasing labor and the chains of time which bind him to the here and now. He desists from labor and soars through heart and mind to spheres of spiritual delight. He breaks the bonds of time as he relives experiences of ages past and envisions with the prophets the end of days.

"Through the holidays, the Jew celebrates the goodness of God, the life of his people, and his own free adventurous spirit and exalted destiny as child and co-worker with God" (ibid., p. 150).

The festivals are the sacred days that express the unique teachings of Judaism, fostering them and transmitting them to the generations to come. Each festival has its distinct philosophy, its own historical referent, and its special observances.

The major festivals are usually categorized in two separate groupings: the שָׁלֹשׁ רְגָלִים, or Three Pilgrimage Festivals (Pesaḥ, Shavu'ot, and Sukkot), and the יָמִים נוֹרָאִים, or Days of Awe (Rosh Hashanah and Yom Kippur).

All three of the Pilgrimage Festivals—

1. commemorate an important event in Jewish history;
2. mark a stage of the harvest and thus are agricultural festivals;
3. impart an essential religious truth;
4. have the same rules regarding prohibited and permitted work.

2. Work on the Festivals

The commandment "Ye shall do no manner of work" (Lev. 23:3), which pertains to the Sabbath, is given without any qualification. The commandment pertaining to the festivals, "You shall do no manner of servile work" (Lev. 23:7, 21, 35, 36), is qualified, however, by the statement: "save that which every man must eat (*okhel nefesh*), that only may be done by you" (Exod. 12:16).

The sages of the Mishnah expressed this distinction succinctly: "The festival differs from the Sabbath only in respect to the preparation of food" (M. *Meg.* 1:5; B. *Bet.* 5:2). Accordingly, they permitted work on the festivals that is connected with the preparation of food, such as baking and cooking, or the labor necessary for these.

In defining *okhel nefesh* the rabbis used several principles. The problem centers around the question of what should be included in the term *preparation of food.*

How far in the process of the preparation may we go? Do we include the cutting of grain in the field for the preparation of bread, or the slaughtering of an animal in the case of meat?

The first principle applied was that the work should not be done on the festival if it could be done before the festival without impairing the quality of the food (*O.H.* 495:1 in Rama ad loc.).

Second, the activities should be avoided if they are of such a nature that they would threaten the sanctity and joy of the festival (Maimonides, *Hil. Yom Ṭov* 1:5; *O.H.* 495 in Taz, 2). Also, so as not to detract from the joy of the festival, too much work or too heavy work is not permitted (*O.H.* 495 in *Mishnah Berurah* 7; *O.H.* 510:8).

In the case of two types of work, הַבְעָרָה (transferring fire) and הוֹצָאָה (carrying), the rabbis established the principle: מִתּוֹךְ שֶׁהֻתְּרָה לְצוֹרֶךְ הֻתְּרָה נַמִּי שֶׁלֹּא לְצוֹרֶךְ (B. *Bet.* 12a)—since it is permitted when necessary, it is permitted even when not necessary. According to Maimonides, this relaxation was motivated by the desire to add to the joy of the festivals (*Hil. Yom Ṭov* 1:4–6).

According to some opinions, anything that can be included in the category of *hana'at haguf* (pleasure derived by the body) is also included in the category of *okhel nefesh,* provided it is דָּבָר הַשָּׁוֶה לְכָל נֶפֶשׁ—something enjoyed by all and not limited to certain individuals (*O.H.* 511:1 in *Mishnah Berurah* 1). Taking a bath and smoking would be examples of the former.

The all-embracing principle behind these regulations is the talmudic decision that "half of it [the enjoyment of the festival] is for the Lord, and half of it for yourselves" (B. *Bet.* 15b).

These general principles result in the following specific rules:

All work prohibited on the Sabbath is prohibited on the festivals, with the exception of certain kinds of work connected with the preparation of food, transferring fire, and carrying (*O.H.* 495:1). Lighting and extinguishing gas and electric ovens in connection with cooking is permitted (*O.H.* 514:1; *Mishpeṭei 'Uzi'el, O.H.* 66b). In the case of gas, it is understood that the pilot light stays lit.

Harvesting and grinding of grain, even if done in the preparation of food for the festival, are not permitted (*O.H.* 495:2). (See the interesting note on grinding coffee beans in *O.H.* 504 in *Sha'arei Teshuvah* 3. This is permitted because freshly ground coffee tastes better and thus the joy of the festival is enhanced.)

Purchasing food is not permitted (*O.H.* 500:1). In an emergency, one may obtain food in a manner that does not look like a formal business transaction (*O.H.* 323:4, 517:1).

Preparation of food during the festival for consumption after the festival is not permitted unless some of it will be eaten during the festival (*O.H.* 503:1). If the festival should occur on a Friday, food may be prepared for the Sabbath only if an *'eruv tavshilin* has been made (see below).

Kneading dough is permitted (*O.H.* 506:3).

Cheese-making and butter-churning are not permitted (*O.H.* 510:5 and Rama ad loc.).

Smoking is permitted for one who usually smokes, but not for one who is not a habitual smoker (*O.H.* 514 in *M.A.* 4; *B.H.* 1).

There are certain types of work which are theoretically permitted on the festivals, but yet give the feeling that they are not in accord with the spirit of the festival. These may be done, but in a manner different than usual. Thus, while carrying is permitted, one should carry a heavy object only in an unusual way (*O.H.* 510:8). In grinding pepper and other spices, one should avoid using the type of grinder normally employed (*O.H.* 504:1). The same law applies to the crushing of grits (*O.H.* 504:3).

3. ʻEruv Tavshilin

If one of the days of the festival occurs on Friday, it is theoretically forbidden to cook in preparation for the Sabbath since the only cooking that is permitted on a festival is of food that will be eaten the same day. However, if one cooks on the festival for the festival itself and some food remains, the remainder may be eaten on the Sabbath (*O.H.* 527:1).

To cook on a festival which occurs on Friday for the following Sabbath, one must prepare an *ʻeruv tavshilin.* An *ʻeruv tavshilin* is a dish that is cooked before the festival and kept until the Sabbath. By doing this we indicate that the cooking necessary for the Sabbath began before the advent of the festival, and thus we may cook on the festival for the Sabbath.

The procedure is to take a cooked or roasted dish and a piece of bread and recite the benediction אֲשֶׁר קִדְּשָׁנוּ בְּמִצְוֹתָיו וְצִוָּנוּ עַל מִצְוַת עֵרוּב and add בַּהֲדֵין עֵרוּבָא יְהֵא שָׁרֵא לָנָא לְמֵפָא וּלְבַשָּׁלָא וּלְאַטְמָנָא וּלְאַדְלָקָא שְׁרָגָא וּלְמֶעְבַּד כָּל צָרְכָנָא מִיּוֹמָא טָבָא לְשַׁבְּתָא (*O.H.* 527:12).

While the obligation of making an *ʻeruv tavshilin* applies to all, a rabbi should add the words לָנוּ וּלְכָל הַדָּרִים בָּעִיר הַזֹּאת so that anyone in the community who forgets or was not in a position to make an *ʻeruv* will still be able to cook for the Sabbath (*O.H.* 527:7, 12).

4. The Second Day of the Festival

According to the Bible, the festivals during which no work was to be done comprised one day of Rosh Hashanah, one day of Yom Kippur, the first and last days of Sukkot, the first and last days of Pesaḥ, and one day of

Shavu'ot (B. *Bet.* 4b). Later, one day was added to each of these, with the exception of Yom Kippur (B. *Bet.* 4b–5a).

This practice was based on the way the calendar was calculated in ancient times. Originally, the beginning of each month was determined by direct observation of the phases of the moon. A council of the Sanhedrin sat in session beginning with the thirtieth of each month to receive witnesses who had seen the "new moon." If the tiniest crescent of the moon had been observed, to the satisfaction of the court, the day was declared Rosh Ḥodesh. If not, then the next day was declared Rosh Ḥodesh (M. *R.H.* 2:5–7).

When the court declared the new moon to be *mequdash* (sanctified), the news was spread to the people by means of beacons lit on the tops of mountains (M. *R.H.* 2:4). When the awaited signal was observed on neighboring mountains, similar fires were lit "until one could behold the whole of the diaspora before him like a mass of fire" (M. *R.H.* 2:4). When the Samaritans deliberately attempted to confuse the Jews by lighting such signals at the wrong time, the practice was discontinued. In its place messengers were sent to convey the news (M. *R.H.* 2:2). This put those who lived far away at a disadvantage. In the case of Rosh Hashanah the disadvantage was particularly strong, since Rosh Hashanah occurs on the first of the month and therefore no time was left for the messengers to arrive. This problem gave birth to the יוֹם טוֹב שֵׁנִי שֶׁל גָּלֻיּוֹת (the second day of the festival observed in the diaspora). Residents of places that the messengers did not reach observed all the festivals for two days since they could not be sure whether the first of the month was on the thirtieth of the previous month or on the thirty-first (B. *Bet.* 4b).

A two-day Rosh Hashanah was sometimes observed even in Jerusalem, for the residents began to observe the festival on the thirtieth day lest the witnesses come and testify that they had seen the new moon that day. If they came late that day, another day had to be observed (B. *R.H.* 30b). Only in the case of Yom Kippur was one day observed since the observance of two days would cause undue hardship.

When the calendar became fixed, the custom of observing two days was retained in the diaspora (B. *Bet.* 4b). In Israel one day was observed, as it is today with the exception of Rosh Hashanah. There is good authority for the theory that Rosh Hashanah was observed for only one day until the thirteenth century (see Wahrman, *Ḥagei Yisra'el Umo'adaw*, pp. 25 f.).

Since the fixed calendar made a second day unnecessary, why was it retained? The Talmud suggests: "Be careful with the customs that you have from your fathers because sometimes the government may pass decrees and we may become subject to error" (B. *Bet.* 4b).

The question has arisen in recent times whether there is still sufficient reason to retain the second day. Would it not be hypothetically possible to restore the original way of determining the calendar? A court in Jerusalem could declare the beginning of the new month, and with modern means of communication, the news could soon be flashed to the entire world. Or perhaps we could rely completely on the fixed calendar, since the fear expressed in the Talmud would not apply today.

Halakhically, there is a difference of opinion in the interpretation of the precaution expressed in the Talmud. According to one opinion, the exhortation הִזָּהֲרוּ בְּמִנְהַג אֲבוֹתֵיכֶם, "be careful with the customs that you have from your fathers," is based on the statement that follows: זִימְנִין דְּגָזְרוּ מַלְכוּת גְּזֵירָה, "sometimes the government may pass decrees." Hence, if there is no reason for the second, the first one becomes irrelevant. However, there is another opinion that these are two separate reasons, and that the admonition to uphold the usages of our fathers stands regardless of the other circumstances. Hence the second day of the festival in the diaspora has become a fixed practice (*Otsar Hage'onim, Bet.*, p. 8; *Beirur Halakhah* of Rabbi Kook to *Bet.* 4b).

The practical considerations are economic and social. However, if a change is to be made, it would be unwise to do it unilaterally (see the responsum by Rabbi Aaron Blumenthal in the archives of the Committee on Law and Standards). It is suggested, however, that the second day should not be a mere repetition of the first, but should be given special significance.

Where a second day is observed, the laws regarding work on the first day also apply to the second (*O.H.* 496:1). The burial of the dead is the main exception to this rule. For those who are occupied with burial, all work connected with a burial is permitted on the second day—יום טוב שֵׁנִי לְגַבֵּי מֵת כְּחוֹל שַׁוְיוּהָ רַבָּנָן (B. *Bet.* 6a; *O.H.* 496:2).

The treatment of the sick is another exception. Medical treatment is permitted on the second day of a festival even when no danger is involved.

Nowadays, since it is not unusual to delay burial for other reasons, since the old hygienic reasons (i.e., the danger of putrefaction) are no longer applicable, and since there is no *niwwul hamet* (insult to the dead) involved, many communities forbid burials on Yom Ṭov Sheini. A contributing reason for this practice is that, under present circumstances, a great deal of *ḥillul yom ṭov* (desecration of the festival) is inevitable in such cases.

In the case of Israelis who are visiting other lands or of people from the diaspora who are visiting Israel, we apply the principle of נוֹתְנִין עָלָיו חֻמְרֵי מָקוֹם שֶׁיָּצָא מִשָּׁם וְחֻמְרֵי מָקוֹם שֶׁהָלַךְ לְשָׁם (M. *Pes.* 4:1). Therefore, both tourists visiting Israel and Israelis visiting the diaspora should observe two days (*O.H.* 496:3). However, one who comes to settle should follow the norm of the land (ibid.). An Israeli visiting the United States must observe the second day by refraining from work but should privately say the weekday 'Amidah and should also put on Tefilin (*O.H.* 496 in *Mishnah Berurah* 13). Similarly, a tourist visiting Israel should say the festival prayers privately at home on the second day without making the observance obvious (*O.H.* 496 in *Sha'arei Teshuvah* 3, ad loc.). A decision of the Law Committee of the Rabbinical Assembly (not unanimous) gave visitors to Israel who wish to follow the prevailing practice of observing only one day the option to do so. This, of course, does not include Rosh Hashanah (see Law Committee archives).

Candles should be lit at the advent of festivals just as they are at the beginning of the Sabbath, but for festivals the blessing is לְהַדְלִיק נֵר שֶׁל יוֹם טוֹב (*O.H.* 514:11). If the festival falls on a Sabbath, the blessing is לְהַדְלִיק נֵר שֶׁל שַׁבָּת וְשֶׁל יוֹם טוֹב. On the second night of Yom Ṭov, candles are lit after the conclusion of the first day; not before. On all festivals except the last two days of Pesaḥ, the blessing over the candles is followed by the שֶׁהֶחֱיָנוּ.

UNIT VII

PESAḤ (I)

Introduction
The Four Parashiyot
Shabbat Hagadol
The Month of Nisan
The Eve of Passover
The Disposal of Leaven
Kashering of Utensils
Forbidden Foods
The First Night of Passover

VII.
Pesaḥ (I)

1. Introduction

We noted in the preceding unit that the Pilgrimage Festivals have a threefold significance: historical, agricultural, and ideological. We can illustrate these as they apply to Pesaḥ (Passover).

As a historical festival, Pesaḥ commemorates the liberation of the children of Israel from Egyptian bondage. The exodus looms large not only for Pesaḥ but also for a number of other Jewish institutions. The phrase זֵכֶר לִיצִיאַת מִצְרָיִם ("as a memorial of the exodus from Egypt") occurs frequently in our liturgy. Many of the mitswot have the memory of the exodus as one of their themes. The Decalogue, in proclaiming the sovereignty of God, describes Him as the God who brought us out of the land of Egypt (Exod. 20:2; Deut. 5:6). The Qiddush for Sabbaths and festivals uses the phrase זֵכֶר לִיצִיאַת מִצְרָיִם, and in the third paragraph of the Shema' we recite: "I am the Lord your God, who brought thee out of the land of Egypt" (Num. 15:41). Thus Pesaḥ is dedicated to the celebration of this historical event and to its memorialization.

As a festival of nature, Pesaḥ is a springtime holiday that has its parallels in the calendars of other peoples. When nature reawakens and the fields bring forth their fruit again, man is impelled to rejoice. The month of Nisan is called חוֹדֶשׁ הָאָבִיב, as it is written: "Observe the month of Aviv and keep the Passover unto the Lord thy God" (Deut. 16:1; the term *'aviv* designates the green ears of grain and thus refers to the beginning of the spring harvest). Consequently Pesaḥ was also called חַג הָאָבִיב, or the spring festival. As time passed, the agricultural theme of the festival was muted and the historical took precedence. However, a number of observances remain to celebrate the rebirth of nature. On the first day of Pesaḥ, at Musaf, we recite the prayer for dew; on the second night we start counting the 'Omer; and on the Sabbath of the festival it is customary to read the Song of Songs with its description of spring. This constitutes our recognition that the forces in the physical environment which make for physical survival and well-being have a divine source.

The historical theme of all the festivals teaches us "that in awakening in the nations the power of historical consciousness, [the Jews] have assumed the responsibility of directing that power into channels of peace and good will" (Kaplan, *The Meaning of God in Modern Jewish Religion,* p. 192). Basing the festivals on historical events gives man a sense of history, and "through his sense of history, man enlarges his field of operation far beyond the range of the three generations of time with which life is usually contemporaneous" (ibid., p. 189).

The Pilgrimage Festivals all center around the early history of our people. To understand a man's personality, psychiatrists probe his mind to learn of his earliest experiences. The experiences of infancy and childhood have a decisive influence on the entire development of a human being. This is true of a nation as well. Our destiny has been shaped by our historical experience.

But Pesaḥ does not focus on the exodus simply as a historical event that took place long ago. In the Haggadah we recite: "One must look upon himself as if he himself had come out of Egypt, personally" (quoted from M. *Pes.* 10:5). The exodus is contemporary for every generation of Jews. Jefferson said: "Eternal vigilance is the price of freedom." Pesaḥ provides that eternal vigilance for the Jewish people.

When Moses first approached Pharaoh regarding the liberation of the Jewish people, the king of Egypt asked: "Who is this God that I should obey Him and free Israel?" (Exod. 5:2). Pharaoh knew of no god who redeems the oppressed. Professor Kaplan has written: "The conception of God as the redeemer of the oppressed has revolutionized the meaning and function of religion, and has placed it at the service of the ethical impulses" (Kaplan, *The Meaning of God,* p. 268). In the words of a contemporary theologian: "What makes the exodus from Egypt the pattern of redemption for all mankind is the interpretation of the prophet who sees God as a redeemer from tyranny; the God of Israel makes history the place where man progresses to freedom" (Maybaum, *The Face of God after Auschwitz,* p. 177).

Kabbalists have understood freedom as the emancipation from the powers of evil and the realm of Satan, who lies in wait for man and tries to enslave him morally. Translated into modern categories of thought, this means moral responsibility as against subjugation to passion, impulse, and instinct. Thus Rabbi Kook writes: "The difference between a slave and a free man is not only a difference in status; that is, that by a matter of chance one person is subject to another person, and another person is not. We can find a wise bondman whose spirit is filled with freedom, and a free man who has the spirit of a slave. Authentic freedom is the exalted spirit to which a man and a people as a whole are elevated so that one is faithful to his inner self, to the image of God that is within him" (*'Olat Re'iyah,* 2:245).

These ideas are not left in the abstract but are expressed in the many observances that cluster around Pesaḥ.

2. The Four Parashiyot

In the six weeks preceding Pesaḥ during the months of Adar and Nisan, there occur four special Sabbaths called שְׁקָלִים, זָכוֹר, פָּרָה, and שַׁבָּת הַחֹדֶשׁ. In addition, the Sabbath immediately preceding Pesaḥ is called שַׁבָּת הַגָּדוֹל. The first four are referred to as the אַרְבַּע פָּרָשִׁיּוֹת and are distinguished by additional readings from the Torah and special lessons from the prophets. Two of these are connected with the celebration of Passover (M. *Meg.* 3:4). (A good summary of the אַרְבַּע פָּרָשִׁיּוֹת can be found in the *Mishnah Berurah* on *O.H.* 681:1, n. 1.)

Shabbat Sheqalim

In ancient days, every male Israelite twenty years and older had to contribute a half-shekel annually to the maintenance of the Temple in Jerusalem. This had to be paid before the first of Nisan. In order to remind the people of this duty, proclamations were made on the first of Adar that the half-shekel was due (M. *Sheq.* 1:1). Inasmuch as Jews came to the synagogue on the Sabbath, it was instituted that on the Sabbath preceding the first of Adar, the Torah reading would include the passage describing the first proclamation of the half-shekel. On that Sabbath two Torah scrolls are removed from the ark. In one we read the portion of the week, and in the other Exodus 30:11–16, which contains this passage (*O.H.* 685:1). If the first day of Adar occurs on a Sabbath, three Torah scrolls are used: the first for the portion of the week, the second for the section for Rosh Ḥodesh (Num. 29:9–15), and the third for the section for Sheqalim (*O.H.* 685:1). Ḥatzi Qaddish is recited on the Sabbaths of the four parashiyot upon completion of the reading from the scroll prior to the one from which the Mafṭir is read.

The Hafṭarah is from II Kings 12:1–17, which is an account of the gifts contributed for the repair of the Temple in the reign of King Jehoash. This Hafṭarah is recited even if Shabbat Sheqalim falls on Rosh Ḥodesh (*O.H.* 685:1).

In a leap year Shabbat Sheqalim occurs on the Sabbath before Adar II, or on Rosh Ḥodesh Adar II if it occurs on the Sabbath.

Shabbat Zakhor

The Sabbath preceding Purim is called Shabbat Zakhor. Again two Torah scrolls are used. In the first the portion of the week is read, and in the second, Deuteronomy 25:17–19, which tells of the battle with Amalek. This portion begins with the word זָכוֹר—hence the name of the Sabbath. The Hafṭarah is from I Samuel 15:1–34, which also tells of a battle with the Amalekites. This material is associated with Purim because of a tradition that Haman was a descendant of the Amalekites since he was called an Agagite, and Agag was king of the Amalekites in the time of Samuel (I Sam. 15:8).

Shabbat Parah

The third of the four Sabbaths is Shabbat Parah. This must always precede the last of the four Sabbaths, Shabbat Haḥodesh. Thus if Rosh Ḥodesh Nisan falls on a Sabbath and it also becomes Shabbat Haḥodesh, Shabbat Parah falls on the last Sabbath of Adar (*O.H.* 685:3–4). If Rosh Ḥodesh Nisan is in the middle of the week, Shabbat Haḥodesh falls on the last Sabbath of the month of Adar and Shabbat Parah precedes it (*O.H.* 685:5).

Again two Torah scrolls are used. From the first we read the portion of the week, and from the second, the laws concerning the red heifer (*parah adumah*) in Numbers 19:1–22. The Hafṭarah deals with the future purification of Israel as described in the Book of Ezekiel (36:16–38).

All Israelites came to the Temple in Jerusalem on Pesaḥ in order to offer the Paschal lamb. They had to be in a state of ritual purity to perform this rite. Since the ashes of the red heifer were used in the process of purification, this passage served to remind those who were not in a state of purity to take the necessary steps.

Shabbat Haḥodesh

The Sabbath before the month of Nisan, or the first of Nisan if it is a Saturday, is Shabbat Haḥodesh. Again two Torah scrolls are used. In the first we read the portion of the week, and in the second, Exodus 12:1–20. If Rosh Ḥodesh Nisan is on Sabbath, three Torah scrolls are used. In the first we read the portion of the week, in the second, the portion for Rosh Ḥodesh (Num. 28:9–15), and in the third, that of Shabbat Haḥodesh. Qaddish is said after the reading of the second scroll. The Hafṭarah is Ezekiel 45:16–46:18, which contains a description of the sacrifices to be brought on the first of Nisan, Pesaḥ, and other festivals in the future Temple. This Sabbath celebrates the arrival of the month of Nisan, during which the liberation of the children of Israel took place.

3. Shabbat Hagadol

In addition to these four Sabbaths, the Sabbath immediately preceding Pesaḥ is called Shabbat Hagadol (*O.H.* 430:1). It received the title "great" because of the importance of the approaching festival. In the opinion of at least one scholar, the Sabbath before each of the festivals was originally called Shabbat Hagadol because of the instruction sought and given respecting the observances of the coming festival (Zunz, *Ritus*, p. 10). The name has been preserved only in the case of the Sabbath before Pesaḥ possibly because in this case the questions were more numerous.

Other explanations have been given. According to tradition, the tenth of Nisan in the year of the exodus was on a Saturday; it was considered a great event, in fact a miracle, that the Israelites could on that day select a lamb for sacrifice without being molested by their Egyptian masters, who, at other times, would have stoned them for such daring (Exod. 8:22; *O.H.* 430:1 in *M.A.*). Another possible reason for the name is that the Hafṭarah speaks of the "great day" of the Lord on which Messiah will appear (Mal. 3:4–24).

A most cogent and yet novel explanation is that the people used to return from the synagogue later than usual on this Sabbath because of the unusually long discourse that was customary on this day. Thus this Sabbath seemed "great," i.e., longer than the other Sabbaths (*Shibolei Haleqeṭ*, sec. 205).

There is no change in the service or the Torah reading on this Sabbath. According to some customs we are to recite part of the Haggadah, from עֲבָדִים

לְכַפֵּר עַל כָּל עֲוֹנוֹתֵינוּ to הָיִינוּ, instead of Psalm 104, normally recited on Sabbath afternoons in the winter (Rama on *O.H.* 430:1).

4. The Month of Nisan

The month of Nisan itself, because of Pesaḥ, partakes of the nature of a festive occasion. Hence, Taḥanun is not said during the entire month, nor is צִדְקָתְךָ said on Shabbat at Minḥah. At funerals, no eulogies are said except for persons of distinction, nor is it the custom to recite צִדּוּק הַדִּין or אֵל מָלֵא רַחֲמִים (*O.H.* 429:2 and Rama ad loc.). In the manual of the Rabbinical Assembly there is a variant of the memorial prayer which is suggested for use on such days. Since the memorial prayer has become so intimately associated with the funeral service that the family would be hurt by its omission, this prayer can provide for a felt need.

Ma'ot Ḥiṭṭin

It is an ancient custom to make special solicitation of funds before Pesaḥ to be used to help those in need. While charity is a mitswah at all times, it was felt that on Pesaḥ particularly, no one should go hungry (Rama on *O.H.* 429:1), and everyone should have the wherewithal for the Sedarim.

5. The Eve of Passover

On the day before Passover, Psalm 100, מִזְמוֹר לְתוֹדָה, and Psalm 20, לַמְנַצֵּחַ, are omitted at the morning service (Rama on *O.H.* 429:2). Psalm 100 is associated with the thanksgiving offering in the Temple, which was not offered on the day before Passover because the loaves that were part of the offering contained ḥamets (*O.H.* 429:2 in *B.H.* 9).

A first-born son should fast on this day to commemorate the deliverance of the first-born Israelites in Egypt (*O.H.* 470:1). In this case first-born refers both to a first-born of the mother and to a first-born of the father (ibid.). It has become customary for the rabbi to make a Siyyum (a public reading and explanation of the concluding passage of a tractate of Talmud, the study of which has been completed) on the morning before Pesaḥ. Since eating at such an occasion is a *se'udat mitswah,* a festive meal which accompanies the performance of certain mitswot, the first-born who are present at the

Siyyum may join in the festivities and eat (*O.H.* 470 in *Mishnah Berurah* 10; *Ḥawot Ya'ir* 7 in the name of Maharshal).

If this day falls on the Sabbath, the same procedure is followed on the preceding Thursday (*O.H.* 470:2). All other matters pertaining to this day should be done one day earlier. Thus, *bediqat ḥamets* is done the night previous (Thursday night), the cleaning and the burning of the ḥamets are done the day previous (Friday), and just enough food is left to suffice for the Friday night meal and for the Saturday morning meal to be eaten while the eating of ḥamets is still permitted.

6. The Disposal of Leaven

The Bible prohibits the eating of ḥamets during the festival of Pesaḥ (Exod. 12:15–20). The word חָמֵץ is translated as "leavened bread." Basically it refers to food prepared from five species of grain—wheat, barley, oats, spelt, and rye—that has been allowed to leaven. To these, Ashkenazic rabbis added rice, millet, corn, and legumes. There are certain differences between the former and the latter that will be explained below.

If any amount of the above becomes mixed with other food, this also becomes ḥamets. This is called *ta'arovet ḥamets.* Most of the products that we consider ḥamets are in this category. Other foods are not considered to be subject to leavening.

Matsah is unleavened bread made from any of these five species of grain. It is customary, however, to make the matsah from wheat flour only. It is essential, of course, that the wheat and flour be given no chance to leaven. Hence the grain used for matsah must be kept perfectly dry.

The rule against leaven applies not only to its consumption (אֲכִילָה), but also to enjoying any benefit thereof (הֲנָאָה) and even to its possession. Therefore, before the advent of Pesaḥ all leaven must be removed from one's premises. Nor should one have leaven in his legal possession.

To satisfy these requirements we must have בְּדִיקַת חָמֵץ, the search for leaven; בִּטּוּל חָמֵץ, the nullification of leaven; בִּעוּר חָמֵץ, the removal or burning of leaven; and מְכִירַת חָמֵץ, the selling of leaven.

The Search for Leaven

The night before Pesaḥ, immediately after sundown, we begin the search for leaven (M. *Pes.* 1:1; *O.H.* 431:1). Our aim is to insure that no leaven has been left behind after the cleaning of the house. Hence, places where no leaven is used during the year do not need to be searched (ibid.).

The procedure is as follows. A candle is lit, the benediction עַל בִּעוּר חָמֵץ is recited, and the house is searched by the light of the candle (*O.H.* 432:1, 433:1). Since by this time the house has been cleaned thoroughly, and the chances of finding any leaven are minimal, it has become customary to put a number of crumbs of bread in places where they can be easily found in order to prevent the recitation of a *berakhah levaṭalah,* a benediction in vain (*O.H.* 432:2; *Tanya Rabbati, Hilkhot Hapesaḥ,* sec. 43; see also comment of Shneur Zalman of Lyady, *Shulḥan 'Arukh* 432:11, who doubts whether there could be a *berakhah levaṭalah* even if no leaven is found).

The crumbs of bread that are found and the leaven left over for breakfast should be guarded lest a new search become necessary (*O.H.* 434:1).

The Nullification of Leaven

After the search for leaven, one recites the formula for *biṭṭul ḥamets* (*O.H.* 432:4). The following morning, between ten and eleven o'clock, the leaven is burned, and again the formula for *biṭṭul ḥamets* is recited—this time with a slight variation. At night we say דְּלָא חֲמִתֵּהּ וּדְלָא בִעַרְתֵּהּ, and in the morning, דַּחֲמִתֵּהּ וּדְלָא חֲמִתֵּהּ, דְּבִעַרְתֵּהּ וּדְלָא בִעַרְתֵּהּ (*O.H.* 434:2, 4).

If a person is leaving on a trip during the thirty days preceding Pesaḥ, and does not plan to be back by Pesaḥ, he should perform *bediqah* without a blessing before departing; prior to the thirty days preceding Pesaḥ no *bediqah* is necessary. Before Pesaḥ arrives, wherever one is, one should recite the *biṭṭul.* If one plans to return just before Pesaḥ, he should make *bediqah* before leaving lest he return too late (*O.H.* 436:1).

Families that go away for the entire Pesaḥ should sell their leaven and lock up the house. They need not do anything additional in preparation for Pesaḥ (*O.H.* 436:2; Zevin, *Hamo'adim Bahalakhah,* p. 252; *Sedeh Ḥemed* under *Ḥamets Umatsah* 9:6).

The Selling of Leaven

One must not have any leaven in his legal possession during Pesaḥ (*O.H.* 445, 446). In a simple economy this was easily managed. If by chance a bit of leaven was left, it could be disposed of without any difficulty. When the economy became more complex, a new solution had to be found. It has been suggested that there was a transition period when leaven was sold, but to a non-Jewish friend with the full knowledge that it was a temporary sale (Zevin, *Hamo'adim Bahalakhah*, p. 246). When this process led to collusion, it was instituted that at least outwardly the sale take a legal form using a formal bill of sale, or שְׁטַר מְכִירָה (ibid., p. 248; *O.H.* 448:3, *M.A.* 4). Now the sale is carried out through the agency of the rabbi in order to insure that the proper form is maintained (*Sedeh Ḥemed* under *Ḥamets Umatsah*, sec. 9).

The procedure is as follows. We use a שְׁטַר הַרְשָׁאָה, an authorization which gives the rabbi power of attorney. Those who wish to sell their leaven sign their names under this agency appointment and authorize the rabbi to act in their behalf. The authorization empowers the rabbi to sell the leaven they own, and the place where it is stored, at terms that he sees fit. The rabbi keeps the authorization and sells the leaven to a non-Jew by means of a *shṭar mekhirah* which contains all the terms of the sale. At the conclusion of Pesaḥ he buys it back. While this transaction is not intended to be a real sale, nevertheless, since all the formal requirements of a legal sale have been met, it satisfies the requirement of the law forbidding the possession of leaven during Passover.

The Burning of Leaven

The leaven that was found during the *bediqah*, as well as any other leaven that was left over, is destroyed by burning (*O.H.* 445:1).

While the prohibition against the use or ownership of leaven begins at noon on the fourteenth of Nisan, the rabbis ordered, as a precautionary measure, that leaven be burned at least an hour earlier (*O.H.* 434:2). After the burning the formula for *biṭṭul ḥamets* is repeated with the variation mentioned above (*O.H.* 434:3). Leaven may not be eaten from two hours before noon. (These hours must be adjusted to the length of the day and daylight savings time, if in effect.)

7. Kashering of Utensils

It is customary to remove the utensils that have been used during the year and replace them with new ones, or with utensils that are used exclusively for Pesaḥ. Today, it is customary to have special dishes for Pesaḥ. However, vessels used during the year may be used for Pesaḥ if they undergo a process of purging known as "kashering" or *hag'alah*. The aim is to cleanse the vessel in such a way that it is purged of any leaven it may have absorbed. The principle behind the procedure is כְּבוֹלְעוֹ כָּךְ פּוֹלְטוֹ—"as the vessel absorbs so does it rid itself of what it absorbed" (B. *Pes.* 30a; Rashi ad loc.).

Therefore, cooking utensils are kashered by boiling, while those used for broiling over an open fire must be heated until they are red-hot or until they become so hot that a piece of paper will be singed if touched to the utensil (*O.H.* 451:4, 5). Utensils used only for cold food may be kashered by rinsing (*O.H.* 451:22).

The process of kashering through boiling is as follows. The utensils to be kashered must first be thoroughly cleansed (*O.H.* 451:3) and should not be used for at least twenty-four hours (Rama on *O.H.* 452:2). They are then immersed in a container filled with boiling water. Some add a red-hot stone to the water so that the heat will be retained and (in the case of a large vessel which cannot be immersed in another) so that the water overruns the rim and cleanses the outside as well (*O.H.* 452:6). The utensils are then rinsed in cold water (*O.H.* 452:7).

The kashering should be completed before ten o'clock in the morning on the fourteenth of Nisan (*O.H.* 452:1, see *B.H.* 1).

Earthenware may not be kashered because it is porous and cannot be completely purged (*O.H.* 451:1). Glassware should be soaked in water for seventy-two hours with the water changed every twenty-four hours (*Ḥayyei Adam, Klal* 125:22; *O.H.* 451:26).

There is a difference of opinion in the case of pyrex dishes. Some authorities classify these as earthenware, which may not be kashered. Others suggest that since pyrex is hard and nonporous, and there is no danger that it will crack while boiling, they may be kashered in the same manner as utensils. The latter opinion has enough support to be considered normative (see *Ḥavalim Bane'imim,* pt. 4, no. 6; *Sha'arim Metsuyanim Bahalakhah,* 3:108).

Metal utensils glazed with nonporous substances, such as agate or teflon, have also aroused controversy because it was not known of what substance the glaze was made. Some authorities have classified them as earthenware (see *Ḥatam Sofer,* pt. 2, no. 113). Today we know that the lining is not made of a porous substance, nor of a substance that would be damaged by boiling. Hence kashering should be permitted (see *She'eilat Mosheh, Y.D.* no. 24: *'Arukh Hashulḥan, Y.D.* 121:27; *Hagahot Maharsham, O.H.* 451:3; *Yad Me'ir* no. 1; *Maharam Schick, O.H.* 238).

Knives, forks, and spoons are kashered in the same way as other metal utensils (*O.H.* 451:3). If the handles are of wood or some other material attached to the blade, kashering is not effective because particles of food may penetrate the joint in such a manner that they can never be removed (ibid. in *M.D.* 5). If the handles are of material that is welded to the blade so that no particles of food can penetrate, they may be kashered.

Tables, closets, and cupboards that have been used for leaven are kashered by pouring hot water over them (*O.H.* 451:20). Today it is customary to cover them before using for Pesaḥ (ibid. in *B.H.* 43).

The covers of vessels, like the vessels themselves, must be kashered (*O.H.* 451:14).

Regarding autoclaving—i.e., kashering with steam rather than water—there is a difference of opinion. One opinion is that only water can serve the purpose (*O.H.* 451:5). Today we know that steam under pressure penetrates more and has a more potent purging effect. Hence it should be permitted (cf. *Maharsham,* pt. 1, no. 94; *Yad Yitsḥaq,* pt. 2, no. 216; *Avnei Neizer, Y.D.* pt. 1, no. 111; *Hagahot Maharsham* on *O.H.* 451:3; *Yad Me'ir,* sec. 1).

Electrical appliances cannot be immersed. If, however, the parts that come in contact with the leaven are detachable, these may be kashered. Thus the beaters and bowl of an electric mixer can be removed and kashered.

Porcelain is in the category of earthenware and may not be kashered. Fine china, though, if not used for twelve months, has the status of new dishes (Medini, *Sedeh Ḥemed* under *Ḥamets Umatsah* 7:2).

Vessels or articles that may be damaged by hot water should not be kashered (*O.H.* 451:7).

Articles which cannot be thoroughly cleansed should not be kashered (Rama on *O.H.* 451:18). While theoretically this principle is valid, there are very few objects that do not lend themselves to modern means of cleansing.

The handles of vessels need kashering as well. Where the handles protrude from the vessel in which they are being kashered, it is sufficient to pour boiling water over them (*O.H.* 451:12 in Rama).

It is customary not to kasher utensils used for the kneading of dough (Rama in *O.H.* 451:17).

8. Forbidden Foods

Leaven may not be eaten during the eight days of Passover, beginning with noon of the day preceding Passover. The practice of stopping two hours earlier is a precautionary measure. Theoretically, the term *ḥamets* refers to the five species of grain which have been subjected to the leavening process. These are wheat, barley, spelt, rye, and oats (B. *Pes.* 35a). To these

Ashkenazic rabbis added rice, millet, corn, and legumes (*O.H.* 453:1 in Rama).

The law against the use of leaven on Passover applies not only to eating (אִסּוּר אֲכִילָה), but also to using it in any way (אִסּוּר הֲנָאָה), to legal possession, and to keeping it on one's premises. The last is an extra precaution that was made only in the case of leaven, inasmuch as one might easily forget and use it (B. *Pes.* 2a in Tosafot, s.v. אור לארבעה עשר; *Torah Shlemah,* vol. 19, supplement, chap. 20).

Leavening is caused when the grain or its products come into contact with water. This excludes moistening with other liquids, such as undiluted fruit juices (*O.H.* 462:1). Hence cakes made with kosher-for-Passover flour and eggs or undiluted fruit juices are not forbidden (*O.H.* 462:4).

There are several kinds of leaven. What was mentioned above—i.e., grain or its products that have come in contact with water—is חָמֵץ בְּעֵין (visible ḥamets). Food that is not leaven in itself but contains an admixture or has come in contact with חָמֵץ בְּעֵין is תַּעֲרוֹבֶת חָמֵץ. Since an admixture of even the smallest amount of leaven (*ḥamets bemashehu*) makes a food forbidden, great care must be exercised with all foods. The articles of leaven that are directly forbidden are few in number and easily shunned. The articles that contain some admixture are very large, however, and expert knowledge is required to make the proper discrimination. Hence there are many articles of food that need a *hekhsher,* certification, to show that they are free of such an admixture.

The rule of *ḥamets bemashehu* applies only when the mixing took place after the start of Pesaḥ, i.e., after sunset. If the admixture took place before this time, the same rule applies here as in the case of admixtures of other forbidden foods, i.e., it is *baṭel beshishim,* annulled in a mixture in which the *ḥamets* constitutes less than one-sixtieth of the total (*O.H.* 447:2).

There is also leaven that has become so hard that it is not fit for consumption. According to most authorities this is also forbidden, except that if it becomes mixed with other food, it is subject to the rules of other forbidden foods (*O.H.* 447:9, 447:12 in *M.A.* and *Mishnah Berurah*).

There are many foods that are not intrinsically *ḥamets.* However, customs have developed in certain localities that certain products are not eaten on Pesaḥ. In some cases the reason for the custom has been forgotten. Today we have an ambivalent attitude toward such customs. We do not want to discourage those who want to continue them because they have become part of the aura of the festival. On the other hand, we cannot say a thing is forbidden when it is not (*Ḥayyei Adam* 127:7). In an age of commercialization, this would become an invitation for a fraudulent *hekhsher*. Furthermore, there are many articles for which a *hekhsher* was warranted in the past but is not needed today.

Sugar is the best example of this. In the codes sugar is forbidden on Pesaḥ (*O.H.* 467:8). In a later code we are told that today, when sugar is processed by machine, there is no suspicion of leaven but nevertheless a *hekhsher* is still necessary (*'Arukh Hashulḥan* 467:15). The suspicion of an admixture of leaven was based on the fear that the sugar was adulterated with flour, which was cheaper, or that the laborers would dip their bread into it when it was in liquid form (Medini, *Sedeh Ḥemed,* sec. *Ḥamets Umatsah* 3:19). The first fear was eliminated in the case of sugar that came in solid cone shapes (*hut-zucker,* as it was called). Any adulteration of *hut-zucker* would be easily recognized.

Today all these fears have been eliminated. Hence, packaged sugar can be used without a *hekhsher*. The same is true with coffee, tea, salt, frozen vegetables, dried fruits, and honey, provided no other ingredient has been added (see *O.H.* 447:6; Hoffman, *Melamed Leho'il, O.H.* resp. 79; *Sedeh Ḥemed, Ḥamets Umatsah* 9 and 3:19; *O.H.* 467:8 in *M.A.* and *M.D.*; *Ḥayyei Adam* 127:2–3).

Some people do not use garlic on Pesaḥ. None of the authorities can find a reason for this (*Sedeh Ḥemed, Ḥamets Umatsah* 6:9; *Eishel Avraham* 464:1). The reason may be that in some regions garlic was harvested with knives that were also used for leaven. The same may be true in the case of cabbage. It has also been suggested that garlic may have been mistaken for a legume. Obviously, in such cases there is no reason to continue the custom today (*Ḥayyei Adam* 127:7).

Legumes and corn are forbidden because they can be confused with grain. String beans, however, are a vegetable and hence permitted (*Eishel Avraham,* resp. 453; *Beit David,* resp. 6; *Yad Yitsḥaq,* sec. 3, resp. 92:2).

Oil made from legumes is permitted (Maharsham, vol. 1, resp. 183). Beverages that contain grain alcohol are forbidden (*O.H.* 442 in *Mishnah Berurah* 3). This includes rye, scotch, bourbon, beer, and many mixed drinks that contain alcohol (*O.H.* 442:5).

Pills and tablets are normally free of leaven, but any chemist or druggist should be able to tell whether the ingredients in a particular preparation are of leaven. Among the more commonly used pills and tablets that are permissible on Pesaḥ are saccharin (see Hoffman, *Melamed Leho'il, O.H.* resp. 79), aspirin in its various forms, and digitalis.

Nowadays, given the easy availability of baby foods, it is not necessary to resort to the use of leaven for feeding infants. Where necessary, however, a special place in the house should be assigned for feeding the infant so that his food will not come into contact with other foods in the house.

Many items were avoided because they might have been prepared in a vessel that was used for leaven, or some leaven might have dropped into it by accident. Hence a *hekhsher* was necessary to indicate that this had not occurred. In large, modern industrial plants, where production is specialized and the containers are cleansed thoroughly and sterilized, these possibilities are completely eliminated.

The only items that need a *hekhsher* are those in which the ingredients may or may not be of leaven. The *hekhsher* of a reliable rabbi is a guarantee that the ingredients used do not, in fact, contain any leaven.

9. The First Night of Passover

The advent of Passover, like that of the Sabbath and the other festivals, is marked by the lighting of candles. The benediction אֲשֶׁר קִדְּשָׁנוּ בְּמִצְוֹתָיו וְצִוָּנוּ לְהַדְלִיק נֵר שֶׁל יוֹם טוֹב is recited before lighting the candles (*O.H.* 263:5, 514:11). On the Sabbath the benediction is לְהַדְלִיק נֵר שֶׁל שַׁבָּת וְשֶׁל יוֹם טוֹב.

The time for Minḥah and Ma'ariv is the same as on Friday evening. The Minḥah is that of the weekday. The Ma'ariv is the same as on the Sabbath, except that where וְשָׁמְרוּ is said on the Sabbath, we substitute another biblical quotation suitable for festivals: וַיְדַבֵּר מֹשֶׁה אֶת מֹעֲדֵי יְהוָֹה אֶל בְּנֵי יִשְׂרָאֵל (Lev. 23:44).

The 'Amidah is also similar to that of the Sabbath. It consists of seven benedictions. The first three and the last three are those of the weekday 'Amidah. For the other thirteen, we substitute one benediction called קְדֻשַּׁת הַיּוֹם, which emphasizes the theme of the festival (B. *Beț.* 17a).

According to Rashi, the name קְדֻשַּׁת הַיּוֹם applies specifically to וַתִּתֶּן לָנוּ, which is the heart of the benediction. It is preceded by אַתָּה בְחַרְתָּנוּ, an introductory prayer parallel to אַתָּה קִדַּשְׁתָּ of the Friday night 'Amidah. In rabbinic tradition, the sanctity of the festivals is derived from the sanctity of the children of Israel, since the dates of the festivals were established and proclaimed each year by a human agency, the highest authority of the Jewish people, the Beth Din of Jerusalem; the Sabbath, however, comes automatically every seventh day without the intervention of any human agency. It is God who sanctified the Sabbath. Hence, in the case of the festivals we speak first of the sanctification of the children of Israel.

This is also the reason for the wording of the conclusion of the קְדֻשַּׁת הַיּוֹם benediction: מְקַדֵּשׁ יִשְׂרָאֵל וְהַזְּמַנִּים. Israel is sanctified first and then the festival.

If the festival occurs on the Sabbath, we say מְקַדֵּשׁ הַשַּׁבָּת וְיִשְׂרָאֵל וְהַזְּמַנִּים because the Sabbath is sanctified independently of the children of Israel (B. *Beṭ*. 17a; *O.H.* 187:1).

If the festival is on a Saturday night, the prayer וַתּוֹדִיעֵנוּ, a form of Havdalah, is recited immediately after אַתָּה בְחַרְתָּנוּ. וַתִּתֶּן לָנוּ, a prayer of thanksgiving for the past, is followed by יַעֲלֶה וְיָבוֹא, a prayer for the future, and by וְהַשִּׂיאֵנוּ, the concluding prayer that we carry away with us the true spiritual benefit of the festival (Abrahams, *Companion to the Authorised Daily Prayer Book*, p. 194).

If the festival falls on a Sabbath we add Shabbat before mentioning the festival: אֶת יוֹם הַשַּׁבָּת הַזֶּה וְאֶת יוֹם חַג הַמַּצּוֹת הַזֶּה and מְקַדֵּשׁ הַשַּׁבָּת וְיִשְׂרָאֵל וְהַזְּמַנִּים. We omit מָגֵן אָבוֹת after the ʻAmidah when Pesaḥ falls on a Sabbath because it was included in order to enable latecomers to the synagogue to complete their prayers before the departure of the rest of the congregation, so that they would not have to walk home alone. On Pesaḥ, the festival of freedom, there was no such fear. וַיְכֻלּוּ, however, is included. Inasmuch as it has been omitted in the ʻAmidah, it must be said afterwards in order to attest to the Sabbath as a memorial to creation.

Qiddush is not recited in the synagogue on the first two nights of Pesaḥ. It was originally added to the public service for the sake of those who would not have the opportunity to recite it at home. On Pesaḥ it is assumed that even the poorest will have wine or will be at a home where Qiddush is recited during the Seder (*O.H.* 487.2).

As for the recitation of לְכוּ נְרַנְּנָה and לְכָה דוֹדִי, customs vary. The most prevalent custom is to omit both and say only Psalm 92 (see *Liquṭei Mehariḥ*, 3:9b).

As on the Sabbath, the service is concluded with ʻAleinu, the mourner's Qaddish, and a closing hymn, usually אֲדוֹן עוֹלָם or יִגְדַּל.

UNIT VIII

PESAḤ (II)

The Seder

VIII.
Pesaḥ (II)

10. The Seder

The scriptural exhortation to tell the story of the exodus to our children (Exod. 13:8) is interpreted as a positive commandment to retell the story each year (Lauterbach, *Mekhilta, Mesekhta D'pisḥa,* 1:17, p. 149; Maimonides, *Sefer Hamitswot, mitswah* 157). Hence we have the Seder.

"The Passover celebration commemorates an event which will probably symbolize for all time the essential meaning of freedom—namely freedom directed to a purpose. When Israel came forth from bondage, it was not simply to enjoy liberty but to make liberty an instrument of service" (Finkelstein, *The Haggadah,* p. i).

"Because Jewish tradition holds that God must be worshipped not only through prayer, but in equal degree, through study and learning, the Passover celebration is arranged primarily as a lesson, in which are mingled Jewish history, literature and religion" (ibid., p. iii). Hence the Haggadah is "an anthology of Jewish literature in almost every one of its multifarious aspects, composed in many ages and under many skies, and moulded by long centuries of usage into an harmonious whole" (Roth, *The Haggadah,* p. v). The name *Haggadah,* which means "telling," is derived from "And thou shalt tell thy son" (Exod. 13:8).

Preliminaries

Whereas the rabbis normally discouraged displays of affluence, in the case of the Seder they urged that the table should be set lavishly with the finest silver and dishes at one's disposal (*O.H.* 472:2; ibid. in Shneur Zalman of Lyady, *Shulḥan 'Arukh*). In many families it is customary for the chief celebrant to wear a white robe known as a Kittel (*sargenes* among German and Alsatian Jews). Many reasons have been given for this practice.

The Kittel is a festive garment that was worn in ancient times at all joyous celebrations. The High Priest wore white garments when officiating in the Temple of Jerusalem (Lev. 16:4), and wearing the Kittel gives the Seder the status of a sacred service in the Temple. According to the kabbalists, white symbolizes the divine attributes of lovingkindness and mercy חֶסֶד וְרַחֲמִים, and thus reminds us that the Holy One showed lovingkindness and mercy to our ancestors in Egypt since not all of them were deserving of redemption. We should exhibit the same mercy and lovingkindness toward our fellow men. Hence the special emphasis on inviting guests who are in modest circumstances to the Seder (Wahrman, *Ḥagei Yisra'el Umo'adaw,* pp. 147 f.).

A strange interpretation of the practice maintains that the Kittel resembles a shroud and is donned as a precaution lest the celebration turn to revelry (*O.H.* 472 in *M.D.* 3).

Dr. Finkelstein has suggested that the Kittel was an adaptation of the festive garment of Jerusalem in the days of the Second Temple. As a matter of fact, many of the practices connected with the Seder derive from the life of the Jews of that period, such as eating an egg and parsley, washing the hands before touching any food, and the reclining posture which becomes free men (copied from the Persians) (Finkelstein, *The Haggadah,* p. iv).

The Seder Plate

The Seder Plate, containing three matsot, bitter herbs, Ḥaroset, parsley or another vegetable, and two dishes—usually a shankbone and a roasted egg, is placed before the one who conducts the Seder (*O.H.* 473:4).

In accordance with the principle of אֵין מַעֲבִירִין עַל הַמִּצְוֹת (i.e., one should not pass over a mitswah when he meets it), the foods on the Seder Plate are so arranged that the first one to be used is nearest to the leader of the Seder, the next one next, and so on (Rama on *O.H.* 473:4). Hence the arrangement is as follows:

1. Top right, the Zero'a (shankbone)
2. Top left, the egg
3. Center, Maror (bitter herbs)
4. Lower right, Ḥaroset
5. Lower left, Karpas (parsley)

The Seder

All the printed Haggadahs have fifteen words which trace the sequence of the Seder service. These are written in rhyme and were devised as a mnemonic. Abudraham quotes a variety of other mnemonic verses. The one in our printed editions has been attributed to Rashi (Kasher, *Haggadah Shelemah*, p. 77). It is as follows: קַדֵּשׁ וּרְחַץ; כַּרְפַּס יַחַץ; מַגִּיד רָחְצָה; מוֹצִיא מַצָּה; מָרוֹר כּוֹרֵךְ; שֻׁלְחָן עוֹרֵךְ; צָפוּן בָּרֵךְ; הַלֵּל נִרְצָה. We shall explain each term and the laws connected with it.

קַדֵּשׁ As with all festival meals, the Seder begins with Qiddush. It consists of three benedictions: one over wine, the second over the festival, and the שֶׁהֶחֱיָנוּ. On the Sabbath we begin with וַיְכֻלּוּ and add the appropriate references to the Sabbath. On Saturday night, before שֶׁהֶחֱיָנוּ, we insert a special Havdalah that consists of two benedictions—בּוֹרֵא מְאוֹרֵי הָאֵשׁ and the regular Havdalah but with the variation necessitated by the festival. Here the separation is not בֵּין קוֹדֶשׁ לְחוֹל (between the holy and the profane) but between קוֹדֶשׁ חָמוּר לְקוֹדֶשׁ קַל (between the holy of a higher degree and the holy of a lesser degree). We therefore add בֵּין קְדֻשַּׁת שַׁבָּת לִקְדֻשַּׁת יוֹם טוֹב הִבְדַּלְתָּ and conclude with הַמַּבְדִּיל בֵּין קֹדֶשׁ לְקֹדֶשׁ (*O.H.* 473:1).

Four Cups of Wine

The cup of wine used for Qiddush also counts as the first of the four cups ordained for Pesaḥ (*O.H.* 472:8, 13, 14).

Many explanations have been given for the four cups of wine. They are said to be symbolic of the four synonymous expressions for redemption used by Scripture (Exod. 6:6–7), or of the four monarchies which are to precede the final redemption (Dan. 7), or of the four figurative cups of punishment which the empire of godlessness is to drain before the event, while the four cups of comfort are administered to Israel (M. *Pes.* 10:1).

A modern commentator has proposed a more simple reason for the four cups. Every Sabbath and festival we have two cups of wine at the meal, one for Qiddush and one for Birkat Hamazon. Since the Haggadah has two more benedictions, one concluding the first part of the Haggadah, גָּאַל יִשְׂרָאֵל, and one concluding the second part, מֶלֶךְ מְהֻלָּל בַּתִּשְׁבָּחוֹת, two more cups were added, the second for the former, and the fourth for the latter (Knebel, *Haggadah shel Pesaḥ*, p. 24).

The Cup of Elijah

The question arose whether a fifth cup of wine should be drunk at the Seder, after Hallel Gadol (Ps. 136), corresponding to the fifth scriptural expression of redemption, וְהֵבֵאתִי (Exod. 6:8). Since the question remains unresolved, we pour a fifth cup but do not drink it. We call this the cup of the Prophet Elijah because when Elijah reappears to herald the coming of the Messiah, he will rule on all unanswered halakhic questions (including the question of whether a fifth cup is required). Our custom thus has been to have four cups (*O.H.* 481:1, but see Maimonides, *Hil. Ḥamets Umatsah* 8:10, and Rama, *O.H.* 481:1, who rule that the fifth is optional).

At least one modern Haggadah suggests that, following the ruling of Maimonides making the fifth cup optional, we should adopt it as our practice in gratitude for the reestablishment of the State of Israel (Silverman, *Haggadah*, p. 66). (For an extensive discussion of the fifth cup, see Kasher, *Haggadah Shelemah*, pp. 94–95.)

A person who never drinks wine, either because it is harmful to him or because he does not like it, should make a special effort on Pesaḥ to drink from each of the four cups (*O.H.* 472:10).

Even children, when they have reached the age of being trained in the performance of religious commandments, should have a small cup of wine before them (*O.H.* 472:15).

Reclining

In ancient times laborers and slaves ate hurriedly, squatting on the ground. The well-to-do, on the other hand, reclined on cushions alongside the table. On the night of Pesaḥ, when there is no distinction between rich and poor, we all recline at the table in the manner of free men.

Customs change, however, and the ancient *triclinium* (dining couch) has long since passed out of use. Thus, when we recline at the Seder table, harking back to the practice of the Jews in Palestine at the time of the Second Temple, we do not use a *triclinium* but sit propped up on cushions. The celebrant leans to his left when drinking the wine or eating the food (see Roth, *Haggadah*, p. xi et al.). Hence, when he sits down after reciting the Qiddush, the celebrant should drink the first cup of wine while reclining to the left (*O.H.* 472:2–3).

וּרְחַץ Immediately after Qiddush the hands are washed. This washing is necessary because we are obliged to wash our hands before touching anything that is dipped in liquid (B. *Pes.* 115a; Ṭur, *O.H.* 473), and the next item in the sequence of the Seder service is the dipping of a vegetable (*O.H.* 473:6). Since this is not the regular statutory washing before meals, the benediction on washing the hands is omitted (see Tosafot, B. *Pes.* 115a, s.v. קול).

Opinions vary as to whether this washing of the hands is obligatory for all the participants or only for the leader of the Seder. Since the reason for the washing obviously applies to all the participants, all should wash (see *Abudraham Hashalem,* p. 219). Most current Haggadahs, however, speak only of the celebrant washing his hands (see *Yosef Omets* 763 and *Leqeṭ Yosher,* p. 88). One scholar has proposed that this is either based on an error (i.e., since the instructions in most Haggadahs are given in the singular, they were interpreted as referring only to the celebrant), or that it is sufficient if the leader alone performs the washing since the practice is only the vestige of an ancient custom (see Goldschmidt, *Die Pessach-Haggada,* p. 20, n. 1; see also Kasher's comments in *Haggadah Shelemah,* pp. 96–97).

כַּרְפַּס A piece of parsley or some other vegetable is given to each person at the table and dipped in salt water. It is eaten after the recitation of the following benediction: בָּרוּךְ אַתָּה יְיָ אֱלֹהֵינוּ מֶלֶךְ הָעוֹלָם בּוֹרֵא פְּרִי הָאֲדָמָה (*O.H.* 473:17). This practice is meant to arouse the curiosity of the children (Ṭur, *O.H.* 473).

Historically, the dipping of the vegetable goes back to the fashion of eating meals a few thousand years ago. The meal began with an hors d'oeuvre, or dish of a slightly pungent flavor, steeped in some liquid of a similar nature. This ultimately became identified with the bunch of hyssop which was dipped in the blood of the first Paschal sacrifice at the time of the exodus and used for marking the doorways of the houses of the children of Israel as a sign to the angel of death (Roth, *Haggadah,* p. 8).

יַחַץ The leader takes the middle matsah and breaks it into two pieces. One portion is left where it is. The larger portion is wrapped in a cloth and hidden somewhere in the room—generally under the tablecloth or between the celebrant's cushions (*O.H.* 473:6 and in *B.H.* 19). The breaking of the matsah represents the bread of affliction—i.e., of the poor man who eats crumbs rather than whole loaves (B. *Pes.* 115b–116a).

We use three matsot at the Seder because on Sabbaths and festivals it is customary to have לֶחֶם מִשְׁנֶה (two loaves of ḥallah) on the table in recollection of the double share of manna which fell in the wilderness on the sixth day (Exod. 16:22; B. *Shab.* 117b). Since one of the matsot is broken in two at the beginning of the Seder, there must be three matsot at the outset so that two whole ones will remain for the meal (*Seder Rav 'Amram,* ed. Goldschmidt, p. 113).

The custom of hiding the Afiqoman and rewarding the child who finds it is intended to keep the children interested until the end of the Seder (Wahrman, *Ḥagei Yisra'el Umo'adaw,* p. 144).

מַגִּיד The story of the exodus is recited. As mentioned above, the telling of the story is one of the commandments connected with the observance of Pesaḥ, hence the Haggadah.

The Haggadah as a whole has two main divisions. The first contains most of the ceremonies, and the recital of historical and expository passages explaining the reason for the Seder celebration. The second part comes after the meal. The passages recited here are hymnal and glorificatory, also expressing our hopes for deliverance.

The first part, which begins after Qiddush and the few preliminary rituals, is referred to as מַגִּיד. It comprises the following sections.

1. Lifting the plate and reciting the introductory passage—הָא לַחְמָא.
2. The display of the plate, and particlularly of the matsah, occasions the child's questions—מַה נִשְׁתַּנָּה after the *qe'arah* (plate) has been put down and the cups filled.
3. The answers follow, with illustrations of the duty to recount the story of the exodus, the description of the four sons, and the exposition of Joshua 24:2–4 and Deuteronomy 26:5–8, leading to an elaboration of the ten plagues. Then follow psalms of thanksgiving and the prelude to the meal with its attendant ceremonies.

Usually it is the youngest son who asks the four questions. In ancient times the questions were spontaneous, and the child had to be prepared in advance if he was not alert enough to ask questions on his own. Later the questions became set with a permanent text which the children had to learn. If the children cannot ask the questions, or if there are no children, the wife may ask them, or another adult, or the celebrant himself reads the questions (B. *Pes.* 116a; *O.H.* 473:7).

It is customary to spill a bit of wine from the cup at the mention of each of the ten plagues. This is also done when the mnemonic of the plagues דְּצַ"ךְ עֲדַ"שׁ בְּאַחַ"ב is said. This practice probably originated in an ancient belief that in so doing we ward off evil—*nolo me tangere* (Roth, *Haggadah,* p. 27). Some explain that since the wine is usually spilled by dipping a finger into the cup, the practice refers to the verse "This is the finger of God" (Exod.

8:15). A more rationalistic explanation is given by Don Isaac Abarbanel. The spilling of the wine is a sign that our cup of joy is not full since our deliverance involved the punishment of others; our joy is made incomplete by the fact that the Egyptians suffered so that we might be liberated.

Before the conclusion of the first part of the Haggadah, marked by the drinking of the second cup of wine, the first two paragraphs of Hallel are recited, as they were during the sacrifice of the Paschal lamb (M. *Pes.* 9:3, 10:6, 7). The usual blessing is omitted (Ṭur, *O.H.* 473 in *Bet Yosef,* s.v. בענין ברכת ההלל). The blessing is recited only when all of Hallel is recited without interruption, or when Hallel is recited by day (see Kasher, *Haggadah Shelemah,* pp. 139 f.).

The first part of the Haggadah ends with the second cup of wine, which is preceded by the blessing on wine (*O.H.* 474:1 in Rama).

רָחְצָה As before every meal, each participant washes his hands and recites the blessing עַל נְטִילַת יָדָיִם (*O.H.* 475:1).

מוֹצִיא מַצָּה After the washing of the hands, the leader takes the matsot from the Seder plate and recites two blessings, the usual הַמּוֹצִיא and the special blessing for matsah (אֲשֶׁר קִדְּשָׁנוּ בְּמִצְוֹתָיו וְצִוָּנוּ עַל אֲכִילַת מַצָּה), and then distributes a piece of the uppermost matsah and a piece of the broken middle matsah to each participant; these are eaten while reclining to the left (*O.H.* 475:1). When a large group is present, the participants can use other matsot. The eating of matsah is an obligation only at the Seder, and is optional during the rest of Pesaḥ The requirement of abstaining from leaven applies to all of Pesaḥ (*O.H.* 475:7; M. *Pes.* 10:5).

מָרוֹר The participants take a piece of bitter herb, usually horseradish root, dip it into the Ḥaroset to reduce its sharpness, and eat it after reciting the blessing אֲשֶׁר קִדְּשָׁנוּ בְּמִצְוֹתָיו וְצִוָּנוּ עַל אֲכִילַת מָרוֹר (*O.H.* 475:1).

כּוֹרֵךְ The leader breaks the bottom matsah into smaller pieces and makes sandwiches of bitter herbs between two pieces of matsah. These are eaten after reciting זֵכֶר לְמִקְדָּשׁ כְּהִלֵּל while reclining on the left (*O.H.* 475:1). Customs vary as to whether Ḥaroset is used here again (ibid. in Rama).

The eating of bitter herbs is a biblical commandment (Exod. 12:8; Num. 9:11). It is a symbol of the bitter servitude our ancestors experienced as slaves in Egypt (M. *Pes.* 10:5).

The Ḥaroset, which lessens the sharpness of the Maror, is a compound of apples, almonds, raisins, and spices, chopped very fine into a paste with the addition of some wine. Its admixture with the Maror, dulling the sharpness of the bitter herbs, may be taken as symbolic of God's lovingkindness, which dulled the bitterness of the Egyptian bondage. The color and general composition of the Ḥaroset remind us of the mortar which the Hebrew slaves used while working on the building projects assigned by their taskmasters.

The principal ingredient of the Ḥaroset, the apple, recalls an ancient legend regarding Pharaoh's heartless sentence against the male Hebrew children. Jewish mothers, fearing for the lives of their infants if they were boys, used to give birth in the secrecy of orchards, unseen by human eyes, and there, we are told, angels came down from heaven to help them. The source of this explanation is a midrashic comment on the verse in the Song of Songs: "I raised thee up under the apple tree; there thy mother brought thee forth" (Song of Songs 8:5; *Exodus Rabbah* 1:16; Rama on *O.H.* 473:5). The other ingredients of the Ḥaroset are also fruits to which the people of Israel have been compared (*O.H.* 473:5 in Rama; detailed explanation in *Qitsur Shulḥan 'Arukh* 118:4; Roth, *Haggadah,* p. ix; see also B. *Pes.* 116a in Tosafot, s.v. צריך).

שֻׁלְחָן עוֹרֵךְ The meal is an integral part of the Seder service. The heart of the service in ancient times was the eating of the Paschal lamb, which had to be consumed within the confines of Jerusalem and in a state of ritual purity. Nowadays the table becomes an altar, and eating performed in the right spirit becomes an act of worship.

A spirit of reverence, therefore, should pervade the meal. Immoderate eating or drinking would be blasphemy (*O.H.* 476:1 in Rama), and loose language should be avoided. By such measures the commonplace is sanctified, becoming an act of divine service (Roth, *Haggadah,* p. 44).

It is customary to start the Seder meal with a hard-boiled egg dipped in salt water. Classical scholars, recollecting the traditional description of a Roman meal (*ab ovo usque ad mala*), consider the egg to be no more than a relic of the customary hors d'oeuvres of the typical meal of ancient times (Finkelstein, *Haggadah,* p. ix; Roth, *Haggadah,* p. ix; Wahrman, *Ḥagei Yisra'el Umo'adaw,* p. 147). It has been pointed out, however, that popular lore throughout the world generally associates eggs with the spring season.

While the egg may be a relic of an ancient custom, it can be given a fresh symbolic value (Roth, *Haggadah,* p. ix). Various explanations in this vein have been offered. Eggs are a symbol of mourning (round things are generally eaten in a house of mourning), and thus the egg at the Seder is said to be a gesture of mourning for the destruction of Jerusalem, added in place of the קָרְבַּן חֲגִיגָה (the special festival offering), which can no longer be offered. This interpretation is emphasized by the fact that the ninth of Av always falls on the same day of the week as the first night of Pesaḥ (*O.H.*

476:2). Hence the salt water at the Seder symbolizes the tears we shed over the destruction of the Temple (Wahrman, *Ḥagei Yisra'el Umo'adaw,* p. 147).

Rabbi Moses Sofer (the "Ḥatam Sofer") offered a more fanciful interpretation. In general, the more a food is cooked, the softer it becomes. With the egg, however, the opposite is the case. This is symbolic of the people of Israel. The more they are oppressed by the nations of the world, the harder they become in their determination not to yield and to remain faithful to the covenant.

The rest of the Seder meal follows the custom of the land regarding festive meals. In certain places, however, roasted meat is forbidden at the Seder because the Paschal lamb was roasted, and roasted meat might be construed as being a קָרְבַּן פֶּסַח (Paschal sacrifice), which is forbidden today. In some other places, there is no restriction on roasted meat but an entire lamb may not be roasted, since it would be too similar to the Paschal lamb (*O.H.* 476:1).

צָפוּן After the meal, the half-matsah that was put aside early in the evening is distributed to the participants, each of whom eats a piece to conclude the meal. This is the Afiqoman. The word *afiqoman* has been given various interpretations. The most logical is that it is the Greek word for "dessert" (Roth, *Haggadah,* p. 44). For us the Afiqoman represents the Paschal lamb, which was traditionally the last thing to be eaten at the Seder so that its taste and recollection would remain uppermost. Therefore nothing is eaten after partaking of the Afiqoman (*O.H.* 478:1). Some Sefardic rites preface the eating of the Afiqoman with the words זֵכֶר לְקָרְבַּן פֶּסַח הַנֶּאֱכָל עַל הַשֹּׂבַע ("in remembrance of the Paschal lamb which is eaten when one is sated") (Goldschmidt, *Haggada,* p. 71). There is a difference of opinion about drinking after the Afiqoman. Some authorities only permit the drinking of water—with the exception, of course, of the last two of the four statutory cups of wine (*O.H.* 478:1 in *Mishnah Berurah*). Others forbid fermented beverages, since drinking these may lead to intoxication (*O.H.* 478:1 in *B.H.*).

בָּרֵךְ The third cup of wine is filled and Birkat Hamazon is recited. It is the usual Grace after meals with the addition of יַעֲלֶה וְיָבֹא and the הָרַחֲמָן for the festival, with רְצֵה on a Sabbath; the cup of wine, which is generally optional, is obligatory at this service (*O.H.* 479:1).

הַלֵּל After the Birkhat Hamazon and the drinking of the third cup, the fourth cup is filled and the rest of Hallel is recited (*O.H.* 480:1). During the Middle Ages שְׁפוֹךְ חֲמָתְךָ, consisting of verses from Psalms 79:6 and 69:25 and Lamentations 3:66, was inserted before the recitation of the second part of

Hallel (Wahrman, *Ḥagei Yisra'el Umo'adaw,* p. 149). The old Haggadahs do not have it (see *Seder Rav 'Amram,* ed. Goldschmidt; Maimonides, *Maḥzor Vitry,* ed. Hurwitz, p. 282). These imprecations seem vengeful and vindictive to us, and unworthy of a festival which includes a number of rituals showing compassion even for the Egyptians. The fact that they date from the Middle Ages, when persecutions of the Jews had become common, explains the mood (see *Abudraham Hashalem* 234).

It is customary to pour an extra glass of wine, known as כּוֹס שֶׁל אֵלִיָּהוּ, Elijah's cup, and keep the door open during the recitation of שְׁפוֹךְ חֲמָתְךָ. This is a symbolic act which shows that we are not afraid, despite the oppressive cruelty we face, and that our faith in the final redemption and the final triumph of righteousness is unshaken (*O.H.* 481:1 in Rama, *B.H.* 3). It has been suggested that originally the door was open throughout the entire Seder. During the Middle Ages, when it was dangerous to do so, the door was kept closed, but it was opened just for this passage (see Wahrman, *Ḥagei Yisra'el Umo'adaw,* p. 149). In Jewish lore, Elijah the prophet has become the harbinger of the coming of the Redeemer. We call this cup the cup of Elijah to reaffirm our faith in his coming to announce the final redemption (ibid., and *Yosef Omets* 788; also, see above p. 123). A commendable effort has been made to use this passage as an occasion for the memorialization of the six million martyrs who perished at the hands of the Nazis and for the heroes of the ghetto uprisings. When recited in relation to these tragic events, the words no longer seem unduly vindictive.

After this, Hallel is continued, starting with לֹא לָנוּ (*O.H.* 480:1). The customary final benediction, מֶלֶךְ מְהֻלָּל בַּתִּשְׁבָּחוֹת, is omitted because the later benediction אֵל מֶלֶךְ גָּדוֹל בַּתִּשְׁבָּחוֹת, serves as the closing benediction for the entire section (see B. *Pes.* 118a in Tosafot, s.v. ר' יוחנן; and in *Abudraham Hashalem,* p. 236; *O.H.* 480:1 in *B.H.* 3).

The Haggadah divides Hallel into two sections because the first part of Hallel, which mentions the exodus, fits the mood of the Haggadah passages preceding the meal, all of which are variations on the same theme, while the second part of Hallel is hymnal and thus fits the songs of praise which are the substance of the second part of the Haggadah (Kasher, *Haggadah Shelemah,* pp. 140 f.; *Abudraham Hashalem,* p. 236).

After Hallel we recite Hallel Gadol (Ps. 136) and Birkat Hashir (B. *Pes.* 118a), which we call נִשְׁמַת (*O.H.* 480:1 in Rama, *B.H.* 3), ending with the benediction מֶלֶךְ אֵל חֵי הָעוֹלָמִים. After this the fourth cup is drunk and the Berakhah Aḥaronah is recited.

נִרְצָה marks the end of the Seder with an appropriate hymn—חֲסַל סִדּוּר

פֶּסַח and לְשָׁנָה הַבָּאָה בִּירוּשָׁלָיִם. Some hymns have been added at the end of the service. We recite וּבְכֵן וַיְהִי בַּחֲצִי הַלַּיְלָה of Yannai on the first night and וּבְכֵן וַאֲמַרְתֶּם זֶבַח פֶּסַח on the second night. In addition there are three other playful songs: כִּי לוֹ נָאֶה, אֶחָד מִי יוֹדֵעַ, and חַד גַּדְיָא. Though the commentators have read profound meanings into these songs, they were simply intended as a means of holding the attention of the children until the very end.

The rest of the evening should be spent in serious discussion or in study consonant with the spirit of the celebration (*O.H.* 481:2).

With the exception of the slight variation mentioned above, the Seder on the second night of Pesaḥ is celebrated exactly as on the first night (*O.H.* 481:2 in Rama).

UNIT IX

PESAḤ (III)

The Morning Service
The Counting of the ‘Omer
The Second Day
The Intermediate Days
The Concluding Days of Pesaḥ

IX.
Pesaḥ (III)

11. The Morning Service

On the first day of Pesaḥ, the morning service to Barekhu is the Sabbath service with minor variations. The proper psalm for the day is recited, and the ḥazzan begins Shaḥarit not with שׁוֹכֵן עַד but with הָאֵל one paragraph earlier. This passage speaks, appropriately, of the power of God which was revealed in the exodus from Egypt (*Levush*, *O.H.* 488:1).

From Barekhu to the 'Amidah the service follows either the weekday or the Sabbath practice, depending on whether it is on a weekday or a Saturday. The 'Amidah is the one recited at Ma'ariv the preceding night, except that שִׂים שָׁלוֹם is recited in place of שָׁלוֹם רָב. In the *Ḥazarat Hashats* we add the Qedushah for the Sabbath and the Birkat Kohanim before שִׂים שָׁלוֹם. On a Sabbath we add the appropriate insertions. Immediately after *Ḥazarat Hashats* the complete Hallel is recited, preceded by the benediction אֲשֶׁר קִדְּשָׁנוּ בְּמִצְוֹתָיו וְצִוָּנוּ לִקְרוֹא אֶת הַהַלֵּל (*O.H.* 488:1). Hallel is followed by Qaddish Shalem.

If the first day of Pesaḥ occurs on a Sabbath, the prayers for Hotsa'at HaTorah are the same as on a regular Sabbath. On a weekday, before בְּרִיךְ שְׁמֵהּ, we add the שְׁלֹשׁ עֶשְׂרֵה מִדּוֹת, thirteen divine attributes (Exod. 34:6–7), which is recited three times; the prayer beginning with רִבּוֹנוֹ שֶׁל עוֹלָם, and the verse וַאֲנִי תְפִלָּתִי, which is also said three times. This practice arose through the influence of the kabbalists of Safed in the sixteenth century, particularly of Isaac Luria (*Liqutei Meharih*, vol. 3, p. 24). It was originally intended only for the month of Elul, but in time it was extended to Rosh Hashanah and Yom Kippur, and eventually to the three festivals as well (see *Ḥemdat Hayamim*, and *Sha'arei Tsion* of Nathan Hannover).

For Qeri'at HaTorah two scrolls are taken from the ark. In the first we read Exodus 12:21–51. Five 'aliyot and no more are distributed, and on a Sabbath, seven, but if it is customary to have more than seven on a Sabbath, the same may be done on a festival that falls on a Sabbath (*Levush, O.H.* 488:3). When the prescribed reading is completed, the second Torah is placed on the reading desk alongside the first and half-Qaddish is recited (ibid.). The first Torah is then lifted, rolled, and covered, and the second is opened for the Mafṭir, which is from Numbers 28:16–25. The Hafṭarah is Joshua 5:2–6:1 (*O.H.* 488:3). The reading from the Torah contains the first scriptural mention of Pesaḥ, and the Hafṭarah records the first mention of Pesaḥ in the Prophets.

After the reading of the Torah and the Hafṭarah is completed, Ashrei is recited and the Torah is returned to the ark. For Hakhnasat HaTorah we recite the same prayers as on the Sabbath, substituting Psalm 24 for Psalm 29 if the festival occurs on a weekday. On a Sabbath we include יְקוּם פֻּרְקָן and מִי שֶׁבֵּרַךְ before אַשְׁרֵי but not אַב הָרַחֲמִים.

The pattern of the Musaf 'Amidah is the same as Shaḥarit. The first and last three benedictions are the same as in the weekday 'Amidah. For the thirteen benedictions that are omitted, we substitute one which begins with אַתָּה בְחַרְתָּנוּ and ends with וְהַשִּׂיאֵנוּ as in Shaḥarit and Ma'ariv. In between we include the biblical passage that describes the sacrificial offerings prescribed for the day.

According to the Talmud, one must add something new in the Musaf 'Amidah (P. *Ber.* 4:6). The additions are וּמִפְּנֵי חֲטָאֵינוּ, which is an appropriate introduction to the biblical passage, and מֶלֶךְ רַחֲמָן, which is a fitting conclusion, because both speak of the rebuilding of the Temple in Jerusalem.

If the festival falls on a Sabbath, the 'Amidah of the festival is retained but with appropriate insertions to indicate that the day possesses the sanctity of both the Sabbath and the festival.

From the Musaf 'Amidah of the eighth day of Sukkot to the Musaf 'Amidah of the first day of Pesaḥ, we add מַשִּׁיב הָרוּחַ וּמוֹרִיד הַגָּשֶׁם between the first and second paragraphs of the second benediction of the 'Amidah. During the months when this phrase is omitted, the Sefardim substitute מוֹרִיד הַטָּל. Both Sefardim and Ashkenazim, however, recite a prayer for dew on the first day of Pesaḥ during the *Ḥazarat Hashats* of the Musaf 'Amidah (*Levush, O.H.* 488:3). The Tefilat Tal that is in use today was written by Kalir.

It is customary for the ark to be opened from the beginning of *Ḥazarat Hashats* until the prayer for dew is completed. It is also customary for the ḥazzan to wear a white robe during the Musaf service, indicating the importance of this prayer.

Another addition in the *Ḥazarat Hashats* of the Musaf 'Amidah is in the

Qedushah. Before the last part (יִמְלֹךְ), we add אַדִּיר אַדִּירֵנוּ, a prayer that the Redeemer establish the Kingdom of God. (It is not said on a regular Sabbath because there is a tradition that the Messiah will not come on the Sabbath.) (*Levush, O.H.* 488:3).

The conclusion of the morning service is the same as on the Sabbath.

While there is less strictness in the observance of the festivals than of the Sabbath, the atmosphere of sanctity must nevertheless be maintained by spending the rest of the day in the type of activity that will enhance the festival.

The Minḥah service for the first day of the festival begins with אַשְׁרֵי and וּבָא לְצִיּוֹן as on the Sabbath, followed immediately by the ʻAmidah. The ʻAmidah is the same as the one recited for Maʻariv except that we now omit מַשִּׁיב הָרוּחַ וּמוֹרִיד הַגָּשֶׁם. In the *Ḥazarat Hashats* the weekday Qedushah is recited.

The Maʻariv is identical with that of the first night except that on the second night we start the counting of the ʻOmer (*sefirat haʻomer*).

12. The Counting of the ʻOmer

We begin with an introductory prayer, לְשֵׁם יִחוּד, declaring the worshipper's intention of performing the Torah's commandment to count the ʻOmer. The biblical passage prescribing the commandment is quoted (Lev. 23:15–16). Then the benediction אֲשֶׁר קִדְּשָׁנוּ בְּמִצְוֹתָיו וְצִוָּנוּ עַל סְפִירַת הָעֹמֶר is recited. The ʻOmer is then counted; i.e., we declare what day of the ʻOmer it is, starting with one the first night and continuing until the number forty-nine is reached on the night before Shavuʻot. The counting is done by days and weeks. For instance, on the nineteenth day, we say: "Today is the nineteenth day, which is two weeks and five days, of the ʻOmer" (*O.H.* 489:4).

In ancient times the ʻOmer accentuated the agricultural aspect of the festival because it was accompanied by the bringing of a measure (*ʻomer*) of the first barley harvest (Lev. 23:10, 15, 16; Deut. 16:9; B. *Men.* 63b–64a). In an agricultural economy the meaning of this observance was obvious; it was one of the rituals that served to show gratefulness to God for his bounty. Only after the people had shown its gratitude by bringing the ʻOmer to the Temple in Jerusalem was the individual allowed to enjoy eating of the produce of the new harvest (Lev. 23:14).

After the destruction of the Temple new meanings were sought which could keep this practice relevant. One obvious meaning suggested itself. The counting of the 'Omer could serve as a vehicle for the expression of our yearning for the restoration of Zion and the rebuilding of the Holy Land, hence, the יְהִי רָצוֹן ... שֶׁיִּבָּנֶה בֵּית הַמִּקְדָּשׁ that follows immediately (see *Me'ir Netiv* under *Sefirat Ha'omer*). Today we translate this into a means of strengthening our resolve to reclaim the soil of the Holy Land and to work for the rebuilding of Zion as a homeland for the exiled and as a center of spiritual life for our people (Silverman, *Haggadah*, p. 63).

Another inspiring meaning is suggested in a Midrash. It was asked why the festival of Shavu'ot, unlike any other festival, depends on the counting of the days preceding it. In answer, it is suggested that when the children of Israel received the glad tidings of their liberation from Egypt, they were also told that fifty days thereafter they would receive the Torah. This news was so thrilling that they started counting the days. This counting then became a prescribed practice for all subsequent generations (*Shibolei Haleqeṭ*, ed. Buber, p. 236; Rabbeinu Nisim, at the end of Alfasi on *Pesaḥim*, s.v. וּמְחַיְּיבִין לְמִימְנֵי יוֹמֵי דְשַׁבְעָה שָׁבוּעֵי). Today we can say that the counting of the 'Omer is a bridge connecting Pesaḥ and Shavu'ot, indicating that we want not only freedom *from* bondage but also freedom *for* a purpose, i.e., to receive the moral law at Mount Sinai and to practice it (see Silverman, *Haggadah*, loc. cit.). The receiving of the Torah was the purpose and goal of the exodus from Egypt.

The counting of the 'Omer should always take place after sundown (Maimonides, *Hil. Temidin Umusafin* 7:22). If the Ma'ariv service was recited before sundown, one should count the 'Omer without a *berakhah* and repeat the counting, but with ~~a *berakhah*,~~ after sundown (*O.H.* 489:3). The custom in such cases is to announce at the service that the people present should count the 'Omer again later in the evening.

If one has forgotten to count the 'Omer during Ma'ariv he may do so all night with the prescribed *berakhah* and even the entire succeeding day, but without a *berakhah* (*O.H.* 489:7).

The 'Omer is counted immediately before 'Aleinu except on Saturday nights or at the end of a festival, when it is recited before Havdalah. Although the 'Omer should logically follow Havdalah, since it is a weekday activity, we reverse the order to show our desire to lengthen the Sabbath, מְאַחֲרִים לָצֵאת מִן הַשַּׁבָּת וּמְמַהֲרִים לָבוֹא ("who are late in departing from the Sabbath and hasten its arrival"), and on Saturday night and the night of the conclusion of the festival we rely on the Havdalah that was already recited in the 'Amidah (*O.H.* 489:9).

The conclusion of the service is identical with that of the first night.

13. The Second Day

On the second night the Seder is conducted exactly as on the first night with the exception of the few slight variations mentioned.

The morning service of the second day is identical with that of the first, except for the variation in the psalm for the day and the reading of the Torah and the Hafṭarah. For the Torah reading, as on the first day, we use two scrolls. In the first we read Leviticus 22:26–23:44 because it discusses the festivals, and particularly because it includes the laws of the 'Omer. In the second scroll the Mafṭir is read, as on the first day, in Numbers 28:16–25. The Hafṭarah is II Kings 23:1–9, 21–25, which describes the Pesaḥ held in the days of King Josiah (*O.H.* 490:1).

In the evening the Minḥah service is the same as the night before. The Ma'ariv service is that of a weekday with the addition of אַתָּה חוֹנַנְתָּנוּ in the fourth benediction of the 'Amidah and יַעֲלֶה וְיָבוֹא in the seventeenth. Beginning with this service, וְתֵן בְּרָכָה is said in the ninth benediction in place of וְתֵן טַל וּמָטָר לִבְרָכָה. After the 'Amidah Havdalah is recited over wine. The benedictions for fire and spices are included on Saturday nights only.

14. The Intermediate Days

The Intermediate Days of Pesaḥ have the status of semiholidays. While work was generally permitted, there were many limitations (*O.H.* 530–548). Today most Jews, apart from the very pious, pursue their daily tasks as on regular weekdays. However, these days retain the positive aspects of the festival. Thus on Pesaḥ we refrain from eating ḥamets during the Intermediate Days as well as during the rest of the festival.

The Shaḥarit, Minḥah, and Ma'ariv services follow the weekday pattern except that we add יַעֲלֶה וְיָבֹא in the seventeenth benediction of the 'Amidah. At grace after meals, we insert יַעֲלֶה וְיָבֹא before וּבְנֵה יְרוּשָׁלַיִם.

After Shaḥarit we recite "half Hallel," i.e., the shortened version omitting לֹא לָנוּ (Ps. 115:1–11) and אָהַבְתִּי (Ps. 116:1–11) (*O.H.* 490:4) to show that these days have less sanctity than the first two (*Levush, O.H.* 490:4). It has also been suggested that since we omit these passages on the last two days of Pesaḥ, it would be improper not to omit them during the Intermediate Days as well.

Hallel is concluded with Qaddish Titqabbel since this is the conclusion of Shaḥarit.

The Torah is read every morning of the Intermediate Days. Two scrolls are used and four 'aliyot are distributed, three for the first scroll, and one for the second. On the first day we read Exodus 13:1–16 in the first scroll; on the second day, Exodus 22:24–23:19; on the third, Exodus 34:1–26; on the fourth, Numbers 9:1–14. In the second scroll the reading is the same for all four days—Numbers 28:19–25. The only change in this order comes when the first of the Intermediate Days falls on a Sabbath. Then we read, with some additions, the portion assigned for the third day, Exodus 33:12–34:26. For the rest of the days we follow the same sequence, but start the first day's reading on the second day (*O.H.* 390:5).

The reading of the Torah is followed by אַשְׁרֵי and וּבָא לְצִיּוֹן, half-Qaddish, and the Musaf 'Amidah of the festival. The conclusion of the service is as on a weekday.

There is a difference of opinion over whether one should put on Tefilin during the Intermediate Days. The Sefardic practice, followed by the Ḥassidim as well, is not to put on Tefilin (*O.H.* 31:2). The Ashkenazic custom is to put them on (ibid. in Rama). The reason for not donning the Tefilin on Sabbaths and festivals is that these occasions are already an *ot* ("sign") in themselves. The difference of opinion regarding Tefilin depends on what characteristic of the festival makes it an *ot*. According to one opinion, it is the abstention from work; according to the other, it is the other themes of the festival, such as not eating ḥamets on Pesaḥ, or eating in the Sukkah, or saying the benediction over the Etrog and Lulav on Sukkot. Those who maintain the former position suggest that Tefilin are obligatory during the Intermediate Days since work is permitted; according to the latter opinion, Tefilin should not be used because the Intermediate Days retain their special characteristics (see Shneur Zalman of Lyady, *Shulḥan 'Arukh* 31:2). In Israel the Sefardic custom is followed by all (see above, unit 1, p. 6).

No weddings should take place during the Intermediate Days (*O.H.* 546:1) because אֵין מְעָרְבִין שִׂמְחָה בְּשִׂמְחָה ("rejoicing may not be mingled with other rejoicing") (ibid. in *B.H.* 1).

We do not mourn for the dead during the Intermediate Days or on the festivals themselves. If there is a death in the family during the Intermediate Days, the family starts the Shiv'ah after the conclusion of the festival. With qeri'ah there are variations in practice. According to one authority it is done immediately, and according to the other we wait until the conclusion of the festival (*O.H.* 547:6). No eulogies are given during the Intermediate Days (*O.H.* 547:1).

On the Sabbath of the Intermediate Days the services are like those on every other Sabbath with the following variations. On Friday night we begin with Psalm 92, מִזְמוֹר שִׁיר לְיוֹם הַשַּׁבָּת. (Some Ḥassidim begin with מִזְמוֹר לְדָוִד.) In the 'Amidah, יַעֲלֶה וְיָבֹא is inserted in the first of the last three benedictions, רְצֵה. After the 'Amidah of Shaḥarit the shortened version of Hallel is recited.

The reading of the Torah has already been mentioned. The prayers accompanying the taking out and returning of the Torah are the same as on every other Sabbath. The Maftir is the same as the reading from the second scroll on the other Intermediate Days. The Hafṭarah is from Ezekiel 37:1–14 because there is a tradition that the resurrection will take place on Pesaḥ (*O.H.* 490:9; ibid. in Ṭur).

At Musaf we recite the festival 'Amidah with the appropriate insertions for the Sabbath (*O.H.* 490:9). In some synagogues it is customary to recite the Song of Songs before the reading of the Torah (Rama on *O.H.* 490:9; *Soferim* 14:18). There is a difference of opinion as to whether a benediction should be recited before the book is read (*Levush, O.H.* 494:2; Rama on *O.H.* 490:9; *Mishnah Berurah* ad loc.; Shneur Zalman of Lyady, *Shulḥan 'Arukh* 494:13, 17). The present practice is not to recite a benediction.

According to rabbinic tradition שִׁיר הַשִּׁירִים is a love song, with God the beloved and the children of Israel the bride. Since Pesaḥ marks the beginning of this courtship (its culmination was *Matan Torah*), the reading of the Song of Songs during Pesaḥ is most appropriate. The Song of Songs is also a song to spring (2:11–13). Pesaḥ is a spring festival both literally and figuratively. Spring means hope and happiness. In this case hope lies in freedom, and happiness in the attachment to the law of God. If the Sabbath falls on the last day of Pesaḥ, the Song of Songs is recited on the last day (*O.H.* 490:9).

At Minḥah the Torah portion to be read is the portion of the next week (Ṭur).

The Ma'ariv is the weekday Ma'ariv with the usual additions for Saturday night (אַתָּה חוֹנַנְתָּנוּ) and for the Intermediate Days (יַעֲלֶה וְיָבֹא), but וִיהִי נוֹעַם and וְאַתָּה קָדוֹשׁ are omitted. These are recited only when followed by שֵׁשֶׁת יְמֵי הַמַּעֲשֶׂה, i.e., six weekdays not interrupted by a festival.

The Havdalah is the regular Sabbath Havdalah, but it is preceded by the counting of the 'Omer, as mentioned above.

15. The Concluding Days of Pesaḥ

The seventh and eighth days of Pesaḥ (in Israel the seventh day) equal the first days in sanctity, and the same regulations apply to them.

The services are exactly the same as during the first days, except that the shortened version of Hallel is recited during the morning services, each day has its own specially assigned reading from the Torah and the Prophets, and memorial services for the deceased are recited on the last day.The שֶׁהֶחֱיָנוּ is omitted from the candle lighting and evening Qiddush.

The shortened form of the Hallel is recited for the following reason. According to tradition, the children of Israel crossed the Red Sea on the seventh day of Pesaḥ. When the ministering angels saw the hosts of Pharaoh drown, they wished to sing praises unto God. God rebuked them, saying: "Shall ye sing praises unto me while my creatures are drowning?" (B. *Meg.* 10b). Hence we shorten the hymns of praise on this occasion. Another suggested reason is that normally the complete Hallel is recited only at the beginning of the festival, as is done on Pesaḥ. Only when the succeeding days have some theme peculiar to themselves do we say the complete Hallel on those days as well. During Sukkot each day saw a different number of sacrifices offered in the Temple, and on each night of Ḥanukkah a different number of candles is lit, giving each day a significance of its own. The complete Hallel is therefore recited on each of these days (B. *Arak.* 10a–b).

The Torah reading on the seventh day is Exodus 13:17–15:26, telling of the crossing of the Red Sea, which took place on the seventh day, and the song that Moses and the children of Israel sang when they were saved. The Maftir is the same as the reading from the second scroll on the Intermediate Days. The Hafṭarah is II Samuel 22:1–51, also a song of deliverance.

On the eighth day the reading is Deuteronomy 15:19–16:17. On a Sabbath the reading starts with 14:22. The Maftir is the same as the day before. The Hafṭarah is Isaiah 10:32–12:6, which speaks of the future deliverance of the children of Israel.

The Memorial Services follow the reading of the Torah and the Hafṭarah. The present-day practice is to have *Hazkarat Neshamot* at the end of each festival, i.e., the eighth day of Pesaḥ, the second day of Shavu'ot, the eighth day of Sukkot, and on Yom Kippur, which, because it is connected to Rosh Hashanah by the Ten Days of Penitence, is considered to be like the last day of a festival.

The custom of remembering the dead in the synagogue is an old one and is based on the belief that such prayers are of help to the dead (*Midrash*

Tanḥuma, Ha'azinu 20:8; *Pesiqta Rabbati* 20). This was done individually by people when they were called up to the Torah and pledged a gift for charity (*O.H.* 284:7 in Rama). In some synagogues this is still the practice. In other synagogues a memorial prayer is recited after the Torah reading, or on the Sabbath at Minḥah after the Torah reading when the names of all those whose Yahrzeit will be held during the coming week are mentioned in a memorial prayer, אֵל מָלֵא רַחֲמִים.

A collective memorial prayer with the entire congregation joining in originally took place only on Yom Kippur. It was recited not only for the dead (*O.H.* 621:6) but also to put the living into a contrite mood (*Kol Bo* 70). Among German Jews this custom is still maintained (*Me'ir Netiv*, p. 144; see also *Siddur Rashi*, ed. Buber, par. 214).

Those whose parents are living customarily leave the place of worship during the יִזְכּוֹר service. Many reasons have been given for this practice: lest we arouse the jealousy of those whose parents are dead; to prevent those who do not have to say יִזְכּוֹר from falling into the error of saying it by mistake, thus tempting fate; lest we be in the awkward position of remaining silent when those around us are worshipping. Obviously some of the above are superstitions, but the custom has nevertheless persisted.

Among the Sefardim no one leaves the service during יִזְכּוֹר. Many Conservative synagogues have adopted the Sefardic custom (see Eliyahu Kitov, *Sefer Hatoda'ah* 1:56).

That the יִזְכּוֹר service has such wide appeal in our day is to be welcomed, for it helps to bind the generations together in filial piety. Death does not end or break this bond. The virtues of the fathers work to mitigate some of the faults of the children, and the virtues of the children work to remove some of the imperfections of the fathers. "Moreover, to pray for the dead is not an unjustifiable corollary of the belief in God's boundless mercy. Unless we are prepared to maintain that at his death the fate of man is fixed irretrievably and forever, that therefore the sinner who rejected much of God's love during a brief lifetime has lost all of it eternally, prayer for the peace and salvation of the departed soul commends itself as of the highest religious obligations" (Singer, *Lectures and Addresses*, p. 72, quoted in Abrahams, *Companion to the Authorised Daily Prayer Book*, pp. ccxxi f.).

The rest of the service is exactly as on the seventh day. The same is true of Minḥah. The Ma'ariv service is a weekday service, with אַתָּה חוֹנַנְתָּנוּ inserted in the fourth benediction.

The festival is concluded with Havdalah on wine, both at the synagogue and at home, as at the end of the first two days. On a Sabbath the benedictions for fire and spices are added.

UNIT X

SEFIRAH AND SHAVU'OT

Sefirah
Shavu'ot

X.
Sefirah and Shavu'ot

1. Sefirah

The period between Pesaḥ and Shavu'ot is called Sefirah ("counting"). The name is derived from the practice of counting the 'Omer, which is observed from the night of the second Seder of Pesaḥ until the eve of Shavu'ot.

The Sefirah period is a time of sadness. According to the Talmud, this is because twelve thousand of Rabbi Akiva's disciples died one year between Pesaḥ and Shavu'ot (B. *Yeb.* 62b; *Otsar Hage'onim, Yebamot,* p. 141). The rabbis explain that this massacre took place because the disciples did not respect each other. Historians connect the event with the Hadrianic persecution, which followed the Bar Kokhba revolt in which Rabbi Akiva was involved (Wahrman, *Ḥagei Yisra'el Umo'adaw,* p. 166).

Some associate the somberness of these days with an even earlier period of Jewish history. The fruits of the field ripen during the time encompassed by Sefirah, and it is, therefore, a period of uncertainty—of hope and prayer that our physical sustenance will be continued in abundance (*Abudraham Hashalem,* p. 241; B. *R.H.* 16a). A contemporary scholar has suggested that this uncertainty was due, in particular, to the fact that in Israel, the hot winds that are so harmful to the crops blow between Pesaḥ and Shavu'ot (Wahrman, *Ḥagei Yisra'el Umo'adaw,* p. 171).

The 'Omer could no longer be brought to the Temple of Jerusalem after the destruction. The counting was continued, however, as a זֵכֶר לְמִקְדָּשׁ (remembrance of the Temple)—hence another reason for sadness (B. *Men.* 66a; *Kol Bo,* chap. 55; Maimonides, *Hil. Sefirat Ha'omer*). It was easy to superimpose other sorrowful memories on such a period, and the Hadrianic persecution was the most prominent of these.

The Crusades added another reason for sorrow, especially for the Jews of Germany, since the massacres perpetrated by the Crusaders also took place at this time of the year (*O.H.* 493:2 in *M.D.* 2).

Another reason for sadness was added in modern times. While the crematoria and gas chambers of the Nazis operated all year round, some notable tragic events took place in the Sefirah period. The Parliament of Israel fixed the twenty-seventh of Nisan as Memorial Day for those slaughtered by the Nazis during World War II. In addition, the day before Israel Independence Day is called Yom Hazikaron for those who died in the War of Liberation. The last great deportation to the gas chambers, that of the Jews of Hungary, took place during the Sefirah period.

These sad events are memorialized by our refraining from participation in joyous events during this period. No weddings should take place, and it is customary not to have the hair cut (*O.H.* 493:2). No event involving music and dancing should be scheduled during Sefirah (*O.H.* 493:1 in *M.A.* 1).

The one interruption in this doleful period is ל״ג בָּעוֹמֶר, the thirty-third day of the counting of the 'Omer, which falls on the eighteenth of Iyar. Evidently on this day there was an interruption in the oppression and hence the requirements of Sefirah were waived.

There are numerous variations in the customs prevailing during this period (*O.H.* 493:3). Some observe mourning up to Shavu'ot, excluding Lag Ba'Omer only (*O.H.* 493 in *M.D.* 2; ibid. in *Sha'arei Teshuvah* 8); some observe mourning only until Lag Ba'Omer (*O.H.* 493:1 in Rama); others start the period of sadness on the first day of Iyar (*O.H.* 493:3) and count until Shavu'ot, with the exception of Lag Ba'Omer; and still others begin on the first day of Iyar and continue until three days before Shavu'ot (*Ḥayyei Adam* 130:11).

In Ashkenazic communities, the most widespread custom has been to observe mourning from Pesaḥ until the three days before Shavu'ot. Exceptions are made on Rosh Ḥodesh Iyar, Rosh Ḥodesh Sivan, and Lag Ba'Omer (see in *Mishnah Berurah, O.H.* 493:15). Some add the fifth of Iyar, which is Israel Independence Day.

The Committee on Jewish Law and Standards of the Rabbinical Assembly, in 1949, adopted the Geonic tradition with the following statement:

"According to Geonic tradition, marriages in the *Sefirah* days were forbidden only from the second day of Passover until Lag B'Omer, and not from Lag B'Omer on (*Otsar Hageonim, Yebamot* 140).

"This tradition was also practiced in the Medieval period in the Jewish communities of France.

"The prohibition against marriages during these thirty-three days applied only to wedding ceremonies accompanied by dancing, singing and music.

"We therefore recommend that the Geonic tradition concerning marriages during *Sefirah* be followed, and that the prohibition be observed from the second day of Pesaḥ until Lag B'Omer. During this period, marriages not accompanied by dancing, singing and music may be performed.

"On those days, during the thirty-three day period, when *Taḥanun* is not recited in the synagogue, as well as on the fifth day of Iyar (Israel Independence Day), marriages of a public and festive nature may be solemnized."

A later decision of the Law Committee shortened the period even more and introduced a new element. On the one hand, the whole basis for the restrictions during the Sefirah period rests on shaky grounds. On the other hand, two other events which happened within our own memory must be memorialized and given significance. These are the martyrdom of the six million victims of the Holocaust and the establishment of the State of Israel. For the one we have declared the twenty-seventh of Nisan as Yom Hasho'ah, and for the other we have declared the fifth of Iyar as Yom Ha'atzma'ut. Both are gaining more and more recognition by Klal Yisrael. Hence it was proposed and passed that no joyous functions be allowed on the weekend before the twenty-eighth of Nisan, and that it be declared a period of mourning for the six million martyrs. Beyond that there should be no prohibition whatsoever (see Law Committee archives).

We should add the caveat expressed by the Rama, who says that in order to avoid separation, we should strive to avoid a situation where some Jews in a city adopt one custom and others, another custom (*O.H.* 493:3). In large communities this may not be applicable, but in small ones it is good advice.

The Warsaw Ghetto Memorial. It has become the custom in many communities to memorialize the martyrs of the Warsaw Ghetto Uprising. There is, as yet, no uniform pattern of observance. However, the day has tended to become a memorial not only for the fighters of the Warsaw Ghetto but also for the six million martyrs. When a pattern finally crystallizes, this day will rival the ninth of Av in solemnity and in the memories it will evoke. As of this writing, the twenty-seventh of Nisan has been accepted as Yom Hasho'ah.

Yom Ha'atsma'ut. The fifth of Iyar has been designated the official day for celebrating Israel's independence, for it was on the fifth of Iyar, 5708, that Israel's independence was declared. In Israel it has become both a national and religious holiday. As the years pass, a tradition of observance is beginning to crystallize. A special service and a guide for observance have been drawn up by the Chief Rabbinate. In time Yom Ha'atsma'ut will certainly take its place alongside Ḥanukkah and Purim.

In the diaspora Yom Ha'atsma'ut has also been recognized as a day of rejoicing. The Rabbinical Assembly has prepared a special service that expresses thanks for the great deliverance and recognition of the interdependence of the Jewries of Israel and the diaspora.

In Israel the day preceding Independence Day is called Yom Hazikaron, a day of remembrance for all those who made the supreme sacrifice during the War of Liberation.

Pesaḥ Sheini

In the time of the Temple, those who could not bring the Paschal lamb at the required time, either for reasons of ritual impurity or because they were traveling and were too far from Jerusalem to arrive in time for Pesaḥ, could bring the Paschal lamb a month later, on the fourteenth of Iyar (Num. 9:6–12). Today the day on which they did this (called Pesaḥ Sheini) is remembered with a slight variation in the service, i.e., Taḥanun is not recited. In some places a piece of matsah is eaten during the day (Singer, *Ziv Haminhagim,* p. 104).

Lag Ba'Omer

The thirty-third day of the 'Omer, which falls on the eighteenth of Iyar, is a semiholiday (*O.H.* 493:2 in Rama). According to tradition, the calamities of the Hadrianic persecution were interrupted on the eighteenth of Iyar, and as a result it was declared a semiholiday (Maharil [Warsaw, 5634], p. 21; [Bnai Brak, 5719], pp. 41–42). Taḥanun is not recited, weddings and joyous occasions are permitted, and one may cut his hair (*O.H.* 493:2 in Rama).

In Israel the day is also observed as הִלּוּלָא דְרַבִּי שִׁמְעוֹן בַּר יוֹחַאי, the Yahrzeit of Rabbi Shimon bar Yoḥai, the alleged author of the *Zohar.* Large numbers of people visit Rabbi Shimon bar Yoḥai's grave in Meron and celebrate the day as a full festival.

The origin of this celebration is attributed to the great kabbalist Isaac Luria. In Lag Ba'Omer he saw not only the cessation of the plague that afflicted Rabbi Akiva's disciples, but also the fact that Rabbi Akiva's surviving students saved the Torah. The student who was most famous in the eyes of the kabbalists was Rabbi Shimon bar Yoḥai, to whom they ascribed the authorship of the *Zohar*. According to tradition, he died on the eighteenth of Iyar. It was an ancient custom to celebrate the Yahrzeit of great people as a holiday (*Otsar Hageonim, Yebamot* 241), and Rabbi Isaac Luria applied this to the Yahrzeit of Rabbi Shimon bar Yoḥai, thus making Lag Ba'Omer even more significant (see Wahrman, *Ḥagei Yisra'el Umo'adaw*, p. 167). Lag Ba'Omer is also called the scholars' festival because of its association with the students of Rabbi Akiva. It is perhaps for this reason that the celebration has been observed mostly by schoolchildren. It used to be customary for children to make bows and arrows and engage in archery on Lag Ba'Omer. This is an obvious reference to the warlike activities of Rabbi Akiva's followers. Later kabbalists saw an association with the rainbow, which is a symbol of redemption, since there is a tradition that the rainbow will appear in the sky as the harbinger of the final redemption (*Benei Yisakhar*, month of Iyar, 1).

Shloshet Yemei Hagbalah

The three days before Shavu'ot are called שְׁלֹשֶׁת יְמֵי הַגְבָּלָה in reference to "And thou shalt set bounds [וְהִגְבַּלְתָּ] unto the people round about" (Exod. 19:12), referring to the three days of preparation enjoined on the children of Israel before they received the Torah at Mount Sinai.

Taḥanun is not recited from the first day of Sivan until the eighth day: the first day because it is Rosh Ḥodesh; the second (termed יוֹם הַמְּיוּחָס) because on the second day the children of Israel were told, "And ye shall be unto me a kingdom of priests and a holy nation" (Exod. 19:6), and also because that same day they received the command to prepare for the acceptance of the Torah (*Mishnah Berurah, O.H.* 494:8); the succeeding three days because they are the Sheloshet Yemei Hagbalah; the sixth and seventh because of Shavu'ot; and the eighth because it is Isru Ḥag (the day following the festival).

Pirqei Avot

Beginning on the Sabbath after Pesaḥ, it is customary to study one chapter of *Pirqei Avot* (also called the *Ethics of the Fathers*) every Sabbath afternoon. According to one source, this custom was originally observed only on the six Sabbaths between Pesaḥ and Shavuot (*Abudraham*

Hashalem, p. 245) since it was considered to be an appropriate preparation for *Matan Torah.* The general practice today, however, is to continue studying *Pirqei Avot* throughout the summer until Rosh Hashanah (*Levush, O.H.* 493:4). It has been suggested that this is because the moral maxims in *Pirqei Avot* serve to counteract the tendency to idleness that is experienced during the long afternoons of the summer months (ibid. in *Abudraham Hashalem,* p. 245, and *Midrash Shmu'el,* introduction).

2. Shavu'ot

Shavu'ot, occurring on the sixth and seventh of Sivan, is the second of the Three Pilgrimage Festivals. Like the other Pilgrimage Festivals, it commemorates an important event in the history of the Jewish people, it has an agricultural reference, marking a stage in the harvest, and it imparts an essential religious truth.

The agricultural reference is the most apparent since Shavu'ot marks the end of the counting of the 'Omer. The agricultural significance of Shavu'ot is also indicated by the first two references to the festival in the Torah: "And thou shalt observe the feast of weeks, even the first fruits of the wheat harvest" (Exod. 34:22); also, "And the feast of harvest, the first fruits of thy labors, which thou sowest in the field" (Exod. 23:16).

Thus two names are given to this festival: Ḥag Haqatsir (harvest festival), because of its agricultural aspect, and Ḥag Hashavu'ot, which does not indicate any characteristic of the festival except the date, i.e., that it comes after the counting of seven weeks (Deut. 16:10–12).

In the Talmud the name 'Atseret is also given to the festival (M. *R.H.* 1:2; B. *Pes.* 68b). Our sages regarded Shavu'ot as the conclusion of the festival of Pesaḥ, and therefore called it 'Atseret, just as the conclusion of the Sukkot festival is called Shemini 'Atseret (*Shir Hashirim Rabbah* 7:2).

According to rabbinic interpretation of the Bible (B. *Shab.* 86b–88a), the Ten Commandments were given on the sixth day of Sivan. Shavu'ot thus is זְמַן מַתַּן תּוֹרָתֵנוּ, commemorating this event and emphasizing the Torah's sanctity.

Torah, in its all-inclusive sense as the heritage of the children of Israel, is literally חַיֵּינוּ וְאֹרֶךְ יָמֵינוּ ("our life and the length of our days"). Sa'adia Gaon said that Israel is a people by virtue of the Torah. It is one element in the Jewish "trinity": קוּדְשָׁא בְּרִיךְ הוּא, אוֹרַיְיתָא וְיִשְׂרָאֵל—"the Holy One Blessed Be He, the Torah, and Israel"(*Zohar, Aḥarei Mot* 73a).

As the Hebrew phrase תּוֹרָה מִן הַשָּׁמַיִם indicates, the Torah is divinely ordained. Its moral laws are both normative and of divine origin, possessing unique validity that we must affirm and emphasize every day.

Professor Kaplan has written: " . . . the moral law must be regarded not as some prudential arrangement or social convention, but as inherent in the very nature of reality. The human mind loses all sense of security, and suffers from failure of nerve the moment it begins to suspect that the moral law is man-made" (*The Meaning of God in Modern Jewish Religion,* p. 302).

The rabbis in the Midrash express the same thought poetically. Rabbi Abahu said in the name of Rabbi Yoḥanan: "When God gave the Torah, no bird sang or flew, no ox bellowed, the angels did not fly, the Serafim ceased from saying, 'Holy, holy,' the sea was calm, no creature spoke; the world was silent and still, and the divine voice said: 'I am the Lord thy God . . . ' " (*Exodus Rabbah* 29:9). When God spoke the world was hushed. This gives us the common denominator in the various interpretations of תּוֹרָה מִן הַשָּׁמַיִם. The validity of the moral law is not conventional or prudential, but divine.

"We should therefore recognize in the doctrine of *Torah min hashamayim* . . . the original prophetic discovery of the moral law as the principal self-revelation of God" (Kaplan, ibid., p. 303).

Whether we consider תּוֹרָה מִן הַשָּׁמַיִם to be a historical fact or a theological concept, the import is that the moral law has divine sanction.

"The unique element in the Jewish religion consisted in the conscious recognition that the chief function of the belief in God was to affirm and fortify the moral law. . . . The outstanding characteristic of the Jewish religion is its *conscious emphasis* upon the teaching that the moral law is the principal manifestation of God in the world" (Kaplan, ibid., p. 302).

Shavu'ot is thus the festival that bids us emphasize the primacy of the moral law and the normative character of Judaism.

Observance

The laws concerning work on Shavu'ot are the same as on Pesaḥ.

The statutory services are also the same, with variations where Shavu'ot is mentioned. Thus in the 'Amidah we say חַג הַשָּׁבֻעוֹת הַזֶּה זְמַן מַתַּן תּוֹרָתֵנוּ, and the reading of the Torah is, of course, especially selected for Shavu'ot. On both days of Shavu'ot two Torah scrolls are removed from the ark. On the first day, in the first scroll, we read Exodus 19 and 20, which tell of the giving of the Ten Commandments. In the second scroll we read Numbers 28:26–31, which tells of the festival of Shavu'ot. The Hafṭarah is Ezekiel 1:1–28, 3:12, which contains the prophet's vision of God.

On the second day we read Deuteronomy 15:19–16:17, which speaks of the festivals. On a Sabbath we read Deuteronomy 14:22–16:17. The Hafṭarah is Habakkuk 2:20–3:19, where the revelation at Sinai is mentioned (*O.H.* 494:1–2; *Levush, O.H.* 494:1).

On the second day יִזְכּוֹר is recited after the Torah reading, as it is on the last day of Pesaḥ, on Shemini 'Atseret, and on Yom Kippur (*Levush, O.H.* 490:9 and 494:2).

Special Observances for Shavu'ot

It is customary to start the evening services of the first night later than usual. This is to satisfy the implication of the verse שֶׁבַע שַׁבָּתוֹת תְּמִימֹת (Lev. 23:15, i.e., we count seven *complete* weeks; therefore we wait to make sure that the forty-ninth day has been completed [*O.H.* 494 in *M.A.* and *M.D.*]).

It was an ancient custom for Jews to remain awake for the entire first night of Shavu'ot to study Torah. The *Zohar* ascribes this custom to particularly pious Jews (*Emor* 98a). In Eastern Europe it was widely observed, and a special text for the occasion, known as תִּקּוּן לֵיל שָׁבוּעוֹת, developed which contained the first and last verses of each Sidrah, the first and last passages of each tractate of the Mishnah, and excerpts from the *Zohar*.

A quaint reason is given for the practice of staying awake on the first night of Shavu'ot. Legend tells that the children of Israel slept so soundly the night before the Torah was given that they had to be awakened with thunder and lightening. We, on the contrary, are up all night and need not be awakened (*O.H.* 494 in *M.A.* and *Shir Hashirim Rabbah*).

The more obvious reason is that we review the Torah to celebrate the anniversary of its giving.

'Aqdamut

The hymn known as 'Aqdamut (because it begins with that word) is a song of praise to God for having chosen Israel and for granting us the Torah, hence its inclusion in the Shavu'ot liturgy (*Levush, O.H.* 494:1).

It was once customary to chant 'Aqdamut responsively at the Torah reading after the first man was called and had said the benediction and the reader had read the first verse of the reading. Now we say it before the first benediction (Singer, *Ziv Haminhagim,* p. 112; *M.D.* on *O.H.* 494). 'Aqdamut was written by Rabbi Meir of Orleans, a cantor in Worms, Germany, who lived in the eleventh century. Evidently its purpose was to strengthen the people's faith during the Crusades.

The Book of Ruth

The Book of Ruth is read on the second day of Shavu'ot. The custom is mentioned in *Masekhet Soferim* (14:16), and the fact that the first chapter of *Midrash Ruth* deals with the giving of the Torah is evidence that this custom was already well established in the period when this Midrash was compiled (Dunsky, *Midrash Ruth,* p. 3).

Many explanations are given for the reading of Ruth. The most quoted rason is that Ruth's coming to Israel took place around the time of Shavu'ot, and her acceptance of the Jewish faith was like *Matan Torah* for the people of Israel (*Abudraham Hashalem,* p. 240; *Levush, O.H.* 494:2). The acceptance of the Torah entails suffering and sacrifice for us just as it did for Ruth (*Yalkut Ruth* 586).

A more logical reason is the desire to have sections from all three divisions of the Bible—i.e., Torah, Nevi'im, and Ketuvim—in the liturgy of Shavu'ot and to show that they are all divine. And why the Book of Ruth? Because in the Talmud (B. *B.B.* 14b) Ruth is counted as the first book in the Ketuvim (Singer, *Ziv Haminhagim,* p. 112).

Since the Book of Ruth ends with the genealogy of David, whose forebear Ruth was, it has been suggested that it is read on Shavu'ot because there is a legend that David died on Shavu'ot (P. *Ḥag.* 2:3, P. *Beṭ.* 2:4, *Ruth Rabbah* 3:2).

A recent scholar has suggested that the custom had its origin in the polemics against the Karaites. The Karaites denied the validity of the Oral Law. According to biblical law, an Ammonite cannot enter the fold of Israel. How, then, was Ruth accepted? The rabbis interpreted the law as referring to males only; hence Ruth could become part of the people of Israel (B. *Yeb.* 76b). But this interpretation is based on the Oral Law, not the Written, and thus it is proof of the validity of the Oral Law. Shavu'ot was an appropriate time to show the equal validity of both the Oral and the Written Law (Maimon, *Ḥagim Umo'adim,* p. 271).

There is a difference of opinion as to whether a benediction should be recited before the Book of Ruth is read (see *Levush, O.H.* 494:2; Rama on

O.H. 490:9; *Mishnah Berurah* ad loc.; Shneur Zalman of Lyady, *Shulḥan 'Arukh* 494:13, 17). The present practice is not to recite a benediction.

The Eating of Dairy Dishes

It is customary to eat dairy dishes on the first day of Shavu'ot. Many reasons have been given for the custom. One derives it from the verse "honey and milk shall be under your tongue" (Song of Songs 4:11), which is made to refer to the Torah, implying that the words of the Torah are as pleasant and acceptable to our ears and hearts as milk and honey are to our tongues (*Kol Bo* 58).

It has also been suggested that just as we have two food items (the shankbone and the egg) at the Seder to represent the two sacrificial offerings brought to the Temple on Pesaḥ, so on Shavu'ot we have two types of food, first milk and later meat, in commemoration of the two special sacrificial offerings that were brought on Shavu'ot (*O.H.* 494:3).

We must mention one more reason which is still taken seriously by many though it seems almost facetious. With the giving of the Torah the dietary laws were established. Hence, when the people came home from Sinai they could not eat meat because they had none that was prepared properly. To prepare new meat properly would take too long. They had no choice, therefore, but to eat milk dishes (*O.H.* 494:2 in *Mishnah Berurah* 12).

A more logical reason, which may be an afterthought, however, connects the custom of eating dairy with restraint and self-control. The Torah is gained by eschewing pleasures and excesses. Meat is the food of those who know no restraint. Ascetics and people who seek self-control usually limit themselves to dairy dishes. Eating dairy dishes on Shavu'ot is a reminder that the Torah is given to him who lives the sober life rather than that of pleasure (Hirshovitz, *Otsar Kol Minhagei Yeshurun,* p. 201).

It is also customary on Shavu'ot to decorate the synagogue with flowers and foliage, and in some places the floors of the synagogue were strewn with fresh grass as a reminder of the agricultural character of the festival (*O.H.* 494:3 in Rama).

In some places the synagogues were adorned with branches and large plants as a reminder that according to the Mishnah (*R.H.* 1:2), the world is judged regarding the fruits of the trees on Shavu'ot. On Shavu'ot we thus pray for God to bless the fruit of the trees (B. *R.H.* 16a). Today, when flowers decorate the pulpit at all times, we simply add to the decorations and vary them.

In Israel many of the old customs are being revived, especially those having to do with the agricultural aspects of Shavu'ot. The bringing of *bikkurim* (first fruits) to the Temple in Jerusalem, as described in the Mishnah, was a gala affair (M. *Bik.* 3:1–8). It was discontinued after the destruction of the Temple, but has been revived in the villages and towns of Israel, where the children bring the first fruits of their fields with special festivities (Wahrman, *Ḥagei Yisra'el Umo'adaw,* p. 1186).

Confirmation

In many synagogues, confirmation services are held either on the first night or the first morning of Shavu'ot. The confirmation service has no roots in Jewish tradition but was instituted in the early nineteenth century in Germany by the Reform movement. It was frankly an importation from the Lutheran Church, but it struck roots in the Jewish community and was accepted by the Conservative synagogues and even by some Orthodox synagogues. There is no uniform service, no uniform age, and no uniform curriculum for preparation. The purpose, however, is to solemnly initiate Jewish boys and girls into their ancestral faith.

There were various motives behind the introduction of this rite. It was supposed to be a substitute for Bar Mitswah, and would thus apply to boys only. Then it was supposed to give equality to women as an equivalent to the Bar Mitswah. Later, when the Bar Mitswah rite was eliminated in the Reform movement, confirmation became the practice for both boys and girls (see *Jewish Encyclopedia,* 4:219).

In America the practice became so widespread that a Reform rabbi has written: "The confirmation ceremony, which generally attracts congregations that overflow the synagogues, is one of the chief contributions that Reform Judaism has made to the evolution of Jewish education and Jewish religious ceremonies in the American synagogues" (*Universal Jewish Encyclopedia,* 3:330).

Recent developments, however, have shaken this confidence. The Bar Mitswah has been reestablished with full force in all synagogues. And now—a contribution of the Conservative movement—the Bat Mitswah rite has been spreading to all segments of Judaism. Thus, all the original reasons for confirmation have disappeared. The protagonists of confirmation are hard put to find new meaning for it so as not to make it a duplication of the Bar and Bat Mitswah ceremonies. Where Bar Mitswah has a basis in tradition, and Bat Mitswah has a basis in the equalization of the sexes, confirmation is a *hora'at sha'ah* (temporary measure) which has lost its momentum (see *CCAR Journal,* June 1966, esp. the articles by Klein, Wolf, and Silverman).

In a number of synagogues confirmation has been eliminated, and instead there is a reconsecration rite with an entirely different purpose in mind.

UNIT XI

SUKKOT

XI. Sukkot

1. Introduction

The festival of Sukkot is the third of the Pilgrimage Festivals. It begins on the fifteenth of Tishre and continues for seven days. The first two of these are celebrated as full holidays with all the prescriptions already mentioned. The five days that follow are *Ḥol Hamo'ed*—weekdays which retain some aspects of the festival. The seventh day (the fifth of the Intermediate Days) is Hosha'nah Rabbah, with special observances of its own. There follow two concluding days which are separate festivals (שְׁמִינִי רֶגֶל בִּפְנֵי עַצְמוֹ) (B. *Suk.* 47a) and bear individual names: Shemini 'Atseret and Simḥat Torah.

Like the other two Pilgrimage Festivals, Sukkot commemorates an event or period in the history of the Jewish people, has an agricultural connotation, and teaches a number of religious truths.

The Bible stresses the historical aspect: "You shall live in booths seven days; all citizens in Israel shall live in booths, in order that future generations may know that I made the Israelite people live in booths when I brought them out of the land of Egypt. I am the Lord your God" (Lev. 23:42, 43). The agricultural theme is indicated earlier: "when you have gathered in the yield of your land, you shall observe the festival of the Lord [to last] seven days" (Lev. 23:29). Sukkot is thus a harvest festival during which we rejoice over the bounty of the harvest and are given an opportunity to thank God for his blessings.

While the Sukkah symbolizes the historical aspect of the festival, the Four Species bring to mind the agricultural: "on the first day you shall take the product of *hadar* trees, branches of palm trees, boughs of leafy trees, and willows of the brook, and you shall rejoice before the Lord your God seven days" (Lev. 23:40).

The names of the festival also reflect these various themes. The name used most often is *Sukkot,* (the Feast of Booths, or Tabernacles); it is also called חַג הָאָסִיף (the Feast of Ingathering) and simply חַג, the festival par excellence. While rejoicing is enjoined for all festivals, in the case of Sukkot an extra measure of enjoyment was prescribed: "And thou shalt rejoice in thy festival . . . and thou shalt be altogether joyful" (Deut. 16:14–16). Hence in the 'Amidah the descriptive phrase for this particular festival is זְמַן שִׂמְחָתֵנוּ.

The three names are also indicative of the religious truths that the festival seeks to impart. We noted that the reason for the Sukkah is: "that I made the Israelite people live in booths when I brought them out of the land of Egypt" (Lev. 23:43). The rabbis were not satisfied with the obvious meaning of this verse. While Rabbi Akiva says סֻכּוֹת מַמָּשׁ, i.e., that the booths mentioned in the Bible were real booths in which the children of Israel dwelt while in the desert, Rabbi Eliezer suggests that they were עֲנָנֵי כָבוֹד, or clouds of glory with which God surrounded the children of Israel to protect them while they wandered in the desert (B. *Suk.* 11b).

The interpretation of Rabbi Eliezer is expanded in the *Pesiqta deRav Kahana.* "Why do the children of Israel make a Sukkah? For the miracles that God wrought for them when they went out of Egypt, surrounding them with clouds of glory and shielding them, as it is said: 'For I make the children of Israel dwell in booths' [Lev. 23:43]. The Holy One, blessed be He, said to them: 'My children, make ye booths and dwell in them seven days that ye may be reminded of the miracles I wrought for you in the desert' " (*Pesiqta deRav Kahana,* ed. Buber, p. 188b). The building of the Sukkah was thus a means of infusing faith in God, particularly in time of distress.

Rabbi Akiva's interpretation, סֻכּוֹת מַמָּשׁ, is obviously more suitable to the modern temper, and it, too, suggests a significant truth. The reminder of the period when the children of Israel sojourned in the desert is a motif that occurs again and again in the Bible. In the Talmud the דּוֹר הַמִּדְבָּר is usually mentioned pejoratively, but in the Bible, particularly in the Prophets, the desert period was considered an ideal time in Jewish history, a time when life was simple but noble. With longing the prophet Jeremiah recalls: "I remember the devotion of your youth, your love as a bride; how you followed me in the wilderness in a land not sown" (Jer. 2:2). When the children of Israel entered Canaan and encountered the vices and corruption of urban civilization, they looked back with nostalgia to the nomadic period of their history, when they were free of these corrupting influences. They saw in this nomadic period a set of standards by which they could purify the civilization of their day. They looked with admiration at the sect known as the Rechabites, who wanted to reproduce the life of the nomads in Canaan itself

(Jer. 35:6, I Kings 10:15). In our day Sukkot should become a call to the ethical life, free from the corruption and vices of the affluent society.

Maimonides also gives the historical aspect a moral and ethical turn when he says that the purpose of remembering the days of the wilderness is "to teach man to remember his evil days, in his days of prosperity. He will thereby be induced to thank God repeatedly and to lead a modest and humble life" (Maimonides, *Moreh Nevukhim* III:47).

A more pietistic tone is struck by the well-known medieval moralist Isaac Aboab, who said: "The Sukkah is designed to warn us that man is not to put his trust in the size or strength or beauty of his home, though it be filled with all precious things; nor must he rely upon the help of any human being, however powerful. But let him put his trust in the great God whose word called the universe into being, for He alone is mighty, and His promises alone are sure" (Isaac Aboab, *Menorat Hama'or* III, 4:6; ed. Mossad Harav Kook, p. 315).

Rightly does Dr. Mordecai Kaplan conclude: "From the foregoing circumstances [that life in the wilderness was purer and freer than life in the civilization of Canaan] it follows that having the Israelites relive their Wilderness experience on the festival of Sukkot [by living in a Sukkah] was bound to place them in a frame of mind which enabled them to detach themselves from the order of life which they had come to accept as normal and to view it critically" (*The Meaning of God in Modern Jewish Religion,* p. 208).

The agricultural theme of the festival is called to mind by its other name: חַג הָאָסִיף. The crops of the field having been gathered, the people rejoiced before the Lord in gratitude for the blessings which He bestowed upon them. When agriculture ceased to be the main occupation of the people, the theme of gratitude to God was still valid. Consequently, the symbolic expression of the agricultural theme through the Four Species received a new meaning.

The Midrash thus made the four species symbolize the need for the unity of the Jewish people that comes when each segment of the people receives due consideration. Therefore the Midrash says: "Just as the Etrog has taste and fragrance, so there are in Israel men who are both learned and doers of good deeds; as the Lulav, whose fruit is palatable but is without fragrance, so there are those who are learned but without good deeds; as the myrtle has a pleasant odor but is tasteless, so there are men of good deeds, but who possess no scholarship; as the willow is neither edible nor of agreeable fragrance, so there are those who are neither learned nor possessed of good deeds" (*Wayiqra Rabbah* 30:12). In binding the species together and pronouncing the benediction over them, we assert that the unity must include all segments of the community; only when each has its proper place, can there be a benediction.

Another comment of the Midrash stresses the unity of the human personality necessary for the moral life. On the verse "all my bones shall proclaim, 'O Lord who is like unto thee?' " (Ps. 35:10) the Midrash comments: "This verse refers to the Lulav. The back of the Lulav is like the backbone of man, the myrtle like the eye, the willow, the mouth, and the Etrog, the heart. Thus David said: 'There are no limbs greater than these for they equal the entire body in importance; hence: all my bones will proclaim . . . ' " (*Wayiqra Rabbah* 30:14).

This psychological insight suggests that the entire personality must be involved in the search for happiness. Happiness is experienced whenever the human being, in all his relationships, participates in the fulfillment of some specific need, or needs, and there is no inner conflict of the type which might lead to the disintegration of personality (Kaplan, *The Meaning of God*, p. 226).

The unity of the human personality and of the Jewish people leads our thoughts to the unity and interdependence of all humanity—i.e., to the Messianic ideal. The Messianic ideal is symbolized, according to the rabbis, by the sacrifice of seventy oxen (Num. 29:13–34), corresponding to the proverbial seventy nations of the world, for whose welfare these were offered on the altar of the Temple in Jerusalem (B. *Suk*. 52b). In this connection the prophet Zechariah invited all the nations of the world to "go up to Jerusalem from year to year to worship the King, the Lord of hosts, and to keep the Feast of Tabernacles" (Zech. 14:16).

Samson Raphael Hirsch also saw in the Sukkah a symbol of universal peace and brotherhood. The Ma'ariv service on Sabbaths and festivals contains the prayer וּפְרוֹשׂ עָלֵינוּ סֻכַּת שְׁלוֹמֶךָ. The term *sukkah* is used in the prayer to symbolize peace and brotherhood, which shall be based not on common economic and political interests, but on the prophetic vision: "On that day the Lord shall be one and His name one" (*Horeb*, pp. 126 f.).

The festival has a third name, חַג—or the festival par excellence. Hence we add the description זְמַן שִׂמְחָתֵנוּ, "the time of our rejoicing," when we mention the festival in the 'Amidah and in the Qiddush. The rabbis said: "The Divine presence is not made manifest to man through melancholy . . . but rather joy" (B. *Shab.* 30b). In the Jewish tradition, happiness is requisite to entering into a conscious relationship with God (Kaplan, *The Meaning of God,* p. 225).

This happiness is best expressed through gratitude to God. The Midrash says: "In the millennium all other sacrifices will be abolished, but not the thanksgiving offering; all other prayers will be abolished, but not the prayer of thanksgiving" (*Wayiqra Rabbah* 9:7). Thus gratitude and thankfulness have supreme value as the essence of religion.

2. Preliminary Observances

The four days between Yom Kippur and Sukkot have a festive touch of their own. Fasting is prohibited and Taḥanun is not recited. If a Sabbath occurs during these four days, neither *Av Haraḥamim* nor *Tsidqatekha* is said. The Temple of Solomon was dedicated during these days, and today pious Jews are occupied with building a Sukkah and acquiring an Etrog and Lulav, hence the more festive mood (*O.H.* 624, end).

3. The Building of a Sukkah

There is an ancient maxim: מִצְוָה הַבָּאָה לְיָדְךָ אַל תַּחֲמִיצֶנָּה ("if an opportunity to perform a mitswah presents itself to you, do not be slow in performing it") (based on comment in *Mekhilta, Masekhta d'Pisḥa, Parasha* 9, ed. Lauterbach, vol. 1, p. 74). Hence, the building of the Sukkah should be started immediately after Yom Kippur (*O.H.* 625:1). Some pious Jews drive in the first nail, so to speak, the night after Yom Kippur so as to proceed directly from one mitswah to another (*O.H.* 624).

The Sukkah is a temporary structure constructed for the festival of Sukkot. It must be erected in the open air, under the sky, not in a room or under a tree (*O.H.* 626:1). It consists of four walls and a removable covering. This covering, called *sekhakh,* must be of material that grows from the soil, has been detached from the ground, and cannot be defiled (*O.H.* 629:1). Hides and the like are excluded because they do not grow from the soil; vines and tendrils are excluded because they are attached to the ground; cloth, utensils, or metal objects are excluded because they can become ritually defiled.The *sekhakh* is usually of cut branches or plants.

The *sekhakh* should be loose enough so that one can see the sky, yet thick enough so that the shadow it casts on the ground exceeds the light thrown by the sun: צִלָּתָהּ מְרֻבָּה מֵחַמָּתָהּ (*O.H.* 631:1, 3). No open space measuring three hand-breadths, or about twelve inches, or longer, may be left (*O.H.* 632:2). There is only one class of objects which, though they conform to the above requirements, may not be used for *sekhakh:* grasses or leaves that dry quickly and start falling, or that have an offensive odor (*O.H.* 629:14).

The walls may be constructed of any material (*O.H.* 630:1), but materials with an offensive odor or that will shrivel within the seven days should not be used (Rama on *O.H.* 680:1). Theoretically two complete walls and part of a third wall satisfy the minimum requirements for a Sukkah, but it is customary to have four walls (*O.H.* 630:5 in Rama), and these should be strong enough to withstand the impact of ordinary winds (*O.H.* 630:10).

The Sukkah should not be constructed in a conic shape—all walls and no *sekhakh*—because the name Sukkah implies that there is *sekhakh* on top (*O.H.* 631:10).

The Sukkah should not be more than twenty cubits high (about thirty feet) (*O.H.* 631:1) because it would then cease to be a temporary dwelling since the walls would have to be exceedingly strong (*O.H.* 631:1 in *M.A.* 1); nor should it be less than ten hand-breadths (approximately three feet) high. It should be at least seven by seven hand-breadths in area (approximately twenty-six inches square)—the minimum space necessary for at least one person (*O.H.* 633:1).

Some people build a permanent Sukkah in their houses by having a removable ceiling in one of the rooms. During the festival the ceiling is removed and *sekhakh* is put in its place. In some cases, the roof is opened by means of pulleys. Both are permissible (*O.H.* 626:1, 3). If it rains the roof may be closed and then reopened when the rain stops (Rama on *O.H.* 631:3).

On the basis of the rabbinic maxim that the commandments should have aesthetic appeal—הִתְנָאֵה לְפָנָיו בְּמִצְוֹת (B. *Shab.* 133b), it has become customary to decorate the Sukkah. Each country uses its own aesthetic forms in fulfilling this requirement (*Sefer Maharil, Hilkhot Sukkah; O.H.* 627:4).

The building of a Sukkah is an obligation for each individual. However, the custom has become widespread to build a Sukkah in a yard near the synagogue for use by all the worshippers, at least for Qiddush or light refreshment. The synagogue Sukkah may be used by those who are observant but find it difficult to build a Sukkah on their own premises. All the laws pertaining to the Sukkah apply here too. We have reason to believe that such communal Sukkahs are not a new development but have precedents as far back as the Middle Ages (see *Shibolei Haleqeṭ*, ed. Buber, p. 314; *Sefer Hamo'adim, Sukkot*, p. 25; Abraham ben Nathan of Lunel, *Sefer Hamanhig*, p. 64).

4. The Four Species

Before the advent of the festival each family should provide itself with the Four Species: citron (אֶתְרוֹג), palm branch (לוּלָב), myrtle (הֲדַסִּים), and willow (עֲרָבוֹת) (*O.H.* 651:1).

The biblical source for this commandment is the verse in Leviticus 23:40: "On the first day you shall take the product of *hadar* trees, branches of palm trees, boughs of leafy trees, and willows of the brook." The willow and the palm branch are mentioned explicitly. The Talmud explains that "the product of *hadar* trees" refers to the Etrog (B. *Suk.* 35a) and that "boughs of leafy trees" refers to the myrtle (ibid. 32b). While the Etrog retained its name, the other three species are together called the Lulav because of the prominence of the palm branch. Hence the blessing for the four species is עַל נְטִילַת לוּלָב (B. *Suk.* 37b). These three species are tied together with leaves from a palm branch (*O.H.* 651:1). Today they are also put into a basketlike structure, woven of palm leaves, that serves to hold them together.

The Lulav should have one palm branch, two willow, and three myrtle twigs (*O.H.* 651:1). They should be tied together in the direction in which they grow, the myrtle on the right of the palm branch, the willow on the left, and the spine of the palm branch facing the holder (*O.H.* 651:1 in *M.A.* 4). The minimum length of the palm branch should be four hand-breadths (sixteen inches). The myrtle and the willow should be at least three hand-breadths (twelve inches). The palm branch should be at least one hand-breadth (four inches) longer than the myrtle and willow (*O.H.* 650:1). The Etrog should be at least as large as an average egg (*O.H.* 648:22).

As with the Sukkah, pious people seek to emphasize the aesthetic aspect of the mitswah so that they can worship God in the beauty of holiness. They go to great lengths to acquire an Etrog and a Lulav that are particularly pleasing to the eye. Especially in the case of the Etrog they try to get a מְהֻדָּר (extra fine). Here shape and color are important factors. The Etrog should taper upward at the top rather than be spherical. The surface should not be smooth like a lemon but rather rough and ridged (בְּלִיטוֹת). The shape should be symmetrical so that the tip (פִּטְמָא) is directly above the stem (עוּקֶץ). There should be no blotches, spots, or discolorations on the skin. It should not be green, but yellow, like a ripe lemon (*O.H.* 648).

The Lulav should be fresh, not dried, reaching straight to the top; the leaves should not spread out nor should the tip be broken off (*O.H.* 645). The myrtle and willow should be green, fresh, and with the leaves intact (*O.H.* 646, 647; for a resume, see *Qitsur Shulḥan 'Arukh*, ed. Feldmann, 2:64).

The other preparations for Sukkot are the same as those for the other Pilgrimage Festivals.

5. Services

The candles are lit in the Sukkah with two benedictions: לְהַדְלִיק נֵר שֶׁל יוֹם טוֹב and the שֶׁהֶחֱיָנוּ. If the first day is a Sabbath, the candles should be lit at the time prescribed for the Sabbath and with the benediction לְהַדְלִיק נֵר שֶׁל שַׁבָּת וְשֶׁל יוֹם טוֹב (*O.H.* 514:11; Singer, *Ziv Haminhagim*, p. 222). If the Sukkah is so built that a wind can blow out the candles, they should be moved into the house immediately after being lit.

Minḥah is the regular weekday service, and Ma'ariv is the same as on the other Pilgrimage Festivals with the variations appropriate to Sukkot. After the services Qiddush is recited in the Sukkah. The regular festival Qiddush is recited, with the appropriate reference to Sukkot. At the end of Qiddush we add two benedictions: אֲשֶׁר קִדְּשָׁנוּ בְּמִצְוֹתָיו וְצִוָּנוּ לֵישֵׁב בַּסֻּכָּה and the שֶׁהֶחֱיָנוּ (*O.H.* 643:1). On Saturday we follow the usual variations appropriate for the day. At home each person recites the Qiddush in his Sukkah as above.

The kabbalists have added a poetic touch to the Sukkot festival. It is written in the *Zohar* that when the children of Israel leave their houses and go into the Sukkah, they are rewarded by receiving the שְׁכִינָה, divine presence, as a guest along with seven faithful shepherds who descend from heaven and enter the Sukkah (*Zohar, Emor* 103b). The seven faithful shepherds are Abraham, Isaac, Jacob, Joseph, Moses, Aaron, and David. It has become customary to invite all of these faithful shepherds, each day a different one of them being the special guest, heading the others in chronological order. Isaac Luria rearranged the order according to the importance of the figures, placing Moses and Aaron before Joseph (Wahrman, *Ḥagei Yisra'el Umo'adaw*, p. 66; Singer, *Ziv Haminhagim*, p. 224).

The meal, and the prayers accompanying it, follows the pattern of the other festivals with one variation: At the end of the Grace after meals we say הָרַחֲמָן הוּא יָקִים לָנוּ אֶת סֻכַּת דָּוִיד הַנֹּפָלֶת.

In the morning the Shaharit service is the regular festival service with the same variations in the 'Amidah as on the night before. Before Hallel we recite the benediction over the Etrog and Lulav.

While one can perform this commandment at any time during the whole day (literally during the day but not at night), it is best to do it in the morning, preferably before Hallel (*O.H.* 652:1). It should be done in the following manner. The Lulav is taken in the right hand and the Etrog in the left hand, held together in the position in which they grow, i.e., tips upward (*O.H.* 651:2). Since a benediction must precede the performance of a commandment, we begin by holding the Etrog in the reverse position, i.e., with its tip downward and the stem upward (*O.H.* 651:5), and the benedictions עַל נְטִילַת לוּלָב and שֶׁהֶחֱיָנוּ are recited. The שֶׁהֶחֱיָנוּ is recited on the first day only, but if the first day is a Sabbath, it is recited on the second day because the Etrog and Lulav are not taken on the Sabbath (*O.H.* 658:2). The Etrog is then reversed so that it is held in the position of its growth, and together the four species are waved in the four directions, upwards and downwards, in this sequence: east, south, west, north, up, down. Each wave is a forward and backward motion and is accompanied by the shaking of the leaves of the Lulav (*O.H.* 651:9–10). All this time the Etrog and Lulav are held together so that they touch each other (*O.H.* 651).

The waving of the Etrog and the Lulav is also done each time the verse הודו is said and at אָנָּא יְיָ (M. *Suk.* 3:9). Since הודו has six words apart from the divine name, each word is accompanied by a wave, and since אָנָּא יְיָ has three words apart from the divine name, each word is accompanied by two waves (*Hayyei Adam* 148:14). The Talmud says: "We wave toward the four points of the world in honor of Him to whom the four corners of the world, upwards and downwards, heaven and earth, belong, proclaiming thereby that the world is God's and that His dominion is everywhere" (B. *Suk.* 37b).

Also, we wave the four species to and fro to ward off harmful winds, upwards and downwards to keep away harmful waters. The ceremony thus becomes a form of prayer through action, recalling the agricultural theme of the festival.

Two Torah scrolls are taken out of the ark accompanied by the usual festival prayers. In the first Torah scroll we read Leviticus 22:26–23:44, which deals with the festivals. Five people are called, and on the Sabbath, seven. From the second Torah scroll we read Numbers 29:12–16, which contains the sacrificial offerings for the day. For the Hafṭarah we read the fourteenth chapter of Zechariah because it speaks of the Messianic days when all mankind will come to Jerusalem, on the Sukkot festival, to worship the Lord of Hosts (*O.H.* 659:1).

The Musaf service is the same as on the other Pilgrimage Festivals, with specific variations for Sukkot.

After *Ḥazarat Hashats* and before Qaddish, the Hosha'not are recited. These hymns begin with הוֹשַׁע נָא, and one is recited each day in an order which varies each year according to the day on which the festival begins. The variation is due to the fact that the contents of each hymn are suited to certain days of the week. Thus אֹם נְצוּרָה, which praises the Sabbath, is always said on the Sabbath; לְמַעַן אֲמִתָּךְ, which speaks of the glory of God, is always said on the first day (except if the first day is a Sabbath, when it is said on the second day); and אֶעֱרוֹךְ שׁוּעִי is always on the third day (except if the third day is a Sabbath) because it speaks of atonement, the theme of Yom Kippur, which always occurs on the same day of the week as the third day of Sukkot.

The ark is opened, a scroll of the Torah is removed, and the ark is left open. The reader takes the Etrog and Lulav and chants the four introductory verses, each beginning with הוֹשַׁע נָא. The congregation repeats each verse after the reader. A procession of all who have an Etrog and Lulav is then formed, and it follows the reader around the bimah while the congregation and the reader recite the hymn for the day responsively. After the procession there is a closing hymn, כְּהוֹשַׁעְתָּ and הוֹשִׁיעָה אֶת עַמֶּךָ. After these the Torah is returned to the ark, the ark is closed, the people in the procession return to their places, and the service continues with the closing Qaddish.

If the holiday falls on a Sabbath, the Hosha'not for the Sabbath are recited but there is no procession. The ark is opened, but no Torah is removed (*O.H.* 660:1, 2). The procession is patterned after the one held in the Temple of Jerusalem, where it took place around the altar. Today the Torah replaces the altar. Since there is no procession, there is no need for taking out the Torah.

On the second day the service is exactly as on the first day with the following variations. At the preceding Minḥah we add וּבָא לְצִיּוֹן before the 'Amidah and recite the festival 'Amidah. Ma'ariv is as the night before, but we recite לֵישֵׁב בַּסֻּכָּה at Qiddush *after* the שֶׁהֶחֱיָנוּ (*O.H.* 661:1). In the morning the Hafṭarah is I Kings 8:2–21, which tells of Solomon's dedication of the

Temple, which took place on Sukkot, and for the Hosha'not there is a different hymn. In the afternoon Minḥah is like the day before, and Ma'ariv is the weekday Ma'ariv with אַתָּה חוֹנַנְתָּנוּ and Havdalah.

6. The Intermediate Days

On Sukkot there are five Intermediate Days. The observance of eating in the Sukkah and the benediction over the Etrog and Lulav apply as on the first two days. In the synagogue we follow the pattern of the Intermediate Days of Pesaḥ with some variations. The complete Hallel is recited every day because the sacrificial service in the Temple of Jerusalem varied each day, making each day a separate festival (*Levush, O.H.* 663:1). Each day we have four 'aliyot and read the sacrificial service for the day, starting on the first day with the sacrifices for the second day, since before the calendar was fixed this might have been the second day. Thus the Kohen is called for וּבַיּוֹם הַשֵּׁנִי, and the Levi is called for וּבַיּוֹם הַשְּׁלִישִׁי. We read וּבַיּוֹם הָרְבִיעִי For the third 'aliyah and for the fourth 'aliyah we go back and read וּבַיּוֹם הַשֵּׁנִי and וּבַיּוֹם הַשְּׁלִישִׁי; inasmuch as the fourth 'aliyah is the special addition in honor of the festival, we read the portion that applies specifically to the day (*Levush, O.H.* 663:1). This pattern is followed on each of the Intermediate Days except on the Sabbath, when we have seven 'aliyot and a Maftir. The Sabbath Torah reading is Exodus 33:12–34:36. For the Maftir we read just two paragraphs of the sacrificial service, depending on the day of the festival. The Haftarah is Ezekiel 31:18–39:16 because of a tradition that the victory at Armageddon will take place during the Sukkot festival (Ṭur, *O.H.* 490).

It is customary to read the Book of Ecclesiastes on the Sabbath of the Intermediate Days, or on Shemini 'Atseret if it falls on a Sabbath (*O.H.* 663:2). Although the mood of the book is cynical, it does teach that one should be content with his lot, that there is no joy in the possession of material wealth, and that everything we have is a gift from God. These themes reflect the mood of this festival (*Levush, O.H.* 663:2). Another explanation is that the fall season was the occasion for bacchanalian orgies and wild celebrations in the ancient pagan world, and the reading of Ecclesiastes, with its somber view of life, was introduced in an effort to counteract this influence (Dunsky, *Midrash Qoheleth,* p. 13). No benediction is recited before the reading.

7. Hosha'na' Rabbah

The last of the Intermediate Days, the seventh day of Sukkot, and officially the last day of the festival—since the following day is Shemini 'Atseret, which is considered a separate festival (B. *Suk.* 47b–48a)—is called Hosha'na' Rabbah. This designation, which does not occur in the Talmud, already appears in the geonic literature (*Seder Rav 'Amram*, ed. Goldschmidt, p. 175). The name becomes regular in the Middle Ages (Abraham b. Nathan of Lunel, *Sefer Hamanhig, Hilkhot Etrog* 38; *Maḥzor Vitry*, ed. Hurwitz, no. 380, p. 442) and is probably derived from the willow twigs, called *hosha'not*, used during the special service of the day. While the Hebrew for "willow twig" is *'aravah*, the name *hosha'nah* became prevalent because of its use during the Hosha'not prayers (B. *Suk.* 31a). Hence the day was called Yom 'Aravah (*She'iltot, Parashah Vayakhel, Shibolei Haleqeṭ*, ed. Buber, sec. 371), Yom Hosha'na' (*Wayiqra Rabbah* 3), and Yom Ḥibbuṭ 'Aravot (M. *Suk.* 4:6).

Tradition has made this day into a sequel to the Days of Awe, lengthening the period of penitence, postponing the day when final sentence is to be rendered, and giving an opportunity to those who have not made full use of the grace afforded by Yom Kippur. Kabbalistic influence gave Hosha'na' Rabbah a status akin to that of Yom Kippur: "The seventh day of the festival is the close of the judgment of the world, and writs of judgment [פִּתְקִין] issue from the sovereign" (*Zohar, Tsaw* 31b).

An authority of the Middle Ages offers this paraphrase of a well-known talmudic statement: "On Hosha'na' Rabbah the closing of the three books that were opened on Rosh Hashanah, and sealed on Yom Kippur, takes place. Hosha'na' Rabbah is the end of the period of atonement" (Abraham b. Nathan of Lunel, *Sefer Hamanhig, Hil. Etrog, O.H.* 38). These authorities suggest that Hosha'na' Rabbah came to be associated with the days of judgment in this manner. According to the Mishnah, on Sukkot the world was judged for water, i.e., whether rain would be plentiful during the coming season or whether there would be drought and famine. It is an easy transition to see this period as a continuation of the preceding solemn days of judgement (ibid.; *Shibolei Haleqeṭ*, ed. Buber; Munk, *The World of Prayer*, 2:283; Levi, *Yesodot Hatefilah*, p. 270).

The services on Hosha'na' Rabbah are similar to those of the other Intermediate Days with the following variations. In Pesuqei Dezimrah we add the psalms that are recited on Sabbaths and festivals before יְהִי כְבוֹד. We do not say נִשְׁמַת but continue the service as on *Ḥol Hamo'ed* (*O.H.* 664:1). For the Torah reading we follow the pattern of festivals and say אֵין כָּמוֹךָ, שְׁמַע יִשְׂרָאֵל, and אֶחָד אֱלֹהֵינוּ (including וְנוֹרָא) (ibid.). It is customary to use the High Holiday melody for this and the Ḥatsi Qaddish before Musaf. In some places it is also customary to say אֵין כֵּאלֹהֵינוּ at the conclusion of the service.

The main variation comes at the Hosha'na' service. Whereas on each day of the festival one Torah scroll is taken out of the ark, and one procession (הַקָּפָה) is made around the bimah with the Etrog and Lulav, on Hosha'na' Rabbah all the scrolls of the Law are taken out of the ark and seven processions are made (B. *Suk*. 45a; *O.H.* 660:1, and in Rama). Additional hymns, penitential in nature, are then recited. During these prayers the Etrog and Lulav are laid aside, and the Hosha'na', consisting of five willow twigs tied together, is held in hand (*O.H.* 664:2, 5). At the end of the service, as the verse קוֹל מְבַשֵּׂר מְבַשֵּׂר וְאוֹמֵר is said, the worshippers strike the willow against the ground or against other solid objects (*O.H.* 664:4). Because of the penitential nature of the day, the reader wears a white robe (Kittel) during the service, as on Yom Kippur (*O.H.* 664:1 in *M.A.*; commentary of Elijah of Vilna, s.v. יש נוהגים). It is also a well-established custom to spend the preceding night in study, as on the first night of Shavu'ot. There are various customs regarding the subject for study. At present there is a printed text, תִּיקּוּן לֵיל הוֹשַׁעְנָא רַבָּה, which contains the prevalent choice (*O.H.* 664:1 in *M.A.*; *Mishnah Berurah, O.H.* 664:1, n. 1).

The beating of the willow is explained in this way. These branches, when shaken or struck, lose their leaves one after the other; so do the trees from which the branches have been cut, and so also all other trees. But the rain and heat sent by God in due time give them fresh life, and they produce new leaves. Our experience is similar. The struggle for life reduces our strength and weakens our health. But faith in God and trust in His providence renew our strength; our health improves, our cares and troubles are diminished, and we feel ourselves restored to fresh life (Friedländer, *The Jewish Religion*, p. 398, n. 1).

8. Shemini 'Atseret

The last two days of Sukkot are called Shemini 'Atseret and Simḥat Torah. In Israel only one day is celebrated, and it includes the features of both.

In the Talmud it is written שְׁמִינִי רֶגֶל בִּפְנֵי עַצְמוֹ ("the eighth day is a separate festival"), and six observances are enumerated that mark it as a separate festival (B. *Suk*. 47b–48a).

The Midrash gives a poetic touch to its interpretation of the significance of the day. When the children of Israel, after having spent a long holiday period in worship and rejoicing, are about to resume their regular daily life, God says to them: "It is difficult for me to part with you. Tarry a while longer. Stay another day." Hence the name Shemini 'Atseret, for the word *'atseret* means "to tarry" or "to hold back" (quoted by Rashi on Lev. 23:36). The Talmud embellishes this even further. While on Sukkot the universal aspect of the festival is stressed through the offering of seventy bullocks to remember the proverbial seventy nations of the world, on Shemini 'Atseret we are concerned solely with the children of Israel. Therefore only one bullock, corresponding to the people of Israel, is offered on this day—stressing the intimate bond between the people of Israel and God (B. *Suk*. 55b).

"Thus on Shemini 'Atseret Israel opens its heart to the pure, unalloyed rejoicing in the deliverance to come. On this Concluding Festival the Messianic rejoicing over peace among the nations and the enjoyment of undisturbed communion with God takes priority over all else. On these two final Festival Days, Israel reconfirms its faith in the future and in the Kingdom of God that is to come, and the rejoicing which now reaches its splendid pinnacle is brightened and glorified by *Simhath Torah,* the rejoicing with the Law, to which Israel owes its survival and by which it will triumph in the end" (Munk, *The World of Prayer,* 2:293).

A most relevant interpretation of the word *'atseret* is given by Rabbi Yaaqov Zevi Mecklenburg. He maintains that it means "to retain." During the holiday season we have experienced a heightened religious fervor and a most devout spirit. This last day is devoted to a recapitulation of the message of these days, with the hope that it will be retained the rest of the year (ibid., 2:294).

Since Shemini 'Atseret is a separate festival, the observances most characteristic of Sukkot—dwelling in a Sukkah, the Etrog and Lulav, and the daily procession around the bimah—are omitted. The Qiddush, however, both of the evening and of the morning, is recited in the Sukkah, with the omission of the benediction לֵישֵׁב בַּסֻּכָּה (*O.H.* 668:1).

The services are as on the first days, with several variations. Where חַג הַסֻּכּוֹת הַזֶּה is said on the first seven days, we substitute שְׁמִינִי חַג הָעֲצֶרֶת הַזֶּה.

There are variations in this phrase, some saying חַג before שְׁמִינִי, some after, and some omitting it altogether; each version emphasizes that Shemini 'Atseret is a separate holiday (*O.H.* 668:1 in Rama).

The Torah reading is the same as on the eighth day of Pesaḥ, Deuteronomy 14:22–16:17, except that we start with עַשֵּׂר תְּעַשֵּׂר even if the eighth day is on a weekday, because the first part (omitted on Pesaḥ if it falls on a weekday) deals with the laws of tithes, charity, and the release of servants, which are done at this time of the year (*O.H.* 668:2). The Maftir is Numbers 29:35–30:1. The Haftarah (I Kings 8:54–66) relates how King Solomon blessed the people on the eighth day of Sukkot and bade them farewell. After the Torah reading we recite *Hazkarat Neshamot* (*Levush* 668:2). Before the 'Amidah of Musaf the reader announces that in the second benediction of the 'Amidah מַשִּׁיב הָרוּחַ וּמוֹרִיד הַגָּשֶׁם should be said. This announcement is made to avoid confusion; for some people might wait until the reader has said it in *Ḥazarat Hashats* during the prayer for rain (*Levush* 668:2).

The prayer for rain corresponds to the prayer for dew that is said on the first day of Pesaḥ. It is said now because Shemini 'Atseret marks the beginning of the rainy season in Israel. Since, as already mentioned, the world is judged for rain at this time, according to the Talmud, it is proper to pray for rain at this time of the year. The prayer gives expression to the natural anxiety felt in Israel for the seasonal rain, the absence of which means famine, thirst, and disease. The prayer is delayed until Shemini 'Atseret because it should not be invoked when fine weather is needed to enable us to dwell in the Sukkah (B. *Suk.* 28b; *Levush* 668:4). Furthermore, the prayer is not "a direct prayer for rain, but praise of Him who causes the rain to fall (גְּבוּרוֹת גְּשָׁמִים) while the daily direct prayer for rain (וְתֵן טַל וּמָטָר) begins about two months later, when the pilgrims that had come from distant countries to Jerusalem for the festival were assumed to have reached their homes" (Friedländer, *The Jewish Religion,* p. 388, n. 2). Since this is a period of judgment, the prayer for rain is recited with a special plaintive melody and the reader wears a white robe (Kittel) as on the High Holy Days (*O.H.* 668:2).

9. Simḥat Torah

Simḥat Torah, the festival of rejoicing with the Torah, is a fitting finale for the holiday season. In the diaspora it falls on the ninth day of Sukkot, and is devoted completely to rejoicing. In Israel, where the eighth day is the last day, the practices of Simḥat Torah are observed on Shemini 'Atseret.

The name Simḥat Torah is not mentioned in the Talmud. It occurs first in the post-geonic literature (Isaac Ibn Ghayyat, *Sha'arei Simḥah*, pt. I, p. 118; Avraham Yaari, *Toldot Ḥag Simḥat Torah*, p. 29) and in the *Zohar* (*Pinḥas* 256b). Since the concluding portion of the Torah is read on this day, it has become an occasion for rejoicing and an opportunity to demonstrate Israel's love for the Torah. Hence the name Simḥat Torah (*Abudraham Hashalem*, p. 300; *O.H.* 669:1 in Rama and in *M.A.* ad loc.).

It has been asked why the reading of the last Sidrah, וְזֹאת הַבְּרָכָה, was assigned to Simḥat Torah. Since the reading of the Torah should be completed during the year, it would have been logical to read it on the last Sabbath of the year, the Sabbath before Rosh Hashanah. Furthermore, on Simḥat Torah, which is a *safeiq shemini*, we should read what is usually read on the last day of a festival, פָּרָשַׁת רְאֵה of כָּל הַבְּכוֹר.

In answer, it is explained that there was, first, the desire to join the joy of *siyyum haTorah* with *siyyum heḥag*. Second, the purpose was to have the Torah portion similar to the Hafṭarah. Originally, the Hafṭarah contained the blessing that King Solomon gave the children of Israel at the conclusion of the festival as they were ready to depart (I Kings 8:16), and the Sidrah וְזֹאת הַבְּרָכָה, the blessings that Moses gave the children of Israel when he was about to depart (*Abudraham Hashalem*, p. 300).

Today, when we have two days for the concluding festival, we adopt a compromise. On the eighth day we read the special portion of the festival and the Hafṭarah from the Book of Kings; on the ninth we read וְזֹאת הַבְּרָכָה, and the Hafṭarah is the first chapter of Joshua, which is a natural continuation of the portion that tells of the death of Moses (see Avraham Yaari, *Toldot Ḥag Simḥat Torah*, pp. 33–34; and Zevin, *Hamo'adim Bahalakhah*, p. 141).

The festivities begin in the evening with Ma'ariv. This is the regular festival service with the difference that after Qaddish we have Haqqafot and the reading of the Torah. The Haqqafot are introduced with אַתָּה הָרְאֵתָ, a collection of biblical verses in praise of God and the Torah. Each verse is read by the reader and then repeated by the congregation (Maharil, *Sukkot*). In some places each verse is read by a different member of the congregation and then repeated by the entire congregation.

When the verse וַיְהִי בִּנְסֹעַ is reached, the ark is opened. When the last verse has been recited, all the scrolls are removed from the ark and are carried in procession (הַקָּפוֹת) in the synagogue. This is done seven times. In each procession each Torah is given to a different person so that as many as possible should have an opportunity to participate. Each Haqqafah is done to the chanting of prescribed hymns. To these are added songs and hymns of a joyous nature (*O.H.* 669:1 in Rama). The children, too, are invited to participate, and are allowed more freedom for their pranks than usual.

After the seven Haqqafot all the scrolls of the Torah except one are returned to the ark. The reader lifts the remaining one and chants שְׁמַע, אֶחָד אֱלֹהֵינוּ and גַּדְּלוּ.

Custom varies about what is read on the night of Simḥat Torah. In some places any parashah that the scroll happens to be rolled to is read. The prevailing custom is to read וְזֹאת הַבְּרָכָה and to call up three people. We conclude with half-Qaddish. The Torah is returned to the ark with the chanting of the appropriate hymns and the service is concluded. At home the same procedure is followed as on the night before, except that Qiddush is recited in the house and not in the Sukkah.

In the morning the Shaḥarit service is the usual festival service, as the day before, up to the completion of Hallel. After Hallel the Haqqafot follow as on the night before. After the Haqqafot all the scrolls of the Torah except three are returned to the ark. Three Torah scrolls are needed, one for the reading of the Sidrah וְזֹאת הַבְּרָכָה, the second for the reading of the first chapter of בְּרֵאשִׁית, and the third for the Mafṭir (*O.H.* 669:1).

The procedure is as follows. Since on Simḥat Torah everyone in the synagogue is called up for an 'aliyah (Rama on *O.H.* 669:1), we read in the first Torah up to וּבְגַאֲוָתוֹ שְׁחָקִים (Deut. 33:26) in five portions. In order to give everyone an opportunity for an 'aliyah, this portion is read again and again (*Levush, O.H.* 669). In a large congregation, in order not to prolong the service unduly, the Torah is read in several places or several people are called for each 'aliyah.

For the last 'aliyah all the children are called up (*Levush, O.H.* 669:1). This honor is usually given to one of the distinguished worshippers, who spreads his Ṭalit like a canopy under which the children stand and recite the blessings. After the second benediction, the congregation recites the blessing which Jacob gave to his grandchildren, the sons of Joseph (Gen. 48:15–16; Rama on *O.H.* 669).

The last part of the Sidrah, which begins with מְעֹנָה אֱלֹהֵי קֶדֶם (Deut. 33:27), is reserved for the Ḥatan Torah, the name by which we call the 'aliyah which completes the reading of the Torah. This 'aliyah is usually given to the rabbi or to a distinguished member of the community. He is called up with a special *piyyuṭ* in praise of the Torah. When the reading is finished, the second Torah is placed on the reading table, and the Magbiah and Golel for the first Torah are called. The second Torah is opened and the first chapter of Genesis is read. Thus we start to read the Torah again just as soon as we finish reading it. The study of the Torah is an unending process (Ṭur, *O.H.* 669; *Abudraham Hashalem,* p. 300). The person who receives this 'aliyah is called the Ḥatan Bereshit. This honor, too, is given to a distinguished member of the congregation, and he, too, is called with a special *piyyuṭ* that sings the praises of God and the Torah.

When the first chapter of Genesis is read, the congregation participates in the readings by saying aloud וַיְהִי עֶרֶב וַיְהִי בֹקֶר. The reader repeats the phrase. At the sixth day, in addition to this phrase, the congregation recites aloud the whole passage of וַיְכֻלּוּ (Gen. 2:1–3) and then the reader chants it (*Liquṭei Mehariḥ,* 3:109).

It is customary in many places to spread a Ṭalit like a canopy over the Ḥatan Torah and the Ḥatan Bereshit.

After the Ḥatan Bereshit has recited the second benediction, the third Torah is placed on the table, half Qaddish is said, and the Torah is rolled. The Mafṭir is the same as on the day before. The Hafṭarah is the first chapter of Joshua. Since the Torah ends with the death of Moses, it is proper to tell how his work was continued by Joshua, his disciple (*Levush, O.H.* 669).

The Musaf service is the usual festival Musaf except that the joyous mood is maintained by the ingenuity of the reader. Latitude is given to merriment, but no vulgarity is permitted, since our joy should be pure and exalted, stemming from our awareness that the Torah is a precious gift, and that it leads to the purification of the heart and the ennoblement of the mind.

It has become a custom in many communities to invite friends home for Qiddush and for continued rejoicing in the spirit of Simḥat Torah. This is done particularly by those who have been given the special honors at the morning services. Minḥah is the usual festival service, and Ma'ariv is the weekday service, with the addition of אַתָּה חוֹנַנְתָּנוּ and Havdalah as on every *Motsa'ei Yom Ṭov.*

UNIT XII

THE DAYS OF AWE (I)

XII.
The Days of Awe (I)

1. Introduction

The term Yamim Nora'im ("Days of Awe") was first used as a designation for the High Holy Day period by the Maharil (1365–1427). While the term now seems quite appropriate, the fact that it came so late in the history of the festivals is evidence that the solemn mood associated with the High Holy Days is the result of a process of development.

Today we know the Yamim Nora'im as a time of contemplation and prayer, meditation and stock-taking, repentance and atonement. Like other sacred moments, it has its periods of preparation and consummation. The preparatory period begins with the month of Elul.

The main themes of this penitential period are the sovereignty of God and repentance. Man is like the ladder of Jacob, which was "set up on the earth, and the top of it reached to heaven" (Gen. 28:12). He is therefore capable either of rising to noble heights or of falling into a life of sin—the choice is his (Maimonides, *Hil. Teshuvah* 5:1). Both choices emerge out of man's nature. Repentance is the remaking of man's nature in the direction of righteous living (ibid. 2:2).

Transposing this into modern terminology we would say: "Man's sin is his clinging to the lower rather than the higher self. His sin may express itself in deeds done and in deeds not done. But every deficiency, every sin, has also a relationship to his Creator. It is a withdrawal from God, from the God whose image he bears. On the other hand, every step forward in his quest for perfection is a return to God" (Bokser, *Judaism,* p. 236).

This is the Teshuvah that signalizes the Days of Awe. It is a call for a return to God.

"The days of Rosh Hoshanah and Yom Kippur summon man to the vision that his real self is the divine image within him, that the meaning of his life be measured in the victory he has achieved in disciplining his baser self and bending it to serve his higher purpose. These days summon him to continue his quest toward the highest and to that end to renounce his sins, his deficiencies. It is because every man can be better than he is that every man needs to renounce deficiency, to overcome sin" (ibid. pp. 235 f.).

"The need for Teshuvah is grounded in one sense on the claim which God has upon man. God is the father, the provider, the gracious giver, of all we have and of all we prize. He yearns for our love not because our love adds anything to His perfection, but because our love for Him is an indication that we have understood our true relationship to Him.

"But the need for Teshuvah is also grounded on the consequences which derive from the alienation of man from God. Man is free, if he will, to turn his back upon his Creator, but he pays a price for this. For our lives are constantly under God's judgment. Life without God is life beset by misery of loneliness and frustration. Sin is a kind of sickness of spirit, the only therapy open to us is to renounce sin and to return to God. Teshuvah is the road to the healing of the spirit" (ibid.).

2. The Month of Elul

Because of the great solemnity surrounding the High Holy Days, a whole month was ordained as a preparatory period. The period concluded on Yom Kippur, and was later extended to Hosha'nah Rabbah, the seventh day of Sukkot. A hint regarding the length of this period is found in the forty days that Moses, according to the biblical account, spent in heaven before receiving the second tablets. These forty days started on the first of Elul and ended on Yom Kippur (*Pirqei DeRabbi Eli'ezer* 46).

A number of customs and observances have been adopted for the month of Elul to accentuate the theme of repentance. The Shofar is sounded every morning, excluding Sabbaths, immediately after the morning services, beginning with the first day of the month and continuing for the rest of the month with the exception of the morning before Rosh Hashanah (*O.H.* 581:3 in Rama).

The Shofar is a call to repentance (Maharil, *Hil, 'Aseret Yemei Teshuvah*). Our devotional literature (סִפְרֵי מוּסָר) connects it with the ascent of Moses to heaven to receive the second tablets. As already mentioned, Moses ascended on the first of Elul (*Maḥzor Vitry*, ed. Hurwitz, pp. 361 f., quoting *Pirqei DeRabbi Eli'ezer;* Ṭur, *O.H.* 581; *Levush, O.H.* 581). On the morning before Rosh Hashanah, the sounding of the Shofar is omitted in order to differentiate between the sounding of the Shofar on Rosh Hashanah, which is prescribed in the Bible, and that of the month of Elul, which was adopted later (*Levush, O.H.* 581:1, *O.H.* 581:3 in *M.D.* 4 and *M.A.* 14; see also in *Mishnah Berurah* 24).

Another practice is the recitation of Psalm 27 at the conclusion of the morning and evening services, beginning with the first day of Elul and concluding on Hosha'na' Rabbah. This practice is based on a Midrash which interprets the first verse of the psalm as follows: " 'The Lord is my light' on Rosh Hashanah, 'my salvation' on Yom Kippur, 'whom shall I fear' on Hosha'na' Rabbah" (*Midrash Tehillim* 27:4).

3. Seliḥot

Seliḥot, or penitential prayers, are recited before the morning service during the month of Elul and between Rosh Hashanah and Yom Kippur (*O.H.* 581:1). The Sefardim begin reciting Seliḥot on the first day of Elul; the Ashkenazim, on the Sunday before Rosh Hashanah. If Rosh Hashanah falls on Tuesday or earlier in the week, the recitation of Seliḥot begins on the Sunday morning of the preceding week (ibid. in Rama). We should have at least four days during which Seliḥot are recited. One of the reasons for this is that a sacrificial offering in the Temple was examined for four days for defects or blemishes that would disqualify it from being sacrificed. Man should consider himself to be like a sacrificial offering on Rosh Hashanah and hence needs four days for self-examination (ibid. in *B.H.* 5). In America it has become customary to hold the first Seliḥot service on Saturday night after midnight. Since people are in the habit of staying up late on Saturday nights, it is easier for them to attend such services than to rise early the next morning. Another commendable custom is to have a study session during the hours preceding the Seliḥot service at which some aspect of the meaning and purpose of the High Holy Days is discussed. Some synagogues have social affairs prior to Seliḥot, but this is a reprehensible practice which should be discontinued. The mood of frivolity is not a fit preparation for penitential prayers.

The Seliḥot service is a collection of penitential prayers, the work of liturgical poets (פַּיְטָנִים) who flourished during the ten centuries following the close of the talmudic era. The structure of the service follows a definite pattern.

Originally the service consisted of several groups of biblical verses, each climaxed by the recitation of the thirteen attributes: יְיָ יְיָ אֵל רַחוּם וְחַנּוּן. In the fifth or the sixth century, אֵל מֶלֶךְ יוֹשֵׁב was composed as a prelude to the recitation of the thirteen attributes (Arzt, *Justice and Mercy,* p. 207). In geonic times the service was further expanded with *piyyuṭim.* At present the standard form is to start with Psalm 145 and end with שׁוֹמֵר יִשְׂרָאֵל, both being followed by Qaddish, the first with Ḥatsi Qaddish and the latter with Qaddish Shalem, in order to correspond to the pattern of the regular service (*Levush, O.H.* 581:1). The collection of biblical quotations, the thirteen attributes and their introductory prayers, the short confession אָשַׁמְנוּ, and some concluding prayers are the constant of each service. The variables are the *piyyuṭim,* as different ones are recited each day.

4. ‘Erev Rosh Hashanah

On the Sabbath preceding Rosh Hashanah the prayer for the new month is omitted. The purpose of this prayer is to announce when the new month begins, and it is not necessary to do so when the beginning of the new month is also Rosh Hashanah (*O.H.* 417 in *Mishnah Berurah, Sha‘ar Hatsiyun* 2). Folklore has added another reason which was once taken very seriously: כְּדֵי לְעַרְבֵּב אֶת הַשָּׂטָן ("in order to confuse Satan"). Satan is waiting for Rosh Hashanah in order to speak ill of the children of Israel before the throne of judgment. The omission of the prayer for the new month will mislead him about the date, and thus he will miss his chance (Isaac Tyrnau, *Sefer Haminhagim,* p. 32).

The day before Rosh Hashanah has a special cluster of customs and observances all its own. The Seliḥot are more extensive than on other mornings (*Levush, O.H.* 581:2). Even a person who is sitting Shiv‘ah, and thus would normally stay home, may leave his house in order to join the congregation in the synagogue to say Seliḥot (*O.H.* 581:1). Folklore suggests that the omission of the blowing of the Shofar at this service will mislead Satan into believing that Rosh Hashanah is past (*M.A.* in *O.H.* 581:3, sec. 14). As in the case of all festivals, Taḥanun is omitted at Shaḥarit and Minḥah on the day before Rosh Hashanah (*O.H.* 581:3).

In some congregations Hattarat Nedarim follows immediately after the morning services. The procedure is as follows. The person who wants to be released from vows that he may have forgotten about should declare so in the presence of three who constitute a court. Then the court releases him from these vows by declaring הַכֹּל יִהְיוּ מֻתָּרִים לָךְ ("you are absolved from all these"). Then follows מְסִירַת מוֹדָעָה, a precautionary declaration against future vows. Both the individual's declaration and the court's response have a formalized text printed in some prayer books. This should not be construed as a general amnesty on vows but rather as bearing only on those of which one is unaware or which one may have forgotten, and only if they pertain to himself and not others (Ṭur, *O.H.* 619; *Shibolei Haleqeṭ,* ed. Buber, 317).

It is customary to replace the regular *parokhet* and the cover of the reading table with white ones until after Yom Kippur, white being a symbol of atonement and grace (Agnon, *Days of Awe,* p. 49).

It is also customary to visit the graves of dear ones on the day before Rosh Hashanah (*O.H.* 581:4 in Rama). In some communities this practice is not limited to the day before Rosh Hashanah but is extended to the entire penitential period. Many congregations have established the fine custom of holding a public memorial service at the cemetery. After the service, or before, each individual visits the graves of his dear ones.

Another highly commendable custom is the practice of contributing to charitable causes on the day before Rosh Hashanah (*O.H.* 581:4 in Rama). Today, with organized philanthropies working all year round, the custom has continued and is applied to charities beyond those for which one is approached by organized bodies.

The practice of sending greeting cards to friends wishing them a happy new year is also commendable. Originally it was customary to wish each one that he be inscribed in the Book of Life (*O.H.* 582:9 in Rama). The circle was later widened by sending such greetings by mail to all friends.

If Rosh Hashanah falls on Thursday and Friday, an *'eruv tavshilin* should be made, as in the case of the other festivals, so that one may cook for the Sabbath on the second day.

5. Rosh Hashanah

"On Rosh Hashanah all the inhabitants of the world pass before Him [in judgment] like a flock of sheep" (M. *R.H.* 1:2).

"All are judged on Rosh Hashanah, and the verdict is sealed on Yom Kippur" (Tosefta, *R.H.* 1:12).

'Rabbi Kruspedai said in the name of Rabbi Yoḥanan: 'Three books are opened on Rosh Hashanah, one for the utterly wicked, one for the perfectly righteous, and one for the intermediates. The perfectly righteous are straightaway inscribed and sealed for life; the wicked are straightaway inscribed and sealed for death; the intermediates are suspended and wait from Rosh Hashanah until Yom Kippur. If they merit, they are inscribed for life; if not—they are inscribed for death' " (B. *R.H.* 16b).

These passages make it apparent that in talmudic times, Rosh Hashanah had already developed into a day of reflection, repentance, and judgment. Whereas in the case of Yom Kippur the Bible tells us: "For on this day shall atonement be made for you to cleanse you; from all your sins shall you be clean before the Lord" (Lev. 16:30), in the case of Rosh Hashanah there is no mention that it is a New Year festival or that it is a day of judgment, but only that it is a *yom teru'ah* or *zikhron teru'ah* (Num. 29:1, Lev. 23:24). The name Rosh Hashanah occurs for the first time in the Mishnah. (The one place where it is mentioned in the Bible—Ezekiel 40:1—refers to Yom Kippur, which comes at the beginning of the year.)

The festival was also known as Yom Hadin and Yom Hazikaron. Each of these names conveys one of the characteristics of Rosh Hashanah, but the name Rosh Hashanah has become prevalent. It is based on tradition that the creation of the world was finished on the first of Tishre (*R.H.* 11a). In the liturgy of the day the two themes, creation and judgment, are combined, הַיּוֹם הֲרַת עוֹלָם, הַיּוֹם יַעֲמִיד בַּמִּשְׁפָּט. This is expanded in the central part of the services.

זֶה הַיּוֹם תְּחִלַּת מַעֲשֶׂיךָ זִכָּרוֹן לְיוֹם רִאשׁוֹן . . .
וְעַל הַמְּדִינוֹת בּוֹ יֵאָמֵר אֵיזוֹ לַחֶרֶב . .
וּבְרִיּוֹת בּוֹ יִפָּקֵדוּ לְהַזְכִּירָם לְחַיִּים וְלַמָּוֶת

From a day of judgment it is a natural step to a period of repentance. The call to repentance has come to be the major characteristic of Rosh Hashanah, and most of the prayers and rituals sound this theme.

As a day of judgment by God and repentance by man, Rosh Hashanah makes God the final arbiter of human destiny. "One interpretation of life, which western civilization has inherited from ancient Greek culture, is that human life is the inevitable working out of a dire doom from which there is no escape. Man may delude himself with the belief that he is free to make of his life what he will, but in actuality he is trapped by a destiny which is deaf to his most heart-rending appeals. The very antithesis of that is the version of life implied in the Jewish religion" (Kaplan, *The Meaning of God,* p. 64).

In the Jewish religion, man's place in "life is conceived not as the working out of a doom but as the fulfillment of a blessing! . . . Evil is an interference; it is not Fate. Man is not trapped; he is tested. 'The die is cast,' says the occidental man; and the Jewish religion retorts, 'But the final issue is with God'" (ibid., pp. 67–68).

Professor Heschel writes: "Man in quest for an anchor in ultimate meaning is far from being a person shipwrecked who dreams of a palace while napping on the edge of an abyss. He is a person in full mastery of his ship who has lost his direction because he failed to remember his destination. Man in his anxiety is a *messenger who forgot the message*" (*Who Is Man?*, pp. 118 f.).

Rosh Hashanah, then, is not an opportunity for mirth. The rejoicing associated with the festival stems from the awareness that life always holds out the promise of better things. Principally, however, it is an occasion for self-examination, a veritable Yom Hadin and Yom Hazikaron, a time when there comes before God "the remembrance of every creature ... man's deeds and destiny, his works and ways, his thoughts and designs and the workings of his imagination." It is not only God who judges our actions; we also are called to judge our own actions and thus find our direction again. Similarly Yom Hazikaron calls us to remember not only great events in the dim past but also incidents in the journey we have made since the year began (Vainstein, *Cycle of the Jewish Year*, p. 97). All this has one main purpose— a call to repentance.

6. Evening Services

At sundown candles are lit with the benediction לְהַדְלִיק נֵר שֶׁל יוֹם טוֹב; on a Sabbath we say שֶׁל שַׁבָּת וְשֶׁל יוֹם טוֹב. This is followed by the שֶׁהֶחֱיָנוּ (*Levush, O.H.* 487). The Minḥah service is the regular weekday service.

The Ma'ariv service is the festival service with the variations required for Rosh Hashanah. On a Sabbath, Ma'ariv is preceded by Psalm 92, and וְשָׁמְרוּ is added after הַשְׁכִּיבֵנוּ as on every Sabbath. The specific passage for Rosh Hashanah is the verse תִּקְעוּ בַחֹדֶשׁ שׁוֹפָר (Ps. 81:4–5), which is interpreted as referring to the blowing of the Shofar on Rosh Hashanah (*Wayiqra Rabbah* 29:6; *Levush, O.H.* 582). This is followed by half-Qaddish. The word לְעֵלָּא is repeated: לְעֵלָּא וּלְעֵלָּא; and the same phrase is used in every Qaddish throughout the entire Ten Days of Penitence (*O.H.* 582 in *M.A.* 4). As with so many of the variations for Rosh Hashanah, it emphasizes the sovereignty of God, who is particularly exalted when He sits on the throne of judgment (*Levush, O.H.* 582:8).

The ‘Amidah, like that of the other festivals, consists of seven benedictions—the first and last three the same as in the weekday ‘Amidah and the middle one referring to the specific festival. The Rosh Hashanah ‘Amidah, however, varies from that of the other festivals in a number of respects. First there is an insertion in most benedictions relevant to the meaning of the day. In the first benediction, before מֶלֶךְ עוֹזֵר, we add זָכְרֵנוּ לְחַיִּים since a prayer for life is most appropriate on a day of judgment (*Levush, O.H.* 582:5). In the second benediction, before וְנֶאֱמָן אַתָּה, we add מִי כָמוֹךָ for the same reason (ibid.). In the third benediction there is a long interpolation consisting of five passages, beginning with וּבְכֵן תֵּן פַּחְדְּךָ. The ending of the benediction is changed from הָאֵל הַקָּדוֹשׁ to הַמֶּלֶךְ הַקָּדוֹשׁ so as to proclaim God as King. This ending is maintained throughout the Ten Days of Penitence (B. *Ber.* 12b; *O.H.* 582:1).

In the מוֹדִים benediction we insert וּכְתוֹב לְחַיִּים טוֹבִים before וְכֹל הַחַיִּים. In the last benediction we insert בְּסֵפֶר חַיִּים before the concluding benediction, which is itself changed from the accepted הַמְבָרֵךְ אֶת עַמּוֹ יִשְׂרָאֵל בַּשָּׁלוֹם to עוֹשֶׂה הַשָּׁלוֹם. The Sefardim retain the usual form. The substitution of the shorter form, עוֹשֶׂה הַשָּׁלוֹם, in the other rites is due to the fact that this form was generally used in Palestine. Since בְּסֵפֶר חַיִּים also originated in Palestine, where such interpolations were encouraged, the entire text was taken over (Arzt, *Justice and Mercy,* p. 117).

The middle benediction, as the name קְדֻשַּׁת הַיּוֹם implies, speaks of the meaning of the day and is structured like the middle benediction of the ‘Amidah of the other festivals. It begins with אַתָּה בְחַרְתָּנוּ, continues with וַתִּתֶּן לָנוּ (but מוֹעֲדִים לְשִׂמְחָה is omitted—*Orḥot Ḥayyim, Hil. Rosh Hashanah,* sec. 2) and יַעֲלֶה וְיָבֹא, and concludes with מְלוֹךְ עַל כָּל הָעוֹלָם, which corresponds to וְהַשִּׂיאֵנוּ of the Pilgrimage Festivals. This final paragraph which expresses the specific significance of the day, the proclamation of the sovereignty of God, was substituted for וְהַשִּׂיאֵנוּ, since the latter has the expression בִּרְכַּת מוֹעֲדֶיךָ, and there is a difference of opinion as to whether Rosh Hashanah should be counted among the Mo‘adim (*Beit Yosef* on Ṭur, *O.H.* 585; Munk, *World of Prayer,* 2:180). For the same reason, מוֹעֲדִים לְשִׂמְחָה is omitted in וַתִּתֶּן לָנוּ and in Qiddush (*Orḥot Ḥayyim, Hil. Rosh Hashanah,* sec. 2). The ‘Amidah is followed by קַדִּישׁ תִּתְקַבַּל. If Rosh Hashanah falls on a Sabbath we mention the Sabbath in the proper places, and before Qaddish we add וַיְכֻלּוּ, מָגֵן אָבוֹת, and רְצֵה בִמְנוּחָתֵנוּ, as we do on every Sabbath.

The Qiddush of Rosh Hashanah is recited, concluding with the שֶׁהֶחֱיָנוּ. On a Sabbath we mention the Sabbath in the appropriate places. As with all other services, we conclude with עָלֵינוּ and אֲדוֹן עוֹלָם, but we add Psalm 27

(לְדָוִד יְיָ אוֹרִי וְיִשְׁעִי), which is also followed by the mourner's Qaddish.

After the service it is customary for worshippers to greet each other with New Year wishes: לְשָׁנָה טוֹבָה תִּכָּתֵבוּ (*O.H.* 582:9). At home we follow the pattern of other festivals with Qiddush over wine, a festive meal, and rejoicing, but without losing sight of the solemnity of the day.

Special customs have developed with regard to the foods eaten at the Rosh Hashanah meals. Certain foods are regarded as symbolic of the day and are accompanied by a prayer. Thus, the bread is not salted when reciting the הַמּוֹצִיא; instead, the bread, and also a piece of apple, is dipped in honey and is accompanied by the prayer יְהִי רָצוֹן שֶׁתְּחַדֵּשׁ עָלֵינוּ שָׁנָה טוֹבָה וּמְתוּקָה (*O.H.* 583:1 in Rama), which dates back to talmudic times (B. *Ker.* 6a). Bitter or sour foods are avoided. In some places the *ḥallot* are baked in the shape of a ladder, as if to indicate that on Rosh Hashanah it is decided "who shall be exalted and who shall be brought low" (*O.H.* 583.1), or in the shape of birds, referring to the verse: "As birds hovering, so will the Lord of hosts protect Jerusalem" (Isa. 31:5). (For other customs, see Wahrman, *Ḥagei Yisra'el Umo'adaw,* pp. 18 f.; *Levush, O.H.* 583; *O.H.* 583; *Abudraham Hashalem*). The custom was to eat foods whose names could be construed as a blessing. When the food was eaten, a prayer appropriate to it was recited. For example, it was the custom to eat the head of a sheep and say יְהִי רָצוֹן שֶׁנִּהְיֶה לְרֹאשׁ וְלֹא לְזָנָב ("may it be thy will that we become heads, not tails") (*O.H.* 583:2). All that remains today is the custom of dipping a piece of apple in honey.

The meal concludes with the regular Birkat Hamazon for a festival. In יַעֲלֶה וְיָבֹא we mention the festival as יוֹם הַזִּכָּרוֹן הַזֶּה and the special הָרַחֲמָן reads: הָרַחֲמָן הוּא יְחַדֵּשׁ עָלֵינוּ אֶת הַשָּׁנָה הַזֹּאת לְטוֹבָה וְלִבְרָכָה.

7. The Morning Service

The solemnity of Rosh Hashanah is expressed in the liturgy. Not only the prayers, but also the traditional Nusaḥ, or musical rendition of the prayers, helps to create this mood. Even the prayers which are not specifically for this festival are intoned to music that is used only for the High Holy Days.

The first parts of the morning service, the Birkhot Hashaḥar and the Pesuqei Dezimrah, are the same as on Sabbaths and festivals. The service begins with a special chanting of Adon 'Olam; while this hymn is recited every day of the year as part of the morning service, it has a special significance on the High Holy Days because of two basic ideas that it expresses. It tells that God's existence and sovereignty are independent of the existent universe, that He fashioned the universe in time, and that He will continue to be after all existence has returned to void. This negates the view that God is only an aspect of the universe. It also declares God's providential concern for each of his creatures and the abiding peace and security that men find in drawing close to their maker (Bokser, *High Holy Day Prayer Book*, p. 219).

Another variation is that before מִזְמוֹר שִׁיר חֲנֻכַּת, the Hymn of Glory, אַנְעִים זְמִירוֹת, is recited responsively. The ark is opened for this hymn and the congregation stands. It is followed by the mourner's Qaddish. While in many synagogues this hymn is recited every Sabbath at the end of the morning services, on Rosh Hashanah it is recited at the beginning and has added significance because of its proclamation of the glory of God.

On the Sabbath the *Ba'al Shaḥarit* begins with *Shokhen 'Ad*, and on the Pilgrimage Festivals he begins with *Ha'el;* on the High Holy Days he begins with *Hamelekh*, giving added emphasis to the supreme kingship of God (*Levush*). There is also a slight textual variation on the High Holy Days. Instead of the usual הַמֶּלֶךְ הַיּוֹשֵׁב we say הַמֶּלֶךְ יוֹשֵׁב. The former is a simple statement of homage; the latter is a declaration that *now*, at this very moment, the King is sitting on His throne in judgment (Munk, *World of Prayer*, 2:184 f.).

Dr. Arzt comments that "the point at which the reader begins to read the concluding words of *Nishmat* strikes an appropriate note for each occasion. On Sabbath, as *Nishmat* is concluded, the reader begins with *Shokhen 'Ad*, celebrating God's eternity as the Creator. On Festivals he begins with *Ha'el*, acclaiming Him as the omnipotent Protector of His people; and on Rosh Hashanah and Yom Kippur he begins with *Hamelekh*, proclaiming Him as Sovereign and Judge" (*Justice and Mercy*, p. 42).

Until the 'Amidah, the Shaḥarit service basically follows the weekday form, except if Rosh Hashanah falls on a Sabbath, when it follows the order of the Sabbath. However, a number of *piyyuṭim* are interpolated after Barekhu in the benediction preceding the Shema', but not in those after the Shema'. We do not interrupt the passage beginning with אֱמֶת וְיַצִּיב because the entire portion describes the reign of God as King of the Universe (see Munk, *World of Prayer*, 2:15; *Liquṭei Meharih*, pt. 3, p. 67b). The 'Amidah is the same as the one recited at the evening service, except that שִׂים שָׁלוֹם replaces שָׁלוֹם רָב.

During *Ḥazarat Hashats* a great number of *piyyuṭim* are interpolated. If the first day of Rosh Hashanah falls on a Sabbath, those that pertain to the blowing of the Shofar are shifted to the second day or are retained with their wording changed to fit the Sabbath; e.g., we substitute יוֹם זִכְרוֹן תְּרוּעָה for יוֹם תְּרוּעָה.

The ark is opened and the congregation stands during the recitation of certain *piyyuṭim,* adding to the solemn atmosphere. Dr. Arzt explains: "It appears that the ark was originally opened to draw attention to a significant interpolation into the standard liturgy. The frequency of such occasions and the designation of the places in the service when the ark is opened are not governed by any mandatory rules. As prayer books were published, the printer indicated a *petiḥah* (opening of the ark) before those *piyyuṭim* which, in his opinion or in the practice of his synagogue, called for a heightened sense of exaltation which would be induced by the opening of the ark and the consequent rising of the entire congregation" (*Justice and Mercy,* p. 41).

Before the concluding Qaddish, said after *Ḥazarat Hashats,* אָבִינוּ מַלְכֵּנוּ is recited (*O.H.* 584:1) with the ark open and the congregation standing (ibid.). The Talmud mentions that Rabbi Akiva recited Avinu Malkenu on fast days. Today it is recited on all fast days, on Rosh Hashanah and Yom Kippur, and during the Ten Days of Penitence. Since it was originally recited on fast days, it is omitted on the Sabbath, when fasting is not permitted (*Orḥot Ḥayyim, Hil. Rosh Hashanah,* sec. 2). Furthermore, it is customary not to make any personal requests on the Sabbath (*O.H.* 584 in *M.A.* 3; Rivash, sec. 512). The *Levush* adds that since Avinu Malkenu corresponds to the eighteen benedictions of the weekday 'Amidah, it would be out of place on the Sabbath (*O.H.* 584:1; *Maṭeh Mosheh,* sec. 801). According to another opinion, Avinu Malkenu corresponds to Taḥanun, and these are not recited on the Sabbath (*Levush, O.H.* 584:1).

On the other festivals it is customary to recite Hallel at this point in the service. It is omitted on Rosh Hashanah because the joyous exultation of the Hallel is not in keeping with the solemnity and seriousness of the day of judgment. The Talmud explains that the ministering angels asked God why the children of Israel do not sing hymns of praise to Him on Rosh Hashanah and Yom Kippur. God answered: "Is it conceivable that Israel should sing hymns of praise even as the King sits on His throne in judgment and the books of life and death are open before Him?" (B. *R.H.* 32b).

8. Torah Reading

The service accompanying *Hotsa'at haTorah* is the same as on the other festivals with one variation—in אֶחָד אֱלֹהֵינוּ we add one word, saying: קָדוֹשׁ וְנוֹרָא שְׁמוֹ, the word וְנוֹרָא, meaning "revered," being an appropriate addition for this period of judgment. As on the festivals, two scrolls of the Torah are taken out of the ark. In the first, Genesis 21:1–34 is read. Five people are called for 'aliyot; seven on a Sabbath.

The second Torah scroll is then put on the table, half-Qaddish is recited, and the Mafṭir is called. For Mafṭir Numbers 29:1–6 is read. The Hafṭarah is I Samuel 1:1–2:10 (*O.H.* 584:2; B. *Meg.* 31a).

According to the Talmud, Sarah, Rachel, and Hannah gave birth on Rosh Hashanah (B. *R.H.* 10b). Hence the portion of the Torah about Sarah and the Hafṭarah about Hannah. The Mafṭir deals with the Rosh Hashanah sacrifice. The benedictions before and after the Hafṭarah follow those of the Sabbath except for the last one, where instead of יוֹם הַשַּׁבָּת we say יוֹם הַזִּכָּרוֹן הַזֶּה (on a Sabbath we say both), and the ending, which reads מְקַדֵּשׁ יִשְׂרָאֵל וְיוֹם הַזִּכָּרוֹן (on a Sabbath we say הַשַּׁבָּת וְיִשְׂרָאֵל וְיוֹם הַזִּכָּרוֹן).

UNIT XIII

THE DAYS OF AWE (II)

The Shofar
The Musaf Service
Tashlikh
Minḥah and Ma‘ariv

XIII.
The Days of Awe (II)

9. The Shofar

If Rosh Hashanah coincides with a Sabbath, the blowing of the Shofar is omitted and the service continues with יְקוּם פֻּרְקָן and מִי שֶׁבֵּרַךְ. This is because the sounding of the Shofar, while not forbidden, might lead to a violation of the Sabbath. For example, someone who wanted to learn how to sound the Shofar might inadvertently carry it, and carrying is forbidden on the Sabbath (B. *R.H.* 29b; *O.H.* 588:5).

The Talmud finds support for this ruling in the fact that the Bible refers to Rosh Hashanah both as *yom teru'ah* (Num. 29:1) and as *zikhron teru'ah* (Lev. 23:24). According to the rabbinical interpretation, when the Shofar is sounded it is *yom teru'ah,* and when the Shofar is not sounded (i.e., on the Sabbath), it is *yom zikhron teru'ah* (P. *R.H.* 4:1).

A historical explanation has also been advanced. In ancient Palestine the Shofar was sounded on the Sabbath only in the Temple and in the city of Jerusalem. After the destruction of the Temple, the sounding of the Shofar on the Sabbath was restricted to the place where the Great Sanhedrin convened. When the Sanhedrin ceased to exist, the sounding of the Shofar on the Sabbath was discontinued (see Kieval, *The High Holy Days,* p. 114).

On a weekday, the sounding of the Shofar follows immediately after the concluding benedictions of the Hafṭarah and thus occupies the central part of the service.

According to Maimonides, although the sounding of the Shofar on Rosh Hashanah is a decree of Holy Writ, it also has a profound meaning, for it seems to say: "Awake, awake, O sleepers from your sleep; O slumberers, arouse ye from your slumbers; and examine your deeds, return in repentance, and remember your Creator. Those of you who forget the truth in the follies of the time and go astray, the whole year, in vanity and emptiness, which neither profit nor save, look to your souls; improve your ways and works. Abandon, every one of you, his evil course and the thought that is not good" (Maimonides, *Hil. Teshuvah* 3:4).

The most comprehensive explanation of the Shofar is that of Sa'adiah Gaon, who gives ten reasons for the sounding of the Shofar.

1. The sound of the Shofar is analogous to the trumpet blasts which announce the coronation of a king. On Rosh Hashanah God created the world and became its sovereign. By sounding the Shofar we acknowledge him as our King.
2. Rosh Hashanah is the first of the Ten Days of Penitence, and the Shofar is sounded to stir our consciences, inducing us to confront our past errors and return to God, who is always ready to welcome the penitent.
3. The Shofar is reminiscent of God's revelation at Sinai, which was accompanied by the sounding of a Shofar. It reminds us of our destiny to be a people of Torah, pursuing the study of Torah and practicing its commandments.
4. The sound of the Shofar is reminiscent of the exhortations of the prophets, whose voices rang out like a Shofar in denouncing their people's wrongdoing, and in calling them to the service of God and man.
5. The Shofar reminds us of the destruction of the Temple, and calls upon us to strive for Israel's renewal in freedom and in fellowship with God.
6. The Shofar, since it is a ram's horn, is reminiscent of the ram offered as a sacrifice by Abraham in place of his son Isaac. It thus reminds us of the heroic faith of the fathers of our people, who exemplified the highest devotion to God of which man is capable.
7. The Shofar urges us to feel humble before God's majesty and might, which are manifested by all things and which constantly surround our lives.
8. The Shofar is a reminder of the Day of Final Judgment, calling upon all men and all nations to prepare themselves for God's scrutiny of their deeds.
9. The Shofar foreshadows the jubilant proclamation of freedom when the exiled and homeless of Israel return to the Holy Land. It calls upon us to believe, at all times and under all circumstances, in Israel's coming deliverance.

10. The Shofar foreshadows the end of the present world order and the inauguration of God's reign of righteousness throughout the world, with a regenerated Israel leading all men in acknowledging that God is One and His name One. (*Abudraham Hashalem,* 269 f.)

Yeḥezkel Kaufmann explains that the blowing of the Shofar is man's means of expressing hope for salvation, awe and praise of God, and acceptance of God's sovereignty from everlasting to everlasting (*Toldot Ha'emunah Hayisra'elit,* 1:584).

Professor Kaplan gives a similarly relevant explanation. The sounding of the Shofar, the most ancient rite in the Rosh Hashanah observances, has been interpreted as a summons to the soul to present itself before God's judgment seat. It has also been construed as the תְּרוּעַת מֶלֶךְ, the salute to the Sovereign, with all its implications of fealty and allegiance. It has functioned, and should still function, in the life of the Jewish people as an invitation to the individual Jew to review his oath of unqualified allegiance and loyalty to those ideals, the realization of which would convert human society into a Kingdom of God (Kaplan, *The Meaning of God in Modern Jewish Religion,* p. 118).

The Talmud and Midrash are replete with homilies on the meaning of the Shofar. Most of these are incorporated in Sa'adiah's ten points. One, which is completely homiletical, is based on a play on words. Rabbi Berechiah comments on the verse תִּקְעוּ בַחֹדֶשׁ שׁוֹפָר "blow the shofar at the new moon," that the word חֹדֶשׁ "new moon" implies חַדְּשׁוּ מַעֲשֵׂיכֶם "renew your deeds," and the word שׁוֹפָר implies שַׁפְּרוּ מַעֲשֵׂיכֶם "improve your deeds." The Holy One, blessed be He, said: "My children, if you will improve your deeds, I will act unto you as the Shofar. Just as you blow into one end of the Shofar and the sound comes out at the other end, so will I rise from the throne of law and sit on the throne of mercy, changing my attribute of law to that of mercy" (ibid., 29:6).

The Shofar service begins with Psalm 47 because the verse עָלָה אֱלֹהִים בִּתְרוּעָה is interpreted by the Midrash as referring to the sounding of the Shofar on Rosh Hashanah (*Wayiqra Rabbah* 29:3). The significance became mystical under the influence of the Lurianic Kabbalah. The name of God occurs seven times in Psalm 47, and the psalm is repeated seven times, corresponding to the seven heavens that God created—Rosh Hashanah being the anniversary of the creation of the world (Singer, *Ziv Haminhagim,* p. 169).

The psalm is followed by seven verses. Six of these form an acrostic, the first letters of which spell קְרַע שָׂטָן ("destroy Satan"), also a Lurianic theme. The introductory verse, מִן הַמֵּצַר, is an appropriate expression of the mood of the occasion and raises the number of verses to seven, a number deemed especially sacred.

The Shofar is covered until the time for sounding it. The person who sounds the Shofar (the *Ba'al Teqi'ah*) is normally not the reader, since if the reader sounded the Shofar he might become confused and lose the place (*O.H.* 585:4), but someone else who is known for his piety and good deeds (Ṭur, *O.H.* 586). Before sounding the Shofar the *Ba'al Teqi'ah* recites two benedictions: לִשְׁמוֹעַ קוֹל שׁוֹפָר and שֶׁהֶחֱיָנוּ (*O.H.* 585:2). לִשְׁמוֹעַ ("to hear") is said rather than לִתְקוֹעַ ("to sound") to emphasize that the mitswah is in listening to the Shofar, not in sounding it (Maimonides, *Hil. Shofar* 1:1).

The Shofar should be—

1. Fit for sounding;
2. Blown at the proper time and place;
3. Sounded in the proper order (Ṭur, *O.H.* 586).

Fit for Sounding

1. In order to be fit, the Shofar must be a ram's horn. Theoretically the horn of any kosher animal except a cow or an ox may be used (*O.H.* 586:1 and in Rama). The accepted practice is to use a ram's horn because of its association with the binding of Isaac (B. *R.H.* 16a; *Tanḥuma, Wayera* 23).
2. The Shofar should be bent or curved in shape to symbolize the bent and humbled spirit appropriate on Rosh Hashanah (B. *R.H.* 26b).
3. The Shofar may not be painted but may be decorated with carved designs (*O.H.* 586:17 and in Rama). However, the outside of the Shofar may be covered with gold, provided that the natural tone of the Shofar is not changed, and if the mouthpiece is not covered with gold (*O.H.* 586:16).
4. The Shofar may not be used if it is cracked along its length unless enough space is left between the crack and the mouthpiece to fulfill the minimum requirement for the size of a Shofar (*O.H.* 586:8 and in Rama); i.e., four thumb-breadths, or about six inches, long (*O.H.* 586:9).
5. The Shofar may not be used if it is cracked around its width and

the crack is more than half its width, unless there is enough space from the crack to the mouthpiece to satisfy the minimum requirement for the length of the Shofar (*O.H.* 586:9).

6. There is no prescription pertaining to the kind of sound a Shofar must produce, and therefore a Shofar may be used whether its sound is "thick" or "thin" (*O.H.* 586:6).

Time and Place

1. The Shofar is sounded immediately after the Hafṭarah benedictions (B. *R.H.* 32b). It is sounded on the bimah, the same place where the Torah is read (*O.H.* 585:1 and in Rama).
2. Originally the Shofar could be sounded at any time during the course of the day (M. *Meg.* 2:5; O.H. 588:1). Since it is meritorious to perform a mitswah as soon as possible because of זְרִיזִין מַקְדִּימִין לְמִצְוֹת ("The zealous come early for the performance of a mitswah") (B. *R.H.* 32b), it was customary to sound the Shofar at dawn (B. *Meg.* 20b in Rashi), and in the synagogue service the Shofar was originally sounded during the Shaḥarit 'Amidah. During the second century C.E., however, the Patriarch Rabbi Simeon ben Gamaliel II ordained that the sounding of the Shofar should be postponed until the Musaf service. He made this decision because the Roman occupation troops in Palestine had once misconstrued the Shofar blasts as a call to revolt and killed many Jews. The delay until Musaf enabled the Romans to observe how the Jews would pray for a considerable period of time before sounding the Shofar, and this apparently convinced them that the sounding of the Shofar was peaceful in nature (P. *R.H.* 4:8; B. *R.H.* 32b in Rashi; Tosafot, *R.H.* 32b, s.v. בשעה). According to the Talmud, the practice of sounding the Shofar at Musaf was continued even after this danger ceased because by the time Musaf is recited, most of the worshippers have assembled in the synagogue and thus will have a chance to hear the Shofar (B. *R.H.* 32b). It was also pointed out that the mention of יוֹם תְּרוּעָה is followed in the Bible (Num. 29:1 f.) by the commandment concerning the Musaf offerings (P. *R.H.* 4:8). The same source adds that children usually do not come to the synagogue earlier than Musaf, and thus they are also enabled to hear the Shofar (ibid.).

   The midrashic literature adds a homiletical explanation. By the time Musaf has begun, the worshippers have already fulfilled several important mitswot, such as donning the Ṭalit, reading the Shema', reading the Torah, and reciting many prayers. If the Shofar is sounded at this time, it will be even more effective in pleading their cause before the throne of glory (*Pesiqta Rabbati*).

The Order of the Sounding of the Shofar

1. There are three types of Shofar blasts. Known collectively as *teqi'ot,* these notes are: *teqi'ah,* a straight, unbroken sound that ends abruptly; *shevarim,* a series of three broken sounds whose combined duration equals that of a *teqi'ah;* and *teru'ah,* a quick succession of short trills made up of nine staccato tones equivalent in combined duration to a single *teqi'ah* (M. *R.H.* 4:9).
2. The Torah mentions the *teru'ah* three times in connection with Rosh Hashanah (Lev. 23:24, 25:9; Num. 29:1; B. *R.H.* 34a). Hence the Shofar should be sounded three times: once after מַלְכֻיּוֹת, once after זִכְרוֹנוֹת, and once after שׁוֹפָרוֹת, the three central sections of the Musaf 'amidah (see below). Since each *teru'ah* must be preceded and followed by a *teqi'ah* (B. *R.H.* 34a), there should be three times three blasts, as prescribed in the Mishnah (*R.H.* 4:9).
3. There is a difference of opinion in the Talmud about the definition of a *teru'ah.* According to one opinion, it is the sound of sighing—גְּנוֹחֵי גְּנַח—i.e., like the *shevarim.* According to another opinion, it should be like the vibrating sound of sobbing—יְלוּלֵי יְלֵיל—i.e., like our *teru'ah.* According to a third opinion, it is both. In order to eliminate any doubts, all three forms are used. We begin with *shevarim teru'ah* three times, continue with *shevarim* three times, and conclude with *teru'ah* three times (B. *R.H.* 34a). Since each of these must be preceded and followed by a *teqi'ah* (*O.H.* 592:1), there is a total of thirty sounds.
4. The practice today is to sound the Shofar in the order of תשר״ת (acronym for תְּקִיעָה, שְׁבָרִים־תְּרוּעָה, תְּקִיעָה), תש״ת (תְּקִיעָה, שְׁבָרִים, תְּקִיעָה), and תר״ת (תְּקִיעָה, תְּרוּעָה, תְּקִיעָה), at *Ḥazarat Hashats* after the concluding benedictions of מַלְכֻיּוֹת, זִכְרוֹנוֹת, and שׁוֹפָרוֹת. These sounds are designated the תְּקִיעוֹת דִמְעֻמָּד, the sounds during which the congregation stands, or the sounds made during the 'Amidah, and they constitute the actual fulfillment of the mitswah of sounding the Shofar. Congregations that use the Sefardic rite follow the same procedure during the silent recitation of the 'Amidah.

5. There is also a sounding of the Shofar immediately after the Torah and Hafṭarah service. This is designated תְּקִיעוֹת דִּמְיֻשָּׁב because the congregation may be seated during the sounding (today, however, it is customary for the congregation to stand). The order of the תְּקִיעוֹת דִּמְיֻשָּׁב is three times תשר״ת, with a prayer following; three times תש״ת, with a prayer following; and three times תר״ת, with a concluding prayer.

   Various reasons for the addition have been proposed (see Singer, *Ziv Haminhagim,* p. 162). The most cogent suggests that while the practice of sounding the Shofar during Musaf was retained even after the reason for its institution was no longer applicable, there was a desire to show that the sounding of the Shofar had once been part of Shaḥarit (see also B. *R.H.* 16b).

   Another plausible reason is that the sounding of the Shofar during Shaḥarit was retained for the sake of the sick and of others who are unable to stay for the long Musaf service. This shortened version takes less time but enables them to hear the prescribed number of sounds (see *Melekhet Shelomoh,* quoting *Ba'al Hama'or* in M. *R.H.* 4:5). Though the תְּקִיעוֹת דִּמְעֻמָּד is the main service, the benedictions preceding the sounding of the Shofar are recited before the תְּקִיעוֹת דִּמְיֻשָּׁב and are not repeated before the תְּקִיעוֹת דִּמְעֻמָּד.

6. The Shofar is also sounded at the conclusion of the service to make a total of one hundred blasts (Tosafot, B. *R.H.* 33b, s.v. שיעור תרועה; *Sefer Hamanhig, Hil. Rosh Hashanah,* sec. 21; *Liquṭei Meharih,* p. 180). Customs vary as to how the hundred blasts are completed. Those who follow the Sefardic practice of having thirty blasts during the silent 'Amidah were shy ten, and added these during the Qaddish Titqabbel that follows the 'Amidah. Those who follow the Ashkenazic rite were shy forty; they added thirty at Qaddish Titqabbel and ten more after the mourner's Qaddish following Aleinu. The thirty blasts follow the sequence תשר״ת, תש״ת, תר״ת three times, and the ten follow the same sequence once. Each set of thirty is concluded with a תְּקִיעָה גְדוֹלָה—a long blast—as a sign that the prescribed sounds of this section have come to an end (Maharil).

7. If the *Ba'al Teqi'ah* who made the benedictions is unable to complete the prescribed sounds, another one may take over, provided that he was present when the benedictions were recited. This ap-

plies even if the first *Ba'al Teqi'ah* was unable to produce even one sound (*O.H.* 585:3).

8. At the conclusion of the תְּקִיעוֹת דִּמְיֻשָּׁב one or more verses from Psalm 89, depending on the rite followed (Maharil), are recited. All rites say the verse אַשְׁרֵי הָעָם יֹדְעֵי תְרוּעָה (Ps. 89:16). Others add the two succeeding verses (*Abudraham Hashalem,* p. 270). This is followed by Ashrei and *Hakhnasat HaTorah,* which is the same as on the other festivals.

10. The Musaf Service

The reader for Musaf should not be the same as the one for Shaḥarit. He begins with הִנְנִי הֶעָנִי, a prayer expressing the cantor's humility and unworthiness to represent the congregation in prayer, and a petition that he be able to perform his mission properly.

Because הִנְנִי is a personal prayer and not part of the prescribed liturgy, it ends with a benediction in which the שֵׁם (mention of the name of God) and מַלְכוּת (mention of the kingship of God, מֶלֶךְ הָעוֹלָם) are omitted. The prayer is recited only before the Musaf 'Amidah, both on Rosh Hashanah and Yom Kippur, but not before the Shaḥarit 'Amidah because of the liturgical rule that there can be no interruption בֵּין גְּאֻלָּה לִתְפִלָּה (between the blessing of redemption and the Amidah) (Arzt, *Justice and Mercy,* p. 162).

This is followed by Ḥatsi Qaddish, chanted according to the special mode unique for this specific Qaddish. Each Qaddish in the service has its own unique mode (נוּסַח) (see Kieval, *The High Holy Days,* p. 136). The silent 'Amidah follows immediately.

The Musaf 'Amidah for Rosh Hashanah is the longest one in the prayer book and is built upon three central sections which sound the main themes of the festival: the מַלְכֻיּוֹת, which stress God's Kingship over all the creatures of the Universe; the זִכְרוֹנוֹת, referring to God's remembrance of the acts of faith performed by our ancestors, and the שׁוֹפָרוֹת, verses concerning the Shofar.

The pattern of the 'Amidah is the same as that of the Sabbath and festivals. However, whereas the Sabbath and festival 'Amidahs have only one central section, the Rosh Hashanah Musaf has these three central sections.

Since Rosh Hashanah is also Rosh Ḥodesh, some authorities felt that Rosh Ḥodesh should have been mentioned in וַתִּתֶּן לָנוּ. However, it is referred to in the next passage (מִלְּבַד עֹלַת הַחֹדֶשׁ וּמִנְחָתָהּ), and this is considered sufficient (*Levush, O.H.* 591:2).

The Malkhuyot, Zikhronot, and Shofarot begin with עָלֵינוּ. The grandeur of this prayer is attested by the fact that it was borrowed from the Rosh Hashanah liturgy, during the thirteenth century, to become the closing prayer of every synagogue service (Elbogen, *Der jüdische Gottesdienst,* p. 80).

Each of the extra sections has an introduction (עָלֵינוּ being, technically, the introduction to מַלְכֻיּוֹת), and a conclusion ending in a benediction. The central part of each section consists of ten verses (M. *R.H.* 4:6): three from the Pentateuch, three from the Prophets, three from the Hagiographa, and a final one again from the Pentateuch (B. *R.H.* 32a). Although in the Bible the Prophets come before the Hagiographa, in the Rosh Hashanah 'Amidah, the verses quoted from the Hagiographa come before the verses from the Prophets. This is because some of the verses from the Hagiographa are from the Book of Psalms, which traditionally is ascribed to David, and thus they are dated earlier than the prophetic writings (Tosafot, B. *R.H.* 32a; *Levush, O.H.* 591:4).

The Talmud gives three opinions on the use of ten verses. According to Rabbi Levi, it corresponds to the ten Hallelujahs with which David praised the Lord in Psalm 150; according to Rabbi Joseph, it corresponds to the Ten Commandments; and according to Rabbi Yoḥanan, it corresponds to the ten divine commands by which the world was created (B. *R.H.* 32a). "Thus the number ten is a most appropriate symbol for Rosh Hashanah, since it recalls to us not only the creation of the world (which came to pass by means of ten commands) but also the moral law (centered around ten basic commandments) which makes it possible for the world thus created to remain in existence. Therefore men sing the praise of their creator with a tenfold Hallelujah and strengthen their own conviction by impressing upon themselves, ten times over the most sacred principles of their faith" (Munk, *World of Prayer,* 2:206).

In the Jerusalem Talmud reasons like the above are ascribed to each of the Malkhuyot, Zikhronot, and Shofarot (*R.H.* 4:7). The verses of Malkhuyot correspond to the ten praises that David said in Psalm 150. The ten verses in Zikhronot correspond to the ten warnings (וִידוּיִים) that the prophet Isaiah issued to the people ("Wash ye, make ye clean"), which are followed by "Come let us reason together." And the ten verses of Shofarot correspond to the ten sacrificial offerings of the day: seven sheep, one bullock, one ram, and one he-goat.

The reason for the sequence is explained in the midrashic literature. Rabbi Nathan said: "Why did the sages deem it fit to say Malkhuyot first and then Zikhronot and Shofarot? So that you make Him sovereign over you first, and then pray for mercy so that you be remembered before Him. With what? With the Shofar of liberation, for Shofar means freedom, as it is said: 'And it shall be on that day that the great Shofar will be sounded' [Isa. 27:13]" (*Sifre Bemidbar* 10:10). These sections of the Musaf refer, then, to the three fundamentals of our religion: (1) the existence of God, who is King of the Universe; (2) divine justice; and (3) revelation (Friedländer, *The Jewish Religion,* p. 404).

A philosopher of the nineteenth century explains that the verses of Malkhuyot relate to God's governing the world, those of Zikhronot, to His judging the world, and those of Shofarot, to His redemption of the world. The governing of the world will reach its perfection with the Kingdom of God of the Messianic era. Therefore the third benediction of the 'Amidah of Rosh Hashanah and Yom Kippur says: "Let this awe be manifest in all thy works and a reverence for thee fill all that thou hast created so that all thy creatures may know thee and all mankind bow down to acknowledge thee." In this fellowship the Kingdom of God will be established in the world. The covenant that God made with Noah is completed with a covenant between God and mankind, the sign and guarantee of God's rule in the world (Hermann Cohen, quoted in *Sefer Hamo'adim, Rosh Hashanah,* p. 56).

The repetition of the 'Amidah is of special importance. First of all, תְּקִיעוֹת דִּמְעֻמָּד take place here. After the concluding benedictions of Malkhuyot, Zikhronot, and Shofarot respectively, the Shofar is sounded. In each case the *Ba'al Teqi'ah* sounds ten blasts in the order תשר״ת, תש״ת, and תר״ת. Some High Holy Day prayer books have only תשר״ת. While there is good authority for this (*O.H.* 592:1; *Levush, O.H.* 592:1), the accepted practice, adopted virtually universally, is the longer order mentioned above.

After the conclusion of each of the series, the congregation recites הַיּוֹם הֲרַת עוֹלָם and אֲרֶשֶׁת שְׂפָתֵינוּ (*O.H.* 592:1 in Rama). The first of these prayers is based on the tradition that the world was created on the first of Tishre. It is appropriate to mention the creation of the world here because the sounding of the Shofar proclaims our acceptance of God's sovereignty (*Levush, O.H.* 592:2). This prayer is recited, therefore, even if Rosh Hashanah coincides with a Sabbath, when the sounding of the Shofar is omitted. The second prayer, אֲרֶשֶׁת שְׂפָתֵינוּ, however, is omitted on the Sabbath because it explicitly mentions God's listening to the sounds of the Shofar blasts, which would not be true on the Sabbath (ibid.; *O.H.* in Rama).

Rabbi Herman Kieval, in his commentary on the Rosh Hashanah liturgy, calls attention to the meaning of this prayer. Abraham Joshua Heschel points out that whereas pagan myths are concerned with the site of creation, their shrines often claiming sanctity on this account, Judaism sanctified the time of creation. Understood in this light, Rosh Hashanah carries the momentous message that the human personality, the "crown of creation," also possesses limitless capacities for renewal. Thus God is quoted by the sages: "My children, I look upon you as if today [Rosh Hashanah] I had created a new creature" (*The High Holy Days*, p. 158).

Another reason for the importance of the repetition of the 'Amidah is that it includes a number of important *piyyuṭim*, most of which have been accepted by congregations throughout the world. They are all woven around the main themes of Rosh Hashanah: repentance and God's sovereignty, justice, and compassion.

At עָלֵינוּ, when the cantor reaches the words וַאֲנַחְנוּ כּוֹרְעִים, it was the custom for the congregation to prostrate themselves, oriental style, as a sign of total allegiance to the King of Kings (*O.H.* 621:4 and in *Levush*). Today in many congregations, only the cantor does this (see Kieval, *The High Holy Days*, p. 155).

Franz Rosenzweig comments: "What distinguishes the Days of Awe from all other festivals is that here and only here does the Jew kneel. Here he does what he refused to before the king of Persia, what no power on earth can compel him to do, and what he need not do before God on any other day of the year, or in any other situation he may face during his lifetime. And he does not kneel to confirm a fault or to pray for forgiveness of sins, acts to which this festival is primarily dedicated. He kneels only on beholding the immediate nearness of God, hence on an occasion which transcends the earthly needs of today" (quoted in Kieval, *The High Holy Days*, p. 155).

The 'Amidah is followed by אֵין כֵּאלֹהֵינוּ, עָלֵינוּ, קַדִּישׁ, Psalm 27, קַדִּישׁ, and אֲדוֹן עוֹלָם.

The meal at home is the usual festival meal, beginning with Qiddush. During the meal, honey is eaten; sour and acidic foods are avoided.

11. Tashlikh

During the afternoon of the first day, or of the second day if the first day coincides with a Sabbath, it is customary to go to the banks of a river, or any body of water, and say such texts as the last three verses of the Book of Micah, which include the phrase וְתַשְׁלִיךְ בִּמְצֻלוֹת יָם כָּל חַטֹּאתָם. Some prayer books (e.g., Singer's) have interpolated a sentence which is not scriptural: וְכָל חַטֹּאת עַמְּךָ בֵּית יִשְׂרָאֵל תַּשְׁלִיךְ בִּמְקוֹם אֲשֶׁר לֹא יִזָּכְרוּ וְלֹא יִפָּקְדוּ וְלֹא יַעֲלוּ עַל לֵב לְעוֹלָם.

The name Tashlikh is derived from the verse וְתַשְׁלִיךְ בִּמְצֻלוֹת יָם.

The custom is not found in the Talmud or in the responsa of the Geonim, but is first mentioned by the Maharil (Rabbi Jacob Moellin, 1355–1427). (See Lauterbach, *Rabbinic Essays,* p. 433, for an exhaustive historical study.)

The symbolism of the act is obvious. Nevertheless, some less obvious explanations have been given. Tashlikh reminds us of the 'Aqedah because the Midrash relates (*Tanḥuma, Wayera* 22) that Satan, in an effort to prevent Abraham from sacrificing Isaac, transformed himself into a deep stream on the road leading to Mount Moriah. Plunging into the stream, Abraham and Isaac prayed: "Save me, O Lord, for the waters are come unto my soul" (Ps. 69:2), whereupon the place became dry again (Maharil, *Levush* 596). The metaphor is that of a drowning person (Abrahams, *Companion to the Authorised Daily Prayer Book,* p. 56). The body of water should have fish in it, according to the custom of certain places. The precariousness of the existence of fish reminds man of his precarious existence and thus puts him in the mood to repent (*Levush, O.H.* 596).

A more rationalistic explanation suggests that Tashlikh gives us a chance to reflect on water's purifying effect on the body and to be reminded that even as the body is purified by water so ought our souls be purified by repentance and the appeal to God's help and mercy (Friedländer, *The Jewish Religion,* p. 405).

12. Minḥah and Ma'ariv

The Minḥah service conforms to the pattern of all festivals, beginning with אַשְׁרֵי and וּבָא לְצִיּוֹן, followed by the silent 'Amidah and *Ḥazarat Hashats.* The 'Amidah is the same as at Shaḥarit and Ma'ariv.

If the first day of Rosh Hashanah coincides with a Sabbath, the Torah is read as on every Sabbath afternoon. The first part of the Sidrah of the following Sabbath, הַאֲזִינוּ (Deut. 32:1–12), is read.

After *Ḥazarat Hashats* we recite אָבִינוּ מַלְכֵּנוּ with the ark open. On the Sabbath it is omitted. The reader then says Qaddish Titqabbel followed by עָלֵינוּ and the mourner's Qaddish.

The Ma'ariv service is the same as the night before. If the first day of Rosh Hashanah coincides with a Sabbath, וַתּוֹדִיעֵנוּ is inserted after אַתָּה בְחַרְתָּנוּ (*O.H.* 599).

The festival meal is the same as the night before except that the שֶׁהֶחֱיָנוּ of Qiddush is recited over a "new" fruit or a new article of clothing donned that night for the first time (*O.H.* 600:2). This practice has been adopted in order to satisfy two views regarding the nature of the second day of Rosh Hashanah. According to one opinion, the second day of Rosh Hashanah is like the second day of any festival, i.e., it is סְפֵיקָא דְיוֹמָא, possibly the festival itself, and therefore the recitation of שֶׁהֶחֱיָנוּ is obligatory. According to the other opinion, the second day of Rosh Hashanah is an extension of the first day (יוֹמָא אֲרִיכְתָּא), and therefore no שֶׁהֶחֱיָנוּ should be recited. In order to satisfy both views, it is customary to provide another reason for the שֶׁהֶחֱיָנוּ, such as a new fruit or a new garment.

On the morning of the second day the services are the same as on the first day, with some variations in the *piyyuṭim* that are recited. There is also a difference in the Torah reading. From the first scroll we read the 'Aqedah (Gen. 22:1–24). The sounding of the ram's horn is connected with the ram sacrificed instead of Isaac. The 'Aqedah passage is thus part of the motif of Zikhronot, and it is also appropriate for Rosh Hashanah since it stresses the theme of "return" and "repentance" (see Kieval, *The High Holy Days,* p. 102). The Hafṭarah is Jeremiah 31:2–20.

Minḥah is the same as on the first day.

The halakhic question regarding the second day of Rosh Hashanah centers about whether it is on a par with the first day and thus is counted as an extension of the first day—יוֹמָא אֲרִיכְתָּא, or whether it is like the second day of the other festivals, which are *sefeiqa deyoma,* hence in the category of יוֹם טוֹב שֵׁנִי שֶׁל גָּלֻיּוֹת. The fact that Rosh Hashanah is observed for two days in Israel would indicate that we have accepted the former. Recent studies, however, have indicated that the observance of two days of Rosh Hashanah in Israel, though the universal practice today (*O.H.* 601.2), was a late development (see *Otsar Hage'onim, Masekhet Yom Ṭov,* p. 4; Levi, *Yesodot Hatefilah,* pp. 254 f.; Arzt, *Justice and Mercy,* pp. 25 ff.; Wahrman, *Ḥagei Yisra'el Umo'adaw,* pp. 23–26).

The Ma'ariv service is that of a weekday, but אַתָּה חוֹנַנְתָּנוּ is added in the fourth benediction. The Havdalah, marking the end of the festival, is the one recited at the end of the Sabbath, but הִנֵּה אֵל יְשׁוּעָתִי and the blessings over spices and light are omitted here as at the end of the other festivals (*O.H.* 601:1 and 491).

UNIT XIV

THE DAYS OF AWE (III)

'Aseret Yemei Teshuvah
Yom Kippur: Introduction
'Erev Yom Kippur
Rituals of Abstinence
Kol Nidrei

XIV.
The Days of Awe (III)

13. 'Aseret Yemei Teshuvah

"Rabbi Kruspedai said in the name of Rabbi Yoḥanan: 'Three books are opened on Rosh Hashanah: one for the thoroughly wicked, one for the thoroughly righteous, and one for the intermediate group. The thoroughly righteous are forthwith inscribed in the Book of Life, the thoroughly wicked are forthwith inscribed for condemnation, while the fate of the intermediate group is suspended from Rosh Hashanah until Yom Kippur; if they merit, they are inscribed in the Book of Life; if not, they are condemned' " (B. *R.H.* 16b).

This passage enables us to understand the purpose of the 'Aseret Yemei Teshuvah, or Ten Days of Penitence—the period between Rosh Hashanah and Yom Kippur. During these ten days, we are all provided with an opportunity to be inscribed in the Book of Life, for all of us are considered to be in the intermediate group (B. *Qid.* 40b). Thus, if we have failed to earn our reward for the coming year by Rosh Hashanah, we are granted a period of grace during which we can still determine our fate.

Maimonides explains that while prayer and repentance are pleasing to God at any time, He finds them especially pleasing during the Ten Days of Penitence and accepts them forthwith. This is true for the prayers and repentance of the individual, but the congregation as a whole is heard whenever its prayers and penitence are wholehearted, as it is written: "What great nation is there that has a God so near to them as the Lord, our God, is whenever we call upon Him?" (Deut. 4:7). For this reason, all Israel endeavors to practice deeds of lovingkindness and to do mitswot and good works even more during the 'Aseret Yemei Teshuvah than during the rest of the year. Moreover, it is generally customary during the ten days to rise at night and go to the synagogue to recite prayers and supplications until dawn (*Hil. Teshuvah* 3:4). The 'Aseret Yemei Teshuvah, then, were considered to be especially propitious for repentance, and thus the verse "Seek the Lord while he may be found, call upon him while he is near" (Isa. 55:6) was interpreted as referring to them (B. *R.H.* 18a). Today we would say that the Ten Days of Penitence are appropriate for serious contemplation and penitence. Coming between the two solemn festivals of Rosh Hashanah and Yom Kippur, they should be a time of increased devotion and earnest self-examination.

The heightened sense of responsibility that should pervade us is stressed in the following talmudic analogy: "A man should always consider himself evenly balanced, i.e., half sinful and half righteous. If he performs one mitswah, happy is he, for he has tilted the scales toward righteousness. If he commits one sin, woe unto him, for he has tilted the scale toward sinfulness."

"Rabbi Elazar the son of Simon said: 'Inasmuch as the world is judged in accordance with the majority of *its* deeds, and the individual is judged in accordance with the majority of *his* deeds, if he performs one mitswah, happy is he, for he has tipped his scales and the scales of the world toward merit. If he commits one sin, woe unto him, for he has tipped the scales toward sinfulness for himself and for the world' " (B. *Qid.* 40a–b). The stress upon the individual's responsibility for his own fate and for the fate of the world is even more meaningful today, for in our impersonal society, the individual often feels himself to be lost in the flow of mass movements.

A number of practices were instituted to enhance the effectiveness of the Ten Days of Penitence as a time for contemplation and self-examination. Seliḥot are recited every morning before the Shaḥarit prayers (*Levush, O.H.* 602:2). In the 'Amidah we insert זָכְרֵנוּ לְחַיִּים in the first benediction, מִי כָמוֹךָ in the second, וּכְתוֹב לְחַיִּים in the eighteenth, and בְּסֵפֶר חַיִּים in the concluding one. For הָאֵל הַקָּדוֹשׁ we substitute הַמֶּלֶךְ הַקָּדוֹשׁ, and for מֶלֶךְ אוֹהֵב צְדָקָה וּמִשְׁפָּט we substitute הַמֶּלֶךְ הַמִּשְׁפָּט (B. *Ber.* 12b; *O.H.* 582:1; *Abudraham Hashalem* 261). After the 'Amidah, at both Shaḥarit and Minḥah, אָבִינוּ מַלְכֵּנוּ is recited with the ark open (*O.H.* 602:1 in Rama).

It was once customary to fast on each of the ten days in order to add to their solemnity (*Levush, O.H.* 602:2; Mordecai at the beginning of *Yoma; Abudraham Hashalem* 261). One authority suggested that weddings should not take place during this period (*Qitsur Shulḥan 'Arukh* 130:4), but his view has not generally been accepted (see Hoffmann, *Melamed Leho'il,* pt. 3, no. 1).

The day after Rosh Hashanah (or the next day if the day after Rosh Hashanah is a Sabbath) is the Fast of Gedaliah, a *ta'anit tsibur* (public fast day) referred to as *tsom hashevi'i* (B. *R.H.* 18b; *O.H.* 602:1 in Rama) because it falls in the seventh month if we count Nisan as the first month. The fast commemorates the murder of Gedaliah, the governor of Judah appointed by Nebuchadnezzar after the fall of Jerusalem (II Kings 25:25). His assassination brought great suffering to the survivors of the war with Babylon and also completed the destruction of the First Commonwealth. The rules and order of prayers for the Fast of Gedaliah are given in the section dealing with public fasts (see below, p. 244 ff.).

The Sabbath between Rosh Hashanah and Yom Kippur is called Shabbat Shuvah because the Haftarah (Hos. 14:2–10) commences with the phrase שׁוּבָה יִשְׂרָאֵל. It is read on this Sabbath because in it the prophet exhorts Israel to return to God. Some authorities suggest that this Sabbath is called Shabbat Teshuvah because it occurs during the 'Aseret Yemei Teshuvah (Singer, *Ziv Haminhagim,* p. 178).

There were originally several different customs regarding the length of the Haftarah for Shabbat Shuvah. Some read only the nine verses from Hosea mentioned above, but this practice contravened the rule that a Haftarah should have at least twenty-one verses (ibid. and in *Levush*). Therefore some authorities added twelve verses from Joel (2:15–27) to complete the required twenty-one. There was, in addition, another objection to reading only the section from Hosea, namely, that it ends on a discouraging note: "but transgressors do stumble therein." As a result, the last verses of Micah (7:18–20), which speak of the forgiveness of sins, were added.

Nowadays, the verses from Micah are added if Sidrah וַיֵּלֶךְ is read on Shabbat Shuvah, and the verses from Joel if the Sidrah is הַאֲזִינוּ. Our practice here is based on the idea that the Haftarah should bear some relationship to the scriptural reading for the day. וַיֵּלֶךְ says: "Then my anger shall be kindled," and Micah includes the phrase: "He retaineth not His anger forever." In הַאֲזִינוּ we read: "My doctrine shall drop as the rain," while Joel has the passage: "And He causes the rain to come down for you" (*Liquṭei Meharih* 3:187).

In view of the serious implications of its contents, and the call to repentance it contains, the Haftarah of Shabbat Shuvah should be read by an honored member of the congregation (Maharil, *Maṭeh Mosheh* 833).

At one time rabbis preached only on Shabbat Shuvah and Shabbat Hagadol. On Shabbat Hagadol they explained the complex laws of Pesaḥ, while on Shabbat Shuvah they exhorted the people to repent in preparation for Yom Kippur (*Maṭeh Mosheh* 833). In time these sermons became scholarly discourses. Because the Shabbat Shuvah discourse was given in the afternoon, neither פִּרְקֵי אָבוֹת (*Ethics of the Fathers*) nor בָּרְכִי נַפְשִׁי (Ps. 104) is said (Singer, *Ziv Haminhagim,* p. 179).

Some congregations say אָב הָרַחֲמִים and צִדְקָתְךָ צֶדֶק on Shabbat Shuvah, and others do not (Singer, *Ziv Haminhagim,* p. 179).

14. Yom Kippur: Introduction

"Rabbi Akiva said: 'Happy are you, Israel. Before whom do you become clean? Who is it who makes you clean? Your father who is in heaven' " (M. *Yoma* 8:9).

Sin and repentance are the themes of Yom Kippur. Sin alienates man from God, and repentance effects a reconciliation. Repentance brings about a change of heart and makes man a new creature, a regenerated personality. Yom Kippur summons man to repent; it summons him to the vision that his real self is the divine image within him, that the meaning of his life is measured in the victory he has achieved in disciplining his baser self and bending it to serve his higher purpose. It summons him to continue his quest toward the highest, and to that end to renounce his deficiencies (see Kaplan, *The Meaning of God,* p. 149; Bokser, *Judaism,* pp. 235 f.).

Since Yom Kippur concludes the Ten Days of Penitence, it forms the climax of this period. In an effort to bring man directly before his Maker, the day is observed in a manner that will remove the worshipper from every aspect of the mundane world. He neither eats nor drinks nor attends to daily affairs. He reviews his past and ponders his future in the presence of the one and only Judge of all flesh.

15. 'Erev Yom Kippur

The day before Yom Kippur is important not only because of its proximity to Yom Kippur, but also because the rabbis gave it a significance of its own. This is reflected in the talmudic dictum that just as it is a mitswah to fast on Yom Kippur, so is it a mitswah to eat on the day before (B. *Yoma* 81b; *O.H.* 604:1).

Thus, whereas the sages sought to heighten the solemnity of Yom Kippur by the long preparatory period, they prescribed that the day immediately preceding it be partially festive as a sign of our confidence in God's mercy (Ṭur, *O.H.* 604; *Levush, O.H.* 604:1). Hence, the Seliḥot recited that morning are comparatively short (*Levush,* ibid.). Taḥanun and Psalm 20 before וּבָא לְצִיּוֹן are omitted (*O.H.* 604:2 and Rama). Psalm 100, מִזְמוֹר לְתוֹדָה, is also omitted because it was recited only when a קָרְבַּן תּוֹדָה was offered in the Temple in Jerusalem; since such an offering was not brought on the morning before Yom Kippur (because the time for its consumption would be shortened), the recitation of the psalm was also omitted. אָבִינוּ מַלְכֵּנוּ, which is said on each of the Ten Days of Penitence, is also omitted. If Yom Kippur coincides with a Sabbath, we say it the day before at Shaḥarit but not at Minḥah (*O.H.* 604:2, in Rama and *M.A.* 2; *Levush, O.H.* 604:2).

A widespread custom which has fallen into desuetude is that of Kapparot. It was the practice to wave a rooster in the case of a male, and a hen in the case of a female, three times in a circular motion around one's head while reciting appropriate prayers. The fowl was then slaughtered in the manner prescribed, and the meat, or its monetary value, was given to the poor.

Although there was a great deal of rabbinic objection to this practice, it became widespread and accepted (*O.H.* 605:1; see also Ṭur 605 in *Bet Yosef,* and Mordecai at the beginning of *Yoma*). Today many people have substituted charitable contributions. Even before, some authorities suggested that where Kapparot cannot be abolished, the ritual should be performed with money rather than with a fowl (*Ḥayyei Adam* 144:4).

Tradition prescribes that festive meals be eaten on the day preceding Yom Kippur. The final meal of the day, the *se'udah hamafseqet,* must be eaten before sundown. Since it is a mitswah to start each holiday a bit earlier than the start of the next day (מוֹסִיפִין מֵחוֹל עַל הַקּוֹדֶשׁ) (B. *Yoma* 81b), the meal should end while it is still day (*O.H.* 608:1). The meal should be festive and satisfying so that one is in condition to fast the next day (*Levush, O.H.* 604:1; Ṭur, *O.H.* 604 and in *BaḤ*). Others suggest a contrary reason. Since we are enjoined to afflict ourselves on Yom Kippur, we eat a hearty meal the day before because that makes the fasting more difficult (*'Arukh Hashulḥan, O.H.* 604:4).

Before the meal one should recite the confession of sins, עַל חֵטְא. This is done at Minḥah. The Minḥah service, which thus must be recited before the final meal, begins like the other weekday Minḥah services of the Ten Days of Penitence. After the final benediction, however, before אֱלֹהַי נְצוֹר, both the short (אָשַׁמְנוּ) and the long (עַל חֵטְא) confessions are recited. At חֲזָרַת הַשׁ״ץ only the regular 'Amidah is recited (*O.H.* 607:5 in Rama).

The reason for this practice is that a hearty meal may induce levity (שֶׁמָּא תִּטָּרֵף דַּעְתּוֹ בַּסְּעוּדָה), preventing a person from reciting the confession. Hence, one must do it before the meal (B. *Yoma* 87b, *Tosefta Kippurim* 4:14; see Lieberman's comments in *Tosefta Kifshutah,* 4:829 f.). Maimonides suggests that this is a precautionary measure lest a mishap occur during the meal and a person die before confessing (*Hil. Teshuvah* 2:7).

It is customary for parents to bless their children before leaving home for the synagogue. In addition to the usual text used on Friday nights, the blessing should contain good wishes for the coming year and a prayer that the children may live ethical and moral lives dedicated to Torah and mitswot (see *Qitsur Shulḥan 'Arukh* 130:16; *Ḥayyei Adam* 144:19).

Candles should be lit just as on Friday nights, with the benediction לְהַדְלִיק נֵר שֶׁל יוֹם הַכִּפּוּרִים. If Yom Kippur falls on a Sabbath, the benediction is לְהַדְלִיק נֵר שֶׁל שַׁבָּת וְשֶׁל יוֹם הַכִּפּוּרִים (*O.H.* 610:1–3 and in Rama). This is followed by the שֶׁהֶחֱיָנוּ (*'Arukh Hashulḥan, O.H.* 610:5).

In addition to these candles, a special memorial light that will burn until the conclusion of Yom Kippur is lit in memory of one's parents. This is called נֵר נְשָׁמָה (*O.H.* 610:3; *Levush, O.H.* 610:3). It used to be customary for each family to bring a large candle into the synagogue (*Qitsur Shulḥan 'Arukh* 131:7). The custom has become obsolete, presumably because it is not feasible today.

The table should be covered as for the Sabbath and festivals (*O.H.* 610:4), and one should be attired as for a holiday. It was once customary for women to be dressed in white for the synagogue services and for men to wear the Kittel as a symbol of purity (*O.H.* 610:4 in Rama). Today at least those officiating at the services wear white robes.

16. Rituals of Abstinence

Yom Kippur is the holiest and most solemn day of the year. Its central theme is atonement and reconciliation. Every act, every ritual, every observance, and every prayer heightens and accentuates the meaning of the day. Yom Kippur is, therefore, the only festival during which the prohibition of work is as severe as on the Sabbath. The exceptions made in the case of the other holidays in regard to cooking, using fire, and carrying do not apply to Yom Kippur (*O.H.* 611:2).

Yom Kippur, however, has additional prohibitions that add to the solemnity of the day. We are forbidden to eat, drink, bathe, anoint ourselves, wear shoes, and have conjugal relations (*O.H.* 511:1; B. *Yoma* 11a).

According to rabbinic tradition (B. *Yoma* 73b ff.), these are included in the biblical commandment to afflict oneself (Lev. 23:27). The reason for their inclusion is that the gratification of our bodily appetites is the principal source of sin. Teshuvah, the return to the right path, must therefore include an earnest attempt to control and, when necessary, to suppress such appetites (Friedländer, *The Jewish Religion,* p. 406).

Fasting, in particular, represents such an attempt. The fasting should begin before sundown and end after nightfall the following day. The obligation to fast begins when a child reaches the age of religious maturity, i.e., girls at twelve, and boys at thirteen (*O.H.* 616:2). Children nine years old or younger should not be allowed to fast even if they want to, lest they suffer therefrom (ibid.). Children more than nine years old should be trained to fast, gradually adding hours each year as they grow older (ibid.).

Sick people should follow the advice of their physician. Even if the patient claims that he can fast in spite of his illness, the advice of the physician should be followed (*O.H.* 618:1). If the patient claims that he cannot fast, we accept his opinion even if the physician disagrees (ibid.). A pregnant woman who wants to eat even though she understands the importance of fasting on Yom Kippur should be allowed to eat until the desire is stilled (*O.H.* 617:2; Maimonides, *Hil. Shevitat 'Asor* 2:9). A woman who has just given birth is considered to be as one dangerously ill for the first three days and is not allowed to fast (*O.H.* 617:4). From the third to the seventh day she is considered as a sick person and treated as described above. After that she is treated like all other persons (ibid.).

Bathing and washing of a pleasurable nature are forbidden (*O.H.* 613:1), but washing the hands and face for hygienic purposes is permitted (ibid.; *Levush* 613:1–3; Ṭur 613). The sick or those who have to bathe for medical reasons are permitted to do so (Ṭur, loc. cit.).

Leather shoes were considered an apparel of luxury. Abstaining from wearing leather shoes on Yom Kippur was therefore considered a suitable form of self-deprivation. Another reason for not wearing leather shoes is that the entire day serves as a vivid reliving of the Temple days. Leather shoes were forbidden in holy places (see Exod. 3:5 and M. *Ber.* 9:5). Kohanim had to remove their shoes when they went up to pronounce the Priestly Benediction (B. *R.H.* 31b; Arzt, *Justice and Mercy,* p. 198).

"Rabbi Moses Isserles (1520–73), the great medieval codifier of Jewish law, explained the practice of not wearing leather shoes on Yom Kippur as an expression of concern for animal welfare. On the holiest day of the year we are to shed the symbol of our predatory nature, the shoes which were made from the skin of a living creature. Wearing shoes is generally permitted, but this permission is a tragic yielding to necessity, and on the holiest day of the year, according to Isserles, we ought to reach out for a higher moral standard than is expected of us on other days" (Bokser, *Judaism*, pp. 170 f.).

Dr. Kaplan reminds us that the prohibitions should not be construed as mortification of the flesh. "Thus, while abstinence from food and drink and other forms of bodily gratification on the Day of Atonement is commanded, self-torture for the purpose of mortifying the flesh is discountenanced.

"When we refrain from indulging our physical appetites for a limited period, in order to devote ourselves for a time more exclusively to demands that rank higher in our hierarchy of values, we are not denying the physical appetites their just place in life; we are simply recognizing the need of putting them in their place" (*The Meaning of God*, p. 169).

The moral implications of fasting and abstinence on Yom Kippur are best expressed in the Hafṭarah following the reading of the Torah in the morning. The prophet exhorts the people that these are not ends in themselves, "the day for a man to afflict his soul" (Isa. 58:5), but rather a reminder:

> To loose the fetters of wickedness
> To undo the bonds of the yoke,
> And let the oppressed go free
> And that ye break every yoke.
> Is it not to deal thy bread to the hungry?
> And that thou bring the poor that are cast out
> to thy house?
> When thou seest the naked that thou cover him
> And that thou hide not thyself from thine own flesh? [Isa. 58:6–7]

17. Kol Nidrei

The Yom Kippur services begin with Kol Nidrei, which must be recited before sunset because it deals with the annulment of vows, and this cannot take place on a Sabbath or on a festival (*O.H.* 619:1 in Rama and in *M.A.* 5).

Because of the extra solemnity of the day, the Ṭalit is donned for the evening prayers, the only evening service of the year when this is done. Since the donning of the Ṭalit is obligatory only during the day, it should be put on while it is still day so that the benediction לְהִתְעַטֵּף בְּצִיצִת may be recited. If it is already night, one should put on the Ṭalit without the benediction (*Levush, O.H.* 619:1; *O.H.* 619 in *Mishnah Berurah* 4).

In some synagogues the service is introduced with the verse אוֹר זָרֻעַ לַצַּדִּיק וּלְיִשְׁרֵי לֵב שִׂמְחָה (Ps. 97:11), which stresses the belief that through sincere repentance and righteousness of heart, light and gladness can be achieved by all (see Ṭur, *O.H.* 619; *Qitsur Shulḥan 'Arukh* 132:1; Vainstein, *Cycle of the Jewish Year,* pp. 110 f.). The ark is opened and two distinguished members of the congregation take out two Torah scrolls. One proceeds to the right of the cantor, and the other to the left. The cantor then recites בִּישִׁיבָה שֶׁל מַעְלָה וּבִישִׁיבָה שֶׁל מַטָּה, עַל דַּעַת הַמָּקוֹם וְעַל דַּעַת הַקָּהָל אָנוּ מַתִּירִין לְהִתְפַּלֵּל עִם הָעֲבַרְיָנִים (*O.H.* 619:1 in *M.D.*). According to Rabbi Mordecai ben Hillel (d. in Germany, 1298), this formula was instituted in the thirteenth century by Rabbi Meir ben Barukh of Rothenburg (d. 1293) to permit transgressors who had been excommunicated because of their defiance of communal regulations to worship with the congregation. This is done, even if the transgressors did not request it, because of a statement in the Talmud by Rabbi Simon the Pious that a public fast in which sinners do not participate is not a fast (B. *Ker.* 6b). The two members of the congregation and the cantor form the court that issues this permission (Ṭur, *O.H.* 619).

It has also been suggested that the transgressors referred to are the Marranos. When they came to the synagogues during the High Holy Days, they aroused the resentment of their brethren, who opposed their admission on the ground that they should have fled from Spain and left behind all their worldly goods rather than submit, even if only outwardly, to conversion. To discourage such opposition to the Marranos, the recitation of this formula was instituted. The word עֲבַרְיָנִים may even be a play on the word *Iberian,* the name applied to the inhabitants of Spain (Wahrman, *Ḥagei Yisra'el Umo'adaw,* p. 50; Vainstein, *Cycle of the Jewish Year,* p. 110).

The reader chants the Kol Nidrei three times (*O.H.* 619:1 in Rama). According to one opinion, this is done in order to assure that latecomers may hear it at least once. A more cogent suggestion is that in the case of *Hattarat Nedarim* ("Absolution of Vows"), which Kol Nidrei actually is, the absolution has to be said three times (*Y.D.* 228:3). The first time, the cantor should chant it softly as one who hesitates to enter the king's palace and fears to approach with a request for a favor; the second time, he chants it somewhat louder; the third time, he raises his voice louder and louder, like one who is accustomed to being a member of the king's court (*Maḥzor Vitry* and Maharil).

The language of Kol Nidrei is Aramaic, evidently because Aramaic was the vernacular in the place where it was composed. In some communities, however, the text was in Hebrew (*Levush, O.H.* 619:1; Ṭur, *O.H.* 619).

After Kol Nidrei the reader and the congregation say וְנִסְלַח לְכָל עֲדַת בְּנֵי יִשְׂרָאֵל וְלַגֵּר הַגָּר בְּתוֹכָם כִּי לְכָל הָעָם בִּשְׁגָגָה (Num. 15:26) three times. This is followed by סְלַח נָא לַעֲוֹן הָעָם הַזֶּה כְּגֹדֶל חַסְדֶּךָ וְכַאֲשֶׁר נָשָׂאתָה לָעָם הַזֶּה מִמִּצְרַיִם וְעַד הֵנָּה, וְשָׁם נֶאֱמַר (Num. 14:19) said by the reader, to which the congregation responds with וַיֹּאמֶר יְיָ סָלַחְתִּי כִּדְבָרֶךָ (Num. 14:20) three times (*O.H.* 691:1 in Rama). The reader concludes with the שֶׁהֶחֱיָנוּ (*O.H.* 619:1). On other holidays this is recited at the conclusion of the Qiddush, but since Qiddush is not recited on Yom Kippur, it is said immediately after the Kol Nidrei (Arzt, *Justice and Mercy,* p. 198). The Torah scrolls are then returned to the ark, the ark is closed, and the members of the congregation return to their places.

The solemnity surrounding Kol Nidrei is due not to its intrinsic meaning but to the fact that it opens the Yom Kippur service. Though not an integral part of the service, its popularity caused its name to be bestowed on the entire service, which is often referred to as the Kol Nidrei service. The popularity of Kol Nidrei is partially due to its melody, probably the best known of all those associated with the synagogue services.

Kol Nidrei itself has a tenuous connection with Yom Kippur, and its origin is shrouded in mystery. It has been suggested that it was composed during the reign of Reccared I (reigned 586–601), a Visigothic king of Spain noted for his persecution of the Jews. He ordered their conversion to Catholicism under very fearful oaths and anathemas. The penalty for disobeying was death. When the forced converts assembled secretly on the eve of Yom Kippur to pray, Kol Nidrei was an expression of their overwhelming grief at having committed apostasy, and their means of seeking absolution from the vows they had been compelled to make to an alien faith. In subsequent centuries, during the persecution of the later Byzantine rulers (700–850), and still later under the Spanish Inquisition (1391–1492), the Kol Nidrei served a similar purpose (Joseph Bloch, quoted in Davidson, *American Jewish Year Book, 1923,* pp. 186 f.). This suggestion has not been accepted by scholars (ibid.; see, however, Levi, *Torat Hatefilah* p. 214).

Whatever its origin, the purpose of Kol Nidrei was to provide release from vows in matters relating to ritual, custom, and personal conduct, from inadvertent vows; and from vows one might have made to himself and then forgotten. It does not refer to vows and promises to other people. One cannot be released from these without the consent of the other party. We must stress this because Kol Nidrei invited attacks against the Jews with the claim that their vows and promises could not be relied upon since Kol Nidrei released them from all vows and promises.

While the Kol Nidrei prayer does release us from vows, it actually stresses the importance of the plighted word. The rabbis discouraged the making of vows (B. *Ned.* 20a; *Y.D.* 203:1), and insisted on their fulfillment once made because of the sacredness of the spoken word (*Y.D.* 203:3). The release from a vow—of the vows that Kol Nidrei is concerned with—was a last resort to compensate for human weakness, which makes us prone to make vows thoughtlessly.

Today the Kol Nidrei service teaches that we should forgive those who, in the heat of strife, acting under strong irritation, have offended us. Hence we say עַל דַּעַת הַמָּקוֹם, etc. We should be careful with regard to vows, and should consider the effect before making them. We should reflect on human weakness, and consider that what we are able to do today may prove impossible for us tomorrow. This reflection should remove all prideful thoughts from our hearts and inspire us with humility (Friedländer, *The Jewish Religion,* p. 408).

"For us today, *Kol Nidrei* can symbolize the need to deepen our sensitivity toward the resolutions which we make in our finest moments of spiritual decision. A feeling of discontent may, in a solemn moment of self-examination, prompt a person to resolve to change his ways. But too often he lacks the tenacity needed for effecting a radical break with strongly entrenched habits. *Kol Nidrei* can serve us as a reminder that only by resolute will and by severe self-discipline can we hope to lessen the distance between what we are and what we ought to be" (Arzt, *Justice and Mercy,* p. 201).

UNIT XV

THE DAYS OF AWE (IV)

Ma'ariv
Shaḥarit
The Reading of the Torah
Musaf
Martyrology
Minḥah
Ne'ilah
Ma'ariv

XV.
The Days of Awe (IV)

18. Ma'ariv

The Ma'ariv service begins with בָּרְכוּ and follows the standard format for festivals, with the usual blessings that accompany the Shema' (*Levush, O.H.* 619:2).

On all other days of the year, the בָּרוּךְ שֵׁם is recited in a whisper, but on Yom Kippur, both in the evening and in the morning, it is said aloud (*O.H.* 619:2). "The reason is that *Barukh Shem* is a singular reminiscence of the solemn service of atonement that was held in the Temple on Yom Kippur. In the 'Avodah section of the Musaf we recall that service with special vividness and repeat the threefold confessions spoken by the High Priest as he recited the Ineffable Name. As the people heard the Name, they knelt, prostrated themselves, and fell on their faces and said, 'Blessed be his glorious sovereign name for ever and ever.' Indeed, *Barukh Shem* rather than *'Amein* was the response to all blessings uttered in the Temple [B. *Ber.* 63a; Tosefta, *Ta'anit* 1:10]. The emphasis given to *Barukh Shem* on Yom Kippur is therefore an added means of reliving and recalling the atonement rites formerly conducted in the Temple" (Arzt, *Justice and Mercy,* p. 224; see ibid. for folkloristic reasons).

Before Ḥatsi Qaddish, the reader and the congregation say: כִּי בַיּוֹם הַזֶּה יְכַפֵּר עֲלֵיכֶם (Lev. 16:30). It is from this verse that the Mishnah derived one of the main principles of atonement. For transgressions against God, Yom Kippur effects atonement; but it does not effect atonement for transgressions against one's fellow man unless one has first conciliated him (M. *Yoma* 8:9).

If Yom Kippur coincides with a Sabbath, Psalms 92 and 93 and the mourner's Qaddish are recited before בָּרְכוּ. Also, וְשָׁמְרוּ is recited before the theme verse כִּי בַיּוֹם הַזֶּה.

The 'Amidah, up to the last benediction, is similar to that of Rosh Hashanah, with the variations appropriate for Yom Kippur. The closing prayer for the middle benediction is also different, in order to make it more suitable for Yom Kippur.

The main difference, however, is that we add the confession after the last benediction, as at Minḥah.

It is customary to beat one's breast both at אָשַׁמְנוּ and at עַל חֵטְא. This is based on a Midrash: "And the living will lay it to his heart" (Eccles. 7:2). Rabbi Meir said: "Why do people beat their hearts [in remorse for their sins]? Because the heart is the seat and source of sin" (*Eccles. Rabbah*, quoted in Arzt, *Justice and Mercy*, p. 221).

After the 'Amidah there is a series of penitential *piyyuṭim*, the confessional is repeated (the confessional is said ten times on Yom Kippur, including the Minḥah preceding כָּל נִדְרֵי), and אָבִינוּ מַלְכֵּנוּ is recited. If Yom Kippur coincides with a Sabbath, we follow the custom for festivals, inserting וַיְכֻלּוּ and מָגֵן אָבוֹת before the *piyyuṭim*, and omitting אָבִינוּ מַלְכֵּנוּ (*O.H.* 619:3 in Rama).

In accord with the solemnity of Yom Kippur, it used to be customary for people to stay in the synagogue for additional prayers and meditations. Some even spent the night in the synagogue (*O.H.* 619:6). While these customs are no longer observed, the idea behind them is still very relevant. The air of solemnity and awe should be maintained even after the services, not only in the synagogue, but also at home.

19. Shaḥarit

The morning service up to Barekhu is the same as on Rosh Hashanah. After Barekhu, the pattern is similar to that of Rosh Hashanah but with variations appropriate to Yom Kippur. This begins with the opening benediction following Barekhu. The 'Amidah is the same as the one said at the Ma'ariv service, except that שִׂים שָׁלוֹם replaces שָׁלוֹם רָב.

The repetition of the 'Amidah is interlaced with appropriate *piyyuṭim*. The confessional is also repeated, as is אָבִינוּ מַלְכֵּנוּ, except on a Sabbath.

20. The Reading of the Torah

The service for taking out and returning the Torah is the same as on Rosh Hashanah. Two Torah scrolls are removed from the ark. From the first we read Leviticus 16, which has a description of the sacrificial service on Yom Kippur. Six people are called to the reading (*O.H.* 601:1)—one more than on other festivals in order to show the greater solemnity of Yom Kippur (*Mishnah Berurah* 620:1). If Yom Kippur coincides with a Sabbath, seven are called.

For the Mafṭir we read Numbers 29:7–11 because it, too, speaks of the sacrifices offered in the Temple on Yom Kippur (*O.H.* 601:1).

The Hafṭarah is Isaiah 57:14–58:14. This passage was chosen because of its concern with the true purpose of fasting. A fast is of no avail, says the prophet, if it does not induce a just and merciful relation with our fellow men.

21. Musaf

Yizkor is recited after the Hafṭarah. According to the tradition, we say Yizkor because the departed are also in need of forgiveness (*O.H.* 621:6). A more rationalistic reason is that Yizkor adds to the solemnity of the day and induces a contrite mood (*Qitsur Shulḥan 'Arukh* 133:21).

If Yom Kippur coincides with a Sabbath, we say יְקוּם פֻּרְקָן and מִי שֶׁבֵּרַךְ before Yizkor (Maharil, *Hil. Yom kippur*). After Yizkor אַב הָרַחֲמִים and אַשְׁרֵי are said, followed by the return of the Torah scrolls to the ark. Musaf begins with הִנְנִי and Ḥatsi Qaddish, followed by the 'Amidah.

The Musaf 'Amidah, with seven benedictions, follows the pattern of festival 'Amidahs. The first three benedictions are the same as in the morning service. The middle benediction has אַתָּה בְחַרְתָּנוּ, וַתִּתֶּן לָנוּ, וּמִפְּנֵי חֲטָאֵנוּ, and the closing prayer אֱלֹהֵינוּ וֵאלֹהֵי אֲבוֹתֵינוּ, as on the Pilgrimage Festivals, with the variations appropriate for Yom Kippur.

The 'Amidah includes the usual interpolations for the Sabbath if Yom Kippur falls on a Saturday. Unique to Yom Kippur, however, is the confessional, which is added to the Musaf 'Amidah as it is to every 'Amidah on Yom Kippur. The *Ḥazarat Hashats* follows the pattern of the Rosh Hashanah Musaf with *piyyuṭim* and Seliḥot; in many instances the *piyyuṭim* are the same as those for Rosh Hashanah.

Two elements of the service are unique to the Yom Kippur Musaf: the 'Avodah and the Martyrology.

The 'Avodah is based on the mishnaic description of the prayers and ceremonies in the Temple on Yom Kippur (M.*Yoma* 1–7). The heart of the

Temple service was the confession recited by the High Priest in the Holy of Holies, first of his own sins, then of the sins of his fellow priests, and then of the sins of the entire community of Israel. In the course of making these confessions, the High Priest would pronounce the Ineffable Name of God (Yom Kippur was the only occasion when this was permitted). Each time he did so, the priests and ordinary people standing outside in the Temple courts prostrated themselves and responded: בָּרוּךְ שֵׁם כְּבוֹד . The 'Avodah ends with the High Priest's prayer for the welfare of the people.

Nowadays the reader prostrates himself when reciting the High Priest's confession. In some places the worshippers do so as well (*O.H.* 621:4 and in *M.D.* 3).

Professor Kaplan, in discussing the meaning of the 'Avodah, suggests that just as the Sanctuary had to be purified and cleansed of the impurities caused by the sins of the people in order to merit God's presence, so our homes, synagogues, schools, and other communal institutions must be purified in order to function properly as the abode of God.

"What the *'Abodah* rite should symbolize is that just as each individual Jew was to assume responsibility for the contamination of the sanctuary and for the elimination from it of God's Presence, so must everyone today recognize his individual responsibility for the corruption of our social institutions and their tendency to defeat the divine purpose of life, and seek by all the means at his command to atone for the evil they do" (Kaplan, *The Meaning of God,* pp. 172–73).

22. Martyrology

After telling of the "glorious" days when Israel enjoyed freedom and independence, and services in the Holy of Holies, the service veers to the opposite mood of Israel in exile, the chief theme of which is martyrdom.

Our Maḥzorim use the story of the martyrdom of the Ten Sages to illustrate the theme. Despite what we are led to believe by the poem אֵלֶּה אֶזְכְּרָה, however, the Ten Sages were not, in fact, martyred simultaneously. The author of the poem, apparently with the intention of heightening the effect on his readers, gathered several episodes of martyrdom among the sages and wove them into a coherent epic of faith.

The background of the events recounted in the poem was the Roman Empire's determination to blot out all resistance in the province of Judaea by forbidding the practice of Judaism and demanding the conversion of the Jews to paganism. According to *Midrash Eleh Ezkerah,* the Ten Sages of Israel were given over to be slaughtered as a punishment for the sin committed by the ten sons of Jacob, who sold their brother Joseph into slavery. The Book of Jubilees suggests that the sale of Joseph took place on Yom Kippur (Jubilees 34:12).

Leopold Zunz wrote: "If there are ranks in suffering, Israel takes precedence of all nations; if the duration of sorrows and the patience with which they are borne ennoble, the Jews can challenge the aristocracy of every land; if a literature is called rich in the possession of a few classic tragedies—what shall we say to a national tragedy lasting fifteen hundred years, in which the poets and the actors were also the heroes?" (Zunz, *Die synagogale Poesie,* p. 9).

If this could be said before the advent of Hitler, what should we say today, we who have witnessed the Nazi Holocaust, next to which all previous persecutions pale into insignificance! The new Maḥzorim have added recent martyrologies that more than match the heroism of the Ten Sages (see the Silverman, Bokser, Harlow, and Reconstructionist Maḥzorim). Lest it be thought that the deaths of these martyrs are mentioned in order to inspire vengeance, we cite the observation of Rabbi Ben Zion Bokser: "It is characteristic of the Jewish liturgy that the reference to catastrophies suffered at the hands of tyrants, moved to another climax than the invocation of wrath against the enemy. It moves to a reaffirmation of the hope in restoration. Various Scriptural promises are cited, assuring us of redemption, of renewal in the Holy Land. And this renewal is pictured as coincidental with a moral regeneration in Israel and all mankind. The life of the martyrs will find its true vindication in the dawn of the Messianic age, when the people of Israel will be renewed in Zion, to establish a vital spiritual life that shall lead all men to God, for God's house shall be 'a House of Prayer for all people' " (Bokser, *High Holy Day Prayer Book,* p. 436).

The Musaf continues with further penitential prayers, the confessional, the rest of *Ḥazarat Hashats,* the hymn הַיּוֹם תְּאַמְּצֵנוּ, and Qaddish Titqabbel.

אֵין כֵּאלֹהֵינוּ is not recited at the conclusion of the Yom Kippur Musaf. It was originally added to the Musaf for Sabbaths and festivals as a substitute for the benedictions of the weekday 'Amidah that are omitted on those occasions, but on Yom Kippur, when the Ne'ilah service, and the many other additional prayers, more than compensate for the omitted blessings, אֵין כֵּאלֹהֵינוּ would be superfluous (*O.Ḥ.* 622:1 in Rama; *M.A.* 1; *M.D.* 3; *Maṭeh Mosheh* 877).

23. Minḥah

The Minḥah service begins with the Torah reading. Normally Minḥah begins with אַשְׁרֵי and וּבָא לְצִיּוֹן, but on Yom Kippur these are deferred until the beginning of the Ne'ilah service (*O.H.* 622:1). This is because the Yom Kippur Musaf is quite lengthy, and it was feared that if these prayers were included in the Minḥah, the recitation of the Minḥah 'Amidah would be delayed beyond the prescribed time (*O.H.* 622:1; *Levush, O.H.* 622:2).

וַאֲנִי תְפִלָּתִי is omitted even if Yom Kippur coincides with a Sabbath. Since וַאֲנִי תְפִלָּתִי was interpreted as David's plea that unlike the heathen kings, who became inebriated and indulged in revelry on their festivals, we praise the Lord after a day of feasting, it is out of place to say it on Yom Kippur, when everyone is fasting (*Levush, O.H.* 622:2; Ṭur 622).

The ark is opened, and the congregants say וַיְהִי בִּנְסֹעַ and בְּרִיךְ שְׁמֵהּ. One Torah scroll is removed from the ark. The prescribed reading is Leviticus 18, which deals with prohibited marriages and the prohibition of illicit relations (*O.H.* 622:2).

The choice of this scriptural reading was prompted by an old custom mentioned in the Mishnah (*Ta'an.* 4:8). The young men of Israel used to select their brides on Yom Kippur, and the young women would dance before them in the vineyards, singing: "Young man, raise your eyes and see what you are choosing; do not set your eyes on beauty, but set your eyes on family" (*Otsar Hatefilot,* p. 1158). The reading of Leviticus 18 was a means of impressing on the young people the need for maintaining Israel's high standards of chastity and family morality. Some commentators, however, suggest that the passage was chosen because it follows closely after, and thus concludes, the Torah portion read at the morning service (Eliyahu Kitov, *Sefer Hatoda'ah,* p. 55).

Three people are called to the Torah. The third also reads the Hafṭarah, which comprises the entire Book of Jonah with the addition of the last three verses of the Book of Micah (Ṭur 622).

The Book of Jonah was chosen because it illustrates the power of repentance (*Levush, O.H.* 622:2; M. *Ta'an.* 2:1) and shows that man cannot escape the presence of God (*Abudraham Hashalem*). The reading is concluded with the usual benedictions up to מָגֵן דָּוִד (*O.H.* 622:2 in Rama). The benediction עַל הַתּוֹרָה is omitted, however, on Yom Kippur, because the offering ritual in the Temple referred to by the words וְעַל הָעֲבוֹדָה ended before Minḥah. In addition, this passage is not read on other fast days, and it was felt that in this respect no distinction should be made in the case of Yom Kippur (*O.H.* 622:2 in *M.A.* 2).

The Torah is returned to the ark. Ḥatsi Qaddish is said, followed by the ʻAmidah, which is the same as the one recited at Shaḥarit. The *Ḥazarat Hashats* includes *piyyuṭim* and Seliḥot which continue the theme of repentance and atonement. אָבִינוּ מַלְכֵּנוּ is not said after Minḥah in order to eliminate the possibility of delaying the Neʻilah service (R. Meir of Rothenburg, *Hagahot Maimuniyot* on *Mishneh Torah, Hil. Shevitat ʻAsor,* end of chap. 3).

24. Neʻilah

Neʻilah is a service specially added on Yom Kippur (B. *Pes.* 54b), though there is some indication that at one time every official fast day had a closing service (B. *Taʻan.* 24a). The name Neʻilah ("closing") is derived either from the closing of the Temple gates, which took place around this time of day, or from the symbolic closing of the gates of heaven at the end of Yom Kippur (P. *Ber.* 4:1). The Neʻilah service thus assumes the character of a final appeal that the twenty-four-hour day of self-deprivation and prayer now coming to a close should have its atoning affect (Arzt, *Justice and Mercy,* p. 272).

Samson Raphael Hirsch views Neʻilah as a recapitulation of the Divine service of the heart to which the entire day has been devoted, and of the message which we must now take with us as we seek to serve God through the activities of day-to-day living (*Horeb,* no. 657; see also *Levush* 623:2).

The service begins with אַשְׁרֵי and וּבָא לְצִיּוֹן. Normally these would have preceded Minḥah, but they are recited before Neʻilah instead, thus separating the two services. The Torah reading makes a similar distinction between Musaf and Minḥah (*Kol Bo* 70; Ṭur, *O.H.* 622 in *Beit Yosef*).

The ʻAmidah up to הַנִּסְתָּרוֹת וְהַנִּגְלוֹת אַתָּה יוֹדֵעַ at the end of אָשַׁמְנוּ is the same as the ʻAmidah of Minḥah except that we substitute the root חתם, "seal," for כתב, "write" (*O.H.* 623:2). Instead of the עַל חֵטְא which follows at Minḥah, two new prayers are said—אַתָּה נוֹתֵן יָד לַפּוֹשְׁעִים and אַתָּה הִבְדַּלְתָּ אֱנוֹשׁ מֵרֹאשׁ. These emphasize the idea that God is always ready to welcome and pardon sinners who repent.

At the *Ḥazarat Hashats* the ark is kept open during the entire service because this is the most important prayer of the entire day (*Levush, O.H.*

623:2, 4). In some synagogues the ark is opened only for important *piyyuṭim,* since the congregants are supposed to stand when the ark is open, and it is difficult for people who have become faint from fasting to stand too long. In either case, by keeping the ark open we give visible expression to the fundamental plea of Ne'ilah: "Open for us the gates of Heaven at the time when the portals close" (Munk, *World of Prayer,* 2:264).

As at the other services, *piyyuṭim* and Seliḥot are interwoven in the 'Amidah during *Ḥazarat Hashats*. The solemnity of the service is imparted not only by the prayers but also by the Nusaḥ, the music that has become characteristic of Ne'ilah.

After the 'Amidah אָבִינוּ מַלְכֵּנוּ is said even if Yom Kippur coincides with a Sabbath. We make this exception because Ne'ilah is the final moment of judgment and a plea for mercy is extremely appropriate (Shneur Zalman of Lyady, *Shulḥan 'Arukh* 623:9).

Yom Kippur comes to an end with the blowing of the Shofar, which marks the conclusion of the fast. It has been suggested that the Shofar is sounded at this point in memory of the Jubilee Year. In Temple times the beginning of the Jubilee was announced on the tenth day of Tishre (Yom Kippur), but since the reckoning of the fifty-year Jubilee cycle is no longer certain, we now do it every year (Rav Hai, quoted in *Abudraham Hashalem*).

Professor Louis Ginzberg saw this practice as an instance of the tendency to preserve vivid reminders of the Temple ritual in the Yom Kippur liturgy. In Temple times, the conclusion of every Yom Kippur, and of every Sabbath as well, was marked by the sounding of the Shofar, and this practice was continued even after the Temple was destroyed (Arzt, *Justice and Mercy,* p. 273).

The sounding of the Shofar is preceded by the recitation of שְׁמַע יִשְׂרָאֵל once, בָּרוּךְ שֵׁם כְּבוֹד three times, and יְיָ הוּא הָאֱלֹהִים seven times. After the Shofar is sounded, the congregants say לְשָׁנָה הַבָּאָה בִּירוּשָׁלָיִם (in Israel, בִּירוּשָׁלַיִם הַבְּנוּיָה). The Ne'ilah service concludes with Qaddish.

Many congregations defer the blowing of the Shofar until after Ma'ariv, a practice prompted by the desire to keep the congregants in the synagogue for the Ma'ariv service. Yom Kippur does not really end until Ma'ariv is concluded and Havdalah has been recited, but many people leave the synagogue once the Shofar has been sounded, and they will not stay for Ma'ariv if it is sounded after Ne'ilah. In addition to this consideration, however, there is good authority for the custom of sounding the Shofar after Ma'ariv (see *Ṭur, O.H.* 624 and *Abudraham Hashalem*).

25. Ma'ariv

The Ma'ariv for the conclusion of Yom Kippur is the same as the one said at the end of Sabbaths and other festivals. Havdalah is recited before עָלֵינוּ and לְדָוִד יְיָ אוֹרִי (Ps. 27). If Yom Kippur coincides with a Sabbath, the Sabbath Havdalah is recited. If it is a weekday, the benediction for spices and הִנֵּה אֵל יְשׁוּעָתִי are omitted (*O.H.* 624:3 in *M.A.* 2).

After the services the worshippers go home in a festive spirit, confident that God has graciously forgiven their sins. They break the fast joyously, since according to the Midrash, at the close of Yom Kippur a heavenly voice proclaims: "Go thy way, eat thy bread with joy, and drink thy wine with a merry heart; for God has already accepted thy works" (Eccles. Rabbah 9:7).

UNIT XVI

THE MINOR FESTIVALS

XVI.
The Minor Festivals

In addition to the major festivals that are prescribed in the Torah, there are several minor festivals of later origin. Since these do not have the sanctity of the major festivals, work is permitted. They are marked by special observances in the synagogue and home, and their meaning is elaborated by additions to the morning and evening liturgy. Chief among these minor festivals are Ḥanukkah and Purim. Both commemorate great deliverances of the Jewish people.

1. Ḥanukkah

"Now on the five and twentieth day of the ninth month, which is called the month of Kislew, in the hundred forty and eighth year, they rose up in the morning, and offered sacrifice according to the law upon the new altar of burnt offerings, which they had made. At the very season and on the very day that the Gentiles had profaned it, it was dedicated with songs, citherns, harps, and cymbals. . . . And so they kept the dedication of the altar eight days. . . . Moreover Judah and his brethren, with the whole congregation of Israel, ordained that the days of the dedication of the altar should be kept in their season from year to year for eight days, from the five and twentieth day of the month Kislew, with mirth and gladness" (I Macc. 4:52–59).

"What is Ḥanukkah? For the rabbis have taught: Commencing with the twenty-fifth day of the month of Kislew there are eight days upon which there shall be neither mourning nor fasting. For when the Greeks entered the Temple, they defiled all the oil that was there. It was when the might of the Hasmonean dynasty overcame and vanquished them that, upon search, only a single cruse of undefiled oil, sealed by the High Priest, was found. In it was oil enough for the needs of a single day. A miracle was wrought and it burned eight days. The next year they ordained these days a holiday with songs and praises" (B. *Shab.* 21b; for variations of the story, see *Pesiqta Rabbati,* ed. Meir Ish Shalom, p. 5a; *Megilat Ta'anit,* ed. Lichtenstein, p. 341).

These passages represent the two strands within the Jewish tradition regarding Ḥanukkah and its meaning, the one preserved in the Apocrypha, in First and Second Maccabees, and the other in the Talmud.

In the apocryphal books, the story of the people of Israel during the Hellenistic period places special stress on the battles and victories of the Hasmonean (Maccabee) family. The war fought by the Hasmoneans is given a religious meaning; it was a struggle against the suppression of Judaism, culminating in the purification and rededication of the Temple of Jerusalem. The rededication took eight days; hence the eight days of Ḥanukkah.

The Talmudic tradition, on the other hand, stresses the miracle of the cruse of oil and mentions the Hasmonean struggle only cursorily. It is remarkable that while the Talmud contains an entire tractate devoted to Purim, Ḥanukkah is not even mentioned in the Mishnah. The talmudic discussion begins with the question מַאי חֲנֻכָּה ("What is Ḥanukkah?"), as if the answer were not very well known.

The early authorities sensed that the Hasmonean victories had already lost their luster by the mishnaic period. Abudraham claims that while the Hasmoneans were initially pious, they sinned by making themselves the rulers of the Jewish state, an office not to be assumed by a priestly family. As Kohanim, the Hasmoneans had no right to take the royal scepter into their hands. Their punishment for this crime was eventually inflicted by Herod, who exterminated virtually all the Hasmoneans who were alive during his reign (*Abudraham Hashalem,* p. 201).

Rabbi Moses Sofer sees Rabbi Yehudah Hanassi as responsible for the omission of Ḥanukkah from the Mishnah. He says that Yehudah Hanassi, who claimed to be a direct descendant of King David, regarded the Hasmoneans as usurpers since they were not members of the Davidic dynasty (Rabinowitz, *Ḥol Umo'ed,* p. 65). It has been suggested that there was also a political reason for the fact that the Maccabees are not mentioned in the Mishnah. The Romans, who dominated Judaea during the period when the Mishnah was compiled, would have interpreted any emphasis on a Jewish war of independence as a sign of rebelliousness, and this might have had dire consequences for the entire community (see Kahana, *Sifrut Hahistoriah Hayisra'elit,* 1:61).

It is apparent that the Hasmonean dynasty had lost its glory by the time of the Mishnah, for the last of the Hasmoneans were guilty of the very things their forebears fought against; as a result, Ḥanukkah was well-nigh forgotten (Kahana, loc. cit.). In time the festival was reestablished, but now the stress was on the miracles that accompanied the rededication of the Temple, not on the victories of the Maccabees. Hence, when the Talmud asked מַאי חֲנוּכָּה the answer did not pertain to the Maccabean victories and rededication of the Temple, but rather to the miracle of the cruse of oil (B. *Shab.* 21a).

The talmudic tradition has obtained to our own day. The message of Ḥanukkah is expressed in the prophetic words of the Hafṭarah of the Sabbath of Ḥanukkah: "Not by might, nor by power, but by My spirit, saith the Lord of Hosts" (Zech. 4:6). In this spirit Dr. Kaplan says: "The striking feature of the celebration of Ḥanukkah is the fact that, although the occasion which it commemorates was incidental to a successful war of independence fought against an oppressive foreign ruler, that occasion itself was neither a victory on the field of battle nor a political transaction that gave official recognition to the hard-won independence of Judaea. Ḥanukkah commemorates the rededication of the Temple at Jerusalem to the God of Israel after it had been deliberately defiled by the Grecian rulers" (Kaplan, *The Meaning of God,* p. 330).

With the rise of Jewish nationalism, Ḥanukkah assumed a new importance; again the stress was shifted, this time back to the wars for political independence. The celebrations that heretofore were conducted at home and in the synagogue took the form of public demonstrations. The heroism of the Maccabees in liberating their country from foreign domination became a source of inspiration for nationalist endeavors (see *Sefer Hamo'adim, Ḥanukkah,* pp. 189–91, article by Joseph Klausner; Schauss, *The Jewish Festivals,* p. 230; Waxman, *Handbook of Judaism,* p. 73; Wahrman, *Ḥagei Yisra'el Umo'adaw,* p. 98).

This stress on the Maccabean struggle for independence reached its peak in Israel, where Ḥanukkah has become a patriotic celebration.

In America the proximity of a Christian holiday, and its prominence on the secular calendar, has influenced the celebration of Ḥanukkah both positively and negatively. The positive influence expresses itself in the greater and more widespread observance of Ḥanukkah. Negatively, Ḥanukkah has become more important to many American Jews than some of the major festivals on the Jewish calendar and is celebrated more and more lavishly in order to compete with the celebration of the non-Jewish holiday.

2. The Observance of Ḥanukkah

Ḥanukkah begins on the eve of the twenty-fifth day of Kislew and lasts eight days. Work is permitted during the eight days, but all signs of sadness are to be avoided. There is no fasting, and at funerals eulogies and צִדּוּק הַדִּין are omitted (*O.H.* 670:1; Rama on *O.H.* 683:1).

Ḥanukkah is marked by the kindling of lights at home and in the synagogue (hence it is also called חַג הָאוּרִים, the Festival of Lights). If oil is used for the Ḥanukkah lights, olive oil is preferred (*O.H.* 673:1). If candles are used, wax candles are preferred. The weight of rabbinic opinion opposes the use of an electric Menorah (*She'arim Metsuyanim Bahalakhah,* 3:240 f., quotes *Levush Mordekhai, Or Zar'ua, Pequdat El'azan, Bet Yitsḥaq,* see also Rabbi Y. E. Henkin in *'Edut Leyisra'el,* p. 122; *Mishpeṭei 'Uzi'el,* 1:25). In addition to the reasons cited in these sources, it should be noted that the use of candles or oil has great esthetic appeal and more sentimental meaning.

One light is kindled on the first night of Ḥanukkah; an additional light is added each succeeding night, so that eight lights are kindled on the eighth night (*O.H.* 671:2). The lights should be kindled after sundown (*O.H.* 672:1). Three benedictions are recited before the kindling of the lights on the first night: לְהַדְלִיק נֵר שֶׁל חֲנֻכָּה, שֶׁעָשָׂה נִסִּים לַאֲבוֹתֵינוּ בַּיָּמִים הָהֵם בַּזְּמַן הַזֶּה, and שֶׁהֶחֱיָנוּ וְקִיְּמָנוּ וְהִגִּיעָנוּ לַזְּמַן הַזֶּה (*O.H.* 676:1); the first two are also recited on each of the seven subsequent nights, but שֶׁהֶחֱיָנוּ is not (*O.H.* 676:1).

The first candle is placed on the right side of the Menorah. The second candle (on the second night) is placed directly to the left of the place occupied by the first candle, and so on, always moving leftward. The kindling starts on the left and moves toward the right. Thus the first candle to be lit each day is the candle added for that day (*O.H.* 676:5). הַנֵּרוֹת הַלָּלוּ is sung while kindling the lights, followed by מָעוֹז צוּר (*O.H.* 676:4). The Menorah should be placed where it is visible from outside the house in order to proclaim the miracle of Ḥanukkah to all passers-by—לְפַרְסוּמֵי נִסָּא (*O.H.* 671:5, B. *Shab.* 24a).

In addition to the candles that are lit for each day, there is a special candle known as the שַׁמָּשׁ. This extra candle is necessary because the Ḥanukkah lights themselves should not be used for kindling other lights—הַנֵּרוֹת הַלָּלוּ קֹדֶשׁ הֵם וְאֵין לָנוּ רְשׁוּת לְהִשְׁתַּמֵּשׁ בָּהֶם. The שַׁמָּשׁ is added, therefore, to be used in lighting the other candles and to provide illumination; it remains lit with the others (*O.H.* 673:1).

Ḥanukkah lights are lit in the synagogue as well as in the home, and the same laws apply. They are lit immediately before Ma'ariv (*O.H.* 671:7). Since the main idea is לְפַרְסוּמֵי נִסָּא, this is not a substitute for kindling the lights at home (ibid.).

For the same reason, it is customary to light candles in the synagogue before Shaḥarit each morning, but without the accompanying benediction (*Ziv Haminhagim,* p. 263, no. 26). This also serves as a reminder of how many candles must be lit in the evening (see Eisenstein, *Otsar Dinim Uminhagim,* p. 141).

On Friday night the Ḥanukkah lights are lit before the Sabbath candles (*O.H.* 678:1). Opinions differ regarding whether the Ḥanukkah candles should be lit before or after Havdalah in the synagogue (*O.H.* 681:2 and *M.D.* ad loc.). Our custom is to light before Havdalah (see *Ḥayyei Adam* 153:37; *Qitsur Shulḥan 'Arukh* 139:18).

3. Ḥanukkah Services

In the liturgy עַל הַנִּסִּים is added before וְעַל כֻּלָּם and in Birkat Hamazon before וְעַל הַכֹּל (*O.H.* 682:1). Taḥanun is not recited on Ḥanukkah, beginning with Minḥah on the eve of Ḥanukkah (*O.H.* 683:1). Complete Hallel is recited every morning after the 'Amidah (*O.H.* 683:1 in Rama). Since there is no Musaf on Ḥanukkah, and Hallel is thus not the end of the Shaḥarit service, only half-Qaddish is recited after Hallel (see *Ziv Haminhagim,* p. 263, no. 26; *Abudraham Hashalem,* p. 202). The complete Hallel is recited each day of Ḥanukkah because each day has its own individuality, as marked by the addition of a candle (*Abudraham Hashalem,* p. 202).

The Torah is read every morning and three people are called to the reading. The reading is from the Sidrah נָשֹׂא (Num. 7); it is known as פָּרָשַׁת נְשִׂיאִים because it tells of the gifts the princes of Israel brought at the dedication of the Tabernacle in the wildnerness.

On the first day the reading starts at the beginning of the chapter (the Sefardim start three verses earlier, with the Birkat Kohanim) and ends with verse 17 (*O.H.* 684:1).

There are variations in the manner in which the portion is divided into 'aliyot. According to one custom, we read up to בַּיּוֹם הָרִאשׁוֹן for Kohen, the first three verses of the next passage for Levi, and the last three verses for Shelishi. According to the other custom, the passage beginning with בַּיּוֹם הָרִאשׁוֹן is kept intact for Shelishi, and the first passage is divided between Kohen and Levi, the first four verses being read for Kohen, and the rest for

Levi (*O.H.* 684:1). The Rabbinical Assembly *Weekly Prayer Book* follows the latter custom.

On the second day the portion begins with verse 18—בַּיּוֹם הַשֵּׁנִי—which describes the offering of the second day. The first three verses are read for Kohen, the second three verses for Levi (*O.H.* 684:1), and the entire passage of בַּיּוֹם הַשְּׁלִישִׁי for Shelishi (Rama on *O.H.* 684:1).

The same order is followed each day except the sixth, which is also Rosh Ḥodesh Ṭevet (*O.H.* 684:3), the day or days of Ḥannukah that fall on a Sabbath, and the last day of Ḥanukkah, when we begin with בַּיּוֹם הַשְּׁמִינִי and complete the chapter up to and including the offering of the twelfth day, and the concluding passage beginning with זאת חֲנֻכַּת הַמִּזְבֵּחַ (*O.H.* 684:1). Because of the reading of this passage, the eighth day of Ḥanukkah is sometimes called זאת חֲנֻכָּה.

On the last day the reading begins with בַּיּוֹם הַשְּׁמִינִי. The paragraph is divided as on the other days: the first three verses for Kohen, the next three for Levi, and from בַּיּוֹם הַתְּשִׁיעִי through the end of the chapter for Shelishi.

On the sixth day, which is always Rosh Ḥodesh, two Torah scrolls are taken from the ark. In the first Torah scroll we read the portion prescribed for Rosh Ḥodesh (Num. 23:1–15), calling three people. In the second Torah scroll we read the prescribed portion for Ḥanukkah, בַּיּוֹם הַשִּׁשִּׁי, calling one person (*O.H.* 684:3). When Rosh Ḥodesh Ṭevet is observed for two days, the service follows the same procedure on the second day of Rosh Ḥodesh as on the first, except that the portion read from the second scroll begins with בַּיּוֹם הַשְּׁבִיעִי.

On the Sabbath two Torah scrolls are taken out. The Sidrah of the week is read from the first. The Mafṭir, which is the prescribed reading for that day of Ḥanukkah, is read from the second (*O.H.* 684:2). The Hafṭarah is Zechariah 2:14–4:4. It was chosen because it mentions the Menorah and also because it contains the verse "Not by might, nor by power, etc.," which has become the motto of Ḥanukkah.

Since Ḥanukkah lasts eight days, it will have two Sabbaths if the first day of the festival is a Sabbath. In such a case, we follow the same procedure on the second Sabbath as on the first, except that the Hafṭarah is from I Kings 7:40–50. This passage has a description of the furnishings of the Temple of Solomon, an appropriate reading on a holiday that celebrates the rededication of the Second Temple.

If Rosh Ḥodesh and the Sabbath coincide, three Torah scrolls are taken out. The Sidrah of the week is read from the first, and six people are given ʿaliyot. The passage for Rosh Ḥodesh (Num. 28:9–15) is read from the second for the seventh 'aliyah. The Qaddish is then recited. The prescribed reading for the sixth day of Ḥanukkah is read from the third. The Hafṭarah is that of Ḥanukkah (*O.H.* 684:3). The services for the day incorporate the special prayers of both Ḥanukkah and Rosh Ḥodesh; i.e., complete Hallel, the Musaf 'Amidah of Rosh Ḥodesh and עַל הַנִּסִּים in each 'Amidah (*O.H.* 682:2). On the Sabbath of Ḥanukkah אַב הָרַחֲמִים and צִדְקָתְךָ צֶדֶק are omitted (Rama on *O.H.* 683:1) since they are omitted on any Sabbath on which, were it a weekday, Taḥanun would not be said (*O.H.* 292:2).

Many festive customs are associated with Ḥanukkah. Special games (dreidl) and special foods (latkes or pancakes) are characteristic of the holiday. In America Ḥanukkah has become an occasion for the exchanging of gifts, especially for children (*Ziv Haminhagim,* pp. 262–63, nos. 24, 25). Plays and celebrations are held in religious schools. At home there is special emphasis on the children's participation in the lighting of the candles (*O.H.* 675:3). The festival thus recalls to us a great act of faith, commemorating the liberation of our people בַּיָּמִים הָהֵם בַּזְּמַן הַזֶּה, "in those days, at this season." Today Ḥanukkah symbolizes the struggle of "the few against the many, the weak against the strong," the eternal battle of the Jewish people for its faith and its existence. To the world it proclaims the eternal message of the prophet Zechariah: "Not by might, nor by power, but by My spirit."

4. Purim

"The Jews ordained and took upon themselves and upon their descendants . . . that these days of Purim should not cease from among the Jews, nor the memory of them perish from among their descendants . . . to observe these days of Purim at their appointed time" (Esther 9:27–31).

The festival of Purim is based on the story in the Book of Esther. While scholars have had difficulty in identifying the time and the characters of the story, there is no doubt that Jewish tradition and the Jewish people have accepted the event as authentic, and the celebration of Purim as based on a firm foundation. Unlike Ḥanukkah, which is postbiblical and is not even mentioned in the Mishnah, Purim is based on a book of the Bible; a tractate of the Mishnah and Talmud is devoted to it as well.

Purim attained great popularity because it reflected the perennial problem of the Jewish people—animosity against the Jew. Haman's accusation—"There is a certain people scattered abroad and dispersed among the peoples . . . " (Esther 3:8)—has been repeated in every age. The celebration of Purim serves to strengthen our people, enabling them to face such accusations with dignity and courage, and inspiring them with the hope of final victory over their enemies.

Elaborating on this point Professor Kaplan says: "Out of the reaction of the Jews in the past to their status as a minority everywhere in the diaspora there evolved a remarkable philosophy of life or system of spiritual values. It is remarkable not only for its influence in sustaining the courage of the Jew in desperate situations, but for its inherent worth. Being in the minority, Jews were expected to accept the life-pattern of a conquered people. They were expected to adopt the standards imposed on them by the majority, with good grace, if they could, or with sullen resentment, if they must. They did neither. Instead they formulated a philosophy of life which prevented the conquest from being consummated" (*The Meaning of God,* p. 363).

The corollary of this is not that we face hatred with faith and courage, but rather that we find meaning in the minority status that so often makes us the target for the slings and arrows of our enemies. "It is therefore necessary," says Professor Kaplan, "as it is appropriate, to make of the Feast of Purim, and of the special Sabbath preceding it, an occasion for considering anew the difficulties that inhere in our position as 'a people scattered and dispersed among the nations.' It is important that Jews know the nature of these difficulties in order that they may the better equip themselves to meet them. Those days should make Jews conscious of the spiritual values which their position as a minority group everywhere in the diaspora should lead them to evolve, and of the dangers which they must be prepared to overcome, if they expect to survive as a minority group" (ibid., pp. 361–62).

It is perhaps for this reason that the rabbis said that even when all the other festivals are abolished, Purim will remain (*Midrash Mishle* 9:2).

5. The Observance of Purim

The Sabbath preceding Purim is called שַׁבָּת זָכוֹר, the Sabbath of Remembrance. It is one of the אַרְבַּע פָּרָשִׁיּוֹת preceding Pesaḥ, discussed in unit 7 in connection with Pesaḥ. Its association with Purim is based on the tradition that Haman was a descendant of the tribe of Amalek. Furthermore, Amalek and Haman had in common the desire to annihilate the Jewish people, and both were frustrated in their designs.

The day before Purim, the thirteenth of Adar, is a fast day. If Purim is on a Sunday, the fast day is observed on the preceding Thursday (*O.H.* 686:2).

The four statutory public fasts will be discussed later (see next unit). They are observed in memory of the tragic events connected with the destruction of Jerusalem and the loss of the Jewish state. The Fast of Esther is a statutory public fast of a similar nature, but it is connected with another calamity that threatened the existence of the Jewish people. The precedent for this fast is found in the Book of Esther. When Mordecai informed Esther of Haman's plans, she asked him to proclaim a three-day fast (Esther 4:16). It is in memory of this that we fast on the day before Purim (*O.H.* 686:1).

Noting that the fast proclaimed by Esther was not on the thirteenth of Adar, some authorities offer a different explanation. When the children of Israel gathered together on the thirteenth of Adar to defend themselves against their enemies, they were in a state of war, and preparations for war always included a public fast (see *O.H.* 686 in *Mishnah Berurah* 2; *Ziv Haminhagim,* p. 275, no. 7).

A modern commentator suggests that the Jews fasted on the thirteenth of Adar because they were so occupied with defending themselves that they had no opportunity to eat (Rabinowitz, *Ḥol Umo'ed,* p. 72; Munk, *World of Prayer,* 2:311).

Since the fast of the thirteenth of Adar is not explicitly mentioned in the Bible, the rabbis were lenient about its observance (*O.H.* 686:7 in Rama; *Ziv Haminhagim,* p. 275).

The primary observance connected with Purim is the reading of the Book of Esther, usually called the מְגִלָּה (Scroll). It is read twice: in the evening, after the 'Amidah of Ma'ariv and before עָלֵינוּ; and in the morning after the Torah reading (B. *Meg.* 4a; *O.H.* 687:1).

The Megillah is read from a parchment scroll that is written the same way a Torah is written—i.e., by hand, and with a goose quill (*O.H.* 690:3). If there is no such scroll available, the congregation may read the Book of Esther from a printed text, without the accompanying benedictions.

The Megillah is chanted according to a special cantillation used only in the reading of the Book of Esther. If no one is present who knows this cantillation, it may be read without the cantillation, as long as it is read correctly (*Qitsur Shulḥan 'Arukh* 141:18). It may be read in the language of the land (*O.H.* 690:9). In practice, however, reading the Megillah in any but the original language is to be avoided (*'Arukh Hashulḥan, O.H.* 690:16). Today in particular, when we seek to emphasize the use of the sacred tongue whenever possible, we should not encourage any deviation from the prevailing practice.

Before the reading, the scroll is unrolled and folded to look like a letter of dispatch, thus further recalling the story of the great deliverance (Maimonides, *Hil. Megillah* 2:12). The reading is preceded by three benedictions and followed by one (*O.H.* 692:1). The three before the reading are עַל מִקְרָא מְגִלָּה, שֶׁעָשָׂה נִסִּים לַאֲבוֹתֵינוּ, and שֶׁהֶחֱיָנוּ. The benediction following the reading is הָרָב אֶת רִיבֵנוּ.

The Megillah must be read standing and from the scroll, not by heart (*O.H.* 690:1, 7). During the reading the following four verses, termed "verses of redemption" (פְּסוּקֵי גְאֻלָּה), are said aloud by the congregation and then repeated by the reader:

אִישׁ יְהוּדִי הָיָה בְּשׁוּשַׁן הַבִּירָה . . . (ב:ה)
וּמָרְדְּכַי יָצָא מִלִּפְנֵי הַמֶּלֶךְ בִּלְבוּשׁ מַלְכוּת . . . (ח:טו)
לַיְּהוּדִים הָיְתָה אוֹרָה . . . (ח:טז)
כִּי מָרְדְּכַי הַיְּהוּדִי . . . (י:ג)

At certain key points in the story the reader raises his voice. These are:

לִהְיוֹת כָּל אִישׁ . . . (א:כב)
וְהַנַּעֲרָה אֲשֶׁר תִּיטַב בְּעֵינֵי הַמֶּלֶךְ . . . (ב:ד)
וַיֶּאֱהַב הַמֶּלֶךְ אֶת אֶסְתֵּר . . . (ב:יז)
רֶוַח וְהַצָּלָה יַעֲמוֹד לַיְּהוּדִים . . . (ד:יד)
יָבוֹא הַמֶּלֶךְ וְהָמָן . . . (ה:ד)

and especially בַּלַּיְלָה הַהוּא נָדְדָה שְׁנַת הַמֶּלֶךְ (ו:א), which is the turning point of the entire story (*Ziv Haminhagim*, p. 277).

The verses enumerating the ten sons of Haman (Esther 9:7–10) are said in one breath to signify that they died together (B. *Meg.* 16b). Another reason has also been suggested: We should avoid the appearance of gloating over their fate, even though it was deserved (Vainstein, *Cycle of the Jewish Year*, p. 135).

It is a widespread Purim custom for the listeners at the Megillah reading to make noise, usually with special noisemakers called graggers, whenever Haman's name is mentioned. This is an outgrowth of a custom once prevalent in France and the Provence, where the children wrote the name on smooth stones, then struck them together whenever Haman was mentioned in the reading so as to rub it off, as suggested by the verse, "the name of the wicked shall rot" (Prov. 10:7; *Abudraham Hashalem*, p. 209; *O.H.* 690:17 in Rama). In some places this practice is discouraged because it makes it difficult for worshippers to hear the reader (ibid. and also in *Mishnah Berurah*, n. 59 and n. 57 thereto of Sha'ar Hatsiyun).

The Megillah should be read in the synagogue in the presence of a minyan. If a minyan is not available it may be read even for one individual (*O.H.* 690:18). Those who cannot attend services in the synagogue may read the Megillah at home (Rama on *O.H.* 690:18).

6. Shushan Purim

"But the Jews that were in Shushan assembled together on the thirteenth day thereof, and on the fourteenth thereof; and on the fifteenth day of the same they rested, and made it a day of feasting and gladness. Therefore do the Jews of the villages, that dwell in the unwalled towns, make the fourteenth day of the month of Adar a day of gladness and feasting" (Esther 9:18–19).

From these verses the sages derived the view that Purim was celebrated on the fifteenth of Adar, as in Shushan, in cities that had been walled since the days of Joshua (M. *Meg.* 1:1; *O.H.* 688:4 and in *M.A.* 4). In the towns of the Ashkenazic diaspora this is academic because there are no cities that ancient (*Levush, O.H.* 688:4). In Jerusalem, however, Purim is observed on the fifteenth of Adar. There are also cities which are in a doubtful category, such as Jaffa, Safed, Akko, Tiberias, and Lydda; in these the Megillah is read on both the fourteenth and the fifteenth of Adar. On the fifteenth it is read only at night and without the accompanying benedictions (*Shanah Beshanah 5727,* p. 59; *O.H.* 688:4).

7. Purim Services

The services on Purim are the same as on other weekdays except for the following variations. עַל הַנִּסִּים is added before וְעַל כֻּלָּם in the 'Amidah and before וְעַל הַכֹּל in the Birkat Hamazon (*O.H.* 693:2, 3); Taḥanun is not said at Minḥah the night before, in the morning, or in the evening (*O.H.* 693:3, 697:1); לַמְנַצֵּחַ is also omitted (*O.H.* 693:3).

The Torah is read in the morning, with three people given 'aliyot. The reading is from Exodus 17:8–16, beginning with וַיָּבֹא עֲמָלֵק (*O.H.* 693:4).

The rabbis sought to understand why Hallel is not recited on Purim (*O.H.* 693:3). The Talmud explains that the redemption represented by Purim was not complete. True, the Jews were saved from the annihilation plotted by Haman, but they still remained subject to Ahasuerus (B. *Meg.* 14a), whereas after the redemption commemorated by Pesaḥ they ceased to be subjects of Pharaoh, and after Ḥanukkah they were no longer subject to Antiochus (*Levush, O.H.* 693:3; *O.H.* in *M.D.* 2). Moreover, the reading of the Megillah performs the function of Hallel (*Levush, O.H.* 693:3). The Talmud also explains that Hallel is not said for events that took place outside the land of Israel (B. *Meg.* 14a).

Shushan Purim is celebrated as a semi-holiday; Taḥanun is not said, and one should not fast, give a eulogy, or say צִדּוּק הַדִּין (*O.H.* 696:3, 697:1).

During a leap year, it is the usual practice to do all things that must be done during the month of Adar during First Adar, in conformity with the principle that "one must not pass by precepts" (B. *Pes.* 64b). Purim, however, is celebrated only during Second Adar (M. *Meg.* 1:4). The Talmud suggests that since Purim and Pesaḥ both celebrate the deliverance of Israel, they should occur close to one another (*Levush, O.H.* 697). First Adar is not neglected completely, however. On the fourteenth and fifteenth of First Adar, Taḥanun is omitted, no eulogy is said, and fasting is not permitted (B. *Meg.* 6b; *O.H.* 697:1). It is therefore called פּוּרִים קָטָן (*'Arukh Hashulḥan, O.H.* 697:2).

Opinions differ as to whether a person who is sitting Shiv'ah should continue to observe Shiv'ah on Purim (*O.H.* 696:4). The prevalent practice is for mourners to come to the synagogue, sit on a regular chair, and wear their shoes. As on the Sabbath, however, they should observe דְּבָרִים שֶׁבְּצִנְעָה, and the day of Purim counts as one of the days of Shiv'ah (Rama on *O.H.* 696:4; *Ḥayyei Adam* 154:36).

There is also a difference of opinion regarding weddings on Purim. Some authorities oppose them on the principle of אֵין מְעָרְבִין שִׂמְחָה בְּשִׂמְחָה, "we do not mix one joyous occasion with another," (B. *Mo'ed Qatan* 8b, 9a; *O.H.* 696:8 in *M.A.* n. 18; *'Arukh Hashulḥan* 696:12; *Maharam Schick, O.H.* 345). Others permit them (*O.H.* 696:8 in *Sha'arei Teshuvah,* n. 12; Ṭur, *O.H.* 698 in *Beit Yosef* and *Ḥayyei Adam* 154:39). The weight of opinion is with the latter position.

8. Purim Customs

"And Mordecai wrote these things, and sent letters unto all the Jews that were in all the provinces of the king Ahasuerus both nigh and far, to enjoin them that they should keep the fourteenth day of the month of Adar, and the fifteenth day of the same, the days wherein the Jews had rest from their enemies, and the month which was turned unto them from sorrow to gladness and from mourning unto a good day; that they should make them days of feasting and gladness, and of sending portions one to another and gifts to the poor" (Esther 9:20–22).

This order by Mordecai provides the basis for all the practices ordained and adopted in connection with Purim, with the exception of the reading of the Megillah.

The "feasting and gladness" are expressed by the סְעוּדַת פּוּרִים, an especially festive meal held in the afternoon before sundown (*O.H.* 695:2). In order to heighten the joy at this meal, the rabbis even allowed an unusual amount of levity. Well known is the statement in the Talmud: "Rava said: A person should be so exhilarated [with drink] on Purim that he does not know the difference between 'cursed be Haman' and 'blessed be Mordecai'" (B. *Meg.* 7b). The later authorities tried hard to lessen the exuberance of this command. Since they could not condone intoxication, they suggested that the passage means that one may drink more than he does usually (*O.H.* 695:2 in Rama). It was also ingeniously suggested that the numerical values of "cursed be Haman" and "blessed be Mordecai" are the same; to be unable to discover this does not require a very high degree of intoxication. (See *Abudraham Hashalem* for other interpretations. The most rational is the one quoted from Ba'al Haminhagot. According to him, there were responsive readings where the responses to the reader were "cursed be Haman" and "blessed be Mordecai." Naturally it was necessary to know when the one was called for, and when the other. Again, one did not have to be highly intoxicated to confuse the responses.)

The permissiveness in regard to imbibing on Purim was explained on the ground that imbibing was very much involved in the story of Purim. Vashti fell from grace when "the heart of the king was merry with wine" (Esther 1:10), which resulted in Esther becoming the queen. When Esther became queen there was a similar banquet (Esther 2:18). Haman's downfall started with the drinking of wine (Esther 7:1, 2; *O.H.* 695:2 in *M. D.*, note 1).

It was customary in Eastern Europe for youngsters at the סְעוּדַת פּוּרִים to be disguised in costumes and to sing humorous Purim songs or render humorous dramatic recitations, usually of their own composition. Each country and each generation, dating back to talmudic times (B. *San.* 64b), had its own form of merrymaking.

In European countries, where a carnival with parades, pantomimes, and masquerades took place at about the same season of the year, the celebration of Purim was influenced by the customs of the environment. Consequently, on this day plays were produced representing scenes from the events related in the Megillah, and at times also from other biblical stories. The amateur players were known as Purim Shpielers (Waxman, *Judaism*, p. 74). Sometimes women were dressed in the garb of men, and vice versa. This would normally have been forbidden, but it was permitted in the case of Purim since the object was merrymaking (Responsa of R. Yehudah Mintz, 16, quoted in *Maṭeh Mosheh* 1014; also *O.H.* 696:8 in Rama; see also Maimon, *Ḥagim Umo'adim*, pp. 121–23).

In America, not counting the reading of the Megillah, the celebration of Purim found its widest expression in the religious schools. It is in the schools that we have Purim plays, carnivals, masquerade contests, and Queen Esther crownings. Some adult organizations also have Purim masquerade balls and parties.

In Israel, Purim, like Ḥanukkah, has experienced a great revival, with emphasis on the national theme. One specific innovation is the עַדְלָיָדַע. The name is based on the talmudic statement mentioned above: עַד דְּלָא יָדַע בֵּין „אָרוּר הָמָן" לְ„בָרוּךְ מָרְדְּכַי". It is an elaborate, well-organized parade with floats, bands, marchers, costumes, and dancing in the streets and squares of the city (Wahrman, *Ḥagei Yisra'el Umo'adaw*, p. 126).

Another practice is that of מִשְׁלוֹחַ מָנוֹת (*O.H.* 695:4). Families, especially the women, exchange gifts of foods and pastries.

The custom of giving gifts to the poor on Purim has become a casualty of our modern system of organized charities. In ages past, it was ordained that on Purim people were to be extra generous, giving to all who asked without question (*O.H.* 694:1, 3). It is still customary in many congregations to put collection plates on a table in the vestibule of the synagogue. The contributions are called מַחֲצִית הַשֶּׁקֶל money, in memory of the half-sheqel that was collected in ancient days around Purim-time for the upkeep of the Temple in Jerusalem.

The only special food for Purim is hamantashen, a three-cornered pastry filled with poppy seed (the original name was *muntashen—mun* being the Yiddish word for "poppyseeds"). In Hebrew this pastry is called אָזְנֵי הָמָן, based on the older name *Haman Ohren* or, in Italian, *Orrechi d'Aman* (*Jewish Encyclopedia*, s.v. "Purim"). In old illustrations Haman is pictured wearing a three-cornered hat, and this may have given rise to the three-cornered pastry.

The many community and family Purims of Jewish history are a unique development connected with Purim. These private holidays were instituted to commemorate great deliverances experienced by individual communities or families. They were celebrated with festivities, and often with the reading of a scroll telling the story of the deliverance (for examples of these scrolls, see Ginsburger, "Deux Pourims Locaux"; on local Purims, see Roth, "Some Revolutionary Purims," and "Supplement," *Jewish Encyclopedia*, s.v. "Purim"; *Ḥagim Umo'adim*, p. 161).

The festival of Purim offers Jews a powerful lesson, teaching them not to despair even when dangers are most threatening and persecution most cruel. Its festivities cheered the Jew in his darkest moments and assured him that deliverance was at hand. No wonder that the sages took literally the Book of Esther's promise that "these days of Purim shall not disappear from among the Jews, nor the memory of them perish from their descendants" (9:28), and therefore said: "All the festivals will cease, but the days of Purim will not cease" (*Midrash Mishle* 9; see also P. *Meg*. 1:6).

UNIT XVII

PUBLIC FASTS

Fasting
The Four Fasts
The Fast of the Seventeenth of Tamuz
The Three Weeks
Tisha'ah Be'av
Other Public Fasts
Individual Fasts

XVII.
Public Fasts

1. Fasting

As an expression of piety, fasting goes back to antiquity. Abstinence from food and drink was also thought to induce a susceptibility to visions and dreams in which one had direct access to the realities of the spiritual world (*Interpreter's Dictionary of the Bible,* s.v. "Fast, Fasting"). Alternately, fasting could be a sign of sorrow; a person who felt alienated from God could not eat because he was so distressed. In some cases, moreover, abstinence from meat and drink was prescribed as preparation for a sacred meal (Smith, *Religion of the Semites,* p. 134).

In biblical times fasts were proclaimed when danger threatened, and also served as a call to penitence and an opportunity for worship and prayer (Esther 4:3, 16; Neh. 9:1; Joel 2:15; Jonah 3:5). Fasting was a sign of mourning when calamity occurred. It was also an ascetic practice, one of a series of purificatory rites (Hastings, *Encyclopedia of Religion and Ethics,* s.v. "Fasting").

Since there is no ascetic strain in Judaism (Moore, *Judaism,* 2:263 ff.), Jewish fasting was rather a manifestation of piety springing from a desire for meritorious living in line with the ethical emphasis of the Bible. Hence the choice of Isaiah 58 as the Hafṭarah for Yom Kippur. According to the Talmud, on fast days an elder would address the people, saying: "My brethren, it is not sackcloth and fasts which cause forgiveness, but repentance and good deeds; for so we find of the men of Nineveh that it is not said of them that God saw their sackcloth and fasts, but that 'God saw their works that they turned from their evil ways' [Jonah 3:10]" (B. *Taan.* 16a).

Judaism includes fasts of three kinds: (1) statutory public fasts, (2) public fasts decreed on special occasions, and (3) private fasts.

There are six statutory public fasts. First in importance is Yom Kippur, the most prominent, and a category by itself because it is the only fast explicitly commanded in the Torah. The other five statutory public fasts, though mentioned in the Bible, were actually ordained by the sages. Of these, the Fast of Esther has already been discussed (see above, p. 233 f.). The remaining four public fasts are Tish'ah Be'av, the seventeenth day of Tamuz, the tenth of Ṭevet, and Tsom Gedaliah. In addition, special public fasts were sometimes imposed by the religious authorities in the face of calamities or governmental decrees that threatened the Jewish community (Maimonides, *Hil. Ta'aniyot* 1:4; *O.H.* 576).

Private fasts were of two kinds: special fasts that an individual vowed in time of danger or as an act of piety (*O.H.* 563, 568, 569, 578, 288), and fasts that were customary in connection with certain events in the life cycle, such as the fast of a bride and groom on their wedding day (*O.H.* 573 in *M.A.* 1), and the fast on the day of a parent's Yahrzeit (*O.H.* 568:7–8 and *Y.D.* 402:12 in Rama).

The four public fasts are all connected with the destruction of Jerusalem and the Temple, and the loss of the Jewish state. Without the longing for a return to Israel that was fostered by these fasts, memories would have grown dim. Mourning for Jerusalem preserved the Jewish people's yearning for the restoration of the holy city, strengthened their historical consciousness, and kept alive the bond that tied them to their past. Thus, Israel's restoration in our time resulted from the harnessing of energies that had been stored in the Jewish soul for centuries. As days of national mourning, the four public fasts still serve to recall the calamities that have befallen the Jewish nation, making each generation, as it were, participate in those misfortunes (Maimonides, *Hil. Ta'aniyot* 5:1).

Dr. Robert Gordis suggests that there is a universal dimension to the four public fasts. The banishment from the holy land was understood as divine retribution visited on the children of Israel because of their lack of faith in the teachings of the Torah. Restoration was promised if the Jewish people would change their ways. The lessons taught by the four fasts tended further to confirm Israel's faith in God's direction of history, and especially in His providential concern with the destiny of the Jewish people. This focuses attention on the Messianic hopes of all mankind, which have long been integral to Judaism (see Gordis, *Judaism for the Modern Age,* p. 207).

The sad but beautiful dirge chanted on Tish'ah Be'av, אֱלִי צִיּוֹן, enumerates the things that we bemoan in connection with the destruction of Jerusalem. One of these is עֲלֵי שִׁמְךָ אֲשֶׁר חֻלָּל. We weep for the desecration of the name of God that results from man's iniquity, and we pray that with the end of exile there will also be an end to גָּלוּת הַשְּׁכִינָה (Maimonides, *Hil.*

Ta'aniyot 5:1; Munk, *World of Prayer,* 2:137; Greenstone, *The Jewish Religion,* p. 115).

2. The Four Fasts

"Thus saith the Lord of hosts: The fast of the fourth month, and the fast of the fifth, and the fast of the seventh, and the fast of the tenth, shall be to the house of Judah joy and gladness and cheerful seasons" (Zech. 8:19).

The Talmud and the codes enumerate a large number of fasts (*O.H.* 580:2). All eventually fell into desuetude (ibid. in *M.A.*), with the exception of the four mentioned by Zechariah and the Fast of Esther. The four fasts mentioned by Zechariah are interpreted in the Talmud as follows: צוֹם הָרְבִיעִי refers to the seventeenth of Tamuz, which falls in the fourth month if we count Nisan as the first month; צוֹם הַחֲמִישִׁי refers to Tish'ah Be'av, which falls in the fifth month; צוֹם הַשְּׁבִיעִי refers to the Fast of Gedaliah, which falls in Tishrei, the seventh month; and צוֹם הָעֲשִׂירִי refers to the tenth of Ṭevet, which comes in the tenth month (B. *R.H.* 18b).

3. The Fast of the Seventeenth of Tamuz

The seventeenth of Tamuz marks the beginning of the destruction of Jerusalem, for it is the day on which the Romans breached the walls encircling the city (M. *Ta'an.* 4:6). During the siege preceding the first destruction of Jerusalem, the wall was breached on the ninth of Tamuz (Jer. 39:2), but both events are commemorated on the same date.

The rabbis mention a number of other calamities that were believed to have occurred on the seventeenth of Tamuz: the breaking of the Tablets by Moses; the cessation of the daily sacrifices (קָרְבַּן תָּמִיד) during the Roman siege of Jerusalem; the burning of the Torah and the erection of an idol in the Temple by Apostomos during the period preceding the Maccabean revolt (M. *Ta'an.* 4:6).

The fast begins at sunrise and concludes at sunset of the same day. This applies to all fasts, with the exception of Yom Kippur and Tish'ah Be'av, both of which begin the preceding night (*O.H.* 550:2, 564).

The fast of the seventeenth of Tamuz also differs from Yom Kippur and Tish'ah Be'av in that fasting is the only restriction imposed; working and bathing as usual are permitted (ibid.; *Qitsur Shulḥan 'Arukh* 121:8).

The seventeenth of Tamuz is marked in the liturgy by additions to the regular daily service as well as some special variations. In the 'Amidah עֲנֵנוּ is added. The individual worshipper adds this prayer in the benediction of שְׁמַע קוֹלֵנוּ before כִּי אַתָּה שׁוֹמֵעַ. The reader says it as an additional benediction between רְאֵה and רְפָאֵנוּ during *Ḥazarat Hashats,* ending it with הָעוֹנֶה בְּעֵת צָרָה (*O.H.* 565:1–566:1).

There are several practices pertaining to the recitation of עֲנֵנוּ. According to one custom, both the congregants and the reader say it at Shaḥarit and again at Minḥah (*O.H.* 565:1; *Qitsur Shulḥan 'Arukh* 20:8). According to another custom, עֲנֵנוּ is said only at Minḥah since it should be said only by those who are fasting, and in the morning it is uncertain whether one will complete the fast, while at Minḥah one knows that he has fasted (*O.H.* 565:3 in Rama). The most prevalent custom, however, and the one followed in the Rabbinical Assembly *Weekday Prayer Book,* is for the reader to say עֲנֵנוּ at Shaḥarit, since he represents the whole congregation and it may be assumed that at least some of the congregants will complete the fast, and for both the individual worshippers and the reader to say it at Minḥah (ibid.; *Ziv Haminhagim* 124).

After the 'Amidah, both at Shaḥarit and at Minḥah, אָבִינוּ מַלְכֵּנוּ is recited (Singer, *Ziv Haminhagim* 124; *Siddur Otsar Hatefilot,* pp. 383 f.).

The Torah is read at both Shaḥarit and Minḥah. The reading, which is the same for both services, begins with Exodus 32:11. Four verses are read for the first 'aliyah. The rest of the chapter is skipped, and so is the next chapter, which tells of the sins of the children of Israel. The second 'aliyah continues with Exodus 34:1–34:3. The congregant called at Minḥah for the third 'aliyah, Exodus 34:4–34:10, also reads the Hafṭarah.

The verses שׁוּב מֵחֲרוֹן אַפֶּךָ (Exod. 32:12), יְהֹוָה יְהֹוָה אֵל רַחוּם וְחַנּוּן (Exod. 34:6), and וְסָלַחְתָּ לַעֲוֹנֵנוּ (Exod. 34:9) are said aloud, first by the congregation, and then by the reader (*Ziv Haminhagim* 124). These verses receive special attention because they are פְּסוּקֵי דְרַחֲמֵי (ibid.); their selection was prompted by the fact that they speak of God's mercy and His readiness to forgive. They are chanted with the cantillation used on the High Holidays as a further reminder that the fast calls for repentance and good deeds.

The Hafṭarah is Isaiah 55:6–56:8, which speaks of God's forgiveness to those who repent and of the redemption of Israel and the world. The benedictions are the same as on the Sabbath except that they conclude with מָגֵן דָּוִד.

If one of the four fasts coincides with a Sabbath, it is postponed until Sunday. The Fast of Esther is observed on the Thursday preceding Purim when Purim is on a Sunday (*O.H.* 550:3). The regular procedure is followed when a fast falls on a Friday (ibid.), but this pertains only to the tenth of Tevet, since the arrangement of the calendar makes it impossible for any of the other fasts to occur on a Friday (ibid. in *M.A.* 5).

Since the rabbis were lenient in formulating the regulations for the four fasts, pregnant women, nursing mothers, and the sick are exempted from the obligation to fast (*O.H.* 550:1 in Rama, and in *M.A.* 2).

4. The Three Weeks

The days between the seventeenth of Tamuz and the ninth of Av are considered days of mourning, for they witnessed the collapse of besieged Jerusalem, beginning with the breaching of the walls on the seventeenth of Tamuz, and culminating with the burning of the Temple on the ninth of Av. Since exactly three weeks passed between these two events, the period is known as the "three weeks." In rabbinic literature it is known as בֵּין הַמְּצָרִים, derived from the verse הִשִּׂיגוּהָ בֵּין הַמְּצָרִים (Lam. 1:3), which was interpreted as referring to the days between the seventeenth of Tamuz and the ninth of Av.

Weddings and other joyous celebrations should not take place during this period (*O.H.* 551:2 in Rama; *Qitsur Shulḥan 'Arukh* 122:1).

A further element of mourning is added during the "nine days" between the first and ninth of Av (M. *Ta'an.* 4:6—"When Av comes in, gladness must be diminished"). During this period the pious refrain from eating meat and drinking wine, except on the Sabbath or at a Se'udat Mitswah (*O.H.* 651:9), such as a Pidyon Haben or upon completing a treatise of the Talmud (*O.H.* 651:10 in Rama), and in addition they do not have their hair cut (*O.H.* 551:3).

The somber mood of the "three weeks" is accentuated by the תְּלָת דְּפֻרְעָנוּתָא, or special Hafṭarot, chanted on the Sabbath. On the first Sabbath the Hafṭarah is דִּבְרֵי יִרְמְיָהוּ (Jer. 1:1–2:3); on the second Sabbath it is שִׁמְעוּ דְבַר יְהֹוָה (Jer. 2:4–28, 3:4, 4:1–2); and on the third, the Sabbath preceding Tish'ah Be'av, it is חֲזוֹן יְשַׁעְיָהוּ (Isa. 1:1–27)—this Sabbath is called Shabbat Ḥazon, from the first word of its Hafṭarah.

If the seventeenth of Tamuz coincides with a Sabbath, there are four Sabbaths during the "three weeks." On the first of these the Hafṭarah is וְיַד יְהֹוָה הָיְתָה (I Kings 18:46–19:21); this passage is also the Hafṭarah of פָּרָשַׁת פִּינְחָס (*O.H.* 428:8; *Ziv Haminhagim* 128).

In some synagogues, during the "three weeks," it is customary to chant

לְכָה דוֹדִי, with the exception of the last two verses to the tune of אֱלִי צִיּוֹן, which concludes the קִינוֹת of Tish'ah Be'av (*Ziv Haminhagim* 128).

On Shabbat Ḥazon the Hafṭarah is chanted almost entirely to the tune of אֵיכָה (*O.H.* 282 in *M.A.* 14; *Ziv Haminhagim* 131). The verse אֵיכָה אֶשָּׂא לְבַדִּי (Deut. 1:12) in the Torah reading is also chanted to this tune.

5. Tish'ah Be'av

The ninth of Av is the saddest day in the Jewish calendar. The rabbis held that it was preordained to be a day of tragedy for the Jewish people. According to the Talmud, God marked the ninth of Av as a day of calamity because of an incident, recounted in Numbers 13–14, which took place on that day during the period of the sojourn in the wilderness. The spies (*meraglim*) sent to Canaan brought back a discouraging report, and the people, displaying ingratitude and a complete lack of faith in God's promises to them, tearfully bemoaned their lot. As a result, God declared: "You wept without cause; I will therefore make this an eternal day of mourning for you [*bekhiyah ledorot*]." It was then decreed that on the ninth of Av the Temple would be destroyed and the children of Israel would go into exile (B. *Ta'an.* 29a).

The destruction of Jerusalem and the loss of the Jewish state are not the only sad events that have occurred on the ninth of Av. The Mishnah enumerates the following: On the ninth of Av it was decreed against our fathers that they should not enter the Land of Israel (Num. 14:29), the Temple was destroyed both the first and the second times, Bethar was captured, and Jerusalem was ploughed up (M. *Ta'an.* 4:6).

It is a tragic coincidence that since the time of the Mishnah, many other calamitous events in Jewish history have occurred on the ninth of Av. On Tish'ah Be'av in 1290, King Edward I signed the edict compelling his Jewish subjects to leave England. The expulsion from Spain occurred on the same day in 1492. Tish'ah Be'av also marked the outbreak of World War I, beginning a long period of suffering for the Jewish people. Not only did this period witness the pogroms and massacres perpetrated against the Jews of Russia, Poland, and other countries of Eastern Europe, but it was also a prelude to World War II and the savage destruction of six million Jews.

Since the reestablishment of the Jewish state, it has been maintained in some quarters that Tish'ah Be'av and the other fasts connected with the destruction of Jerusalem have lost their meaning and should be discontinued. Some even claim that with the establishment of the Jewish state the prophecy of Zechariah has been realized, and therefore we should fulfill the second part of the prophecy, observing the fast days as festivals. (A sad precedent for this is Shabbetai Zvi's proclaiming Tish'ah Be'av a festival of joy.)

The opponents of this view insist that the fasts must still be observed since the redemption of Israel is not yet complete. For many years they supported their arguments by pointing out that even the city of Jerusalem was not wholly in Jewish hands, while much of the ancient land of Israel also remained under enemy domination.

Notwithstanding the changes in the political situation following the war of 1967, with Jerusalem now integrated into the State of Israel and the rest of the land under Israeli control, at least for the time being, there was and is no need for such apologetics. Though the fasts are a challenge for חַדֵּשׁ יָמֵינוּ כְּקֶדֶם, "renew our days as of old," the events commemorated by Tish'ah Be'av cannot be undone, and it is necessary to remember them, whether to establish continuity with our past, or, as Maimonides suggested, as a constant stimulus for repentance and good deeds.

Dr. Robert Gordis, after an extensive discussion of the question, concludes that the fast must be retained. "In sum," he writes, "Tisha B'av can perform these basic functions for Jews living in the middle of the twentieth century, with the state of Israel before them as a reality. It can keep Jews mindful of the tasks which lie ahead in the areas of Jewish religious rebirth and of ethical living, both in the state of Israel and throughout the world. It can focus attention upon the universal aspects of the Messianic hope, which have long been integral to Judaism. Finally, it can help to remind Jews of the long record of sacrifices and sufferings of past generations, and thus prevent the cultural degeneracy which would follow from the ignoring of the achievements of Galut or Diaspora" (Gordis, *Judaism for the Modern Age,* p. 210).

The fast of Tish'ah Be'av begins the night before, as does the fast of Yom Kippur, and therefore the last meal before the fast must be eaten before sunset. This meal, called the סְעוּדָה הַמַּפְסֶקֶת because it marks the boundary between the periods of eating and fasting, was characterized by certain mourning customs. As at the meal served to mourners after a funeral, it was customary to eat special foods that were signs of mourning, such as eggs and lentils. Some pious people went so far as to dip the bread in ashes and sit on the ground during the meal (*O.H.*·552 in Rama). While these expressions of mourning have fallen into desuetude, we retain the mood by keeping the meal modest and simple.

At Minḥah Taḥanun is not recited. If the day before Tish'ah Be'av falls on a Sabbath, צִדְקָתְךָ is omitted at Minḥah (*O.H.* 552:12 in Rama).

Before the Ma'ariv service the Parokhet is removed from the ark as a sign of mourning (*O.H.* 559:2 in Rama). As another sign of mourning, the congregants remove their shoes if they are made of leather (*O.H.* 554:16). It was once customary not to wear leather shoes during the whole of Tish'ah Be'av, but the practice is now limited by some to the time and place of the service (*O.H.* 554:17).

Ma'ariv is recited in a subdued voice and a mournful tone (*O.H.* 559:1 in Rama). The 'Amidah is followed by the complete Qaddish, including תִּתְקַבֵּל.

After Qaddish the worshippers sit on the ground or on stools (*O.H.* 559:3 in Rama) for the reading of אֵיכָה—the Book of Lamentations (*O.H.* 559:1–2). It is chanted in a special plaintive cantillation, and it is customary for the reader to raise his voice at the beginning of each chapter. The last verse, הֲשִׁיבֵנוּ אֵלֶיךָ, is recited aloud by the congregation, and then repeated by the reader (*O.H.* 559:1 in Rama). The chanting of אֵיכָה is followed by Qinnot, sorrowful hymns that emphasize the import of Tish'ah Be'av and lament the tragic events associated with it (*O.H.* 559:2). The Qinnot are followed by וְאַתָּה קָדוֹשׁ. On a Saturday night, when וְאַתָּה קָדוֹשׁ is recited the whole year, וִיהִי נוֹעַם is omitted (*O.H.* 559:2). וְאַתָּה קָדוֹשׁ is added after the Qinnot because it is necessary to follow the recitation of these lamentations with a prayer for the coming of the Messiah, who will put an end to our mourning. The introductory passage (וּבָא לְצִיּוֹן גּוֹאֵל), however, is not said because there is a tradition that the deliverance will not come at night (*Shibbolei Haleqeṭ* 267). Another reason for the omission is that this passage speaks of the Covenant of the Torah, and Tish'ah Be'av is one of the rare occasions when Torah study is not permitted (Munk, *World of Prayer,* 2:331; *O.H.* 554:1).

The complete Qaddish follows, but the verse תִּתְקַבֵּל is omitted, as in the prayers in a house of mourning (*O.H.* 559:4 in Rama). The same form is followed in the Qaddish after Shaḥarit but not at Minḥah. The reason for the omission is that in the Book of Lamentations we say שָׂתַם תְּפִלָּתִי (Lam. 3:8). If the gates of prayer are closed, it would be a contradiction to say תִּתְקַבֵּל (Kitov, *Sefer Hatoda'ah* 2:378).

In accordance with a tradition originating with Rabbi Meir of Rothenburg (ca. 1215–1293), the Ṭalit and Tefilin are not worn at Shaḥarit (*O.H.*

553:1), as an additional sign of mourning. The Tefilin are termed פְּאֵר, or "ornaments," and the Book of Lamentations says: "The Lord has cast down תִּפְאֶרֶת יִשְׂרָאֵל," which was interpereted as referring to the Tefilin (Munk, *World of Prayer,* 2:327).

The Shaḥarit service itself follows the pattern of the regular weekday service, except that the reader says עֲנֵנוּ before רְפָאֵנוּ during the repetition of the 'Amidah, as on all public fasts, and the Birkat Kohanim is omitted (*Qitsur Shulḥan 'Arukh* 124:3).

After the 'Amidah, neither Taḥanun nor אָבִינוּ מַלְכֵּנוּ is said. The Torah is taken from the ark and Deuteronomy 4:25–40 is read. Three people are called up, with the last also reading the Hafṭarah, Jeremiah 8:13–9:23, which is chanted according to the tune of אֵיכָה (*O.H.* 559:4 in Rama, and in *M.A.* 6).

After the Torah is returned to the ark, the worshippers sit on the ground or on low stools and recite Qinnot, followed by אַשְׁרֵי. The psalm לַמְנַצֵּחַ is omitted, but וּבָא לְצִיּוֹן is said, with the verse וַאֲנִי זֹאת בְּרִיתִי omitted because it mentions the studying of the Torah, which is not permitted on Tish'ah Be'av (*Qitsur Shulḥan 'Arukh* 124:3). After וּבָא לְצִיּוֹן the complete Qaddish without תִּתְקַבַּל is recited. The service ends with עָלֵינוּ, followed by the mourners' Qaddish. The psalm for the day is omitted. In places where אֵין כֵּאלֹהֵינוּ is said at the morning service, it is omitted on Tish'ah Be'av (*O.H.* 559:4 in Rama).

At Minḥah the Ṭalit and Tefilin are put on, and the prayers that were omitted in the morning (such as the psalm for the day) are recited. After אַשְׁרֵי the Torah is taken out and three people are called, the third also reading the Hafṭarah. Both the Torah reading and the Hafṭarah are the same as on the other public fasts. In the 'Amidah נַחֵם is added before the closing benediction of וְלִירוּשָׁלַיִם עִירְךָ, and עֲנֵנוּ before כִּי אַתָּה שׁוֹמֵעַ. The reader repeats these in the repetition of the 'Amidah but says עֲנֵנוּ as a separate benediction before רְפָאֵנוּ, as on the other public fasts (*Qitsur Shulḥan 'Arukh* 124:19). The Ma'ariv is the regular weekday service, and it marks the end of the fast. At the meal after the fast one should still abstain from meat and wine, since the burning of the Temple continued until the next day (*O.H.* 558; *Qitsur Shulḥan 'Arukh* 124:20).

Tish'ah Be'av is subject to the same limitations as Yom Kippur: abstention not only from food but also from bathing, anointing oneself, wearing leather shoes, and conjugal relations (*O.H.* 554:1). In addition, because of the joy it affords, the Sages forbade all study of sacred literature, with the exception of books that fit the mood of the day, such as the Book of Job, the parts of the Talmud and Midrash that tell of the destruction of Jerusalem, and parts of the Book of Jeremiah (*O.H.* 554:1, 2).

If Tish'ah Be'av falls on a Sabbath it is postponed to Sunday, since on the Sabbath one may neither fast nor mourn publicly (*O.H.* 551:3; 288; *Y.D.* 400:1).

If it falls on a Sunday, צִדְקָתְךָ is not recited at Minḥah of the Sabbath preceding it. In the Ma'ariv of Saturday night אַתָּה חוֹנַנְתָּנוּ is said; so is בּוֹרֵא מְאוֹרֵי הָאֵשׁ, but the Havdalah on wine is postponed until Sunday night. When Havdalah is said on Sunday night, the benedictions on light and spices are omitted (*O.H.* 556).

If there is a funeral on Tish'ah Be'av, the צִדּוּק הַדִּין is not said (*O.H.* 559:10 in Rama).

A mourner who is sitting Shiv'ah may go to the synagogue both morning and evening for אֵיכָה and Qinnot (*O.H.* 559:6).

Just as the weeks preceding Tish'ah Be'av are marked by practices that accentuate the sorrowful mood of the period, so the weeks following are marked by some practices that encourage a mood of comfort and consolation. During the seven weeks following Tish'ah Be'av we read Hafṭarot that comfort the children of Israel with the promise of the restoration of Zion. These are called שְׁבַע דְּנֶחָמְתָא. The first Sabbath after Tish'ah Be'av is called שַׁבָּת נַחֲמוּ because the first of these seven Hafṭarot begins with נַחֲמוּ נַחֲמוּ עַמִּי (Isa. 40:1) (*Ziv Haminhagim*, p. 137; *O.H.* 428:8).

6. Other Public Fasts

There are two other statutory public fasts, the Fast of Gedaliah and the Fast of the tenth of Ṭevet. The Fast of Gedaliah takes place on the third of Tishrei, the day following Rosh Hashanah, and it commemorates the slaying of Gedaliah ben Aḥikam, whom Nebuchadnezzar appointed governor of Judah after the first destruction of Jerusalem (Jer. 40:7–41:3; II Kings 25:22–26; B. *R.H.* 18b). Gedaliah's death was the final blow to any remaining hopes that the effects of Babylonian domination might be alleviated and that the Jewish state might survive.

The tenth of Ṭevet marks the beginning of the siege of Jerusalem by the forces of Nebuchadnezzar (B. *R.H.* 18b). It is thus connected with the destruction of Jerusalem.

Since its historical basis is tenuous, a suggestion has been made that we give new meaning to the tenth of Ṭevet by proclaiming it a commemoration of the six million who perished in the Nazi Holocaust. So far the response to this proposal has not been encouraging.

All the regulations pertaining to the seventeenth of Tamuz were prescribed for these fasts as well (*O.H.* 549:1; 550:1, 2).

In addition to the statutory public fasts, special public fasts were ordained when a particularly grave situation warranted an appeal for mass prayer and repentance (Maimonides, *Hil. Ta'aniyot,* 1:4; *O.H.* 576). In ancient times, the people were called upon to fast whenever danger threatened (Esther 4:3, 16; Neh. 9:1; Joel 2:15; Jonah 3:9). Since occasions of distress were frequent, we find many instances where the leaders of the community decreed fasts. Such special fasts were sometimes limited to one community or to a single country. The rules and regulations were the same as those applying to the statutory public fasts.

There are also some fasts that were widely observed at one time but have now become obsolete or are observed only by the very pious.

Fasting on the day before Rosh Ḥodesh was once widespread, particularly in Eastern Europe, and there was also a special service at Minḥah. This monthly fast was called Yom Kippur Qaṭan, and as the name signifies, it was a day of penitence. Yom Kippur Qaṭan is not mentioned in the Talmud or in the *Shulḥan 'Arukh* of Caro, and the observance is ascribed to the kabbalist Moses Cordovero (*Seder 'Avodat Yisra'el,* p. 319; *Peri Ḥadash, Laws of Rosh Ḥodesh* 417).

Some extremely pious individuals used to observe three days of fasting after Pesah and after Sukkot (*O.H.* 492:1). The usual practice was to wait for the end of Nisan or Tishre and fast on the first Monday, first Thursday, and second Monday of the following month. These fasts served as a penitence for any levity the people might have indulged in during the holiday festivities, just as Job did penance after his children's festivities (Job 1:5; *O.H.* 492:1 in *M.A.*). According to some authorities, these fasts were instituted because the change of the seasons following Pesaḥ and Sukkot brings with it the danger of disease, or ushers in a period when it is appropriate to pray for sufficient rain or dew (*Ziv Haminhagim* 252; *Maṭeh Mosheh* 716).

7. Individual Fasts

Certain fasts are not obligatory on the community but merely on certain individuals at certain times. For example, it is considered a mitswah to fast on the day of a parent's Yahrzeit (*Y.D.* 376:4 in Rama). Similarly, since the wedding day is a Yom Kippur for the bride and groom, and their sins are forgiven (P. *Bik.* 3:3), it is a praiseworthy custom for them to fast before the wedding ceremony (*Even Ha'ezer* 61:1; *O.H.* 573 in *M.A.* 1). A more sobering explanation is that the bride and groom may perform the marriage rites in an improper mood if they celebrate too much beforehand (*B.H.* ad loc. in *Even Ha'ezer; Mishnah Berurah* on *O.H.* 573:8). Nowadays we would add that the practice helps impress the bride and groom with the solemnity of marriage.

In former times, the members of the burial society (*ḥevra qadisha*) fasted on the day prior to the society's annual dinner, generally the seventh of Adar, the anniversary of the death of Moses, or the fifteenth of Kislew. They also visited the cemetery to ask pardon of the deceased if they had not shown proper reverence during the burial (see Eisenstein, *Otsar Dinim Uminhagim,* p. 122; *Sefer Hamo'adim,* p. 42).

In addition, a person who dropped a Torah scroll was obliged to fast; in certain places, those who saw the Torah fall were also obligated to fast (*Qitsur Shulḥan 'Arukh* 28:12; *O.H.* 44 in *M.A.* 8).

The fast of the first-born, Ta'anit Bekhorim, has already been mentioned in connection with Pesaḥ (see above, p. 109).

Individual fasting was also customary as an act of piety during a crisis or as an exhibition of sorrow or prayer during periods of suffering. For instance, David fasted when his child was sick (II Sam. 12:16). Nehemiah fasted when he learned of the sorry state of Jerusalem (Neh. 1:4). Ezra fasted when he heard about the deteriorating situation of the newly returned Jewish community (Ezra 9:3–6). Ahab fasted when he received evil tidings (I Kings 21:2–7).

Such individual fasts are mentioned frequently in the Talmud (B. *Git.* 55b; B. *Pes.* 68b; B. *M.K.* 25a; B. *B.M.* 33a). Although they deepened the piety of the people and helped them to develop self-discipline, the rabbis discouraged the practice where it led to asceticism (Maimonides, *Hil. Ta'aniyot* 3:1).

Today such fasts are rare and are practiced only by people of extreme piety.

UNIT XVIII

ROSH ḤODESH

XVIII.
Rosh Ḥodesh

I. Introduction

"The waxing and waning of the moon remind the pious of Israel's renewal. Even in its darkest wanderings, Israel, like the moon itself, is never lost; and Israel's return into the light is assured, so long as its children loyally cling to the paths which God's word hath shown unto them" (S. R. Hirsch, quoted in Hertz, *Authorised Daily Prayer Book,* p. 995).

"The waning of the moon was conceived by Kabbalists as a symbol of the exile of the Shekhina and the diminution of the power of holiness during the Exile, and its renewal as a symbol of the return to perfection in the age of Redemption."

In ancient days Rosh Ḥodesh was regarded as an important holiday and observed with great seriousness. It was a day for solemn convocation (Isa. 1:13), with special sacrifices (Num. 28:11–15) and with the sounding of the trumpets at the Sanctuary (Num. 10:10). It was a day of rejoicing (ibid.), family festivity (I Sam. 20:5), and cessation from work (Amos 8:5). It also had its solemn aspects (Isa. 1:13) since people sought religious instruction (II Kings 4:23) and worshipped (Isa. 66:23). Quite clearly, then, Rosh Ḥodesh was a major festival in biblical days, and it is often mentioned in association with the Sabbath and the Festivals.

Rosh Ḥodesh is now counted among the minor festivals, however, because in the course of the centuries, and especially after the destruction of the Temple, it lost its festive character. The only observances still associated with Rosh Ḥodesh are liturgical; there are no restrictions on work and no special rituals (*O.H.* 417:1). In former times pious women used to refrain from working on Rosh Ḥodesh (ibid.)—a custom based on the tradition that the women of the generation of the desert were rewarded with a festival of their own because they refused to cooperate when their husbands asked them to give their jewelry for the golden calf (*'Arukh Hashulḥan* 417:10, quoting *Pirqei DeRabbi Eli'ezer;* P. *Ta'an.* 1:6). Today, though, Rosh Ḥodesh differs from an ordinary weekday only in the order of the service, but it remains important because of its connection with the Jewish calendar.

2. The Jewish Calendar

Rosh Ḥodesh is the beginning of the new month. The length of a month in the Jewish calendar is determined by the time it takes for the moon to make one revolution around the earth as determined by the conjunction of the sun, moon, and earth in a line. This is called the מוֹלָד, i.e., the "birth" of the "new" moon. Such a revolution is completed in 29 days, 12 hours, 44 minutes, 3½ seconds. The technical formula used in Hebrew is כ״ט, י״ב, תשצ״ג; i.e., 29 days, 12 and 793/1080 hours, the hour being divided into 1,080 parts (חֲלָקִים).

Since a calendar month does not begin in the middle of the day because months are counted by days, not hours (B. *Meg.* 5a), it is necessary to add half a day to one month or subtract half a day from the next. As a result, the months alternate between twenty-nine and thirty days in length. The thirty-day month is מָלֵא, i.e., full or long; the twenty-nine-day month is חָסֵר, i.e., defective or short. There are some variations, however, due to factors that will be explained below. Nisan, Siwan, Av, Tishrei, Shevaṭ, and Adar I in a leap year are always מָלֵא; Iyar, Tamuz, Elul, Ṭevet, Adar II, and Adar in a nonleap year are always חָסֵר. Ḥeshwan and Kislew are sometimes full and sometimes defective. When a month is thirty days, the Rosh Ḥodesh of the next month is celebrated for two days because the thirtieth day of the month that has just passed is counted as the first day of Rosh Ḥodesh, and the first day of the next month, as the second day. Consequently, Nisan, Siwan, Av, Tishrei (only the first day of Rosh Hashanah is counted as Rosh Ḥodesh) always begin with one day of Rosh Ḥodesh; Iyar, Tamuz, Elul, Ḥeshvan, Adar I, and Adar II always begin with two days; Kislew and Ṭevet begin with either one day or two. For a concise summation, see the accompanying table, on p. 258.

These variations result from the solar-lunar structure of the Jewish calendar. The year in the Jewish calendar consists of twelve lunar months, but the festivals follow the solar year, since several of them (Pesaḥ, Shavu'ot, Sukkot) must take place in certain seasons, and the seasons are determined by the earth's annual revolution around the sun. Since the lunar year is roughly 354 1/3 days in length, while the solar year is roughly 365½

LENGTH OF MONTHS IN JEWISH CALENDAR

Month	Length	Days of Rosh Ḥodesh
Tishrei	30 days	1
Ḥeshwan	29 or 30	2
Kislew	29 or 30	1 or 2
Ṭevet	29	1 or 2
Shevaṭ	30	1
Adar	29	2
Adar I*	30	2
Adar II*	29	2
Nisan	30	1
Iyar	29	2
Siwan	30	1
Tamuz	29	2
Av	30	1
Elul	29	2

*Adar I and Adar II occur only during a leap year.

days, or about eleven days longer, the festivals would eventually fall in the wrong seasons if their occurrence followed the cycle of lunar months. For example, Pesaḥ would be celebrated eleven days earlier each succeeding year, and as a result would eventually be in the winter, and then in the autumn and summer, in violation of the biblical prescription that Pesaḥ must take place in the month of Aviv (Deut. 16:1), i.e., in the spring. Similarly, Shavu'ot must occur at the time of the early harvest and Sukkot in the fall.

To prevent this difficulty, the lunar calendar is regularly adjusted to keep it in conformity with the solar year. This is done through the periodic addition, or intercalation, of a thirteenth month, known as Second Adar, or Adar II, immediately after the normal month of Adar, which in leap years is known as First Adar, or Adar I. Since the discrepancy between the solar and lunar years amounts to 207 days every nineteen years, the "leap month" of Adar II is added to the third, sixth, eighth, eleventh, fourteenth, seventeenth, and nineteenth year of every nineteen-year period.

Now to explain why Ḥeshwan and Kislew are sometimes מָלֵא and sometimes חָסֵר. Neither the ordinary years nor the leap years are uniform in length. The ordinary years fluctuate between 353, 354, and 355 days, and the leap year fluctuates between 383, 384, and 385 days. The reason is as follows: The beginning of the astronomical month, we said, is the moment of the conjunction of the sun and the moon, i.e., the Hebrew מוֹלָד, when the moon is exactly between the earth and the sun, hence invisible. The first day of Tishrei, for instance, is fixed on the day of the מוֹלָד of Tishrei. There are, however, four exceptions, i.e. דְּחִיּוֹת, when we "postpone" the first day of Tishrei to the day after the מוֹלָד:

1. דְּחִיַּת אַדּ"וּ; לֹא אַדּ"וּ רֹאשׁ: Rosh Hashanah, the first day of the new year, may not occur on Sunday, Wednesday, or Friday. If Rosh Hashanah were on Sunday, Hosha'na' Rabbah would be on Saturday, and this must be avoided because it would prevent the proper celebration of the day. If Rosh Hashanah were on Wednesday, Yom Kippur would be on a Friday, and this would cause undue hardship because there would be two days in a row with severe restrictions. If Rosh Hashanah were on a Friday, Yom Kippur would be on a Sunday, and again we would have two days in a row with severe restrictions. Therefore, if the מוֹלָד is on either Sunday, Wednesday, or Friday, the first day of Tishrei is postponed to the following day.
2. דְּחִיַּת מוֹלָד זָקֵן: If the מוֹלָד of Tishrei occurs at noon or later, Rosh Ḥodesh is declared to be the following day. Thus, if the מוֹלָד is Monday at noon or later, Tuesday is declared to be Rosh Ḥodesh. The reason is that if the מוֹלָד is before noon, it is certain that the new crescent will be visible in some part of the world before sunset of the same day. If, however, the מוֹלָד occurs after midday, the new crescent will not be visible before sunset of the same day. This is called דְּחִיַּת י"ח because it is after the eighteenth hour from the night before. If the following day is Sunday, Wednesday, or Friday, days on which the first day of Tishrei may not occur, it is further postponed to the next following day, so that the first of

Tishrei is the third day counting from and including the day of the מוֹלָד.

3. דְּחִיַּת ג״ט ר״ד: If the מוֹלָד of Tishrei in an ordinary year is on Tuesday at 3 204/1080 A.M. or later, the first of Tishrei is postponed to Thursday. It cannot be on Tuesday because then the next year's מוֹלָד of Tishrei would be on Saturday afternoon, and Rosh Ḥodesh would have to be postponed to Sunday because of זְקֵן מוֹלָד, and then again to Monday because of לֹא אַדּ״וּ רֹאשׁ. This would make the year in question 356 days long, which is more than the statutory limit of 355.

4. דְּחִיַּת ב׳ ט״ו תקפ״ט: This occurs if the מוֹלָד of Tishrei in a year succeeding a leap year is on a Monday (יוֹם ב׳) after 9:00 A.M. (i.e., the fifteenth hour from the beginning of the night before) and 589/1080 (תקפ״ט) parts. If this year were to begin on Monday, Rosh Hashanah of the preceding year would have fallen on Tuesday noon, and would have been postponed to Wednesday because of מוֹלָד זְקֵן, and then again to Thursday because of דְּחִיַּת אַדּ״וּ. This would make the current year 382 days, which is lower than the statutory limit of 383.

In the old texts these four דְּחִיּוֹת were put into the form of a jingle

לֹא אַדּ״וּ רֹאשׁ
מוֹלָד זָקֵן בַּל תִּדְרוֹשׁ
ג״ט ר״ד בְּשָׁנָה פְּשׁוּטָה גְרוֹשׁ
ב׳ ט״ו תקפ״ט אַחַר הָעִבּוּר עָקוֹר מִלְּשָׁרוֹשׁ

To compensate for these postponements from the astronomical new year, a day is added to one year and taken from the next. The addition is made in the month of Kislew, and the subtraction from the month of Ḥeshwan. It has been suggested that these months were chosen because among the Babylonians, from whom the Jews borrowed the names of the months, these months were sometimes twenty-nine days long and sometimes thirty (Feldman, *Rabbinical Mathematics and Astronomy,* p. 187). Hence, when both months are defective, the year has 353 days; when both are full, the year has 355 days, and when one is defective and one is full, the year has 354 days. During leap years, a parallel variation takes place between 383, 384, and 385 days.

A few more terms merit definition because they occur in printed calendars.

The Larger Cycle (מַחֲזוֹר גָּדוֹל) is of twenty-eight years duration. Theoretically, the first supposed תְּקוּפַת נִיסָן, i.e., vernal equinox, occurred at the beginning of the fourth day, i.e., on Tuesday at 6:00 P.M. Each Tequfah occurs seven and one-half hours later than the preceding one. Every twenty-eight years Tequfat Nisan will begin at the same time, i.e., Tuesday at 6:00 P.M. When this occurs, the blessing of the sun (בִּרְכַּת הַחַמָּה or קִדּוּשׁ) is recited on Wednesday morning.

The character of the year is designated by three letters, the first indicating the day of the week on which the first of Tishrei occurs; the second indicating whether the year is שְׁלֵמָה ("full," i.e., 355 days), חֲסֵרָה ("defective," i.e., 353 days), or כְּסִדְרָהּ ("regular," i.e., 354 days); and the third indicating the day on which the first day of Pesaḥ will fall. Thus, 5734 is designated as ה, ש, א; ה means that the first day of Tishrei is on Thursday; ש that the year is full, i.e., 355 days with both Ḥeshwan and Kislew being thirty days; and א that the first day of Pesaḥ will be on a Sunday; and the year is פְּשׁוּטָה, i.e., ordinary and not a leap year.

3. Shabbat Mevarekhim

In ancient days Rosh Ḥodesh was determined by direct observation. Witnesses watched for the reappearance of the moon and reported it to the Sanhedrin. The witnesses and their testimony were carefully examined, and if satisfied with their reliability the Sanhedrin announced the first of the month, solemnly declaring it to be מְקֻדֶּשֶׁת, or sanctified—i.e., a day to be observed as Rosh Ḥodesh (M. *R.H.* 2:5–7).

Later, when the Jewish calendar was definitively regularized and systematized by Hillel II around 360 C.E., it became the custom to announce the arrival of Rosh Ḥodesh at the time and place most appropriate for such public announcements—i.e., after the Torah reading and before אַשְׁרֵי at the service on the Sabbath preceding Rosh Ḥodesh (*Abudraham Hashlem* 193; *Siddur Otsar Hatefilot*, p. 720). In the course of time, this announcement underwent a striking change, and instead of being merely a proclamation of the new moon, it came to be regarded as the blessing of the coming month (Hertz, *Authorised Daily Prayer Book*, p. 509). The Sabbath when these prayers are recited is called Shabbat Mevarekhim, and the prayers are called Birkat Haḥodesh, or more popularly, in the Yiddish, Rosh Ḥodesh Bentchen.

The Birkat Haḥodesh originally consisted of merely a simple announcement of the date (i.e., the day of the week) when the new month would begin (*Abudraham Hashalem*, 193). Later, prayers were added. The resulting unit has the hope of Israel's redemption as its central theme. The monthly reappearance of the moon became the symbol of Israel's redemption. Just as the moon emerges from its total eclipse into brightness, so will Israel be redeemed from its exile and brought back to the land of its fathers (Millgram, *Jewish Worship*, p. 765; *Soferim* 19:9).

This prayer is preceded by יְהִי רָצוֹן, a petition composed by Rav (B. *Ber.* 16b), which was recited after the morning prayers. The sentence "to renew unto us this coming month for good and for blessing" was inserted in order to make יְהִי רָצוֹן appropriate for Birkat Haḥodesh. It was introduced into the Ashkenazic prayer book in the nineteenth century, and thus is the most recent addition to the traditional Siddur (Berliner, *Randbemerkungen*, pp. 63 f.).

It is customary to recite all of Birkat Haḥodesh standing, in remembrance of the original sanctification of the new moon by the court of Jerusalem, which was done while standing (*O.H.* 417:1 in *M.A.*; *'Arukh Hashulḥan* 417:8).

Before מִי שֶׁעָשָׂה נִסִּים, one of the officiants announces the time of the מוֹלָד. It is customary to hold the Torah during this service, and the reader takes it when he announces the date of Rosh Ḥodesh.

When the Birkat Haḥodesh is recited on the Sabbath, except during the Sefirah period, אַב הָרַחֲמִים is omitted; so is צִדְקָתְךָ at Minḥah; and memorial prayers are not recited (see Baer, *Seder 'Avodat Yisra'el*, p. 232).

4. Yom Kippur Qaṭan

During the sixteenth century, the famous kabbalist, Rabbi Moses Cordovero, began the practice of fasting on the day before Rosh Ḥodesh, which he called Yom Kippur Qaṭan (Baer, *Seder 'Avodat Yisra'el*, p. 319) because, like Yom Kippur, it was to be a day of atonement (*M.A., O.H.* 417:3). Cordovero's practice spread among the pious, and the observance of Yom Kippur Qaṭan came to include the recitation of psalms and penitential prayers as well as fasting. The service for Yom Kippur Qaṭan is found in any complete Siddur along with Minḥah. If there are ten at the service who are fasting, the Torah portion for fast days, וַיְחַל משֶׁה (Exod. 32:11–14, 34:1–10), is read. If Rosh Ḥodesh is on a Sabbath, Yom Kippur Qaṭan is observed on the preceding Thursday.

There is no Yom Kippur Qaṭan on the day preceding Rosh Ḥodesh of the following four months:

1. Ḥeshwan, because the major Yom Kippur was celebrated in the preceding month.
2. Ṭevet, because the day before Rosh Ḥodesh is the fifth day of Ḥanukkah, a festival during which fasting and reciting penitential prayers are not permitted.
3. Iyar, because the day preceding Rosh Ḥodesh is the next-to-last day of Nisan, and fasting is not permitted during Nisan.
4. Tishrei, because the day before is the eve of Rosh Hashanah, and the recitation of penitential prayers is not permitted (*Ziv Haminhagim*, p. 6).

5. Liturgy

Taḥanun is not recited at Minḥah on 'Erev Rosh Ḥodesh.

During the Ma'ariv 'Amidah, יַעֲלֶה וְיָבֹא is inserted into the seventeenth benediction (רְצֵה), as during the intermediate days of Pesaḥ and Sukkot. יַעֲלֶה וְיָבֹא is the מֵעֵין הַמְּאוֹרָע, the specific prayer that indicates the significance of the day, and it is repeated in every 'Amidah of Rosh Ḥodesh except that of Musaf.

During the early part of the service, at Birkhot Hashaḥar, after the Qorbanot, the Torah portion read on Rosh Ḥodesh, Numbers 28:9–15, is recited as a reminder. The Sefardic rite omits it since it is included in the Torah reading (*O.H.* 421). The Rabbinical Assembly *Weekday Prayer Book* follows the Sefardic custom.

After the 'Amidah, half-Hallel is recited. The reason for saying the incomplete Hallel is that its recitation is merely a *minhag* (custom) and not a *din* (religious law) (B. *'Arak. 10b;* Maimonides, *Hil. Ḥanukkah* 3:7; *Abudraham Hashalem,* 194. While the recital of Hallel on Rosh Ḥodesh is mentioned in the Talmud (B. *Ta'an.* 28b), the authorities differ on the question of whether a benediction is necessary, since saying Hallel on Rosh Ḥodesh is only a *minhag* (ibid. in Maimonides; *Abudraham Hashalem,* 194). We follow the opinion of the Rama (*O.H.* 422:2), reciting the benedictions before, and concluding with יְהַלְלוּךָ, which is a closing benediction. This is followed by the complete Qaddish, as is the custom at the conclusion of

Shaḥarit. When there is no Musaf service, as on Ḥanukkah, only half Qaddish is recited (*O.H.* 423 in *B.H.* 1).

After Hallel the Torah is read, with four people called (*O.H.* 423:1). The reading is Numbers 28:1–15. The first 'aliyah is verses 1–3; the second repeats verse 3 and continues to verse 6 inclusive; the third continues to the end of verse 10; the fourth continues to the end of verse 15 (*O.H.* 423:2; for an explanation of this division, see *Mishnah Berurah* on *O.H.* 423:2). There is no Hafṭarah when Rosh Ḥodesh falls on a weekday (*O.H.* 423:1).

The Torah reading is followed by אַשְׁרֵי and וּבָא לְצִיּוֹן. Psalm 20, which usually follows אַשְׁרֵי, is omitted on Rosh Ḥodesh. Some congregations return the Torah to the ark before אַשְׁרֵי and some after (*O.H.* 423:3 in *Mishnah Berurah* 5). From the standpoint of expediency, it is better for the congregation to say אַשְׁרֵי and וּבָא לְצִיּוֹן while the *golel* prepares the Torah for its return to the ark.

It is customary to remove the Tefilin before Musaf since this part is like a festival service, when Tefilin are not worn (*O.H.* 423:4).

The Musaf 'Amidah is structurally the same as the Musaf 'Amidah of the Pilgrimage Festivals, with the central prayer reflecting the significance of the day; the sacrifices mentioned are those that were prescribed for Rosh Ḥodesh. The concluding portion, the petition חַדֵּשׁ עָלֵינוּ אֶת הַחֹדֶשׁ הַזֶּה, includes twelve pleas for comfort corresponding to the twelve months of the year; in a leap year a thirteenth plea וּלְכַפָּרַת פָּשַׁע is added (see Baer, *Seder 'Avodat Yisra'el*, p. 240; Abrahams, *Companion to the Prayerbook*, p. 189).

Psalm 104 is added after the psalm of the day (*O.H.* 423:3). There is an old tradition that Rosh Ḥodesh had a special psalm of its own. Since we no longer know which psalm it was, however, Psalm 104 has become customary because its nineteenth verse reads: "Who appointed the moon for seasons." The oldest source for the practice is in *Orḥot Ḥayyim I*, 69c, no. 2 (Elbogen, *Der jüdische Gottesdienst*, p. 126).

If Rosh Ḥodesh falls on a Sabbath, the procedure is the same, with the following variations:

1. Two Torah scrolls are taken from the ark. The portion of the week is read from the first; the Mafṭir (Num. 28:9–15) from the second.
2. There is a special Hafṭarah, Isaiah 66:1–24, chosen because of its twenty-third verse: "And it shall come to pass that from one new moon to another, and from one Sabbath to another, shall all flesh come to worship before Me, saith the Lord" (*O.H.* 425:3; *Mishnah*

Berurah 4). Verse 23 is repeated at the end of the Hafṭarah to insure that the reading will end with words of comfort and encouragement (ibid.).

3. No memorial prayers (הַזְכָּרוֹת) are recited and אַב הָרַחֲמִים is omitted.
4. In the Musaf 'Amidah, אַתָּה יָצַרְתָּ, which is almost identical with וּמִפְּנֵי חֲטָאֵנוּ of the Festival 'Amidah, is said instead of the weekday רָאשֵׁי חֳדָשִׁים לְעַמְּךָ נָתַתָּ.
5. צִדְקָתְךָ is omitted at Minḥah.

If Rosh Ḥodesh is on a Sunday, I Samuel 20:18–42 is read as the Hafṭarah on the preceding Sabbath. Its connection with Rosh Ḥodesh is based on its opening words: "And Jonathan said unto David, 'Tomorrow is the new moon: and thou wilt be missed, because thy seat is empty.' "

The sixth day of Ḥanukkah is always Rosh Ḥodesh. When Kislew is thirty days long, the seventh day is also Rosh Ḥodesh. If it is a weekday, two Torah scrolls are taken from the ark. The portion prescribed for Rosh Ḥodesh (Num. 28:1–15) is read from the first, and three people are called up. A fourth person is called for the reading of the prescribed portion for the sixth day of Ḥanukkah (Num. 7:42–47; 7:48–53 on the seventh day) from the second Torah scroll.

If the sixth day of Ḥanukkah is a Sabbath, three Torahs scrolls are taken from the ark. The Sidrah of the week is read from the first, and six people are called. The passage for Rosh Ḥodesh (Num. 28:9–15) is read from the second Torah scroll for the seventh 'aliyah. The portion for the sixth day of Ḥanukkah is read in the third Torah scroll. The Hafṭarah is the one for Ḥanukkah (*O.H.* 684:1). The services for the day incorporate the special prayers of Rosh Ḥodesh (*O.H.* 425:3), and עַל הַנִּסִּים in each 'Amidah (*O.H.* 682:1, 2).

If Rosh Ḥodesh Adar is a Sabbath, it is also Shabbat Sheqalim. The same procedure is followed: three Torah scrolls are taken from the ark, the first for the portion of the week; the second for the Rosh Ḥodesh reading; and the third for the Shabbat Sheqalim reading (Exod. 30:11–16) (*O.H.* 685:1). The Hafṭarah of Sheqalim (II Kings 12:1–17) is read (ibid.).

Three Torahs scrolls are also needed when Rosh Ḥodesh Nisan falls on a Sabbath, since that Sabbath is also Shabbat Haḥodesh. The portion of the week is read in the first Torah scroll, the passage for Rosh Ḥodesh in the second, and the passage for Shabbat Haḥodesh (Exod. 12:1–20) in the third. The Hafṭarah is Ezekiel 45:16–46:18, prescribed for Shabbat Haḥodesh (*'Arukh Hashulḥan, O.H.* 685:6).

In all the above cases, Rosh Ḥodesh takes precedence when it coincides with a Sabbath, but yields, as far as the Mafṭir and Hafṭarah are concerned, when it conflicts with any other occasion (*O.H.* 425:4). Priority is given to Rosh Ḥodesh as far as sequence is concerned; i.e., the Rosh Ḥodesh portion is read before the portion for the other special occasion, on the principle of תָּדִיר וְשֶׁאֵינוֹ תָּדִיר, תָּדִיר קוֹדֵם "whatever occurs more frequently comes first." Since the reading for the other special occasion comes last, and the Mafṭir reads the Hafṭarah, it determines the Hafṭarah (*'Arukh Hashulḥan, O.H.* 425:4, 684:4, 685:4).

The special character of the Jewish calendar poses one further problem. As mentioned above, Rosh Ḥodesh Kislew and Rosh Ḥodesh Ṭevet may be either one day or two. It was explained that this is due to the length of the preceding months, Ḥeshwan and Kislew, which may be either twenty-nine or thirty days long. If a death occurs on the first day of Rosh Ḥodesh Kislew (i.e., the thirtieth day of Ḥeshwan), and Ḥeshwan will have only twenty-nine days in the following year, when should the Yahrzeit be observed? The following is the rule. If a death occurs on the first day of Rosh Ḥodesh when Rosh Ḥodesh is two days, and the first Yahrzeit is in a year when Rosh Ḥodesh is only one day, the Yahrzeit should be fixed permanently for the twenty-ninth of the preceding month. If, however, the first Yahrzeit occurs when Rosh Ḥodesh is two days, the Yahrzeit should be fixed so that it is always on a Rosh Ḥodesh—on the first day when it is two days, and on the one when it is one day, so as to avoid confusion (*O.H.* 568 in *B.H.* 16, *M.A.* 20).

If a death occurs on the first day of Rosh Ḥodesh Adar II (i.e., the "leap month," which, as explained above, only occurs in seven years of the nineteen-year cycle), the Yahrzeit in the following year should not be observed on the twenty-ninth of Adar, which is, in fact, closest to the anniversary of the death, but rather on the first day of Adar, because the month of Adar (in non-leap years, when there is only one Adar) is regarded as standing in place of Adar II in such cases (ibid.).

6. Qiddush Levanah

According to rabbinic tradition, a person who witnesses an important or stirring phenomenon is obliged to pronounce a benediction (B. *Ber.* 54a ff., 59b). Since a pious Jew offers praise and thanksgiving to the Creator whenever he becomes aware of the miracle of creation, the appearance of the new moon, with its blessings of light and hope, obviously calls for a benediction (*O.H.* 426:1; Maimonides, *Hil. Berakhot* 10:16; Millgram, *Jewish Worship*, p. 266): hence, Qiddush Levanah, a service recited when the moon is clearly visible in the sky; it is found in all complete, traditional Sidurim.

While the Qiddush Levanah is an all but forgotten ritual, it embodies much that might be appealing to contemporary Jews and to the spirit of our age. As one contemporary scholar has commented: "The service of *Kiddush Levanah* has a mystic, haunting air about it. On a clear moonlit weekday evening, immediately after the Maariv service, the congregation assembles in front of the synagogue and proceeds with the service. There is no reader. Yet it is a public service, because a quorum of ten men is required" (Millgram, *Jewish Worship*, p. 267).

Since the prayers must be recited when the moon is clearly visible (*O.H.* 426:1 in Rama; and in *M.A.* 1), they should be said during the second phase of the moon, i.e., from the seventh to the fifteenth day of the month inclusive (*O.H.* 426:3, 4). Obviously it should be done at night (ibid. 1), in the open air (ibid. 4) or before an open door or window (*M.D.* 4; *M.A.* 14). Saturday night is preferable (if it occurs before the tenth of the month), because people are still in a festive mood and in festive garb (ibid. 2 and in Rama).

Qiddush Levanah should not be said before Tish'ah Be'av or before Yom Kippur (ibid.), but it was considered proper to say it immediately after the conclusion of the Yom Kippur service, because at that time, as on Saturday night, we are in a festive mood. It should not be said at the conclusion of the fast of Tish'ah Be'av (ibid.). It should be recited standing (B. *San.* 42a; Maimonides, *Hil. Berakhot* 10:17; *O.H.* 426:2).

7. Qiddush Haḥamah

The Talmud states: "Our rabbis taught: He who sees the sun at its turning point (בִּתְקוּפָתָהּ), the moon in its power, the planets in their orbits, and the signs of the Zodiac in their orderly progress, should say: 'Blessed be He who has wrought the work of creation.' And when does this happen? Abaye said: Every twenty-eight years when the cycle begins again, and the Nisan [vernal] equinox falls in Saturn on the evening of Tuesday, going on Wednesday" (B. *Ber.* 59b).

Every twenty-eight years at the Nisan (vernal) equinox, the sun begins a new cycle. When this cycle begins, the equinox occurs early Tuesday night. On the following day, the first Wednesday of the Nisan period, in the morning, upon seeing the sun, the benediction "Who has wrought the works of creation" is recited. It is customary to pronounce the benediction after the morning services (*O.H.* 229:2; see also Maimonides, *Hil. Berakhot* 10:18).

Neither the codes nor the standard complete prayer books add to this. Rabbi Moses Schreiber, in his responsa, *Ḥatam Sofer* (*O.H.* Resp. 56), gives a complete order of the service recited at the beginning of the larger cycle (מַחֲזוֹר הַגָּדוֹל), comprising Psalm 148, the benediction עוֹשֶׂה מַעֲשֵׂה בְרֵאשִׁית, the hymn אֵל אָדוֹן, and Psalm 19, and concluding with עָלֵינוּ and קַדִּישׁ (see also *Mishnah Berurah* on *O.H.* 429:8). More lengthy services are found in *Sedeh Ḥemed* (vol. 8, p. 1 [1962 ed.], vol. 4, after Ḥanukkah [1st ed.]) as well as in Tucazinsky, *Quntres Birkat Haḥamah,* and Segner, *Or Haḥamah* (see also *Encyclopaedia Judaica* 15:518).

The last Birkat Haḥamah took place on April 8, 1953 (23 Nisan 5713), and the next one will be on March 18, 1981 (12 Adar II 5741).

UNIT XIX

THE LAWS OF MOURNING (I)

Biqqur Ḥolim
Preservation of Life
'Aninut
Autopsies
Transplanting Tissue
Cremation
Embalming
Preparation for Burial
Funeral
At the Cemetery
Suicide

XIX. The Laws of Mourning (I)

"Yea, though I walk through the valley of the shadow of death, I will fear no evil, for Thou art with me" (Ps. 23:4).

When Rabbi Yoḥanan finished the Book of Job he used to say: "The end of man is to die and the end of a beast is to be slaughtered, and all are doomed to die. Happy is he who was brought up in the Torah, and whose labor was in the Torah, and who has given pleasure to his Creator, and who grew up with a good name; and of him Solomon said: 'A good name is better than precious oil; and the day of death than the day of one's birth' [Eccles. 7:1]" (B. *Ber.* 17a).

"Death cannot be and is not the end of life. Man transcends death in many altogether naturalistic fashions. He may be immortal biologically through his children; in thought through the survival of his memory; in influence, by virtue of the continuance of his personality as a force among those who come after him, and ideally through his identification with the timeless things of the spirit.

"When Judaism speaks of immortality it has in mind all these. But its primary meaning is that man contains something independent of the flesh and surviving it, his consciousness and moral capacity, his essential personality—a soul" (Steinberg, *Basic Judaism,* p. 160).

Life is sacred. Its beginning and its end are mysteries. Both birth and death touch the fringe of the divine and have therefore been invested with meaningful religious rites. The sacredness of human life extends to both body and soul because הַנְּשָׁמָה לָךְ וְהַגּוּף פָּעֳלָךְ—both are the handiwork of God (High Holy Day liturgy, Seliḥot service). Hence, our concern when the mortal body reaches its end.

This concern gives expression both to יְקָרָא דִּשְׁכִיבָא (B. *B.B.* 100b; B. *San.* 46b, 47a), respect and reverence for the dead, and to יְקָרָא דְּחַיֵּי (B. *San.* 46b, 47a), concern for the bereaved.

Our sages expressed this reverence for the dead by saying that the Shekhinah stands at the head of a dying person (B. *Shab.* 12b). The lack of such reverence in modern society, despite the current popularity of lavish funerals, is a phenomenon bemoaned by Margaret Mead: "We more and more hustle the dead off the scene without ceremony, without an opportunity for young and old to realize that death is as much a fact of life as is birth" (quoted in Lerner, *America as a Civilization,* p. 619). In contrast, Jewish tradition prescribes that when death occurs, those present, and those who hear it about, should say בָּרוּךְ דַּיַּן הָאֱמֶת "blessed be the righteous Judge" (M. *Ber.* 9:2; B. *Ber.* 54a; *O.H.* 222:2), thus affirming an awareness that God's governance of the universe includes death no less than life; and that death does not negate divine providence but instead is, in its own way, an illustration of it. While the modern recoil from death betrays a lack of sensitivity to death's implications for the spirit, Judaism has surrounded death with practices that include tender regard for the dying, deep concern for the family, and the affirmation of basic religious principles.

Rabbi Bokser writes: "Man is mortal. He abides in the world for but a limited time, and then his sun sets, and his breath departs from him. But his mortality does not necessarily degrade him. On some levels . . . he has the power to transcend his mortality, and he can enter into life eternal. But death, in its own grimness and terror, has a positive aspect in the scheme of divine providence. For death is the price of life" (Bokser, *Judaism,* p. 63).

There are a number of observances incumbent upon the living and the dying before death occurs.

1. Biqqur Ḥolim

The rabbis considered the mitswah of Biqqur Ḥolim, visiting the sick, important enough to be numbered among the things for which a man enjoys the fruits in this world while the principal remains for him in the world to come (Daily Prayer Book, incorporating M. *Pe'ah* 1:1 and B. *Shab.* 127a).

Sensing that visiting the sick alleviated their pain, the sages imbued this social obligation with religious significance (B. *Ned.* 40a). On the other hand, since they were also alert to the fact that visits could at times cause pain and suffering (ibid.), they instituted a series of rules for the practice of Biqqur Ḥolim.

It is a mitswah to visit the sick (Maimonides, *Hil. Aveil, Y.D.* 335:1). One should visit the sick of all peoples without regard to race, color, or creed (*Y.D.* 335:9). One should not visit the sick immediately after they have fallen ill, lest they become frightened, but this does not apply to relatives and close friends of the patient. It is best to wait until the third day, but if the illness is serious, one should not wait at all (*Y.D.* 335:1).

Since it is the comfort of the patient that is desired, one should be careful that his visit does not cause discomfort. The visitor should not come in the early hours of the morning or the late hours of the evening; in the morning the attendants are usually occupied with the patient, and in the evening the patient is usually tired (B. *Ned.* 40a; see *Y.D.* 335:4 for other reasons). One should not visit a sick person when his needs are being attended to (Maimonides, *Hil. Aveil* 14:5). One should not be the bearer of sad news to a sick person and should not weep for the dead in his presence, for it surely will distress him and retard his recovery (*Y.D.* 337).

If a near relative becomes seriously ill, it is permitted to violate the Sabbath, if necessary, in order to visit him and cheer him up (*Kol Bo 'al Aveilut,* p. 22). One should not stay too long, since that might make the patient uncomfortable (Abrahams, *Hebrew Ethical Wills,* p. 40). In all cases, one should be guided by the patient's doctor or nurse in determining how long to stay or whether to visit at all.

The primary purposes of visiting a sick person were to make him comfortable, cheer him up, and pray for his recovery. The visitors should pray for the patient's recovery and have a מִי שֶׁבֵּרַךְ recited for him in the synagogue at the reading of the Torah (*Y.D.* 335:10).

In our day this meritorious act of visiting the sick has been relegated to the rabbi and religious functionaries of the synagogue. While this has the virtues of our age of specialization, since the rabbi usually knows better what to do in such situations, and in addition the patient derives comfort from his feeling of confidence in the rabbi, the traditional requirement that the obligation devolves upon everyone is to be preferred and should be encouraged. The Biqqur Ḥolim society, first mentioned by Rabbi Nissim Gerondi (ca. 1360) and formerly a feature of every Jewish community (see *Encyclopaedia Judaica,* 14:1498), should also find a place in the contemporary congregation.

2. Preservation of Life

Human life is precious, and its preservation takes precedence over every other consideration. This includes the obligation to visit the sick and the permission to violate the Sabbath to help a person afflicted with a dangerous illness (*O.H.* 328:2). It also includes the obligation of forbearance from doing anything that might hasten the death of a sick person, no matter how serious the illness (Maimonides, *Hil. Aveil* 4:5). Hence, euthanasia is forbidden under any circumstances.

However, if death is certain, and the patient suffers greatly, it is permissible to desist from postponing death by artificial means (B. *A.Z.* 18a; B. *Ket.* 104a; *Y.D.* 339:1 in Rama; Rosner, "Jewish Attitude Toward Euthanasia").

As death draws near, the patient should be encouraged to say וִדּוּי (confession) (*Y.D.* 338:1). Care should be taken that this does not distress the patient. It should be explained that saying Vidui does not mean that death is imminent (ibid.). A short form of the Vidui is the following: מוֹדֶה אֲנִי לְפָנֶיךָ יְיָ אֱלֹהַי וֵאלֹהֵי אֲבוֹתַי שֶׁרְפוּאָתִי וּמִיתָתִי בְּיָדֶךָ. יְהִי רָצוֹן מִלְּפָנֶיךָ שֶׁתִּרְפָּאֵנִי רְפוּאָה שְׁלֵמָה וְאִם אָמוּת תְּהֵא מִיתָתִי כַּפָּרָה עַל כָּל חֲטָאִים וַעֲוֹנוֹת וּפְשָׁעִים שֶׁחָטָאתִי וְשֶׁעָוִיתִי וְשֶׁפָּשַׁעְתִּי לְפָנֶיךָ וְתֵן חֶלְקִי בְּגַן עֵדֶן וְזַכֵּנִי לָעוֹלָם הַבָּא הַצָּפוּן לַצַּדִּיקִים (*Y.D.* 338:2; for a different version, see Hertz, *Authorised Daily Prayer Book,* p. 1064).

A number of practices that were once observed in connection with death and dying are no longer applicable, among them lighting a candle when a person dies (*Kol Bo 'al Aveilut,* p. 23; *Gesher Haḥayyim,* 2d ed., 1:49; *Ṭur, Y.D.* 352:4), closing the eyes of a corpse, pouring out the water from containers in neighboring houses (*Y.D.* 339:5), placing the corpse on the ground (*Y.D.* 339:1), etc. Nowadays, since most deaths occur in hospitals, these customs are no longer feasible. Other ancient customs that were given prominence in מַסֶּכֶת שְׂמָחוֹת, the talmudic tractate on mourning laws and customs, have been discontinued in the diaspora because of concern about the possible Gentile reaction to their observance (see Zlotnick, *Tractate Mourning,* p. 12; Zimmels, *Ashkenazim and Sephardim,* pp. 217–18). There are other customs, however, that are still meaningful and feasible and therefore still appropriate for modern observance.

A dying person should not be left alone because he should not feel abandoned in his last moments, and also because of the sobering effect death has on the living (*Y.D.* 339:4). Since the body is the abode of the spirit, it is entitled to respect and reverence even after the spirit has departed from it. Therefore a corpse should not be left alone; someone should always be present to guard it. Of the various reasons given for this practice, the only one still applicable is that it is a sign of respect (B. *Ber.* 18a; *Y.D.* 373:5 in Rama).

The principle of Kevod Hamet (respect for the dead) has gained new relevance in connection with a number of current problems, including autopsy, embalming, cremation, exhumation, transplantation of parts of the human body, and viewing the body prior to the funeral.

3. 'Aninut

The period between death and burial is called 'aninut, and the bereaved person is called 'onen. The 'onen is exempt from the performance of all positive religious obligations, such as reciting the morning and evening prayers and putting on Tefilin (*Y.D.* 341:1). At the same time he is forbidden to drink wine, eat meat, or indulge in luxuries (*O.H.* 341:1). If his 'aninut should fall on a Sabbath or a festival, he is permitted to eat meat and drink wine and is obligated to fulfill all the mitswot except his sexual obligations to his spouse (*Y.D.* 341:1).

The reason for these prescriptions is twofold. First, there is the principle of הָעוֹסֵק בְּמִצְוָה פָּטוּר מִן הַמִּצְוָה (B. *Suk.* 26a; B. *Soṭah* 44b): since the bereaved is obligated to attend to the needs of the deceased, there should be nothing to distract him from these obligations. Second, it is considered a breach of Kevod Hamet to do anything but attend to the deceased. Hence, a mourner is not permitted to perform his religious obligations even if he wants to (Asheri on *Ber.* 17b; for other views, see Rashi ad loc., and Maimonides, *Hil. Aveil* 4:6; see also *Hagahot Maimuniyot,* n. 4).

Today when organized groups or commercial firms take care of burial needs, and the participation of the family is minimal, such exemptions are not necessary. Rather, the solace and comfort derived from prayer and the performance of religious duties would suggest that we should encourage such activities (*Semaḥot* 10:1; *Y.D.* 341:1, 3; *Qitsur Shulḥan 'Arukh* 196:5). The laws of 'aninut, as well as all the laws of mourning, apply to the seven close relatives: spouse, father and mother, son and daughter, brother and sister of one father (*Y.D.* 374:4).

4. Autopsies

The question of autopsies is not new, but contemporary medical advances have relied increasingly upon knowledge gained from post-mortems, and this has led to abuses where autopsies have become a matter of routine, without proper concern for the burial of the parts of the body. To prevent this, the following rules should be observed.

Routine autopsies are forbidden because they violate the principle of Kevod Hamet. An autopsy is permitted—

1. when the physician claims that it could provide new knowledge

that would help to cure others suffering from the same disease;
2. when the law requires it in order to determine the cause of death.

In either case, however, it must be certain that all parts of the body will be properly buried after the autopsy (*Rabbinical Assembly Proceedings*, 1939, p. 157; Klein, "Responsum on Autopsy").

5. Transplanting Tissue

Modern medical science has made it possible to save the eyesight of a living person by transplanting the eye of a deceased person and to heal certain diseases by transplanting tissue from other people. Is the mutilation of the corpse necessitated by such procedures to be regarded as Nivul Hamet (disgrace to the dead)?

The weight of opinion is that it is not. On the contrary, there can be no greater Kevod Hamet than to bring healing to the living. Therefore a person may will his eye, or other organs or tissues of his body, for transplantation in other bodies for healing purposes. As for the objection that burial does not take place, the fact that a transplanted tissue will ultimately receive burial with the demise of the beneficiary satisfies this requirement (see Klein, "Responsum on Autopsy").

6. Cremation

The Jewish way of burial has been to place the body in the earth. Hence, cremation is frowned upon. The questions that arise in a case of cremation are:

1. Should the ashes be buried in the congregational cemetery?
2. Should a rabbi officiate at such a funeral?

A great number of authorities forbid the burial of ashes in a Jewish cemetery because this would encourage the practice of cremation (see *Duda'ei Hasadeh*, sec. 16; *Maḥazeh Avraham*, vol. 2, *Y.D.* 38; and Lerner, *Ḥayyei 'Olam*). Others permit it and even permit a service at the burial (Rules of the Burial Society of the United Synagogue of London, quoted in

Rabinowicz, *A Guide to Life,* p. 29; see also Rabbi Eliyahu ben Amozegh, *Ya'aneh Va'eish*).

The Law Committee of the Rabbinical Assembly has ruled that cremation is not permitted. When it is done by the family in disregard of Jewish practice, a rabbi may officiate only at the service in the funeral parlor; the ashes may be buried in a Jewish cemetery and appropriate prayers may be said, but not by a rabbi, lest his participation be interpreted as approval (*Rabbinical Assembly Proceedings,* 1939, p. 156; Law Committee Archives).

7. Embalming

While there are instances of embalming in the Bible (see Gen. 50:26), the later authorities forbade the practice because it involves Nivul Hamet and infringes on Kevod Hamet and the preservation of the body.

Today, for sanitary reasons and by requirement of the civil law, it sometimes becomes necessary to embalm a body. In such cases embalming is permitted as Kevod Hamet, i.e., to prevent putrefaction from setting in, and to keep the body from becoming malodorous. Since in most cases burial no longer takes place on the day of death, this is now almost always necessary. The only method of embalming that is permitted in such cases, however, is one that leaves the body intact (*Gesher Haḥayyim* 1:73; *Kol Bo 'al Aveilut,* p. 51).

Embalming is also permitted when burial must be delayed, as, for example, when the body is shipped a long distance, or if a person dies at sea and the delay is intended to prevent the usual burial at sea. If the method used in such cases involves removing parts of the body, as, for instance, when the blood is drawn out, these should be buried in their container (ibid. and Law Committee Archives; *Gesher Haḥayyim,* 1:95–96).

8. Preparation for Burial

Ṭahorah, the washing, or purification, of the body, usually performed by the members of the Ḥevra Qadisha, is another expression of reverence for the dead. The Ṭahorah is accompanied by the recitation of prayers and psalms appropriate for the occasion. All parts of the body, from head to foot, are washed thoroughly with warm water, including the orifices and the spaces between the fingers and toes. The body is turned from side to side to make sure that the water reaches every part, but it is never allowed to lie face downward (*Qitsur Shulḥan 'Arukh* 197:2; *Gesher Haḥayyim,* 1:95–96).

Formerly, a room was set aside for the Ṭahorah in a chapel at the cemetery (*Kol Bo 'al Aveilut* 87), but nowadays, when most funerals take place in funeral parlors, it is done on the premises of the establishment.

Pious Jews should do the purification (*Kol Bo 'al Aveilut,* p. 87), but when this is impossible, it may be done by non-Jews under Jewish supervision (*Melamed Leho'il,* vol. 2, *Y.D.* 112, quoted in responsum on Ṭahorah by R. Sanders Tofield, Law Committee Archives).

If a person was mutilated, and the blood soaked into his clothes, he is buried without Ṭahorah in the blood-stained clothes he was wearing at the time of death (*Y.D.* 364:4).

If the family does not permit the Ṭahorah, the deceased should nevertheless be accorded all the honors due the dead (*Kol Bo 'al Aveilut,* p. 89).

Tradition frowns upon dressing up the deceased in fine clothing (*Y.D.* 352:1) and prescribes the use of תַּכְרִיכִין, plain linen shrouds (ibid. 2 and B. *M. Q.* 27b). According to the Talmud, this practice was instituted both to protect the poor from embarrassment and also because a funeral is not a proper occasion for showing off one's wealth (Shakh, ibid.)

In addition to the shrouds, a man should be buried in his Ṭalit, especially if he wore it regularty while alive (*Y.D.* 351:2). Some authorities maintain that one of the fringes of the Ṭalit should be rendered ritually defective (*pasul*) before the burial (*Gesher Haḥayim* 2:14; *Y.D.* 351:12 in Rama).

The purpose of burial is to return the body to the earth in conformity with the verse "for dust thou art and to dust thou shalt return" (Gen. 3:19). In many communities it was customary not to use a coffin since burial without a coffin would hasten the process of "returning to dust" (*Kol Bo 'al Aveilut,* p.181). The prevailing custom, however, is to put the body in a coffin (אָרוֹן). As with the shrouds, ostentation is discouraged, and the coffin should be as simple as possible, preferably of plain boards (ibid.).

Tradition also frowns on viewing the body and on leaving the coffin open (B. *M.Q.* 27a). The recent innovation of having the body on exhibition the night before the funeral mocks the tradition that the funeral is an occasion for paying respect to the dead, and that consoling the mourners begins after the burial. It is also an affront to the bereaved family, since the obligation of receiving visitors in the funeral home taxes them with social formalities at a time when their hearts are heavy with sorrow (see Tofield, "Viewing the Dead," Law Committee Archives).

The prescribed practice is that burial should not be delayed (*Y.D.* 357:1). In former times, this meant that the burial, whenever possible, took place on the day of the death (*Y.D.* 357:1 in *Pitḥei Teshuvah,* no. 1). According to some scholars, this was a hygienic measure necessitated by the warm climate of the region in which the custom originated. It would seem, however, that it was actually an element of Kevod Hamet, since leaving a corpse unburied was considered to be a humiliation of the dead. Because of the importance of Kevod Hamet, a delay in burial was permitted only if it was for purposes of honoring the dead, such as to provide time for procuring the shrouds and coffin or to await the arrival of relatives (*Y.D.* 357:1).

Nowadays, however, it is virtually impossible to have the burial on the day of the death. Moreover, if the burial were held on the same day, the effect would be the opposite of Kevod Hamet, since there would be insufficient time to make the necessary preparations; and often the next of kin live at a distance, and thus would be unable to attend. Hence, honoring the dead sometimes requires delaying the burial until the next day, or even longer, in some cases, if the next of kin live very far away (*Y.D.* 357:1). As a general rule, however, the burial should not be delayed any longer than necessary.

קְרִיעָה, or rending one's garment, is an ancient mourning practice. In biblical times it was customary to rend one's garment upon hearing sad news, especially news of the death of a dear one (II Sam. 1:11; Gen. 37:24). The Talmud prescribes that anyone who witnesses a death must rend his garment (B. *M.Q.* 25a; *Y.D.* 340:5). The present law requires Qeri'ah only for those relatives for whom one must observe the mourning period (*Y.D.* 340:1). The rending is done while standing (ibid.) and is preceded by the benediction דַּיַּן הָאֱמֶת (*Y.D.* 339:3). Originally this benediction was recited at the moment of death or upon learning of the death, and in fact it is still customary to say בָּרוּךְ דַּיַּן הָאֱמֶת upon learning of the death but בְּלִי שֵׁם וּמַלְכוּת—without mentioning either the name of God or His sovereignty (*O.H.* 223:2 in *B.H.* 6; *Gesher Haḥayyim* 1:48). For a very practical reason, however, the Qeri'ah is now done at the funeral—all the mourners are present, and normally there is someone there who knows the procedure (*Kol Bo 'al Aveilut,* pp. 26–33; *Gesher Haḥayim* 1:55–63).

If a funeral takes place on a day that is a festival, the Qeri'ah is postponed until after the festival's conclusion (*Y.D.* 340:31). Opinions differ as to whether Qeri'ah should be performed if the death occurs during the intermediate days. The general practice today is not to perform Qeri'ah in such cases except if the deceased is one's mother or father.

There is a further distinction in the way Qeri'ah is performed for a parent and for other relatives. The garment is rent on the right side for other relatives, but on the left side for a parent, because the left is nearer to the heart, and the idea is to expose the heart (*Y.D.* 340 in Shakh 19). Moreover, Qeri'ah is not required for other relatives if one learns of the death more than thirty days after it occurred, but the obligation to perform Qeri'ah for a parent continues regardless of the interval (*Y.D.* 340:18). Qeri'ah is not necessary, however, in the event of the death of a child less than thirty days old (*Y.D.* 340:30).

Nowadays, for social reasons, only the very pious actually rend their usual garments. Some people tear a necktie, since a necktie is considered a garment. The general practice, however, is to make a cut in a ribbon pinned to one's outer garment. This is considered acceptable, since as an expression of grief it serves the same purpose as rending one's actual garment (Tofield, "The Rite of Keriah by Means of a Ribbon," Law Committee Archives; cf. *Kol Bo 'al Aveilut,* p. 28, which frowns on this practice and recommends a second Qeri'ah without a *berakhah* during the Shiv'ah).

9. Funeral

There is no standard or fixed service for funerals, but all prayer books and rabbinic manuals have a form. While there are many variations, they all have certain elements in common. There is usually a service to be conducted at home and a service to be conducted at the cemetery with Tsidduq Hadin, a prayer acknowledging divine justice.

The form generally followed at home, and in most cases at the funeral parlor as well, is to recite a psalm, read a scriptural passage, and chant the memorial prayer אֵל מָלֵא רַחֲמִים (see Harlow, *Rabbi's Manual,* pp. 101–21).

It is customary to give the eulogy before the memorial prayer. The Talmud declares pithily: "Just as the dead shall be called to account, so shall the eulogizers be called to account" (B. *Ber.* 62a), implying that just as it is wrong to overpraise in a eulogy, so it is wrong not to eulogize a deserving person properly.

While in the immediate past eulogies were reserved for the distinguished, today, as an expression of the democratic spirit of our era, eulogies are delivered at all funerals. To be sure, it is forbidden to exaggerate and attribute virtues to one who never had them, but it is also permitted to be charitable in offering praise. Furthermore, the eulogy may also serve as an opportunity to moralize and dwell on the meaning of life so that וְהַחַי יִתֵּן אֶל לִבּוֹ "so that the living shall reflect" (Eccles. 7:2) (*Semaḥot* 3:5–6; *Gesher Haḥayyim* 1:120).

If the deceased was a spiritual or communal leader, the practice in some communities is to bring him into the synagogue for the funeral service (*Y.D.* 340:20). The practice is open to abuse; care should be taken to limit it to the deserving.

The eulogy is omitted when the funeral takes place on a day when Taḥanun is not recited. It is also omitted at funerals that take place on Friday afternoon or on the afternoon of the day before a festival (*O.H.* 420:2 in Rama, 670:1, 697:1). It is before or after this service that the mourner performs Qeri'ah.

The use of flowers at funerals—myrtles, to be exact—is mentioned in the Talmud (B. *Ber.* 53a, *B.Q.* 16b; *O.H,* 526:4), but is discouraged in current practice, both from a desire to keep funerals simple and in opposition to the introduction of alien and pagan customs. People who wish to express sympathy for the bereaved family in a tangible way should contribute to the favorite charity of the deceased or to the synagogue where he or she worshipped.

There is a difference of opinion about the order of the procession when the coffin leaves the house or the funeral parlor. In some places the mourners lead, followed by the coffin, carried by the pallbearers, and then by the rest of the people (*Y.D.* 358:3). In other places the coffin is carried out first (*Qitsur Shulḥan 'Arukh* 197:8). In many places today, the practice is for the family to lead, followed by the rest of the people, and finally by the coffin. This is more a matter of convenience.

In former times, the pallbearers carried the coffin to the cemetery on their shoulders, especially if the deceased was a man of distinction. An exception was made where the cemetery was so far that this would have been difficult. Today, since practically all cemeteries are far, the pallbearers carry the coffin from the funeral parlor to the hearse and from the hearse to the grave. Whenever possible, it is customary for the hearse to stop in front of the synagogue where the deceased worshipped.

10. At the Cemetery

At the gates of the cemetery, the pallbearers remove the coffin from the hearse and carry it to the grave. Several stops are made on the way to the grave (*Y.D.* 358:3 in Rama). The prevailing custom is to pause seven times while reciting Psalm 91. On days when Tsidduq Hadin is omitted, no stops are made (Ṭur, *Y.D.* 376). The seven stops are symbolic of the seven times the word הֶבֶל (vanity) occurs in the Book of Ecclesiastes (B. *B.B.* 100b) and also of the seven stages of life (*Eccles. Rabbah* 1:1). It has been suggested, as well, that the pause on the way to the grave gives the mourners time to reflect upon human existence and to comprehend the vanities that are often mistaken for a meaningful life (Gordon, *In Times of Sorrow,* p. 4).

After the coffin has been placed in the grave, the traditional requirement is that a few spadefuls of earth be put over it before the service (*Y.D.* 375:1). In some communities the coffin is covered with a carpet simulating grass. In others, it is simply lowered into the grave.

The graveside service begins with the Tsidduq Hadin. As a justification of the divine judgment, this prayer conveys the essential message of the burial service (*Qitsur Shulḥan 'Arukh* 198:14). On days when Taḥanun is not said, Psalm 16 is recited instead of Tsidduq Hadin (*Qitsur Shulḥan 'Arukh* 199:9). The memorial prayer אֵל מָלֵא רַחֲמִים follows, and the mourners then say Qaddish. The service usually ends with the verse "The Lord hath given, and the Lord hath taken away; blessed be the name of the Lord" (Job 1:21).

After the service the people present make two lines and the mourners pass between them. As the mourners pass, the people offer their condolences with the traditional formula: הַמָּקוֹם יְנַחֵם אֶתְכֶם בְּתוֹךְ שְׁאָר אֲבֵלֵי צִיּוֹן וִירוּשָׁלָיִם.

Before leaving the cemetery those present should wash their hands. The practice in some places is to wash the hands before entering the house (*Qitsur Shulḥan 'Arukh* 199:10). This is a symbolic way of saying that our hands are clean as far as the death of the departed is concerned, for we have done everything in our power to keep him in life or to ease his distress (see *Ḥesed Le'avraham* 24; *Y.D.* 376:4 in *Ḥiddushei R. 'Akiba Eger*).

It is also customary to pluck some grass on leaving the burial grounds and to say: "And they blossom out of the city like grass of the earth" (Ps. 72:16) and "He remembereth that we are dust" (Ps. 103:14). Both passages are emblematic of both the frailty of life and the hope of resurrection (ibid. in *Qitsur Shulḥan 'Arukh* 199:10); see also Abrahams, *Companion to the Authorised Prayer Book,* p. 229; *Y.D.* 376:4 in *B.H.* 4).

A Kohen, because of the sacredness of his role in the service at the Temple in Jerusalem, was vested with special sanctity and subject to a number of restrictions. One of these was the regulation that he must not come into physical contact with the dead, which included a prohibition of being under the same roof with a dead body. Thus the Torah enjoins: "There shall none defile himself for the dead among his people" (Lev. 21:1). Since these regulations are still operative, a Kohen may not approach nearer than four cubits to a grave and may not enter a house in which there is the body of a dead Jew (*Y.D.* 371:1, 5). The Torah lifts these restrictions when the deceased is one of the seven close relations for whom the Kohen has to observe Shiv'ah (*Y.D.* 373:3 and also Lev. 21:2).

Since work is forbidden, burials should not take place on festivals. However, because of the strong emphasis on not delaying burial, the following rules were adopted:

On the first day of a festival, all the work usually forbidden on a festival is permitted in the case of a funeral if it is done by non-Jews. On the second day of a festival, all the work connected with the funeral is permitted without any restrictions. This applies to all the people connected with the burial (*mit'asqim*), but not to those who come simply to pay their respects (*O.H.* 526:4).

Today, since we are not as particular about immediate burial, and since a burial on a festival usually brings about a great deal of unnecessary Ḥillul Yom Ṭov (desecration of the holiday), some have suggested that we delay burial until after the festival (see Rabinowicz, *Guide to Life*, p. 43, where he quotes this rule of the London Ḥevra Qadisha: "It is an accepted custom in the Anglo-Jewish community not to arrange any funerals either on the first or the second day of Yom Ṭov").

11. Suicide

The rabbis ruled that no rites whatsoever should be observed for a suicide. This means that there should be no rending of clothes, and no eulogizing, but people should line up to comfort the mourners and the mourners' blessing should be recited, out of respect to the living. The general rule is that the public should participate in whatever is done out of respect for the livng, but it should not participate in whatever is done out of respect for the dead (*Semaḥot* 2:1; *Y.D.* 345:1).

Suicide was considered a moral wrong. Deliberate destruction of one's own life was rebellion against God. Only He who gave life may take it (B. *A.Z.* 18a). Suicide has been defined as follows: "Who is to be accounted a suicide? Not one who climbs to the top of a tree or to the top of a roof and falls to his deah. Rather, it is one.who says: 'Behold, I am going to climb to the top of the roof, or to the top of the tree, and then throw myself down to my death,' and thereupon others see him climb to the top of the tree or to the top of the roof and fall to his death. Such a one is presumed to be a suicide, and for such a person no rites whatsoever should be observed" (*Semaḥot* 2:2; *Y.D.* 345:2).

The later authorities qualified the definition even further. The only suicide for whom mourning is not observed is one who killed himself out of a cynical disregard for life; this excludes one who killed himself because he could not cope with his problems (B. *Giṭ.* 57b; Tosafot, s.v. קפצו; see also *Kol Bo 'al Aveilut,* p. 319, sec. 50).

Nowadays, since it is known that most cases of suicide result from temporary insanity caused by depression, we observe all the rites of mourning (see *Gesher Haḥayyim* 1:71–73).

We also take into consideration the fact that any humiliation of the dead adds to the anguish of the living, and the punishment of suicide affects them rather than the victim. This is a valid consideration, since even the early authorities permit everything that is done out of respect for the living (*Y.D.* 345:1; *'Arukh Hashulḥan, Y.D.* 345:5).

UNIT XX

THE LAWS OF MOURNING (II)

Shiv'ah
Sheloshim
The First Year
Sabbath and Festivals during Shiv'ah
Timely and Distant News
Qaddish
Yahrzeit
The Tombstone
The Cemetery
Exhumation
Addenda

XX.
The Laws of Mourning (II)

12. Shiv'ah

The sages of the Talmud declared: "Do not comfort a person when his dead lies before him" (M. *Avot* 4:18). At the time of death, the bereaved is in a state of shock and cannot be reached by comforting words. After the funeral, when he becomes aware of his loss, he is open to consolation. The rite of Shiv'ah serves to tide him over during this painful period until he is able to resume his normal life. A number of prescribed observances aid in this process; they are obligatory on the following relatives of the deceased: father, mother, son, daughter, brother, sister, husband, wife (*Y.D.* 374:4).

The Shiv'ah period begins immediately after the burial and lasts seven days (*Y.D.* 375:1). If the burial is to take place at a great distance—for instance, in the Holy Land—the Shiv'ah begins when the vehicle carrying the deceased leaves on its journey.

The seventh day of the Shiv'ah period does not have to be a complete day, for on the principle of מִקְצָת הַיּוֹם כְּכֻלּוֹ (B. *M.Q.* 19b), a small part of the final day is enough. Therefore, the mourners sit but a short while after Shaḥarit on the seventh day and then rise, while the people present offer them the traditional condolence: הַמָּקוֹם יְנַחֵם אֶתְכֶם בְּתוֹךְ שְׁאָר אֲבֵלֵי צִיּוֹן וִירוּשָׁלָיִם.

It is customary to cover the mirrors in a house where Shiv'ah is being observed. Many reasons have been offered for this practice (*Duda'ei Hasadeh*, no. 78). The one most cogent today is that a mirror, as a symbol of human vanity, is out of place in a house of mourning (*Kol Bo 'al Aveilut*, p. 262; see also Gordon, *In Times of Sorrow;* A. Klein, *Laws of Mourning*).

Since light is a symbol of the soul, as suggested by the verse "The soul of man is the lamp of the Lord" (Prov. 20:27), and since the soul is attached to the body as the flame is to the wick (*Gesher Haḥayyim*, vol. 1, p. 198:1), a candle is kept burning throughout the seven days of Shiv'ah (*Kol Bo 'al Aveilut*, pp. 261–62). For sentimental reasons, wax or tallow candles are preferred, but an electric light is permitted. Electric bulbs with designs appropriate for Shiv'ah are available, and one of these should be used, because the special design makes it apparent that the light has been lit specifically as a memorial for the dead (*Gesher Haḥayyim,* vol. 1, p. 198:1).

The mourners' first meal after returning from the cemetery (the Se'udat Havra'ah) should be prepared and served by friends or neighbors (B. *M.Q.* 27b; *Y.D.* 378). Since at this point the mourners would not normally think about food, it is an act of kindness for others to feed them (Ṭur, *Y.D.* 378 in *Perishah* 1). In addition, the mourners may be experiencing a sense of guilt, as well as a feeling of loneliness or of being forsaken by God and man, and the Se'udat Havra'ah provides comfort and consolation, reminding them that there are other people who care.

The Se'udat Havra'ah usually includes round foods, such as eggs or lentils. Eggs are a symbol of life and hope (*O.H.* 552:3). In addition, as symbolic representations of גַּלְגַּל הַחוֹזֵר בָּעוֹלָם—the wheel of fate from which no one escapes, round foods assuage the mourner's sense of guilt, reminding him that death is the fate of all human beings.

The importance of this lesson is reflected in the traditional story of the bereaved woman who came to a saint and told him that her bereavement had robbed her of all peace of mind, while her friends' efforts at consolation merely increased her sorrow. The saint advised her to bake a cake, using materials gathered only from inhabitants of the town who had never experienced sorrow and bereavement. The anguished woman went from house to house, but in each case she was unable to accept even a single grain of wheat. That night, weary with disappointment, she returned to the saint to report her failure. Suddenly it dawned on her that the failure was the remedy. She realized that she had not been singled out, but rather that sorrow is the fate of all mortals.

While observing Shiv'ah, the mourners should sit on low stools as a sign of mourning. It was once customary to sit on inverted beds (*Semaḥot* 6:1). After this fell into disuse, it became customary to sit on the floor (*Y.D.* 387:1–2); the elderly and the ill were permitted to use cushions. Nowadays the prevailing practice is to sit on low stools.

The mourners should stay at home during the seven days of Shiv'ah, and services, both morning and evening, should be conducted in the house where Shiv'ah is being observed (*Y.D.* 376:3 in Rama). It is preferable to observe Shiv'ah in the home of the deceased (*Qitsur Shulḥan 'Arukh* 207:5). Members of a family who are observing ("sitting") Shiv'ah together but live in separate dwellings may go home to sleep. During the day, however, the mourners should stay together in the house where Shiv'ah is being observed (*Kol Bo 'al Aveilut,* p. 262).

Taḥanun is omitted from services conducted in a house of Shiv'ah because its main theme, רַחוּם וְחַנּוּן חָטָאתִי, would tend to make the mourners feel guilty rather than comfort them. Psalm 20 before וּבָא לְצִיּוֹן is also omitted because its contents and tone are not appropriate to a house of mourning (*O.H.* 131:10 in *M.A.* 10). The verse וַאֲנִי זֹאת בְּרִיתִי is omitted in וּבָא לְצִיּוֹן (*Kol Bo 'al Aveilut,* p. 280; *Gesher Haḥayyim,* vol. 1, p. 204:4). Birkat Kohanim is not recited before Sim Shalom (*O.H.* 128:42; *Gesher Haḥayyim,* vol. 1, p. 204:8).

Opinions differ as to whether the verse תִּתְקַבַּל of Qaddish Shalem should be recited in a house of mourning. According to some customs, it should be said as usual, while others omit it. Some compromise, omitting it if the mourner leads the service but saying it as usual if someone else acts as leader (*Kol Bo 'al Aveilut,* p. 280; *Gesher Haḥayyim,* vol. 1, p. 206:8).

Since Hallel, which normally forms part of the service for Rosh Ḥodesh and Ḥanukkah, includes sentiments that may be saddening to mourners, such as "The dead praise not the Lord, neither any that go down into silence" and "This is the day which the Lord hath made; we will rejoice and be glad in it," it should not be said in a house where Shiv'ah is being observed. An alternative practice has the mourners leave the room while the other worshippers recite Hallel. Some authorities maintain that on Ḥanukkah Hallel must be recited, even in a house of mourning (*Kol Bo 'al Aveilut,* pp. 282–83; *Gesher Haḥayyim,* 1:205–6).

Psalm 49 is recited at the end of the service, both morning and evening, because it offers a message appropriate for the Shiv'ah period (*Gesher Haḥayyim,* 1:207).

If it is impossible to assemble a minyan at the house where Shiv'ah is being observed, the mourners are permitted to go to the synagogue for services and to say Qaddish (*Kol Bo 'al Aveilut,* pp. 286 ff.).

Mourners are also permitted to attend Sabbath services at the synagogue, but a mourner may not accept an 'aliyah (*Y.D.* 393:3, 400:1; *Kol Bo 'al Aveilut,* pp. 333, 338) and may not act as Sheliaḥ Tsibur (*Y.D.* 376:4) except if he is one professionally. If a mourner is accidentally called up to the Torah, he should not refuse the 'aliyah (*Kol Bo 'al Aveilut,* p. 338).

Public mourning observances are suspended on the Sabbath. However, since mourners remain obliged to observe all mourning rules pertaining to things done in privacy, the Sabbath is counted as one of the days of mourning (*Y.D.* 400:1).

Mourners should not attend to business or go to work during the Shiv'ah period (*Y.D.* 380:1, 3). If a mourner is of modest means, however, and must work in order to sustain himself, he is permitted to return to work on the third day of Shiv'ah. This means that three days is the minimum mourning period, but as with the seventh day, part of the day (even one hour) counts as a whole day (*Y.D.* 393:1 in Rama; *Sedeh Ḥemed,* vol. 5, *Aveilut* 38). If abstention from work would result in severe financial loss, the mourner is permitted to work (*Y.D.* 380:5 in Rama), but it is preferable that the work be done by others (*Y.D.* 380:5).

A physician is permitted to see his patients during the Shiv'ah period, even if there are other physicians available, because a patient has more confidence in his own physician (*Kol Bo 'al Aveilut,* p. 29, no. 36; *Y.D.* 380 in *Pitḥei Teshuvah,* n. 1).

Work connected with housekeeping, such as sweeping the floor, washing dishes, and making beds, is permitted (*Semaḥot* 11:9). Participation in festivities, attendance at weddings, and listening to music are prohibited (*Y.D.* 393:2).

Since leather shoes were considered a luxury, they are forbidden during the Shiv'ah period (*Y.D.* 380:1, 382:1) except when walking outside. Indoors a mourner should wear either socks or cloth slippers; this does not apply to a sick person, or to anyone else who might sustain injury if he does not wear shoes (*Y.D.* 382:2, 3, 4). Bathing and anointing oneself are permitted only for hygienic reasons but not for pleasure (*Y.D.* 381:1, 2).

Mourners should not cut their hair or shave during the Sheloshim, or thirty days (*Y.D.* 390:1; see below, p. 291, for exceptions). Excepts for brides and girls of marriageable age, women should not use cosmetics (ibid.). Conjugal relations are forbidden during the Shiv'ah period (*Y.D.* 383:1).

Social greetings present a problem. According to some authorities, such greetings are forbidden if they involve an elaborate ritual with an etiquette of its own, but informal greetings, such as the modern "good morning" and "how do you do," are permitted (*Y.D.* 385 in *B.H.* 2). Very pious mourners, however, do not greet other people during the whole Shiv'ah period, and respond to greetings only from the third day on (*Y.D.* 385:1).

Jewish tradition regards the comforting of mourners as a meritorious act (B. *Soṭ.* 14a) and prescribes that this obligation be fulfilled when it will offer the mourners the greatest consolation. Attending the funeral and accompanying the deceased to his final resting place—לְוָיַת הַמֵּת—are not only means of paying respect to the dead but also acts of comfort to the mourners. The first act of condolence takes place when the mourners leave the grave, passing through an aisle formed by two rows of well-wishers, who offer the traditional condolence: הַמָּקוֹם יְנַחֵם אֶתְכֶם בְּתוֹךְ שְׁאָר אֲבֵלֵי צִיּוֹן וִירוּשָׁלָיִם (*Kol Bo 'al Aveilut,* p. 216).

Visiting the mourners during the Shiv'ah period, usually referred to as

Niḥum Aveilim, is another means of offering comfort. Such visits should not be turned into social events; they are occasions for expressing sympathy, not for indulging in vulgar small talk.

Gifts brought or sent to the house of Shiv'ah should be suitable. Flowers and candy, currently the most popular items, are not, since they usually result in waste. Close friends may send food, but the most appropriate gift is a contribution to the favorite charity of the deceased or to the synagogue where he or she worshipped.

Friday night, when the mourners come to the synagogue, is another occasion for offering condolences. The traditional custom has the mourners stay in an anteroom outside the sanctuary until the congregation has completed לְכָה דוֹדִי. The mourners enter the sanctuary just before the recitation of Psalm 92 and the congregation greets them with הַמָּקוֹם יְנַחֵם אֶתְכֶם (*Gesher Haḥayyim,* vol. 1, p. 239:5). Some congregations that have a late Friday night service (see p. 59) have adopted a variant of the preceeding practice. Since the Sabbath has already commenced before the beginning of the late service, the mourners enter the sanctuary when the service begins rather than before Psalm 92. After לְכָה דוֹדִי the leader of the service announces that so-and-so has died and the bereaved have come to worship, and asks the congregants to join him in offering condolences to the mourners with the traditional formula mentioned above.

13. Sheloshim

The mourning period is arranged to help the bereaved person recover from the state of shock caused by the death of one dear to him. The most intense mourning takes place during the first three days of Shiv'ah; the mourning is only slightly less intense during the remaining days of Shiv'ah. When Shiv'ah concludes, the mourner returns to work, but he continues to observe certain restrictions during the Sheloshim, the period of thirty days following the burial. Among these, he may not attend weddings, dances, and parties or participate in any other form of merriment (B. *M.Q.* 22b). In addition, he may not listen to instrumental music or play a musical instrument (*Kol Bo 'al Aveilut,* p. 361), unless he earns his livelihood by playing an instrument or is playing it in order to learn (ibid.), and he may not listen to the radio, watch television, or attend a movie, theatrical performance, or concert.

It has been asked whether radio and television programs that are informative rather than entertaining are included in these restrictions. The same question applies to the theater and to concerts of serious music. The latter are included in the restriction because they are usually gala affairs not in consonance with mourning; the former are permitted.

In former times, all mourners were enjoined not to shave or cut their hair until the conclusion of the Sheloshim (B. *M.Q.* 27b), and those who were mourning the death of a parent were urged to go without shaving or cutting their hair until rebuked by friends and acquaintances for untidiness (B. *M.Q.* 14a, 22a). Many authorities have commented that it is not necessary to adhere to this rule in places where being unshaven is considered untidy (*Kol Bo 'al Aveilut,* p. 352). Nowadays, the prevailing custom is to resume shaving after the conclusion of the Shiv'ah period.

A mourner may not get married during the Sheloshim (Ṭur, *O.H.* 392). An exception is made in the case of a bride or groom whose wedding preparations had already been made before the death occurred (*Y.D.* 342:1). If at all possible, however, the wedding should be postponed at least until after the Shiv'ah (ibid.). If a man is in mourning for his wife, he must wait until the three Pilgrimage Festivals have passed before remarrying (*Y.D.* 392:2), unless there are small children who need care (ibid.).

14. The First Year

All the preceding restrictions are extended to twelve months (even in a leap year) for those who are mourning the death of a parent (B. *M.Q.* 22b; *Gesher Haḥayyim,* 1:249). In addition, they recite the mourner's Qaddish at every service for eleven months (*Y.D.* 376:4).

15. Sabbath and Festivals during Shiv'ah

The Mishnah established the principle that the Sabbath is counted among the days of mourning and does not cut off the mourning period; a festival, however, cuts off the mourning period and is not counted among the days of mourning (B. *M.Q.* 19a; *Semaḥot* 7:1). Therefore, the Sabbath is counted as one of the days of Shiv'ah even though public mourning is not observed; when the Sabbath ends, the mourners resume the omitted public observances until the Shiv'ah is completed.

If, however, the mourning period begins even a moment before the beginning of a festival, it is counted as if the mourner had observed the full seven-day period, and he does not have to resume the mourning observances after the conclusion of the festival (*Y.D.* 399:1).

The reason for this distinction is that Shiv'ah can be observed without a festival intervening, but it can never be observed without a Sabbath intervening. Were the Sabbath to cut off the Shiv'ah, there could never be seven continuous days of mourning, since a Sabbath occurs every seven days. As a result, only the festivals cut off the mourning period (P. *M.Q.* 3:5). Moreover, the commandment "to rejoice" (Deut. 16:14), which applies to festivals, cannot be fulfilled during mourning (B. *M.Q.* 14b), while the term "delight" עֹנֶג (Isa. 58:13) is used to describe the Sabbath day, during which private mourning is permitted (Zlotnick, *Tractate Mourning, Semaḥot,* p. 127).

The days of the festival count as part of the Sheloshim, however. For example, if there is a death before Pesaḥ, whatever time elapses before the onset of the festival is counted as equivalent to the full seven-day Shiv'ah period. Pesaḥ counts for eight additional days, and thus fifteen days remain for the completion of the Sheloshim.

On the other hand, a festival cuts off the Sheloshim if the Shiv'ah period was completed before the onset of the festival. For example, if a death occurs before Rosh Hashanah, the Shiv'ah is cut off by Rosh Hashanah, and the Sheloshim is cut off by Yom Kippur (*Y.D.* 399:3). Since even a small part of the seventh day of Shiv'ah is counted as a whole day, a festival cuts off the Sheloshim even if the seventh day is 'Erev Yom Ṭov (Rama on *Y.D.* 391:3).

The case of Sukkot requires special attention. As in the preceding examples, the festival cuts off the Shiv'ah, and whatever time elapses between the beginning of Shiv'ah and the onset of the festival is counted as seven days. Sukkot itself also counts for seven days. In addition, Shemini 'Atseret, the day immediately following the seventh day of Sukkot (see above, p. 168 ff.), is also counted as seven days, on the principle that it is regarded as a festival by itself—שְׁמִינִי רֶגֶל בִּפְנֵי עַצְמוֹ (*Y.D.* 399:11).

However, Shiv'ah cannot begin during the intermediate days of a festival. Thus, if a death occurs during the intermediate days of Sukkot (i.e., less than seven days before the onset of Shemini 'Atseret), the situation is the same as it would be if the death had not occurred prior to the beginning of a festival except that Shiv'ah and Sheloshim begin on the night following the festival (*Y.D.* 399:13).

The festivals do not affect the twelve-month period.

16. Timely and Distant News

If news of a death reaches those who are obligated to observe the mourning period less than thirty days after the death occurred, it is termed a שְׁמוּעָה קְרוֹבָה ("timely tidings"), and all the laws and customs of mourning must be observed from the moment the news is received.

If the news is received more than thirty days after the death, it is termed a שְׁמוּעָה רְחוֹקָה ("delayed tidings"), and the mourner is required to observe only one hour of mourning, during which he does not wear leather shoes and sits on a low stool (*Y.D.* 402:1). He is exempted from all other observances, such as Qeri'ah (except in the case of a parent's death) and the Se'udat Havra'ah (*Y.D.* 402:3, 4).

17. Qaddish

The meaning of the Qaddish prayer is explained in the unit dealing with the daily prayers (see above, p. 38 f.)

A person who is in mourning for a parent must recite the Qaddish at all public services, morning and evening, for eleven months. Originally Qaddish was recited for twelve months, since it was maintained that the memory of the dead remains fresh for twelve months (B. *Ber.* 58b). However, since twelve months was also regarded as the maximum period of punishment for the wicked in the heavenly courts, a mourner's saying of Qaddish for twelve months might be interpreted as implying that he felt his parent deserved the maximum penalty. As a result, the period was reduced to eleven months, even in a leap year (*Y.D.* 376:4 in Rama). The custom of saying Qaddish for eleven months is still observed even though this reasoning is no longer cogent.

The Qaddish is a form of Tsidduq Hadin, and in reciting it the mourner affirms God's justice and the meaningfulness of life (*Gesher Haḥayyim,* vol. 1, p. 316:1).

It was formerly the custom, particularly among the Ashkenazim, for the mourners saying Qaddish to follow an order of precedence based upon their standing in the community (*Y.D.* 376:4 in Rama). The prevailing custom today is for all the mourners to say the Qaddish together without any distinction being made between them (*Gesher Haḥayyim,* vol. 1, p. 324:1; *Yesodei Yeshurun,* 1:242).

If the deceased left no children, or if his children find it too difficult to attend daily services, another person may be asked to say Qaddish (*Kol Bo 'al Aveilut,* p. 376). This dispensation should be discouraged, since it is subject to abuse and has often been commercialized, degrading and vulgarizing a custom of great sanctity. In many cases, bereaved persons have treated the obligation to say Qaddish lightly, taking advantage of the dispensation even when attending daily services to say Qaddish poses no difficulty for them.

Traditionally, only the male children observed the saying of the Qaddish (see *Pitḥei Teshuvah* on *Y.D.* 376:3, n. 3; and *Sedeh Ḥemed,* vol. 5, under *Aveilut,* sec. 160). Today it is widely accepted for a daughter to recite the mourners' Qaddish, especially on the Sabbath and even if there are male children.

18. Yahrzeit

Jewish tradition added a further ritual to help meet the crisis of bereavement—the recurrent commemoration of the anniversary of a death. Each year, on the anniversary of death, we keep the Yahrzeit, a solemn day of remembrance in prayer and meditation. The chief expression of the Yahrzeit is the recitation of the Qaddish (Bokser, *Judaism,* p. 251).

The Yahrzeit occurs on the anniversary of the death, not of the burial (*O.H.* 568:8 and in *M.D.* 4; *Y.D.* 402:12 in Rama and in *M.D.* 9; *Gesher Haḥayyim,* 1:345). Opinions differ as to whether this also applies to the first Yahrzeit, especially if the burial took place three days or more after the death (*Y.D.* 402:12 in *M.D.* 9). Since there is ample support for the custom of always observing the Yahrzeit on the date of the death, it would be less confusing to adopt this practice.

On the day of the Yahrzeit, the mourner attends all the services, beginning with the Ma'ariv of the night before and ending with the Minḥah of the day itself (*Y.D.* 376:4 in Rama). It is proper for the mourner to act as leader of the service.

On the Sabbath preceding the Yahrzeit, the mourner is called up to the Torah (*Levush, O.H.* 133; *Kol Bo 'al Aveilut,* p. 399), and at that time the memorial prayer אֵל מָלֵא רַחֲמִים is chanted for the deceased. Since any number of deceased persons may be mentioned in the same memorial prayer (*Kol Bo 'al Aveilut,* p. 399), many large synagogues have adopted the custom of saying the memorial prayer after the Torah reading at Minḥah for all whose Yahrzeit will take place during the ensuing week.

A light is lit in memory of the deceased on the eve of his Yahrzeit and allowed to burn throughout the Yahrzeit (*Qitsur Shulḥan 'Arukh* 221:1); an electric light may be used (*Gesher Haḥayyim,* 1:343).

If the date of the Yahrzeit falls in the month of Adar, it is observed during Adar I in a leap year, on the principle אֵין מַעֲבִירִין עַל הַמִּצְוֹת. If the death occurred in either of the two months of Adar in a leap year, the Yahrzeit, in each succeeding leap year, is observed in the same Adar in which the death occurred (*O.H.* 568:7).

As explained in the discussion of the Jewish calendar (see above p. 259 f.), Rosh Ḥodesh Kislew and Rosh Ḥodesh Ṭevet may be either one or two days, due to the fact that the preceding months, Ḥeshwan and Kislew, respectively, are sometimes twenty-nine days and sometimes thirty. If a death occurs on the first day of either Rosh Ḥodesh Kislew or Rosh Ḥodesh Ṭevet, and for calendrical reasons that day, in the year of the death, is actually the thirtieth of the preceding month, when should the Yahrzeit be observed in a year when the month has only twenty-nine days?

If the death occurs on the first day of Rosh Ḥodesh when Rosh Ḥodesh has two days, and the first anniversary of the death is in a year when Rosh Ḥodesh is only one day, the Yahrzeit should be fixed permanently on the twenty-ninth of the preceding month. If, however, the first anniversary of the death also occurs when Rosh Ḥodesh is two days, the Yahrzeit is fixed to always occur on Rosh Ḥodesh (the first day when Rosh Ḥodesh is two days) so as not to cause confusion (*O.H.* 568 in *B.H.* 16).

If a person forgets to observe a Yahrzeit and thus does not say Qaddish, he should observe the Yahrzeit when he remembers it (*Kol Bo 'al Aveilut,* p. 394).

If a person does not know the exact date of the death, he should choose a date and from then on observe it as the Yahrzeit (*O.H.* 568 in *B.H.* 17 and in *M.A.*).

19. The Tombstone

The use of tombstones is an ancient custom, dating back to biblical times (Gen. 35:20; II Sam. 18:18; M. *Sheq.* 2:5). The tombstone is erected at the head of the grave. Its purpose is to keep the memory of the deceased alive as well as to identify the grave (*Kol Bo 'al Aveilut,* p. 379; *Yad Yitsḥaq,* pt. 3, no. 38).

The usual practice is to erect the tombstone no sooner than one year after the death, since to do it earlier would be an indication that the memory of the deceased is fading and artificial means are required to revive it (*Ḥiddushei R. 'Akiva Eger, Y.D.* 376:4; *Tanna Devei Eliyahu Rabbah* on *O.H.* 17; for other customs regarding the time to erect the tombstone, see *Kol Bo 'al Aveilut,* p. 379).

In former times, the inscription on the tombstone was an elaborate tribute to the virtues of the occupant of the grave. Nowadays simplicity is preferred; contemporary inscriptions generally include no more than the Hebrew name of the deceased, his father's name, and the date of death according to the Jewish calendar. The top of the tombstone generally bears the letters פ״נ, standing for פֹּה נִקְבָּר or פֹּה נִטְמָן, "here lies" (the Sefardim use the letters מ״ק, standing for מְקוֹם קְבוּרַת or מְקוֹם קֶבֶר, "the tombstone of the grave of"), and the bottom, the letters תנצב״ה, standing for תְּהִי נִשְׁמָתוֹ צְרוּרָה בִּצְרוֹר הַחַיִּים, "may his soul be bound up in the bond of life." Despite the objections of some authorities, the inclusion of the secular date and the name of the deceased in the vernacular are now almost universally accepted practices (*Kol Bo 'al Aveilut,* p. 380, n. 2).

There is no legal objection to having a photograph of the deceased on the tombstone but it should be discouraged as being in poor taste and out of place in a cemetery (for a discussion of the subject, see *Kol Bo 'al Aveilut,* p. 380).

If a tombstone has been placed on the grave, and the family desires to replace it with another, they may do so; the old tombstone, with the original inscription excised, may be used for another grave (*Maḥazeh Avraham,* no. 19; *Kol Bo 'al Aveilut,* p. 383).

A Levite's tombstone often has a ewer carved over the inscriptions as a symbol of his function in the Temple, which included laving the hands of the priests before they gave the Priestly Benediction. The tombstones of Kohanim are marked by a carving of the hands raised in the Priestly Benediction.

In Western European countries and in America, it has become the custom to "consecrate" the tombstone with a service. Since in America the tombstone is covered with a cloth, which is removed by the family during the service, the ritual has been called the "unveiling."

The unveiling usually takes place twelve months after the death. While there is no traditional basis for this service, except for the custom of visiting the grave on the day of Yahrzeit, it is now an accepted and meaningful practice. It offers additional opportunity for the officiant to pay tribute to the deceased as well as to speak to the living about the meaning of life and death. Participants should take care to insure that the unveiling does not become a social event.

20. The Cemetery

Proper burial is considered so important that the community as a whole is held responsible for the proper burial of an unclaimed body; a Kohen is permitted to defile himself to carry out such a burial (*Semaḥot* 4:16; *Y.D.* 374:1, 3). For this reason, an unclaimed body is called a מֵת מִצְוָה. In large cities, this function is carried out by a special organization, usually called חֶסֶד שֶׁל אֱמֶת.

To insure that the dead are buried properly, and need not be sent to another community or be buried among non-Jews, it is an established practice for even the smallest Jewish community to have a cemetery of its own (*Kol Bo 'al Aveilut,* p. 162).

When the community is unable to buy a separate cemetery but can purchase ground in an area set aside for all burials, both Jewish and non-Jewish, the Jewish section should be set apart with a fence or other form of barrier (*Kol Bo 'al Aveilut,* p. 163).

A new cemetery should be dedicated with a service and special rites before any burial takes place (*Maharam Schick, Y.D.* 357; *Peri Hasadeh,* pt. 3, no. 81).

People should comport themselves with dignity while at a cemetery (*Y.D.* 368:1); they should not step on graves (ibid. 364 in Shakh, sec. 3) unless there is no other way of getting to another grave (ibid. in Ṭaz, sec. 1), and should not allow cattle to graze in the cemetery or use the grass growing in it (B. *San.* 46a.).

The graves should not be too close to each other nor should one coffin be placed on top of another (*Y.D.* 352:4). Usually six handbreadths should be left between one grave and another, and three handbreadths between coffins buried on top of each other (ibid.); when there is a shortage of space, a thin solid partition between the two coffins is sufficient (*Y.D.* 362 in *Pitḥei Teshuvah,* sec. 3).

21. Exhumation

The general rule on exhumation was stated in the earliest rabbinic literature: Neither a corpse nor the bones of a human being may be transferred, whether from an inferior place to an honored place, or, needless to say, from an honored place to an inferior place except if they are being transferred to a family tomb; even if this means transfer from an honored place to an inferior place, it is permitted, for it honors the deceased (P. *M.Q.* 2:4, *Semaḥot* 13.7).

Except in the following cases, therefore, exhumation is to be shunned as disrespectful to the dead.

1. When the body is exhumed in order to be transferred to a grave in the Land of Israel.
2. If the body was originally buried with the intent that it be on a temporary basis.
3. If the grave is not secure from animals, vandals, or water seepage.
4. If the body is exhumed in order to transfer it to a family plot. Opinions differ on whether a body may be transferred to a family plot in which no one has been buried as yet (*Kol Bo 'al Aveilut,* p. 232; responsum of Rabbi Jack Segal, Law Committee Archives). Since the sainted Rabbi Kook permits it, even if no one is buried there as yet, we may follow his ruling.
5. If for some reason a body was buried in a non-Jewish cemetery (e.g., a soldier buried in a military cemetery), it may be transferred to a Jewish cemetery (*Ḥakḥam Tsevi,* no. 50). This is optional, not compulsory (*Minḥat El'azar,* vol.II, pt. 4, no. 53).

The vacated grave may be used for the burial of another person (*Rashba,* vol. 1, no. 537). Some authorities require that it not be used by relatives of the deceased, for that would mean deriving benefit from the dead, which is forbidden (*Shevet Sofer* 104).

22. Addenda

It is customary to name children after deceased relatives. Among some Sefardim, children are also named after living relatives (*Kol Bo 'al Aveilut,* p. 34; see also *Yehudah Ya'aleh, Y.D.* no. 247).

Mourners do not occupy their regular seats in the synagogue during the twelve months of mourning but sit a few rows farther back (*Y.D.* 393:4). The rabbi, however, need not change his special seat since this concerns not only him but also the honor of the congregation (*Maharam Schick,* no. 389).

If a body is sent a great distance for burial, the Shiv'ah period begins when the mourners accompanying the coffin leave the coffin. Thus, when a body is put on a ship or a plane, the mourners begin the Shiv'ah when they leave the ship or the plane. If part of the family accompanies the coffin, the beginning of the Shiv'ah period is determined by the actions of the leader or most important member of the family. If he goes with the body, the Shiv'ah begins after the burial; if he stays home, it starts when he departs from the body (*Y.D.* 375:2).

However, if a person is informed of a death by telegram or telephone, and is also informed of the time of the burial, the mourning period begins after burial, as it does for those who are present at the burial (*Gesher Haḥayyim,* 1:184).

If the burial is delayed unduly because of some emergency, and the body is stored until the emergency is over, the Shiv'ah period begins when the coffin is closed. Examples of such emergencies are a town under siege and, in our day, a grave-diggers' strike (*Y.D.* 375:4).

If a person drowns in מַיִם שֶׁיֵּשׁ לָהֶם סוֹף, a body of water whose shores can be seen from all sides, or is mangled by a wild beast, and the body is missing, the mourning period begins when the search for the body is given up (*Y.D.* 375:7). If the body is found later on, it is not necessary to observe an additional mourning period, except that the children, if they are present at the burial, observe the day of the burial as a period of mourning; if they are not present, they only have to do Qeri'ah (ibid., see also in Shakh, who maintains that the other relatives who are present at the burial also observe mourning that day).

If parts of the body are found piecemeal, the period of mourning begins when the head and the greater part of the body are recovered, or when the search for the rest is given up (ibid.).

If a married man is lost in a body of water שֶׁאֵין לָהֶם סוֹף, whose shores cannot be seen from all sides, such as the ocean, the problem is complicated because the wife's status as a widow is involved. If mourning is required, the woman may think she is allowed to remarry, and this is not the case. One authority suggests that if the rabbinic authorities are discussing her status, she should observe the laws of mourning, because she will follow the decision of the rabbis, and the fact that she observes the mourning period will not prejudice her status (*Gesher Haḥayyim,* 1:306).

There are various customs regarding visits to the grave. Among the Sefardim, it is the custom to visit the grave after the Shiv'ah, after the

Sheloshim, and on the Yahrzeit (*Gesher Haḥayyim,* 1:306). The Ashkenazim do not visit the grave until after the Sheloshim.

Graves should not be visited on Rosh Ḥodesh, on the intermediate days of Festivals, on Purim, and certainly not on the Sabbath or on a Festival (*Gesher Haḥayyim,* 1:307). On the other hand, some people do go on Rosh Ḥodesh and Purim. The general principle, however, is to discourage too frequent visits to the cemetery.

If a burial takes place in America in the afternoon, and in Israel, because of the time difference, it is already evening and thus the next day on the calendar, which day should the mourner observe as the Yahrzeit? He should follow the time in the place where he is and not where the burial took place (see *Kol Bo 'al Aveilut,* p. 311).

Since Judaism puts the emphasis on life, one should not indulge in more mourning than is required (B. *M.Q.* 27b; *Y.D.* 394:1). "He will destroy death forever; and the Lord God will wipe tears away from all faces" (Isa. 25:8). "He gives strength to the weary, fresh vigor to the spent" (Isa. 40:25).

UNIT XXI

THE DIETARY LAWS (I)

SHEḤIṬAH

Introduction
Permitted Creatures and Animals
Clean and Unclean Fowl
Fish
Insects and Reptiles
Cheeses and Wines
Sheḥiṭah
The Knife

XXI. The Dietary Laws (I) Sheḥiṭah

I. Introduction

The dietary laws loom large in Jewish life. They are referred to many times in the Torah apart from the full chapter devoted to them in Leviticus (Lev. 11) and part of a chapter in Deuteronomy (Deut. 14:4–21). They are elaborated in the Talmud in a large treatise, *Ḥullin*, which deals with them almost exclusively. In the post-talmudic literature, they are discussed in every code, the *Ṭur* and the *Shulḥan 'Arukh* both devoting over a third of one section, *Yoreh De'ah*, to this codification.

Efforts have been made to give a rationale for the dietary laws. The most persistent—hailing back to Maimonides (*Guide* 3:48)—is that they were originally hygienic measures. Thus, Maimonides says: "I maintain that the food forbidden by the law is unwholesome. There is nothing among the forbidden foods whose injurious character is doubted except pork and fat. But also in these cases is the doubt unjustified" (*Guide* 3:48). Today, this explanation is often given by those who wish to discard the dietary laws on the grounds that we can achieve the same health measures by other means.

The inadequacy of the medical rationale was pointed out by Isaac Abarbanel: "God forbid that I should believe that the reason for forbidden foods is medicinal! For were it so, the Book of God's Law would be in the same class as any of the minor brief medical books. . . . Furthermore, our own eyes see that people who eat pork and insects and such . . . are well and alive and healthy at this very day. . . . Moreover, there are more dangerous animals . . . which are not mentioned at all in the list of prohibited ones. And there are many poisonous herbs known to physicians which the Torah does not mention at all. All of which points to the conclusion that the Law of God did not come to heal bodies and seek their material welfare but to seek the health of the soul and cure its illness" (Abarbanel on Leviticus, quoted in Cohn, *Royal Table*, p. 17).

The sources, the Bible in particular, never mention such reasons. Rather, it is usually suggested that the laws have some connection with holiness. Thus we read in Leviticus: "I am the Lord your God; sanctify yourself, and be holy; for I am holy. . . . For I am the Lord that brought you up out of the land of Egypt, to be your God; ye shall therefore be holy, for I am holy" (Lev. 11:44–45). This is repeated in Deuteronomy: "for thou art a holy people unto the Lord thy God" (Deut. 14:21).

The Torah regards the dietary laws as a discipline in holiness, a spiritual discipline imposed on a biological activity. The tension between wanton physical appetites and the endeavors of the spirit was traditionally explained as the struggle between יֵצֶר הַטּוֹב, the good inclination, and יֵצֶר הָרַע, the evil inclination—the two forces that contend with each other for mastery of the soul.

To transpose this into a modern key, it is the struggle between our higher self and our lower self, between the animal in us and the urge to strive upwards, which is part of the process of evolution. The arena of struggle in this evolutionary process is biological. All these appetites remain in the realm of the physical. Religion strives to lift them out of the merely physical into the realm of the spirit.

To illustrate: Eating is one of the important functions of life. It begins as a biological act, a means of satisfying hunger. When we invite a friend for dinner, a new dimension is added to eating; it becomes a social act. It helps to cement friendship. When a meal takes place in connection with שִׂמְחָה שֶׁל מִצְוָה, the joy of observance of a commandment, it becomes a solemn act that helps add significance to an occasion. On the Sabbath, or even more, on Pesaḥ at the Seder, eating becomes a religious act, an act of worship, with the table becoming an altar of God.

Religion thus raises the biological act into the dimension of the holy. Hence the connection in the Torah between the dietary laws and holiness.

Rabbi Samuel H. Dresner suggests that the dietary laws have as their purpose the teaching of reverence for life. He says: "Human consumption of meat, which means the taking of animal life, has constantly posed a religious problem to Judaism, even when it has accepted the necessity of it. The Rabbis of the Talmud were aware of the distinction between man's ideal and his real condition, regarding food" (Dresner and Siegel, *Jewish Dietary Laws,* p. 24). Since it was felt that man must eat meat, the act was surrounded with regulations which would prevent him from being brutalized and instead would cause him to develop reverence for life. Rabbi Dresner continues: "We are permitted to eat meat, but we must learn to have reverence for the life we take. It is part of the process of hallowing which Kashrut proclaims. *Reverence for Life,* teaching an awareness of what we are about when we engage in the simple act of eating flesh, is the constant lesson of the laws of Kashrut" (ibid., p. 27).

This would explain the purpose of the dietary laws as a whole. There are additional reasons which apply to parts of the laws or to one specific practice. We shall mention them in the appropriate sections below.

2. Permitted Creatures and Animals

In Leviticus 11:2, the Torah enumerates the identifying marks of the animals we may and may not eat, and in Deuteronomy 14:4 it lists the names of the permitted animals; among the domesticated animals, these include cattle, sheep, goats (buffalo, yak), and among the undomesticated animals, the deer family, i.e., stag, moose, hart, elk (antelope, gazelle, eland).

In the case of חיות ("beasts," i.e., undomesticated animals), the rabbis added a number of other distinguishing marks: forked horns or, failing that, horns that are circular in cross-section, composed of layers rather than of solid bone, and with certain deep indentations near the base (B. *Ḥul.* 59a f.).

These distinguishing marks become necessary when it is not certain whether a particular species of beast is one of those enumerated in the Bible. No such identification is required for beasts that are listed in the Bible (*Y.D.* 80:2). Furthermore, certain laws that apply to cattle do not apply to beasts, and vice-versa. The fat of clean beasts, for example, may be eaten, while certain fats of cattle may not be eaten (B. *Ḥul.* 59b; *Y.D.* 80:1,5,6). Also, the blood resulting from the slaughter of beasts must be covered with earth or with something similar (Lev. 17:13).

3. Clean and Unclean Fowl

The Torah does not prescribe any identifying marks for birds; instead, it enumerates the species that are forbidden—a total of twenty-four according to the reckoning in the Talmud (B. *Ḥul.* 63b). The implication is that those not listed are permitted. The rabbis of the Talmud, however, deduced four distinguishing marks of birds that are permitted. A permitted bird has a crop; the sac in the gizzard can be peeled off; it has an extra toe—i.e., in addition to the three front toes, it has another toe in the back; it is not a bird of prey (דּוֹרֵס וְאוֹכֵל). According to one opinion, a bird that divides its toes when it rests, i.e., two toes in front and two in the back, is not permitted (M. *Ḥul* 3:6).

Despite these identifying marks, it has become the accepted practice that only those birds that have been traditionally accepted as permitted may be eaten (*Y.D.* 82:3 in Rama). They are: chickens, turkeys, ducks, geese, and pigeons. Pheasants have been considered permitted in many places (*Melamed Le'ho'il,* vol. 2, no. 16, but see also *Yad Halevi, Y.D.* no. 39, which forbids it; for an up-to-date list, see Loewinger, "'Of Ṭahor," pp. 258–77).

4. Fish

The fish that may be eaten are those that have fins and scales (Lev. 11:9–10; Deut. 14:9–10). The actual determining factor is scales because every fish that has scales has fins also—but the reverse is not true (*Y.D.* 83:3).

The scales should be removable by hand or with a scraping instrument without tearing the skin (*Y.D.* 83:1 in Rama). The scales need not be permanent; if the fish has scales during any stage of its life, and then sheds them, it is permitted (*Y.D.* 83:1). (For a list of permitted and forbidden fishes, see Dresner and Siegel, *Jewish Dietary Laws;* a slightly different list is given in *Kashruth: Handbook for Home and School,* published by the Union of Orthodox Congregations. Dresner and Siegel hold that swordfish and sturgeon are kosher; the authors of the UOC pamphlet classify them as unkosher. For a discussion of the reasons for permitting these fishes, see I. Klein, "Swordfish," and Graubart, "Sturgeon," in the archives of the Rabbinical Assembly Committee on Law and Standards.)

5. Insects and Reptiles

The Torah forbids שְׁקָצִים וּרְמָשִׂים—i.e., creeping things (Lev. 11:20), but it enumerates several species of locusts that are permitted (Lev. 11:22). The Talmud lists the following distinguishing marks: "All that have four legs, four wings, leaping legs, and wings covering the greater part of the body, are clean. R. Jose says: It must also bear the name 'locust'." (M. *Ḥul.* 3:6).

Our brethren from Yemen claim to be expert at the identification of permitted locusts and have eaten them. In Western countries, the eating of locusts of any kind has traditionally been forbidden on the grounds that we are no longer able to distinguish between clean and unclean locusts (*Y.D.* 85:1 in Ṭaz, sec. 1).

6. Cheeses and Wines

The controversy over the kashrut of cheeses is an old one, dating back to the time of the Talmud (M. *A.Z.* 2:4, 5; M. *Ḥul.* 8:5; B. *Ḥul.* 116b). Cheese is made from curdled milk. Since the curdling agent was rennet, which is extracted from the walls of a calf's stomach, cheese was forbidden as a mixture of dairy and meat. According to some authorities, however, the use of rennet does not affect the kashrut of cheese because rennet no longer has the status of food and instead is comparable to a mere secretion (פִּירְשָׁא בְּעַלְמָא). This controversy appears again and again among the posqim (see Rabbenu Tam in B. *A.Z.* 35a, s.v. חדא קתני; Maimonides, *Hil. Ma'akhalot 'Asurot* 4:13, 14, 19; *'Arukh Hashulḥan, Y.D.* 87:42). Some halakhic authorities demand a hekhsher for certain cheeses, implying that those without a hekhsher are not kosher; other authorities maintain that all cheeses are permissible and no hekhsher is necessary.

The Committee on Law and Standards of the Rabbinical Assembly has decided to follow the lenient opinion. First of all, it reasons, the חֲשָׁשׁוֹת (fears) expressed by those who require a hekhsher applied only in former times, when cheesemaking was a cottage industry and there was no way to control the ingredients used. Under these conditions, there was always the danger that an individual farmer who made cheese might use the milk of a nonkosher animal or might add lard to the mixture. Today however, at least in America, cheesemaking is a major industrial enterprise regulated by the Pure Food and Drug Law, which requires that most food products bear a label listing their ingredients.

Furthermore, the rennet used in many of the hard cheeses does not impair their kashrut, both for the talmudic reason stated above and also because the substance from which the rennet is extracted is thoroughly dried and treated with strong chemicals, and this process makes the rennet a דָּבָר חָדָשׁ (new substance) or comparable to a piece of wood (עֵץ בְּעַלְמָא). Thus, all cheeses that are subject to the Pure Food and Drug Act should be considered kosher (see I. Klein, responsum on cheese in Law Committee Archives, and in *Responsa and Halakhic Studies,* pp. 43–58).

The permissibility of יֵין נֶסֶךְ (wines of the gentiles) is also a controversial subject. *Yein nesekh* was originally prohibited because it was used for libations in idol worship, and anything used in idol worship is forbidden to Jews. The rabbis considered this interdict to be a biblical commandment (see Dan. 1:5; B. *A.Z.* 29b; Maimonides, *Sefer Hamitswot,* no. 194; *Y.D.* 123–35.

In our day, however, there is no *yein nesekh* since there is no longer any idol worship (B. *A.Z.* 57b in Tos., s.v. לאפוקי מדרב; *Y.D.* 123:1 in Rama). Rather, we are concerned nowadays with סְתָם יֵינָם—ordinary wines made or handled by gentiles. The Talmud forbids such wines as a precautionary measure to prevent socializing with gentiles since it might lead to intermarriage (B. *A.Z.* 31b) or because those who use such wines might be exposed to the religious influence of gentiles and thus be persuaded to apostatize. A hekhsher on wine, therefore, indicates that no gentiles were directly involved in any stage of the wine-making process (i.e., from the pressing of the grapes through the bottling and sealing of the wine).

At the request of the Committee on Law and Standards of the Rabbinical Assembly, Rabbi Israel Silverman made a study of the question and reported his findings in a responsum. Rabbi Silverman found that winemaking in the United States is fully automated (his study did not cover imported wines, many of which are not produced by automated processes), and no human hand comes in contact with the wine from the moment the grapes are put into containers and brought to the winery until the wine appears in sealed bottles. Wines manufactured by this automated process may not be classified as wines manufactured by gentiles and thus do not come under the interdict against the use of סְתָם יֵינָם.

Rabbi Silverman called attention to several additional considerations, however. Since it is a mitswah to support Israel, he suggested, we should give priority to wines imported from Israel, all of which are kosher according to the traditional standard, as indicated by the hekhsher they bear. Moreover, he deemed it advisable, for psychological reasons, that only wines with a hekhsher be used in religious ceremonies (e.g., for Qiddush or Havdalah). Similarly, on Pesaḥ only wines marked Kosher Lepesaḥ should be used.

The committee accepted Rabbi Silverman's findings (see, however, the responsum of Rabbi Jacob Radin for an opposing opinion).

7. Sheḥiṭah

Those animals, beasts, and birds that are permitted must be slaughtered in a prescribed manner called Sheḥiṭah. Essentially this consists of a highly trained person (called a shoḥeṭ), equipped with a special kind of knife, cutting both the windpipe (trachea) and the food pipe (esophagus) in the case of animals, and at least one of these in the case of fowl.

The use of a special method of slaughtering has been explained as the fulfillment of the commandment of צַעַר בַּעֲלֵי חַיִּים—prevention of cruelty to animals. Maimonides writes: "The commandment concerning the killing of animals is necesary because the natural food of man consists of vegetables and the flesh of animals; the best meat is that of animals permitted to be used as food. No doctor has any doubts about this. Since, therefore, the desire of procuring good food necessitates the slaying of animals, the law enjoins that the death of the animal should be the easiest. We are not permitted to torment the animal by cutting the throat in a clumsy manner, by pole-axing or by cutting off a limb whilst the animal is alive" (*Guide* 3:48; see also commentary of Naḥmanides to Gen. 1:29 and comment of *Sefer Haḥinukh,* sec. 48 [Chavel ed., p. 564]). Modern science has borne out the claim that Sheḥiṭah is the most humane method of slaughter (see Dembo, *Jewish Method of Slaughter;* Berman, *Sheḥiṭah,* pp. 431 ff.).

The persistent efforts of some humane societies to promote anti-Sheḥiṭah laws on grounds of compassion for animals often has its source not in compassion for animals but rather in hostility to the children of Israel. The stubborn claim that Sheḥiṭah constitutes cruelty to animals ignores expert opinions to the contrary (see Lewin, Munk, and Berman, *Religious Freedom,* pp. 16, 121–66).

The most recent attacks have been leveled not against Sheḥiṭah itself but against the method of preparing the animal for Sheḥiṭah, which is called hoisting and shackling. While the sight of hoisting and shackling is not very edifying, the degree of pain and discomfort to the animal has been grossly exaggerated. Nevertheless, changes are being made through the introduction of a specially designed pen which puts the animal into position for Sheḥiṭah without any pain or discomfort (S. Rubenstein, *Kashruth,* pp. 12 ff.).

The question of stunning the animal before slaughter, either by electricity or by anesthesia, has been on the agenda for a number of years. While some authorities see no objection to some of the proposed methods (Federbusch, *Binetivot Hatamud,* pp. 209 ff.), the overwhelming majority has ruled that stunning is contrary to the rules of Sheḥiṭah (ibid.; Lewin, Munk, and Berman, *Religious Freedom,* pp. 179 ff.; Sassoon, *Critical Study of Electric Stunning; Seriei Eish,* vol. 1, pp. 1–172; vol. 3, sec. 90).

It has been suggested that the purpose of Sheḥiṭah is to indicate a reluctance to allow the eating of meat altogether. In Genesis it is written: "And God said: Behold, I have given you every herb yielding seed, which is upon the face of the earth, and every tree, in which is the fruit of a tree yielding seed—to you it shall be for food" (Gen. 1:29). Meat is not mentioned here among the foods permitted to man. Only after the flood was Noah told: "Every moving thing that liveth shall be for you; as the green herb have I given you all" (Gen. 9:3). The implication is that man ideally should not eat meat because it entails taking the life of an animal. Later on there was an effort to limit the use of flesh to sacrifices. How else can we explain the following biblical passage: "When the Lord thy God shall enlarge thy border, as He hath promised thee, and thou shalt say: 'I will eat flesh,' because thy soul desireth to eat flesh; thou mayest eat flesh, after all the desire of thy soul. If the place which the Lord thy God shall choose to put His name there be too far from thee, then thou shalt slaughter of thy cattle and of thy flock, as I have commanded thee, and thou shalt eat within thy gates, after all the desire of thy soul" (Deut. 12:20–21)?

The permission to eat meat was thus a compromise. Hence the eating should, at least, be controlled by refraining from eating certain parts of the animal, especially the blood, and by special regulations governing the preparation of the meat (see Dresner and Siegel, *Jewish Dietary Laws,* pp. 21–23).

The Talmud summarizes the laws of Sheḥiṭah as follows: "One may not eat of the slaughtering of any טַבָּח [butcher] who does not know the rules of Sheḥiṭah. And these are: pausing, pressing, burrowing, deflecting, and tearing" (B. *Ḥul.* 9a). In talmudic times, the *ṭabaḥ* was both butcher and shoḥeṭ. Among our Yemenite brethren, it continued to be so until recently. In the Western countries, however, the ritual slaughtering of animals became a profession in its own right, restricted to persons of great piety who were specially trained for it.

A shoḥeṭ is required to have a license to practice. This license (קַבָּלָה) is granted by a recognized scholar (*Y.D.* 1:1 in Rama); it is granted only to a person who has been trained in the theory and practice of Sheḥiṭah, and has passed a thorough examination in both. Only persons of great piety are eligible. After the examining scholar is satisfied with the applicant's piety (*'Arukh Hashulḥan, Y.D.* 1:23), he examines him concerning Sheḥiṭah and Bediqah (see below), including his expertise in preparing the knife as required for Sheḥiṭah (ibid.).

Anyone who satisfies the preceding requirements is eligible to become a shoḥeṭ. Theoretically, therefore, women are also eligible (B. *Ḥul.* 2a; *Y.D.* 1:1). The accepted custom, however, is that women do not enter this occupation (*Y.D.* 1:1). Most frequently it is explained that women would have an untoward emotional reaction to the act of slaughtering. There have been exceptions, however, where women were permitted (*Simlah Ḥadashah* 1:13; see also Berman, *Sheḥiṭah,* p. 134).

8. The Knife

The חַלִּיף, or slaughtering knife, must be razor sharp and perfectly smooth, and must have no dents or nicks, since these would tear the flesh and cause unnecessary pain. The knife must be examined before and after the Sheḥiṭah to make sure that it is without blemish (פְּגִימָה) during the Sheḥiṭah (*Y.D.* 18:3, 12). The Talmud prescribes that it be examined *Abisra, Aṭufra, W'atlata Ruḥata*—with the flesh of the finger and with the fingernail, and that the examination must be of the three edges of the knife; i.e., the sharp edge and also the sides of this edge must be examined (B. *Ḥul.* 17b; *'Arukh Hashulḥan, Y.D.* 18:12). If the slightest dent or nick (פְּגִימָה) is felt, it is forbidden to use the knife (*Y.D.* 18:10).

It has become the custom to use a special knife exclusively for Sheḥiṭah (*Y.D.* 18:14 in Rama).

The knife should be at least twice as long as the diameter of the neck of the animal or fowl to be slaughtered (*Y.D.* 8:1 in Rama). The knives used today generally have a twenty-inch blade for sheep and goats, and a five-inch blade for fowl.

Before the Sheḥiṭah the shoḥeṭ recites the blessing אֲשֶׁר קִדְּשָׁנוּ בְּמִצְוֹתָיו וְצִוָּנוּ עַל הַשְּׁחִיטָה (*Y.D.* 19:1).

The Sheḥiṭah is restricted to the neck below the larynx, and preferably below the first ring of the trachea up to the point where the trachea begins to divide into branches, or up to the upper side of the left lung (*Y.D.* 20:1, *Ḥokhmat Adam* 10:1). In the case of the esophagus, it is from the top of the tube to the point where it takes on a hairy appearance (*Y.D.* 20:2).

In the slaughtering of animals and beasts, the cuts should be made horizontally across the throat, severing the trachea and the esophagus (*Y.D.* 21:1). With fowl, the severance of one of the two is sufficient (ibid.). In either case, it is sufficient if a greater part of the organ is severed.

The Talmud prescribes five regulations pertaining to the process of cutting.

1. *Shehiyah*—pausing, or delay. The knife must be drawn quickly across the neck of the animal, beast, or bird without a stop. The smallest delay or pause renders the Sheḥiṭah defective and the animal not kosher (*Y.D.* 23:2 in Rama).
2. *Derasah*—pressing. The blade must be applied with a to-and-fro motion, not with a chopping or striking motion (*Y.D.* 24:1).
3. *Ḥaladah*—burrowing. The blade must not be inserted between the trachea and the esophagus and used with an upward thrust; nor may the blade be inserted under the skin in any fashion (*Y.D.* 24:7, 8).
4. *Hagramah*—cutting out of the specified zone, or deflecting. As was explained above, the cut must be made below the larynx, preferably below the first hard ring of the trachea and up to the place where the bronchial tubes begin to branch (*Y.D.* 24:12).
5. *'Aqirah*—tearing out. The trachea and esophagus must be cut with the blade and not torn out or lacerated in any way. Thus, if the trachea was cut properly, and it is then found that the esophagus was ripped out from the jawbone at the root, the Sheḥiṭah is not valid and the animal may not be eaten. In the case of birds, if one of the two organs is ripped out after the first is cut properly, the Sheḥiṭah is proper, since for birds the severance of only one organ is necessary (*Y.D.* 24:15).

After the Sheḥiṭah has been completed, the shoḥeṭ must examine the carcass to determine whether the greater part (רוֹב) of the two pipes, in the case of animals and beasts, and at least one pipe in the case of fowl, have been severed (*Y.D.* 25:1).

When beasts or birds are slaughtered, the blood that flows from the cut must pour upon a bed of dust (עָפָר) and be covered with dust (Lev. 17:13; *Y.D.* 28:1, 5). This ritual should be preceded by the blessing עַל כִּסּוּי הַדָּם בֶּעָפָר (*Y.D.* 28:2).

This special attention to the blood is explained in the Bible in Leviticus 17:4, where blood is identified as the life-giving element in the body. "There is no clearer visible symbol of life than blood. To spill blood is to bring death. To inject blood is often to save life. The removal of blood which Kashrut teaches is one of the most powerful means of making us constantly aware of the concession and compromise which the whole act of eating meat, in reality, is. Again, it teaches us reverence for life" (Dresner and Siegel, *Jewish Dietary Laws*, p. 29).

Rabbi Hertz notes that the prohibition of the consumption of blood also tamed man's violent instincts by weaning him from blood and implanting within him a horror of all bloodshed (Hertz, *Pentateuch and Haftorahs,* comment on Lev. 17:10). About the covering of the blood, he says: "The blood being the symbol of life, it had to be treated in a reverent manner, in the same way that a corpse must not be left exposed. The covering with dust was the equivalent of burial in the case of a dead body" (ibid., comment on Lev. 17:13).

Why, then, was this law not applied to animals (בְּהֵמוֹת) as well as to beasts (חַיּוֹת) and fowl? It is because the exhortation to act reverently in regard to blood is not likely to be forgotten in the case of animals, since they were brought as sacrifices on the altar, and their blood had to be sprinkled thereon. The reminder is only needed for those creatures that could not be brought as sacrifices (*Sefer Haḥinukh,* mitswah 187).

UNIT XXII

THE DIETARY LAWS (II)

LAWS OF ṬEREFOT: THE RESPIRATORY SYSTEM

Structure of the Lungs
Defects in the Lungs
Coloration of Lungs
Texture of Lungs
Perforations in the Lungs
Blisters, Cysts, Swellings
The Principle of Tarte Lere‘uta (Double Fault)

XXII.
The Dietary Laws (II)
Laws of Ṭerefot: Respiratory System

After the slaughtering, an animal, beast, or fowl must be examined to determine whether or not it is rendered *ṭerefah* by certain physical blemishes or pathological conditions.

The word *ṭerefah* originally meant an animal torn by beasts of prey, as in the passage "Ye shall not eat any flesh that is *ṭerefah* [torn] of beasts in the field" (Exod. 22:30). It has come to be the designation for meat that is not ritually fit for consumption by Jews, i.e., the opposite of kosher. Maimonides comments: "We have already explained in the *Laws Concerning Forbidden Foods* that the *ṭerefah* mentioned in the Torah refers to an animal about to die; the word *ṭerefah* is employed here only because Scripture speaks in terms of the most common occurrence, for instance, when the animal is torn by a lion or a similar beast of prey, and is left fatally injured but not yet dead" (*Hil. Sheḥiṭah* 5:1).

The Mishnah, after enumerating eighteen defects that make an animal *ṭerefah*, concludes with this general rule: "If it could not continue alive in a like state, it is *ṭerefah*" (M. *Ḥul.* 3:1). Maimonides expands the number of defects to seventy (*Hil. Sheḥiṭah* 5:2). 'Ulla, a third-century Amora, classifies all the defects under eight categories (*B. Ḥul.* 43a; *Y.D.* 29). "'Ulla said: Eight categories of *ṭerefah* were communicated to Moses on Sinai: *derusah* [clawed], *nequbah* [perforated], *ḥaserah* [missing], *neṭulah* [removed], *qeru'ah* [torn], *nefulah* [fallen], *pesuqah* [severed], and *shevurah* [fractured]." All these categories will be explained in detail further on.

Since it may be assumed that most cattle are in a sound condition (Shakh on *Y.D.* 39:1), it is not necessary to inspect an animal for any kind of *ṭerefah* not known to be present (*Y.D.* 39:1). An exception is made in the case of cattle and beasts, the lungs of which are examined to determine whether there are any adhesions (*sirkhot*).

1. Structure of the Lungs

The lungs of cattle have one large and three smaller lobes on the right side, and one large and two smaller lobes on the left side. Each lobe has a distinctive shape. Between the two halves of the lung, slightly toward the right, there is a small additional lobe which rests in a pocket (*aninute de-varda*), the infra-cardiac lobe.

Since the most frequent defect or disease in cattle is pulmonary, the lungs must be examined carefully. The animal is cut open at the front, a hand is inserted, and the lung is examined manually for possible adhesions (*sirkhot*). The lungs are inspected again upon removal from the body cavity. If they are smooth to the touch—i.e., if the hand does not meet any obstructions (hence the term glatt [i.e., smooth] kosher), and, of course, provided there are no other defects in the lungs which would make the animal *ṭerefah*—the animal is declared kosher. As will be explained below, some of the adhesions that may be found on the lungs do not affect the status of the animal.

2. Defects in the Lungs

We mentioned that the lungs are examined for adhesions. An adhesion is a band of collagen fibers arising pathologically from the organization of fibrinous exudates (Levin and Boyden, *Kosher Code*, p. 76, n. 2).

According to Rashi, an animal with an adhesion on its lung is *ṭerefah* because whenever there is an adhesion, there is also a perforation which causes the adhesion. Through this perforation the lung absorbs liquids of all kinds, and these, when thickened, ooze through the hole and set, thereby forming a membrane which will eventually become loosened. According to Tosafot, although there is no hole now, an adhesion that is not of the natural order (see below) will become loosened by the movement of the animal, and thereby a perforation will develop (*Y.D.* 39 in Ṭaz, sec. 3, and Shakh, sec. 10). This principle provides the basis for understanding the rules concerning adhesions.

The following adhesions do not make an animal unkosher:

1. *Sirkha teluyah,* a pendent adhesion growing out of the lung with the other end not attached to anything (*Y.D.* 39:8), provided that

the lung is sound (i.e., no swelling) at the place where it is attached.

2. An adhesion between two adjacent lobes, provided that the adhesion is on the half nearer the base of each lobe, and between the adjacent surfaces (*Y.D.* 39:4).
3. If the adhesion emanating from the lung is attached at the other end to another organ nearby in that part of the chest where no possible movement of the organ might pull the adhesion away. Thus, if the adhesion is attached to the spine, or to the fat that surrounds the aorta, or to the trachea, or if the small lobe has an adhesion at its base, the animal is not affected.

In all the preceding cases, no examination is necessary. All other adhesions make the animal potentially *ṭerefah*. In such cases, the spot where the adhesion occurs is gently massaged. If it fails to come off, the animal is *ṭerefah*. If it does come off, the lungs are inflated and the spot is tested for a possible perforation; the animal is kosher if a drop of liquid placed on the spot does not bubble (*Y.D.* 39:1, 39:13 in Rama and in Shakh, ad loc.).

The following irregularities in the shape of the lungs make the animal *ṭerefah:*

1. The lungs have three smaller lobes on the right and two on the left. If the number is reversed, the animal is *ṭerefah* (*Y.D.* 35:2).
2. One extra lobe, either on the right or on the left, in the rows of the lobes (*bedare de'una*), or protruding toward the spine (i.e., dorsally), does not affect the kashrut of the animal, but if toward the heart (i.e., ventrally), the animal is *ṭerefah* (*Y.D.* 35:3).
3. If the lobes of the lungs are not differentiated but appear as one piece, the animal is *ṭerefah* (*Y.D.* 35:8). If there is a trace of a subdivision, however, it is kosher (Shakh, sec. 44). In young goats and sheep the lobes are rarely differentiated, but they are nevertheless kosher (*Y.D.* 35:8 in Rama). These laws do not apply to fowl, inasmuch as the lungs of many species are never differentiated into lobes, while in other species the lobes are of an indeterminate number (*Y.D.* 35:10).

3. Coloration of Lungs

If the color of the lungs is unnatural, it is sometimes considered a defect and sometimes not. An animal is *ṭerefah* if its lungs are—

1. black as ink (*Y.D.* 38:1);
2. yellow like an egg yolk, gold, wax, or an etrog (ibid.);
3. flesh color (ibid.);
4. saffron color (ibid.);
5. white like the white of an egg (ibid. in Rama).

An animal is not *ṭerefah* if its lungs are green, blue, or red (*Y.D.* 38:4).

The discolorations that make an animal *ṭerefah* do so only if the color remains after the lungs are inflated and massaged (*Y.D.* 38:2), and only if the discoloration is in the texture of the membrane, and not because of material, such as pus, underneath (*Y.D.* 38:3, esp. in Rama).

4. Texture of Lungs

Lungs that are as hard as wood to the touch render an animal *ṭerefah* (*Y.D.* 36:10). The animal is also *ṭerefah* if the lungs are light in weight (ibid. and Shakh, sec. 28).

If the lungs are so brittle that chips fall off when the lung is scratched with the fingernail and the scratch remains visible—even if only a small part of the lung is affected—it is a sign that the lungs are dry, and therefore the animal is *ṭerefah* (*Y.D.* 36:13 in Rama).

If the lung is found to be puffed up, the animal is *ṭerefah*, because of uncertainty whether the puffy area is simply a swelling or an addition to the lung (*Y.D.* 36:12; Maimonides, *Hil. Sheḥiṭah* 8:8 [see ibid. 7:18 for a different version]; Levin and Boyden, *Kosher Code*, p. 60, n. 34, consider this condition to be an extreme case of emphysema).

If the flesh of the lung is fluidlike, the rule is as follows: If the outer membrane and the bronchi are intact, the animal is kosher; if not, it is *ṭerefah*. To test whether the bronchi are intact, the liquid in the lung is poured into a dark-colored vessel (lined with lead) and the fluid is examined to see whether it contains white threads. The presence of such threads is an indication that the bronchi have decayed. If the liquid is turbid or putrid, the animal is also *ṭerefah* (*Y.D.* 36:7). The practice today is not to rely on these tests except in cases of great financial loss (*Simlah Ḥadashah* 36:18; Katzenelson, *Hatalmud Weḥokhmat Harefu'ah*, pp. 159 f., identifies this condition as bronchiectasis, a fatal disease which in humans has only recently responded to surgery).

If the lung is decayed to such a degree that it disintegrates when it is hung up, the animal is *ṭerefah* (*Y.D.* 36:11). Medically, this is a case of multiple abscesses (see Levin and Boyden, *Kosher Code*, p. 60, n. 33).

In cases where the lung is entirely shrunk, the Talmud and the early authorities make a distinction between shrinkage induced by natural causes and shrinkage induced by man, the former being kosher and the latter being *ṭerefah* (B. *Ḥul.* 54a, 55b; *Y.D.* 36:14). A test is also prescribed (*Y.D.* 36:15), but the Rama maintains that we cannot depend on it except where the probabilities are that the cause was natural. Veterinarians claim that the test is a valid one—i.e., if the shrinking of the lung is permanent, due to a sclerosis, the lung will sink in water; if not, it will expand, rise to the surface, and float. But there is no corroboration for a distinction between natural and artificial causes.

If, when the lungs are inflated, a certain part, no matter how small, does not inflate because a passage is plugged (a case known as atelectasis), the cause of the obstruction is sought by cutting the membrane near the spot with a knife. If a secretion is found, but otherwise that part of the lung looks the same as the rest of the lung, the animal is kosher (*Y.D.* 36:9) because the obstruction is temporary and the secretion would pass out if the animal were alive (Shakh, ad loc.). If no secretion is found, a feather or a straw is placed on the spot; if it moves during inflation the animal is kosher, for this proves that the air can come through (*Y.D.* 36:9 in Rama). The Rama further suggests that in the case of such an obstruction, the lung may be placed in tepid water, or tepid water may be poured through the windpipe and shaken, or the spot strongly massaged. The water should then be poured out and the lungs inflated; if the spot inflates, the animal is kosher (*Y.D.* 36:9).

If the lung is already cut, and the plugged place can be inflated with a tube, the animal is kosher (*Y.D.* 36:9).

The animal is also kosher if the secretion has the appearance of pus, because this means that the secretion is a tubercle (calcified area), and tubercles do not make an animal *ṭerefah* (*Y.D.* 36:9, 37:3).

5. Perforations in the Lungs

As already noted, an animal that has certain adhesions on its lungs is *ṭerefah* because these adhesions indicate a perforation or potential perforation of the lungs. Perforations in the vital organs make an animal *ṭerefah* because matter from these organs may ooze into the body cavity and cause poisoning, or the deterioration of the organ itself may lead to the death of the animal (Katzenelson, *Hatalmud Weḥokhmat Harefu'ah,* pp. 92–96). Therefore, if the lungs are perforated through both membranes which form the sac in which the lungs are enclosed, the animal is *ṭerefah* (*Y.D.* 35:1, 36:1).

There is a difference of opinion as to whether the perforations must face each other (*Y.D.* 36:1, opinions of Caro and Rama). According to a third opinion, the animal is *ṭerefah* even if the perforations do not face each other but are on the same side of the lungs (Ṭaz, sec. 1). The logic of the third opinion is that there is little chance for anything to get through if the perforations are not on the same side.

If part of the substance of the lung is missing, but there is no perforation of the membranes, according to one opinion the animal is kosher (*Y.D.* 36:8). According to the Rama, the established practice is that the animal is *ṭerefah* if the deficiency is noticeable from the outside when the lungs are inflated, and it takes the shape of a semicircle (like a bent *kaf*), so that a thumb can be put into the depression. Otherwise, it is kosher (*Y.D.* 36:8; see Shakh for other opinions).

If a sound is heard when the lungs are inflated, indicating a possible perforation, a straw or some liquid is placed on the spot. If it moves, it is an indication that there is a perforation, and the animal is therefore *ṭerefah*. If the place cannot be found, the lungs are tested by placing them in a container filled with warm water and inflating them. If the water bubbles, it is an indication that there is a perforation; if not, it is an indication that only one of the two membranes has been pierced and the noise is due to air moving between the two membranes. The animal is therefore kosher (*Y.D.* 36:4).

If the presence of a needle is felt in the flesh of the lungs, the needle may have reached its present place via the trachea without having pierced any of the organs, or it may have penetrated the walls of the lungs from the outside and thus perforated at least the membranes of the lungs. To determine what happened, we attempt to inflate the lungs; if the lungs inflate, it indicates that there are no perforations (*Y.D.* 36:16). The Rama limits this test to cases where a great financial loss is involved. By the same logic, the animal is kosher if the needle is found in the main bronchus, since it is assumed that it got there without piercing any organ (*Y.D.* 36:17).

If the membranes of the lungs were perforated but the perforation was closed up by another membrane growing over it, the animal is nevertheless *ṭerefah* because the covering membrane is bound to be destroyed (*Y.D.* 36:3; Rashi on B. *Ḥul.* 43b).

6. Blisters, Cysts, Swellings

The word *bu'a* in the Talmud is variously translated as "cyst," "blister," and "swelling" (see p. 252, Soncino trans. of B. *Ḥul.* 47a; Levin and Boyden, *Kosher Code,* p. 65, n. 1; trans. of H.Z. Rappaport, *Y.D.* 37:1). In the discussion that follows, the term "cyst," adopted in the Soncino translation, will be used, but it should be understood to include pathological swellings of all kinds.

A lung with a cyst on it is kosher (*Y.D.* 37:1 in Rama). If two cysts are close to each other, the animal is *ṭerefah* (*Y.D.* 37:3). If there is one cyst but it looks like two, it should be perforated and examined. If the fluid empties at one place, it is one cyst, and the animal is kosher; if not, it is two cysts and therefore the animal is *ṭerefah* (*Y.D.* 37:3). There is a difference of opinion regarding the reason for this rule. According to Rashi, the fact that a second cyst appeared so close to the first is an indication that there is a perforation in the lungs. Another authority holds that if there are two cysts close to each other, they will jostle each other and cause a perforation to develop (*Simlah Ḥadashah* 37:6).

If there are growths on the lungs—i.e., hard tubercles with no fluid in them, or abscesses (*mursa*) covered with a membrane and not protruding above the surface of the lungs—the animal is kosher even if they are close to one another (*Y.D.* 37:3). According to the Shakh, this applies only if the membrane is the color of the lungs. Otherwise, we apply the same law as when two cysts are close to each other. Here, "close to one another" means that when the lungs are inflated the space between the two cysts is less than two hair-breadths, and that this space has the color of the lungs (*Y.D.* 37:3 in Rama).

Cysts on the extremities of the lungs (*shippulei*) or on a furrow (*ḥarits*) or on a fold (*qemet*) are like two cysts that are close to each other, and the animal is therefore *ṭerefah* (*Y.D.* 37:3).

7. The Principle of Tarte Lere'uta (Double Fault)

Neither a pendent adhesion emerging from a cyst nor a cyst on a defective part of the lung makes an animal *ṭerefah;* but the combination of these two defects does (*Y.D.* 37:2). This is the source of the principle that two defects, either of which by itself would not cause the animal to be considered *ṭerefah,* make the animal *ṭerefah* when they occur together (*Y.D.* 37:2 in

Ṭaz, sec. 3; for a detailed discussion of this principle, see *'Arukh Hashulḥan, Y.D.* 19–14; also Rappaport, pp. 18–21; Eisenstein, *Otsar Dinim Uminhagim*, p. 385).

Another example of this principle is the rule that the animal is kosher if the upper membrane of the lung is missing but the inflation of the lung indicates that the other membrane is intact. If, however, a cyst is found where the upper skin is peeled off, the animal is considered *ṭerefah* (*Y.D.* 36:2).

Together with the laws concerning the lungs it is logical to treat the other parts of the body that are part of the pulmonary system. First is the mouth. An animal is kosher if its lower jaw is missing, provided that the defect does not interfere with its ability to eat—i.e., the animal can still be fed by others.

The animal is *ṭerefah* if its upper jaw is missing, however, because in this case the respiratory organs become exposed to the cold air, and this may lead to respiratory diseases (*Y.D.* 33:2; Shakh, sec. 3; *Levush, Y.D.* 33).

The animal is also *ṭerefah* if the windpipe was severed through most of its cavity—i.e., most of its internal circumference, in the area prescribed for slaughtering, or above it, i.e., in the larynx (*Y.D.* 34:1).

UNIT XXIII

THE DIETARY LAWS (III)

LAWS OF ṬEREFOT:

BONE STRUCTURE AND DIGESTIVE SYSTEM

The Skull
The Spinal Column and Spinal Cord
The Ribs
The Legs
The Digestive System
The Pharynx and Esophagus
The Stomach
The Intestines
The Liver, Gallbladder, Pancreas, and Spleen

XXIII.
The Dietary Laws (III)
Laws of Ṭerefot:
Bone Structure and Digestive System

The bone structure includes the skull, spinal column, ribs, forelegs, and hindlegs.

1. The Skull

The skull is the spherical bone that shelters the brain. Any defect in the skull may affect the brain. Hence, if most of the skull was crushed—i.e., many bruises but no open hole (Rashi on *B. Ḥul.* 52b)—the animal is *ṭerefah* (*Y.D.* 30:1). The term "most of the skull" means most of the circumference (*rov heqeifah*) or most of the "height" of the skull (*rov govhah*).

There is a difference of opinion regarding the meaning of these terms. According to one definition, "height" refers to the space between the level of the eyes and the level of the horns, and "circumference," to the whole upper part of the head, beginning with the level below the eyes and extending to the level of the horns (Ṭur). The other maintains that "height" refers to the front part of the skull, from the space beneath the eyes up to the horns, while "circumference" circles the entire skull, front and back (*Y.D.* 30:1; Ṭaz. 1).

If the skull is broken through so that a portion the size of a *selah* (one-third of a *tefaḥ*, or 3 3/4 inches [see Shakh 5; Feldman, *Rabbinical Mathematics*, p. 222]) is missing, the animal is *ṭerefah* (*Y.D.* 30:2). The same law applies if there are smaller holes which add up to the size of a *selah* (ibid.). This applies to large animals, such as an ox. Smaller animals are *ṭerefah* if the skull has holes of proportionate size (*Tevu'ot Shor* 30:3). The reason for these rules is not that the injury to the skull per se makes the animal *ṭerefah*, but rather that such an injury will lead to a perforation of the membrane of the skull.

The brain itself has two membranes (*meninges*), an upper (*dura mater*) and a lower (*pia-arachnoidea*). If the lower membrane is perforated, the animal is *ṭerefah* (*Y.D.* 31:1). If the upper membrane is perforated, according to Caro, the animal is kosher (ibid.); but according to Rama, it is *ṭerefah*, unless there would be a substantial financial loss (ibid.). Later authorities maintain that there should be no distinction between the two membranes (*'Arukh Hashulḥan, Y.D.* 31:2; *Ḥokhmat Adam* 15:6; for other differences of opinion, see Ṭur, *Y.D.* 31).

The animal is kosher if a small portion of the brain is soft or decayed (*Y.D.* 31:2), but if it is liquified like water or softened like wax, the animal is *ṭerefah* (ibid.).

If there is water in the brain, but it is completely surrounded by the substance of the brain, and there is a loss of brain substance equal to the quantity of water, the animal is kosher. The same is true if the water is in a sac (ibid.).

The brain, and the laws regarding it, extend to and include the two beanlike structures (*occipital condyles*) at the base of the skull. Below this point the laws of the spinal cord apply (*Y.D.* 31:4).

2. The Spinal Column and Spinal Cord

The spinal column consists of vertebrae through which the spinal cord (*medulla spinalis*) passes. These vertebrae are divided into: *vertebrae colli,* the seven vertebrae of the neck; *vertebrae dorsi* (or *thoracis*), the thirteen vertebrae to which the ribs are attached; *vertebrae lumbarum,* six in number, which have no ribs attached to them but have vestigal ribs—i.e., they are larger than the other vertebrae with protrusions larger than those of the other vertebrae; *vertebrae sacrum,* the four or five vertebrae that are near the pelvic bones; *vertebrae coccyges,* the small vertebrae that are at the very end.

Injury to the spinal column itself does not make an animal *ṭerefah*. The resulting injury to the spinal cord is the determining factor. If the skin that envelops the spinal cord is cut in most of its circumference, the animal is *ṭerefah* (*Y.D.* 32:1). If the cord itself—i.e., the substance (*moaḥ*) within the skin—has become fluid like water or melted like wax, it is tested by holding the cord underneath the injured part; the animal is *ṭerefah* if the piece immediately above the hand cannot stand upright but bends (*Y.D.* 32:3).

The same is true if the cord cannot stay upright because of excessive density and heaviness (*Y.D.* 32:3; see also Maimonides, *Hil. Sheḥiṭah* 9:2).

In the following cases of injury the animal remains kosher:

1. When the skin of the spinal cord is cut lengthwise (*Y.D.* 32:2), since, in spite of the cut, the contents of the skin are still well protected (see the case of the windpipe, *Y.D.* 34:7).
2. When the spine is broken but the cord remains intact (ibid.).
3. When the contents are crushed and therefore hang loose and move about (ibid.).
4. When the substance of the cord is severed but the skin that envelops it is intact (*Y.D.* 34:1; Shakh 2).
5. When a small amount of the marrow is missing, causing an empty space within the marrow (*Y.D.* 34:4).

The spinal cord begins at the base of the skull and ends with the tail. The above laws, however, apply only up to the place where the lumbar and sacral nerves leave the cord. This is referred to as the third branching of the cord (*parashah shelishit*). Beyond that, the continuing cord is not halakhically considered to be part of the spinal cord (*Y.D.* 32:5).

As for the nerves that branch off from the cord, if one of the two branches of the first and second forkings is severed, the animal is *ṭerefah*. If one of the two branches of the third forking is severed, the animal is kosher (*Y.D.* 32:5).

3. The Ribs

There are twenty-two large ribs attached to the *vertebrae dorsi*, eleven on each side (Katzenelson, *Hatalmud Weḥokhmat Harefu'ah*, pp. 192, 277). If more than half of these (i.e., at least twelve) are broken in their upper half (i.e., between the midpoint of the rib and the spine), the animal is *ṭerefah* (*Y.D.* 54:1).

If one of the large ribs (i.e., one of the twenty-two mentioned above), is torn out with half of a vertebra, the animal is *ṭerefah* (*Y.D.* 54:3). The Shakh, following the *Halakhot Gedolot*, considers the animal *ṭerefah* where a rib was torn out at its root, even if the vertebra to which it is attached remains whole, if there would be no great financial loss (*Y.D.* 54:4).

If the above are missing naturally, not because they were torn out by force, the animal is kosher (*Y.D.* 54:4 in Rama). If one of the vertebrae was torn out completely, even a vertebra which has no ribs attached to it, the animal is *ṭerefah* (*Y.D.* 54:4). (In the case of vertebrae that have ribs attached to them, this is academic, since it is impossible to tear out a vertebrae without the ribs attached to it.)

If the small ribs which have no marrow are broken, the animal is kosher (*Y.D.* 54:2). These are the small vestigial ribs attached to the *vertebrae lumbarum.*

4. The Legs

There is a great difference between the rules regulating the hindlegs and those regulating the forelegs. The hindlegs are more important to the animal because the movements of the body are more dependent on them; hence, the bone structure is more complicated, and the ligaments and muscles are the strongest in the body. For the same reason, damage to the hindlegs is more injurious to the animal.

If one of the forelegs was dislocated at its root, or was completely cut off, the animal is kosher (*Y.D.* 53:1); there is no fear that the injury may have caused a puncture in the lungs, since the shoulder blade, to which the foreleg is attached, is thick and strong, and it protects the lungs (Shakh, ibid., sec. 1).

If, however, there is clotted blood over the ribs, it is an indication that the lungs were injured (*Y.D.* 53:1). Some authorities would make the animal *ṭerefah* even if no clotted blood appears over the ribs (*B.H.* 1), due to fear that there may be a perforation in the lungs. Later authorities modify this, declaring the animal kosher if the cartilage (*gid*) binding the bone to its sockets has not decayed (*Simlah Ḥadashah, Hil. Ṭerefat Ha'atsamot* 7:1). Another recent authority suggests that since under any circumstances the fear that the lungs may have been punctured is an added severity, the lungs should be examined by placing them in water and inflating them. If no bubbles appear, it is an indication that the lungs were not punctured, and the animal should be declared kosher, at least where there would otherwise be a substantial financial loss (*'Arukh Hashulḥan, Y.D.* 53:4).

The leg itself is forbidden because of אֵבֶר מִן הַחַי (*Y.D.* 53:1, 62:3). If there is simply a fracture, and most of it is covered with skin and flesh, the leg too is permitted; since it can heal again, it is not considered to be detached from the body (*Y.D.* 62:3).

The hindleg consists of three parts: (1) the lower part, called the canon bone (the shin); (2) the middle part, called the shank or tibia; (3) the upper part, called the thigh bone or femur.

The joint between the lower and the middle part is the *'arqom,* or hock. Above the hock, at the base of the middle part, is the *tsomet hagidin,* the juncture of the tendons—i.e., a group of flexor tendons that converge upon the hock. The joint between the middle and upper parts is the *arkuvah,* or knee.

The animal is kosher if the bone is severed in the lower part, no matter where (*Y.D.* 55:1). The animal is *ṭerefah* if the bone is severed in the upper part (ibid.). It is also *ṭerefah* if the bone is cut at the juncture of the sinews in the middle part. Regarding cuts above the juncture, opinions differ. Our practice is to consider any severance of the bone above the hock as making the animal *ṭerefah* (ibid. in Rama). The animal is also *ṭerefah* if the thighbone is dislodged from its socket, where it is attached to the body, and the ligaments that bind the thighbone to the socket are decayed. According to the Rama, in cases where there would be no substantial financial loss, such a dislocation is always *ṭerefah,* even if the ligaments are not decayed (ibid.).

5. The Digestive System

The digestive system begins with the mouth and ends with the anal opening. Since the mouth was discussed earlier in connection with the pulmonary system (see p. 321), we begin with the areas next to the mouth, and continue with the pharynx—*tarbets haweshet* or *beit habeli'ah;* the esophagus or gullet—*weshet;* and the stomach, which in the ruminants is a very complicated affair with four compartments: (1) the rumen or paunch—*keres hapenimi;* (2) the reticulum or honeycomb bag—*beit hakosot;* (3) the omasum or manyplies—*hemses;* and (4) the abomasum or true stomach—*qeivah.*

The food, when first swallowed, travels in the form of a coarse pellet into the paunch, the largest of the four compartments. There it is softened and passed into the reticulum, where it is moulded into "curds" of convenient size. Later these are passed into the mouth by regurgitation. After mastication they are swallowed again, passing into the third stomach, or manyplies, and then into the fourth compartment, or true stomach.

From the stomach the food goes into the duodenum (*rosh me'i*) and then into the intestines (*daqin* or *hadra dekanta*) and finally into the rectum (*karkashta* or *ḥalḥolet*). We should also mention the *saccus caecus*, which according to some scholars is the *sanya divei* of the Talmud. In anatomical texts the intestinal tract has a number of subdivisions, but in the Talmud they all come under the term *daqin*.

From the very beginning, the food that goes through the alimentary canal is treated by and mixed with the body juices and secretions. Hence, a perforation in any of the organs of digestion would allow the admixture of food and secretions to enter the body cavity and cause poisoning or peritonitis (Katzenelson, *Hatalmud Weḥokhmat Harefu'ah*, p. 97). As a result, a puncture in any of these organs, with some very few exceptions to be mentioned below, makes the animal *ṭerefah*.

6. The Pharynx and Esophagus

The pharynx is a muculo-membranous sac which belongs to both the digestive and respiratory tracts. It is somewhat funnel-shaped, the large anterior part joining the mouth and nasal cavity, while the small end is continued by the esophagus (Sisson and Grossman, *Anatomy of the Domestic Animals*, p. 407; cf. Talmud and Rashi: the Talmud asks what the *tarbets haweshet* [pharynx] is, and answers that it is *mavla'ta*, which Rashi interprets as follows: "It is the chamber of swallowing [the pharynx], very close to the opening of the gullet" [B. *Ḥul.* 43b]).

The esophagus extends from the pharynx to the stomach. If either the pharynx or the esophagus is perforated, the animal is *ṭerefah* (*Y.D.* 33:3). The esophagus has two skins—the outer one is red, the inner one, white. If these are reversed and the outer one is white and the inner red, or if both are completely white or completely red, the animal is *ṭerefah* (*Y.D.* 33:5). The change in color means that one of the skins is diseased (Shakh 9). The Ṭaz quotes authorities who claim that the animal is kosher if both skins are white (sec. 10; see also *Ḥokhmat Adam* 16:7, who claims that according to the established custom the animal is *ṭerefah*; on the other hand, see *'Arukh Hashulḥan* 14:33 to the contrary).

If the perforation is such that the hole in one skin is not against the hole in the other skin, the animal is nevertheless *ṭerefah*; since the esophagus contracts and expands, the two holes may sometimes face each other (B. *Ḥul.* 43a; *Y.D.* 33:4; see also Ṭaz 5).

The animal is also *ṭerefah* if the esophagus is separated from the windpipe so that they are detached throughout most of their length (*Y.D.* 33:10).

The reason suggested is that if the esophagus is loose it makes proper Sheḥiṭah impossible, as in the case where the organ was forcibly torn away from the jaw (*'iqqur*) (see *Y.D.* 24:16; B. *Ḥul.* 44a in Tosafot, s.v. *weha'ika*).

If a thorn is embedded in the skin of the esophagus, even if the skin is not punctured through and through, the animal is *ṭerefah*, because the skin may have been punctured but subsequently healed (*Y.D.* 33:9). The Rama disagrees, maintaining that the animal is *ṭerefah* only if there is a drop of blood on the other side, opposite the thorn (ibid.). As usual, the Ashkenazic tradition follows the opinion of the Rama.

7. The Stomach

The stomach is the large dilation of the alimentary canal between the esophagus and the intestines. In the ruminants it has four compartments as noted above. The animal is *ṭerefah* if the skin of any of the four stomachs is perforated (*Y.D.* 48:1, 2, 7). There are two exceptions to this rule. The second and third compartments are attached to each other by a common wall. In the center of this wall there is an opening, connecting the two stomachs. The animal is not *ṭerefah* if this wall is perforated, because this perforation would not interfere with the proper functioning of the respective organs nor would it allow their contents to get into the body cavity (*Y.D.* 48:7).

The other case is the following: In certain places fatty material clings to the organ and plugs up any holes that may be present. Thus, for example, the abomasum has a curved form, both sides being covered with fat; but only the fat on the concave side clings to the flesh and therefore plugs up any possible hole, thus preventing the animal from becoming *ṭerefah*. On the other hand, the fat on the convex side does not cling to the flesh, and therefore any perforation on that side does make the animal *ṭerefah* (*Y.D.* 48:1). As a general principle, fat that is kosher usually clings to the flesh and therefore plugs a hole in the organ to which it is attached, while fat that is not kosher does not cling to the flesh, and therefore does not plug properly any hole in the organ to which it is attached (B. *Ḥul.* 49b; *Y.D.* 64).

If a sharp object—a needle or a splinter, for example—is found in any of the stomachs, the animal is kosher (*Y.D.* 48:8, 6).

8. The Intestines

What the books of anatomy subdivide into duodenum, small intestine, large intestine, and caecum, the Talmud and the codes include in the one term *daqin*. Only the rectum has a name of its own to distinguish it from the other parts of the alimentary canal that follow the stomach. The terms used are *karkashta* and *ḥalḥolet*. This lack of subdivision makes no material difference because all of this is treated alike in the Halakhah. A perforation of the walls of any part of the tract makes the animal *ṭerefah* (*Y.D.* 46:1). Moreover, the animal is *ṭerefah* even if congealed fluids plug the perforation tightly (ibid.). It is not *ṭerefah*, however, if the hole is stopped by fat that is kosher (ibid.), or where the folds of the intestines are such that the wall of one is close to the other and plugs any perforation (*Y.D.* 46:3).

If a sharp object, such as a needle or a splinter, is found in the intestines, the animal is *ṭerefah*, inasmuch as where the intestines are coiled it is likely that the sharp object had pierced the wall (*Y.D.* 46:4). The Shakh (sec. 11) makes a distinction based upon the position of the sharp object, maintaining that the animal is kosher if the object is lying lengthwise, and if a great loss would otherwise be involved.

The animal is also *ṭerefah* if its rectum is punctured, except if the perforation is at the point where the rectum reaches the area between the pelvic bones and the spinal column; in this latter case, the animal is kosher even if the larger part of the rectum was removed, so long as two fingerbreadths in large animals or one fingerbreadth in sheep, remain intact (*Y.D.* 46:5; *Ḥokhmat Adam* 19:8).This is because the rectum is so closely surrounded by bones that even if it is perforated, its contents will not enter the body cavity and cause poisoning.

One other rule must be added which, though it concerns an area which is not part of the alimentary canal, is directly connected with an organ which is part of the digestive system: the belly wall, a layer of flesh that covers most of the abdomen. Part of the rumen is held tight by the thoracic bones in the chest, and part protrudes from the thoracic cavity and is held by this layer of flesh. A large animal is *ṭerefah* if this flesh is torn to the length of one handbreadth (*Y.D.* 48:3); a small animal is *ṭerefah* if most of the length of the flesh is torn, even if it is less than a handbreadth (ibid.). Maimonides explains that such a rent would permit the rumen to protrude from the body and be hurt (*Hil. Sheḥiṭah* 9:5; *'Arukh Hashulḥan, Y.D.* 48:19, 25).

The animal is *ṭerefah* even if the tear does not extend right through the thickness of the flesh but through most of it (ibid. in *Y.D.* and in Maimonides). The Shakh, however, is inclined to be lenient when the rent is not completely through the flesh, in cases where a great financial loss is involved (sec. 4).

9. The Liver, Gallbladder, Pancreas, and Spleen

Anatomy texts include the liver, gallbladder, pancreas, and spleen in the digestive system because, though not part of the actual alimentary canal, they are directly involved in the process of digestion.

The liver produces materials that help in the digestive process, a vital function biologically. Hence, the animal is *ṭerefah* if it has been removed (*Y.D.* 41:1; Katzenelson, *Hatalmud Weḥokhmat Harefu'ah,* p. 97, maintains that this rule is academic since the animal will die if a large part of the liver is removed). If, however, a small portion—i.e., the size of three olives: one where the liver is attached to the gallbladder, one where it is attached to the diaphragm, and one where it is attached to the kidneys—remains intact, the animal is kosher (*Y.D.* 41:1; Shakh 3).

Modern medicine would be stricter here, since it maintains that a liver reduced to this size would not sustain life, for a liver will restore itself only when not less than a fourth of its substance remains, and then only if the portal vein and common bile ducts are intact (see Levin and Boyden, *Kosher Code,* p. 99, n. 2).

If the liver becomes so dry that it chips off when scratched with a fingernail, the animal is *ṭerefah* subject to the same modifications that obtain when the liver is missing. Therefore, if a small portion, the size of three olives and distributed as above, is left intact, the animal is kosher (*Y.D.* 41:3). If two of the above-mentioned vital places, each the size of an olive, are dry, the animal is *ṭerefah* (*Y.D.* 41:3 in Rama).

The same law applies in the case of cirrhosis of the liver; i.e., if the liver is hard as stone but the three vital areas mentioned above remain normal, the animal is kosher (*Y.D.* 41:3 in Rama). The Shakh (sec. 5) is inclined to be lenient here in a case of great financial loss, but the later authorities disagree (*'Arukh Hashulḥan, Y.D.* 41:14; see also Miller, *Meat Hygiene,* p. 114, according to whom such a liver would not pass U.S. government inspection).

The animal is *ṭerefah* if the liver is so soft that blood oozes out, even if the vital areas remain normal, because these areas will also deteriorate (*Y.D.* 41:3). The Shakh and the Ṭaz both disagree, ruling that the animal is kosher if the vital areas are intact (Shakh 4; Ṭaz 2; see also *'Arukh Hashulḥan, Y.D.* 41:17).

If a needle is found in the liver, the animal is *ṭerefah*, because in order to get there the needle must have punctured some vital organ (*Y.D.* 41:6). While the text makes a distinction based upon the orientation of the thin and thick ends of the needle, I am inclined to agree with *Knesset Hagedolah* that today we cannot make such distinctions (see Levin and Boyden, *Kosher Code,* p. 103, n. 14).

The gallbladder's function is to store the bile manufactured by the liver. The bile is necessary for the proper absorption of the fats from the small intestines. Therefore, the animal is *ṭerefah* if the gallbladder has been punctured (*Y.D.* 42:1). But if the puncture is at the point where the gallbladder lies against the liver, and is thus plugged by the surface of the liver, the animal is kosher (ibid.). However, if the liver is perforated opposite the puncture in the gallbladder, the animal is *ṭerefah* (ibid.; Shakh 2).

If the gallbladder is missing, either congenitally or because it has been removed, the animal is theoretically *ṭerefah* (*Y.D.* 42:2). However, the animal is kosher if the liver tastes bitter; if it does not, there is another test. The liver is broiled over charcoal and tasted again. If it tastes bitter, the animal is kosher; if not, it is *ṭerefah* (*Y.D.* 42:3).

If there are two gallbladders, the animal is *ṭerefah*—on the principle that "every addition is deemed equal to a loss" (B. *Ḥul* 58b)—but it must be certain that there really are two gallbladders. One of them is punctured and examined to determine whether it empties into the other. If it does, this proves that in reality there is only one gallbladder, and therefore the animal is kosher (*Y.D.* 42:4). If it does not empty into the other, another test is applied. One gallbladder is inflated, and the other is watched to see if it becomes inflated as well, or water is poured into one and the other fills up. If it does, the animal is kosher. It is possible for the other to fill with air or water, though in the first test the other bladder did not react, because bile is thick, hence did not pour into the other, though they are really one (*Y.D.* 42:5).

The codes, following the Talmud (B. *Ḥul.* 49a), speak of "pits" found in the gallbladder, ruling that if they are shaped like a date, which does not have a sharp point, the animal is kosher; but if they are shaped like an olive pit, which has a sharp point, the animal is *ṭerefah* (*Y.D.* 42:9). Either they have already perforated the walls of the gallbladder or they will yet do so (see *Bet Yosef* and *'Arukh Hashulḥan* 42:26). Katzenelson explains that the discussion here is about what we now call gall stones (*Hatalmud Weḥokhmat Harefu'ah,* pp. 183 f.). Evidently the authorities who discussed this matter were unaware that these do not enter the gallbladder but are developed *in situ.* Hence, today the second reason is applied—i.e., if sharp, these stones are bound to perforate the gallbladder (Levin and Boyden, *Kosher Code,* pp. 111–13).

There is no mention of the pancreas in the Talmud. Some have identified it with the *yoteret hakaved* of the Bible (Exod. 29:3) and with the *etsba' hakaved* of the Mishnah (*Tam.* 4:3; see Katzenelson, *Hatalmud Weḥokhmat Harefu'ah,* p. 46). Most commentators and translators disagree. The Revised Version translates the biblical term as "appendage of the liver"; the new Jewish Publication Society Version, as "protruberance of the liver." As for *etsba' hakaved,* Danby translates it as "lobe of the liver." The *Encyclopedia Mikrait* identifies *etsba' hakaved* as the caudate lobe (see also Preuss, *Biblisch-talmudische Medizin,* p. 109; Levin and Boyden, *Kosher Code,* pp. 99–100).

According to Levin and Boyden, *ṭavḥaya* designates the pancreas (loc. cit., n. 4). This term is found in the Rama (*Y.D.* 64:15) and is quoted from the *Kol Bo,* a code dating from the late thirteenth or early fourteenth century. It refers to the meat that is popularly called "sweetbreads" in English and *grashitse* in Yiddish.

Now we can define our terms: *yoteret hakaved* and *etsba' hakaved* are the caudate lobe; *ḥatsar hakaved* and *ṭarpesh hakaved* refer to the diaphragm; *ṭavḥaya* refers to the pancreas.

The only regulation concerning the pancreas is that the membrane and the fat covering it must be removed (*Y.D.* 64:15; *'Arukh Hashulḥan, Y.D.* 64:39).

UNIT XXIV

THE DIETARY LAWS (IV)

CIRCULATORY SYSTEM; FOWL

The Heart
The Liver and Spleen
The Kidneys
The Urinary and Reproductive Organs
Injuries
Injuries Caused by Falling
A Flayed Animal
The Flesh of a Living Animal
Fowl

XXIV.
The Dietary Laws (IV)
Circulatory System; Fowl

The circulatory system includes the heart, the blood vessels, and some organs that have an indirect connection with the circulatory system, such as the liver, spleen, and kidneys. Some of these organs have already been treated in the sections dealing with the pulmonary system (unit 22) and the digestive system (unit 23). Here, therefore, we shall limit our discussion to the heart, blood vessels, and kidneys.

1. The Heart

The heart is the central organ not only of the circulatory system but of the entire animal. Its function is to pump blood through the blood vessels into every part of the body. It consists of powerful muscle tissue and acts like a pump, with four chambers that are filled with blood and emptied by the action of the muscles.

While the number of chambers mentioned in the Talmud and codes is at variance with the number given in modern books of anatomy (see Levin and Boyden, *Kosher Code*, p. 94, n. 2; Katzenelson, *Hatalmud Weḥokhmat Harefu'ah*, p. 54; Preuss, *Biblisch-talmudische Medizin*, p. 115; cf. B. *Ḥul.* 45b), this does not affect the rules of kashrut pertaining to the heart.

If the wall of the heart is perforated through and through—i.e., the perforation penetrates entirely through the wall of the heart into one of the chambers—the animal is *ṭerefah* (*Y.D.* 40:1). Even if the perforation is plugged by the fat surrounding the heart, the animal is still *ṭerefah* because the fat does not hug the heart too closely (ibid. in Rama). Such a perforation may be due either to a heart ailment that weakens the heart muscles, which then yield to the pressure of the blood, or to the animal's being stabbed by a sharp instrument. In the first case, death is immediate; in the second case, death is not immediate, but the animal cannot live very long. It is in the latter case that our ruling applies (Katzenelson, *Hatalmud Weḥokhmat Harefu'ah*, p. 94).

If the perforation does not reach one of the chambers of the heart, the source of the perforation must be examined. If it is due to disease, the animal is kosher; if it was caused by a sharp object, such as a thorn or a needle, the animal is *ṭerefah* (*Y.D.* 40:2). The reason for this distinction is that a sharp object must have entered from the outside and punctured some other organ in its passage (*Y.D.* 49:4; *Darkhei Teshuvah* 40:15). Therefore, if the sharp object is so located that it could have entered without puncturing any organ in its passage, the animal is kosher (*Y.D.* 40:3 in Rama; Shakh 6). If the animal is found to have two hearts, or, academically, no heart at all, the animal is *ṭerefah* (*Y.D.* 40:5).

These rules pose a problem today because of the current advances in medical science. What is the rule if the heart has been removed, but the animal is kept alive by an artificial substitute or by a transplanted heart? Furthermore, would a heart that has been transplanted be in the category of *eiver min haḥai?*

If the aorta or the pulmonary artery is punctured, the animal is *ṭerefah* (*Y.D.* 40:4). The ancients considered these to be part of the heart and therefore subject to the same rule (Levin and Boyden, *Kosher Code*, p. 97, n. 11). Medically, such a puncture would cause hemorrhage and excessive internal bleeding.

2. The Liver and Spleen

The ancients believed the liver to be the organ that produces blood. Its reddish color, and the fact that two blood vessels, the portal vein and the hepatic artery, convey blood into it, giving it a larger supply of blood than other organs, lent credence to such a belief.

Since the function of the liver is to manufacture bile for digestion, it was treated with the digestive system in the preceding chapter. So was the spleen, since physiologists include it in the digestive system, even though its function is to filter the blood.

3. The Kidneys

The kidney is a compound tubular gland which serves the general function of stabilizing the blood, ridding it of nitrogenous wastes and undesirable salts through a process of filtration. Along with the skin and lungs, it helps to maintain the constant volume of the blood by eliminating excess water which serves as the filtrate. Depending on the needs of the animal, a portion of the filtrate is reabsorbed. Whatever is not reabsorbed is excreted as urine.

In the sides of the kidney, toward the median line of the body, is a large depression called the hilum, which leads to a large cavity called the sinus (Miller, *Meat Hygiene*, pp. 183 ff.).

According to the Mishnah, the animal is kosher if the kidneys are missing (B. *Ḥul.* 54a). The codes, however, read: "Therefore, if an animal is born with one or three kidneys, the animal is kosher" (*Y.D.* 44:1). Katzenelson comments that an animal could not live more than two days if both kidneys were missing or were removed, and he suggests, therefore, that the reading in the Mishnah should be in the singular (*Hatalmud Weḥokhmat Harefu'ah*, pp. 105 f.).

Similarly, if the kidney is perforated or part of it is cut, even up to the hilum, the animal is kosher (*Y.D.* 44:1). However, if the kidney is diseased and its flesh becomes nephrosed, and the disease reaches the white matter inside the kidney (the sinus), the animal is *ṭerefah* (*Y.D.* 44:2), for the obvious reason that a diseased kidney is worse than a missing or perforated one since it can lead to the inflammation of the neighboring organs and the body cavity (*'Arukh Hashulḥan, Y.D.* 44:2, 3).

If a secretion (pus) is found in the kidney, even if it is not putrid; or if ill-smelling water is found, and the fluid reaches the white part of the kidney (sinus or pelvis), the animal is *ṭerefah* (ibid.). If the water is clear, however, or if the kidney is filled with blood, even if these reach the hilum, the animal is kosher (ibid.).

If the water is not clear, and has the color of honey, though it is not turbid, the animal is *ṭerefah* (ibid. in Rama; this is identified as a case of hydronephrosis—see Levin and Boyden, *Kosher Code*, p. 119, n. 8).

If the kidney is diseased in its white matter (the sinus or the pelvis), the animal is *ṭerefah* even if the rest of the organ is sound (*Y.D.* 44:3).

If stones are found in the kidneys, the animal is kosher (*Y.D.* 44:4).

If a kidney is reduced in size so that it is not larger than a bean in a small animal and not larger than a grape in a large animal (for these sizes, see *Maharam Schick, Y.D.* 57), the animal is *ṭerefah* if this defect is due to disease, but kosher if it is congenital. How can we distinguish between the two? If the membrane covering the kidney is shrunk (i.e., wrinkled, showing that the matter inside is shrunken), it is due to disease (intestinal nephritis); if it is not shrunk (i.e., the membrane fits perfectly over the flesh), it is congenital (congenital aphrasia) (*Y.D.* 44:5).

If the natural color of the kidney has changed, and the change pervades the organ up to the white matter (pelvis), the animal is *ṭerefah* (*Y.D.* 44:8; *'Arukh Hashulḥan*, *Y.D.* 44:25).

4. The Urinary and Reproductive Organs

If the uterus is missing, whether in cattle or in fowl, the animal is kosher (*Y.D.* 45:1). If, however, it is punctured or decayed, the animal is *ṭerefah* (ibid. in Rama; see, however, *'Arukh Hashulḥan*, *Y.D.* 45:3–7; and *Ḥokhmat Adam* 19:2).

Later authorities tend to be strict in the case of fowl if the organ in which the eggs develop is missing, and declare the fowl *ṭerefah* if no large loss is involved (*Ḥokhmat Adam* 19:1).

If the fetus is found decayed in the uterus, the animal is *ṭerefah* if no great loss is involved (*Ḥokhmat Adam* 19:2).

If the bladder is missing, or is punctured or decayed, the animal is *ṭerefah* (*Y.D.* 45:2 in Rama).

5. Injuries

This section will treat defects that do not result from disease or congenital deficiencies but rather were brought about by external causes that directly impair the animal.

If cattle or fowl have been clawed by predatory wild beasts or by birds of prey, the animal is *ṭerefah* (*Y.D.* 57:1). The reason given by the traditional authorities is that predatory animals have poison in their claws or talons which they inject into their victims (see Rashi and Tosafot on B. *Ḥul.* 42a). Maimonides is the only one among the standard codifiers who does not mention this (see *Hil. Sheḥiṭah* 5:4–8). Katzenelson claims that modern science does not know of any such poison, and therefore suggests that the word *zihara* in the Talmud (B. *Ḥul.* 53a), which has been translated as "poison," does not mean poison but rather "reddishness," i.e., the reddishness that results from the impact of a striking claw or talon. The impaired tissue can develop into gangrene (Katzenelson, *Hatalmud Weḥokhmat Harefu'ah*, pp. 102, 192).

There is a gradation in the animals and the force of their clawing and the resultant damage. A large beast has enough force in its claws to injure the largest cattle. A small beast has no effect on large cattle and can inflict injury only on small animals and birds.

Thus, if a lion, or its equivalent, claws even the largest ox, he makes the ox *ṭerefah* (*Y.D.* 57:1). A wolf, however, has no effect upon cattle but can injure smaller species, such as sheep (ibid.). A cat, a marten, or a fox can effectively injure only small animals, such as young goats, lambs, and fowl (ibid.).

Birds of prey, if they attack fowl, make them *ṭerefah*, but they cannot affect animals of any size. A hawk, however, if it strikes young goats and lambs, causes them to become *ṭerefah* (*Y.D.* 57:2).

A dog is not considered a predatory beast; therefore, if it attacks an animal, the animal does not become *ṭerefah* (*Y.D.* 57:1).

6. Injuries Caused by Falling

If an animal or a fowl falls from a height of ten handbreadths (*Y.D.* 59:1), and it gets up immediately and walks four cubits, it is kosher; if it does not walk, it should be allowed to rest for twenty-four hours. If it rises and walks, it is kosher; if not, it is *ṭerefah* (*Y.D.* 58:1). If the animal was thrown suddenly by force, the above rules apply even if it fell from a height of less than ten handbreadths (ibid.). The animal is *ṭerefah* in all the above instances because of the possibility that its internal organs have been crushed (*Y.D.* 58:3). The same rule applies if an animal or fowl is struck by a falling hard object that is heavy enough to cause internal injury (*Y.D.* 58:2 in Rama).

If the animal jumped of its own accord, it is kosher even if it jumped from a greater height, because an animal usually estimates the height from which it can jump without causing injury to itself (*Y.D.* 58:11).

7. A Flayed Animal

If an animal loses its hide, whether flayed by hand or because of disease, it is *ṭerefah* (*Y.D.* 59:1). Katzenelson explains that this refers only to the removal of the epidermis. The animal is kosher only if some parts of the skin remain intact because then it can heal. If the entire skin down to the flesh is removed, then even if a large part is left unhurt, the animal cannot live (*Hatalmud Weḥokhmat Harefu'ah*, p.111).

If a strip the width of a *sela'* along the whole length of the spine, and a piece of skin the size of a *sela'* over the navel, and the size of a *sela'* at the top of every joint remain intact, the animal is kosher (*Y.D.* 59:1).

If the hide has been removed from one of the above areas, the animal is kosher; if from all the above areas, though the rest of the hide is intact, the animal is *ṭerefah* (ibid. and in Rama).

8. The Flesh of a Living Animal

It is forbidden to eat flesh cut from a living animal—*eiver min haḥai* (Gen 9:4; *Y.D.* 62:1). Obviously, this is prohibited as an act of cruelty. Even where no cruelty is involved, however, such flesh is still *ṭerefah*. Thus, if a limb is torn from the body of an animal, but still remains hanging, though it is detached to such a degree that it cannot grow back to the body, it may not be eaten even after the animal has been properly slaughtered. If it can grow back, it is still considered part of the body, and it may be eaten after the animal has been properly slaughtered (*Y.D.* 62:3).

9. Fowl

While the principles regulating the kashrut of cattle apply in general to fowl as well, there are variations and additions because of the differences in anatomy. In discussing these, we shall follow the same order as in the discussion of cattle.

Whereas the lungs of cattle must be examined for defects, such examination is not necessary for fowl (*Y.D.* 39:1).

A fowl is kosher even if its beak is missing (*Y.D.* 33:1 in Rama). There is a question, however, whether the ruling of Maimonides that an animal is *ṭerefah* if its upper jaw is missing (*Y.D.* 33:2) also applies to fowl (see ibid. in *B.H.* 1). The final decision is that it does (see *Peri Megadim* ad loc.).

If the windpipe (trachea) is perforated like a sieve, the area of perforation should be cut out and placed against the orifice of the windpipe; if it covers the greater part of the orifice, the fowl is *ṭerefah* (*Y.D.* 34:4). If a piece of the windpipe is missing, theoretically we should take the size of an *isar*, which is the norm in cattle, and follow proportionately in the case of fowl (ibid. in Rama). In practice, however, especially since the size of an *isar* is no longer known, the same procedure is followed as when the windpipe is perforated like a sieve (ibid. in Shakh 10). The lungs of fowl are relatively small and do not have lobal divisions (*Y.D.* 35:10); this eliminates all the rules that have to do with the lobes.

The digestive tract of the fowl differs from that of cattle in the following ways: The beak, unlike the mouth of cattle, has no teeth, and the bird therefore swallows its food without chewing it. From the mouth the food goes into the gullet or esophagus, which leads into the crop (*zefeq*). The crop is actually an enlargement of the gullet and serves as a storage pouch in which the food is softened. From the crop the food travels via the proventuculus, a thickened tube, into the gizzard (*qurqevan.*). In this passage the food is mixed with an acetic gastric juice. The gizzard is an oval-shaped organ with thick muscle walls that grind or crush the food. The food, when ground to a homogeneous mass, passes into the duodenum. The rest of the tract follows the pattern of cattle.

The rules concerning the esophagus are the same as in the case of cattle except in the following instances:

When geese have been force-fed in order to produce the maximum amount of fat, the esophagus must be inflated and examined for punctures (*Y.D.* 33:9 in Rama; *Ḥokhmat Adam* 16:10). Some authorities forbid such force-feeding (ibid. in Rama).

If the top of the crop (i.e., the part which moves with the gullet when the fowl stretches its neck) is punctured, the fowl is *ṭerefah*. If any other part of the crop is punctured, the fowl is kosher (*Y.D.* 33:11). If the crop is missing, even though enough remains to make it possible for the food to pass from the gullet to the gizzard, the fowl is *ṭerefah* (ibid.). If the tube connecting the crop and the gizzard (proventiculus) is punctured, the fowl is *ṭerefah* (ibid. in Rama).

The gizzard consists of muscle wall and an inner membrane as a lining. If it is punctured so that the hole goes directly through both, the fowl is *ṭerefah*. If both are punctured but the perforations are not congruous, the fowl is kosher. This is unlike the case of the esophagus, where it would be *ṭerefah*, because in this case the wall is hard, and if the holes are not congruous there is no chance for them to become congruous and allow the food to come into the body cavity and cause poisoning (*Y.D.* 49:1). Even if the holes are congruous, but the fat on the gizzard plugs the hole, the fowl is kosher (*Y.D.* 49:2).

If a needle is found in the wall of the gizzard, and is completely insulated by the flesh of the gizzard, the fowl is kosher on the assumption that the needle has come there in such a way that no vital organs were punctured in its passage (*Y.D.* 43:11 and in Shakh, ad loc.).

The skeletal structure of the fowl may be divided into two parts, axial and appendicular. The axial comprises the skull, vertebral column, ribs, and sternum. The appendicular skeleton includes the bones of the limbs, which are so modified as to conform to the peculiar physiological requirements during locomotion.

If the skull of a fowl was perforated, the fowl is *ṭerefah* (*Y.D.* 30:2 in Rama). The rules regarding the spinal column are affected by the structure of the spine, which differs from that of cattle. Thus it is only the cervical vertebrae, the number of which varies in the different species (the fowl has fourteen; those with longer necks have more), that are separate as in cattle. The thoracic and lumbosacral vertebrae are practically all fused into one solid mass of bone.

There is, therefore, a difference of opinion regarding how far the spinal cord must be severed to make the fowl *ṭerefah*. According to one opinion, it is up to the place where the wings are connected to the body; according to the other opinion, where the bone which is joined to the body ends; i.e., either the humerus of the wing or the scapula in the body, the bladelike bone which is over the thoracic vertebrae (*Y.D.* 32:5). The latter ruling is followed except where great material loss is involved (Rama, ad loc.).

If the wings are fractured or cut off, the fowl is theoretically kosher, even if the fracture is close to the body. However, since the wings are attached to the body close to where the lungs are located, there is always the possibility that the fracture may have caused a perforation of the lungs. Hence, if the fracture is less than the breadth of a thumb from the body, the fowl is *ṭerefah* (*Y.D.* 53:2).

If the wing is dislodged, the ruling is the same as when the foreleg of cattle is dislodged, and the fowl is *ṭerefah* (*Y.D.* 53:3 and Shakh, ad loc.).

Some authorities rule that in the case of fowl, even if only one rib (not the majority of ribs, as in the case of cattle) was broken in half near the spine, the fowl is *ṭerefah*. This is like the case of a fractured wing, where the fowl is declared *ṭerefah* because the lungs may have been punctured (*Levush*, *Y.D.* 53; Shakh on *Y.D.* 53:3). Others maintain that the analogy is not a valid one because the wings are generally in motion and the possibility of a puncture is always present; but the ribs are not in motion (*Y.D.* 53 in Ṭaz, sec. 2). Hence, the fowl is *ṭerefah* only if the break is a jagged one with sharp points that may puncture the lungs. Even then, if a large monetary loss is involved, or if the food is needed for the Sabbath and it is close to the Sabbath, the lenient ruling is followed (*'Arukh Hashulḥan, Y.D.* 54:8).

A fracture in the leg of a fowl is subject to the same rulings that pertain to cattle, with one exception. Cattle have three converging tendons located in the middle bone (tibia), but fowl have sixteen; if the greater part of any one of these is severed, the fowl is *ṭerefah* (*Y.D.* 56:8).

Defects in the spleen or the kidneys do not make a fowl *ṭerefah* (*Y.D.* 43:6, 44:10). Later authorities, however, maintain that a fowl is *ṭerefah* if its spleen is perforated (*Y.D.* 43; Shakh 9; Ṭaz 9; *Ḥokhmat Adam* 18:6), unless great financial loss is involved.

If the gall of a fowl is missing, the rule is the same as in cattle, except that some birds (e.g., the pigeon) have no gall (*Y.D.* 42:8; Levin and Boyden, *Kosher Code*, pp. 110 f., n. 11).

If the placenta where the eggs lie is lacking, the fowl is *ṭerefah* (*Y.D.* in *B. H.* 45:1; *Ḥokhmat Adam* 19:1). Capons (i.e., male fowl that have been castrated—though this is forbidden) are kosher (*Y.D.* 46 in *B.H.* 8). If the eggs in the placenta are found to be putrid, the fowl is kosher (*Ḥokhmat Adam* 19:3). If a needle is found in the placenta among the eggs, the fowl is *ṭerefah* (*Ḥokhmat Adam* 19:5).

Fowl that have been clawed by smaller predators, such as weasels, cats (but not dogs), or vultures, are *ṭerefah*. Theoretically, such fowl should be examined to see whether the clawing caused poisoning; but because we do not consider ourselves experts in such examinations, all cases are ruled to be *ṭerefah* (*Y.D.* 57 in Shakh 10).

The clawing is considered to be effective if the bird of prey is the size of the fowl attacked or larger, except in the cases of the hawk, falcon, or eagle, where clawing is effective even if the fowl attacked is larger than itself, if it is of a species similar in size to the species of the attacking bird (*Y.D.* 57:3). The falcon is unique among predatory birds in that its clawing is effective on all species, even those larger than its own species (ibid. in Rama).

A fowl that has suffered a fall, or has been stepped on or knocked against a wall or kicked by an animal, or that has been struck by a hard object so that it cannot walk, should be allowed to rest for twenty-four hours. If it recovers its normal ability to walk, it is kosher; otherwise it is *ṭerefah* (*Y.D.* 58:2, 3).

If a fowl strikes the surface of a body of water with force, and it nevertheless swims its full length against the current, or if it swims its full length ahead of other objects flowing with the current, thus showing that it is moving on its own and not carried by the current, it is kosher; otherwise it is *ṭerefah* (*Y.D.* 58:7), unless it is able to walk (*'Arukh Hashulḥan*, *Y.D.* 58:17).

A fowl that has lost all its feathers is *ṭerefah*, except where the loss is due to an excess of fat in its body (*Y.D.* 59:2 in Rama).

A fowl that has fallen into a fire and been rescued may not be used until its internal organs are examined. If those organs which are usually red, such as the heart, liver, spleen, and gizzard, have turned greenish; or if the crop or intestines have turned red, the fowl is *ṭerefah* (*Y.D.* 52:1). The fowl is also *ṭerefah* if the colors are normal but change upon boiling (*Y.D.* 52:3). The reverse is also true. If they regain their normal color upon boiling, the fowl is kosher (*Y.D.* 52:2).

UNIT XXV

THE DIETARY LAWS (V)

PORGING AND KASHERING

Porging
The Removal of Forbidden Fat
Soaking
Salting
Broiling

XXV.
The Dietary Laws (V)
Porging and Kashering

1. Porging

After the animal is slaughtered, it is subjected to a procedure called *niqqur* or porging (in Yiddish, *treibern*). The purpose of porging is to—

1. remove the residual blood that did not drain during Sheḥiṭah;
2. remove the forbidden fats;
3. remove the sciatic nerve (*gid hanasheh*), which is also forbidden.

The various stages of porging are carried out in the abattoir, the butcher shop, and the home of the consumer. Nowadays, the part that the consumer formerly did at home is often done by the butcher.

The part of the procedure that takes place at the abattoir is carried out under the supervision of the shoḥeṭ or of a specially trained functionary called a *menaqqer* or porger.

The kosher butcher holds a special position in the Jewish community. He is not just another merchant; he is also the guardian of a religious institution—kashrut. He holds a position of trust because the people of the community depend on him to sell strictly kosher meat. Thus, he must not only be trustworthy and religiously observant but must also possess the knowledge and skill necessary to dress the meat in the manner prescribed by Jewish law and practice before he sells it to the consumer (*Y.D.* 64:21 in Rama).

Since it is difficult to learn porging from a book, the kosher butcher must acquire the skill by practice under the supervision of a competent, experienced instructor (*Y.D.* 65:8 in Rama).

The reason for the removal of blood has already been discussed (see unit 21). It is the concern of the shoḥet when he slaughters the animal, of the butcher when he porges the animal, and of the consumer, or rather the housewife, when the final preparations for cooking are made.

When the shoḥeṭ severs the organs in the neck, most of the blood is drained from the body of the animal—most, but not all. To continue the process of removing the blood, certain veins, sacs, and membranes in which the blood tends to gather must be removed.

Such veins are found in the forelegs, shoulders, lower jaws, tongue, neck, tail, and the fat of the entrails (*Y.D.* 65:1). There are also veins to be removed from the gallbladder, spleen, and kidneys; but since this pertains to the removal of the forbidden fat on these organs, it will be treated below.

The meninges (the sacs that encase the brain) and the testicles must be sliced in order to remove the blood that is in them. The heart and the liver must be treated specially (see below).

In addition to all this, the meat must be salted, soaked, and rinsed as the final stages in the removal of the blood. This will also be discussed below.

In the case of fowl, it is customary to cut between the knee joints, and to remove or cut through the veins in the throat (*Y.D.* 65:3 in Rama, and 22:1).

2. The Removal of Forbidden Fat

Forbidden fat (*ḥelev*) is found only in cattle and sheep but not in fowl or beasts (*Y.D.* 64:1). It can be identified by the following characteristics: (1) it adheres loosely to the flesh (*totav qerum w'niklaf*); (2) it always acts like a sheath and is never surrounded by muscle tissues (*ushelo yehei basar ḥofeh oto*) (Ṭur, *Y.D.* 64; *Y.D.* 64:4).

The fat must be removed from the stomach, both ends of the intestines, the kidneys, the liver, the spleen, the diaphragm, the omentum majus, and the area of the hindquarters.

The biblical prohibition of the *gid hanasheh* or sciatic nerve (Gen. 32:33) applies to cattle, sheep, and beasts but not to fowl (*Y.D.* 65:5). The removal of the sciatic nerve from the hindquarters is very difficult, requiring the skill of an expert porger. Since the average butcher does not have sufficient skill, it has become the custom in Jewish communities not to use the hindquarters at all, but to sell them to non-Jews, thus making it unnecessary to porge these parts of the animal. This is important because much of the forbidden fat is found in the hindquarters, including the fat on the flanks (*kesalim*) and loins (*motnayim*) (*Y.D.* 64:6, 7).

Among our Oriental brethren, the hindquarters have always been porged and used. In some European Jewish communities of the past, specially qualified porgers were licensed to prepare the hindquarters properly for the kosher trade. This was quite rare, however. Today, in Israel, the question has come up in full force. Because of the general shortage of meat, and because the disposal of the hindquarters to the non-Jewish trade is not as feasible in Israel as it was in the European communities, it has become the practice to have the hindquarters porged by experts licensed to do so. Thus, meat from the hindquarters is readily available in Israel (see Lewinger, *Madrikh Lehilkhot Niqqur,* p. 8).

The fat in the large tails of the sheep found in the Near East is permitted (Ṭur, *Y.D.* 64), but certain veins must be removed (*Y.D.* 64:5); for a detailed guide to porging, see Ṭur, *Y.D.*, at the end of 265, quoting Ba'al Ha'iṭur; Eisenstein, *Otsar Dinim Uminhagim,* s.v. Niqqur; Lewinger, *Madrikh Lehilkhot Niqqur,* Adler, *Sefer Niqqur Hama'asi Batemunot.*

Even after blood has been removed by porging, there is still some blood that was absorbed in the flesh. This blood can be removed by two methods: (1) broiling over an open fire, (2) salting.

Blood in the flesh is prohibited only if it has left its original place. Theoretically, therefore, raw meat may be eaten without salting (*Y.D.* 67:1) as long as the surface blood is washed off and the veins removed (*Y.D.* 67:2). In cooking, however, blood will certainly leave its original place; hence, the need for salting or broiling.

3. Soaking

Before salting, the meat should be washed (rinsed) and soaked in water for half an hour (*Y.D.* 69:1 in Rama). Many reasons have been given for this soaking. The most logical ones are: (1) it removes the blood that is on the surface; (2) it softens the meat and makes it possible for the salt to draw out the blood (*Y.D.* 69:1 in Shakh 1).

It has become the practice to soak the meat in a special vessel that is not used for any other purpose (ibid.). The water should cover the meat completely. If some blood gathers in one part of the meat or clots because of a wound, that piece should be cut off before the soaking (*Y.D.* 67:4).

Soaking should take place no more than three days after the slaughtering. If the meat is not soaked or at least rinsed within the three days, the blood will become so coagulated that salting will not remove it (*Y.D.* 69:12). This rule is very important today when much of our meat is brought in from afar. For example, meat brought by truck from Iowa to New York may be on the road for more than three days. In such cases, arrangements are made for the meat in transit to be rinsed properly under competent rabbinical supervision before three days have passed. The date the animal was slaughtered is stamped on the meat, and the supervising rabbi gives the driver a certification stating the exact time the meat was rinsed.

The soaking should take about a half-hour, though the meat is permitted if it was rinsed and washed thoroughly and then salted (*Y.D.* 69:1 in Rama). If the soaked meat is cut again prior to salting, it must be resoaked (*Y.D.* 69:1).

If the meat was soaked for more than twenty-four hours, both the meat and the vessel are forbidden on the principle of *kavush kimevushal;* soaking for twenty-four hours is tantamount to cooking, and the unsalted meat that is cooked becomes forbidden (*Y.D.* 69:1 in Rama).

If the meat, after soaking but before salting, is pickled in vinegar in order to "freeze" the blood that is in it, the rule is as follows: If the meat becomes reddish, it is an indication that the blood was not frozen but rather has left its place. Hence, the vinegar and the meat are both forbidden except for broiling. If the meat is intended for cooking, it must be cut up and salted (*Y.D.* 67:5). If it does not become red, the vinegar is permitted and the meat may even be consumed raw (ibid.).

4. Salting

After soaking, the meat is salted. It should be salted liberally on all sides so that no spot is left without salt (*Y.D.* 69:4). A fowl should be opened and salted inside and outside, and its inner organs should be removed and salted separately (ibid.). Meat that has a concave surface (e.g., an opened fowl or a side of beef) should be placed on the salting board with the concave side downward to prevent the accumulation of blood (*Y.D.* 70:1 in Rama; *Ḥokhmat Adam* 30:14). The vessel on which the meat is salted should be so constructed that it will allow the blood to drain off, as, for example, a vessel with a perforated bottom, or with a smooth, grooved, inclined surface (*Y.D.* 69:16).

The salt used should be neither very fine nor very coarse. Fine salt melts too quickly, and coarse salt rolls off the surface of the meat (*Y.D.* 69:3). Today, most markets sell packaged salt especially ground for the kashering of meat. If no salt is available the meat should be broiled, and then it may be cooked (*Y.D.* 69:21).

The salt is left on the meat for an hour (*Y.D.* 69:6 in Rama). In cases of emergency, or if it is necessary to rush because of the nearness of Sabbath, twenty-four minutes, or even eighteen minutes, is sufficient (*Ḥokhmat Adam* 30:9). The same rule applies if the period of salting was erroneously terminated after twenty-four, or eighteen, minutes (ibid.). After the hour, the meat is rinsed thoroughly three times in order to remove the salt (*Y.D.* 69:7 in Rama).

If the meat was salted without preliminary soaking, it may not be eaten, except if a substantial monetary loss is involved (*Y.D.* 69:2). If the meat was rinsed and then salted, but was not soaked, it is permitted (*Y.D.* 69:1 in Rama).

If the meat was salted in a vessel without a perforated bottom, the vessel may not be used (*Y.D.* 69:16). Any meat salted in the vessel that touches the juices gathered in the vessel may not be eaten; the other pieces may be eaten (*Y.D.* 69:18 in Rama).

If the meat was salted, but not rinsed afterward, and then it was cooked, it is permitted if there is additional meat in the pot equal in volume to the unrinsed piece of meat. The reason is that a piece of meat is generally at least thirty times the volume of the salt that is on it. If there is an equal amount of meat in the pot, it would add up to sixty times the volume of the salt and thus cause it to be *baṭel beshishim* (*Y.D.* 69:9).

If the meat was salted on only one side, and this is discovered before twelve hours have passed, and it has not yet been rinsed or cooked, the other side should be salted. If more than twelve hours has elapsed, the meat must be broiled. If it has been rinsed, even before the passage of twelve hours, the meat must be broiled because rinsing closes the pores and a subsequent salting will not remove the blood (*'Arukh Hashulḥan, Y.D.* 69:31).

If the meat is salted properly but not rinsed, and is left in this state until it becomes dry, it is permitted because in this case the piece of meat certainly possesses sixty times the volume of the salt (*'Arukh Hashulḥan, Y.D.* 69:56). But one should not allow this to happen; if it does, the meat should be washed thoroughly before it is used (ibid.).

If the meat is frozen, it should not be salted until it is restored to its normal softness. If it is frozen during the salting, it should be salted again after it thaws and kept in the salt the required hour. If the meat is not salted again but stays in the original salt the required time, it is permitted. "Required time" means a complete hour after the thawing (*Y.D.* 69:11 in Shakh). According to one opinion, the hour includes the time the meat was in the salt before it froze (*Peri Ḥadash,* quoted in *B.H.* 8; also *'Arukh Hashulḥan, Y.D.*

69:17–19). If time is short, as on Friday or because guests are coming, the thawing may be hastened by putting the meat in warm water, but definitely not in hot water (*Y.D.* 68:11).

A current question posed by modern technology concerns meat that is put into a deep freeze. Must the meat be "kashered" (i.e., soaked and salted) before it is put into the deep freeze, since the law requiring that it be washed before three days have passed applies here too; or do we say that the time the meat is in the deep freeze does not count because all activity within the frozen meat stops? An authority quoted in *Ba'eir Heiṭeiv* (*Y.D.* 69:8) would forbid the use of meat not "kashered" before freezing (but see *'Arukh Hashulḥan, Y.D.* 69:79, who permits it). Recent authorities, concluding that the modern deep freeze is quite different from the kind of freezing discussed by the earlier authorities, have allowed meat that was in a deep freeze to be kashered and cooked. Rabbi Chayim Ozer Grodzensky allowed it with frozen meats sent to Germany in 1934, and the Israeli Rabbinate allows it with frozen meats imported from other countries. We would suggest that housewives who put meats into a deep freeze should, as a rule, kasher them first and then freeze them. In cases of emergency, however, and where the meat was accidentally not kashered, we permit the kashering of the meat after it is taken out of the deep freeze (see Law Committee Archives, L81 and O80, P60).

If, after salting, a piece is cut from the meat, it is not necessary to salt the cut surfaces again (*Y.D.* 69:5). If the meat is cut during the salting, the cut surface must be washed and salted immediately (ibid. in Shakh 24).

It is permitted to salt many pieces of meat together even if one is on top of another (*Y.D.* 70:1).

If kosher and non-kosher meat are salted together, or if non-kosher meat is salted and the kosher meat is unsalted, and they touch each other, the surface of the kosher meat must be scraped where it touched the non-kosher meat (*Y.D.* 70:3). In the reverse case, rinsing the kosher meat is sufficient (*Y.D.* 70:3).

The head. Since the meninges have blood vessels and the brain also contains blood, there would be no way for the blood to drain if the head as a whole were salted. Therefore, the head should be split open, the brain removed, and the meninges pierced. The head and brains should then be salted separately (*Y.D.* 71:1, 3). If keeping the head intact is desired, the skull and the sac of the brain should be pierced, and then it should be salted. The opening in the skull should be downward (*Y.D.* 71:3).

The feet. Since hoofs are like containers and prevent the drainage of blood, they should be cut open. The feet may then be salted in their entirety even over the hide (*Y.D.* 71:2; *Ḥokhmat Adam* 31:3).

The heart. Since the heart obviously has a large accumulation of blood and ordinary salting will not remove it completely, salting should be preceded by cutting off the tip, slicing open the heart, and draining the blood. The heart may then be cooked (*Y.D.* 72:1; Ṭaz 1; *Ḥokhmat Adam* 31:4). If this procedure was not followed before salting, it may be done after the salting (*Y.D.* 72:2). If it was omitted and the heart was washed, the contents of the pot are forbidden unless the meat in the pot is sixty times the volume of the heart (ibid.). If an entire fowl is cooked, and its heart was not sliced open, the fowl is permitted, on the assumption that a fowl has a volume at least sixty times that of its heart; the heart itself, however, remains forbidden (*Y.D.* 72:3 in Rama). This applies only if the heart is not attached to any other piece of meat. If it is, the attached piece becomes prohibited, and the pot must contain sixty times the volume of the heart and the attached piece to render its contents permissible (*Y.D.* 72:3 in Rama).

The liver. The liver is covered by a set of special rules. Since it contains an excessive amount of blood, it must be broiled (*Y.D.* 73:1). Before broiling, the liver must be cut lengthwise and crosswise (*sheti va'eirev*) or punctured many times. It is then salted a bit and broiled over an open fire (*Y.D.* 73:5 in Rama; see also Ṭaz 2 and 5); since the broiling must take place on a surface that will permit the blood to drain off (e.g., a grid or a spit), the liver should not be wrapped in foil for broiling (*Ḥokhmat Adam* 34:16). The liver may be cooked after the broiling, but it should be rinsed first (*Y.D.* 73:1). "Broiled" means broiling to the point that it is edible (ibid. in Rama and in Shakh 2; see below under "Broiling"; see also, Efrusi, *Sha'arei Halakhah*, pt. 1, p. 18).

Modern electric broilers have posed a problem because the electric coil is on top. The first question is whether the heated wire coil constitutes an open fire comparable to live coals or gas flames; the second, whether the fire above is as effective in drawing out the blood as a fire below. One of the sources mentions the case of a heated oven where there is no fire underneath and the liver hangs in mid-air and is broiled. This is permitted as long as the dripping of the blood is not obstructed (*'Arukh Hashulḥan, Y.D.* 73:19; *Pitḥei Teshuvah, Y.D.* 73:1). An electric broiler is analogous and should, therefore, be permitted.

If the liver is pickled in vinegar or scalded in boiling water after the removal of the blood vessels in which blood may be gathered, it should theoretically be permitted because this process prevents the blood from moving from its place, and blood that has not left its original place is permitted. But the early authorities (geonim) have forbidden this practice (*Y.D.* 73:2).

Bones. Bones that have marrow in them must be salted in the same manner as meat (*Y.D.* 71:3 in Ràma). If they have meat attached to them, they may be salted together with the meat; otherwise, they must be salted separately (*Y.D.* 71:3 and Shakh 11).

The lungs. The lungs should be split open, especially the trachea, since there might be blood gathered in them. Since this custom was established as an extra precaution, the lungs are permitted if they are salted and cooked without having been split open (*Y.D.* 72:4; Shakh 20).

The digestive organs. The digestive organs themselves contain very little blood, but the fat that surrounds them is full of blood vessels, and these must be removed. Aside from the cow's upper stomach, which must be salted, none of the digestive organs theoretically requires salting. Despite this it is customary to salt them; nonetheless, they may be eaten, cleared of the fat and cooked without salting (*Y.D.* 75:1).

The entrails should be salted on the outer side, where the fat and the blood are found. If salted only on the inside, it is as if they were not salted at all (*Y.D.* 75:1 in Rama) because the walls of the intestines, which contain very little blood, act as a barrier between the salt and the fat, which is the real object of the salting due to the many blood vessels it contains. If this error in the salting procedure is noticed prior to the cooking, the entrails should be resalted on the outer side (ibid.). If they have already been cooked, the entire contents of the pot are forbidden (ibid.).

The stomach of a suckling calf is sometimes filled with milk; the milk should be removed, and the stomach should then be salted in the same manner as any other meat (*Y.D.* 90:4 and in Rama).

Kidneys and testicles. The kidneys and testicles contain a considerable amount of blood. Opinions differ whether they should be salted and cooked or broiled. The prevalent custom is to broil them. After the broiling, of course, it is permitted to cook them (*Y.D.* 74:1; Shakh 2; *Ḥokhmat Adam* 31:9).

The spleen. Though its color would seem to indicate that the spleen, like the liver, has a great amount of blood, it is salted in the same manner as ordinary meat (*Y.D.* 74:1; *Ḥokhmat Adam* 31:8).

The fat. All edible fats, whether of cattle or fowl, are like meat in regard to soaking and salting (*Ḥokhmat Adam* 34:23).

The gizzard. The gizzard must be cut open so that any food in the process of digestion can be removed. It is then salted in the same manner as any other meat (*Ḥokhmat Adam* 34:21).

The udder. The problem with the udder is that it contains milk. It will therefore be treated in detail with the laws concerning meat and milk (see chap. 26). Here we mention the rule that the udder may not be cooked but only broiled. Before broiling, however, it must be cut open with two slits, perpendicular to each other, and pressed free of milk (*Y.D.* 90:3).

Eggs. Eggs found in a chicken, whether unfinished and still attached to the placenta or completely finished with a hard shell, must be salted. They should be salted separately, not with other meat (*Y.D.* 75:1 in Rama; Ṭaz 5; *Ḥokhmat Adam* 31:13).

5. Broiling

Broiling is in itself a means of drawing out the blood. Therefore, no prior kashering is required if the meat is to be broiled (*Y.D.* 76:1). However, it has become the custom to wash the meat a bit and put some salt on it immediately before broiling (*Y.D.* 76:2 in Rama). If the washing and salting before broiling were inadvertently omitted, the meat is nevertheless permitted (ibid.). The broiling should be done only on a grid which allows the blood to drip freely, or on a spit (*'Arukh Hashulḥan* 73:19).

Unkashered chopped meat should not be broiled if other ingredients, such as eggs or flour, are mixed with the meat because they obstruct the flow of the blood (*Ḥokhmat Adam* 35:12).

If the meat is broiled without prior kashering (regular soaking and salting), no vessel should be put underneath it to catch the drippings of fat unless it is already broiled sufficiently to be edible (*Y.D.* 76:6)—usually this is when it is half-broiled; i.e., when there is a change in color and a crust is formed. After broiling, the meat should be removed from the spit or grid and the accumulated surface blood should be washed off (*Y.D.* 76:2 in Rama). The spit or grid on which unkashered meat has been broiled should be cleaned and heated in the fire before reusing (*Y.D.* 76:4; Shakh 23; Ṭaz 10).

By the same token, grids and spits used for broiling meat or liver not kashered previously, should not be used for broiling meats that have been kashered; also, a grinder used for non-kashered meat should not be used for kashered meat. However, meat should always be kashered before it is ground. Some butchers have two grinders, one for kashered meat and one for non-kashered meat. Care should be taken not to confuse the two.

After the minimum broiling, the meat, though not kashered by soaking and salting, may be cooked.

It is forbidden to scald fowl or meat before kashering it, because that prevents the draining of the blood. It has been customary to singe chickens before kashering them in order to remove the roots of the feathers that did not come out during the plucking. Care should be taken that this be done over a fire that gives little heat, such as straw, and that the fowl be moved around over the fire to prevent heating (*Y.D.* 68:9).

A new problem has arisen in this connection. Machines have replaced human chicken-pluckers, but machine plucking necessitates dipping the fowls in heated water, and this, of course, is forbidden, because it interferes with the flow of the blood. If, however, the water is not hot (i.e., not far above 115° F.), such machines should be considered permissible (see Law Committee Archives, vol. T, pp. 4–7, and I. Klein, *Responsa and Halakhic Studies,* pp. 84–87).

UNIT XXVI

THE DIETARY LAWS (VI)

MEAT AND MILK;

MIXING OF KOSHER AND NON-KOSHER FOODS

XXVI.
The Dietary Laws (VI) Milk and Meat; Mixing of Kosher and Non-Kosher Foods

The separation of milk and meat is the most prominent distinguishing mark of the Jewish home. Most of the laws connected with the consumption of food are the concern of the shoḥeṭ, the butcher, and the grocer, all of whom are involved before the food reaches the home. With the separation of milk and meat, the family becomes directly involved and the kitchen receives its Jewish character.

Neither the Bible nor the Talmud gives any rationale for these laws. Maimonides ascribes their origin to Jewish disgust at the fertility rites practiced by the pagan cults of Canaan (*Guide* 3:48). One of these rites was the cooking of a kid in its mother's milk. Dr. Nelson Glueck reports that this practice is still found among the Bedouins of today, not as a pagan rite but as an act of hospitality to a distinguished guest (see also Finkelstein, *Pharisees* 1:58–60, 2:831–32, n.; *Encyclopedia Miqra'it,* 1:89; Baron, *Social and Religious History,* 1:328, n. 22).

To us this regulation reflects reverence for life and the teaching of compassion. To seethe a kid in its mother's milk is callous. Professor Abraham Joshua Heschel expresses it thus: The goat—in our case, more commonly the cow—generously and steadfastly provides man with the single most perfect food that he possesses, milk. It is the only food which, by reason of its proper composition of fat, carbohydrates, and protein, can by itself sustain the human body. How ungrateful and callous we would be to take the child of an animal to whom we are thus indebted and cook it in the very milk which nourishes us and is given us so freely by its mother (see Ibn Ezra on Exod. 23:19; Dresner and Siegel, *Jewish Dietary Laws,* p. 70).

1. Sources

The laws concerning the consumption and cooking of milk and meat together are based on one verse which is repeated three times in the Torah, "Thou shalt not seethe a kid in its mother's milk" (Exod. 23:19, 34:26; Deut. 14:21). The Talmud interprets this prohibition to include all kinds of meat, not only that of a kid, explaining that a kid is mentioned specifically because cooking a young goat in its mother's milk was the prevalent custom (B. *Ḥul.* 113b; *Y.D.* 87:2). The term *meat,* however, is limited to its popular connotation; it does not include fish, or locusts in places where it is permitted to eat locusts (*Y.D.* 87:3).

The rabbis noted that the prohibition is mentioned three times; they interpreted this to indicate that it refers not only to cooking, but also to eating and to the derivation of any benefit (הֲנָאָה) from the cooked mixture. Thus it is forbidden to cook milk and meat (the very act of cooking), to eat the cooked mixture, or to derive any benefit therefrom. A dish that combines meat and milk may not even be fed to one's dog, but must be disposed of. Since the Bible speaks of "cooking," this stringency prohibiting any benefit from a mixture applies only when the milk and meat have been cooked together, not just mixed (*Y.D.* 87:1, and Rama).

2. Eating Milk and Meat

Milk and meat, or products derived therefrom, may not be eaten together, or even one after the other at the same meal. Therefore, if a person eats meat, he must wait until the next meal before eating cheese or drinking milk. Since a precise interval of time is not specified in the Talmud, customs vary. In certain localities the waiting period was six hours; in others, it was as little as one hour. The prevalent custom is to wait six hours (*Y.D.* 89:1 in Rama).

The reason for this waiting period is that meat leaves a taste in the mouth that lingers for a long time, and eating a milk product before the meat has had a chance to be digested would be tantamount to eating them together. Also, particles of meat become lodged between the teeth, and they are not dissolved by salivary action until at least six hours have elapsed (*Y.D.* 89 in Ṭaz 1).

If, however, one eats a milk product, he may eat meat after it without an intervening waiting period (ibid. 2). According to some authorities, aged or hard cheeses are subject to the same rule as meat, and if one partakes of these, he must wait six hours before eating meat (ibid. in Shakh and Ṭaz).

Since meat may not be cooked in a vessel used for cooking milk, and vice versa (*Y.D.* 93:1), it has become the established practice to have two sets of dishes, one for meat foods and the other for dairy. However, food cooked in a vessel reserved for meat is not considered a meat dish, and if one eats such a dish he may partake of milk and its derivatives immediately afterward (*Y.D.* 89:3 in Rama).

If one wishes to eat meat after milk, or milk after meat, even after the prescribed interval, the tablecloth that was used for the first must be replaced and the bread that was on the table must be removed. All the dishes should be removed; even the knife used for cutting bread at the meal should be changed. This means that there must be separate knives for cutting bread at meat meals and dairy meals (*Y.D.* 89:4 and in Rama). If the salt shakers are the open type, separate shakers should be used for milk meals and meat meals, since otherwise someone might accidentally dip his food in the salt rather than pour the salt over it (*Y.D.* 88:2 in Rama).

Because meat and milk are forbidden when mixed, extra precautions are necessary to prevent errors. If two persons who know each other should chance to eat at the same table, one eating meat and the other dairy, they must place an object between them to serve as a barrier or a reminder that they must not eat of each other's food (*Y.D.* 88:1). Strangers, however, who ordinarily do not partake of each other's food, need no such reminder (ibid.).

Also, a milk dish should not be cooked in an oven where meat is being roasted, if the dishes are uncovered and the oven is closed, because the vapor arising from the milk will enter the meat. The situation would be the same as if some milk had fallen upon the meat, and the meat would have to measure sixty times the volume of the milk to annul it (*Y.D.* 92:8).

3. Accidental Mixing

Before giving the detailed rules regarding the accidental mixing of forbidden and permitted foods (*ta'arovet*), we should define a number of relevant terms—presented here in Hebrew alphabetical order.

Ein mevaṭlin issur lekhatḥilah—it is not permitted willfully to annul a prohibited article of food by dropping it into a vessel with sixty times its volume of permitted kosher food; nor is it permitted to add to a mixture that has already occurred accidentally that does not have sixty times the volume of the forbidden food, in order to complete the required amount for the annulment (*Y.D.* 99:5). But should such an annulment be effected accidentally, the mixture is permitted (ibid.).

Issur davuq—a forbidden piece of food which is organically attached to a permitted piece. An example is a piece of forbidden fat attached to meat that is kosher.

Afilu be'elef lo bateil—literally, "it cannot be annulled even by a thousand times its volume." Actually, it means that the article cannot be annulled at all.

Efshar lesoḥato—when it is possible to squeeze out a forbidden substance that has been absorbed by a permitted food, does the substance resume its status of a permitted food? (see also *Ḥatikhah na'aseit neveilah;* see B. *Ḥul.* 108 f. and Tosafot and Rashi ad loc.).

Bateil beshishim—it becomes annulled by a substance sixty times its volume. This principle applies to cases of forbidden foods that are accidentally mixed with permitted food. If the permitted food has sixty times the volume of the forbidden food, the latter becomes annulled and has no effect on the permitted food (see B. *Ḥul.* 97a f., 98a ff.).

Beriah—literally, "a creature." The rule is that *afilu be'elef lo bateil*—it does not become annulled even by a thousand times its volume, and the principle of *bateil beshishim* does not apply. That means that it can never be annulled (see B. *Ḥul.* 100a). A *beriah* is subject to the following conditions:

1. It must be something that originally possessed life (see B. *Mak.* 17a).
2. It must have been prohibited from the beginning of its existence.
3. It must be something which loses its distinctive name if it is not whole.
4. It must be whole (see Tosafot, *Ḥul.* 96a, s.v. *Mai Ta'ama*).

Bishul—literally, "cooking" or "boiling." When used in the codes, it includes frying, roasting, boiling, or any process where the use of fire or heat is involved.

Basar—literally, "meat." It includes the flesh of kosher animals unless the flesh of non-kosher beasts or birds is explicitly included. Also included are matured eggs that are still in the fowl. Excluded are fish, locusts, hides, dry bones, horns, and hoofs (*Y.D.* 87:3, 6, 7).

Geridah—scraping. When a forbidden food touches a permitted food, the permitted food must sometimes be scraped at the point of contact (*Y.D.* 96 and in Shakh 21).

Davar ḥarif—a food or substance with a sharp taste, such as radishes, onions, or condiments. A *davar ḥarif* may cause an otherwise disgusting flavor (*noten ta'am lifgam*) to become pleasing (*noten ta'am leshevaḥ*).

Davar sheyesh lo matirin—a thing that becomes, or is, forbidden but will eventually be permitted. Such articles of food cannot be annulled—*afilu be'elef lo bațeil* (see below, p. 374 f. for the classical example, and *Y.D.* 102:1).

Ḥozer wene'or—a forbidden article of food that fell into permitted food more than sixty times its volume and was thus *bațeil beshishim* is "re-awakened" if more of the same forbidden food is added, making the permitted food less than sixty times its volume, and the mixture therefore becomes forbidden (*Y.D.* 99:6 and in Shakh 21).

Ḥalav—literally, "milk," usually refers to the milk of living kosher animals unless specified otherwise. Excluded are the milk of non-kosher animals, milk of kosher animals that has been extracted after the animals were slaughtered, and the milk of humans (*Y.D.* 87:6).

Ḥatikhah hare'uyah lehitkabed—a portion that may be served to guests is *afilu be'elef lo bațeil* (*Y.D.* 101:1; B. *Ḥul.* 100a and Tosafot ad loc.). Such a portion must be forbidden per se and not because it became forbidden through mixture or contact with forbidden food. Also, it must be cooked and ready to be served (*Y.D.* 101:2, 3).

Ḥatikhah na'aseit neveilah—literally, "the piece itself becomes carrion." This principle refers to the case where a piece of permitted food has absorbed from forbidden food enough not to be *bațeil beshishim*. That piece of food in turn becomes forbidden in its entirety (like carrion) so that if it falls accidentally into a vessel with kosher food, we need sixty times the volume of the entire piece, not just of the amount of the forbidden food that has been absorbed (*Y.D.* 92:3, 4; B. *Ḥul.* 96b, 108a).

Ta'am ke'iqqar—"the flavor is tantamount to the substance." For example, if a forbidden article of food accidentally falls into a vessel containing permitted food and is then removed, but the taste of it is felt, it is as if the substance itself were present (B. *Pes.* 44b; B. *Ḥul.* 108a, and Rashi ad loc.).

Kavush kimevushal—soaking for twenty-four hours is as damaging as cooking. If two articles of food, one forbidden (*țerefah*) and one permitted (kosher), were soaked together for twenty-four hours, it is as if they were cooked together, and the mixture is permitted only if it has sixty times the volume of the forbidden food, exclusive of the forbidden article itself (*Y.D.* 105:1). Soaking in salt water, even for a short period, is tantamount to cooking. A short period is defined as the interval in which the mixture could be placed on the fire and brought to a boil (*Y.D.* 105:1; B. *Ḥul.* 97b, 111b; B. *Pes.* 76a).

Kedei neṭilah—paring the thickness of a finger. When forbidden food touches permitted food, the permitted food sometimes has to be pared at the point of contact to the amount of the thickness of a finger (see B. *Pes.* 75b f.; *Y.D.* 96:1).

Keli rishon—a vessel, containing food, that is directly on the fire, or removed from the fire but still hot enough to repel a hand that touches it (*hayad soledet bo*) (P. *Shab.* 3:4; B. *Shab.* 40b).

Keli sheini—a vessel that is not on the fire into which food has been poured from a *keli rishon* (ibid.).

Min bemino—a homogeneous mixture; i.e., a piece of meat that is permitted becomes mixed up with forbidden pieces of meat (B. *Ḥul.* 96b f.; *Y.D.* 98).

Min beshe'eino mino—a heterogeneous mixture; e.g., a vegetable that falls into a vessel with forbidden soup (ibid.).

Maliaḥ keroteaḥ—a substance that is salted so much that it becomes inedible is considered as if it were hot (*Y.D.* 91:5; Rama 105:9; B. *Pes.* 76a).

Notein ṭa'am—literally, "imparts a flavor." For example, if a forbidden substance accidentally falls into a vessel with kosher food and the forbidden food imparts a flavor to it, the kosher food becomes forbidden (M. *Ḥul.* 7:3–4; B. *Ḥul.* 98a).

Notein ṭa'am bar notein ṭa'am—literally, "a taste born of a taste," is permitted. For example, if fish is fried in a meat frying pan, it may be served in a milk dish because there are three stages of *notein ṭa'am* here: (1) the meat imparting the meat flavor to the frying pan, (2) the imparting of the meat flavor from the frying pan to the fish, (3) the imparting of the meat flavor from the fish to the milk dish. Since there is no prohibition involved in the first two stages, not enough potency is left in the flavor to forbid the third stage (*Y.D.* 95:1; B. *Ḥul.* 111a).

Notein ṭa'am lifgam—literally, "imparts a disgusting flavor." For example, if a forbidden article of food accidentally falls into permitted food and the article has a disgusting taste in itself (e.g., putrid food), or if it is not disgusting in itself but becomes disgusting when mixed with this food and has a deteriorating effect on it, the food remains permitted (*Y.D.* 103:1); B. *A.Z.* 65b, 67b).

'Irui mikeli rishon—liquid poured directly from a *keli rishon.*

Qelifah—literally, "paring." If forbidden food touches permitted food under certain circumstances, the permitted food must be pared at the point of contact (B. *Pes.* 75b). The difference between *qelifah* and *geridah* is that in the former the paring has to come off in one piece (*Y.D.* 96 in Shakh 21).

Tata'ah gavar—literally, "the nether conquers," i.e., it is assumed that when one substance falls into another, one being hot and the other cold, the lower is dominant and imparts its temperature to the substance above it (B. *Pes.* 76a).

4. The Accidental Mixing of Milk and Meat

If meat touches cheese, and both are cold and dry, no harm is done to either. If one of them is moist, the points of contact should be rinsed with water (*Y.D.* 91:1 and Shakh 1). If moist meat or cheese comes into contact with bread, the bread should be eaten only with the kind of food it touches (*Y.D.* 91:3).

If a piece of meat accidentally falls into a pot of milk, the rules are as follows:

1. If both the meat and the milk are cold, the meat should be removed immediately and rinsed; then both may be eaten (*Y.D.* 91:4).
2. If both are hot, both become forbidden; see below about *baṭeil beshishim* (ibid.).
3. If one of them is hot and the other cold, the principle of *tata'ah gavar* is applied, and therefore, if the nether substance is hot, it is as if both substances were hot and the rule given in item (2) above is followed. If the lower substance is cold, it is as if both substances were cold and the rule given in item (1) above is followed (*Y.D.* 91:4). The meat, however, must be pared (*Y.D.* 91:4) because it takes a bit of time for the lower substance to cool the upper one, and during this interval it absorbs (B. *Pes.* 76a, quoted in Ṭaz 6, Shakh 7).

Further, if meat accidentally falls into hot milk, but is immediately removed, the milk is permitted on the principle of *baṭeil beshishim* if the volume of the milk is sixty times the volume of the meat (*Y.D.* 92:1). We need this even though the meat has been removed, because of the principle of *ṭa'am ke'iqqar*. The piece of meat itself is not edible because it absorbed the milk.

If a drop of milk accidentally falls on a piece of meat cooking in a pot, two factors must be considered:

1. The position of the piece of meat upon which the drop of milk fell—i.e., whether it is on the surface or completely immersed.
2. Whether the contents of the pot were stirred immediately after the milk fell upon the piece of meat.

If the meat is on the surface and the contents of the pot were not stirred, the meat is forbidden, on the principle of *ḥatikhah na'aseit neveilah*, unless its volume is sixty times the volume of the milk.

If the contents of the pot were subsequently stirred, they must amount to sixty times the volume of the piece of meat in order for the principle of *baṭeil beshishim* to apply.

If the contents were not stirred at all, then it is sufficient to pare *kedei neṭilah,* at the point of contact of another piece of meat that touched the piece of meat upon which the milk fell (*Y.D.* 92:2; Shakh and *Peri Megadim* ad loc.).

If the piece of meat upon which the milk fell is submerged, even partially, the pot's entire contents are measured to determine whether it is sixty times the volume of the milk, as is necessary for the application of *baṭeil beshishim* (ibid. in Shakh 4, and *Hokhmat Adam* 44:1).

If a drop of milk falls on the outside of a pot that is on the fire, it must be determined whether the spot touched by the milk is below or above the level of the contents of the pot. If below, it is as if it fell into the pot itself, because it is assumed that it is bound to seep through the wall of the pot; therefore, if the contents are sixty times the volume of the milk, no harm is done (*Y.D.* 92:5). If above the level of the contents, only the spot where the milk falls becomes forbidden. The procedure to follow is to let the pot cool and then empty the contents via the other side (ibid. and in Shakh 20).

If a drop of milk falls on the outside of the pot on a spot that is reached by the fire, no harm is done because the fire burns it out immediately (*Ḥokhmat Adam* 45.8; *Y.D.* 92:6). If a large amount of milk spills on the pot, then even if it is reached by the fire, the rule is the same as if the milk had fallen below the level of the contents (ibid.).

If the milk falls on the cover of a pot of meat boiling on the fire, and the steam constantly reaches the cover, it is as if the milk had fallen on the pot below the level of the contents. If the pot is not boiling, its contents are not affected. If the cover itself is hot, however, it becomes forbidden; if it is not hot, it simply needs rinsing (*Y.D.* 92:7 in Rama).

If a milk spoon is dipped into a pot of hot meat soup, or a meat spoon is dipped into a pot with hot milk, the contents of the pot are forbidden unless their volume is sixty times the volume of the part of the spoon that was immersed in the food (*Y.D.* 94:1, 2).

If the spoon had not been used for at least twenty-four hours prior to the dipping, the contents of the pot are unaffected because a vessel not used for twenty-four hours is in the category of *notein ṭa'am lifgam* (*Y.D.* 94:1 in Rama). In either case, the spoon itself becomes forbidden (ibid.).

5. Meat and Milk Dishes

Since meat may not be cooked in a pot used for dairy, and dairy foods may not be cooked in a pot used for meat, one should have separate dishes for milk and meat (*Y.D.* 93:1; *'Arukh Hashulḥan* 88:10–11).

Inasmuch as a glass dish needs no kashering if used for both milk and meat, it is often asked whether one set of glass dishes is sufficient for both meat and dairy meals. The same question has been asked about the type of glassware (e.g. Pyrex) used for cooking and serving hot foods. The consensus is that two sets of dishes are required even in the case of glassware (see responsa on this question by Rabbi J. L. Feinberg and Rabbi Isaac Klein in Law Committee Archives).

If meat is cooked in a dairy pot, or vice-versa, and the pot has been used within the preceding twenty-four hours, the food thus cooked becomes forbidden (*Y.D.* 93:1). If twenty-four hours have passed since the pot's last previous use, the food is permitted on the principle of *notein ṭa'am lifgam* (ibid.).

In all the above cases, any vessel that becomes forbidden (except an earthenware vessel) may be kashered by following the procedure elaborated in the discussion of the laws of Pesaḥ (see unit 7). Glass dishes, however, need no kashering.

If hot meat is cut with a dairy knife, the same rule applies: i.e., the meat is forbidden unless it has a volume equal to sixty times the volume of the part of the blade that came into contact with the meat; the knife itself needs kashering (*Y.D.* 94:7). As in the case of vessels, if the knife was not used for twenty-four hours prior to the accidental cutting of the meat, we do not need sixty times the volume of the blade. All that is necessary is to pare the meat *kedei qelifah* at the point of contact with the knife and the knife needs scrubbing and wiping (ibid.).

6. Accidental Mixing of Dishes

Dairy and meat dishes should not be washed together. If they are, the following rules apply:

1. If both have been used within twenty-four hours prior to the washing, and both dishes are soiled and the water used for washing is hot (i.e., it is in a *keli rishon*), each makes the other forbidden, and in order to be used again, they must be kashered (*Y.D.* 95:3 in Rama).
2. If the water is cold (i.e., it is from a *keli sheini*), the dishes are unaffected (ibid.).
3. Likewise, if the vessels are clean and have not been used for twenty-four hours or more, they remain unaffected (*Y.D.* 95:3 and in Rama).
4. If one of the utensils is soiled, and the other, clean, only the clean one is affected and needs kashering (*Y.D.* 95:3 in Shakh 10).
5. If the dishes are washed in the same vessel, not together but rather one after another, they are not affected (*Y.D.* 95:3 in Rama).
6. If the water is poured (*'irui*) from a *keli rishon* into a vessel that contains both milk and meat dishes, opinions differ as follows:
   a. The dishes are unaffected.
   b. They become forbidden, with the exception of cases involving substantial loss.
   c. If the dishes can be kashered, the strict rule is followed; if they cannot be kashered, the lenient rule is followed and the dishes are considered to be unaffected (*Darkhei Teshuvah* 95:73).

A related question presented by modern technology pertains to the use of dishwashing machines. May the same dishwasher be used for milk and meat dishes, or are separate machines necessary?

We accept the opinion that it is permitted to use the same dishwashing machine, and even the same racks, for both milk and meat dishes, with the following provisos:

1. That the milk and meat dishes are not washed together.
2. That the machine is allowed to run a full cycle between the washing of milk and meat dishes (Efrati, *Sha'arei Halakhah,* sec. 4, pp. 29–33).

There are some opinions that separate racks are required for milk and meat dishes if the racks are not of metal (Law Committee Archives, vol. 5, pp. 52–53). The latest authorities, however, do not regard racks made of nonferous material as *keli ḥeres,* which may not be kashered, but as *keli even* (stoneware), which may be kashered (Efrati, loc. cit.).

Thus far we have dealt with the accidental mixing of milk and meat where cooking and heat are involved. There are also cases of accidental mixing where no heat is involved, but which, for specific reasons, are subject to the same rulings.

1. *Maliaḥ keroteaḥ*—meat salted to the point of inedibility is considered to be hot; if it is accidentally mixed with milk, it needs sixty times its volume to annul it (*Y.D.* 91:5; 105:9 in Rama). In such cases, the principle of *tata'ah gavar* does not apply (*Y.D.* 91:5).
2. *Kavush kemevushal*—a forbidden food that is cold and was soaked for twenty-four hours in a permitted food is subject to the same ruling that would apply if they were cooked together (*Y.D.* 105:1).
3. Soaking in brine and vinegar is considered the same as cooking if the food remained in these for the same amount of time that would be required for it to come to the boil if put on the fire (ibid.).

These rules about the accidental mixing of milk and meat apply generally to all cases of a forbidden food accidentally being mixed with a permitted food. One fact must be taken into consideration, however: the mixing of milk and meat is unique in that each of the two, the milk and the meat, is permitted when by itself; only when they are mixed do they become forbidden. The other cases involve mixtures where one of the two is forbidden by itself.

This results in variations in the application of certain rules. For example, the principle of *notein ṭa'am bar notein ṭa'am* is applicable only in cases involving meat and milk (*Y.D.* 95 in Ṭaz 1).

According to some authorities, the principle of *ḥatikhah na'aseit neveilah* only applies to the accidental mixing of meat and milk but not to other mixtures of forbidden foods (*Y.D.* 92:4). We follow the authorities that do not make this distinction (ibid. in Rama; see *'Arukh Hashulḥan, Y.D.* 92:23 ff., for a full discussion of the subject).

7. Annulment by Sixty Times the Volume

In accidental mixtures, as already mentioned, the principle of *bațeil beshishim* is applied—i.e., if a forbidden food accidentally falls into a pot wherein a permitted food is cooking, the permitted food is unaffected and remains edible if it is at least sixty times the volume of the forbidden food.

Originally, in such situations, a Gentile was asked to taste the mixture and to tell whether the forbidden substance imparted its flavor to the permitted food. The principle of *bațeil beshishim* was resorted to when no Gentile was available or when the flavors of the two substances could not be distinguished, as in the case of a homogeneous mixture (*min bemino*). Later authorities decided that the original method was unreliable and applied the principle of *bațeil beshishim* to all cases (cf. B. *Ḥul.* 97a f.; *Y.D.* 98:1).

This rule, while derived from a biblical source (see B. *Ḥul.* 98a f.; Maimonides, *Hil. Ma'akhalot Asurot* 15:21), is actually based on the assumption that no ordinary substance has the potency to impart its flavor to another substance sixty or more times its volume (*Ḥokhmat Adam* 51:6).

In all these cases of accidental mixing, the forbidden substance, if it can be identified, must be removed (*Y.D.* 98:4 in Rama). Even if the forbidden substance is removed, it is still necessary to have sixty times its volume, on the principle of *ța'am ke'iqqar.*

The remedy of *bațeil beshishim* applies to accidental mixing. It is not permitted to deliberately drop a piece of forbidden food into a vessel containing permitted food sixty times its volume in order to cause the forbidden food to be annulled. Furthermore, even if the initial mixing occurred accidentally, but the permitted food was not sixty times the volume of the forbidden food, adding to the permitted food in order to attain the sixty-to-one ratio is prohibited (*Y.D.* 99:5).

There are some noteworthy exceptions to the principle of *bațeil beshishim.* Some of these are merely variations on the principle; others are real exceptions to the rule.

Variations

The udder of a cow that accidentally falls into a vessel of boiling meat food becomes annulled by fifty-nine times its volume (cf. B. *Ḥul.* 96b).

While the udder is the source of the problem, because of the milk absorbed in it, it is nevertheless meat, and when joined with fifty-nine times its volume makes up the required sixty (*Y.D.* 90:1, 98:8; see also Maimonides, *Hil. Ma'akhalot Asurot* 15:18, where the reason given is that the rule was made more lenient because the milk in the udder is forbidden only rabbinically and not biblically).

If an egg is prohibited because it contains a chick (cf. B. *Ḥul.* 98a and Tosafot ad loc.) there must be sixty-one permitted eggs in order to annul the forbidden one. The reason is that eggs vary in size, and in order to be sure that there is sixty times the volume of the forbidden egg, there should be sixty-one eggs (*Y.D.* 86:5; *B.H.* 10; and 98:7). Again Maimonides gives a different reason: an egg that is about to hatch is a separate creature, and the rabbis, therefore, made a distinction in this case (see *Hil. Ma'akhalot Asurot* 15:19).

If a prohibited dry food article is accidentally mixed with a permitted dry food article (*yaveish beyaveish*) of the same species (*min bemino*), only twice the prohibited substance is necessary in order to annul it (*Y.D.* 109:1). If the prohibited substance is accidentally mixed with a permitted food of a different species (*min beshe'eino mino*), the principle of *bateil beshishim* still applies (ibid.).

For other variations, see *Y.D.* 294; *Y.D.* 323:1 in Rama; Maimonides, *Hil. Ma'akhalot Asurot* 15:13–14.

Exceptions

The exceptions to the principle of *baṭeil beshishim* may be subdivided into two categories:

In one category are those food articles to which the reason for the principle of *baṭeil beshishim* does not apply. The reason for the principle is the assumption that ordinary articles of food do not impart their flavor to substances sixty or more times their volume. Experience, however, has proven that certain articles with a sharp flavor or certain other qualities do affect substances more than sixty times their volume. Thus condiments like vinegar, salt, and pepper (*devarim de'avidei leta'ama*) that accidentally fall into a pot of permitted food cannot be annulled (*Y.D.* 98:8; *Ḥokhmat Adam* 53:29; B. *A.Z.* 69a; B. *Ḥul.* 97b).

A coagulant (*davar hama'amid*) that affects substances more than sixty times its volume is not subject to the principle of *baṭeil beshishim* (*Y.D.* 87:11 in Rama). Thus, cheese in which the coagulant is rennet from the stomach of a non-kosher animal is forbidden even if the amount of rennet in the cheese is less than one-thousandth the amount of milk (ibid.). However, many authorities claim that since rennet comes from the thoroughly dried wall of the stomach, it has ceased to be a food and thus is no longer forbidden (Law Committee Archives; for details, see I. Klein, "The Kashrut of Cheeses").

The other category includes substances that have a special importance inherent in their nature and therefore cannot be annulled. These are *beriah* (a creature), *ba'al ḥai* (a living thing), *ḥatikhah hare'uyah lehitkabeid* (a portion fit to be served to guests), and *davar shebeminyan* (things that are important because they are sold individually by number and not in bulk or by weight). Another item which is not subject to the principle of *baṭeil beshishim* for a most logical reason is *davar sheyesh lo matirin* (things that are forbidden which will eventually become permitted). Let us explain each case individually.

The case of *beriah* is subject to the following conditions (*Y.D.* 100:1):

1. It must be an entity which at one time possessed life. Thus a grain of wheat would not be included (see Rosh on B. *Ḥul.* 100a).
2. It must be an entity which was prohibited from the beginning of its existence. This would exclude, for instance, a fowl which has become forbidden because it was slaughtered improperly (ibid. in Rashi).
3. It must be an entity that would lose its identity, its distinctive name, if it is dismembered. Thus forbidden fat, though it may be an entity, is not *beriah* because when it is cut into pieces, each piece will still be called by its original name (ibid. in Rosh and Ran).
4. The entity must be whole. Part of a *beriah* is not covered by the rule of *beriah* (ibid.).

Even when all these conditions are present, the rule that it cannot be annulled, *afilu be'elef lo baṭeil,* applies only when the creature is present in a mixture and cannot be identified. If it can be identified, it should be removed, and the flavor that it imparted is *baṭeil beshishim* (*Y.D.* 100:2).

Examples of a *beriah* are ants, unclean fowl, and a limb torn from a living animal (ibid.).

The case of *ba'al ḥai* is similar to *beriah,* yet quite different (*Y.D.* 110:6; *Ḥokhmat Adam* 53). While a *beriah* is a dead creature, here the main characteristic is that it is alive. An example is a live chicken or animal that has a blemish that renders it *ṭerefah* while still alive; e.g., a fowl with a damaged esophagus (*Y.D.* 33:8); or cattle that have been clawed by a beast of prey (*Y.D.* 57). If these became mixed accidentally with others of their species, all become forbidden, and no annullment is possible (see B. *Zev.* 73a).

If these are slaughtered unwittingly, they lose their status of *ba'al ḥai* and are *baṭeil beshishim.* Nor do they now enter the category of *beriah,* inasmuch as this includes only creatures that were prohibited from the beginning of their existence (*Y.D.* 100:1).

The category of *ḥatikhah hare'uyah lehitkabeid* (a portion fit to serve guests) comprises many items (*Y.D.* 101:1). The authorities enumerate a long list. A prominent example would be a whole chicken, dressed, cooked, and ready to be carved. If this chicken is forbidden and becomes mixed with kosher food, it is not *baṭeil beshishim.* It is evident, however, that these things are subject to change, varying with time and place. What is a delicacy today may be considered inferior tomorrow, and vice-versa. The rabbi who is presented with such a question must exercise his own judgment in each case (*Y.D.* 101 in Shakh 12, 13).

The following restrictions are to be noted:

1. The food article must be forbidden intrinsically, i.e., a thing forbidden of itself and not because it has absorbed prohibited food (*Y.D.* 101:2). A mixture of meat and milk is forbidden intrinsically (*Y.D.* 101:2).
2. The substance must be whole, not torn or crushed. If it loses its wholeness it is *baṭeil beshishim* (*Y.D.* 101:6).

The next category is *davar shebeminyan* (a thing which is sold by the piece and not in bulk, i.e., it is counted individually because each unit is important in itself). This too has criteria which vary with time and place. The Talmud and codes enumerate seven specific items (B. *Bes.* 3b, *Ḥul.* 100a; Maimonides, *Hil. Ma'akhalot Asurot* 16:3–4). However, it is obvious that the importance of these varies with time and place (*Hil. Ma'akhalot Asurot* 16:9).

The last of the categories is *davar sheyesh lo matirin* (things that will eventually be permitted by themselves). The reason is obvious: Since it will be permitted automatically, why resort to the remedy of *baṭeil beshishim?* The classic example is the egg laid on a festival, which may not be eaten on the day it was laid but may be eaten on the morrow (*Y.D.* 102:1). Another example is the case of an article that a person vowed not to partake of which becomes mixed with others. This is a case of *davar sheyesh lo matirin* and is not *bațeil beshishim* because the person who made the vow can lift the prohibition by consulting a sage, or because the vow may be a temporary one (*Y.D.* 102:4 in Rama).

This rule applies only if the mixture is homogeneous (*min bemino*) but not if it is heterogeneous (*min beshe'eino mino*) (*Y.D.* 102:1). The logic of this distinction, which is made only in the case of *davar sheyesh lo matirin*, is as follows: The reasoning behind the rule that *davar sheyesh lo matirin* cannot be annulled is that the forbidden material will become permitted again. This remedy must be patent and obvious. Where the mixture is heterogeneous, it would not be patent and obvious, because the mixture would not be designated by the part that is known as *davar sheyesh lo matirin*, but by the other material which is not so designated. If we should forbid it, there will be confusion about the reason (*Y.D.* 102:1 in Shakh 4; Țaz 5; *Ḥokhmat Adam* 53:20). The Țaz rejects this explanation, adding that in this case we simply follow the opinion of the authority who holds that there is no annulment in homogeneous mixtures.

Another modification of the rule is the following: If a forbidden substance was not identified as a separate entity before it became mixed up, it is not subject to the rule of *davar sheyesh lo matirin;* for instance, crushed grapes in a vat from which wine is issuing, and which are left in that state over the Sabbath. Normally, wine issuing on the Sabbath may not be drunk on that Sabbath but may be drunk after its conclusion. Hence, the wine is in the category of *davar sheyesh lo matirin*, and if it gets mixed up with other wine, it should not be *bațeil beshishim*. In this case, however, if there already was wine in the vat before the advent of the Sabbath, and additional wine keeps oozing into it from the grapes, one may drink from that wine since at no time could the forbidden liquid be distinguished as a separate entity (*Y.D.* 102:4 in Shakh 12 and Țaz 11; *Ḥokhmat Adam* 53:27).

8. Substances That Impart a Disgusting Flavor

The principle of *notein ta'am lifgam* is that if a forbidden article of food accidentally falls into a vessel in which permitted food is being cooked , and imparts a flavor that is disgusting to the taste, the permitted food is unaffected and there is no need for annulment by sixty times the volume of the forbidden food (*Y.D.* 103:1).

The following distinctions should be noted:

1. There are substances that are themselves disgusting to the taste, such as loathsome creatures.
2. There are substances that by themselves are not disgusting to the taste but impart a disgusting taste when mixed with other foods (*Y.D.* 103:1; B. *A.Z.* 65b). Examples are the flavors of animal fat in wine and of meat in olive oil (*Y.D.* 103:4).
3. Objects that impart a weakened flavor because of external factors. For example, a vessel that becomes forbidden because non-kosher food has been cooked in it; if this vessel had not been used for twenty-four hours or more (*eino ben yomo*), the kosher food that was cooked in it remains unaffected because the flavor the vessel may impart to the food is in the category of *notein ṭa'am lifgam* (*Y.D.* 103:5).

Generally speaking, the principle of *notein ṭa'am lifgam* applies to forbidden food that accidentally falls into a vessel with kosher food. There are several distinctions to remember, however.

If a vessel has not been used for twenty-four hours or more and is then used for kosher food, the food, as we said, remains unaffected because of the principle of *notein ṭa'am lifgam*. If, however, the kosher food is a *davar ḥarif* (food with a sharp taste), no distinction is made between a vessel used within twenty-four hours and one not used within the last twenty-four hours because the sharpness of the food arouses even a weakened flavor (*Y.D.* 103:6; *Y.D.* 122 in Rama).

Another distinction has to do with forbidden substances that cannot be annulled. These substances, if they are intrinsically disgusting to the taste, are subject to the ruling of *notein ṭa'am lifgam*. If they are not intrinsically disgusting, but impart a disgusting flavor when mixed with another substance, they retain their status as substances that cannot be annulled (*Y.D.* 103:1). The logic is that a disgusting flavor has no effect in mixtures where the imparting of the flavor (*netinat ṭa'am*) of a forbidden food determines the status of a food article. Where it is not the taste that determines, but another factor, such as being a *davar ḥashuv,* the presence of a disgusting flavor does not make any difference and, hence, the food is still forbidden (*Y.D.* 103:1 in Rama).

9. Doubtful Cases

When doubt arises about the permissibility of an article of food, the general principle is that *sefeqa de'oraita leḥumra*. If the doubt concerns an article forbidden in the Torah, it is resolved by a strict ruling; if it concerns an article forbidden by postbiblical authorities, then *sefeqa derabbanan lequla*—we follow the lenient ruling and permit it.

For example, an animal that was not slaughtered properly (e.g., if it was slaughtered with a knife whose blade was dented) is considered an *issur de'oraita*. Therefore, if a doubt arises (e.g., if the knife was examined before the slaughtering and found to be smooth, and was examined again after the slaughtering and found to have a dent—the doubt is whether the dent was caused by the skin of the neck and thus before the slaughtering, thereby causing the animal to become *ṭerefah,* or by the bones of the nape, after the severing of the esophagus and windpipe, thus making the animal kosher), the rule is *leḥhumra* and the animal is *ṭerefah* (*Y.D.* 18:1).

On the other hand, consider the example of a *ḥatikhah hare'uyah lehitkabeid* (a portion fit to serve for guests). The ruling that such a portion *afilu be'elef lo baṭeil* is rabbinic. Therefore, if doubt arises whether a food article is in this category, the principle of *sefeqa derabbanan lequla* is followed and the article is *baṭeil beshishim* (*Y.D.* 101:1 in Rama).

Connected with these rulings is the principle of *kol qavua' kemeḥetsah 'al meḥetsah damei* (all that is stationary and established is considered as half and half) (B. *Ket.* 15a). Thus, if a person bought some meat from a meat market, in a place where there are markets that sell kosher meat and markets that sell non-kosher meat, and he does not know at which market he shopped, the rule is that no matter what the ratio of kosher to non-kosher shops, even if nine sell kosher meat and only one sells non-kosher meat, we account it as if the ratio were one to one, i.e., five kosher, and five non-kosher, and thus we rule that the meat is *ṭerefah* (*Y.D.* 110:3).

Corollary to this is the principle *kol deparish meiruba parish* (anything that has become separated, has become separated from the majority). Therefore, if a piece of meat is found not in an established stationary place but abandoned or lost, we rule that it originated in a place that is of the majority. If the majority of meat markets deal in kosher meat, the found meat is considered as coming from one of them (ibid.).

If a person bought meat from a kosher meat market, and then some *ṭerefah* meat was found there, and now it cannot be identified, the rule is that the meat bought before the discovery of the *ṭerefah* meat is permissible because the principle of *qavua'* cannot be applied before the *ṭerefah* meat was discovered, and instead the principle of *kol deparish meiruba parish* holds. If the meat was bought after it became known that there was *ṭerefah* meat in the shop, it is forbidden because then the principle of *qavua'* applies (*Y.D.* 110:5).

This leads us to the principle of *sfeq sfeqa*—double doubt. If one of the above pieces that we ruled to be forbidden is accidentally mixed up with other permitted pieces, it is *baṭeil berov*—it becomes annulled if the volume of the permitted food merely exceeds the volume of the forbidden food, because of the principle of *sfeq sfeqa*—i.e., it is questionable whether the forbidden piece is itself forbidden or not. Even if it should be forbidden, now that it has fallen into another mixture we are again in doubt with each piece whether it is the forbidden or the permitted one (*Y.D.* 110:4). The Rama, however, does not consider this a true case of *sfeq sfeqa* since the first doubt (*safeq*) has already been resolved (see there and in Shakh for detailed rules of what constitutes *sfeq sfeqa*.)

UNIT XXVII

THE LAWS OF MARRIAGE (I)

XXVII.
The Laws of Marriage (I)

1. Introduction

According to Jewish tradition, the marital state is the ideal condition for man (used here in the generic sense as including woman). The Bible says: "It is not good for man to be alone" (Gen. 2:18), and the Talmud reiterates: "Any man who has no wife lives without joy, without blessing, and without goodness" (B. *Yev.* 62b).

This view persisted through all the vicissitudes of Jewish history and still obtains in our day. Thus, a comparatively modern authority says: "Marriage is that relationship between man and woman under whose shadow alone there can be true reverence for the mystery, dignity and sacredness of life" (Hertz, *Pentateuch,* p. 930). He continues: "Scripture represents marriage not merely as a Mosaic ordinance, but as part of the scheme of Creation, intended for all humanity. Its sacredness thus goes back to the very birth of man" (ibid.).

The same concept is expressed by a contemporary scholar: "Judaism regards marriage and not celibacy as the ideal human state, because it alone offers the opportunity for giving expression to all aspects of human nature" (Gordis, *Sex and the Family in the Jewish Tradition,* p. 33).

This sentiment is echoed in secular sources. Thus we read: "From a legal perspective marriage is a mode for the organization and control of behavior in society. It has served to formalize patterns of sexual relationship and characterize the expression of biological needs so as to minimize the challenge to social order of incessant rivalry and strife. It has afforded a vehicle for the distribution of property and for the determination of privileges and responsibilities in its use. It has served as a unit for economic organization, exploitation and development. It has regularly been the primary tool for acculturation, for the social, moral and ethical development and the tool necessary for assimilation into society. And marriage has been an agreement, with God or with society, to regularize the function of procreation and insure the perpetuation of the human race" (Ploscow and Freed, *Family Law,* p. 3).

Marriage has therefore become a mitswah in the Jewish tradition. Whereas the Torah says: "*If* a man taketh a wife unto himself" (Deut. 22:13), the code says: "Every man is *obligated* to marry a woman" (*E.H.* 1:1).

The primary reason for marriage is to propagate the race (ibid.). This is Halakhah. But the Aggadah expands on it. Thus we read: "Whoever weds a suitable woman, Elijah kisses him and God loves him" (*Derekh Erets Rabbah* 1). "Let a man be scrupulous about honoring his wife, because whatever blessing prevails in a man's house is there because of his wife" (B. *B.M.* 59a). "Whoso loves his wife like himself and honors her more than himself shall attain the scriptural promise: 'Thou shalt know that thy tent is in peace' [Job 5:24]" (B. *Yev.* 62b; B. *San.* 76b). "He who marries a good woman is as if he fulfilled the whole Torah from beginning to end" (*Yalquṭ Shim'oni, Ruth* 606).

The mystical literature speaks in the same vein. We find in the Zohar: "The Shekhinah dwells in a house only at the time when a man marries and lives with his wife" (Gen. 122a). Also: "A man who does not marry is not a complete person" (Lev. 34a).

And to quote another modern author: "It is true, undoubtedly, that marriage rests in part upon a biological, an economic, a psychological, a legal and social basis. But according to the teachings of Judaism marriage is something more than a biological mating; something more than an economic partnership; something more than a legal entity; something more than a psychological association. The title of the tractate in the Talmud dealing with marriage is '*Qiddushin.*' This is the term employed in every code of Jewish Law. This term is derived from the Hebrew word *Qadosh* which means holy or sacred. Marriage, therefore, according to the teachings of Israel, is a consecration, a sanctification of life. Its purpose is to hallow and to sanctify conduct. This concept of marriage is expressed in the very words that from ancient days the bridegroom utters in wedding his bride: '*Harei at mequdeshet li*'; 'Be thou consecrated unto me' " (Goldstein, *The Meaning of Marriage*, p. 117).

And Dr. Gordis summarizes: "From its inception Judaism has always recognized two purposes in marriage, both spelled out in the opening pages of Scripture.

"The first is the fulfillment of the first commandment: 'Be fruitful and multiply' (Gen. 1:28).

"The second function of marriage is that of companionship" (*Sex and the Family*, pp. 33 f.).

The laws governing family life play a prominent role in Jewish survival.

In their extraordinary life without state and country, without a language and government, under oppression and persecution, dispersed among the nations, our people made desperate efforts to preserve their uniqueness and the cultural and spiritual treasure they had inherited. In these efforts the family unit served as a mighty fortress. What has been said about the Sabbath—that more than Israel preserved the Sabbath, the Sabbath preserved Israel—may undoubtedly be said of the Jewish family as well (see Dykan, *Dinei Nissu'in Wegeirushin,* p. 24).

Marriage has a double aspect—the moral and religious on the one hand, and the purely legal on the other. The first deals with its significance for the individual and society; the second deals with the obligations the parties to the marriage assume toward each other which are enforceable in the courts, such as maintenance, property rights, dowry, inheritance, etc.

The Jewish law of marriage, to be sure, stresses the religious aspect, as the term *qiddushin* indicates, and as is attested by the religious rites that surround its celebration; but it also considers marriage to be a contract between two parties of equal legal capacity, creating mutual rights and duties that terminate either with the death of one of the parties, by mutual consent, or at the insistence of one of the parties following the breach by the other of one of the warranties or fundamental conditions of the contract (see Shiloh, "Marriage and Divorce," p. 492).

In Israel the rabbinic courts have the authority to deal with both aspects of marriage. In the diaspora, since we are subject to the law of the land, the legal aspects of marriage have only academic interest for us. We shall, therefore, restrict ourselves here to the religious and moral aspects of marriage.

2. Forbidden Marriages

Before dealing with marriage itself, we should discuss those cases where marriage is forbidden, either because of consanguinity, marital status, physical condition, religious status, or moral infraction (*E.H.* 15:1–26).

The codes enumerate a theoretical list of relatives who are forbidden to marry each other because of consanguinity. In comparison, the New York State Domestic Relations Law, section 5, entitled, "Incestuous and Void Marriages," provides as follows:

"A marriage is incestuous and void whether the relatives are legitimate or illegitimate between either:

"1. An ancestor and a descendant;
"2. A brother and sister of either the whole or the half blood;
"3. An uncle and niece or an aunt and a nephew."

Jewish law is in agreement with this list with the exception of item 3. According to Jewish law, not only is an uncle permitted to marry a niece, but it is even considered meritorious to contract such a marriage (B. *Yev.* 62b). Rashi and Tosafot (ad loc.) explain that this is "because the affection a man has for his sister will be extended to her daughter." Doubtless, however, the real reason lies in Jewish anthropology and in the family structure of the Jewish community.

In addition to the relationships enumerated above, the following restrictions also apply:

1. It is forbidden to marry a person who is already married (*E.H.* 17:1; see below under "Polygamous Marriages," p. 388 ff.).
2. It is forbidden to marry a person born of an incestuous or adulterous marriage (*E.H.* 4:1, 13; see below, p. 385).
3. It is forbidden for a man whose privy member has been cut off to marry (Deut. 23:2; *E.H.* 5:1). Castration was very common in ancient times, but if the defect was natural (i.e., by birth or because of sickness), the party was eligible for marriage (*E.H.* 5:10).
4. It is forbidden for a man to remarry a woman he has already divorced if she has subsequently been married to another man who then died or divorced her (Deut. 24:1–4). The Bible calls this תּוֹעֵבָה—"an abomination"—in order to condemn the easy passage of a woman from one man to another, since this must always entail some degradation of the wifely ideal, and might lead to virtual adultery, though the formality of the law would be observed (Hertz, *Pentateuch,* p. 850, quoting Naḥmanides and Sforno). Apt also is Koenig's comment: "Woman is a moral personality and not a *thing* that a man may hand over to another and then take back again at pleasure" (ibid.).
5. It is forbidden for a Kohen to marry a divorcee or a proselyte (*E.H.* 6:1). Both of these have been permitted under certain conditions by the Law Committee of the Rabbinical Assembly (Friedman, "Committee on Jewish Law and Standards," pp. 55–61; Kreitman, "The First Ten Years of the Committee on Law and Standards," p. 75; see below, p. 387 f.).

The prohibited marriages listed above are not all on the same level. The law distinguishes between forbidden marriages according to the degree of consanguinity. Certain degrees are forbidden to the extent that if the parties do marry, their act has no effect—i.e., their marital status under the law is not affected, and any child born of their union is considered to be illegitimate (אֵין קִדּוּשִׁין תּוֹפְסִין).

On the other hand, there are some degrees of consanguinity where it is forbidden to marry, but if a marriage takes place, it does have legal effect—i.e., the couple are legally married, but they are not permitted to live together and the marriage *must* be dissolved with a *get* (קִדּוּשִׁין תּוֹפְסִין).

In all cases of consanguinity forbidden in the Torah—referred to as עֲרָיוֹת, i.e., consanguinity of the first degree—any act of marriage is invalid, i.e., אֵין קִדּוּשִׁין תּוֹפְסִין. Thus, no legal act is necessary to dissolve such a marriage, and any children born of the union are bastards (מַמְזֵרִים). This includes marriages—

1. between parents and children or between grandparents and grandchildren (Lev. 18:7, 10);
2. between brothers and sisters of the same mother and/or father (Lev. 18:9, 11);
3. with a stepmother, stepfather, stepson, or stepdaughter (Lev. 18:8);
4. with a brother's wife, except in cases of Levirate marriage (Lev. 18:16);
5. with a wife's sister while the wife is alive even if the husband has divorced her (Lev. 18:8);
6. with an aunt, whether paternal or maternal (Lev. 18:13, 14);
7. with the wife of an uncle (Lev. 18:14);
8. with a son-in-law or a daughter-in-law (Lev. 18:15);
9. with a woman who is already married to another man (Lev. 20:10).

In addition to consanguinity of the first degree, the law also distinguishes שְׁנִיּוֹת לַעֲרָיוֹת—i.e., consanguinity of the second degree. Marriages in this category are also forbidden, but if the prohibition is disregarded and a marriage takes place, it is regarded as valid (i.e., קִדּוּשִׁין תּוֹפְסִין); the courts, however, are obliged to dissolve all such marriages with a *get*. Most of these cases are farfetched possibilities that have no basis in reality, such as marrying a grandmother or a great-grandmother and the like, but some are relevant and thus should be mentioned. Among these are the prohibitions on marrying the wife of a maternal uncle or the wife of a paternal uncle if the uncle and the father are both sons of the same mother. This category also includes certain marriages that are forbidden because of unseemliness.

1. A woman who was divorced because she committed adultery is forbidden to marry the man with whom she was adulterous.
2. A man is forbidden to remarry a woman whom he has divorced if she has subsequently been married to another man who then died or divorced her (Deut. 24:1–5; *E.H.* 10:1).
3. It is forbidden to marry a *mamzer* (bastard). This prohibition is based on the biblical commandment "A bastard shall not enter into the assembly of the Lord" (Deut. 23:3). It has been the source of a great deal of concern on ethical grounds, especially in Israel. Why should children suffer for the sins of their parents? While the rabbis would not initiate legislation that is contrary to the Torah, they sometimes alleviated a difficult situation by limiting the applicability of the law, and that was the course they followed in regard to *mamzerut* (bastardy). First, it must be understood that the definition of illegitimacy in Jewish law differs from the generally accepted one of any child born out of wedlock. In Jewish law a bastard is a child born of an incestuous union (Maimonides, *Hil. Issurei Bi'ah* 15:1; *E.H.* 4:13). Second, Jewish law assumes that all children born to a married couple are legitimate (B. *Qid.* 76b; *E.H.* 2:2). The rabbis interpreted this to mean that all births, even to a woman accused of adultery, are assumed to be due to the husband, stretching the rule to include cases where we would usually claim that the husband is not the father (*E.H.* 4:14–15). Cases of real bastardy, therefore, are very rare, and as a result, the applicability of the law is limited.
4. In order to establish paternity, and to safeguard the health of a newborn child, divorcees and widows should not marry until three months have elapsed after the divorce or the death of the husband, not counting the day of divorcement or death and the day of marriage (*E.H.* 13:1). This law applies even in cases where the paternity of the child can be determined, e.g., when the first husband is away or in jail, or if the woman cannot bear a child (ibid.), on the principle of לֹא פְּלוֹג ("no distinctions are to be made"). The need for the continuation of this law is in doubt. Three months

was once regarded as the period necessary for pregnancy to become apparent, but nowadays pregnancies can be determined much sooner through the use of the Aschheim-Zondek test or other biochemical means, and thus the principle of לֹא פְּלוּג is irrelevant.

5. For related reasons, a man should not marry a woman who is pregnant or who is nursing a child (*E.H.* 13:11). Nowadays, due to the use of bottle-feeding and to the shorter period devoted to nursing, this rule is academic.
6. In the following cases, marriage is forbidden because of a question regarding motivation:
   a. A woman whose husband is reportedly dead, and thus is permitted to remarry, may not marry the man whose testimony that her husband is dead forms the basis for her right to remarry. If they do marry, however, they are not required to dissolve the marriage (*E.H.* 12:1).
   b. A woman is not permitted to marry the man who acts as the agent to deliver her *get* in cases where it is necessary for him to testify that the *get* was written and signed in his presence. In this case also, if they marry in disregard of the prohibition, they are not required to dissolve the marriage (ibid.).

The Bible introduces the list of forbidden marriages with this admonition: "After the doings of the Land of Egypt, wherein ye dwelt, shall ye not do; and after the doings of the Land of Canaan, whither I bring you, shall ye not do, neither shall ye walk in their statutes" (Lev. 18:3). Later in the same chapter, the Bible calls these practices defilements and abominations.

This moral revulsion does not cover all the cases we have mentioned. Later authorities have offered the following additional explanations:

1. It is accepted that a defect in a family is perpetuated if the partners in a marriage are close relations.
2. There is also a natural revulsion to intimate relationships between relatives, although some claim that this revulsion is the result of socialization.
3. If the sexual urge is easily satisfied among persons of the same household who are in constant proximity, this would lead to sexual excesses. The rules of consanguinity control the passions and bring about a normal sex life.

4. There are two kinds of love, the love engendered by family ties that brings mutual aid to both partners, and the love that comes from physical attraction. The mixing of the two brings in its wake many problems.
5. Marriage between close relations is apt to cause jealousy and strife between the various members of the family (Dykan, *Dinei Nissu'in Wegeirushin,* p. 176).

Marriages involving Kohanim (priests) are regulated by a number of special restrictions in addition to the general laws covering all Israelites. The Torah prohibits Kohanim from marrying women of certain specified categories (see below), and ordains that any Kohen who makes such a marriage loses his priestly status (Lev. 21:6–7). These prohibitions were related to the Kohen's role in the Temple service, as explained in the Bible: "They [the Kohanim] shall be holy unto their God, and not profane the name of their God; for the offerings of the Lord made by fire, the bread of their God, they do offer; therefore they shall be holy" (Lev. 21:6). In order to ensure the holiness of the Kohanim, the Torah commands that "they shall not take a woman that is a harlot or profaned; neither shall they take a woman put away from [divorced by] her husband; for he is holy unto his God" (Lev. 21:7). These prohibitions are repeated in Ezekiel, with one variation: "Neither shall they take for their wives a widow, nor her that is put away; but they shall take virgins of the seed of the house of Israel" (Ezek. 44:22).

Thus the Bible prescribes that an ordinary priest is forbidden to marry a divorcee, a profaned woman, or a harlot. In addition, a high priest is not permitted to marry a widow. The rabbis added that he is also forbidden to marry a woman who has performed Ḥalitsah—the ceremony obtaining release from the obligation of Levirate marriage (*E.H.* 6:1). The Book of Ezekiel mentions that only a woman born of Jewish parents is eligible to be the wife of a Kohen. The talmudic understanding of the word for "harlot" also encompasses the meaning "proselyte," and this suggests that maidens not born of Jewish parents were barred from marrying priests because of the low standards of morality prevalent among the non-Jewish peoples of the period.

In all the cases listed above, the act of marriage was effective if a Kohen married in disregard of the prohibitions, and thus any children born of the union were legitimate. The courts, however, were obliged to force the couple to terminate the marriage through divorce (*E.H.* 6:1). Since the destruction of the Temple there has been no sacrificial service, but the sanctified status of the Kohanim remains in force because of the belief in the eventual rebuilding of the Temple and the restoration of the Temple service.

In the past, the restrictions on priestly marriages offered no difficulty, since only those pertaining to divorcees and proselytes were relevant, and divorces were rare, while proselytes were practically nonexistent. In our day, however, when both have become commonplace, there are difficulties in enforcing the law, and it has caused great resentment, especially in Israel, where only the rabbinic courts are authorized to perform marriages. To this is added the fact that the reason for the sanctified status of priests is no longer cogent.

The Law Committee of the Rabbinical Assembly has ruled, therefore, to allow such marriages but to make them modest and unostentatious, and also to instruct the Kohen to forgo his priestly privileges. This decision was based on the fact that the priestly status of most Kohanim is doubtful. Moreover, in the case of proselytes, the reason for the prohibition is embarrassing and borders on Ḥillul Hashem. Since the children of such a union are legitimate according to traditional law, no harm is done even to those who wish to abide by the strict prescriptions. This in no way prejudices the retention of those practices that still give special status to a Kohen: to be called up first to the Torah, to officiate at a Pidyon Haben, and to avoid entering a house where there is a dead body, since the talmudic reason of מִפְּנֵי דַרְכֵי שָׁלוֹם ("to promote peace") can be extended to include all of them. (See Dykan, *Dinei Nissu'in Wegeirushin* p. 195, for a discussion of the subject. For the view of the Rabbinical Assembly see Friedman, "Committee on Jewish Law and Standards—*Teshuvah,*" and Klein, "The Marriage of a Kohen and a Giyoret").

3. Polygamous Marriages

According to biblical and talmudic law, polygamy is permitted (*E.H.* 1:9). In the eleventh century C.E., a synod convoked by Rabbi Gershom ben Yehudah (960–1030), styled "Light of the Exile," issued an edict against polygamy which thereafter became known as חֵרֶם דְּרַבֵּנוּ גֵרְשׁוֹם (*E.H.* 1:10; *'Arukh Hashulḥan, E.H.* 1:23; Finkelstein, *Jewish Self-Government in the Middle Ages,* p. 25).

The text of the ordinance has not been preserved, so we do not know its actual scope or the immediate occasion that called it forth. There is no reference to it after its promulgation until the time of Rashi (Finkelstein, *Jewish Self-Government*, p. 24).

The provisions of the ban and its alleged text come to us from general legal sources and are as follows: It was an ordinance of the *qehillot* that a man should not marry two women. Plural marriage is not permitted except with the approval of a hundred rabbis from three communities and three lands, and they should not approve such a marriage unless there is a compelling reason to permit it. The *ketubah* should be deposited in the hands of a trustee either in pledge or in money (*Otsar Haposqim*, I, 1:14).

There are differences of opinion as to the extent of the ban's authority. The fact, however, is that it was accepted in all Ashkenazic communities (*'Arukh Hashulḥan, E.H.* 1:23). The Sefardic communities in the Moslem countries of the East continued to consider plural marriages lawful until 1950, when an act of the Chief Rabbinate of Israel extended the ban on polygamy to them as well (Schereschewsky, *Dinei Mishpaḥah*, pp. 72 ff.).

The reason for issuing a ban against the practice rather than an outright prohibition was that the later authorities could not consider such marriages invalid since the Bible and the Talmud considered them valid. Hence, if a polygamous marriage was contracted it was legally binding, but it had to be dissolved by a *geṭ*.

In some cases the ban can be lifted since there is a question whether it applied if a mitswah was involved. For example, if a married man became subject to Levirate marriage and wished to marry his widowed sister-in-law, would the ban prevent him from doing so (*E.H.* 1:10)? Today this question is academic because it has long been established that Ḥalitsah is resorted to in all cases of Levirate marriage (*E.H.* 165:1). Even in those Oriental communities where the choice between Levirate marriage and Ḥalitsah survived to our own day, Ḥalitsah was made mandatory by a decree of the Chief Rabbinate of Israel in 1950 (Dykan, *Dinei Nissu'in Wegeirushin*, p. 153; Scherechewsky, *Dinei Mishpaḥah*, p. 213).

The question of lifting the ban also comes up in the case of a woman who has been married for ten years without bearing children. This was considered grounds for divorce (*E.H.* 1:10). If the woman refuses to accept a divorce—and one of the *taqqanot* of R. Gershom was that her consent was necessary—would the ban prevent the husband from marrying another woman? This too is now academic because childlessness is no longer recognized as grounds for divorce (*E.H.* 1:3 in Rama).

The only case that is relevant today is where the wife is legally incapable of accepting a *get* (e.g., a woman who is mentally ill) or when a divorce is legal but the woman refuses to accept it, as in the case of a rebellious woman (*E.H.* 1:10).

4. Engagement, Betrothal, and Nuptials

The history of Jewish marriage sheds light on many present-day marital practices. We shall delve into their historical development to the extent that it bears directly on current usage.

Marriage never took place without preparation. Usually the families of the two prospective partners entered into negotiations, but the consent of the parties concerned was also considered (Gen. 24:50–58).

In talmudic times marriage involved three steps:

1. שִׁדּוּכִין—engagement
2. אֵירוּסִין—betrothal
3. נִשּׂוּאִין—nuptials

שִׁדּוּכִין would correspond to what is now termed "engagement." However, while engagement is simply an announcement that two persons have agreed to be married—i.e., a festive occasion without any legal significance—Shiddukhin, in talmudic times, was a prerequisite for marriage. Thus the Talmud tells us: "Rav punished [with flogging] a person who entered into marriage without Shiddukhin" (B. *Qid.* 12b). This was incorporated into law (*E.H.* 26:4).

The event of Shiddukhin was the occasion at which marriage promises were expressed by the parties concerned, and the terms of the marriage, such as the time, place, and size of the wedding, as well as the obligations of the contracting parties, such as dowry and maintenance, were discussed. The terms arrived at were binding and were put into writing in a document called the תְּנָאִים (terms of contract), hence the name תְּנָאִים for this occasion.

In the document, a penalty (קְנָס) was attached to the violation of any of the terms of the contract, or for the breaking of the engagement; hence the name *Knass-Mahl* for engagement in Central and Eastern Europe, and the term *Farknasst* (Abrahams, *Jewish Life in the Middle Ages,* p. 193).

While the Tena'im was a formal legal contract with stipulated terms and penalties, it did not effect any change in the legal or religious status of the parties to the contract. It was, therefore, revocable under certain conditions without in any way infringing upon the status of the parties concerned (*E.H.* 50:5). However, the public did attach a stigma to the breaking of an engagement, and in certain places it was considered a moral breach to be shunned more than divorce (Falk, *Jewish Matrimonial Law,* p. 112). Jewish folklore reflected this high regard for the sanctity of the engagement with a number of apt sayings (Elzet, *"Miminhagei Yisra'el,"* 354). The legal status, however, remained unchanged (Elman, *Jewish Marriage,* p. 69).

When an engagement was broken, a legal action could be brought by the aggrieved party. Sometimes one party had a legitimate reason for "breaking" the engagement, as when the other party had been guilty of unseemly conduct (*E.H.* 50:5). Action was usually brought when there had been an exchange of gifts (*E.H.* 50:4). This corresponds to "Gifts in Contemplation of Marriage" in general law, where the rule is, as in Jewish law, that the gifts must be returned (McKinney, *Consolidated Laws,* Civil Rights Law, bk. 8, §80-b).

The breaking of an engagement by one of the parties raises the question of breach of promise. This would involve claims for expenses incurred by the aggrieved party, the humiliation suffered, and the resulting pain and anguish (Dykan, *Dinei Nissu'in Wegeirushin,* p. 79).

Today the engagement party has only social significance. The young man usually presents his fiancee with a ring, which she wears as a sign that she is engaged to be married. There is no legal obligation, written document, or recorded promise, but only an occasion to publish the news that the couple will be married in the near future. Even in this case, however, there is the question, if the engagement is broken, whether the ring and other gifts must be returned. This too comes under the subject of "Gifts in Contemplation of Marriage."

The Jewish wedding of today is a combination of two acts which were once performed separately, usually with an interval of twelve months between them. These were termed אֵירוּסִין (betrothal) and קִדּוּשִׁין (nuptials).

Betrothal, the אֵירוּסִין of the Talmud, consisted of the recitation of the בִּרְכַּת אֵירוּסִין over a cup of wine, with the groom giving a ring, or an item worth at least a *peruṭah,* to the bride and reciting the formula: הֲרֵי אַתְּ מְקֻדֶּשֶׁת לִי בְּטַבַּעַת זוֹ כְּדַת מֹשֶׁה וְיִשְׂרָאֵל. This act is also called *qiddushin,* and it establishes the binding relationship between the bride and the groom. The bride is now forbidden to any other man, but she is not yet permitted to live with the groom as his wife (*E.H.* 55:1).

Nuptials, the נִשּׂוּאִין of the Talmud, was the bringing together of the bride and groom under the Ḥuppah, the recitation of the Seven Benedictions, and, after this, the provision of a few moments of privacy for the newlywed couple (יִחוּד) (*E.H.* 55:2).

Today the two acts have been joined into one ceremony, with only the reading of the *ketubah* separating them (for the history of this development, see Falk, *Jewish Matrimonial Law,* pp. 36 ff.; Epstein, *Jewish Marriage Contract,* p. 16).

5. Prerequisites for a Marriage: Consent and *Ketubah*

There are two prerequisites for a Jewish marriage ceremony.

First, both parties must consent to the marriage and enter it of their own free will (*E.H.* 42:1; *'Arukh Hashulḥan, E.H.* 42:3). In ancient times marriages were arranged by the parents and other members of the family. In talmudic times, while such marriages were recognized as legal, they were strongly discouraged (B. *Qid.* 43b f.; Maimonides, *Hil. Ishut* 3:19). Furthermore, even when the father gave his daughter into marriage, her consent was required (B. *Qid.* 43b f.; Maimonides, *Hil. Ishut* 3:19; *E.H.* 37:8). If another member of the family gave an orphaned girl into marriage, the rabbis established the institution of מֵיאוּן, which gave her the right, before coming of age, to summarily terminate the marriage without formal divorce by merely declaring her refusal. Her husband's consent to the separation was not necessary (*E.H.* 155:1).

The institution of *mi'un,* though never abolished formally, gradually became obsolete in the West for the simple reason that child marriage—with some notable exceptions—went out of fashion completely. In the Orient child marriages continued to our own day (see Dykan, *Dinei Nissu'in Wegeirushin,* pp. 202 f.). This practice was ended in 1950 (5710), when the Chief Rabbinate of the State of Israel declared the minimum legal age for marriage to be sixteen (Dykan, *Dinei Nissu'in Wegeirushin,* p. 381; Schereschewsky, *Dinei Mishpaḥah,* pp. 49–50, 398).

The second prerequisite is that the *ketubah* must be written before the marriage ceremony (*E.H.* 61:1 in Rama and 66:1). The *ketubah* is a memorandum of the obligations which a husband assumes toward his wife at the time of marriage (*E.H.* 66:1–11, 69:1; Epstein, *Jewish Marriage Contract,* pp. 53 f.). These include the provision of food, clothing, and other necessities as well as a commitment to engage in conjugal relations. It also pledges the wife a fixed amount as settlement in the event of the dissolution of the marriage.

The purpose of this financial settlement, according to the Talmud (B. *Ket.* 82b), was to serve as a deterrent to divorce. The husband was confronted with a serious financial obligation if he should consider exercising his prerogative of terminating the marriage. (Another deterrent was added by the synod convoked by R. Gershom in the eleventh century, which gave the woman the right to refuse to accept the *get* from her husband [*Otsar Haposqim* 1:14, p. 32].)

Nowadays, in the diaspora, where secular governments have jurisdiction over all matters pertaining to marriage, and the woman's interests are safeguarded by the civil law, the only function of the *ketubah* is to perpetuate an ancient tradition (Epstein, *Jewish Marriage Contract,* pp. 1 f., 5). In Israel, however, where Jewish marriage laws are in force, the *ketubah* retains its time-honored function, and changes have been made in its terms to suit contemporary conditions (Dykan, *Dinei Nissu'in Wegeírushin,* p. 393).

In the Conservative Movement, the *ketubah* has been given a new function and new value by the addition of a paragraph to the traditional text. In an effort to solve the 'Agunah problem in cases where the husband refuses to give his wife a *get* (see below, unit 32), Prof. Saul Lieberman, at the request of the Joint Law Conference, added the following clause to the old text:

"And in solemn assent to their mutual responsibilities of love, the bridegroom and bride have declared: As evidence of our desire to enable each other to live in accordance with the Jewish Law of Marriage throughout our lifetime, we, the bride and bridegroom, attach our signature to this *ketubah* and hereby agree to recognize the *Beth Din* of the Rabbinical Assembly of America or its duly appointed representatives, as having authority to counsel us in the light of Jewish tradition which requires husband and wife to give each other complete love and devotion and to summon either party at the request of the other, in order to enable the party so requesting to live in accordance with the standards of the Jewish Law of Marriage throughout his or her lifetime. We authorize the *Beth Din* to impose such terms of compensation as it may see fit for failure to respond to its summons or to carry out its decisions."

The new clause represents a private agreement between bride and groom entered upon prior to marriage. Since American courts have consistently enforced privately agreed upon stipulations, it was hoped that they would do so in the case of the private agreement represented by the new clause. With this clause added, it was thought, it would be possible to bring a civil action against a recalcitrant husband who refused to comply with the terms of his wife's *ketubah*. Some recent judicial decisions, however, have made it uncertain whether the courts will in fact enforce the agreement, since they tend to shy away from cases involving purely religious obligations.

A marriage is not invalidated by the absence or loss of the *ketubah*, but since a couple must not live together without their marriage contract (*E.H.* 66:1, 3), a missing *ketubah* should be replaced by the substitute document called כְּתוּבָּה דְאִירְכְּסָא (*E.H.* 66:3; Judah b. Barziloi, *Sefer Hashetarot*, pp. 35 f.).

6. Other Requirements

The *ketubah* must be signed by two witnesses who are present at the wedding ceremony (*E.H.* 42:2).

The two witnesses must be pious Jews and eligible to give testimony (*E.H.* 42:5). Nowadays, to avoid possible embarrassment to the wedding guests if they do not meet these requirements, the rabbi and the cantor or sexton sign as witnesses.

Usually, the function of witnesses is to attest to the validity of the witnessed act if it is challenged. If the act is not challenged, it is valid even if it did not take place before witnesses. In the case of marriage, however, the act is invalid without witnesses, even if it is unchallenged and both parties agree that it has taken place, because the witnesses are not merely sources of evidence but are part of the instrument that effects marriage (*E.H.* 42:2; *'Arukh Hashulḥan, E.H.* 42:18; Schereschewsky, *Dinei Mishpaḥah*, p. 36).

Opinions differ as to whether a marriage is valid (thus requiring a *geṭ* for its dissolution) if only one witness signed the *ketubah* and was present at the ceremony. All authorities agree, however, that in cases of hardship, where requiring a *geṭ* would cause difficulty (e.g., where the husband refuses to grant a *geṭ*), the marriage is considered null and void (*E.H.* 42:2 in Rama; *'Arukh Hashulḥan, E.H.* 42:13; Schereschewsky, *Dinei Mishpaḥah*, pp. 36 f.; R. Joshua Maimon, "Bedin Miqaddeish Be'eid Eḥad").

The marriage ceremony must be public, i.e., it must take place in the presence of a minyan (*E.H.* 34:4). The Talmud mentions the need of a minyan for the groom's blessings, which correspond to our Seven Benedictions (B. *Ket.* 7a), but not for the betrothal. The practice is to require a minyan for the entire ceremony (*E.H.* 34:4). The minyan includes the groom, the witnesses, and the officiants. The Talmud explains that the presence of a minyan lends solemnity to the occasion and publicizes the event (see *Otsar Hage'onim, Ket.*, p. 14 and in the notes; *Otsar Haposqim*, 12:12; Freimann, *Seder Qiddushin Wenessu'in*, p. 16; Dykan, *Dinei Nissu'in Wegeirushin*, p. 92).

The need for publicizing marriages arose when malpractice became rampant and secret marriages frequent. Ibn Adret and others ordained special *taqqanot* to require a minyan (Freimann, *Seder Qiddushin Wenissu'in*, pp. 10, 50). During the critical years following the expulsion from Spain, when misrepresentation was comparatively easy in the new communities established by the refugees, it became necessary to publish marriages. Many individual communities in North Africa and Turkey made *taqqanot* of their own, even declaring any marriage without the presence of a minyan to be null and void (Freimann, *Seder Qiddushin Wenissu'in*, pp. 102–5, 160).

There are many differences of opinion about the extent of the requirement of a minyan. The majority opinion maintains that a marriage performed without a minyan is valid. The requirement is only לְכַתְּחִלָּה (*E.H.* 34:4).

Today, when the civil authorities control the status of the parties to a marriage and attach a penalty to misrepresentation, the chances for misrepresentation are minimal. Since all marriage licenses are matters of public record, the requirement of publicity is superfluous. The other reason given in the Talmud, that it lends dignity and solemnity to the event, is still relevant. Hence, wherever possible a minyan should be required (see Kaplan, *Divrei Talmud*, 1, p. 168, for cases where a minyan is not required).

The groom must give the bride an object that has the value of at least a *perutah* (*E.H.* 27:1).

This harks back to the days when the groom paid a price for the bride and marriage was a transaction. The Mishnah mentions three ways of legally acquiring a wife: with money, with a deed, and with intercourse (*Qid.* 1:1). Very early in the development of marriage the first of the three became universal. The giving of something has become figurative rather than substantive, but we still abide by the rule that it must be an object of value. Today it is almost universally the custom to give a ring (*E.H.* 27:1 in Rama, 32:2) although in some Oriental communities a coin is still used (Gelis, *Minhagei Erets Yisra'el*, p. 33, n. 29). The ring should be of precious metal but unjeweled so that the bride can roughly estimate its value; otherwise, since she may overestimate the worth of the object in return for which she agrees to be "acquired" as a wife, the validity of the "transaction" (and the marriage) may be in doubt (*E.H.* 31:2).

At the giving of the ring the groom recites the formula הֲרֵי אַתְּ מְקֻדֶּשֶׁת לִי בְּטַבַּעַת זוֹ כְּדַת מֹשֶׁה וְיִשְׂרָאֵל (*E.H.* 27:1 in Rama and *B.H.* 3). The term מְקֻדֶּשֶׁת לִי ("consecrated unto me") indicates the religious nature of what originally was merely a business transaction. Hence the term *qiddushin* for marriage, which in Jewish tradition is taken as a state of holiness. As Dr. Robert Gordis says: "The moral imperative of Judaism is to strive to reestablish the sense of sanctity of marriage as the noblest estate in which a man and a woman can find themselves. Man fulfills himself most truly in marriage, because marriage permits love to be united with responsibility, stamps it with the attribute of permanence and exemplifies the truth that sex and love are indivisible. It is preeminently in marriage that sex becomes holy and love becomes real" (*Sex and the Family,* p. 45).

A new *minhag* is the double-ring ceremony: the groom gives the bride a ring, reciting the required formula, and the bride reciprocates, giving a ring to the groom. This is sometimes done without any accompanying statement and sometimes with the recitation by the bride of an appropriate passage, such as the verse אֲנִי לְדוֹדִי וְדוֹדִי לִי ("I am for my beloved and my beloved is for me") (Song of Songs 6:3; see rabbinic manuals for other texts).

Some authorities object to this practice since it is a deviation from the traditional pattern, especially if the formula used by the bride is the same as the one used by the groom. Legally, however, there can be no objection. Once the traditional formula has been recited the betrothal is binding, and whatever is added is of no legal significance (B. *Ned.* 87a).

The bride and the groom must be of the proper age.

Child marriages were very common in ancient days. Since marriages were arranged by parents and the consent of the parties was not necessary, age was not a factor in coming to an agreement. The physical factor related only to the consummation of the marriage. Hence, there was usually a waiting period between the agreement and the consummation.

It is logical to assume that when a boy and a girl reached the age of puberty, and the sex urge demanded satisfaction, ancient society deemed marriage to be the answer. In time, other elements became factors in marriage: climate, social conditions, economic conditions, and even political conditions.

While the Bible permits child marriage, the Mishnah and the Talmud discourage it. The Mishnah suggests eighteen as the age for a male to marry

(*Avot* 5:2). For a female no specific age is given, but the Talmud prescribes that a father may not give his daughter into marriage until she grows up and says: I want so-and-so (B. *Qid.* 41b; see also Maimonides, *Hil. Ishut* 3:19; *E.H.* 37:8).

The later authorities felt that eighteen was too advanced an age and suggested an earlier age (*E.H.* 1:3; see also B. *Qid.* 29b f.). The accepted rule was thirteen for a boy and twelve and a half for a girl (*E.H.* 1:3, 37:8, 43:1).

In spite of these rules, there were periods when earlier marriages were advocated (*E.H.* 37:3 in Rama). The main source for this deviation is the following statement in the Tosafot: "And as to the custom that prevails among us to betroth our daughters before they are twelve years old [which is contrary to talmudic teaching], we are compelled to follow this course by the fate of our exile, which we are made to feel more painfully every day. Thus, if a man have it in his power to endow his daughter with a dowry, who can tell but that the following day he will be robbed of his fortune, and his daughter might forever remain unmarried" (B. *Qid.* 41a in Tosafot, s.v. אסור לאדם).

In Moslem countries the Jews followed the custom of the land and had early marriages. Again the consummation followed after a long lapse of time (Freimann, *Seder Qiddushin Wenissu'in,* pp. 24, 83, 116).

Sometimes, after periods of severe persecution, child marriages were encouraged to replenish the loss of life. At other times there were threats or rumors of laws that would forbid Jews to marry before reaching a comparatively advanced age, and panicky parents hastily married off their young children before the law went into effect.

Oriental Jews practiced child marriage until the Chief Rabbinate of Israel, at an assembly of rabbis, declared it forbidden for a member of the Jewish people to betroth a girl under sixteen. This ban also applied to the father of the girl; he is forbidden to give his daughter who is below the above-mentioned age (Dykan, *Dinei Nissu'in Wegeirushin,* p. 381).

In Western countries we are subject to the laws of the land, which prescribe the proper age for marriage.

An authorized person must perform the ceremony.

According to the Talmud, one who is not versed in the laws of divorce and marriage should not have anything to do with them (B. *Qid.* 13a). On the other hand, since marriage is not an affair of the state in Jewish law but a private transaction between the bride and the groom, the requirement of an officiant is not obligatory (Dykan, *Dinei Nissu'in Wegeirushin,* p. 87). The talmudic requirement of an expert refers only to rendering decisions about questions of marriage (*'Arukh Hashulḥan, E.H.* 49:8).

Nonetheless, it was felt that someone versed in the subject should supervise the proceedings to ensure compliance with the law (ibid.). At times precautionary measures were necessary to prevent clandestine weddings. The custom was therefore established that a rabbi or his appointee act as the officiant (מְסַדֵּר קִדּוּשִׁין) (ibid.).

In Israel it is the law of the land that only a duly ordained rabbi, appointed by the Chief Rabbinate, may officiate at a wedding (Dykan, *Dinei Nissu'in Wegeirushin,* p. 382).

In America the situation regarding officiants at weddings was once quite chaotic, and for many years anyone who called himself a religious functionary was free to perform marriage ceremonies. Since then, however, most states have enacted laws that only a duly ordained rabbi or minister can officiate at a wedding. In some states cantors are also empowered to conduct weddings.

In this case the advice of the Talmud—"Go see what the practice of the people is" (B. *Ber.* 45a)—is an excellent guide. The people in general have decided that only a rabbi may officiate at a wedding.

7. Minhagim (Marriage Customs)

Many customs have developed around the marriage ceremony, serving to enhance its joy, solemnity, and meaningfulness, and emphasizing its sanctity. A number of these customs have become an integral part of the wedding ritual; if they are omitted, however, the validity of the marriage is not impaired.

Aufruf

Many of the Minhagim books describing marriage observances and celebrations mention the custom of calling the groom up to the Torah on the Sabbaths before and after the wedding.

The custom of giving the groom an 'aliyah on the Sabbath before the wedding still prevails and has retained its Yiddish name, *Aufruf* (also *Oifrufenish, Ufruff*). If the groom is able, he is given the honor of Mafṭir (Werdiger, *Sefer 'Eidut Leyisra'el,* pp. 2–5). Today it is also customary for the rabbi to bless the bride and groom either when the groom is called up to the Torah or at the end of the service.

The *Aufruf* does not have to be on the Sabbath immediately preceding the wedding, if this should prove inconvenient, and it may be done earlier (Ehrenreich, *Sha'arei Efrayim*, p. 10) or at the Monday or Thursday Torah reading.

The *Aufruf* used to be celebrated by the women in the gallery throwing nuts, raisins, and candies at the groom (Werdiger, *Sefer 'Eidut Leyisra'el*, p. 5). While one great authority protested against this practice because it meant soiling and wasting food (*M.B.* 171:19), the custom persisted and is still practiced in many places (Elzet, "Miminhagei Yisra'el," p. 356; Routtenberg and Seldin, *Jewish Wedding Book*, p. 127).

Fasting on the Wedding Day

It has long been customary for the bride and groom to fast on their wedding day until after the marriage ceremony (*E.H.* 61:1 in Rama; *'Arukh Hashulḥan, E.H.* 61:21). While the custom originated in medieval Germany (it is first mentioned by Eleazar Rokeach), it was adopted by practically all Jewish communities (Zimmels, *Ashkenazim and Sephardim*, p. 176). Many reasons for the custom have been advanced, and most are plausible. Among those that still have relevance are the following:

1. The wedding day ends one phase of life and begins another. Hence, like Yom Kippur, the threshold of the new year, it is an occasion for repentance and prayer, marked by fasting and the recital of the Yom Kippur "confession" by the bridal couple at Minḥah before the ceremony (P. *Bik.* 3:3; *O.H.* 562:2 in Rama).
2. Fasting gives the day a solemn and serene character, prevents cheap merrymaking, and lets the bride and groom enter the marriage ritual in a sober and serious frame of mind (*E.H.* 61:1 in *B.H.* 5).

It is customary to break the fast immediately after the marriage ceremony even if it is early in the day (*'Arukh Hashulḥan* 61:21). If the bride and groom find it difficult to fast, they should not (ibid.). If the marriage occurs on a day when fasting is proscribed, such as Rosh Ḥodesh, the bride and groom do not fast (ibid. and *O.H.* 573). If the wedding is at a late hour, the bride and groom may break the fast before the ceremony, provided they do not indulge in intoxicating liquors (*Ḥokhmat Adam* 129:2).

Ritual Immersion by the Bride

The laws concerning ritual immersion for a married woman after her menstrual period are treated below in the sections dealing with טָהֳרַת הַמִּשְׁפָּחָה ("family purity"; see units 36–37). Here we simply mention that the bride, prior to her wedding, is initiated into the practice of going to the miqweh for ritual immersion. While this is in conformity with the laws governing family purity, it carries the additional significance of preparing her to enter marriage in a state of physical and mental purity.

Visiting the Graves of Parents and Reciting Memorial Prayers

If one or both parents of either the bride or the groom is dead, it is customary to visit the grave before the wedding and/or to recite the memorial prayer (אֵל מָלֵא רַחֲמִים) at the wedding ceremony (Elzet, "Miminhagei Yisra'el, p. 357; Bergmann, *Hafoqlor Hayehudi,* p. 35).

In some places the memorial prayer is recited at the services in the synagogue at the reading of the Torah.

At one time it was customary to recite the memorial prayer during the wedding service under the Ḥuppah. No doubt this practice was a dramatic and effective way to remember the deceased; on the other hand, while due tribute was paid to the departed parent, the joy of the wedding was marred. As a result, the fashion has changed, and the memorial prayer is now usually recited prior to the wedding ceremony in the presence of the immediate family, usually in the rabbi's study.

Qabbalat Qinyan

The text of the *ketubah* concludes with the declaration: "And we have acquired from . . . the groom, for . . . this maiden due authority by means of an instrument legally fit to transact all that is stated and explained above, and everything is valid and established."

The words "acquired . . . by means of an instrument" refer to the formal act that was required to validate a legal transaction. Such a validation, called קַבָּלַת קִנְיָן, was necessary before the witnesses could sign the *ketubah* (*E.H.* 66:1 in Rama); it was usually performed by קִנְיַן סוּדָר; i.e., the parties to the transaction took hold of a kerchief. Today the rabbi asks the groom to take hold of a kerchief extended to him and explains that by doing so he agrees to be bound by the conditions specified in the *ketubah* (*Naḥalat Shiv'ah* 12:69; Werdiger, *'Eidut Leyisra'el*, pp. 12 ff.).

Badecken

Many of the Minhagim books tell how the dignitaries of the community would accompany the bridegroom on the wedding day, greeting and welcoming the bride, and placing a veil over her face.

This custom was known as the *Badecken*, i.e., covering the face, of the bride (Werdiger, *'Eidut Leyisra'el*, pp. 56 f., *Liquṭei Mehariḥ*, 3:130; Elzet, "Miminhagei Yisra'el," p. 360). Its origin is ascribed to the biblical story about Rebecca. When she saw Isaac for the first time, "she took the veil and covered herself" (Gen. 24:65). The covering of the bride with a veil is also mentioned in the Mishnah (*Ket.* 2:1).

Today, when the bride and groom are on the same premises, the *Badecken* takes place immediately before the procession to the Ḥuppah. The groom puts the veil over the bride's face in the presence of the parents and the members of the immediate family. The officiant then pronounces the blessing bestowed upon Rebecca before she left her home, "O sister! may you grow into thousands of myriads" (Gen. 24:60), and the blessing given to daughters generally, "May the Lord make you as Sarah, Rebecca, Rachel, and Leah" (Werdiger, *'Eidut Leyisra'el*, pp. 56 f.; *Liquṭei Mehariḥ* 3:130).

A number of interpretations of the custom have been proposed:

1. It is an indication of modesty and piety (see *E.H.* 31:2 in Rama).
2. It serves to distinguish the virtues of Jewish womanhood; the bride's beauty is reserved for her husband.
3. It reminds us of the first woman to be betrothed to a man of Jewish birth (Elman, *Jewish Marriage*, p. 144; Jakobovits, *Jewish Marriage Service*, p. 9).

The Bride's Walking Around the Groom

A custom rarely seen today is that of the bride walking around the groom upon coming under the Ḥuppah. In some places the bride is led in procession around the groom seven times corresponding to the seven verses in the Bible that contain the phrase "and when a man take a wife." In other places the bride circles the groom three times, corresponding to the passage where the phrase "And I betroth thee" occurs three times (Hos. 2:21–22; Werdiger, *'Eidut Leyisra'el,* p. 61; Routtenberg and Seldin, *Jewish Wedding Book,* p. 90; *Lequṭei Meharih̩* 3:291).

The Ḥuppah

The Ḥuppah is a symbolic marriage chamber, indicative of the bride's leaving her father's house and entering her husband's domain as a married woman (*E.H.* 55:1, in Rama). Today, since the whole wedding service takes place under the Ḥuppah, it is an integral part of the ceremony (ibid.).

Essentially the Ḥuppah is a canopy supported by four staves (ibid.). It can be a simple cloth or Ṭalit, an elaborate, richly embroidered canopy, or a bower of leaves and flowers.

In European countries the Ḥuppah was usually erected under the open sky as a symbol of good fortune, so that the seed of the couple might be like the stars of heaven (*E.H.* 61:1 in Rama). Some strict traditionalists still adhere to this practice. It is amazing that having the Ḥuppah in the synagogue was once opposed on the ground that it was an imitation of the Gentiles (Aloni, *Quntres Haqiddushin Beyisra'el,* p. 32; *Ḥatam Sofer, E. H.* 65). Today the Ḥuppah is erected wherever the wedding is held, whether synagogue, house, hotel, or commercial wedding parlor. Obviously preference should be given to the synagogue as the place most likely to lend solemnity to the occasion.

The Sephardim have the additional custom of putting a Ṭalit over the heads of the bride and groom during the service (*Sefer Hamanhig,* p. 92; Gelis, *Minhagei Erets Yisra'el,* p. 329).

The Ring

The use of a ring in the marriage ceremony is not obligatory. Any article is legally permissible, but it must be an item of some value since it represents the purchase price with which, in antiquity, a man purchased his wife from her father.

Wedding rings are not mentioned in the Talmud since they came into use much later. The earliest reference is in the seventh century, in the geonic period (see Harkavy, *Teshuvot Hage'onim,* p. 30). Adret, in fourteenth-century Spain, while discussing the general use of the ring for betrothal, also records cases where fruits and a prayerbook were used, thus indicating that the ring was not the sole item (Epstein, *Responsa of Adreth,* p. 83). Some Oriental Jewish communities still use these items (Gelis, *Minhagei Erets Yisra'el,* p. 334, note to par. 33). In the Occidental countries, the use of the ring has been well established since the Middle Ages. The best evidence thereto is the fact that in the marriage service published in prayerbooks, the text of the formula for betrothal was הֲרֵי אַתְּ מְקֻדֶּשֶׁת לִי בְּטַבַּעַת זוֹ (for a complete discussion, see Werdiger, *'Eidut Leyisra'el,* pp. 37 ff.).

The ring must be of some value (שָׁוֶה פְּרוּטָה) and must be made of plain metal, without stones, in order to eliminate any possible uncertainty in the bride's mind as to its true value. If gems were involved, there could be a substantial variation in value among rings, and this might cause the bride to have reservations (*E.H.* 31:2).

In time the ring became merely a symbol, but the above requirement was retained.

The use of the ring permits a number of homiletical interpretations. The following are the more popular ones (*Dover Shalom,* commentary on service in *Otsar Hatefilot,* p. 510):

1. Being circular, and therefore without end, the ring is a symbol of eternity, and a token of the permanence and unending happiness which we hope and pray will characterize the marriage.
2. The solid, unbroken metal ring symbolizes the harmony of the newlywed couple, which hopefully will not be marred in any way.
3. The use of a plain band without precious stones indicates, at the sacred moment of marriage, our belief that rich and poor are alike in marital happiness when marriage is based on mutual understanding and affection, and is consecrated and governed by a religious and moral way of life.
4. Like a circle, the ring both includes and excludes. On the one hand, it is a circle around the newlywed couple, symbolizing a union in which complete intimacy, love, and confidence are reserved for husband and wife, with all others excluded. On the other hand, as a symbol of inclusiveness, it points to the concern for society and the community that must characterize the family, for the family does not operate in a vacuum but rather is a unit in society, and its morality and values contribute to the welfare and health of society as a whole.

The Breaking of the Glass

After the Seven Benedictions are recited, a glass is placed on the floor, and the groom steps on it and breaks it (*E.H.* 65:3 in Rama). The custom dates back to an incident recorded in the Talmud. One of the sages, observing that the rabbis present at a wedding were very gay, seized a costly goblet worth four hundred *zuzim* and broke it before them. This had a sobering effect (B. *Ber.* 31a), and the breaking of the glass is similarly intended to temper the joy of the occasion by reminding those present of the destruction of Jerusalem and of the other calamities that have befallen the children of Israel. In the same spirit, the following verses from Psalms are recited at some Sefardic weddings: "If I forget thee, O Jerusalem, let my right hand lose her cunning. Let my tongue cleave to the roof of my mouth, if I remember thee not; if I set not Jerusalem above my chiefest joy" (Ps. 137:5–6) (Gelis, *Minhagei Erets Yisra'el,* p. 332).

According to folklorists, the practice may have an anthropological origin, e.g., to make noise in order to scare away the demons that are jealous of human happiness and eager to cause harm in moments of joy, or it may have been a sign of good luck (Bergmann, *Hafoqlor Hayehudi,* p. 333; for an exhaustive discussion of the origins, which are quite irrelevant to the practice today, see Lauterbach, "The Ceremony of Breaking a Glass at Weddings").

Güdemann proposes an explanation that is mentioned by few other writers on the subject but nonetheless seems plausible. The breaking of the glass, he maintains, was simply a symbol that the transaction was legal and proper (*Geschichte des Erziehungswesens,* 3:122).

In some places the person who drank the wine or held the goblet threw it to the ground and smashed it (Werdiger, *'Eidut Leyisra'el,* p. 36).

More recently, efforts have been made to pour new wine into old bottles. It has been suggested that the breaking of the glass reminds the bride and groom that even at the moment of their greatest joy they must not forget their obligations to society, which still has many people not as fortunate as they. It should be noted that for this very reason, in the not so distant past, it was customary at lavish weddings to set aside a special table for the indigent (Bergmann, *Hafoqlor Hayehudi,* p. 36).

Yiḥud

Immediately after the wedding service, the bride and groom repair to a private room, where they break their fast with a light meal (Werdiger, *'Eidut Leyisra'el,* p. 65; *'Arukh Hashulḥan, E.H.* 55:11; *Qitsur Shulḥan 'Arukh* 143:1; *E.H.* 55:1 in Rama).

It is obvious that this privacy was most meaningful in past ages, when bride and groom were not permitted to be alone with each other before the marriage. Today it is still an expression of the radical change which has been effected in the personal status and relations of the married partners.

UNIT XXVIII

THE LAWS OF MARRIAGE (II)

The Marriage Ceremony

When May Marriages Not Be Performed?

Civil Marriage

Marriages to Karaites, Benei Israel, Falashas, and Samaritans

Conditional Marriage

Marriage of the Mentally Incapacitated

Fictitious Marriage

Barrenness and Sterility

Family Planning

Abortion

Artificial Insemination

XXVIII. The Laws of Marriage (II)

1. The Marriage Ceremony

The order of the marriage ceremony is found in the standard prayerbooks and rabbinic manuals. Here is a brief outline of present practice.

Before the marriage ceremony begins, the *ketubah* is signed and Qabbalat Qinyan is performed in the rabbi's study. The rabbi instructs the bridegroom to confirm the terms of the *ketubah* by the symbolic act of acquisition, which consists of the rabbi taking a handkerchief and extending it to the groom, who grasps the other corner. By doing so, the groom agrees to be bound by the terms of the *ketubah*. The witnesses then sign the *ketubah* and the groom veils the bride. If one of the parents is deceased, it is customary to chant the אֵל מָלֵא רַחֲמִים in the presence of the immediate family.

The bride and groom then march in procession to the Ḥuppah. Under the Ḥuppah, the bride stands to the right of the groom. When they arrive under the Ḥuppah they are welcomed by appropriate chants.

The service begins with the first two benedictions, the בִּרְכַּת אֵירוּסִין (betrothal benedictions), over a cup of wine. After the bride and groom drink from the cup, the groom puts the ring on the forefinger of the bride's right hand while pronouncing the marriage formula. The *ketubah* is then read, separating the two parts of the service to show that they were once separate rituals. Then follow the seven benedictions (שֶׁבַע בְּרָכוֹת) over a second cup of wine. There should be a separate cup for each set of benedictions (*E.H.* 62:9). The bride and groom drink from the wine, a glass is broken, and the service closes with a benediction by the officiant.

There is no objection to adding prayers, explanations, and appropriate messages to the service, provided there is no interruption within each set of benedictions.

2. When May Marriages Not Be Performed?

Marriages should not be performed—

1. on Sabbaths and Festivals, because they involve acts (e.g., signing the *ketubah*) that are in violation of the Sabbath and Festival laws (Maimonides, *Hil. Ishut* 10:14, *Hil. Yom Ṭov* 7:16);
2. during the intermediate days of Pesaḥ and Sukkot, because, on the principle of אֵין מְעָרְבִין שִׂמְחָה בְּשִׂמְחָה ("rejoicing should not be merged with rejoicing"), the joy of the festive period should not be overshadowed (see B. *M.Q.* 8b; *E.H.* 64:6; *O.H.* 546:1 in Ṭaz and *M.A.* ad loc.);
3. during periods of national mourning, such as the days of Sefirah (counting of the 'Omer; see above, p. 142 ff.) between Pesaḥ and Shavu'ot (*O.H.* 493:1) and the "three weeks" between the seventeenth of Tamuz and the ninth of Av (*O.H.* 551:2; see above, p. 246 f.)

There are many differences in practice regarding the seven weeks of Sefirah (*O.H.* 493:3). Some observe the entire period, with the exception of Lag Ba'Omer, as a time of mourning during which weddings may not take place (*O.H.* 493 in Ṭaz 2; ibid. in *Sha'arei Teshuvah* 14). According to others, the mourning period starts on the first of Iyar and, with the exception of Lag Ba'Omer, continues until Shavu'ot (*O.H.* 493:3 in Rama). Still others also begin on the first day of Iyar but conclude three days before Shavu'ot (*Ḥayyei Adam* 131:11).

In the Ashkenazic communities, the most prevalent custom is to refrain from performing marriages from Pesaḥ until three days before Shavu'ot. Exceptions are made on Rosh Ḥodesh Iyar, Rosh Ḥodesh Siwan, and Lag Ba'Omer (*M.B.* 493:15 f.). In recent years some have added the fifth of Iyar—Israel Independence Day.

Because of these variations, as well as a number of social and economic factors, the Committee on Jewish Law and Standards of the Rabbinical Assembly has adopted the following policy:

"According to Geonic tradition, marriages in the *Sephirah* days were forbidden only from the second day of Passover until Lag B'Omer, and not from Lag B'Omer on (*Otzar Hageonim, Yebamoth* 140). This tradition was also practiced in the medieval period in the Jewish communities of France.

The prohibition against marriages during these thirty-three days applied only to wedding ceremonies accompanied by dancing, singing and music.

"We therefore recommend that the Geonic tradition concerning marriages during *Sephirah* be followed, and that the prohibition be observed from the second day of Passover until *Lag B'Omer*. During this period, marriages not accompanied by dancing, singing and music may be performed.

"On those days, during the thirty-three day period, when *Tahanun* is not recited in the synagogue, as well as on the fifth day of Iyar (Israel Independence Day), marriages of a public and festive nature may be solemnized" (see Law Committee Archives).

The three weeks from the seventeenth of Tamuz to Tish'ah Be'av mark the period from the breaching of the walls of Jerusalem to the destruction of the Temple by the Romans. During this mourning period, no weddings may take place (*O.H.* 551:2 in Rama).

With the establishment of the State of Israel and the reunification of Jerusalem, questions have been raised, both in Israel and the diaspora, as to whether this three-week prohibition of marriage should be revised. The Committee on Law and Standards of the Rabbinical Assembly has adopted the following policy:

1. Marriages are prohibited on the seventeenth of Tamuz and the ninth of Av.
2. Marriages are permitted from the eighteenth of Tamuz until the last day of Tamuz.
3. Only very small weddings, conducted in the rabbi's study, are permitted from the first to the eighth of Av (Segal, "Weddings during the Three Weeks").

Regarding all these revisions, both those pertaining to Sefirah and those pertaining to the three weeks, we should like to reiterate the caveat of the Rama: To prevent communal fragmentation, all groups within a community should adopt the same custom (*O.H.* 493:3). Thus, in any community where a change would cause dissension (e.g., in a small town, where any deviation from tradition would be very noticeable), the unity of the community should be taken into consideration when changes are contemplated.

3. Civil Marriage

The problem of civil marriage arose during the era of Emancipation. In the West, people were given the choice of being married under religious auspices or by civil authorities. In some countries it was mandatory to be married civilly regardless of whether or not there was a religious marriage (see Freiman, *Seder Qiddushin Wenissu'in,* pp. 356–84; Cohen, "Appendix on Civil Marriage").

The real question is not whether a civil marriage is valid, but whether a *geṭ* is required for its dissolution. There is a wealth of literature on the subject (Cohen, loc. cit.; Rudner, *Mishpeṭei Ishut,* pp. 132–42; Schereschewsky, *Dinei Mishpaḥah,* pp. 83–95; *Minḥat Yitsḥaq, E.H.* 12:66).

The Rabbinical Assembly has favored the opinion that a *geṭ* is required for the dissolution of a civil marriage. In cases where the requirement of a *geṭ* would pose a threat of *'iggun,* we take into consideration the opinions of those who consider civil marriages null and void (I. Klein, "The Case of Civil Marriage").

4. Marriages to Karaites, Benei Israel, Falashas, and Samaritans

While at present the question of marriage with members of the Karaite, Benei Israel, Falasha, and Samaritan groups is academic outside the State of Israel, cases of marriage with Karaites and with members of Benei Israel are beginning to appear.

The codes are very explicit about the Karaites. The *Shulhan Arukh* categorically forbids marriage with a Karaite (*E.H.* 4:37); the law regarding Karaites has an extra severity in that even if a Karaite should wish to convert to Judaism, he may not be accepted since all Karaites are *safeq mamzerim* (ibid.). This law was reiterated in a decision of the Chief Rabbinate of Israel exactly as it appears in the *Shulhan 'Arukh* (Chief Rabbinate of Israel, *Benei Israel,* p. 7; Elon, *Ḥaqiqah Datit,* p. 179).

It is known, however, that this attitude was not unanimous. At times when relations between the Karaites and the Rabbanites were friendly, marriages were contracted between them (Elon, *Ḥaqiqah Datit,* p. 173). Certainly, the ban against the admission of Karaites as proselytes was far from unanimous (ibid.; Goldman, *Life and Times of Rabbi David Ibn Abi Zimra,* pp. 52–57). In the Middle Ages, in many cases, marriage was permitted (Elon, *Ḥaqiqah Datit,* p. 180). While in the past few centuries the Karaites disassociated themselves from Klal Yisra'el, today they have reversed the process and have even suffered martyrdom for Klal Yisra'el. In Israel, although the official policy has been to forbid such marriages, exceptions have been made that may indicate a new trend (ibid. and *Otsar Haposqim,* vol. 1, sec. 174:1,

p. 206). At present, the once widespread Karaite sect is concentrated in Israel. Its members consider themselves Jews, but form a separate religious community and, at their own request and insistence, have judicial autonomy in family law (see Falk, "News in Israeli Family Law," 46; Ben Zvi, *The Exiled and the Redeemed,* pp. 129–37).

The case of the Benei Israel, while not new, has gained considerable attention in Israel in recent years. The Benei Israel are our brethren from India. They have settled in large numbers in Israel. The cause of the problem regarding marriage with the Benei Israel is similar to that with the Karaites; since they were not versed in the laws of divorce, they were in the category of *safeq mamzerim.* Their case is different, however, in that the Benei Israel never seceded from Klal Yisra'el and always considered themselves an integral part of the Jewish people. There is a strong suspicion that for the sources of the problem we should look into the caste system of India rather than into Halakhah. It is therefore understandable why the Chief Rabbinate of Israel, on the fifth of Ḥeshwan 5722, issued a declaration to the effect that there is no foundation for forbidding marriage with members of Benei Israel (Elon, *Ḥaqiqah Datit,* p. 176; *Benei Yisra'el,* p. 5).

The Falashas of northern Ethiopia, who claim to be of Jewish descent, keep many precepts of the Torah but are quite unfamiliar with talmudic law. As a result, there is a question about their status as Jews. Rabbi Abraham Isaac Kook, the first Chief Rabbi of Israel, referred to the Falashas as "part of our people who because of the trials and tribulations of the *galut* have been far removed from us both in distance and in views" (Goldstein, *Israel at Home and Abroad*). The current practice in Israel is to accept them as proselytes (see *Jerusalem Post Weekly,* Dec. 25, 1972, p. 4; see, however, Waldenberg, *Tsits Eli'ezer,* 10:113–16).

The Samaritans have been completely outside the fold of Klal Yisra'el from the days of the Tannaim (B. *Ḥul.* 6a) and were adjudged to be non-Jews (Goldman, *Rabbi David Ibn Abi Zimra,* p. 57). In present-day Israel they have their own separate religious community.

5. Conditional Marriage

The problem of the 'Agunah, and ways to alleviate her plight, was touched upon in the discussion of the *ketubah*. It is discussed more extensively in the section treating the laws concerning the dissolution of marriage (see unit 32).

6. Marriage of the Mentally Incapacitated

Since marriage requires the consent of both parties, the contractants must be mentally mature and morally responsible. This requisite would automatically invalidate any marital union by persons who are incapable, whether from immaturity or unsoundness of mind, of grasping the implications of married life and carrying out the provisions of the marriage contract. The Talmud includes deaf-mutes, imbeciles, and minors in this category (see Rosenblatt, "Jewish Law of Marriage and Divorce Applying to the Mentally Incapacitated").

1. Marriages involving minors are discussed in unit 30.
2. Marriages involving imbeciles, whether male or female, are invalid. If such a marriage is contracted, a *geṭ* is not required for its dissolution (*E.H.* 44:2); if the marriage was contracted during a period of lucidity, however, it is valid (*E.H.* 121:3, 44:2 in Rama; Sheftelowitz, *Mishpaṭ Hamishpaḥah,* p. 27). The case of a marriage where both partners were of sound mind when they married, but one of them subsequently develops imbecility, is treated in the section dealing with the divorce laws (see below, unit 33). In cases where the husband is afflicted with imbecility, but the wife was unaware of his condition before the marriage because he has lucid moments, and as a result it is now difficult to arrange for a *geṭ*, the marriage may be dissolved on the grounds of *qiddushei ṭa'ut*—"marriage based on error" (Feinstein, *Igrot Mosheh, E.H.* 1, resp. 80).
3. Although deaf-mutes are included in the category of mentally incapacitated, the sages ordained that marriages between deaf-mutes or between deaf-mutes and persons with normal hearing are valid (*E.H.* 44:1).

In modern times, with the establishment of special schools that have enabled deaf-mutes to lead more or less normal lives, the classification of mutes as mentally incapacitated has come into question (see Rabinowitz,

"Deaf Mute," in *Encyclopaedia Judaica;* also Fogelman, *Bet Mordekhai,* no. 65; *Maharam Schick,* no. 79; *Divrei Malki'eil,* vol. 6, no. 35).

In 1940 the Committee on Jewish Law of the Rabbinical Assembly ruled that when a deaf-mute is married, the declaration at the time of *qiddushin* is made in sign language, and the reading of the *ketubah* is dispensed with. Before the ceremony, the rabbi should inform the deaf-mute in writing that the act of marriage is effected by the delivery of the ring accompanied by the proper declaration in sign language. After the ceremony, the witnesses should communicate in writing with the bridegroom to ascertain whether he has followed the instructions correctly (Boaz Cohen, "Report of the Committee on Jewish Law," p. 31; see also Schwartz, "To Open the Ears of the Deaf").

7. Fictitious Marriage

The question of fictitious marriages, i.e., marriages contracted in order to achieve an objective for which marriage is a prerequisite, pertains to a recent phenomenon which is poignantly indicative of the adverse social conditions under which some Jews must live. The most typical cases involve marriages contracted for purposes of immigration and emigration. It has been decided that such marriages are legal and binding, and thus that a *geṭ* is required for their dissolution. When it is impossible to obtain a *geṭ*, the rabbis have endeavored to find ways of dissolving the marriage without one (Dykan, *Dinei Nissu'in Wegeirushin,* pp. 97–99; Stern, "Sha'ar Halakhah," p. 321; *Tsofnat Pa'aneaḥ,* vol. 1, resp. 13).

8. Barrenness and Sterility

Since children were considered a blessing in Jewish society, sterility was regarded as a curse (Deut. 7:14), and a marriage was deemed a failure if it did not result in the birth of offspring (B. *Yev.* 61b, 62a). In consequence, the Talmud maintains that if a couple has lived together for ten years without bearing children, the object of the marriage has been defeated and the husband must divorce his wife (B. *Yev.* 64a). In another place the Talmud adds that it is incumbent on the court to compel him to do so (B. *Ket.* 77a). This opinion was accepted by the codes (*E.H.* 154:10), but the practice subse-

Bath Spa University

Title: Halloween
ID: 00248862
Due: 23/2/2009,23:59

Title: A guide to Jewish religious practice
ID: 00015025
Due: 12/3/2009,23:59

Total items: 2
19/02/2009 17:05

Thank you for using the
3M SelfCheck™ System.

quently fell into abeyance (*E.H.* 1:3 in Rama), and barrenness is no longer considered grounds for divorce.

9. Family Planning

The Jewish attitude on birth control is not characterized by the rigid opposition usually associated in the public mind with traditional religious doctrine. While it is recognized that the curtailment of birth is an interference with a divinely ordered process, it is also recognized that sometimes such interference is necessary and proper, and is to be recommended in order to further this divinely ordered process. Thus it may be sanctioned where the natural process would jeopardize life and health in family or society.

Jewish tradition extolled the vocation of parenthood. Nevertheless, in some circumstances it held it morally right to curtail childbirth. In the face of peril to the life and health of the mother or the child, the rabbis permitted the woman, on the advice of a physician, to use a contraceptive in order to avoid pregnancy. Some authorities went beyond this and declared the use of a contraceptive obligatory (Bokser, "Birth Control," p. 79; Gordis, *Sex and the Family*, pp. 36 ff.; Feldman, *Birth Control in Jewish Law*; Feinstein, *Igrot Mosheh, E.H.* 1, resp. 62–65).

According to Jewish law, it is also permitted to sterilize a woman, either temporarily or permanently, if her life would be imperiled by pregnancy or if it is apparent that children born to her would be afflicted with a fatal congenital disease or with mental abnormality (ibid. and Klein, *Responsa and Halakhic Studies*, p. 163; Jakobovits, *Jewish Medical Ethics*, pp. 159 ff.; Feldman, *Birth Control*, pp. 240 ff.).

It is the general opinion that the pill is the least objectionable contraceptive from the point of view of Jewish law (Feinstein, *Igrot Mosheh, E.H.* 2, resp. 17; Waldenberg, *Tsits Eli'ezer*, vol. 9, 51:3:14, p. 223, and vol. 10, 25:10:1, p. 135; Feldman, *Birth Control*, p. 244; Jakobovits, *Jewish Law Faces Modern Problems*, pp. 67–71; Levy, "Hagelilah Limni'at Heirayon," pp. 167–70).

10. Abortion

The question of abortion, though not new, has become an acute problem in our day, and there is an extensive literature on it. As the artificial termination of a pregnancy before the birth of a child, abortion necessarily involves the death of the embryo or the fetus. The questions involved are: Is abortion permitted—

1. when the mother's life is threatened?
2. when the mother's health is imperiled?
3. in cases of rape and adultery?
4. if there is a danger that the child will be born malformed?
5. where the woman does not wish to have another child?

Where the mother's life is threatened, the law is clear and explicit: the mother's life must be saved, even at the cost of the life of the fetus of the unborn child, at any stage of the pregnancy as long as the child is in the womb (M. *Ohal.* 7:6). Once part of the child is out, i.e., the head or the greater part of the rest of the body, it is not touched because a life may not be saved at the expense of another life (M. *Nid.* 3:5). According to Maimonides, the child is sacrificed because it has the status of a pursuer (רוֹדֵף), one who threatens the life of another, and hence its life may be taken (*Hil. Rotseaḥ* 1:1; also *Ḥoshen Mishpaṭ* 425:2).

When the mother's health is imperiled, a distinction is made between the early and late stages of pregnancy. In the early stages, therapeutic abortion is permitted on the grounds that the child is *pars viscerum matris,* i.e., a limb of the mother (עוּבָּר יֶרֶךְ אִמּוֹ הוּא), which may be removed for the health of the rest of the body.

Opinions differ about what constitutes the early stages of pregnancy, with definitions ranging from forty days to three months (*Ḥawot Ya'ir,* resp. 31; *Peri Hasadeh,* vol. 2, resp. 69).

Some authorities would extend the permissibility of therapeutic abortion to any maternal need (Waldenberg *Tsits Eli'ezer,* vol. 9, no. 51:3). This would include cases of incest or rape (*She'eilat Ya'avets,* vol. 1, no. 43) where shame or embarrassment to the mother from the continuance of the pregnancy are considered threats to her health (Rosner, *Modern Medicine and Jewish Law,* pp. 73 f.; see also *Ḥawot Ya'ir,* no. 31).

There is a consensus of opinion that mental health is on a par with physical health; since mental pain is as severe as physical pain, it is taken into account in determining the permissibility of therapeutic abortion (Feldman, *Birth Control,* p. 236; *Minḥat Yitsḥaq, E.H.,* resp. 116; R. Zalman

Yosef Alony, "Meni'at Haheirayon"; *Darkhei Teshuvah,* 179:35). We would therefore conclude that abortion in the early stages of pregnancy is permissible in a case where a pregnant woman's physical or mental health is threatened by her fear that she may bear a deformed child as a result of having been exposed to German measles or to certain drugs, such as thalidomide (Feldman, *Birth Control,* p. 293; Jakobovits, *Jewish Law Faces Modern Problems,* pp. 72–76, Rosner, *Modern Medicine and Jewish Law,* p. 74).

When abortion is desired for reasons of convenience, however, it is forbidden (Jakobovits, *Jewish Medical Ethics,* pp. 170–91; Feldman, *Birth Control,* pp. 251–94; Klein, *Responsa and Halakhic Studies,* pp. 27–33, and "Abortion and Jewish Tradition;" Feinstein, *Igrot Mosheh, E.H.* 2, resp. 12; Unterman, "Be'inyan Piqquaḥ Nefesh shel 'Ubbar"; Zweig, "'Al Happalah Mel'akhutit," p. 36; Weinberg, "Happalat 'Ubbar Be'ishah Ḥolanit," p. 193).

11. Artificial Insemination

Though the question of the permissibility of artificial insemination is comparatively new, considerable literature has developed around it (Epstein, "Report of the Committee on Jewish Law," p. 157; Feinstein, *Igrot Mosheh, E.H.* 1, resp. 10; *Otsar Haposqim,* vol. 1, 1:42; Kreuzer et al., "Hazra'ah Mel'akhutit"; Neumark, "Kashrut Hayelud," p. 295; Feuchtwenger, "He'arah," p. 385, 395; Yudelowitz, "Beiur Halakhah," p. 57; Grossberg, "Quntras Harefu'ah," p. 314; Waldenberg, *Tsits Eli'ezer,* vol. 9, resp. 51:4, pp. 240–59; Weiss, *Minḥat Yitsḥaq, E.H.* 50).

The consensus of opinion is:

1. In no instance may artificial insemination be considered adultery since there is no adultery without physical intercourse. This ruling removes the stigma of adultery from those who submit to artificial insemination, and the stigma of illegitimacy from children born therefrom. Adultery and illegitimacy apply only in cases where there is lust, broken faith, and physical intercourse (Feinstein, *Igrot Mosheh, E.H.* 1, resp. 10).
2. When the donor is a stranger (AID—artificial insemination from donor), there are other considerations, both legal and moral, e.g.,

the question of the child's paternity, and the possibility of mating brother and sister (see Fletcher, *Morals and Medicine,* pp. 129 ff., for other considerations).

3. When the husband is the donor (AIH—artificial insemination from husband), the problem pertains to onanism (Gen. 38:9, 10). The consensus of opinion is that this discharge, though not the result of natural intercourse, cannot be called onanism since it is used for purposes of conception (*Otsar Haposqim,* 1:12; Feinstein, *Igrot Mosheh,* E.H. 1, resp. 10; Klein, "Science and Some Ethical Issues," pp. 166–69).

UNIT XXIX

RITUAL CIRCUMCISION

XXIX.
Ritual Circumcision

1. Texts

"God further said to Abraham: 'As for you, you shall keep My covenant, you and your offspring to come, throughout the ages. Such shall be the covenant, which you shall keep, between Me and you and your offspring to follow: every male among you shall be circumcised. You shall circumcise the flesh of your foreskin, and that shall be a sign of the covenant between Me and you. At the age of eight days, every male among you throughout the generations shall be circumcised. . . . Thus shall My covenant be marked in your flesh as an everlasting pact' " (Gen. 17:9–13).

"God spoke to Moses saying: 'If a woman . . . bear a man-child . . . on the eighth day the flesh of his foreskin shall be circumcised' " (Lev. 12:1–3).

"Of all the signs and symbols in the Jewish tradition, none is more widely known than circumcision. Countless gentiles almost intuitively associate circumcision with the Jew. And countless Jews, who in every other regard are estranged from synagogue and tradition, whose link to fellow Jews is tenuous indeed, are faithful at least to this mitswah.

"Circumcision for the Jew is the sign of the b'rit, the covenant between God and Israel, established first with Abraham and then renewed at Sinai, to be passed on through every generation until the end of time.

"Circumcision does not 'make' a person Jewish, for he is Jewish already by birth. The circumcision rather testifies that he who bears this sign sealed in his flesh is under the covenant which is what gives meaning to life. Through the covenant he is bound to all of the children of Israel, and through them to God; through the covenant he is made aware of how he sinfully falls short; through the covenant he is promised the coming of the Messiah . . . and life eternal.

"The circumcision of the foreskin is but an outer sign of the circumcision of our inner hearts that we are called upon to perform; as it is written 'Circumcise yourselves to the Lord and take away the foreskin of your heart.'

"Why is the sign of the covenant sealed into the organ of generation? To indicate that just as life is passed on from one generation to another, so is the covenant passed on. Yes, circumcision is for us a sign that the Lord who called to Abraham our father, calls yet to us of Abraham's seed, summoning us in this wonderful, and terrible command-invitation to renew the covenant. 'This is my covenant with them,' says the Lord. 'My spirit is upon you and my words which I have put into your mouth shall not depart from your mouth, nor from your descendants' mouth from now unto eternity' (Isa. 59:21)" (Matt, "Circumcision," p. 2).

2. Introduction

The rite of circumcision is cardinal in Judaism. According to the Bible, it is the sign of the covenant between God and the Jewish people, which began with Abraham (Gen. 17:9–13). While in modern times many Gentiles have adopted circumcision on medical and hygienic grounds, to the Jew it has always had a religious significance. It is the indelible mark of his Jewishness.

The rabbis said that every mitswah for which the children of Israel were willing to risk their lives remained with them (B. *Shab.* 139a), and they gave circumcision as the example. Indeed, throughout their long history Jews were often forbidden to perform the rite of circumcision. And yet today it is the only rite that is observed by virtually all Jews. It has thus become one of the strongest forces contributing to Jewish survival.

The great value of the rite lies in its high spiritual concept. It is the abiding symbol of the consecration of the children of Abraham to the God of Abraham. The fact that it is performed on the generative organ imparts to it the mystery of life and its perpetuation. The devotion with which this vital and fundamental institution is observed remains unbounded.

3. Procedure

Maimonides describes the process of ritual circumcision in these terms: "How is circumcision performed? The entire foreskin which covers the glans [עֲטָרָה] is cut so that the whole of the glans is exposed. Then a thin layer of skin [mucous membrane] beneath the foreskin is torn with the fingernail and turned back with the flesh of the glans completely exposed. Thereafter one sucks the wound until the blood is drawn from the more remote places so that no danger to the child's health may ensue. . . . After this has been done, a plaster bandage or similar dressing is applied" (*Hil. Milah* 2:2). This is quoted in the subsequent standard codes (Ṭur, *Y.D.* 264; *Y.D.* 264:3).

4. Anatomy of the Membrum

The membrum, as it extends from the body at the *pubis,* is a cylindrical organ consisting of three shafts of sinus tissue, two lying alongside each other on the dorsal side (*corpora cavernosa penis*), and the third (*corpus cavernosum penis*) on the ventral side. The glans, a cone-shaped or, better, mushroom-shaped, tissue, is the continuation of the ventral shaft; its posterior end (corona) covers the anterior ends of all three shafts. Just behind the corona the skin forms a fold (frenelum) and extends over the glans. This is the foreskin (prepuce; עָרְלָה in Hebrew), which is cut off at circumcision. Underneath the foreskin is a membrane that covers the glans.

The operation of ritual circumcision consists of three steps:

1. מִילָה, the cutting off of the foreskin.
2. פְּרִיעָה, the tearing off and folding back of the mucous membrane to expose the glans.
3. מְצִיצָה, the suction of the blood from the wound.

5. Instruments

Theoretically, any cutting instrument can be used in the performance of ritual circumcision (*Y.D.* 264:2; Maimonides, *Hil. Milah* 2:1). The custom now is to use either a doctor's scalpel or a knife that is reserved exclusively for circumcisions. To make sure that the officiating *mohel* does not cut into the glans, a shield with a slit in it is placed on the foreskin, and the foreskin is cut above it.

In recent years the introduction of new instruments has aroused controversy. The best known of these instruments are the Gumco Circumcision Clamp, named after its manufacturer, the Gumco Company, and the Yellen Clamp, named after the late Dr. Hiram Yellen of Buffalo, New York, the physician who designed it. The advantage of the Yellen Clamp is that it reduces the possibility of hemorrhage to a minimum and restricts the chance of infection, and thus the wound heals perfectly in thirty-six hours (Yellen,

"Bloodless Circumcision of the Newborn"). The medical profession has adopted it as offering the safest method (Williams, *Williams' Obstetrics*, 14th ed., p. 490; "Circumcision," *Medical Times*).

The Gumco Clamp met with a great deal of opposition from Orthodox rabbis on the grounds that (1) it provides for a bloodless operation, thus eliminating the דַּם בְּרִית (blood of the covenant); (2) it requires a prior incision, which causes unnecessary pain and, since it is not part of the ritual circumcision, constitutes a violation of the Sabbath if the circumcision takes place on a Sabbath; (3) the process takes longer than the traditional method; and (4) it eliminates *peri'ah* and *metsitsah*, both of which are integral parts of the ritual (Bloom, *Berit 'Olam*, p. 185).

Defenders of the clamp claim that it does not preclude the presence of blood and that *peri'ah* and *metsitsah* are not actually eliminated (ibid.; Bloom, "Dinei Milah"; Rabbinical Assembly Law Archives).

Another widely used instrument is the Mogen Clamp. It is said to have all the advantages of the Gumco clamp and in addition meets most of the objections of the Orthodox rabbis. No prior incision is needed, nor does the circumcision procedure take as much time as it does when the Gumco Clamp is used (Bronstein, "New Clinically Proven Mogen Circumcision Instrument," p. 67).

Strict traditionalists still prefer the old method, claiming that with an expert *mohel*, and if the baby is normal and healthy, it is still the fastest and hence the least painful means of circumcision. In addition, it has the aura of tradition (Bloom, loc. cit.).

6. Peri'ah

The second step in the ritual is פְּרִיעָה, the tearing of the soft membrane that covers the glans, and the rolling back of the corona so that the glans is completely exposed.

Traditionally this was performed by the *mohel* with his fingernails. The practice was not universal, however, even in pre-modern times. Already in the Middle Ages we know of the use of an instrument to tear the membrane (Eisenstein, *Otsar Dinim Uminhagim*, p. 221; *Maharam Schick*, *Y.D.* 240). In Eastern Europe and America, however, the use of the fingernails prevailed (Eisenstein, loc. cit.; see also Hoffmann, *Melamed Leho'il*, pt. 2, resp. 81).

The use of the clamp, however, makes *milah* and *per'iah* one process.

7. Metsitsah

Metsitsah is the third step in ritual circumcision. It consists of applying suction to the wound in order to prevent infection.

Opinions differ as to whether *metsitsah* is an integral part of the circumcision ritual or a health measure. If it is a ritual, it is subject to procedural regulation (*Ot Ḥayyim Weshalom, Hil. Milah,* p. 288; Sternbuch, *Dat Wehalakhah,* pp. 57–68); if a health measure, any procedure that enhances its purpose should be permitted (Homa, *Metsitsah,* pp. 7, 12). This difference of opinion has given rise to much controversy regarding the legitimacy of certain methods used in the performance of *metsitsah.*

The prevalent method in the past was direct suction by mouth. This was challenged on hygienic grounds, citing cases where the child was infected by germs from the mouth of the *mohel,* and where the *mohel* was infected by the child (see Homa, *Metsitsah*).

As a result, devices were introduced that eliminated direct contact between the *mohel*'s mouth and the child. Most commonly, a glass tube was used to draw off the blood, the suction being provided by mouth or by a suction device.

Another method was the application of a swab or cotton wool to the wound to absorb the free blood in the tissue (Bloom, *Berit 'Olam,* p. 140; Jakobovits, *Jewish Medical Ethics,* pp. 196 and 338, n. 39).

Since the majority opinion holds that *metsitsah* is not part of the ritual but merely a health measure, medical considerations should determine which method is most advisable (Bloom, *Berit 'Olam,* p. 140). The direct method is absolutely inadmissible (Homa, *Metsitsah*). The other methods are all legitimate, those utilizing an orally sucked tube or pipette being more acceptable inasmuch as the *mohel*'s mouth is still involved, though indirectly (see Bloom, *Berit 'Olam,* pp. 135–64 for the history of the controversy; *Ot Ḥayyim Weshalom,* pp. 286 ff.; Sternbuch, *Dat Wehalakhah,* pp. 57–68, for the strictly traditional view; and Homa, *Metsitsah,* for the medical discussion and the general practice today).

8. Time

Circumcision should take place on the eighth day after birth (Lev. 12:3; Gen. 17:12; *Y.D.* 262:1). The whole day, beginning with sunrise, is permissible, but the morning is preferable so as to show zeal in the performance of the mitswah (ibid.). A circumcision must not be performed at night; if it was done at night, it is necessary to draw an additional drop of blood from the organ (הַטָּפַת דַּם בְּרִית) during the day (ibid. in Rama).

Opinions differ concerning the procedure to follow in the event of a circumcision which was performed before the eighth day. Some authorities maintain that an early circumcision is valid if it was done properly (*Y.D.* 262:1); others hold that it must be validated by drawing a drop of blood (הַטָּפַת דָּם) on the eighth day (Shakh, *Y.D.* 262:2, 264:6; *Ḥokhmat Adam* 149:13). Nowadays, through ignorance or for convenience, many circumcisions take place before the eighth day—often this occurs because doctor and parents want the circumcision done in the hospital before the baby is taken home. In order to discourage this practice, we would insist that such circumcisions are valid only if a drop of blood is drawn on the eighth day (see Klein, responsum on הַטָּפַת דָּם, Rabbinical Assembly Law Archives). Moreover, if a child is circumcised before the eighth day, and his parents refuse to validate the circumcision by הַטָּפַת דָּם, he should not be named at services in the synagogue, unless there are extenuating circumstances (see Bokser, statement on Berit Milah [Oct. 15, 1963], Rabbinical Assembly Law Archives).

If the eighth day falls on a Sabbath or Festival, the circumcision may not be postponed (*Y.D.* 266:2). If the circumcision is performed later than the eighth day, however, it may not be done on a Sabbath or Festival. The mitswah of circumcision supersedes that of Sabbath or Festival only when it is performed at the prescribed time (ibid.).

For the same reason, if a child is born on the eve of a Sabbath or Festival during twilight, the circumcision is not performed on the Sabbath or Festival, but the day after. Since it is uncertain whether twilight should be counted as part of the preceding or the succeeding day, it cannot be determined whether or not the Sabbath or Festival is the eighth day, and Sabbaths and Festivals may be superseded only when it is clear that they are the eighth day (*Y.D.* 264:4, 266:8).

A new problem has arisen. If the *mohel* cannot come on the Sabbath unless he rides, should the circumcision be postponed to the next day to avoid unnecessary violation of the Sabbath, or should we insist on performing the circumcision on the eighth day on the principle that מִילָה דוֹחָה שַׁבָּת—the mitswah of circumcision supersedes that of the Sabbath? We are fully aware that only those procedures in the circumcision are permitted that cannot be done before the Sabbath, and certainly the *mohel* could come to the place where the circumcision will take place before the Sabbath (see *'Arukh Hashulḥan, Y.D.* 266:5).

There are valid reasons for both of these alternatives. On the one hand, there is a need to insist on the importance of having the circumcision on the eighth day (מִילָה בִּזְמַנָּהּ) because of the growing practice of having it at other times. On the other hand, if the *mohel* is permitted to ride because we insist on the eighth day, other forms of Sabbath violation will be involved. Furthermore, there are precedents for postponing a circumcision for other reasons (see Shapira, *Ot Ḥayyim Weshalom,* pp. 382 f., for other cases where postponement may be necessary).

If the child is ill and the physician advises a postponement, the circumcision is postponed for as long as the physician deems necessary. If the child is seriously ill, the circumcision is postponed until seven days after he has recovered (*Y.D.* 262:2). If the child is born circumcised, it is necessary to draw a drop of blood. This ritual is not permitted on the Sabbath or on a Festival (*Y.D.* 263:4, 266:10).

The Talmud and codes speak of cases of מֵתוּ אֶחָיו מֵחֲמַת מִילָה, where two brothers of the child have died as a result of circumcision (*Y.D.* 263:2–3; B. *Yev.* 64b). In such cases, circumcision is not permitted until it is certain that the child will not be similarly affected. This situation has been interpreted as referring to cases of hemophilia (Jakobovits, *Jewish Medical Ethics,* pp. 198 f.; Zimmels, in *Magicians, Theologians and Doctors,* p. 90 and p. 224 in notes, suggests that there are other reasons for such prohibitions). The whole question is academic since in all such cases we depend on the physician's decision in ruling whether the child is healthy enough to be circumcised.

The codes mention that a child who dies before attaining the age of eight days should be circumcised over his grave with a flint or a reed and should be given a name as a memorial (*Y.D.* 263:5, 353:6). In such cases we should follow Maimonides, who does not mention the practice at all.

9. Who May Circumcise

The obligation to circumcise rests upon the father. If he is qualified, he has the prior responsibility (*Y.D.* 260). If he is not qualified, he appoints someone who is (*Y.D.* 265:9). The accepted practice is to appoint a *mohel*—a person specially trained in the theory and practice of circumcision.

Nowadays, a *mohel* is required to have medical certification and a license to practice. Where there is a properly organized Jewish community, he must have a certificate from the communal rabbinic authorities attesting to his piety as well as to his knowledge of the religious rules concerning circumcision.

It often happens in America, especially in smaller Jewish communities, that no qualified *mohel* is available. In such cases a physician is called upon to perform the circumcision. The physician must be Jewish, must know the procedure and the required prayers, and must have a reverential attitude toward the performance of the mitswah (see Bokser, statement on Berit Milah). It is customary to invite the rabbi to supervise the procedure and conduct the service (ibid.). When a *mohel* is available, however, the rabbi should insist on a *mohel*.

Is a woman eligible to be a *mohel?* According to the law, yes, but customarily only men become *mohalim* (*Y.D.* 264:1). However, since there are now many female doctors, there certainly can be no objection to a woman doctor enjoying equality with a male doctor in performing the mitswah.

Is a Gentile doctor qualified? No, because only a member of the faith, who is subject to its precepts, is eligible. A circumcision performed by a Gentile physician is valid, but only if a drop of blood is drawn as described above (*Y.D.* 264:1 and in Rama; see also Novak, *Law and Theology in Judaism,* ser. 1, pp. 69, 71, on cases where only a Gentile doctor is available).

10. The Service

The essentials of the service are the blessing recited by the *mohel*, the blessing recited by the father, the blessing over the wine, the prayer for the welfare of the child and his family, and the namegiving (*Y.D.* 265:1).

Many *minhagim* have developed around the ritual, enhancing its beauty and meaning. Their use has been limited by the custom of having the circumcision performed by a doctor in the hospital. Now that more and more circumcisions are taking place in the home, it is possible to reinstate these rituals. We shall present the full traditional procedure in the hope that as much of it as possible will be adopted.

Before the *berit* the parents select three friends or relatives whom they wish to honor and designate them the *kvatter* (godfather), *kvatterin* (godmother), and *sandaq*. The *kvatterin* brings the child into the room where the circumcision will take place and hands him to the *kvatter*. The *kvatter* hands the baby to the *mohel*. After saying the introductory prayer, the *mohel* places the child on the *sandaq*'s lap. Sometimes he places the child on a table and the *sandaq* holds the child's hands and legs firmly so that the *mohel* may proceed without interference.

It is customary to light two candles in the room where the circumcision will take place.

If possible, there should be a minyan at the circumcision, but this is not an absolute requirement and the circumcision may be performed without it (*Y.D.* 265:6).

Those present stand during the service, except for the *sandaq*, who remains seated (*Y.D.* 265:1 in Rama).

When the *mohel* is ready to begin he calls out: "*kvatter*." The godmother brings the baby in on a pillow and hands it to the godfather. The people present welcome the child, saying: "בָּרוּךְ הַבָּא."

The *mohel* recites a prayer mentioning the covenant with Abraham, takes the child from the godfather and places it on the *sandaq*'s lap, and recites the prayer זֶה הַכִּסֵּא שֶׁל אֵלִיָּהוּ זָכוּר לַטּוֹב.

When all circumcisions were performed in the synagogue, there was a special chair for the *sandaq* called כִּסֵּא שֶׁל אֵלִיָּהוּ, the throne, or chair, of Elijah. As the "angel of the covenant" (Mal. 3:1), Elijah is, in particular, the guardian of the child at the covenant of circumcision (see *Pirqei de Rabbi Eli'ezer,* end of chap. 29, with reference to I Kings 19:10). Hence the special chair in his honor (*Y.D.* 265:11).

Next, the *mohel* recites the blessing עַל הַמִּילָה and performs the circumcision as prescribed. The father then recites the blessing לְהַכְנִיסוֹ בִּבְרִיתוֹ שֶׁל אַבְרָהָם אָבִינוּ. Those present respond: כְּשֵׁם שֶׁנִּכְנַס לַבְּרִית כֵּן יִכָּנֵס לְתוֹרָה וּלְחֻפָּה וּלְמַעֲשִׂים טוֹבִים. Then follows the blessing over the wine and a prayer for the well-being of the child and the family. In the last prayer the child is given his Hebrew name. When the verse בְּדָמַיִךְ חֲיִי is said, a piece of gauze is dipped into the wine and applied to the child's lips.

The wine is then given to the parents to drink, the baby is returned to the mother, and the ceremony is concluded.

It is followed by a Se'udat Mitswah. The grace after the meal includes special prayers for the welfare of the child, its father and mother, and the *mohel*.

11. Namegiving

It is customary to name a male child at the circumcision and a female child at the service in the synagogue. The naming of a boy is part of the circumcision service. In the case of a girl, the father comes to the service on a day when the Torah is read and is honored with an 'aliyah. A מִי שֶׁבֵּרַךְ is recited for the health of mother and child, and in it the child is named.

The prevalent custom in the Ashkenazic communities is to name children after deceased relatives but never after living persons. Among the Sefardim a child can be named after a living person, usually the grandfather or father (Bloom, *Berit 'Olam*, p. 230).

In some communities the mother has the privilege of choosing the name for the first child (Gottlieb, *A Jewish Child Is Born*, p. 110). In others, the privilege is the father's (Bloom, *Berit 'Olam*, p. 232). If the child is to be named after a person of the opposite sex, the nearest equivalent name of the correct gender is used. Examples are Ḥayyah and Ḥayyim; Barukh and Berakhah; Tsevi and Tseviyah; Dan and Dinah.

In ancient times names were given in connection with significant events in the family (Exod. 2:22, Gen. 35:18, etc.), the community (Isa. 7:14), or the world (Gen. 10:25). In present-day Israel this custom has been restored, and as a result, the names of many Israelis are linked to events affecting the new state.

Among the Ḥassidim it was customary to name children after the *tsaddiq* to whom the family was devoted. Today some families have substituted the names of civic or moral leaders.

There is no normative regulation regarding the naming of children or the names to be chosen. Custom and sentiment are the determining factors.

Naming a child has always been a significant experience. In the case of Jewish names, there is the added significance of Jewish identification. The rabbis said that one of the reasons for the redemption of the children of Israel from Egyptian bondage was the fact that they had retained their Jewish names (*Lev. Rab.* 32:5).

Over the centuries, Jews outside Israel have adopted the custom of using a name in the language of the country in which they live. This name is sometimes the translation of the Hebrew name and sometimes merely has an assonance with it, but it may have no relationship at all to the Hebrew name. Some people use their Hebrew names for all purposes and do not have an additional secular name.

12. Redemption of the Firstborn

"The first issue of the womb of every being, man or beast, that is offered to the Lord shall be yours [the priest's]; but you shall have the first-born of man redeemed, and you shall also have the firstling of unclean animals redeemed. Take as their redemption price [for the human first-born] from the age of one month up, the money equivalent of five shekels by the sanctuary weight, which is twenty gerahs" (Num. 18:15–16).

"In very ancient times, the first-born son in every Israelite family was vested with special responsibilities. From the day of his birth he was consecrated to the vocation of assisting the priest in the conduct of worship.

"Later, when a tabernacle was built in the wilderness, this vocation of the first-born was transferred to the Levites, a priestly tribe. The Torah then decreed that every father release his first-born son from the duties incumbent upon all first-born sons by redeeming him from a Kohen. The ancient obligation of the first-born son thus continues to be recalled. This practice, ordained as a recollection of the Exodus from Egypt, further serves to make vivid for us the liberation from bondage of the people of Israel, an event which has been an inspiration to all freedom loving people" (Harlow, *Rabbi's Manual,* p. 14).

Undoubtedly, the original reason for the redemption of the firstborn was the feeling that he belonged to God or was dedicated to God. It expressed the pious awareness that our first obligation is always to God. In very ancient times, among primitive peoples, this may have meant that the firstborn was sacrificed. Among the children of Israel, it meant that the firstborn was given to the priest to assist him in the sanctuary. His redemption was a means of retaining the idea of our primary obligations to God while at the same time keeping the firstborn son home with the family.

The ceremony of פִּדְיוֹן הַבֵּן (redemption of the firstborn) is widely practiced and has a great deal of appeal for American Jewish families. Alas, the cause has been more sociological than religious.

The birth of a child is an important and joyous event, even in our sophisticated society, and families often wish to solemnize it with proper celebrations. Traditionally the Se'udat Mitswah at the circumcision was held for that purpose. Today an elaborate celebration at the circumcision is often impractical and difficult. Hospital administrators usually discourage large groups from attending circumcisions conducted on the hospital premises and often restrict the number allowed to attend. Nor is a hospital an appropriate place for a celebration, even of modest proportions.

Moreover, even if the circumcision takes place at home, it is usually in the morning, during working hours, and few people can attend. Furthermore, the mother is still too weak to entertain.

The celebration of a Pidyon Haben provides an opportunity to make up for this deficiency. The alert rabbi will take advantage of the situation and use it as an additional means to enrich the Jewish home with meaningful ritual.

Every firstborn son of an Israelite mother must be redeemed. In other words, a child must still be redeemed even if he has an older brother born to his father from a previous marriage (*Y.D.* 305:1). Conversely, it is not necessary to redeem a son who is firstborn to the father but not to the mother (i.e., if a man marries a woman who already has a child from a previous marriage, any son issuing from their marriage need not be redeemed [ibid.].

If a woman gives birth to a son after a previous pregnancy that was terminated by a miscarriage, the child does not have to be redeemed unless the miscarriage took place within forty days of conception or if the fetus had not yet developed into human form (*Y.D.* 305:23; see also M. *Nid.* 3:7).

A child born by Caesarean operation does not have to be redeemed because there has been no "opening of the womb" (*Y.D.* 305:24). Moreover, if a woman has a normal birth subsequent to a delivery by Caesarean section, the second child also does not have to be redeemed, even though his birth "opened the womb," because he is not in fact a firstborn (*Y.D.* 305:24; see also M. *Bek.* 8:2).

The firstborn of a Kohen or a Levite is exempt from redemption. The same rule applies to the firstborn of a daughter of a Kohen or Levite who is married to an Israelite (*Y.D.* 305:18).

The redemption should take place only after the child is a full thirty days old. This means that it takes place on the thirty-first day after birth (*Y.D.* 305:11). If the thirty-first day falls on a Sabbath or a Festival, the redemption should be postponed to the following day (ibid.).

The custom is to have the redemption during the day (*'Arukh Hashulḥan, Y.D.* 305:44). If for some reason it did not take place on the thirty-first day, it should be done immediately, on the night following (ibid.).

If the thirty-first day falls during the intermediate days of Pesaḥ or Sukkot, the redemption is not postponed (*Y.D.* 305:11 in Rama; *'Arukh Hashulḥan* 305:46; *Ḥokhmat Adam* 150:9).

Since it is often difficult to have an affair during the daytime on a weekday, especially when the days are short, the question has arisen whether it is permitted to have the redemption the preceding night, on the assumption that in the Jewish calendar that night is already counted as the thirty-first day. The authorities permit this, since, unlike a circumcision, which must take place during the day, the holding of a Pidyon Haben in the daytime is merely a custom. All that is required is that the child be a month old, i.e., 29 days, 12 hours, and 793/1080 (about ¾) of an hour (*'Arukh Hashulḥan, Y.D.* 305:45; *Yad Halevi,* resp. 193; *Ḥokhmat Adam* 508:8). Some authorities do not require this exact time and permit the Pidyon Haben to take place anytime during the night of the thirty-first day.

It is customary to use five silver dollars for the redemption since silver dollars are considered equivalent to the shekels of the Bible. When it is difficult to get silver coins (e.g., if the government withdraws them from circulation), the equivalent amount will serve as well. It has been estimated that a silver vessel weighing ninety-six grams is the equivalent (*Qitsur Shulḥan 'Arukh Hashalem,* ed. Ḥayyim Yeshayahu Hakohen, p. 35 at the end of the book; see also Noeh, "Middot Weshi'urei Torah," p. 94; Hoffmann, *Melamed Leho'il,* pt. 2, resp. 100, says 105 grams).

The service for the redemption of the firstborn is found in all standard Siddurim and rabbis' manuals. For new variations of the service, see Nathan Gottlieb, *A Jewish Child Is Born,* pp. 55–60, and Rabbi Hershel Matt, "Circumcision," p. 1. These have the virtue of retaining the traditional formulae while adding responsive readings in which all the guests may participate.

UNIT XXX

ADOPTION

XXX.
Adoption

1. Introduction

"And Pharaoh's daughter said to her: 'Take this child away and nurse it for me, and I will give thee thy wages.' And the woman took the child and nursed it. And the child grew, and she brought him unto Pharaoh's daughter, and he became her son" (Exod. 2:9–10).

"And he brought up Hadassah, that is, Esther, his uncle's daughter; for she had neither father nor mother, and the maiden was of beautiful form and fair to look on; and when her father and mother died, Mordecai took her for his own daughter" (Esther 2:7).

"This teaches you that whoever brings up an orphan in his home, Scripture ascribes it to him as though he had begotten him" (B. *San.* 19b).

Adoption is defined in law as the legal proceeding whereby a person takes another person into the relation of a child and thereby acquires the rights and responsibilities of a parent in respect of the other person (New York State Domestic Relations Law, §110, in McKinney, *Consolidated Laws of New York,* bk. 14, p. 255).

The institution of adoption is mentioned as far back in history as the Code of Hammurabi (see Hastings, *Encyclopaedia of Religion and Ethics,* s.v. "Adoption"). In ancient times it reached its fullest development among the Romans, and was a common and accepted practice (Justinian's *Digest,* bk. I, title vii) very similar to the practice that obtains today. Since from the religious viewpoint the Romans regarded the ending of a family line as a disaster, families without issue were motivated to adopt by the desire to have a successor who would continue the family line. In addition, adoption conferred status on a child, since a child, or even an adult, who was adopted assumed the status of the adoptive parents in every respect (see Buckland, *Manual of Roman Private Law,* pp. 74 ff.; Jörs, *Geschichte und System des Römischen Privatrechts,* pp. 208 f.). The most famous example is the case of the adoption of Octavian by Julius Caesar.

The modern procedure for adoption is similar in many ways to the

Roman but quite different in motivation. Today adoption results from a charitable interest in helping the parentless or, more often, from the desire of childless parents to raise a family (Jolowicz, *Roman Foundations of Modern Law,* pp. 194 f.).

2. Adoption in Jewish life

In Jewish life adoption in the above sense is a recent phenomenon. In Israel a law of adoption was passed only in 1960 (Alony, *Rights of the Child in the Laws of the State of Israel,* p. 193).

This does not mean that there was no adoption among Jews before that date. In the literature we often find compassionate persons taking an orphaned child into the house (as Mordecai did with Esther) or bringing up a foundling whose parentage was unknown (as Pharaoh's daughter did with Moses), but we do not find the establishment of an artificial kinship with a *vinculum juris* of its own and requiring court action. While Roman adoption transferred the child from an old kinship to a new one, in Jewish tradition the adopted child retained the status of its natural parent, and the adoptive parents were like legal guardians—a contractual relationship. Hence there was no adoption in the accepted sense among the Jews, there is no Hebrew word for it (אִמּוּץ, used today, is newly coined), and there is no mention of it in the standard codes.

The current practice is for a couple, usually childless, to take for their own a child of other parents who for certain reasons wish to give it for adoption. While the adoptive parents want the child because of their desire to have a family, the state enters the proceeding to protect the interests of the child, and therefore surrounds adoption with rules and regulations to achieve that purpose (Witmer et al., *Independent Adoption*). From the Jewish point of view, we are interested in both the matters mentioned above and also the religious implications and requirements involved in adoption. The questions of maintenance, education, inheritance, and the fitness of the adoptive parents are treated by the law of the land. As Jews we must be particularly concerned with the following questions:

1. May Jewish parents adopt a child whose natural parents are not Jewish, even if the latter consent?
2. May a child whose parentage is unknown be adopted?
3. If the parents are Jewish, does the child retain the natural father's

name or that of the adoptive father, e.g., when he is called to the Torah, do we say "Isaac the son of (the natural father's name)" or "(the adoptive father's name)"?

4. In legal documents, such as a *ketubah* or a *geṭ*, do we use the name of the natural father or the adoptive father?
5. If the natural father is a Kohen or a Levite, and the adoptive father is not, or vice-versa, what is the status of the child?
6. If the adopted child is a *bekhor* (firstborn), are the adoptive parents obligated to have a Pidyon Haben?
7. If the natural parents are not Jewish and the child is converted, do we use ben or bat Avraham Avinu as with other proselytes, or the name of the adoptive father?
8. When the adoptive parents die, is the adopted child obliged to sit Shiv'ah and say Qaddish?
9. May an adopted child marry a member of the family of his adoptive parents?

Though adoption is a legal fiction whereby a person who is a member of one family becomes a member of another family, in classical law, and in the laws of the West today, the fiction became a fact, and "an adopted child assumes towards adoptive parents the status of a natural child, and assumes towards natural parents the status of a stranger so far as legal obligations are concerned and adoptive parents become clothed in law with responsibilities of natural parents" (McKinney, *Consolidated Laws of New York*, Domestic Relations Law, bk. 14, p. 314). In Jewish tradition, however, the fiction remains a fiction; ties of blood and kinship can neither be destroyed nor created. Therefore, an adopted child has the same status as his natural father. For example, if his natural father is a Kohen or a Levite, he is also; the status of his adoptive father is irrelevant.

On the other hand, Jewish law has not lost sight of the fact that emotional as well as legal ties are involved in adoption. The adoptive parents come to look upon the adopted child as their own. Their relationships with him become as strong as those of biological parents with their natural offspring. As we shall see below, a number of rules have been adopted with this consideration in view.

3. Halakhic Stipulations

Before discussing the halakhic stipulations we should define a few terms.

מַמְזֵר (bastard)—one born of an unlawful, incestuous, or adulterous marriage. This is not synonymous with the term "illegitimate," which includes children born out of wedlock (*E.H.* 4:13; B. *Yev.* 49a; M. *Kid.* 3:12).

אֲסוּפִי—a foundling picked up from the street; the identity of its father and mother is unknown (M. *Qid.* 4:2; *E.H.* 4:30).

שְׁתוּקִי—a child whose mother's identity is known but not that of its father (M. *Qid.* 4:2).

The law specifies that a *mamzer* may not marry a member of the Jewish community (Deut. 23:3). *Shetuqi* and *asufi* are in the category of *safeq mamzer* (doubtful *mamzer*)—according to the Torah, they may marry a member of the Jewish community (B. *Qid.* 73a), but the rabbis forbade it (ibid.).

To which category do children given into adoption belong? The overwhelming majority of children given into adoption today are the offspring of unwed mothers who are not in a position to take care of them, or who give them up for other reasons. This eliminates them from the category of *mamzer*.

The mother may be either Jewish or Gentile. If she is Jewish and married, we assume that the child was sired by the husband (רֹב בְּעִילוֹת אַחַר הַבַּעַל, B. *Soṭ.* 27a), even when there is only a remote chance of this (Rivash, resp. 446). If she is not married, we assume that the natural father was not of a category that would make the intercourse incestuous.

If the mother is not Jewish, and the law of the land does not forbid the adoption of her child by a Jewish family, the child is required to undergo conversion as prescribed in the rules of conversion (see *Noda' Biyehudah, E. H.* 7).

If the child is of unknown parentage, a very rare situation today, we assume that the parents belong to the majority of the population, which in the diaspora is Gentile.

Theoretically, if the natural parents are Jewish, the adopted child should bear his natural father's name when we use the patronymic "son of so and so"; if the natural parents are not Jewish, and the child is converted as prescribed, it should be called Avraham ben Avraham Avinu. Nevertheless, it is permitted to use the name of the adoptive father instead in order to avoid awkward and embarrassing situations (Feinstein, *Igrot Mosheh, Y.D.* 161).

The same is true regarding the use of the name in legal documents, such as the *ketubah* and the *geṭ* (Hakohen, "Imuts Yeladim," p. 69).

It is also the obligation of the adoptive father to have his adopted child circumcised and to recite the blessing that the father normally recites

(Tumim, in *Hapardes,* Nisan 5700, p. 15; *Migdal 'Oz, Y.D.* 261:1).

If the adoptive father dies, the adopted son is obligated to say Qaddish for him (ibid.).

A serious problem is posed by marriage and kinship. When the identity of the natural parents is unknown, there is a danger that a brother and sister may chance to marry, or that the child may be a *mamzer.* There is also the question whether the adoptee may marry members of the family of his adoptive parents.The first apprehension is not taken into account because the possibility of such occurrences is extremely remote (*Noda' Biyehudah, E.H.* 7).

As to the question of the adopted child's kinship to the adoptive family, there is a difference of opinion. Theoretically, only blood relations are forbidden to marry each other because of consanguinity, and the adopted child is not a blood relation. Some authorities, however, raise the question of unseemliness. People who saw them grow up as sisters and brothers and see them get married will consider it an incestuous marriage (Hakohen, "Imuts Yeladim," pp. 79 f.).

In the areas of the obligations of the adoptive parents in matters of maintenance, inheritance, succession, and so forth, we follow the law of the land (ibid.).

UNIT XXXI

LAWS CONCERNING PROSELYTES

XXXI.
Laws Concerning Proselytes

1. Texts

"Dearer to God is the proselyte who has come of his own accord than all the crowds of Israelites who stood before Mount Sinai. For had the Israelites not witnessed the thunder, lightning, quaking mountains, and sounding of trumpets, they would not have accepted the Torah. But the proselyte, who saw not one of these things, came and surrendered himself to the Holy One, blessed be He, and took the yoke of heaven upon himself. Can anyone be dearer to God than this man?" (*Tanḥuma,* ed. Buber, *Lekh Lekhah* 6 f., 32a).

"One who is about to become a proselyte is not received at once. Rather, he is asked: 'What has induced you to convert? Do you not know that this nation is downtrodden more than all other nations?'" (*Geirim* 1:1).

"R. Samuel b. Naḥmani said in the name of R. Yudah b. R. Ḥanina: Three times the Bible says 'Return' [in the case of Ruth the Moabitess], for the three times that one must discourage him who seeks to become a proselyte; but if he continues to press to be received, then he is received. But R. Isaac said [quoting Job 31:32]: 'The stranger [proselyte] did not lodge in the street.' Always discourage with the left hand and draw near with the right" (*Ruth Rabbah* 2:1).

"Evil after evil comes upon those who receive proselytes" (B. *Yev.* 109b).

2. Attitudes Regarding Proselytes and Conversion

The attitude of Judaism regarding proselytes and conversion from other faiths is varied and runs the gamut from extreme opposition to the highest reverence. On the one hand, the Talmud claims that "proselytes are as hard for Israel as a sore" (B. *Yev.* 47b). On the other hand, we find the statement:

"Beloved are proselytes [by God], for [Scripture] everywhere uses the same epithet of them as of Israel" (*Geirim* 4:3).

The reason proselytes are held in such high regard is expressed beautifully in the Midrash: "The Holy One, blessed be He, loves proselytes exceedingly. We likewise should show favor to the proselyte who left his family, his father's house, his people, and all the gentile peoples of the world, and came to us. He therefore deserves special protection" (*Bemidbar Rabbah* 8:2). An even higher encomium is given in the following passage: "The Holy One, blessed be He, did not exile Israel among the nations save in order that proselytes might join them" (B. *Pes.* 87b).

Evidently there was ambivalence about proselytization and proselytes. While there is ample historical evidence that proselytization was carried on in the Hellenistic period (Moore, *Judaism,* 1:229, 323), the rabbinic sources are silent about such activities and only discuss the desirability of accepting converts and whether they were "good for the Jews." The admonition that "every Israelite should endeavor actively to bring men under the wings of the Shekhinah even as Abraham did" (*Avot Derabbi Natan,* ed. Schechter, version 1, chap. 12, p. 27a) is more homiletical than practical.

Professor George Foot Moore explains the situation as follows: "Speaking generally the tone of the utterances about proselytes is friendly, though not unduly enthusiastic. This is the more to be noted because the Jews' experience with proselytes must at times have been decidedly discouraging. It can hardly be doubted that in perilous times many apostatized. In the outside lands, at least, many went over to Christianity. In the persecution under Hadrian they were under strong temptation to clear their own skirts by turning informers. It would be nothing surprising if under such circumstances the rabbis should have looked askance at all proselytes. There is, however, little evidence of such a temper" (Moore, *Judaism,* 1:342).

From talmudic times until very recently, the prevailing attitude was to discourage proselytism. Since the Christian emperors of Rome had made conversion to Judaism a capital crime, proselytism posed a threat not only to the convert but also to the Jewish community. This attitude became the rule. The rise of Islam was responsible for a similar situation in Moslem countries. As late as the beginning of the twentieth century, the *'Arukh Hashulḥan,* in the title of its chapter dealing with the laws of conversion, includes the instruction that they apply only to יָמִים קַדְמוֹנִים (days of old) because today "it is forbidden by the law of the land for us to accept proselytes" (*Y.D.* 268).

Nowadays new factors have entered into the problem. On the one hand Judaism, as of yore, is demonstrating its appeal to many searching souls who are seeking answers to the basic questions of life and faith, and have not found them in the religion of their fathers. These are the classical גֵרֵי צֶדֶק (righteous proselytes), and they pose no problem, either halakhically or practically. The dangers and risks such conversions entailed in the past have largely disappeared. Most of our present-day candidates for conversion, however, are motivated by the desire to marry a Jewish mate rather than by conviction (see Frieman, "Conversion or Convenience?"; Blumenthal, "Questionnaire on Conversion"). The sources state clearly that conversion for the sake of marriage is not valid (*Geirim* 1:3; *Y.D.* 268:12). The general practice, however, is to accept such conversions as long as there is some indication during the preparation for conversion that the candidate—though the initial impetus for conversion came from the desire to marry a Jewish partner—has now developed a sincere desire to embrace Judaism (see *Aḥi'ezer,* pt. 3, nos. 27, 28; *Encyclopedia Talmudit,* 6:427; Goodblatt, "Converting Because of Marriage Motives").

Today, with both types of candidates on the increase, the rabbi approached by a prospective convert has both a challenge and an opportunity. Experience has taught us that many converts become more loyal devotees of their new faith than those born into it. Also, in cases where the object is marriage, the Jewish partner becomes more serious about his own faith, a more devout Jew, and more observant of the tenets of Judaism.

3. Procedure

The Talmud gives the following description of the conversion procedure: "Our rabbis taught: If at the present time a man desires to become a proselyte, he is addressed as follows: 'What reason have you for desiring to become a proselyte; do you not know that Israel at the present time is oppressed, despised, harassed, and overcome by afflictions?' If he replies, 'I know and yet am unworthy,' he is accepted forthwith, and is given instruction in some of the minor and some of the major commandments. He is also told of the punishment for the transgression of the commandments. . . . And as he is informed of the punishment for the transgression of the commandments, so is he informed of the reward granted for their fulfillment. . . . He is not, however, to be persuaded or dissuaded too much. If he is accepted, he is circumcised forthwith. . . . As soon as he is healed, arrangements are made for his immediate immersion, when two learned men must stand by his side and acquaint him with some of the minor commandments and some of the major ones. When he comes up after his immersion he is deemed to be an Israelite in all respects.

"In the case of a woman proselyte, women make her sit in the water up to her neck, while two learned men stand outside and give her instruction in some of the minor commandments and some of the major ones" (B. *Yev* 47a).

This, by and large, is the procedure that we still follow today, with variations due to social and political changes. Today too, when the candidate applies for conversion, the rabbi should question him thoroughly so that he may become acquainted with the candidate's motives for conversion, his family background, and the degree of his involvement in his present religion (*Y.D.* 268:2). The candidate should not be accepted immediately. He should be informed of the difficulties he might face as a Jew, the obstacles to be overcome in casting his lot with the Jewish people, and the new responsibilities he would have to assume (B. *Yev.* 47b; *Geirim* 1:1–2). Discussions with conversion candidates should also include sociological findings about mixed marriages and the many difficult problems confronting mixed families.

If the candidate persists after these discussions, we no longer follow the talmudic suggestion to acquaint him with some of the laws and then proceed immediately to the conversion ritual. Instead, it has become customary to require a period of training. There is no prescription for the length of the period, and practices vary. The common denominator, however, is that hasty conversions are not allowed except in cases of emergency (see *Rabbinical Assembly Manual,* p. 68; Frieman, "Conversion or Convenience?"). The rabbi who prepares the proselyte should exercise judgment in determining his readiness. In larger cities there are special conversion classes with a prescribed curriculum. This is a good practice, but only as a supplement to the work of the individual rabbi.

Only when the candidate has completed these prescribed studies, and the rabbi is satisfied with his sincerity, do we proceed to the ritual of conversion.

A male must be circumcised. If he has already been circumcised, as is very common today, then a drop of blood is drawn (*Y.D.* 268:1).

In a case where fear of pain is considerable, the circumcision of an adult may be performed while the subject is under anesthesia (Yosef, "Be'inyan Hardamah," p. 1).

At the circumcision, the *mohel* recites the following two benedictions:

1. בָּרוּךְ אַתָּה יְיָ אֱלֹהֵינוּ מֶלֶךְ הָעוֹלָם אֲשֶׁר קִדְּשָׁנוּ בְּמִצְוֹתָיו וְצִוָּנוּ לָמוּל אֶת הַגֵּרִים.
2. בָּרוּךְ אַתָּה יְיָ אֱלֹהֵינוּ מֶלֶךְ הָעוֹלָם אֲשֶׁר קִדְּשָׁנוּ בְּמִצְוֹתָיו וְצִוָּנוּ לָמוּל אֶת הַגֵּרִים וּלְהַטִּיף מֵהֶם

דַּם בְּרִית שֶׁאִלְמָלֵא דַּם בְּרִית לֹא נִתְקַיְּמוּ שָׁמַיִם וָאָרֶץ שֶׁנֶּאֱמַר: אִם לֹא בְרִיתִי יוֹמָם וָלָיְלָה חֻקּוֹת שָׁמַיִם וָאָרֶץ לֹא שָׂמְתִּי. בָּרוּךְ אַתָּה יְיָ כּוֹרֵת הַבְּרִית. (*Y.D.* 268:5 and Ṭaz)

According to one opinion, the second benediction should be preceded by a blessing over wine just as at a regular circumcision (*Y.D.* 267 in Shakh 22; *Netiv Lageir,* p. 46; Ṭur 267 in *Perishah;* the *Rabbinical Assembly Manual* omits it). No blessing is recited if there is only *haṭafat dam* (*Y.D.* 268:1).

When the circumcision has healed, the male convert is brought to the miqweh for immersion. A female convert is brought to the miqweh for the same purpose as soon as she has completed her program of studies to the satisfaction of the rabbi, and has declared her intention to fulfill the requirements of conversion (*Y.D.* 268:2).

At the miqweh the candidate for conversion disrobes, immerses himself completely while nude, then says: בָּרוּךְ אַתָּה יְיָ אֱלֹהֵינוּ מֶלֶךְ הָעוֹלָם אֲשֶׁר קִדְּשָׁנוּ בְּמִצְוֹתָיו וְצִוָּנוּ עַל הַטְּבִילָה (*Y.D.* 268:5) and the שֶׁהֶחֱיָנוּ (ibid. in *Piṭhe Teshuvah* 1). The reason the blessing is recited after the immersion rather than before, as is the usual procedure with blessings recited on the performance of a mitswah, is that the proselyte cannot say "who commanded us" before he has accepted the obligations of his new faith by immersing himself (Felder, *Naḥalat Tsevi,* 1:47).

The immersion is followed by the candidate's official acceptance into the faith. This ceremony is usually conducted in the synagogue in the presence of a rabbinic tribunal. The convert is then given a Jewish name and declared to be a member of the Jewish people.

According to authoritative sources, a *Bet Din* of three is necessary to validate each of the steps, circumcision, *haṭafat dam,* immersion, and Qabbalat Mitswot—the official acceptance of the faith (*Y.D.* 268:3). Actually, it is the final act, Qabbalat 'Ol Mitswot, that is decisive and requires a *Bet Din* (B. *Yev.* 45 in Tosafot, s.v. מי לא טבלה; *Y.D.* 268:3). Since today this is done as a separate ritual after the immersion, a *Bet Din* is required only at the final ceremony. At the circumcision or *haṭafat dam,* and at the immersion, two witnesses are sufficient (*Encyclopedia Talmudit,* s.v. *Gerut;* Felder, *Naḥalat Tsevi,* 1:52).

In the case of the immersion of a female proselyte, the requirement is satisfied by the presence of two male witnesses outside the miqweh proper who listen while the convert immerses herself and recites the blessing under the guidance of a pious woman; or while she immerses herself in the presence of two pious women (according to some authorities, even one) who then testify that proper immersion has taken place (Yashar, *Netiv Lageir,* p. 45).

The very strict insist that a female convert immerse herself in the presence of two male witnesses, but to protect her from exposure to the men, she is first immersed and then covered with sheets.

Occasionally it is not feasible for a proselyte to be immersed in the nude (e.g., when, in the absence of a miqweh, an ocean, lake, or river is used). In such cases the use of a loose-fitting bathing-suit made of porous material is permitted; this is not considered to be a *ḥatsitsah* (barrier).

Where neither a miqweh nor a natural body of water is available, the Law Committee of the Rabbinical Assembly has permitted the use of a swimming pool. In the discussion of the laws concerning the miqweh (see unit 37), we shall explain how a swimming pool may be made into a kosher miqweh (Kreitman, "May a Swimming Pool Be Used as a Mikvah?"). Whenever possible, however, a regular miqweh should be used, not only because it is acceptable to all but also for psychological reasons. The atmosphere and associations should provide an experience of ritual purification (ibid., p. 222).

4. Miscellaneous Laws

Since Abraham is considered to be the father of all proselytes (*Tanḥuma,* ed. Buber, *Lekh Lekhah* 32), it is customary for proselytes to be called the son, or daughter, of our father Abraham (*E.H.* 129:20 and *Bet Yosef* on *E.H.* 129; see also Felder, *Naḥalat Tsevi,* 1:31, 124).

In most cases, a male convert is given the Hebrew name Avraham ben Avraham Avinu, and a female convert, the name Sarah bat Avraham Avinu. A convert need not necessarily be given the Hebrew first name Avraham or Sarah (see Felder, *Naḥalat Tsevi,* 1:127), but the patronymic "ben" or "bat Avraham Avinu" is insisted upon for purposes of identification (*E.H.* 129:20; *Bet Yosef* on *E.H.* 129).

Conversion must be voluntary, but since a child is not in a position to act on its own, the child of a non-Jewish mother who is adopted by Jewish parents is converted עַל דַּעַת בֵּית דִּין (by advice and consent of the court). This is permitted because it is deemed a privilege (זְכוּת) for a child to be converted to Judaism (*Y.D.* 268:7).

If the child is a male, he should be circumcised as soon as his adoptive parents decide that he is to be converted. Whether male or female, immersion should not take place until it is felt that the child will not be frightened by the experience.

There are two provisions pertaining to the conversion of an infant: (1) since the immersion completes the conversion, it must take place in the presence of a rabbinic tribunal, a *Bet Din* of three members (*Y.D.* 268: *Pitḥei Teshuvah* 3); (2) since the conversion is עַל דַּעַת בֵּית דִּין and not voluntary, the convert has the option of annulling it on attaining the age of majority—i.e., twelve for girls, thirteen for boys (*Y.D.* 268:7). This privilege is forfeited if it is not exercised immediately (*Y.D.* 268:8).

An adult proselyte, however, does not have the right of annulment, since his conversion was voluntary, and he remains a Jew even if he becomes an apostate (*Y.D.* 268:2, 12).

Related to this is the question of the status of an apostate Jew who wishes to repent. Theoretically, an apostate never ceases to be a Jew. Nevertheless, there is a feeling among the authorities that readmission to the Jewish community must be marked by a ritual akin to the conversion of a Gentile. Here, too, we must first be convinced of the candidate's sincerity. He should be required to declare his repentance before a court of three. He then should undergo immersion in a miqweh and be readmitted formally into the Jewish community (*Y.D.* 268:12 in Rama; *Melamed Leho'il,* 2, resp. 84; Cohen, and Drob, "Supplement on Jewish Law," p. 9; Rabbinical Assembly Law Archives, 2; H323).

According to traditional law, a Kohen is not permitted to marry a proselyte (*E.H.* 6:8). This leads to a problem if a Kohen is married to a non-Jewish woman and she decides to convert. However, the prohibition deals with a Kohen who wishes to marry a proselyte, and our problem presupposes a couple who are already married. Essentially, the question comes down to determining whether it is a greater transgression to live with a Gentile woman or to live with a proselyte (*Aḥi'ezer,* pt. 3, no. 28). There is good reason to permit the conversion even if a rabbi would have been prohibited from officiating at the wedding in the first place (Cohen, "Report of the Chairman of the Committee on Jewish Law," p. 44; Rabbinical Assembly Law Archives, N 76). The Law Committee of the Rabbinical Assembly has adopted the ruling that a marriage between a Kohen and a proselyte should be permitted (Klein, "The Marriage of a Kohen and a Giyoret"). Hence the above ruling is academic except for those who wish to be *maḥmirim* (followers of the stricter ruling).

If a woman converts while pregnant, the child does not require conversion, even if it was conceived before the conversion, because at the time of birth its mother was already Jewish (*Y.D.* 268:6).

The child of a Jewish mother and a Gentile father is accounted as a Jew in every respect and does not have to be converted (*E.H.* 4:19). When the child is named, it is named after the mother, e.g., Abraham ben Sarah (Rabbinical Assembly Law Archives, B4). The child of a Jewish father and a Gentile mother, even if brought up in the Jewish faith, requires circumcision and immersion in a miqweh under the supervision of a *Bet Din* of three (Rabbinical Assembly Law Archives, 9 257 f., K 263, O 358, P 215).

Conversions conducted by Reform rabbis have been the subject of much controversy. The question should be divided into two parts:

1. Do we recognize the authority of a Reform rabbi to preside at a conversion?
2. Do we recognize Reform conversion, or any conversion performed without circumcision and immersion?

The first question is also asked by our Orthodox colleagues regarding Conservative rabbis, and the ruling is in the negative (see Feinstein, *Igrot Mosheh, Y.D.* 160). Since no legal authority requires the members of the *Bet Din* who supervise a conversion to be *musmaḥim* (traditionally ordained), we should not be overscrupulous; מִפְּנֵי דַרְכֵי שָׁלוֹם (to follow the ways of peace) and מִשּׁוּם תִּקּוּן הָעוֹלָם (for the betterment of the world), we should recognize the authority of Reform rabbis and not cause division in the House of Israel (Cohen, "Report of the Chairman of the Committee on Jewish Law," p. 43).

It is the second question, the absence of circumcision and immersion, that poses the real problem.

A few of our colleagues would recognize all conversions performed by any rabbi (with the exception of one where there was no circumcision) in order to prevent further fragmentation in the House of Israel (Blumenthal and Fink, "Converts of Questionable Status," p. 109).

The majority opinion is that circumcision or *haṭafat dam* and immersion should be required of all proselytes, and that proselytes converted without these cannot be recognized. The only concession is in special cases that would come under the category of שְׁעַת הַדְּחָק—i.e., where a traumatic experience would be involved, and where the status of children would be affected, we say that inasmuch as immersion requires no declaration of intention (כַּוָּנָה) (*Y.D.* 268:3), we accept as a valid immersion any act of bathing in a natural body of water (ocean, lake, or river), and count it as valid for conversion. But this is permitted only in special cases. Ordinarily, the prescribed immersion is required of a female proselyte, and circumcision and immersion of a male proselyte (Bohnen,"Converts of Questionable Status").

Another question that comes up again and again pertains to candidates for conversion who are forbidden to undergo circumcision for medical reasons. In line with the traditional tendency to discourage proselytism, most of the traditional authorities do not permit conversion in such cases (see Weinberg, *Seridei Eish,* pt. 2, no. 102; Frank, *Har Tsevi, Y.D.* 220; Kook, *Da'at Kohen,* no. 150). There are, however, dissenting opinions that permit such conversions (see opinion of Rabbi Tsevi Kahn of Montreal, "Bidevar Tevilat Geirim"; Rabbi Pinchas Hirschprung, also of Montreal, in a *teshuvah* to Rabbi Abraham H. Oler of Brooklyn, New York; and Horowitz, *Imrei Dawid,* no. 93).

It is also frequently asked whether a proselyte may say Qaddish for his deceased Gentile parent. Since theoretically a proselyte is like a newborn child (B. *Yev.* 48b) who has no kin, he has no obligations to those who were his kin before his conversion. However, the authorities permit him to say Qaddish, and some even claim that it is his obligation to do so (see *Leqeṭ Haqemaḥ Heḥadash, O.H.,* chaps. 46–87, p. 316, subsec. 78; Walkin, *Zeqan Aharon* 2, *Y.D.,* no. 87.).

UNIT XXXII

THE DISSOLUTION OF MARRIAGE (I)

The ‘Agunah
Appendix

XXXII.
The Dissolution of Marriage (I)

1. The 'Agunah

Marriage may be dissolved either through the death of one of the partners or through divorce. Under normal circumstances, death presents no problem. When it occurs it dissolves the ties that bound the partners together. There are, however, a number of qualifications.

1. If the wife survives her husband, she must wait at least three months before remarrying in order to establish the paternity of any child born after his death (B. *Yev.* 41a f.; *E.H.* 13:1).
2. If the wife is nursing, she may not remarry until the child is weaned, usually at twenty-four months (*E.H.* 13:1). The age of weaning varies according to the custom of the land (Feinstein, *Igrot Mosheh, E.H.* 1, resp. 6, 9). Today the period of nursing is much shorter than in the past, and if, as in most cases, the child is bottle-fed, the whole matter is academic (see, however, *Ḥatam Sofer,* who claims that this is a case of *piqquaḥ nefesh,* where we take into consideration even a minute minority; see also *Otsar Haposqim* 2:149, which allows marriage after fifteen months, and *'Arukh Hashulḥan, E.H.* 13:30).

Out of respect to the deceased, certain customs have developed regarding the time lapse between the death of the partner and remarriage (*Y.D.* 392:2), usually a year, or the passage of the three Pilgrimage Festivals. If such circumstances as financial hardship must be taken into consideration, the waiting time is shortened (ibid. in *Pitḥei Teshuvah; 'Arukh Hashulḥan, Y.D.* 392:1–6).

When death occurs under abnormal circumstances, the 'Agunah problem presents itself. An 'Agunah is a woman whose husband has disappeared. According to Jewish law, she remains tied to her husband until his death is established. There is no Enoch Arden law in Jewish jurisprudence.

The problem of 'Agunah also arises when a husband refuses to grant his wife a divorce, and when a husband becomes mentally ill and, because legally incapacitated, is incompetent to grant a divorce.

The 'Agunah problem in these cases derives from the nature of Jewish marriage. In Jewish law, the marital relationship is based on a private contract between husband and wife, and any legal action must be initiated and executed by the parties concerned. The court's function is merely to see that the terms of the contract are carried out. Even if a court rules that the wife has the right to demand a divorce, it is the husband who must grant the divorce and not the court. The courts are not empowered to grant a divorce if he refuses or disappears (Schereschewsky, *Dinei Mishpaḥah,* p. 254; for further discussion of the cases mentioned in the preceding paragraph, see unit 33).

To alleviate the situation and relieve the hardships suffered by the 'Agunah, the rabbis permitted many relaxations of the rules of evidence (*E.H.* 17:1 f.). At the same time, they had to avoid the risk of giving a married woman permission to contract a second marriage that might be adulterous, since the children of the second marriage would then be *mamzerim.* In fact, it was because they assumed a woman would be most careful about contracting such a marriage, with its serious consequences, that the rabbis felt they could risk being lenient in applying the rules of evidence (B. *Yev.* 89a). For this reason they lifted most of the restrictions usually governing evidence. Thus, one witness, rather than the usual two, is sufficient to establish the death of a husband (*E.H.* 17:3), and this one witness may be a relative, a woman (ibid.), the wife herself (*E.H.* 17:43), a slave, or even a heathen if his testimony is unsolicited (*meisiaḥ lefi tumo*) (*E.H.* 17:1), even though all of these are witnesses whose testimony would not be valid in ordinary cases. The only restrictions are:

1. A wife's evidence is only valid if her relationship with her husband at the time of parting was amicable; if not, any evidence she offers is inadmissible (*E.H.* 17:48).
2. It was assumed that five female relations of the 'Agunah (the mother-in-law, the mother-in-law's daughter [the 'Agunah's sister-in-law, i.e., her husband's sister], the co-wife, the sister-in-law [the husband's brother's wife], and the husband's daughter) were prone to harm her and therefore might deliberately give false

evidence (*E.H.* 17:4; see, however, *Heikhal Yitsḥaq,* vol. 2, resp. 12, who claims that the restrictions on the five female relations are no longer valid).

Moreover, the evidence of the one witness is valid even if he himself did not personally witness the death but was informed of it by someone else (*E.H.* 17:3).

In addition, a written document recording the death of the husband is sufficient evidence to permit an 'Agunah to marry (*E.H.* 17:11). While it was originally required that such a document must have a Jewish source (ibid. in Rama), most authorities today agree that the documents of non-Jewish governmental authorities are reliable (*Ḥatam Sofer, E.H.* 1:43; *Maharsham,* vol. 2, resp. 32; *Divrei Ḥayyim,* vol. 2, *E.H.*, resp. 55).

Despite these leniencies, the rabbis were strict about the nature of the evidence, i.e., it must establish the husband's death as a fact and not as a probability, and the identity of the decedent must be established beyond doubt (*E.H.* 17:29). Thus, if the face of a decedent was battered beyond recognition, identification by clothing is not sufficient since people sometimes borrow garments (*E.H.* 17:24). There is much controversy on this matter, however, and it was pointed out that certain garments are not lent to others (see *Pitḥei Teshuvah* ad loc., sec. 95; *Otsar Haposqim,* 5:89–95; Herzog, *Heikhal Yitsḥaq, E.H.*, vol. 1, 29:5).

The vast literature on the subject of the person who has disappeared and is claimed to be dead may be divided into the following subheadings:

1. A person who went on a trip and is claimed to have been killed or to have died.
2. A person who drowned or suffered shipwreck.
3. A soldier who was killed in battle or is missing in action.
4. A person who was a victim of persecution, a pogrom, or the Nazi Holocaust.

In all these cases, even if the body is found, the problem of establishing its identity beyond any doubt remains (*E.H.* 17:29). The following rules of identification apply:

1. If the body is intact, it can be identified by people who were acquainted with the dead person (*E.H.* 17:27).
2. If the body is no longer recognizable, it can be identified by the

presence of scars and other distinguishing marks (*E.H.* 17:24).

3. Identification by clothing is questionable; some authorities point out that the decedent might have borrowed someone else's clothing (*E.H.* 17:24); others disagree (see *Pitḥei Teshuvah* ad loc., sec. 95; *Otsar Haposqim,* 5:196–202). In the case of a soldier, it may be assumed that he was wearing his own uniform (*Heikhal Yitsḥaq,* vol. 1, resp. 29:5). Personal documents found on the body (e.g., a passport) are also valid for identification (*Otsar Haposqim,* 5:89 ff.).
4. Since governmental declarations are accepted as valid, methods of identification currently used by the government (e.g., fingerprints, dental X-rays) are also regarded as valid identification.

If the body is not found, several guidelines are applied to determine whether or not survival was possible in the particular situation.

Thus, for example, the Talmud makes a distinction between falling into a lion's den and falling into a snake pit. In the former case survival is possible, since the lions may not be hungry or for other reasons; in the latter case death is certain (B. *Yev.* 121a; *E.H.* 17:29). Similarly, if a person fell into a furnace or a boiling cauldron, he is assumed to be dead (*E.H.* 17:30), but death is not certain if he was crucified (ibid.).

The second guiding principle is that of תְּרֵי רוּבֵּי or "double majority" (*Otsar Haposqim,* 7:4; see responsum of R. Edward Gershfield in Law Committee Archives). The first case mentioned is that of a man who fell off a bridge into a river that was frozen. The first majority is that most people who fall from such a height to a hard surface do not survive. The second majority is that those who drown under such circumstances (i.e., in a river covered with ice) do not survive.

The third guiding principle is that of אָבַד זִכְרוֹ, i.e., a long time passes and nothing is heard from him or about him (ibid.; *Otsar Haposqim,* 7:24 ff.).

The authorities applied these principles to each of the four categories mentioned above.

1. The case most frequently mentioned in the Mishnah and discussed in the Gemara (*Yev.,* chaps. 15 and 16) is that of a missing traveler who is thought to be dead but whose body has not been recovered or cannot be identified. A typical modern instance would be the crew and passengers of a plane that crashed in a desolate area. In his responsum, Rabbi Gershfield applies all three principles to declare the woman a widow (*Otsar Haposqim,* 6:321 ff., 7:21). The same approach can be utilized in many other instances

where bodies were not recovered or have been maimed beyond recognition, e.g., in cases of trainwreck or where people were lost in the desert.

2. In cases of supposed death by drowning, where the victim was seen falling into a body of water, the Mishnah and codes rule that a distinction must be made between water with a visible end (מַיִם שֶׁיֵּשׁ לָהֶם סוֹף)—i.e., where the entire expanse of water can be seen, e.g., a pond, a small lake, a well—and water without a visible end (מַיִם שֶׁאֵין לָהֶם סוֹף)—i.e., where the entire expanse of water cannot be seen, e.g., an ocean (M. *Yev.* 16:4; *E.H.* 17:32, 34). In the former instance, if a time long enough for death by drowning to occur passes without the person reappearing, he is assumed to be dead, since if he were alive he would have been seen emerging from the water. In the latter instance, however, it cannot be assumed that he is dead since he may have emerged from the water on a faraway shore.

In modern times, when ocean voyages became more frequent, this distinction created many problems, and with the tremendous increase in immigration to America by sea, the rabbinic authorities came to the conclusion that it was no longer valid. If a person who fell into water without a visible end survived, modern means of communication would easily enable him to get in touch with his next of kin (*Ḥatam Sofer, E.H.*, resp. 58, 65; Spektor, *'Ein Ya'aqov,* 22:3:20, p. 230, and vol. 2, resp. 1; *Be'eir Yitsḥaq, E.H.* 18; *Otsar Haposqim,* 7:14).

3. Cases of soldiers killed in battle or missing in action became a significant problem with the beginning of the period of emancipation, when Jews became eligible for military service along with all other citizens. The codes rule that a soldier cannot be assumed to be dead unless there is a witness to his death in battle or subsequent burial (*E.H.* 17:50). More recent authorities have ruled that information furnished by the government is valid in establishing the death of a soldier (*Otsar Haposqim,* 8:79 f.; *Ḥatam Sofer,* 1, *E.H.*, resp. 43; *Maharsham,* vol. 2, resp. 32).

Nowadays there is usually no problem, since all soldiers wear "dog tags" for identification, special units of the army are charged with identifying and burying the dead, and the government informs the next of kin of any mishap (*Otsar Haposqim,* 5:202). When soldiers are missing in action, there is no problem if the belligerent powers provide lists with the names of prisoners of war. There is a problem, however, when such lists are not provided, or when, as sometimes happens, prisoners are held even after the cessation of hostilities.

The rabbinic authorities have concluded that the use of preventive measures is the most effective way of dealing with such problems. The

Talmud provides the precedent: "Rabbi Shmuel bar Naḥmani said in the name of Rabbi Yonatan: 'Whosoever went out to war, in the wars of the house of David, writes a writ of divorcement for his wife' " (B. *Shab.* 56a). Rashi comments: "It was a conditional writ of divorcement that would become effective retroactively if the soldier should die."

Based on this, and taking into consideration the complex laws of divorce and of agency appointment, various rabbinic bodies during World War II drew up legal documents to be signed by departing soldiers that would empower a court to issue a writ of divorcement to the soldier's wife if he should not return within a specified time after the declaration of peace or the cessation of hostilities. Three such documents are reproduced in the appendix to this chapter, one issued by the Rabbinical Assembly, another by the Chief Rabbinate of Israel, and the third by the London *Beth Din* (see *Heikhal Yitsḥaq,* vol. 2, resp. 35–41).

4. Though Jewish history is replete with persecution and martyrdom, the magnitude of the Holocaust, with its unutterable savagery, begs comparison. The initial impetus for the relaxation of the laws of evidence in cases of 'Agunah resulting from such cruelties and tragedies came from a similar event, the Roman massacre at Tel Arza during the Bar Kokhba revolt (132–35 C.E.). The Mishnah tells how Rabban Gamliel allowed the wives of the victims to remarry on the testimony of a single witness. On this basis it was established that the testimony of one witness suffices to allow remarriage in similar circumstances (M. *Yev.* 16:7). During and after the Chmielnicki massacres (גְּזֵרַת ת״ח) in the seventeenth century, *taqqanot* were enacted to help the surviving 'Agunot (Kahana, *Sefer Ha'agunot,* p. 57).

Thus, those who sought a solution for the 'Agunot resulting from the Nazi Holocaust had many precedents to go by. In several countries, the rabbis drew up guidelines to help in solving the problem (*Otsar Haposqim,* 7:247–60; Feuerwerger, *'Ezrat Nashim, Taqqanot 'Agunot,* vols. 1–3; Waldenberg, *Tsits Eli'ezer,* vol. 3, resp. 25; Herzog, *Heikhal Yitsḥaq,* vol. 1, resp. 24–28; *Minḥat Yitsḥaq,* vol. 1, resp. 1; Breisch, *Ḥelqat Ya'aqov,* vol. 1, resp. 17–21; Kahana, *Sefer Ha'agunot,* p. 57).

First, lists of survivors were published, with all possible sources of information mobilized in their compilation. When a man's name did not appear on any of the lists, the following principles were applied:

1. If he had been seen among those who went into the gas chambers, he was assumed to be dead, since in such cases death was certain.
2. If, during the "selection" on his arrival at the concentration camp,

he had been told to go to the left, he was also assumed to be dead, since those on the left were sent to the gas chambers, while those on the right were assigned to labor battalions and thus had at least a temporary respite.

3. If, while in a concentration camp, he had been sent to the camp hospital, he was also assumed to be dead, since the practice of the Nazis was not to heal sick people in the camp hospitals but to hasten their deaths.
4. Anyone who was known to have been in a ghetto or a labor camp and did not return was assumed to be dead, since inmates of ghettos and labor camps were subjected to conditions under which survival was virtually impossible.

2. Appendix

שטר מנוי שליחות

אני החותם מטה ממנה בצווי בעל פה וע״י חתימת ידי בשטר זה את הסופרים האלה: **מיכאל ב״ר דוד**, או **מרדכי צבי ב״ר יהושע זאב**, או **אפרים ב״ר שמואל יצחק הלוי**, או **יצחק שלמה ב״ר מרדכי**, להיות כל אחד מהם שליח לכתוב גט כריתות לאשתי בת
בפני הבית דין של אסיפת הרבנים באמריקא מיסודו של בית המדרש לרבנים באמריקא אשר בניו יורק, או בפני בית דין הממונה על ידם, שלש שנים לאחר פטור אנשי הצבא של ארצות הברית מעבודתם. וגם אני נותן רשות לכתוב אפילו עד מאה גיטין לשמי ולשמה ולשם גירושין עד שיגיע אחד מהם ליד אשתי בת
ותתגרש בו ממני כדת משה וישראל.

וכן אני ממנה בצווי בעל פה וע״י חתימת ידי למטה את **מנחם ב״ר חיים**, **ראובן ב״ר חיים אריה**, **משה ב״ר אביגדור הלוי**, **שלמה ב״ר משה**, שאם ירצו בית דין יהיו כל שנים מהם עדי חתימה על הגט הנ״ל אשר יכתוב אחד מהסופרים הנ״ל בפני בית דין הנ״ל או בפני הבית דין הממונה על ידם, וכל אחד מהסופרים הנ״ל אשר יכתוב את הגט הנ״ל ימסור את הגט הנ״ל אחר כתיבתו ליד **מיכאל ב״ר דוד**, או **מרדכי צבי ב״ר יהושע זאב**, או **אפרים ב״ר שמואל יצחק הלוי**, או **יצחק שלמה ב״ר מרדכי**, להיות כל אחד מהם שלוחי להוליך את הגט אחר כתיבתו לאשתי בת ולתת אותו לידה ותהא ידו של כל אחד מהם כידי ועשייתו כעשייתי ונתינתו כנתינתי ופיו כפי ודבורו כדבורי, ונותן אני לכל אחד מהם כח ורשות לעשות שליח בחריקאי ושליח שליח אפילו עד מאה שלוחים, אפילו בלא אונס ואפילו בכתב ועל פי דואר למסור את הגט לאשתי בכל מקום שימצאנה אחד מהם או שלוחו של כל אחד מהם או שליח שלוחו עד מאה שלוחים, ותיכף כשיגיע הגט לידה מיד אחד מהם או מיד שלוחו של כל אחד מהם או מיד שליח שלוחו אפילו עד מאה שלוחים תהא היא מגורשת בו ממני ומותרת לכל אדם.

ומה שאלך ואשוב ואתייחד עם אשתי בת
מהיום ועד שתתגרש ממני כדת משה וישראל לא יבטל על ידי זה המנוי שאני ממנה בהרשאה זו על דבר כתיבת הגט וחתימתו ומסירתו ליד אשתי בת
כי על מנת כן עשיתי את כל המנויים האלו.

והנני מקבל עלי בחרם ובשבועות התורה על דעת בין דין הנ״ל שלא לבטל את הגט ולא את השליחות, ומבטל אני כל מודעות ומודעי דמודעי שעשיתי ושאעשה מיומא דנן ולעלם, ופוסל אני כל עד שיעיד עלי שום עדות שיגרום לבטל את הגט או את השליחות ונאמנת עלי אשתי שלא פייסתיה, וכל המנויים ויתר הדברים הנ״ל אמרתי בפי לפני העדים החתומים בשטר זה ולשם זה חתמתי בעצם חתימת ידי.

ביום לירח שנת פה בעיר

בן בפנינו העדים החתומים מטה הגיד

הבעל בן כל

הדברים הכתובים בשטר הרשאה זה בעל פה לשם צווי ומנוי על כתיבת הגט וחתימתו ומסירתו ליד

אשתו בת

ככתוב בהרשאה זו וחתם בעצם כתב ידו, וקנינא מ

בן על מנוי השליחות ועל הבטולים במנא דכשר

למקניא ביה דלא כאסמכתא ודלא כטופסי דשטרי, ובאנו על החותם על כל מה דכתיב ומפורש לעיל, שריר בריר וקיים.

נאום עד

נאום עד

נעשה במעמד הרב

כתבת

The Rabbinical Assembly of America

Agency Appointment

I,

residing at

husband of

of

BEING MINDFUL of the uncertainty of future events and desiring to protect my beloved wife, do hereby

APPOINT:

Michael ben David, known as Michael Higger; Ephraim ben Samuel Isaac Halevi, known as Mordecai H. Lewittes; and Isaac Solomon ben Mordecai, known as Isidore S. Meyer, each or any of them as a scribe, and authorize and direct them, or any of them to write

A GET, to wit, a bill of divorcement according to the Law of Moses and Israel, in my behalf, directed to, and for my wife *three years after the general demobilization of the armed forces of the United States*

AT THE INSTANCE of my wife, with the approval and under the authority of the central *Beth Din* of the Rabbinical Assimbly of America, at New York, N.Y., or such other *Beth Din,* as it may designate.

I FURTHER APPOINT any two of the following persons to act as witnesses to the execution of this *Get,* and authorize and direct them to affix their signatures thereto, as witnesses, as required by the *Beth Din,* to wit, Menahem ben Hayyim, known as Max Arzt; Moshe ben Abigdor Halevi, known as Moshe Davis; Reuben ben Hayyim Aryeh, known as Robert Gordis; and Shelomoh ben Moshe, known as Simon Greenberg.

I FURTHER APPOINT the following persons to act as my agents, to wit: Michael ben David, known as Michael Higger; Ephraim ben Samuel Isaac Halevi, known as Edward Horowitz; Mordecai Tsebi ben Joshua Zeeb, known as Mordecai H. Lewittes; and Isaac Solomon ben Mordecai, known as Isidore S. Meyer, and do hereby authorize any one of them, to deliver this *Get* in my behalf, unto my wife; each of these agents having the authority to appoint a substitute agent orally or in writing, who in turn shall have full and complete powers of an agent appointed herein, including the power to designate a substitute.

[I DO HEREBY direct my agent, as afore described, to deliver this *Get* in my behalf, to my wife, wherever he may find her, in accordance with the Law of Moses and Israel, to the effect that our marriage shall thereby be terminated in accordance with the Law of Moses and Israel.

I DO SOLEMNLY SWEAR that I shall never claim that the marital relations now existing between myself and my wife have invalidated, or may ever invalidate in any manner or form, the stipulations, appointments, authorizations, or directions made herein. My wife's testimony shall be conclusive as to whether I may have revoked this instrument, or any part thereof, by an act of which, only she and I may have been the witnesses.

I FURTHER SOLEMNLY SWEAR that I will not revoke the stipulations, appointments, authorizations and directions contained herein.]

I HAVE SOLEMNLY MADE the foregoing stipulation, appointments, authorizations and directions by word of mouth and in writing.

IN WITNESS WHEREOF, I hereby subscribe my name hereto this day of , 19 , corresponding to

....

....

....

We hereby certify that the husband above mentioned made the stipulations, appointments, authorizations and directions by word of mouth and in our presence, and in the presence each of each of us, and duly executed and signed this instrument, in the presence of each of us, and we affixed our signatures hereto as witnesses in his presence.

....

....

Done under the
authority of Rabbi..

....

A Get executed and delivered pursuant to this instrument is in no sense a divorce, annulment, separation, or dissolution of marriage, under the laws of the United States of any one of the States.

....

הרשאה לגט ליוצאי מלחמה

אני הח״מ בן

למשפחת מעיר חייל בצבאות ישראל מס׳ היוצא למלחמה. הריני ממנה מעכשיו את כל היהודים יושבי הערים ירושלים, ת״א, חיפה, בגבולותיהן העירוניים ביום הקמת מדינת ישראל שכל אחד מהם יכתוב גט לאשתי

בת נולדה למשפחת ושכל שנים מהם הכשרים לעדות יחתמו על הגט ושכל אחד מהם הכשר להולכה יתן את הגט לאשתי הנזכרת ויכתוב ויחתמו ויתן אפילו עד מאה גיטין עד שיוכשר אחד מהם בכתיבה וחתימה ובנתינה לדעת הרב המסדר את הגט. גט זה ייכתב וייחתם ויינתן ע״י הנ״ל רק אחרי שיתברר לרבנים הראשיים לארץ ישראל שיהיו בימים ההם, או לאחד מהם, שנתקבלה הודעה מהשלטונות הצבאיים שאני בכלל האבודים, או שהידיעות ע״ד העדרי מן העולם ח״ו לא תהיינה מספיקות לדעות הנ״ל או לדעת אחד מהם להתיר את אשתי מכבלי העיגון, ורק אחרי עבור לפחות שנה מאותו היום שישוחררו החיילים היהודים השבויים מידי האויב. ובפירוש אני מגיד בלב גמור ומוחלט, שאפילו אם בימים שבינתיים, היינו מהיום הזה דלמטה עד זמן שתבוא הידיעה הרשמית שאני בכלל באובדים או שתבואנה ידיעות על דבר העדרי ח״ו מן העולם כנ״ל, אשוב לאשתי פעם או יותר ואתייחד עמה בחיי אישות כדרך בעל ואשתו לא תתבטל בשום אופן השליחות הנ״ל, ואשתי תהא נאמנה כמאה עדים לאמר שלא בטלתי את השליחות הנ״ל והנני מקבל עלי בחרם ובשבועת התורה שלא לבטל את השליחות הנ״ל ולא את הגט.

ולראי׳ אני חותם היום לחדש שנת

נאם:

בפנינו עדים הח״מ אמר הבעל כל הנ״ל וחתם על הנ״ל

היום יום לחדש שנת

נאום:

נאום

Beth Din, London
Court of the Chief Rabbi
בית דין צדק
דק"ק לונדון והמדינה

בעזהי"ת אני החתום מטה

הריני ממנה את בני ישראל הנמצאים בלונדון שכל אחד מהם יכתוב גט לאשתי לשמי ולשמה ולשם גרושין ושכל שנים מהם יחתמו על הגט לשמי ולשמה ולשם גרושין ושכל אחד מהם יתן את הגט לאשתי הנזכרת אחרי שנים מיום דלמטה אם לא באתי עד סוף שנים מיום דלמטה למקום שאשתי תדור שם בעת ההיא כשאני חפשי לגמרי מעבודת הצבא ואפילו אם לא באתי בתוך הזמן האמור באופן האמור מחמת אונס דלא שכיח כלל הנני מצוה את כל בני ישראל הנמצאים בלונדון שכל אחד מהם יכתוב גט ושכל שנים מהם יחתמו וכל אחד מהם יתן אפילו עד מאה גטין עד שיגיע גט אחד ליד אשתי ותתגרש היא ממני כדת משה וישראל והגט אחר כתיבתו וחתימתו יתן הסופר לאחד מבני ישראל הנמצאים בלונדון שכל אחד מהם הנני ממנה להיות שליחי להוליך הגט אחר כתיבתו וחתימתו לאשתי וליתן אותו לידה ותהא ידו כידי ועשייתו כעשייתי ונתינתו כנתינתי ופיו כפי ודבורו כדבורי ונותן אני לו רשות לעשות שליח בחריקאו ושליח שליח אפילו עד מאה שלוחים ואפילו בכתב על ידי הפוסט ואפילו בלא אונס למסור הגט לאשתי בכל מקום שימצאנה הוא או שלוחו או שליח שלוחו עד מאה שלוחים ותיכף כשיגיע הגט בידה מידו או מיד שלוחו או מיד שליח שליחו אפילו עד מאה שלוחים תהא היא מגורשת בו ממני ומותרת לכל אדם ובפירוש אני מצהיר בלב גמור ומוחלט כי מה שאלך ואשוב בתוך שנים מיום דלמטה כנהוג באנשי צבא שחופשה ניתנת להם מזמן לזמן והם הולכים ובאים ואפילו אם אתייחד עמה אז בחיי אישות כדרך בעל ואשתו לא יבוטל על ידי זה המנוי שאני ממנה בהרשאה זו על כתיבת הגט וחתימתו ומסירתו ליד אשתי וגם נאמנת לומר שלא פייסתיה והנני מקבל עלי כחרם ובשבועת התורה שלא לבטל את השליחות ולא את הגט ולראיה חתמתי בעצם חתימת ידי

בפנינו עדים החתומים מטה הגיד בעל פה כל הדברים האמורים למעלה בהרשאה זו לשם מינוי על כתיבת הגט וחתימתו ונתינתו ליד אשתו באופן האמור בהרשאה זו ובפנינו חתם למעלה על הרשאה זו ליתר תוקף בעצם חתימת ידו ולראיה חתמנו אנו

Agency Appointment

I,

residing at

husband of

being mindful of the uncertainty of future events and desiring to protect my beloved wife do hereby appoint all the Jews of London (metropolis of England) to act for me in the following manner:

1. That any one of the Jews of London shall write a Get (Jewish Bill of Divorcement) for my wife on my behalf in order to divorce with this Get my said wife.

2. That any two of them shall sign this Get on my behalf and on her behalf for the purpose of divorcing my wife with this Get.

3. That any one of them shall be my deputy to hand the Get to my wife, and all this in case I shall not have returned after five years from to-day for any reason whatsoever, being entirely free from military service to the place where my wife shall then reside.

4. That the scribe should hand the Get after it having been written and duly signed to any one of the Jews in London (England) any one of whom I appoint herewith as my delegate to hand over the Get to the hands of my wife.

5. That any Jew to whom the Get was handed over by the scribe as mentioned above shall have the power to appoint at his discretion another delegate and this other delegate a further one and so up to one hundred and that these delegates can also be made by letter through the postal service.

6. That any action or declaration with regard to the Get of any of these delegates shall be considered as my action or declaration.

7. That as soon as the Get shall have reached the hands of my wife from any one acting on my behalf on the authorisation set out before, my wife shall thereupon be religiously divorced from me and free to all, as according to the Law of Moses and Israel.

And I hereby declare:

(1) That after the expiration of 5 years from to-day both the declaration of my wife that I have not returned to her free from war service and that we have not prior to the writing of the Get come to a mutual understanding to cancel the stipulated arrangements shall be accepted.

(2) That my return on leave to my wife and my resumption of marital relationship shall not in any way interfere with the above appointments and declarations.

And I hereby most solemnly swear not to cancel any of the above instructions and appointments and accordingly hereunto attach my signature this (date).

Witnessed by:

UNIT XXXIII

THE DISSOLUTION OF MARRIAGE (II): DIVORCE

XXXIII.
The Dissolution of Marriage (II)
Divorce

1. Introduction

"When a man taketh a wife, and marrieth her, then it cometh to pass, if she finds no favor in his eyes, because he hath found some unseemly thing in her, that he writeth her a bill of divorcement and giveth in her hand, and sendeth her out of the house . . . " (Deut. 24:1).

"Over him who divorces the wife of his youth, even the altar of God sheds tears" (B. *Giṭ*. 90b).

"Rabbi Yoḥanan said, 'He that putteth her [his wife] away is hated of God' " (ibid.).

There is a tradition that the greatest glory of Aaron the high priest was his work in reconciling discontented husbands and wives and inducing them to live together in harmony (*Avot Derabbi Natan, Tanna Devei 'Eliyahu Rabbah* 30).

"While Judaism does not consider divorce a sin, it recognizes it as a tragedy. Each divorce is a tombstone on high hopes once held by two young people—hopes that have dissolved in bitterness and hostility. The unhappiness of the adult partner is only one part of this massive burden of misery. There are hundreds of thousands of innocent victims of discord, the children of divorce, who lack the security and guidance of two parents and a stable home" (Gordis, *Sex and the Family in the Jewish Tradition,* p. 25).

"Judaism in its continuous concern for human life and fulfillment stresses the sanctity of matrimonial ties, but concomitantly believes in man's freedom of choice and inherent respect for one's total independence. It therefore permits the marital dissolution, after ascertaining that the welfare of the parties is mutually endangered by continuing to use marriage as a source of misery and human degradation, instead of a vital source of happiness and communion" (Fried, *Jews and Divorce,* pp. 17 f.).

As these texts demonstrate, Jewish law permits the dissolution of marriage through divorce. There are two fundamental differences between the Jewish law of divorce and that of many other legal systems.

First, a Jewish divorce is an act of the parties to the marriage, in contradistinction to other systems of law, where divorce derives from a decree of the court, and the parties concerned have no part in its validation. In Jewish law, the function of the court, in the absence of agreement between the parties, is to decide whether and on what terms one party may be obliged to give, or the other to receive, a *get*. But even after the court has thus decided, the parties remain married until such time as the husband actually delivers a *get* to his wife. The court also has the function of ensuring that all the formalities required by the law are carried out properly (see Schereschewsky, *Dinei Mishpaḥah,* p. 254; Dykan, *Dinei Nissu'in Wegeirushin,* pp. 106 f.).

Second, unlike other legal systems, Jewish law does not require the implication of one of the parties to the divorce in some kind of guilt. The consent of both parties suffices to warrant the divorce, without any need for the court to establish responsibility for the breakup of the marriage. The partners must consent of their free will, however, and not out of fear that they may be obliged to fulfill some obligation which they undertook in the marriage agreement in the event of their not being divorced (ibid.).

2. Grounds for Divorce

In the diaspora, the question of grounds for divorce is academic. The couple seeking a *get* has usually obtained a civil divorce. The *get* simply consummates the separation, making it possible for them to remarry in accordance with Jewish law. To deny a *get* after a civil divorce has been granted would make us guilty of putting a stumbling block before the blind (Lev. 19:14) since it would not deter many people from remarrying.

Only in the State of Israel is the question of grounds actual, since in the area of marriage and divorce, the norms of Jewish law are the law of the land.

The grounds for divorce can be listed under four subdivisions:

1. Cases of mutual consent, where both parties agree to the divorce.
2. Cases where the husband sues for divorce, claiming the wife is the guilty party.

3. Cases where the wife petitions for divorce, and the husband, being the guilty party, is compelled to give her a divorce.
4. Cases of divorce enforced by the court without the petition of either party.

We shall explain these in detail.

1. While according to biblical and talmudic law the husband may grant his wife a divorce without her consent, today we follow the decree of Rabbenu Gershom, who, with his synod, ordained that the wife's consent is required (*E.H.* 119:6 in Rama; Finkelstein, *Jewish Self-Government in the Middle Ages,* pp. 29 f.).

When one of the parties has legitimate grounds for divorce, or where the court considers a divorce necessary, the parties can be compelled to submit. The question remains, however: If the consent of both parties is necessary, how can we compel a person to give a *get* against his will? The advice that "they subject him to pressure until he says 'I am willing' " (B. *Yev.* 106a) would conflict with the principle that "A *get* given under compulsion is invalid" (B. *Git.* 88b.). Maimonides answers this question as follows:

"And why is this *get* not null and void, since it is the product of duress, whether exerted by heathens or by Israelites? Because duress applies only to him who is compelled and pressed to do something which the Torah does not obligate him to do, for example, one who is lashed until he consents to sell something or give it away as a gift. On the other hand, he whose evil inclination induces him to violate a commandment or commit a transgression, and who is lashed until he does what he is obligated to do, or refrains from what he is forbidden to do, cannot be regarded as a victim of duress; rather, he has brought duress upon himself by submitting to his evil intention. Therefore, this man who refuses to divorce his wife, inasmuch as he desires to be of the Israelites, to abide by all the commandments, and to keep away from transgression—it is only his inclination that has overwhelmed him—once he is lashed until his inclination is weakened and he says 'I consent,' it is the same as if he had given the *get* voluntarily" (*Hil. Geirushin* 2:20; see also *B.B.* 48a; Amram, *Jewish Law of Divorce,* pp. 57 f.).

It is understood in these cases that any minor children must be provided for; that the property rights of the parties, especially of the wife, must be fairly and honestly adjudged; and that the proper formalities must be observed so that no doubt is cast on the validity of the divorce (*E.H.* 134 gives the laws of a *get* given under duress; see also Schereschewsky, *Dinei*

Mishpaḥah, pp. 255 ff.; Horowitz, *Spirit of Jewish Law,* p. 277; Amram, *Jewish Law of Divorce,* p. 39).

2. The husband may sue for divorce on the following grounds:

1. If the wife has committed adultery or there is a strong suspicion of adultery (*E.H.* 11:1).
2. If the wife apostatizes from Judaism, or displays such disregard of Jewish ritual law as to cause him to transgress against his will (*E.H.* 115:1); in this case, divorce is permitted but not mandatory (*E.H.* 115:4).
3. If the wife's public behavior flouts the code of moral decency (*E.H.* 115:4).
4. If the wife refuses to allow him to exercise his conjugal rights for one year (*E.H.* 77:2). The codes distinguish between refusal prompted by spite (*moredet*) and refusal because the husband has become loathsome; in the former case, an attempt at reconciliation is made, and a *geṭ* is issued only if it fails.
5. If the wife is barren and incapable of bearing children (*E.H.* 154 in *Pitḥei Teshuvah,* n. 29).
6. If the wife suffers from an incurable disease that makes cohabitation impossible or dangerous (*E.H.* 117:2). Illnesses like leprosy are grounds for divorce (*E.H.* 117:1). The authorities differ on whether the husband can sue for divorce if the wife is afflicted with epilepsy (see *'Arukh Hashulḥan, E.H.* 154:5; Schereschewsky, *Dinei Mishpaḥah,* pp. 263 f.; *Otsar Haposqim,* 1:61–62). With modern methods of treatment, most epileptics are now able to lead practically normal lives.
7. If the wife becomes mentally ill (for a further discussion of mental illness in regard to divorce, see below, p. 499 f.).
8. If the wife refuses to live with him in the dwelling place he had clearly designated at the time of marriage; or if he decides to settle in the Land of Israel and she refuses to accompany him; or if they live in the Land of Israel and he wishes to move to Jerusalem, and she refuses to accompany him (*E.H.* 75:1, 4). The place of residence is determined by the husband since it is presumed that the couple so agreed in advance; the wife cannot object to her husband's changing their residence unless there was an agreement, either express or implied, that they would not move without her

consent (*E.H.* 75:1). However, the husband must have good reasons for deciding on a change against the will of his wife, e.g., for purposes of health or livelihood, or because the matrimonial peace at their existing home is disturbed by his or her relatives (Rivash 81, 82). If the wife has a good reason for refusing, e.g., the move would be to a less desirable place (*E.H.* 75:2) or is fraught with danger, her refusal is not grounds for divorce (*E.H.* 75:5).

9. If the wife has certain physical defects, diseases, or anomalies (*E.H.* 117:4). These are grounds for divorce only if present before the marriage; if they developed subsequently, the husband cannot claim them as grounds for divorce (*E.H.* 117:1) unless they are such that living together would be fraught with danger, e.g., if the wife has a communicable disease, or if the ailment interferes with his conjugal rights—in such cases, they are grounds for divorce even if they appeared after the marriage (ibid.; see *Otsar Haposqim,* 1:56–62, where the ailments are enumerated, and the effects of modern medicine are taken into account). However, even if the woman had these defects before the marriage, they are grounds for divorce only if there was no way for the husband to discover them before the marriage; if they could be discovered, and he did not protest, it may be assumed that he accepted them, and thus they cannot be presented as grounds for divorce (*E.H.* 117:5). Similarly, if he did not protest immediately after the marriage, it may be assumed that he had become reconciled to the defects (*E.H.* 117:10).
10. If the wife is sterile. The rules governing the dissolution of a marriage after ten years if there are no children are discussed above (see p. 414 f.). If it is established that the woman is barren and incapable of bearing children, the husband may sue for divorce if he has no children and thus has not yet fulfilled his obligation to be fruitful and multiply (*E.H.* 154:6, discussing the case of a husband's sterility, certainly applies as well when the wife is sterile; see also Schereschewsky, *Dinei Mishpaḥah,* p. 281).

3. The wife may sue for divorce on the following grounds:

1. If the husband's conduct is immoral. When an accusation that the husband is guilty of infidelity and of consorting with dissolute women is supported by his own admission or by witnesses, the

court compels him to grant a divorce (*E.H.* 154:1 in Rama).

2. If the husband is habitually cruel to her. According to the Rama, "A man who beats his wife commits a sin, as though he has beaten his neighbor, and if he persists in this conduct, the court may castigate him and place him under oath to discontinue this conduct; if he refuses to obey the order of the court, they will compel him to divorce his wife at once (though some are of the opinion that he should be warned once or twice) because it is not customary or proper for Jews to beat their wives; it is a custom of the heathen" (*E.H.* 154:3).
3. If the husband contracts a loathsome chronic disease, e.g., leprosy, or if his entire body is stricken with boils (*mukat sheḥin*), making family life difficult. The following provisos apply:
   a. If he contracted the disease or boils before the marriage and did not reveal them to her, it is a clear case of deception and he is compelled to grant a divorce.
   b. If he did reveal them, and she married him nevertheless, she may still sue, claiming she originally thought she would be able to live with him but has now discovered that she cannot.
   c. If the disease or boils developed after the marriage, she can still sue if it interferes with their marital life and makes conjugal relations difficult. This includes not only loathsome diseases but also blemishes and defects, e.g., if both his hands or both his legs have been amputated, or if he has become blind (*E.H.* 154:4); the last claim should be reconsidered, since nowadays blind people receive training which enables them to function normally (*E.H.* 154:1; Schereschewsky, *Dinei Mishpaḥah,* p. 264).
4. If, after the marriage, the husband engages in an occupation that makes him physically disgusting to such a degree that cohabitation is impossible. As examples, the sources mention gathering dog's dung, smelting copper, and tanning hides (B. *Ket.* 77a; *E.H.* 154:1). One wonders what the corresponding occupations would be today, and whether the use of modern deodorants and soaps would make a difference. The same rule applies to a husband who develops a malodorous disease that results in putrid oozings from his mouth and nose (ibid.).
5. If the husband is sterile. Since the obligation to be fruitful and multiply applies only to men, it would seem that this should not

be grounds for divorce by the wife. However, a husband's sterility is grounds for divorce if the wife claims that she wishes to have a child in order to have its support and comfort in her old age (*E.H.* 154:6; *'Arukh Hashulḥan, E.H.* 154:45).

6. If the husband persistently refuses to engage in sexual intercourse (*E.H.* 154:3, 76:11, 77:1). The term מוֹרֶדֶת is applied to a woman who refuses to participate in conjugal relations; some authorities apply the term מוֹרֵד (the masculine of מוֹרֶדֶת) to a man who refuses. He is subject to the same rules as his female counterpart (Rabbenu Asher to *Ket.* 63, secs. 30–34; Schereschewsky, *Dinei Mishpaḥah,* p. 173).
7. If the husband apostatizes from Judaism. Where the Jewish court has authority, the husband can be compelled to grant a *geṭ*. This question is discussed in *E.H.* 154:1.
8. If the husband refuses to support the wife:
   a. If he refuses from malice, the court may compel him to support her (*E.H.* 154:3).
   b. If he refuses because he is not able, and this disability stems from his refusal to work or from his squandering of his property (ibid.).
9. If the husband must flee the country because he committed a crime (*E.H.* 154:9).

4. There are also cases where the courts can compel the parties to submit to divorce even if neither petitions for it. According to Jewish law, a *geṭ* may be granted only with the consent of both parties, and neither may be coerced. We have already explained that this rule applies only if the courts force the couple to submit to a divorce illegally (see above, p. 468). Where divorce is prescribed by law, however, the court may compel the parties to give or accept a *geṭ*. Thus, in the following cases the court may enforce a divorce even without the consent of either husband or wife:

1. The cases known in canon law as *impedimentum impedens,* i.e., where the marriage is forbidden, and thus must be dissolved, but is nonetheless valid if contracted, and thus a *geṭ* is required for its dissolution. This is in the category of קִדּוּשִׁין תּוֹפְסִין and includes marriages between second-degree forbidden relatives (*E.H.* 154:20, 44:7), marriages between a Kohen and a divorcee ac-

cording to traditional law (*E.H.* 6:1, but see above, p. 383), and marriages involving a childless widow who has not submitted to Ḥalitsah (*E.H.* 159:2).
2. If the wife committed adultery, and the husband does not sue for divorce as he has a right to (*E.H.* 115:8).
3. If considerations of health preclude sexual intercourse, unless the parties agree to desist from cohabitation (*E.H.* 154:1).

5. Finally, there are cases of separation where a *geṭ* is not required, viz., where the marriage that was contracted has no validity whatsoever (termed *impedimentum diniment* in canon law):

1. A marriage between relatives of the primary forbidden degree of consanguinity (*E.H.* 44:6).
2. A marriage involving a previously married woman who has not obtained a *geṭ* from her first husband (*E.H.* 17:58).
3. In addition, according to some opinions, a husband may remarry without giving his wife a *geṭ* if she leaves him and becomes an apostate (*E.H.* 1:10 in Rama). Some authorities, however, insist that the woman must be given a *geṭ*. They maintain that while the husband may remarry without a *geṭ*, since Rabbenu Gershom's decree against polygamy is waived in such instances, the woman remains forbidden—the purpose of the *geṭ* is to give her the status of a divorcee so that she will not incur the guilt of adultery if she remarries (*Otsar Haposqim,* 1:76).
4. In the case of a מוֹרֶדֶת (i.e., a woman who refuses to have conjugal relations with her husband in order to spite him, or who deserts him), according to some authorities, the husband may marry another woman (a) without a *geṭ* (Isserlein, *Pesaqim Ukhetavim,* no. 256); (b) with a הֶתֵּר מֵאָה רַבָּנִים, as in the case of a woman who becomes insane (*E.H.* 1:10; *Otsar Haposqim,* 1:73; see below, p. 499); (c) by giving her a *geṭ* עַל יְדֵי זִכּוּי (see below, p. 496 ff., for explanation and details).

UNIT XXXIV

THE DISSOLUTION OF MARRIAGE (III)

DIVORCE PROCEEDINGS

Preliminaries
The Officiating Rabbi
The Sofer
The Witnesses
The Material
Writing the Geṭ
The Text of the Geṭ
The Date
The Place
The Names
Witnesses
Dies Iuridicii: Days When a Geṭ May Not Be Granted
Detailed Procedure
Appendix

XXXIV.
The Dissolution of Marriage (III)
Divorce Proceedings

1. Preliminaries

Since it is a mitswah to bring a husband and wife together (see B. *Ned.* 66b, *Giṭ.* 90a; Amram, *Jewish Law of Divorce,* pp. 47, 79), divorce proceedings may take place only after all efforts at reconciliation have proven futile. Where a civil divorce has occurred in accordance with the law of the land, it is regarded as evidence that there is no possibility of reconciliation.

The persons involved in the granting of a *geṭ* are the officiating rabbi, the *sofer* (scribe), the witnesses, and the man and woman to be divorced.

2. The Officiating Rabbi

It is an old established rule that only an expert in the laws of marriage and divorce may grant a *geṭ* (B. *Qid.* 13a; *E.H.* 154 in *Seder Hageṭ*, sec. 1). Since the rules regulating divorce proceedings require precision, the insistence on expertise reduced mistakes and misunderstanding to a minimum, and settled with reasonable certainty the legal status and mutual obligations and rights of the parties. In addition, it ensured that the granting of a *geṭ* was too difficult for just anyone to undertake (Amram, *Jewish Law of Divorce,* p. 143).

Some authorities require that a *geṭ* be issued by a *Bet Din* of three (see *Sedeh Ḥemed,* chap. 1, sec. 1, where he marshals the authorities, and mentions places where the insistence upon a *Bet Din* prevailed and places where a single expert sufficed). Hence, it is a matter of *minhag*. In Israel a *Bet Din* is generally required. In America the prevalent custom is not to require a *Bet Din* (see also Felder, *Naḥalat Tsevi,* 2:31.)

3. The Sofer

Any Jew is legally qualified to write a *geṭ* (*E.H.* 123:1). Even persons who are otherwise legally disqualified—e.g., deaf mutes, idiots, and minors—are permitted to write a *geṭ* if supervised by a competent person (*E.H.* 123:4); indeed, a woman about to be divorced is permitted to write her own *geṭ*, and she would be legally divorced if after writing it she gave it to her husband, and he then delivered it to her in accordance with the laws of divorce (*E.H.* 123:1). Nevertheless, since many complex rules and regulations govern the preparation of a *geṭ*, it has become the practice to have it written by a *sofer* (a duly qualified scribe). If he does not have the necessary expertise, he may still write the *geṭ* under the close guidance and supervision of the officiating rabbi.

There are several questions regarding the *sofer*.

1. May he serve as one of the witnesses?
2. May the officiating rabbi, if he has the necessary skill, also act as *sofer?*
3. May a relative of the husband or the wife be the *sofer?*

In answering the first question, we call attention to an explicit ruling that a *sofer* may not act as a witness (*E.H.* 130:18; *Seder Hageṭ*, sec. 3). Since there are, however, some weighty dissenting opinions (Maimonides, *Hil. Geirushin* 9:27; Ṭur, *E.H.* 130 near end; *Knesset Hagedolah, E.H.* 130:31; *'Arukh Hashulḥan, E.H.* 130:41), it is permitted in emergencies and בְּדִיעֲבַד (post facto).

Regarding the rabbi acting as *sofer*, the shortage of scribes must be taken into consideration, as well as the fact that the few available scribes are concentrated in metropolitan areas. Of necessity, therefore, some rabbis have acquired the requisite scribal skills. The renowned Rabbi Shalom Mordecai Schwadron, when asked whether a rabbi may serve as scribe, ruled that it is permitted in places where there is no *sofer* (*Meharsham,* vol. 2, no. 56).

As for a relative acting as *sofer*, it is permitted if undue hardship would otherwise be caused (*E.H.* 130:1 in Rama). The same rule applies to the officiating rabbi (ibid. and *Qav Naqi* 6:2).

4. The Witnesses

The qualifications for serving as a witness are discussed at length in the section of the *Shulḥan 'Arukh* that deals with witnesses testifying in court (*H.M.* 33 and 34) and will be given in some detail below. Here we mention merely that the witnesses must not be related to the wife or the husband, to each other, or to the officiating rabbi, and should be pious, reliable, and of good repute. This applies both to the witnesses who sign the *geṭ* and to the witnesses who are present when it is delivered (*E.H.* 130:1 in Rama; *'Arukh Hashulḥan* 130:1–6).

5. The Material

Originally the *geṭ* was written on parchment. Any material normally used for writing is acceptable, however, and nowadays heavy white paper is used (*E.H.* 124:2 in Rama; *'Arukh Hashulḥan, E.H.* 124:18).

Any writing fluid may be used provided it leaves a permanent impression which cannot be erased (*E.H.* 125:1). Today special ink is available, prepared specifically for scribes.

It is customary for the scribe to use a goose quill, just as in the writing of a Torah (*E.H.* 125:22 in *B.H.; 'Arukh Hashulḥan* 125:36). It has been asked whether a *geṭ* may be written with a metal pen, and whether it may be printed, either with a hand print or with a typewriter.

The use of a metal pen is explicitly forbidden (*E.H.* 125:4 in Rama; *'Arukh Hashulḥan, E.H.* 125:36). Later authorities, however, have permitted the use of a metal pen if a goose quill cannot be obtained, or if it is not possible to obtain the services of an expert scribe who is adept in the use of a quill (Weinberg, *Seridei Eish,* vol. 3, resp. 37).

Although the question regarding printing is academic, some authorities discussed it seriously. Most forbid it on the grounds that it cannot be called "writing" since the whole text is printed with one impression. Some permit it, nevertheless (see *'Arukh Hashulḥan, E.H.* 125:37; Fano, *She'eilot Uteshuvot,* resp. 93). The question of using a typewriter is more relevant. The authorities that permit printing would certainly permit typing, but most recent authorities forbid it (see *'Arukh Hashulḥan, E.H.* 125:38; Price, *Mishnat Avraham,* 1:170). The traditional method has the merit of making the proceedings impressive and solemn. This is especially important today, when the civil divorce takes precedence in the eyes of the public and divorce proceedings are often unsavory.

6. Writing the Get

Before the *get* is written, the paper must be lined: twelve lines for the text of the *get*, and two half-lines for the signatures of the witnesses. The paper must also be lined on the margins to ensure that the writing is even and that all the lines are of the same length. The lining may not be done with anything that leaves a mark (e.g., a crayon, a pencil, or a pen); nowadays a sharpened wooden stylus is used. Moreover, it must be done on the reverse side of the paper, i.e., not on the surface on which the *get* is written (*E.H.* 125:10–13). The writing should hang from the lines, i.e., the tops of the letters should touch the line.

The *sofer* must leave a margin on both sides of the text of the *get* as well as at the top and the bottom. The Rama suggests about half a finger's breadth (less than half an inch) on the margins, and a finger's breadth (less than an inch) on the top and bottom of the text (*E.H.* 125:12 in Rama). It is also customary for the length of the paper to be greater than its width (*E.H.* 125:13).

7. The Text of the Get

On the ..... day of the week and ..... day of the month ..... in the year ..... since the creation of the world, the era according to which we are accustomed to reckon in this place, to wit, the town of ..... that is near River ....., do I ..... son of ..... of the town of ..... (and by whatever other name or surname I or my father may be known, and my town and his town) thus determine, being of sound mind and under no constraint; and I do release and send away and put aside thee ..... (and by whatever other name or surname thou and thy father are known, and thy town and his town) who have been my wife from time past hitherto; and hereby I do release thee and send away and put thee aside that thou mayest have permission and control over thyself to go to be married to any man whom thou desirest, and no man shall hinder thee in my name from this day forever. And thou art permitted to be married to any man. And these presents shall be unto thee from me a bill of dismissal, a document of release, and a letter of freedom, according to the law of Moses and Israel.

..... the son of ..... a witness
..... the son of ..... a witness

Note that the essential data of the *get* are the date, the name of the place where the *get* is written, the names of the divorcing parties, the proper formula indicating the complete separation of husband and wife, and the signatures of the witnesses (*Giṭ.* 9:3; *E.H.* 126–30).

Meticulous care is necessary. The spelling of the whole text must be correct, without any deviation, however slight. The only exceptions allowed are slight deviations, such as the omission or addition of a letter, that do not change the sense of a phrase or the meaning of a word (for examples, see *E.H.* 126:49 and *'Arukh Hashulḥan, E.H.* 126:61).

The letters must be distinct and not touching each other (*Qav Naqi* 67:1, sec. 14). It is customary to have the date, the place, and the names included in the first six lines (ibid. 74:1). It is also customary to extend the words כְּדַת מֹשֶׁה וְיִשְׂרָאֵל ("according to the Law of Moses and Israel") so that they occupy the last line completely (*E.H.* 126:18).

8. The Date

The date used in the *get* is the standard date in the Jewish calendar, giving the day of the week (*E.H.* 126:2–3), the day of the month (*E.H.* 126:3–8), and the year since creation (*E.H.* 126:5, 127:1; *'Arukh Hashulḥan, E.H.* 127:38, 44; *Hagahot Maimuniot* to *Hil. Geirushin* 1:27).

For a guide to the correct spelling and form of the dates, see below, p. 491.

A predated *get* is not valid (*E.H.* 127:2). A postdated *get*, however, is valid since it does not take effect until the date occurs (*E.H.* 127:9; *'Arukh Hashulḥan, E.H.* 127:9, 11).

9. The Place

The name of the town where the *get* is written and signed must be mentioned in the *get* (*E.H.* 128:1). The town is usually identified by the bodies of water that are adjacent to it, such as rivers . . . מָתָא דְּיַתְבָא עַל נְהַר, the ocean עַל . . . כֵּיף יַמָּא, or springs . . . עַל מֵי מַעְיָנוֹת (*E.H.* 128:4–6).

It is frequently asked whether a *get* written in a suburb should use the name of the mother city or the name of the suburb (*'Arukh Hashulḥan, E.H.* 128:15, 16; Felder, *Naḥalat Tsevi,* 2:155). The sources distinguish between sections of a city that have their own names and towns that are outside the city limits. Obviously the suburbs of today are in the second category because they are duly incorporated as towns or villages with separate governments. Thus it is proper to include the name of the suburb in the *get*. For purposes of more accurate identification, however, it would be proper to add . . . הַסְּמוּכָה לְמָתָא or . . . שֶׁבְּצַד (ibid.).

10. The Names

We have already mentioned that Jewish law promoted and advocated precision in the writing of a *get* in order to minimize mistakes and misunderstandings, and to settle with reasonable certainty the legal status and mutual obligations and rights of the parties. For this reason, the law is most insistent upon the correct writing of the text in general and of its components in particular, and especially on the authenticity of the names and their correct spelling.

In determining the names of the parties, it is necessary to consider both their official names and the names of their parents as well as any nicknames or added names by which they may be known.

In the diaspora, the matter is complicated by the fact that most Jews have a secular everyday name, generally in the language of the land, as well as the Jewish name they were given at birth. Which of these should have priority, the name by which a person is best known, which in the diaspora is a non-Jewish name, or the Jewish name given at birth, which is generally used only on religious occasions, e.g., when called to the Torah, in the *ketubah,* or when mentioned in a מִי שֶׁבֵּרַךְ?

A further complication is peculiar to America and occurs most commonly with girls: the name habitually used as the Jewish name was given in Hebrew school rather than at birth. In most such cases, the child originally received a Jewish name of non-Hebraic origin and a zealous Hebrew teacher substituted an authentic Hebrew name, which the recipient has used ever since. Is such a name to be taken into consideration?

Before we answer these questions, it will be useful to define certain terms:

1. שֵׁם הָעֲרִיסָה—the name given at birth; it may be—
   a. שֵׁם הַקּוֹדֶשׁ—a Hebrew name, usually of biblical origin, e.g., מֹשֶׁה, אַבְרָהָם, רִבְקָה, שָׂרָה, etc. one authority includes Aramaic names in this category (see *Get Mesudar,* commentary *Pesher Davar,* p. 2, n. 2);

b. שֵׁם לַעַז—a name of non-Hebraic origin, e.g., לֵיבּ, הִירשׁ, גָאלְדֶע, זָלַאטֶע, etc.

2. שֵׁם עִקָּר and שֵׁם טָפֵל—as the terms indicate, the main name, to which priority is given, and the name that is adjunct to it.
3. שֵׁם עֶצֶם and שֵׁם כִּנּוּי—the first term refers to a person's real name; the second to his nickname or added name. These terms also refer to the following: most names are given individually or in conjunction with other names; e.g., אַבְרָהָם, יִצְחָק, and יַעֲקֹב can be used individually or in combinations like אַבְרָהָם יִצְחָק, יַעֲקֹב יִצְחָק, etc. Some names, however, are never used alone but are always combined with another name; e.g., פאליק is always combined with יְהוֹשֻׁעַ. The first element of such a pair is called שֵׁם עֶצֶם; the second, שֵׁם כִּנּוּי.
4. שֵׁם שֶׁנִּשְׁתַּכַּח—a name given at birth that has subsequently fallen into complete disuse.

With these definitions in mind, we can list a few general rules:

1. The Hebrew name given at birth, the שֵׁם הָעִבְרִיסָה that is used mainly for religious purposes, is always the שֵׁם עִקָּר, even if the person is generally known by his English name for legal purposes and for signatures (Henkin, supplement to *Peirushei Ivra*). The English name is added as the שֵׁם טָפֵל, preceded by the word הַמְכוּנֶּה or דְּמִתְקְרֵי for a man and by דְּמִתְקַרְיָא for a woman.
2. When the שֵׁם עִקָּר is Hebrew and the שֵׁם טָפֵל is English or any non-Hebraic name, הַמְכוּנֶּה is used. When both are Hebrew or of non-Hebraic origin, דְּמִתְקְרֵי is used (*E.H.* 129:16 in Rama).
3. The names of the fathers of both the husband and the wife must also be mentioned and are subject to the same rules. If the English name is similar to the Hebrew (e.g., Abraham for אַבְרָהָם), it need not be mentioned (*E.H.* 129:14 in Rama).
4. Titles (e.g., rabbi, doctor, etc.) may not be used; but if the husband is a Kohen or a Levite, this is added after his father's name (*E.H.* 129:7).
5. In the English name, the middle name, which is usually designated only by an initial, may be omitted (Henkin, supplement to *Peirushei Ivra*).
6. Opinions differ regarding the use of surnames. The general practice nowadays is to omit them (ibid.; ee also *Maharsham,* vol 1, no. 83; Breisch, *Ḥelqat Ya'aqov,* vol. 1, no. 161; *Darkhei Mosheh* on *E.H.* 129:19).

7. If the parties do not know their Hebrew names, the names they use for their signatures are used.
8. If the father of either of the pa ties is not Jewish, the name of the mother is used. If he is an apostate, his Jewish name is used nonetheless (*E.H.* 129:5).
9. If a person was given two names, both are used.
10. The correct spelling of names was once a cause of great concern but today is a comparatively simple matter due to the availability of books on the subject. The following are recommended: Münz, *Geṭ Mesudar;* Schechter, *Beit Midrash Shem Wa'eiver;* Henkin, *Pierushei Ivra.*

11. Witnesses

The *geṭ* is validated mainly by the witnesses to its delivery, the עֵדֵי מְסִירָה, but it must also be signed by witnesses, the עֵדֵי חֲתִימָה, and they are subject to the rules covering the qualification of witnessess (*E.H.* 130:1; *'Arukh Hashulḥan, E.H.* 130:2), viz.,

1. They must not be related to the parties to the divorce or to each other.
2. They must be pious and law-abiding.
3. They must be adult males.
4. They must not be involved or interested parties (*Ḥ.M.* 33–35; *Qaw Naqi* 5:10).

The witnesses may sign the *geṭ* only after the ink with which it is inscribed is completely dry (*E.H.* 130:22). They write their names and their father's names, but not their surnames (*E.H.* 130:11), immediately beneath the last line of the *geṭ*, leaving less than two lines' space therefrom, one signature under the other (*E.H.* 130:1 in Rama). Further regulations are given below in the discussion of the procedures for granting a *geṭ* (see p. 484 f.).

12. Dies Iuridicii: Days When a Geṭ May Not Be Granted

Since the giving of a *geṭ* is a legal action in a court of law, it may only take place on days when the courts are permitted to be in session. In addition, divorce proceedings may not take place—

1. on Sabbaths and festivals, because the preparation of a *geṭ* involves such forbidden acts as writing (*E.H.* 136:7; the writing of a *geṭ* is permitted, however, during the intermediate days of Pesaḥ and Sukkot [*M.Q.* 3:3; *O.H.* 545:5], though there are some dissenting opinions [*Sedeh Ḥemed,* under *Geṭ,* no. 1, sec. 11]);
2. on Fridays and on days before the advent of festivals, since they might interfere with the Sabbath or festival preparations (*E.H.* 154 in *Seder Hageṭ*, sec. 1), except בִּשְׁעַת הַדְּחָק (emergency cases);
3. at night, since the giving of a *geṭ* is a form of court litigation that may not be carried out at night (*Seder Hageṭ*, secs. 88–89), except בִּשְׁעַת הַדְּחָק (*Sedeh Ḥemed,* under *Geṭ,* no. 1, sec. 25).

13. Detailed Procedure

The following procedure is based on the *Seder Hageṭ* given after chapter 154 of *Even Ha'ezer* and on the English text prepared by Professor Boaz Cohen ז"ל.

1. *Rabbi to Husband:* Do you, *Ploni ben Ploni* (so-and-so, son of so-and-so), give this *geṭ* of your own free will without duress or compulsion?

2. *Husband:* Yes

3. *Rabbi:* Perhaps you have bound yourself by uttering a vow or by making any binding statement which would compel you to give a *geṭ* against your will.

4. *Husband:* No.

5. *Rabbi:* Perhaps you have once made a statement which would invalidate the *geṭ*, or you have uttered or done something to render the *geṭ* null and void, and have forgotten it, or you were under the erroneous impression that such acts do not render the *geṭ* null and void; will you therefore please make void all such remarks and acts of yours in the presence of witnesses.

6. *Husband:* Hear ye witnesses: In your presence I declare null and void any previous declaration that I may have made which may invalidate this *geṭ*. I also declare any witness that may hereafter testify to such a statement as disqualified.

7. Sofer *to Husband:* You, *Ploni ben Ploni,* I am presenting to you as a gift these writing materials, the paper, the pen, and the ink, so that they become your property.

8. *Husband accepts the writing materials, lifts them up for the purpose of acquiring them, and says:* Ye witnesses, listen to what I will say to the *sofer.*

9. *Then, addressing the* sofer *he says:* You *sofer, Ploni ben Ploni,* I give you this paper, ink, and pen, and all the writing material, and I order you that you write for me, *Ploni ben Ploni,* a *get* to divorce my wife, *Plonit bat Ploni* (so-and-so, daughter of so-and-so), and write this *get lishmi, lishmah, ulesheim geirushin* (in my behalf, in her behalf, and with the intent of effecting divorcement), and write even as many as a hundred *gittin* if necessary, until one valid *get* is written and signed according to the laws of Moses and the children of Israel. I hereby authorize you to make any corrections in the document that may be necessary.

Sofer: So I shall do.

10. *Husband to each witness in the hearing of the other:* You *Ploni ben Ploni* act as witness and sign the *get* which the *sofer Ploni ben Ploni* shall write specifically for me, *Ploni ben Ploni,* and for my wife, *Plonit bat Ploni,* and sign as many as a hundred *gittin* if necessary until one valid *get* is written and signed and delivered according to the laws of Moses and the children of Israel.

11. *The witnesses each say:* So I shall do.

12. *The husband then hands over the writing materials to the* sofer.

13. *The* sofer *says to the witnesses:* Hear ye witnesses: All these preparations that I make and all the writing that I shall do, I shall do in the name of the husband, *Ploni ben Ploni,* to divorce his wife, *Plonit bat Ploni,* and I am writing it *lishmo, lishmah, ulisheim geirushin.*

14. *The* get *is written. The witnesses must be present during the writing of the first line.*

15. *The witnesses as well as the scribe are required to note a distinguishing mark on the* get.

16. *When the* get *is finished and the ink is dried, the witnesses read it; before signing it, they say to each other:* You *Ploni ben Ploni,* witness that I am signing this *get lesheim Ploni ben Ploni,* who ordered us to sign a *get* to divorce his wife, *Plonit bat Ploni,* and I am signing it *lishmo, lishmah, ulsheim geirushin.*

17. *Then the rabbi says to the* sofer:

a. *Rabbi:* You, *sofer Ploni ben Ploni,* is this the *get* that you have written?

Sofer: Yes.

b. *Rabbi:* Do you have any special mark by which you can identify this *geṭ?*

    Sofer: Yes and this is it (*points it out*).

c. *Rabbi:* Did *Ploni ben Ploni*, the husband, give you the writing materials in the presence of the witnesses?

    Sofer: Yes.

d. *Rabbi:* Did the husband tell you to write the *geṭ?*

    Sofer: Yes.

e. *Rabbi:* Did he tell you to write it *lishmo, lishmah, ulsheim geirushin?*

    Sofer: Yes.

f. *Rabbi:* Did he order you in the presence of witnesses?

    Sofer: Yes.

g. *Rabbi:* Did you write it *lishmo, lishmah, ulsheim geirushin?*

    Sofer: Yes.

h. *Rabbi:* What did you say before you started writing this *geṭ?*

    Sofer: I said: I write this *geṭ* in the name of the husband, *Ploni ben Ploni*, to divorce with it his wife, *Plonit bat Ploni*, and I write it *lishmo, lishmah, ulsheim geirushin.*

i. *Rabbi:* Did you say so in the presence of witnesses?

    Sofer: Yes.

    Rabbi: Were the witnesses present at least during the time you wrote the first line?

    Sofer: Yes.

18. a. *Rabbi to Witnesses:* Did you witnesses hear the husband, *Ploni ben Ploni*, order the *sofer* to write a *geṭ* for his wife, *Plonit bat Ploni*, and to write it *lishmo, lishmah, ulsheim geirushin?*

    Witnesses: We did.

b. *Rabbi:* Did you hear him say that he would write it *lishmo, lishmah, ulsheim geirushin?*

    Witnesses: We did.

c. *Rabbi:* Were you present when he wrote the first line?

    Witnesses: We were.

d. *Rabbi to each witness separately:* Is this your signature?

    Witness: Yes.

e. *Rabbi:* Did you sign it *lishmo, lishmah, ulsheim geirushin?*

    Witness: Yes.

f. *Rabbi:* Did the husband tell you to do so?
Witness: Yes.

g. *Rabbi:* Did the other witness see you sign the *get?*
Witness: Yes.

h. *Rabbi:* What did you say before you signed?
Witness: I said: I am signing this *get* in the name of the husband, *Ploni ben Ploni,* to divorce with it his wife, *Plonit bat Ploni,* and I am signing it *lishmo, lishmah, ulsheim geirushin.* So I said and so I signed.

The rabbi repeats this with the second witness. Then the get *is read again to see that it is correct. Then the rabbi says to husband:*

Rabbi: Again I wish to ask you whether you give this *get* of your own free will?

Husband: I do.

Rabbi: Did you bind yourself by any statement or by any vow in a way that would compel you to give this *get* against your free will?

Husband: No.

Rabbi: Again I wish to ask you that perhaps you did make such a statement and have forgotten it or made it erroneously. Will you therefore cancel all such statements and declare them null and void?

Husband: You witnesses hear that I declare in your presence null and void all previous declarations which I may have made, which may invalidate this *get*. I also declare any witness that may testify to such a statement as disqualified.

Rabbi to Wife: Are you accepting this *get* of your own free will?

Wife: Yes.

Rabbi: Did you bind yourself by any statement or vow that would compel you to accept this *get* against your will?

Wife: No.

Rabbi: Perhaps you have unwittingly made such a statement that would nullify the *get*. In order to prevent that, will you kindly retract all such declarations.

Wife: I revoke all such statements that may nullify the *get*, in the presence of you the witnesses.

The rabbi says to those present: If there is anyone who wishes to protest, let him do so now.

Husband to witnesses: You be also witnesses to the delivery of the *get*.

The rabbi now tells the wife to remove all jewelry from her hands, and to hold her hands together with open palms upward in a position to receive the get.

The sofer *folds the* geṭ *and gives it to the rabbi. The rabbi gives the* geṭ *to the husband, who, holding it in both hands, drops it into the palms of the wife and says:* הֲרֵי זֶה גִּיטֵּךְ וְהִתְקַבְּלִי גִּיטֵּךְ וּבוֹ תְּהִי מְגֹרֶשֶׁת מִמֶּנִּי מֵעַכְשָׁיו וַהֲרֵי אַתְּ מֻתֶּרֶת לְכָל אָדָם "This be your *geṭ*, and with it be thou divorced from me from this time forth so that you may become the wife of any man."

The wife receives the geṭ, *lifts up her hands, walks with it a short distance, and returns. She returns the* geṭ *to the rabbi.*

The rabbi reads the geṭ *again with the witnesses.*

The rabbi again asks the sofer *and witnesses to identify the* geṭ *and the signatures.*

The rabbi then says: Hear all ye present that Rabbenu Tam has issued a ban against all those who try to invalidate a *geṭ* after it has been delivered.

The four corners of the geṭ *are then cut, and it is placed in the rabbi's files. It is suggested that for further proof the files should also include the English names and the addresses of all the parties involved (husband, wife, witnesses, and* sofer*) and the secular date.*

The rabbi then issues written statements (פְּטוֹר) *to the husband and wife to certify that their marriage was dissolved according to Jewish law.*

14. Appendix

Bet Din of the Rabbinical Assembly of America
Certificate of Divorcement in Hebrew

תעודת גירושין

להיות לראיה ביד האשה

שקבלה גט פטורין מבעלה

בדת משה וישראל.
והיא מותרת להנשא לכל אדם

ועל זה באתי על החתום ביום לחדש בשנת תש״ פה
נוא יארק

ראש בית דין לכנסת הרבנים באמריקה

Beth Din of the Rabbinical Assembly of America
Certificate of Decree of Divorce

On the day of at the Beth Din of the Rabbinical Assembly of America, came duly to be heard the petition of of praying that the marriage heretofore existing between him and his wife of be terminated and declared null and void.

Whereas the said parties had obtained a civil decree of divorce in the State of , And whereas the petition of the husband for divorce was heard and the scribe had duly written the Bill of Divorce according to Jewish statutes and the writ had been duly delivered by the husband to the wife, the court declared the said marriage dissolved and the wife hereby divorced from her husband.

It shall be lawful for the said to marry any other Jewess.

Signed:

Boaz Cohen, Chairman
Beth Din of the Rabbinical
Assembly of America

Date:

Guide to Correct Spelling of Dates

ימי השבוע

באחד בשבת, בשני בשבת, בשני בחד יו״ד, בשלישי, ברביעי, בחמישי, כל חד בתרי יודין בששי בחד יו״ד.

יום אחד לחדש, שני ימים לחדש, שלשה, ארבעה, חמשה, ששה, שבעה, שמנה, תשעה, עשרה ימים, מכאן ואילך יכתוב יום: אחד עשר יום, שנים עשר יום, שלשה עשר יום, ארבעה עשר יום, חמשה עשר יום, ששה עשר יום, שבעה עשר יום, שמנה עשר יום, תשעה עשר יום, עשרים יום, אחד ועשרים יום, שנים ועשרים יום, שלשה ועשרים יום, ארבעה ועשרים יום, חמשה ועשרים יום, ששה ועשרים יום, שבעה ועשרים יום, שמנה ועשרים יום, תשעה ועשרים יום.

אם ר״ח שני ימים יכתוב ביום א׳ דר״ח דרך משל בר״ח אייר יכתוב: יום שלשים לחדש ניסן שהוא ראש חדש אייר, באדר של שנה מעוברת יכתוב יום שלשים לחדש אדר הראשון שהוא ראש חדש אדר השני, ביום שני דר״ח יכתוב יום אחד לחדש אייר או יום אחד לחדש אדר השני וכן כולם.

במנין הימים כותבים לשון זכר שני ולא שתי וכו׳ הכל כדלעיל.

שמות החדשים

ניסן מלא יו״ד. אייר מלא שני יוד״ן. סיון מלא יו״ד. תמוז מלא וי״ו. אב, אלול מלא וי״ו. תשרי בלא יו״ד בין ת׳ לשי״ן. מרחשון חד תיבה ובחד וי״ו. כסלו חסר יו״ד. טבת, שבט, אדר, אם השנה מעוברת יכתוב בראשון אדר הראשון ובשני אדר השני, ואם כתב באדר ראשון סתם אדר כשר אבל אם כתב בשני סתם פסול, ולכתחלה יש ליזהר להזכיר אדר הראשון.

מנין השנים

שנת חמשת אלפים ואחת, ושתים, ושלש, וארבע, וחמש, ושש, ושבע, ושמנה, ותשע, הכל בלא ה״ה לבסוף דבמנין השנים כותבין בלשון נקבה חוץ משמנה דאין חילוק בין לשון זכר לנקבה דבכולן כותבין בה״א לבסוף חסר וי״ו [מ״מ יש חילוק במבטא שמנה הנו״ן בקמץ לזכר שמנה הנו״ן בסגל לנקבה], אחת עשרה, שתים עשרה, שלשה עשרה, ארבע עשרה, חמש עשרה, שש עשרה, שבע עשרה, שמנה עשרה, תשע עשרה, עשרים, ע״כ יכתוב גם בשנים מנין המועט קודם ומעשרים ואילך מנין המרובה קודם עשרים ואחת. עשרים ושתים, עשרים ושלש, עשרים וארבע, עשרים וחמש, עשרים ושש, עשרים ושבע, עשרים ושמנה, עשרים ותשע, שלשים וכו׳, ארבעים, חמשים ,ששים, שבעים, שמנים, תשעים.

UNIT XXXV

THE DISSOLUTION OF MARRIAGE (IV)

DELIVERY OF THE GEṬ

Delivery Through an Agent
The Case of *Kitvu Utenu*
Geṭ al yedei Zikui
Heter Me'ah Rabbanim
Appendix

XXXV.
The Dissolution of Marriage (IV) Delivery of the Geṭ

1. Delivery Through an Agent

In the preceding chapter, we outlined the procedure whereby a husband delivers a *geṭ* directly to his wife in the presence of two witnesses. If the wife is not present when the *geṭ* is written, the husband may appoint an agent (שָׁלִיחַ) to deliver the *geṭ* personally, or, if this is not feasible, may authorize him to duly appoint another agent to deliver the *geṭ* to the wife. The second agent is authorized to appoint a third agent if he himself is not able to deliver the *geṭ*, etc. Each of these is called the שָׁלִיחַ לְהוֹלָכָה, or agent for delivery.

The wife may also appoint an agent to act on her behalf in receiving the *geṭ* from her husband. She has the choice of appointing the agent as a שָׁלִיחַ לְהוֹלָכָה, an agent for delivery, or a שָׁלִיחַ לְקַבָּלָה, an agent for acceptance. The difference is that in the case of an agent for delivery, whether appointed by the husband or the wife, the wife becomes divorced only when the *geṭ* actually reaches her hand; in the case of an agent for acceptance, she becomes divorced as soon as the *geṭ* reaches the hand of the agent she has appointed (*E.H.* 140:1, 3, 5).

The accepted practice is not to appoint an agent for acceptance except in emergencies (*E.H.* 141:29 in Rama; *B.H.* and *Pitḥei Teshuvah* ad loc.).

Nowadays, when a *geṭ* must be delivered through an agent, two agents are appointed: one, the שָׁלִיחַ רִאשׁוֹן, is located where the *geṭ* is written, and the other, the שָׁלִיחַ שֵׁנִי, is located where the *geṭ* will be delivered.

The husband appoints the agent before telling the *sofer* to write the *geṭ*. The formula of appointment is as follows:

Rabbi to shaliaḥ: You *shaliaḥ*, be it known to you that being the *shaliaḥ* will make it impossible for you to marry the woman to be divorced.

Husband to witnesses: Be ye witnesses that I am appointing this man as the *shaliaḥ* to deliver this *geṭ* to my wife.

Husband to shaliaḥ: I, *Ploni ben Ploni,* appoint you, *Ploni ben Ploni,* to be my *shaliaḥ* to bring this *geṭ* to my wife, *Plonit bat Ploni,* and to give it into her hands, you or your *shaliaḥ*, or the *shaliaḥ* of your *shaliaḥ*, even to the hundredth *shaliaḥ*, even if this should not be an emergency; and I give permission to you or to your *shaliaḥ*, or the *shaliaḥ* of your *shaliaḥ*, even up to a hundredth *shaliaḥ*, to deliver this *geṭ* into her hands wherever you shall find her. Your hand shall be as my hand, your action as my action, your mouth as my mouth, your word as my word, and your delivery as my delivery. As soon as this *geṭ* will be delivered into her hands by you or your *shaliaḥ*, or the *shaliaḥ* of your *shaliaḥ*, even up to a hundredth *shaliaḥ*, she shall be divorced from me and be free to marry any other man, and I accept upon myself, under a biblical oath, that I shall not invalidate this *geṭ* or the *shaliaḥ*.

The procedure then follows that for an ordinary *geṭ*, except that the *shaliaḥ* should be present when the husband orders the *sofer* to write the *geṭ* and the witnesses to sign it and to stay until the first line has been written, and also when the witnesses affix their signatures (*E.H.* 154 in *Seder Hageṭ*, sec. 24, and in Rama).

There is also a variation in the formula when the husband gives the *geṭ* to the agent. Before the husband gives him the *geṭ*, the rabbi addresses the witnesses to sign on the authorization (עֵדֵי הַרְשָׁאָה): "Be ye witnesses that the husband is giving this *geṭ* to the *shaliaḥ* and hear that he is giving it *lishmo, lishmah, ulsheim geirushin.*"

The husband then gives the *geṭ* to the agent and says: "You, *Ploni ben Ploni,* take this *geṭ* to my wife, *Plonit bat Ploni,* and give it into her hand wherever you may find her, and your hand shall be as my hand, your action as my action, your mouth as my mouth, your word as my word. I give you permission to appoint another *shaliaḥ* in your place, and a *shaliaḥ* of this *shaliaḥ* even unto a hundred, even if this should not be necessary because of an emergency, until this *geṭ* will reach her hand from your hand or from the hand of your *shaliaḥ*, and let her be divorced from me and permitted to marry any man."

The agent then presents the *geṭ* before a *Bet Din,* which nowadays is usually constituted of the rabbi who arranged the *geṭ* and two colleagues or other knowledgeable persons.

If the שָׁלִיחַ רִאשׁוֹן appoints a שָׁלִיחַ שֵׁנִי, this is done in the presence of the *Bet Din;* its members sign the agency appointment (הַרְשָׁאָה) of the *shaliaḥ sheini,* and he then delivers the *geṭ* to the wife. The procedure is as follows:

Rabbi to agent: What is your pleasure?

Agent: I, *Ploni ben Ploni,* am the appointed agent of *Ploni ben Ploni,* who was appointed by the husband *Ploni ben Ploni* to convey this *geṭ* to his wife, *Plonit bat Ploni,* wherever I shall find her as described in the *harsha'ah.*"

The rabbi then reads the *harsha'ah* and the *geṭ*. The procedures pertaining to an ordinary *geṭ* are followed, with two exceptions: (1) the agent acts in place of the husband; (2) the formula used when delivering the *geṭ* is as follows: "Behold, this is thy *geṭ* that thy husband, *Ploni ben Ploni,* has sent you, and with it be thou divorced now from your husband, and lo, thou art permitted to marry anyone. And I am the agent appointed by the *Bet Din.*"

It is often asked whether a *geṭ* may be sent through an agent when the husband and wife live in the same city but are unwilling to meet each other (*E.H.* 154:29 in *Seder Hageṭ*). There is no objection to this arrangement if the granting of the *geṭ* would otherwise be hindered (*Pitḥei Teshuvah* in *E.H.* 141:55, subsec. 53).

2. The Case of Kitvu Utenu

If the husband is in a place where there are no facilities for the granting of a *geṭ*, or if he is in a hurry to depart and cannot wait for the execution of the regular procedure, the device termed כִּתְבוּ וּתְנוּ may be employed. The procedure is as follows: The husband orally appoints the *sofer,* the witnesses, and the agent of delivery to write and deliver the *geṭ* to his wife. These appointments may also be made in writing (for the text, see Waldenberg, *Tsits Eli'ezer,* 10:236); some authorities suggest that any written appointment should be in the vernacular to ensure that it is understood by all the parties concerned. A text for such appointments prepared by Professor Boaz Cohen and the form currently used by the *Bet Din* of the Rabbinical Assembly are found in the appendix to this chapter (see pp. 503 and 505).

It has been asked whether this arrangement could be accomplished by telephone. Since there is a difference of opinion, we permit it בִּשְׁעַת הַדְּחָק (Waldenberg, *Tsits Eli'ezer,* 10:47; Liebes, "Be'inyan Minnui Sofer").

3. Geṭ Al Yedei Zikui

One of the enactments of the חֵרֶם דְּרַבֵּנוּ גֵּרְשֹׁם was that a woman may not be divorced without her consent. This led to the question whether such consent must be explicit or implicit, i.e., apparent from some of her actions—

e.g., if she became an apostate, or if she left her husband and married someone else without a *get*, or, what is more frequent today, was granted a civil divorce but is not interested in receiving a *get*.

The following problems are involved. In the above cases, if the man remarries without obtaining a divorce, he is violating the חֵרֶם דְּרַבֵּנוּ גֵּרְשֹׁם. Since the ban was not all-inclusive and is lifted in some cases, may it be waived in some of the above cases, either by means of הֶתֵּר מֵאָה רַבָּנִים or by claiming that it was never intended for such cases (see *Mishpeṭei 'Uzi'el, E.H.*, no. 1)?

In some cases, utilizing the principle of זָכִין לְאָדָם שֶׁלֹּא בְּפָנָיו (i.e., that we may confer a benefit upon a person when he is not present), there is also the possibility of the husband or the *Bet Din* appointing a שָׁלִיחַ לְקַבָּלָה to accept a *geṭ* on the wife's behalf.

In many cases this principle cannot be applied to the appointing of a *shaliaḥ leqabbalah*, since the granting of a *geṭ* confers a חוֹבָה (disadvantage) as well as a זְכוּת (benefit)—i.e., while it permits the wife to remarry, which is a benefit, it also deprives her of the right to live with her divorced husband, which is a loss, and hence the *zekhut* is incomplete. However, if the wife has already obtained a civil divorce, the right to live with the husband no longer exists, since it is forbidden by civil law (דִּינָא דְמַלְכוּתָא). In such cases, the principle of זָכִין לְאָדָם שֶׁלֹּא בְּפָנָיו can be applied, since the *zekhut* conferred upon the wife by the granting of a *geṭ* will be complete (Rudner, *Mishpeṭei Ishut*, p. 107; *Mishpeṭei 'Uzi'el, E.H.*, no. 1).

Moreover, in some cases a wife who refuses to consent can be considered a מוֹרֶדֶת, a rebellious woman, and thus the husband can be allowed to remarry without a *geṭ* and without a *heter me'ah rabbanim* (see *E.H.* 77:2 in Rama; Rashdam, *Y.D.* 140, 142–44; Feinstein, *Igrot Mosheh, E.H.*, no. 2, 120; for further discussion, see below, p. 498).

According to the Rama, the custom in some communities, if the wife apostatized, was to divorce her by a means of a גֵּט עַל יְדֵי זִכּוּי (*E.H.* 1:10; there is an extensive literature on this subject, including the following: *Otsar Haposqim*, 1:75; Schmelkes, *Beit Yitsḥaq, E.H.* 1, no. 104; *'Arukh Hashulḥan, E.H.* 1:30, 31; Spektor, *'Ein Yitsḥaq, E.H.*, no. 1; Rashdam, *Y.D.*, nos. 120, 110; *Mishpeṭei 'Uzi'el, E.H.*, no. 1; Reisher *Shevut Ya'aqov*, sec. 1, no. 120; Feinstein, *Igrot Mosheh, E.H.*, no. 115:2; Stern, "Sha'ar Halakhah," p. 400; Rudner, *Mishpeṭei Ishut*, p. 117; Panet, *Avnei Tsedeq, E.H.*, no. 26).

Since the weight of opinion is to allow a גֵּט עַל יְדֵי זִכּוּי, this has become the current practice. For the woman's sake, so that she will be eligible to remarry under Jewish law, its use has been advocated in cases where the husband can be allowed to remarry without a *get*, as when the wife is declared a מוֹרֶדֶת (*Otsar Haposqim*, 1:76).

The procedure is the same as with a regular *get*, except that at the end, instead of giving the *get* to his wife, the husband appoints a שְׁלִיחַ לְקַבָּלָה, gives him the *get*, and says: "You, *Ploni ben Ploni*, acquire this *get* in behalf of my wife, *Plonit bat Ploni*, and receive in her behalf, and by your acceptance, my wife, *Plonit bat Ploni*, shall be divorced from me, as of now, and be permitted to any man." The agent replies: "I acquire this *get* to get possession of it on behalf of *Plonit bat Ploni*, your wife."

While it facilitates the granting of a *get* where the woman is unjustifiably recalcitrant, this procedure poses an ethical problem: the husband is given an advantage that is not given to the wife, since in a case where the husband refuses to grant a *get*, there is no waiving of the חֵרֶם דְּרַבֵּנוּ גֶּרְשֹׁם. By law the husband must personally order the writing of the *get*, and if he refuses, there is no other recourse. In Israel the courts are empowered to penalize a man who refuses to grant a *get*. If he refuses to yield even when penalized, and there are such cases on record, we still face the problem of freeing the woman from becoming an ʻAgunah.

This is an age-old problem with many ramifications, some of which have already been treated under the subject of ʻAgunah (see above, chap. 32). We discussed the classic difficulties caused by an "act of God," i.e., where the situation is not of our making but is the result of a lack of knowledge as to whether the husband is dead or still alive. As for the problem created by recalcitrance, while it is understandable that the rabbinic authorities were extremely scrupulous in matters of marriage and divorce, it is yet amazing that they were reluctant, and still are reluctant, to use the instruments that talmudic law made available to remedy this situation: annulment and premarital agreement.

There have been many valiant efforts to find ways of reestablishing the use of these instruments, but they invariably meet with a solid wall of opposition from the rabbinate (see Freimann, *Seder Qiddushin Wenissu'in*; Lubetzky, *Ein Tenai Benissu'in;* Berkovits, *Tenai Binissu'in Uvaget;* Kasher, "Beʻinyan Tenai Benisu'in"; *teshuvah* on *tenai beqiddushin* in Law Committee Archives; Greenberg, "And He Writes Her a Bill of Divorcement").

The latest effort on the part of the Rabbinical Assembly was in 1968, when the Law Committee adopted an antenuptial agreement signed by the man and the woman in which they agree that if the marriage should end with a civil divorce, and one of the parties refuses to agree to the granting of a *geṭ*, the marriage should retroactively become null and void (see below, p. 507, for the form used; see also the *teshuvah* in the Law Committee Archives).

This still leaves the problem of those who have not signed such a prenuptual agreement. Further, there are many who have no halakhic objections to this solution, but on aesthetic grounds, and because of אַל תִּפְתַּח פֶּה לְשָׂטָן (so as not to invite misfortune), are reluctant to discuss matters of divorce just before the wedding.

A perfect solution will come when a way is found to empower the *Bet Din* to issue an annulment in such cases.

4. Heter Me'ah Rabbanim

Another difficult situation arises when either husband or wife becomes afflicted with mental illness and can no longer function as a normal spouse. According to Jewish law, a person stricken with insanity has no legal capacity and thus cannot contract marriage; if contracted, such a marriage is null and void (B. *Yev.* 112b; *E.H.* 44:2). The problem arises when two normal persons contract a marriage, meeting all the legal requirements, and subsequently one of them is stricken with insanity.

Even in the era when Jewish law permitted a husband to divorce his wife without her consent, the talmudic sages would not permit divorce in such cases, lest people take advantage of a stricken woman once she was no longer under her husband's protection (B. *Yev.* 113). It is evident, however, that it would be unjust to tie a person down permanently to a partner stricken with insanity, especially where the welfare of a family is involved. Hence, in the case of a husband, the law has been very lenient in its interpretation of insanity, ruling that if he has moments of sanity—and sanity, too, is interpreted broadly—and orders a *geṭ* be written, the *geṭ* may be written and is valid (*E.H.* 121:3).

In the case of a wife, a waiver of the חֵרֶם דְּרַבֵּנוּ גֵּרְשֹׁם is invoked by means of a הֶתֵּר מֵאָה רַבָּנִים (see *E.H.* 1:10 in Rama, and in *B.H.* 22, quoting the *Kol Bo* and the BaḤ; see also *Beit Shmuel*, ibid., subsec. 23). A document is drawn up by the *Bet Din* (see below, p. 508, for a text) describing the condition, as attested by competent physicians, that makes it difficult to live with the woman, and the grounds for the man's urgent need to remarry. This document must be approved and signed by a hundred rabbis.

It is understood in such cases that the rights of the patient are not prejudiced and the obligation of proper care is not minimized in any way. The hundred signatories need not all be ordained rabbis; lay persons who are knowledgeable in the law are also eligible (*E.H.* 1:10; *Otsar Haposqim,* vol. 1, p. 8, sec. 14). Since the signatures may be solicited by mail, the signers need not be present at the *Bet Din* (*Maharam Shick, E.H.* 2). The signatories must reside in at least three different countries or provinces; in the United States, it is accounted valid if they reside in three different states (*Kol Bo*).

Some authorities required that a *geṭ* be written and deposited with a third party, to be delivered to the woman if she should become normal again (*Kol Bo;* BaḤ on *E.H.* 1:10). In general, however, this procedure is not followed nowadays.

5. Appendix

הרשאה ראשונה

בפנינו עדים חתומי מטה בשבת לירח בשנת חמשת אלפים
ושבע מאות לבריאת עולם למנין שאנו מנין כאן בנו יארק, מתא דיתבא על כיף ימא ועל
נהר האדסן, מסר הבעל גט כריתות ביד
להוליכו לאשתו וליתן אותה לידה וכך
אמר הבעל הנזכר לעיל לשלוחו הנזכר לעיל הולך גט זה לאשתי
ותן אותו לידה בכל מקום שתמצאנה ותהא־ידך כידי ועשייתך כעשייתי ופיך כפי ודיבורך
כדיבורי ונתינתך כנתינתי ונותן אני לך רשות לעשות שליח בחריקאך ושליח שליח ושליח אחר
שליח אפילו עד מאה שלוחים ואפילו בלא אונס ואפילו על ידי הבי דואר עד שיגיע גט זה לידה
ותיכף שיגיע גט זה ביד אשתי הנזכרת מידך או מיד שליח שלוחך אפילו עד מאה
שלוחים תהא מגורשת בו ממני ומותרת לכל אדם והגט שנעשה עליו הנזכר לעיל שליח להולכה ככל
הכתוב למעלה נכתב ונחתם בנו יארק מתא דיתבא על כיף ימא ועל נהר האדסן בשבת
לירח בשנת חמשת אלפים ושבע מאות לבריאת עולם ועדיו החתומים בו
ובפנינו ביטל הבעל הנזכר לעיל כל מודעות שמסר על גט זה וגם
בפנינו קבל הבעל הנזכר לעיל בכל חומר ובשבועת התורה שלא לבטל את הגט ולא את השליחות
ומה שראינו ונעשה בפנינו כתבנו וחתמנו והכל שריר וקים.

נאום עד

נאום עד

במותב תלתא בי דינא כחדא הוינא וחתמו באנפנא תרי סהדי ואשרנוהו וקיימנוהו כדחזי.

נאום דיין

נאום דיין

נאום דיין

הרשאה שניה

במותב תלתא בי דינא כחדא הוינא בשבת לירח בשנת חמשת אלפים ושבע מאות לבריאת עולם למנין שאנו מנין כאן בנוא יארק מתא דיתבא על כיף ימא ועל נהר האדסן ואתא לקדמנא ובידו גט ששלח הבעל לגרש בו את אשתו והביא לפנינו הרשאה מקויימת שעשאו הבעל הנזכר לעיל שליח להוליך גט זה לאשתו הנזכרת לעיל ונכתב בהרשאה שנותן לו רשות לעשות שליח ושליח שליח אפילו עד מאה שלוחים ואפילו בלא אונס ואפילו שלא בפניו ואפילו על ידי הבי דואר ועל פי כח זה מנה בפנינו את להיות שליח בחריקאו וכך אמר בפנינו אני ממנה על פיכם ובפניכם את בכל מקום שיהא נמצא להיות שליח בחריקאי להוליך גט זה להאשה וליתן אותו לידה בכל מקום שימצאנה ותהא ידו כידי ופיו כפי ודבורו כדיבורי ושלוחו כשלוחי ונתינתו כנתינתי ונותן אני לו רשות לעשות שליח בחריקאו אפילו עד תשעים ותשעה שלוחים אפילו שלא בפניו אפילו על ידי בי דואר אפילו בלא אונס עד שיגיע הגט לידה בכל מקום שימצאנה ותיכף כשיגיע גט זה לידה מידו או מיד שלוחו או מיד שליח שלוחו אפילו עד תשעים ותשעה שלוחים תהא מגורשת בו מבעלה ומותרת לכל אדם וגט זה בפני נכתב ובפני נחתם וגט זה שנעשה עליו שליח להולכה ככל הכתוב למעלה נכתב ונחתם בנוא יארק מתא דיתבא על כיף ימא ועל נהר האדסן בשבת לירח שנת חמשת אלפים ושבע מאות לבריאת עולם ועדיו החתומים בו וסימני הגט הם אלו ובפנינו בטל השליח הראשון שנזכר לעיל כל מודעות אם מסר על שליחות זה גם קבל עליו בחרם ובשבועת התורה שלא לבטל לא את השליח ולא את השליחות ומה שראינו ושמענו ונעשה על פינו ובפנינו כתבנו וחתמנו והכל שריר וקיים.

נאום דיין
נאום דיין
נאום דיין

Text of Dr. Boaz Cohen
גט כתבו ותנו

I,

residing at

husband of

residing at

Appoint

as scribe, and authorize and direct him to write

A GET, to wit, a bill of divorcement according to the Law of Moses and Israel, in my behalf, directed to, and for my wife.

AT THE INSTANCE of my wife, with the approval and under the authority of the central Beth Din of the Rabbinical Assembly of America, at New York, New York, or such other Beth Din, as it may designate.

I FURTHER APPOINT the following persons to act as witnesses to the execution of the GET, and authorize and direct them to affix their signatures thereto, as witnesses as required by the Beth Din, to wit

I FURTHER APPOINT the following person to act as my agent to wit and do hereby authorize him to deliver the GET in my behalf, unto my wife; this agent having the authority to appoint a substitute agent orally or in writing, who in turn shall have full power to designate a substitute.

I DO HEREBY direct my agent, as afore described, to deliver this GET to my wife, wherever he may find her, in accordance with the Law of Moses and Israel.

I FURTHER SOLEMNLY SWEAR that I will not revoke the stipulations, appointments, authorizations and directions contained herein.

I HAVE SOLEMNLY MADE the foregoing stipulations, appointments, authorizations and directions by word of mouth and in writing.

IN WITNESS WHEREOF, I hereby subscribe my name hereto this day of corresponding to

....
Husband's Name

....
Residence

....
City and State

....
Rabbi

We herby certify that the husband above mentioned made the stipulations, appointments, authorizations and directions by word of mouth and in our presence, and in the presence of each of us, and duly executed and signed this instrument, in the presence of each of us, and we affixed our signatures hereto as witnesses in his presence.

....
Witness

....
Witness

....
Rabbi

Agency Appointment for Jewish Divorce

I,

residing at

husband of

residing at

appoint known as
,as Scribe, and authorize and direct him to write a GET, that is a Bill of Divorce according to the Law of Moses and Israel, for me and my wife, for the purpose of Divorce.

I further appoint:

to act as witnesses to the execution of this GET, and authorize and direct them to affix their signatures thereto, as required by the Beth Din.

I further appoint , known as
as my agent, and authorize him to deliver this GET in my behalf to my wife, wherever he may find her, in accordance with the Law of Moses and Israel. This agent shall have authority to appoint a substitute agent, orally or in writing, who in turn shall have full power to designate substitutes without limitation.

I solemnly swear that I will not revoke the appointments, authorizations and directions contained therein. I have made the foregoing appointments, authorizations and directions by word of mouth and in writing, in witness whereof I hereby subscribe my name this day of (secular date) corresponding to (Hebrew date).

....

(Signature of Husband)

We certify that the above mentioned husband made the appointments, authorizations and directions by word of mouth in our presence, and signed this instrument in the presence of each of us, and we affixed our signatures hereto as witnesses in his presence.

....
(Rabbi)

....
(Witness)

....
(Witness)

Antenuptial Agreement

On the..day of..........., 19......, corresponding to

.... 57......, in..,

the Groom Mr...

and the Bride, M..,

of their own free will and accord enter into the following agreement with respect to their intended marriage

The groom made the following declaration to the bride:

"I WILL BETROTH AND MARRY YOU ACCORDING TO THE LAWS OF MOSES AND ISRAEL, SUBJECT TO THE FOLLOWING CONDITIONS.

a. IF OUR MARRIAGE BE TERMINATED BY DECREE OF THE CIVIL COURTS AND IF BY EXPIRATION OF SIX MONTHS AFTER SUCH A DECREE I GIVE YOU A DIVORCE ACCORDING TO THE LAWS OF MOSES AND ISRAEL (A GET) THEN OUR BETROTHAL (KIDDUSHIN) AND MARRIAGE (NISSUIN) WILL HAVE REMAINED VALID AND BINDING.

b. BUT IF OUR MARRIAGE BE TERMINATED BY DECREE OF CIVIL COURT AND IF BY EXPIRATION OF SIX MONTHS AFTER SUCH A DECREE I DO NOT GIVE YOU A DIVORCE ACCORDING TO THE LAWS OF MOSES AND ISRAEL (A GET) THEN OUR BETROTHAL (KIDDUSHIN) AND MARRIAGE (NISSUIN) WILL HAVE BEEN NULL AND VOID."

The bride replied to the groom:

"I CONSENT TO THE CONDITION YOU HAVE MADE."

We the undersigned, acting as a Beth Din, witnessed the oral statements and signatures of the groom and the bride.

....
(RABBI)

....

....

היתר מאה רבנים

הנה נועדנו יחדיו החתומים לעיין בדינא דהאי גברא משה בר׳ שמואל הכהן להתירו מחרם דרבינו גרשום למען יכול לישא אשה על אשתו פייגל בת ר׳ יצחק הלוי שנשתטית.

גופא דעובדא הכי הוה. בשנת תרע״ג לקח האיש משה בר שמואל הכהן את פייגל בת ר׳ יצחק הלוי לו לאשה בניו בריטען קאנעקטיקוט. בשנת תרע״ז נשתטית עד שהביאו אותה לבית משוגעים והיתה שם כחצי שנה. למרות עצת הרופאים הוציאו אותה משם. בשנת תר״פ הביאו עוד הפעם לבית המשוגעים והיא עוד שם עכשיו. בשנת תרצ״ט קבל הבעל גט על פי חוקי המדינה בערכאות קאנעקטיקוט מטעם שאשתו נשתגעה ועל פי עדות רופאים מומחים שאין לה שום תרופה והבעל קבל עליו לשלם סכום של שלשה דולר בכל שבוע כל ימי חיי אשתו לפרנסתה בבית החולים.

אמיתת הדברים הנ״ל נתברר לפננו מתוך הגט של דיניהם ומתוך דין וחשבון של הרופאים שהעידו בפני הערכאות ומתוך כתב תעודה של רופא המשוגעים שמסר לנו הבעל.

אחרי עיון הסכמנו להתיר למר משה בר שמואל הכהן לישא אשה על אשתו על פי הטעמים ובקיום התנאים אשר לפנינו. בשלחן ערוך אבן העזר סימן א. סעיף י׳. אמר הרמ״א דבנשטתית יש להתיר לו לישא אחרת. והכל בו כתב דאין להתיר חר״ג אלא עפ״י היתר מאה רבנים משלשה קהילות ומשלש מדינות. וכמה פוסקים הסכימו לזה. כמובא בפתחי תשובה. ור׳ יואל סירקיש כתב קבלתי עם שם הרב מוהר״ר שכנא ז״ל שהתיר לישא אחרת הלכה למעשה דבמקום מצות פו״ר לא תיקן ר״ג כל עיקר. גם חכמי ורנקבורט כתבו תשובה ארוכה ע״ז ונמנו להתיר והסכימו עמהם כל חכמי אשכנז ורוסיא והיינו דוקא ליחד לה כתובה וליתן גם ליד אחד להיות שליח להולכה שיהיה בידו הגט וכתובה עד שתשתפה ומכל מקום כל זמן שלא נשתפית חייב ליחד לה בית בפני עצמה ושישמרה ממנהג הפקר וליתן מזונותיה וחייב בתנאי כתובה כדברי הרמ״א ז״ל. מיהו ראיתי מרבותי שקבלו גם הם מגדולי עולם שיציעו הענין לפני הגדולים שבאותו דור ויסכימו בהיתר זה ולחתמו מאה רבנים על אותו הסכמה. ומיהו הערוך השלחן שהוא פוסק אחרון כתב: וכמה מהגדולים כתבו שאין צריך כלל להשלשת הגט ואיזה תועלת יש בו והרי עד שתשתפה אינה מגורשת ולכשתשתפה יכתוב לה אז גט ואי משום שלא ירצה אז ליתן לה גט א״כ מה מועיל השלשתו הלא ביכלתו לבטל את הגט והרי אז יכופו ליתן גט... וכן המנהג אצלנו.

הנה הבעל הסכים לתת גט פטורין כדת משה וישראל על הוצאותיו כשתשתפה וליתר שאת נתן וועקסיל בחתימת ידו בעד השלמת סך הכתובה וגם הבטיח לשלם שלשה דולר בכל שבוע בעד פרנסת אשתו:

לכן הסכמנו להתיר בלי שום פקפוק בצרופא דמאה רבנים להבעל הנ״ל לישא אשה על אשתו על סמך הבטחתו לתת גט לכשתשתפה ועל סמך הוועקסיל בעד השלמת הכתובה דנדוניא ותוספת כתובה במשולש בידי הרב יצחק קליין ויען שאין שום חשש שתצא מבית החולים במצבה הנוכחי וגם ישלם את הסך הנ״ל כל זמן שהיא תהיה שמה מבקשים אנו מאה רבנים דג׳ מדינות אשר יגיעו דברינו אליהם שיצטרפו עמנו לדבר מצוה ולמעוטי תקלה ופרצה בישראל.

פה ספרינגפילד ד׳ שבט תש״ב

____

____

____

על פי הכתוב ומפורש לעיל הננו מסכימים גם כן להתיר להבעל הנ״ל לישא אשה על אשתו הנ״ל.

UNIT XXXVI

FAMILY PURITY (TOHORAT HAMISHPAḤAH) (I)

Introduction
Niddah
Laws of Niddah
Ṭevilah

XXXVI.
Family Purity (I)

1. Introduction

"Do not come near a woman during her period of uncleanness to uncover her nakedness" (Lev. 18:19).

"If a man lies with a woman in her infirmity and uncovers her nakedness, he has laid bare her flow and she has exposed her blood flow; both of them shall be cut off from among their people" (Lev. 20:18).

"Rabbi Akiba said: 'Happy are you, Israel! Before whom do you make yourselves pure? Before your Father in Heaven. As it is written: "The miqweh [hope] of Israel is the Lord" [Jer. 17:13]. Just as the miqweh makes clean those who are unclean, so the Holy One makes Israel clean'" (M. *Yoma* 8:9).

"All things die and are reborn continually. The plant which bows its head to the earth leaves its life capsulized in the dormant seed. In our own bodies, death and regeneration proceed cell by cell. Our fingernails grow, die, and are discarded; our hair also. Our skins slough off dead cells, while a tender new layer forms below the surface. Within us our organs repair and renew themselves repeatedly. Throughout each teeming and dying body, moreover, flows an undying spirit. It is confined to no single area, but, as the sages taught, it 'fills the body as the ocean fills its bed.' That spirit is the soul. Only a conscious being has a soul. Of what is such a being conscious? He is aware of himself. He is aware also of his own growth processes and of his history. Our consciousness tells us that we are created beings and so are mortal. Our soul tells us that we are the image of the Creator and so cannot be mortal. Our knowledge of ourselves, then, is paradoxical. How do we reconcile it and make ourselves whole? Jews solve the paradox with the ritual cycle of *tumah* and *taharah*, in which we act out our death and resurrection" (Adler, in *Jewish Catalog*, p. 167).

Of the laws of *ṭum'ah* and *ṭohorah*, to which so much space is devoted in the Torah and the Talmud, only the laws governing טָהֳרַת הַמִּשְׁפָּחָה (family purity) are still relevant. This is not by accident. A prominent Jewish scholar writes: "The preservation of the menstrual laws alone, with their restrictive regulations entirely unimpaired, is not to be explained as being due to their having become ingrained into the sexual habits of the Jewish people, still less on grounds of their supposed hygienic justification. It is rather a conscious emphasis on, and an attempt at the inculcation in a particularly significant area of human interest, of that self-discipline which must be—in all aspects of life—an integral element in the Jewish ideal of cultivating 'holiness' (Kedushah)" (Loewe, *Position of Women in Judaism,* p. 48).

Hence, we must treat these laws from the aspect of holiness and wholesome family relationships.

The much heralded "sexual revolution," which our generation sees as espousing a "new" philosophy of sex, is in reality old-fashioned libertinism with an academic degree attached to it. The "new morality" is neither new nor morality, but rather the old immorality that reappears from time to time and seeks legitimation. It creates more problems than it solves. In many cases it leads to the undermining of the fabric of the family and the vulgarization of sex, or at best its trivialization. Hence, there is the urgency of reaffirming the traditional Jewish sexual morality.

Modern man is heir to two conflicting traditions neither of which is Jewish: on the one hand, the rebirth of the old paganism with its absolute-pleasure principle, which found its extreme expression in the sacred prostitutes of Canaan and the debaucheries of ancient Rome; and on the other, the Christian reaction to the excesses of paganism and its unbridled sexual laxity—sex became identified with original sin, and celibacy was regarded as the ideal form of life.

Modern man, while opting for pagan libertinism, also suffers a guilty conscience because of his Christian heritage. The children of Israel identify with contemporary civilization and are thus beneficiaries of its triumphs and victims of its aberrations. In the sexual area they are innocent sufferers, because Judaism is free of both extremes. It rejects the espousal of uncontrolled sexual expression that paganism preaches, and also Christianity's claim that all sexual activity is inherently evil (see Gordis, *Sex and the Family in the Jewish Tradition;* Lamm, *A Hedge of Roses;* also *Our Bodies, Ourselves,* p. 24).

Jewish marriage is based on a healthy sexual viewpoint that rejects the two extremist principles, and so are the regulations governing the conjugal relationship between husband and wife, *ṭohorat hamishpaḥah,* the purity of family life. We shall expand on this under three headings: *niddah, ṭevilah,* and miqweh.

2. Niddah

Niddah is the term applied to the menstrual woman, who is forbidden to have any intimacy with her husband. It literally means "separation," i.e., she who is separated or isolated from her husband.

The laws of *niddah* are based on Leviticus 15:19–33, 18:19, and 20:18. These laws appear under two aspects. On the one hand, they are an integral part of the extensive code dealing with ritual defilement; on the other, they bear the aspect of moral purity. We have already mentioned that while the laws of ritual defilement are not operative today, those of *niddah* have been retained, but it is the ideal of moral purity that is stressed.

Before explaining the rules, we must describe the anatomy of the female reproductive organs and the physiology of menstruation.

The female reproductive organs are commonly divided into two groups, the external and the internal. The former are the vulva and the vagina; the latter, the uterus, tubes, and ovaries.

The vagina is a musculomembranous canal which connects the vulva with the uterus.

The uterus is a hollow, pear-shaped, thick-walled, muscular organ which is situated in the pelvis, almost at a right angle to the vagina, with the bladder below and in front of it. It is divisible into a *corpus,* or body, and a *cervix,* or neck.

The Fallopian tubes are two musculomembranous canals which transport the ova from the ovaries to the uterus.

The ovaries are two ovoid bodies which constitute the genital glands of the female (see Novak, *Novak's Textbook of Gynecology,* pp. 14–16).

Menstruation (or cutamenia) has been defined as physiological bleeding from the endometium (the lining of the uterus) that recurs periodically in regular patterns. The elaborate preparation for possible pregnancy, which is initiated by endocrine stimulation to provide for local tissue growth and blood vessel alteration, as well as histochemical changes within the genital tract, also produces effects that are manifest throughout the whole organism. The primary aim is the nidation of the ovum. Menstruation is nature's way of expressing her frustration as well as her persistence (Parsons and Sommers, *Gynecology,* p. 198).

The length of the menstrual period follows a fairly constant pattern for any given woman. The average is 4.6 days, with variations from 2 to 8 days (ibid., p. 202).

One of the most striking features of menstruation is the change in emotional stability. Most women exhibit increased nervousness at this time (ibid., p. 203).

A clinical impression also exists that the body has less resistance to infection during menstruation (ibid., p. 204).

Since physiological changes take place in the woman prior to menstruation, she is able to feel or sense when her period is approaching; as it were, she is warned. This warning is sometimes accompanied by pain.

3. Laws of Niddah

Most women experience their menstrual flow at regular, fixed times, such as the identical day of the month, or at a specified interval of days, or in the wake of an outward physical happening, and the like.

A woman who has a regular period should cease having intercourse with her husband as soon as she feels the approach of menstruation (*Y.D.* 184:2).

The appearance of a speck of blood issuing from the womb (uterus), whether or not at the regular period, renders a woman a *niddah* (*Y.D.* 183:1).

Any reddish color, whether it be dark or rosy, in fact any color inclined toward being red, even if it be blackish, is considered menstrual flow (*Y.D.* 188:1). This is due to the fact that while the composition of the menstrual discharge is chiefly blood, the discharge also contains endometrical desquamation in varying stages of degeneration, some of it viable cervical mucus, degenerated vaginal epithelium, and a variety of bacteria. Since 75 percent of the menstrual discharge is blood, it is characteristically dark red (Parsons and Sommers, *Gynecology,* p. 203).

The menstrual flow comes from the uterus; therefore, if there is reason to believe that a discharge came from another source, e.g., from a wound in the vaginal canal or in any other part of the reproductive organs, it is ascribed to the wound (*Y.D.* 187:5).

If there are stains on a woman's undergarments or bedding, and there is suspicion that it issued from the uterus, she is rendered a *niddah* (*Y.D.* 190:11). Here too, if the stain can be ascribed to another source, it is (*Y.D.* 190:18).

A woman is rendered a *niddah* only by a flow of blood and not by any other fluid, even if it issues from the uterus (*Y.D.* 188:1).

The menstrual period is regarded as lasting a minimum of five days, the day on which the flow starts counting as the first day.

After these five days, or after the cessation of the menstrual flow in cases where menstruation lasts longer, the woman counts seven "clean days," i.e., seven full days of twenty-four hours each, during which there is no menstrual flow, and then immerses herself in a miqweh (*Y.D.* 196:1). The first day begins at sunset, and it is not counted unless the woman made the proper examination for the presence of blood (ibid.).

If a woman sees menstrual blood during these seven days, she must start to count the seven days again, until seven uninterrupted days pass without a flow (*Y.D.* 196:10).

During the days of menstruation and the seven "clean days" it is proper for husband and wife to sleep in separate beds (*Y.D.* 195:6).

A bride becomes subject to the laws of *niddah* immediately before marriage. Therefore, either when the last menstrual flow before her wedding has ceased, or immediately prior to the wedding, she should observe seven clean days, then go to the miqweh for immersion. This should be taken into consideration when setting the date of the wedding (*Y.D.* 192:1–4).

If there is blood because of the breaking of the hymen when the marriage is consummated, the bride becomes a *niddah* on the nuptial night and must count four (not five) unclean days and seven clean days (*Y.D.* 193:1).

Birth also renders a woman *niddah*. She begins to count the seven clean days as soon as there is no longer any blood flow and no blood stains. Before she may go to the miqweh for the required immersion, however, there is a minimum of seven days in the case of a male child and of fourteen days in the case of a female child (*Y.D.* 194:1). This does not apply to birth by Caesarean section (*Y.D.* 194:14).

A miscarriage is accounted as a birth only if it occurs more than forty days after conception. If it occurs sooner, it is considered as if the woman is seeing blood under normal circumstances (*Y.D.* 194:2).

Pregnant women and some nursing mothers do not have menstrual periods. Hence, beginning three months after the onset of pregnancy, even a woman with a regularly recurring period is not subject to the laws of *niddah*, but she still must be careful and, like a woman who does not have a regular menstrual period, must watch for any appearance of bloodstains (*Y.D.* 189:33). Today, since reliable pregnancy tests make it possible for a woman to find out much earlier whether she is pregnant, the three months that were deemed necessary for making certain that pregnancy had occurred may no longer be necessary.

In the case of a nursing mother, the sources give twenty-four months as the period during which there is no menstruation (*Y.D.* 189:33). Later authorities deem this law inapplicable. Today the nursing period is often much shorter (see Sternbuch, *Torat Hamishpaḥah,* p. 36). Medical science sheds light on the subject as follows: The mammary glands secrete increasingly large quantities of milk for six to nine months. Later the output diminishes gradually, and it ceases twelve to eighteen months after delivery. If the child continues to be nursed, and sucks vigorously, lactation is kept up for a longer time. If the offspring are not nursed, the mammary glands rapidly undergo involution, and the same process takes place whenever lactation is suspended. The gland retrogresses and in a few days returns to a condition similar to that which existed before pregnancy (Hoosay, *Human Physiology,* pp. 705 f.).

After her menopause, a woman ceases to menstruate. The change occurs gradually. The reproductive organs undergo changes that cause a diminished flow of shorter duration at periods spread further apart (Parson and Sommers, *Gynecology,* pp. 1045 ff.). The codes speak of the passing of three periods without the appearance of menstrual blood as a sign that menstruation has ceased (*Y.D.* 189:28).

4. Ṭevilah

When the state of *niddah* ceases, the woman is required to immerse herself in a miqweh; if she does not immerse herself, she is not released from the restriction of *niddah* (*Y.D.* 197:1).

The טְבִילָה (immersion) should take place on the night after the completion of the seven clean days. A woman should not immerse herself in daytime even if it is already the eighth or ninth day, except in an emergency, e.g., if it is dangerous to go to the miqweh at night (*Y.D.* 197:3, 4).

Before the immersion, the woman must cleanse herself thoroughly so that no foreign body clings to her and prevents the water from coming into direct contact with her body (*Y.D.* 199:1). There should not be the slightest particle of dirt or foreign object on her body nor may her hair be tangled (*Y.D.* 199:1–2).

Since many women nowadays dye their hair and polish their fingernails, the question was raised whether hair dye and fingernail polish constitute a barrier between the water and the woman's body. Knowing how difficult it would be to make women remove their nail polish or hair-coloring agents, the later *posqim* have taken the lenient view, ruling that hair dye and nail polish become part of the body to which they are applied, and thus immersion without their removal is permitted (*Y.D.* 198:17; Ṭaz, ibid., no. 21; Shakh, ibid., sec. 21; *Aḥi'ezer,* vol. 3, resp. 33; Stern, "Sha'ar Halakhah," p. 327).

In places where it would be embarrassing for a woman to immerse herself in the nude, a loose-fitting garment may be worn (*Y.D.* 198:46 in Shakh, sec. 56).

The woman should immerse herself in a posture that permits the water to come in contact with every part of her body. Therefore, she should not stand erect or bend too much, because in both postures certain folds of the body remain unexposed to the water. Rather, she should stoop slightly, with her legs slightly spread, and then immerse herself (*Y.D.* 198:38).

If someone holds on to a woman during the immersion, the hold should be loose so that the water may come between the hand of the holder and the woman immersing herself (*Y.D.* 198:28).

As with all religious commandments, there is a blessing to be recited at the immersion: אֲשֶׁר קִדְּשָׁנוּ בְּמִצְוֹתָיו וְצִוָּנוּ עַל הַטְּבִילָה. The practice is for the woman to immerse herself once, recite the blessing, and then immerse herself again (*Y.D.* 200:1 in Rama and in Shakh, sec. 1, and the Sheloh quoted in *B.H.* 1).

UNIT XXXVII

FAMILY PURITY (II)

THE MIQWEH

XXXVII.
Family Purity (II)
The Miqweh

A miqweh, as the term is currently used, is a gathering of water for ritual immersion. Nowadays ritual immersion is required for conversion to Judaism and for a *niddah*.

In order to be suitable for such immersions, a miqweh must satisfy the following requirements:

1. It must contain at least forty *se'ah* of water (*Y.D.* 201:1).
2. It must be constructed in such a manner as to permit complete immersion in one act (*Y.D.* 201:1).
3. The container (i.e., the hollow that contains the water) may not be a portable receptacle; rather, it must be built permanently into the ground, making it an integral part of the earth (*Y.D.* 201:10).
4. The minimum forty *se'ah* of the miqweh must be "natural" water, i.e., its source must be natural (*Y.D.* 201:3).

Now to explain:

1. Forty *se'ah* is equivalent in our measurements to about 191 gallons (*She'arim Metsuyanim Bahalakhah* 162:14:1; Telushkin, *Ṭohorat Hamayim,* p. 21). This is an amount sufficient for a person to immerse himself completely.
2. In order to enable a person to immerse himself completely in one act, the sources prescribe that the dimensions of the miqweh must be equivalent to one cubit by one cubit to the height of three cubits (*Y.D.* 201:1). This is equivalent to 24½ inches by 24½ inches to a height of 77½ inches (actually, to be practical, 24 by 24 by 72; *Ṭohorat Hamayim,* p. 142). In order to make complete immersion in one act possible and comfortable, the level of the water should be about 10 to 12 inches above the navel of the person immersing,

usually about 3½ feet deep (*She'arim Metsuyanim Bahalakhah* 162:14:2; Miller, *Secret of the Jews,* p. 345).

3. A portable receptacle may not be used for a miqweh because of the principle that no object that can contract impurity (מְקַבֵּל טוּמְאָה) can be used in connection with a miqweh (*Y.D.* 201:6). It would not be considered a natural body of water and would go counter to the idea of immersion being a symbol of life since *ṭum'ah* is the symbol of death.
4. By "natural water" we mean to exclude "drawn water" (מַיִם שְׁאוּבִים), i.e., a miqweh artificially filled by bucket, or by metal tubing that brings the water above the ground and directly into the miqweh (*Y.D.* 201:3). This only applies to the first forty *se'ah.* Thus, if a miqweh is filled with a little less than forty *se'ah* of natural water, to which three *log* of drawn water is added, it becomes disqualified (*Y.D.* 201:15). If, however, the miqweh already contains the required forty *se'ah* of natural water, the addition of any amount of drawn water does not disqualify it (*Y.D.* 201:15). This rule applies only to water and not to other liquids. Hence, if a miqweh is filled with a little less than forty *se'ah* of natural water, and then some other liquid, such as wine or milk, or ice or snow (which then melts) is poured into it to complete the required forty *se'ah,* it does not become disqualified thereby (*Y.D.* 201:29, 30).

The natural sources of water would be the following:

1. Rainwater.
2. Springs: this would include natural bodies of water, such as rivers, lakes, and oceans.
3. Snow: of course the forty *se'ah* must be measured after the snow has melted.
4. Ice, both natural and artificial. It is understood that immersion does not take place in the ice or snow. Rather, they are put into receptacles and transported to a miqweh. In this case, care must be taken that the receptacles have holes in them to prevent any accumulation of water from the melting of the ice or snow, because such water is drawn water and would disqualify the miqweh (*Y.D.* 201:7). When the ice or snow is already in the miqweh, it is allowed to melt.

There is a difference of opinion regarding artificial ice. Some authorities forbid it since before it was frozen it was already in the category of drawn water and freezing does not change its status (Deutsch, *Peri Hasadeh,* vol. 3, resp. 253; *Imrei Yosher,* vol. 1, resp. 148). Most authorities, however, regard such water as natural (*Divrei Malki'el,* vol. 3; resp. 60, 67, 68; Grodsensky, *Aḥi'ezer,* vol. 3, resp. 33; Grünfeld, *Meharshag, Y.D.,* resp. 62; Zweig, *Porat Yosef,* vol. 1, resp. 8; Telushkin, *Ṭohorat Hamayim,* pp. 54–56).

It is wise to follow the suggestion that while artificial ice is permitted, it should be resorted to only when absolutely necessary. Otherwise rainwater should receive priority (*Avnei Neizer,* quoted in *Darkei Teshuvah, Y.D.* 201, subsec. 141).

It has been explained that natural water is required because water is a symbol of the life forces of the universe; by using it we therefore affirm that God alone is the author of life, and to Him and Him alone do we turn for continued life for us and our descendants after us. Man is not the absolute master of his life and destiny (see Lamm, *Hedge of Roses,* p. 88).

The channels which bring the natural water into the miqweh must be built in such a way that the means used are not objects that can contract ritual uncleanness (*Y.D.* 201:48). The most obvious example for this rule is the case of מַיִם שְׁאוּבִין, when the water is poured in by means of a vessel. It excludes, however, a number of other means, which we shall mention later.

With these principles and rules in mind, we can now proceed with instructions for the construction of a miqweh, taking into consideration both the requirements of Jewish law and what is feasible today, particularly in America (see accompanying illustrations for clarification of the following explanation).

The most common source of water for a miqweh is rainwater (*Y.D.* 201:42) from rooftops conveyed into a storage chamber (בּוֹר) built into the ground. The water stored in the *bor* must amount to at least forty *se'ah,* and it must be conveyed into the *bor* in such a way that it does not become drawn water (מַיִם שְׁאוּבִים) in the process (*Y.D.* 201:36, 44, 46, 48, 49). This can be effected by means of הַמְשָׁכָה, i.e., by the use of a continuous length of plastic, rubber, or concrete pipe without fittings. Many authorities permit the use of metal pipes, even with fittings and bends of 90 degrees, since these are not intended to gather water but rather to transfer it, and as such are not in the category of objects that can contract ritual impurity (see Telushkin, *Ṭohorat Hamayim,* pp. 148, 204 ff.). However, for the last 15 inches, the water should travel through a concrete trough 5 inches wide—which certainly, according to all opinions, cannot contract any ritual impurity. This is proper הַמְשָׁכָה, or transferring the water (*Y.D.* 201:45).

Usually, however, this chamber is not the one used for immersion. It is used for storing the water, and alongside it another structure is built which has a pool in which the ritual immersions (טְבִילָה) take place (*Y.D.* 201:17).

This may be filled with water from any source, usually from the local water supply system.

The water in the storage compartment is then connected to the water in the *ṭevilah* compartment by an opening in the wall separating the two compartments. The diameter of this opening should be at least 1½ inches (כִּשְׁפוֹפֶרֶת הַנּוֹד). The two waters thus mix, and thereby the water in the *ṭevilah* compartment is rendered fit for ritual immersion, since it is like water added to a miqweh that has the required forty *se'ah*.

This process can be repeated; i.e., the *ṭevilah* compartment may be emptied for hygienic reasons, refilled, and connected again with the water in the storage compartment. This process is termed הַשָּׁקָה (lit. "causing to kiss").

Another method is that after the storage compartment has been filled with the required amount of natural water, water from the local water system is allowed to flow directly into the storage compartment and to overflow into the *ṭevilah* compartment. This method is called זְרִיעָה (sowing).

A third method combines the הַשָּׁקָה and זְרִיעָה systems by having three compartments. The third compartment is just below the chamber that was described above, and it is also filled with the required forty *se'ah* of natural water in the prescribed manner. The waters in the upper and lower compartments are in permanent contact by means of a connecting hole. From here the above-described זְרִיעָה system is followed. The advantage of having a third chamber is that it combines the הַשָּׁקָה and זְרִיעָה systems, and thus it is always certain that there is a permanent supply of the required forty *se'ah* of natural water (see Telushkin, *Ṭohorat Hamayim; She'arim Metsuyanim Bahalakhah; Encyclopedia Talmudit,* s.v. "Hashakah").

The question of whether a swimming pool satisfies the requirement of a miqweh has been coming up more and more frequently. The problem arises especially in communities that do not have a regular miqweh, or in places where the miqweh is under sectarian or private control, and the policy of those who are in control makes it difficult for others to use it.

There is a distinction between private swimming pools, which are often built above ground, and public swimming pools, which are permanent structures built into the ground, very much like a miqweh.

We shall limit ourselves to public swimming pools, since as a rule these are built as permanent structures and attached to the ground. The water therein is conveyed in conveyers, not by hand, animal, or manpower, and they do contain the quantity of water required for a miqweh. There is no doubt that a swimming pool can be built to meet the strictest requirements of a miqweh. As a matter of fact, however, there are some authorities who maintain that public swimming pools are already constructed in a matter that meet the requirements of a miqweh (see R. Isaac Herzog, quoted in Telushkin, *Ṭohorat Hamayim,* p. 226; Miller, *Secret of the Jew,* p. 362 [Miller is not known as a halakhic authority, but his book was endorsed by Dr. Bernard Revel]; Kreitman, "May a Swimming Pool Be Used as a Mikvah?"). While the general practice has been to disqualify public swimming pools because of certain legal objections (see Telushkin, *Ṭohorat Hamayim,* loc. cit.; Rubenstein in *Miqweh Anthology,* p. 18), I believe that Rabbi Kreitman's answers to these strictures are valid. The Law Committee has accepted his responsum on the subject.

There are, however, some other objections to the use of a swimming pool.

1. There is the psychological point that people are more apt to consider the immersion a religious experience or a religious ritual if it takes place in a body of water specifically appointed for such a purpose, i.e., a miqweh.
2. There is also a practical consideration. The public nature of swimming pools involves an element of embarrassment which may lead to hasty immersions that do not fulfill the requirements of the law, or at least that are not done in the proper frame of mind. Some authorities apply these objections not only to swimming pools but also to lakes, oceans, and rivers (see Telushkin, *Ṭohorat Hamayim,* pp. 13, 14; *Qitsur Shulḥan 'Arukh* 162:5; *Y.D.* 198:34).
3. A third objection, which applies only when a pool is used for conversions, is that a deviation from the generally accepted practice may later cause hardship for the convert.

We should, therefore, insist on the use of a miqweh, resorting to the use of a swimming pool only when a miqweh is not available.

* * * *

"Rabbi Ḥananya ben 'Akashya said: 'God wanted to confer merit upon Israel; therefore did He give them an elaborate Torah with many commandments' " (M. *Mak.* 3:16).

Bibliography

This bibliography is arranged in two parts. The first lists books and articles in English and European languages (including Yiddish) and is arranged by author. The second list is limited to Hebrew references and is arranged by title.

Part I: English

Abrahams, Israel. *A Companion to the Authorised Daily Prayer Book.* London: Eyre & Spottiswoode, 1922.

———. *Hebrew Ethical Wills.* 2 vols. Philadelphia: Jewish Publication Society, 1926.

———. *Jewish Life in the Middle Ages.* 1896. Reprint. New York: Meridian Books, 1958.

Adler, Morris; Agus, Jacob; and Friedman, Theodore. "Responsum on the Sabbath." *Proceedings of the Rabbinical Assembly* 14 (1950), 112–137.

Adler, Rachel. "Tumah and Taharah—Mikveh." In *The Jewish Catalog,* by Richard Siegel, Michael Strassfeld, and Sharon Strassfeld, pp. 167–171. Philadelphia: Jewish Publication Society, 1973.

Agnon, Shmuel Yosef. *Days of Awe.* New York: Schocken Books, 1948.

Alony, Shulamith. *Rights of the Child in the Laws of the State of Israel.* Tel Aviv, 1964.

Amram, David Werner. *The Jewish Law of Divorce.* 2d ed. New York: Hermon Press, 1968.

Arzt, Max. *Justice and Mercy: Commentary on the Liturgy of the New Year and the Day of Atonement.*)ew York: Holt, Rinehart & Winston, 1963.

Baron, Salo W. *A Social and Religious History of the Jews.* 16 vols. to date. New York: Columbia University Press, 1952–.

Ben-Zvi, Itzhak. *The Exiled and the Redeemed.* Philadelphia: Jewish Publication Society, 1963.

Berliner, Abraham. *Randbemerkungen zum Täglischen Gebetbuche (Siddur).* 2 vols. Berlin: M. Poppelauer, 1909–12.

Berman, Jeremiah J. *A Study in the Cultural and Social Life of the Jewish People.* New York: Bloch, 1941.

Blumenthal, Aaron H. "Questionnaire on Conversion." *Conservative Judaism* 24:4 (Summer 1970), 43–47.

———, and Fink, Leon. "Converts of Questionable Status." *Proceedings of the Rabbinical Assembly* 30 (1966), 109–110.

Bohnen, Eli. "Converts of Questionable Status." *Proceedings of the Rabbinical Assembly* 30 (1966), 105–108.

Bokser, Ben Zion. "Birth Control." *Conservative Judaism* 16:2–3 (Winter–Spring 1962), 79–82.

———. *The High Holy Day Prayer Book.* New York: Hebrew Publishing Co. 1959.

———. *Judaism: Profile of a Faith.* New York: Knopf, 1963.

———. "The Sabbath Halachah—Travel and the Use of Electricity." *Proceedings of the Rabbinical Assembly* 14 (1950), 156–164.

Boston Women's Health Book Collective. *Our Bodies Ourselves.* 2d ed. New York: Simon & Schuster, 1976.

Brav, Stanley Rosenbaum, ed. *Marriage and the Jewish Tradition.* New York: Philosophical Library, 1951.

Bronstein, Harry. "The New Clinically Proven Mogen Circumcision Instrument." *American Journal of Obstetrics and Gynecology,* September 1956, p. 67.

Buckland, W. W. *A Manual of Roman Private Law.* 2d ed. Cambridge: At the University Press, 1957.

"Circumcision (Ablation)." *Medical Times* 80 (April 1952), 238–241.

Cohen, Boaz. "Report of the Chairman of the Committee on Jewish Law." *Proceedings of the Rabbinical Assembly* 10 (1946), 41–51.

———. "Report of the Committee on Jewish Law 'Jewish Law'." *Proceedings of the Rabbinical Assembly* 7 (1940), 27–35.

———. "Appendix on Civil Marriage." *Proceedings of the Rabbinical Assembly* 6 (1939), 141–145.

———, and Drob, Max, eds. "Supplement on Jewish Law." *Bulletin of the Rabbinical Assembly* 4 (January 1941), 9–12, 20.

Cohn, Jacob. *The Royal Table.* New York: Bloch, 1936.

Davidson, Israel. "Kol Nidre." *American Jewish Year Book 5684,* vol. 25 (1923–24), 180–194.

de Groot, J. M. M., et al. "Adoption." *Encyclopaedia of Religion and Ethics* 1, 105–115.

Dembo, Isaak Alexandrovich. *The Jewish Method of Slaughter.* London: Kegan, Paul, 1894.

Drachman, Bernard. "Habdalah." *Jewish Encyclopedia* 6, 118–119.

Dresner, Samuel H., and Siegel, Seymour. *The Jewish Dietary Laws.* New York: Burning Bush Press, 1959.

Dunsky, Samson, ed. and trans. (Yiddish). *Midrash Rabbah: Qoheleth.* Montreal, 1967.

———, ed. and trans. (Yiddish). *Midrash Rabbah: Ruth.* Montreal, 1962.

Elbogen, Ismar. *Der jüdische Gottesdienst in seiner geschichtlichen Entwicklung.* Leipzig, 1913.

Elman, Peter, ed. *Jewish Marriage.* London: Soncino Press, 1968.

Encyclopaedia Judaica. 16 vols Jerusalem: Keter Publishing House, 1972.

Encyclopaedia of Religion and Ethics. See Hastings, James, ed.

Epstein, Isidore. *The Responsa of Rabbi Solomon ben Adreth of Barcelona.* London: K. Paul, Trench, Trubner, 1925. Reprint. New York: KTAV, 1968.

Epstein, Louis. "Report of Committee on Jewish Law." *Proceedings of the Rabbinical Assembly* 6 (1939), 154–160.

———. *The Jewish Marriage Contract.* New York: Jewish Theological Seminary, 1927.

Falk, Ze'ev Wilhelm. *Jewish Matrimonial Law in the Middle Ages.* London: Oxford University Press, 1966.

———. "News in Israeli Family Law." *Dinei Israel* 3 (1972), 45–53.

Feldman, David M. *Birth Control in Jewish Law.* New York: New York University Press, 1968.

Feldman, William Moses. *Rabbinical Mathematics and Astronomy.* London: M. L. Cailingold, 1931. Reprint. New York: Hermon Press, 1965.

Finkelstein, Louis, ed. *Haggadah of Passover.* Trans. by Maurice Samuel. New York: Hebrew Publishing Co., 1942.

———. *Jewish Self-Government in the Middle Ages.* New York: Jewish Theological Seminary, 1924. Reprint. New York: Feldheim, 1964.

———, ed. *The Jews: Their History, Culture, and Religion.* 3d ed. 2 vols. New York: Harper & Bros, 1960.

———. *The Pharisees: The Sociological Background of Their Faith.* 3d ed. 2 vols. Philadelpia: Jewish Publication Society, 1962.

The Five Megilloth and Jonah: A New Translation. Intro. by H. L. Ginsberg. Philadelphia: Jewish Publication Society, 1969.

Fletcher, Joseph F. *Morals and Medicine.* Princeton: Princeton University Press, 1954.

Freid, Jacob, ed. *Jews and Divorce.* New York: KTAV, 1968.

Friedländer, Michael. *The Jewish Religion.* London, 1891. Reprint. New York: Pardes, 1946.

Friedman, Theodore, chairman. "Committee on Jewish Law and Standards, Teshuvah." *Proceedings of the Rabbinical Assembly* 18 (1954), 50–61.

Frieman, Donald. "Conversion or Convenience?" *Conservative Judaism* 24:4 (Summer 1970), 36–42.

Ginsburger, M. "Deux Pourims Locaux." *Hebrew Union College Annual* 10 (1935), 445–450.

Ginzberg, Louis. *Geonica.* 2 vols. New York, 1909. Reprint. New York: Hermon Press, 1968.

Goldman, Israel M. *The Life and Times of R. David Ibn Abi Zimra.* New York: Jewish Theological Seminary, 1970.

Goldschmidt, Ernst Daniel. *Die Pessach Haggada.* Berlin: Schocken, 1937. Jerusalem, 1947.

Goldstein, Israel. *Israel at Home and Abroad (1962–1972).* Jerusalem: R. Mass, 1973.

Goldstein, Sidney Emanuel. *Meaning of Marriage and Foundations of the Family.* New York: Bloch, 1940.

Goodblatt, Morris S. "Converting Because of Marriage Motives." *Conservative Judaism* 28:3 (Spring 1974), 30–40.

Gordis, Robert. *Judaism for the Modern Age.* New York: Farrar, Straus, & Cudahy, 1955.

———. *Sex and the Family in the Jewish Tradition.* New York: United Synagogue, 1967.

Gordon, Albert I. *In Times of Sorrow.* New York: United Synagogue, 1949.

Gottlieb, Nathan. *A Jewish Child Is Born.* New York: Bloch, 1960.

Greenberg, Simon. "And He Writes Her a Bill of Divorce." *Conservative Judaism* 24:3 (1970), 75–141.

Greenstone, Julius Hillel. *The Jewish Religion.* Philadelphia: Jewish Chautauqua Society, 1929.

Grunfeld, Isidor. *The Sabbath.* New York: Feldheim, 1959, 1972.

Güdemann, Moritz. *Geschichte des Erziehungswesens und der Kultur der abendländischen Juden.* 3 vols. Amsterdam: Philo Press, 1966. Vol. 3: *. . . der Juden in Deutschland.*

Guthrie, H. H., Jr. "Fast and Fasting." *Interpreter's Dictionary of the Bible* 2, 241–244.

Harlow, Jules, ed., for Rabbinical Assembly of America. *The Rabbi's Manual.* New York, 1965. (Hebrew title: *Liqqutei Tefillah*)

Hastings, James, ed. *Encyclopaedia of Religion and Ethics.* 13 vols. New York: Charles Scribner's Sons, 1912.

Hertz, Joseph Herman. *The Authorised Daily Prayer Book.* New York: Bloch, 1948.

———, ed. *The Pentateuch and Haftorahs.* London: Soncino, 1936.

Heschel, Abraham Joshua. *The Earth Is the Lord's.* New York: Henry Schuman, 1950. Reprint. New York: Harper Torchbooks, 1966.

———. *God in Search of Man.* New York: Farrar, Straus, & Cudahy, 1956.

———. *The Sabbath.* New York: Farrar, Straus, & Cudahy, 1951. Reprint. New York: Harper Torchbooks, 1966.

———. *Who Is Man?* Stanford: Stanford University Press, 1965.

Hirsch, Samson Raphael. *Horeb: A Philosophy of Jewish Laws and Observances.* London: Soncino, 1962.

Homa, Bernard. *Metsitsah.* London: 1966.

Houssay, Bernardo A. *Human Physiology.* New York: McGraw-Hill, 1955.

Horowitz, George. *The Spirit of Jewish Law.* New York: Central Book Co., 1953.

Idelsohn, Abraham Z. *Jewish Liturgy and Its Development.* New York: Holt, Rinehart & Winston, 1932.

Interpreter's Dictionary of the Bible. Ed. George A. Buttrick et al. 4 vols. and supplementary volume. New York and Nashville: Abingdon Press, 1962.

Jakobovits, Immanuel. *Jewish Law Faces Modern Problems.* New York: Yeshiva University Press, 1965.

———. *Jewish Medical Ethics.* New York: Philosophical Library, 1959.

———. *Order of the Jewish Marriage Service.* New York: Bloch, 1959.

Jewish Encyclopedia. 12 vols. New York and London: Funk &Wagnalls, 1902–7.

Jolowicz, Herbert F. *Roman Foundations of Modern Law.* Oxford: Clarendon Press, 1957.

Jörs, Paul. *Geschichte und System des Römischen Privatrechts.* Berlin: Julius Springer, 1927.

Joseph, Morris. *Judaism as Creed and Life.* New York: Bloch, 1920.

Justinian. *The Digest of Justinian.* 2 vols. Trans. Charles H. Monro., Vol. 2: ed. W. W. Buckland. Cambridge: At the University Press, 1904–9.

Kaplan, Mordecai. *Judaism as a Civilization.* 1934. Reprint. New York: Schocken Books, 1967.

———. *The Meaning of God in Modern Jewish Religion.* New York: Reconstructionist Press, 1937.

Karp, Abraham J. *The Jewish Way of Life.* Englewood Cliffs, N.J.: Prentice-Hall, 1962.

Kieval, Herman. *The High Holy Days: A Commentary on the Prayer Book of Rosh Hashanah.* New York: Burning Bush Press, 1959.

Klein, Andrew. *Laws of Mourning.* New Haven: Cong. Bnai Jacob, n.d.

Klein, Isaac. "The Case of Civil Marriage According to Jewish Law." *Proceedings of the Rabbinical Assembly* 5 (1933–38), 474–86.

———. "The Kashrut of Cheeses." *Conservative Judaism* 28:2 (Winter 1974), 34–46.

———. "The Marriage of a Kohen and a Giyoret." *Proceedings of the Rabbinical Assembly* 32 (1968), 219–223.

———. *Responsa and Halakhic Studies.* New York: KTAV, 1975.

———. "Swordfish." *Proceedings of the Rabbinical Assembly* 30 (1966), 111–115.

———. "Abortion and the Jewish Tradition." *Conservative Judaism* 24:3 (Spring 1970), 26–33.

———. "A Teshuvah on Autopsy." *Conservative Judaism* 13:1 (Fall 1958), 52–58.

Klein, Joseph. "The Covenant and Confirmation." *CCAR Journal* 13:6 (June 1966), 24–30.

Krauss, Samuel. "The Jewish Rite of Covering the Head." *Hebrew Union College Annual* 19 (1945), 121–168.

Kreitman, Benjamin. "The First Ten Years of the Committee on Law and Standards." *Proceedings of the Rabbinical Assembly* 22 (1958), 68–80.

———. "May a Swimming Pool Be Used as a *Mikvah?*" (Hebrew). *Proceedings of the Rabbinical Assembly* 33 (1969), 219–221.

Lamm, Norman. *A Hedge of Roses.* New York: Feldheim, 1966.

Landman, Isaac. "Confirmation." *Universal Jewish Encyclopedia* 3, 329–330.

Landsberg, Max, and Kohler, Kaufmann. "Confirmation, The Rite of." *Jewish Encyclopedia* 4, 219–220.

Lauterbach, Jacob Zallel. "The Ceremony of Breaking a Glass at Weddings." *Hebrew Union College Annual* 2 (1925), 351–380.

———. *Rabbinic Essays.* Cincinnati: Hebrew Union College Press, 1951.

———, *Studies in Jewish Law, Custom, and Folklore.* New York: KTAV, 1970.

———. "Worshipping with Covered Heads." In *Responsa of the CCAR,* ed. Jacob D. Schwarz, pp. 202–218. New York: Union of American Hebrew Congregations, 1954. Originally published in vol. 37 (1928) of *CCAR Yearbook,* 589–603.

Lerner, Max. *America as a Civilization.* New York: Simon & Schuster, 1957.

Levi, Leo. "On the Astronomical Aspects of Twilight in Halakha." In *'Ateret Tsevi: Jubilee Volume Presented in Honor of the 80th Birthday of Rabbi Dr. Joseph Breuer,* ed. Marc Breuer and Jacob Breuer, pp. 251–262. New York: Feldheim, 1962.

Levin, Solomon Isaac, and Boyden, Edward Allen. *The Kosher Code of the Orthodox Jew.* 1940. Reprint. New York: Hermon Press, 1969.

Lewin, Isaac; Munk, Michael L,; and Berman, Jeremiah J. *Religious Freedom: The Right to Practice Sheḥitah.* New York: Research Institute for Post-War Problems of Religious Jewry, 1946.

Loewe, Raphael. *The Position of Women in Judaism.* London: S.P.C.K. in conjunction with the Hillel Foundation, 1966.

MacCulloch, J. A. "Fasting (Introductory and Non-Christian)." In *Encyclopaedia of Religion and Ethics* 5, 759–765.

McKinney, William M. *The Consolidated Laws of New York.* Brooklyn: Edward Thompson.

Maimonides, Moses. *The Guide of the Perplexed.* Trans. and with notes by Shlomo Pines. Chicago and London: University of Chicago Press, 1963.

Malter, Henry. "Purim." *Jewish Encyclopedia* 10, 274–279.

Matt, Herschel. "Circumcision." *Program Notes of the Rabbinical Assembly* (November 1963), 1 f.

Maybaum, Ignaz. *The Face of God after Auschwitz.* Amsterdam: Polak & Van Gennep, 1965.

Metzger, Bruce M., ed. *The Apocrypha of the Old Testament.* New York: Oxford University Press, 1965.

Miller, David. *The Secret of the Jew.* Privately published. Oakland, Calif., 1930.

Miller, Albert R. *Meat Hygiene.* Philadelphia, 1958.

Millgram, Abraham Ezra. *Jewish Worship.* Philadelphia: Jewish Publication Society, 1971.

Moore, George Foot. *Judaism in the First Centuries of the Christian Era.* 3 vols. Cambridge: Harvard University Press, 1927.

Munk, Elie. *The World of Prayer.* 2 vols. New York: Feldheim, 1961–63.

Neulander, Arthur. "The Use of Electricity on the Sabbath." *Proceedings of the Rabbinical Assembly* 14 (1950), 165–171.

Novak, David. *Law and Theology in Judaism, First Series.* New York: KTAV, 1974.

Novak, Edmund R.; Jones, Georgeanna Seeger; and Jones, Howard N. *Novak's Textbook of Gynecology*. Baltimore: Williams & Wilkins, 1975.

Parsons, Langdon, and Sommers, Sheldon C. *Gynecology*. Philadelphia: W. B. Saunders, 1962.

Pieper, Josef. *Leisure: The Basis of Culture*. New York: Pantheon Books, 1952.

Ploscowe, Morris, and Freed, Doris J. *Family Law*. Boston: Little, Brown, 1963.

Preuss, Julius. *Biblisch-talmüdische Medizin*. 1911. Reprint. New York: KTAV, 1971.

Rabbinical Assembly of America. *Rabbinical Asembly Manual*. Ed. Isador Signer. New York, 1952.

———. (*Sabbath Prayers*) *Seder Tefillot Yisra'el Leshabbat Uleshalosh Regalim*. New York: Rabbinical Assembly and United Synagogue, 1964, c. 1946.

———. *Weekday Prayer Book, Tefillot Liyemot Ḥol*. New York: Rabbinical Assembly, 1962.

Rabinowicz, Harry M. *A Guide to Life: Jewish Laws and Customs of Mourning*. 2d ed. London: Jewish Chronicle Publications.

Rabinowitz, Louis Isaac. "Deaf Mute." *Encyclopaedia Judaica* 5, 1419–1420.

Rappaport, H. Z. *The Basic Laws of Kosher Meat Inspection (Or Leyoreh De'ah)*. Port Ewen, N.Y.: Blossom Publications, 1963.

Rosenblatt, Samuel. "Jewish Law of Marriage and Divorce Applying to the Mentally Incapacitated." *Proceedings of the Rabbinical Assembly* 21 (1957), 141–150.

Rosenzweig, Franz. *The Star of Redemption*. Trans. William W. Hallo. New York: Holt, Rinehart & Winston, 1971.

Rosner, Fred. "Jewish Atttitude Toward Euthanasia." In *Modern Medicine and Jewish Law*. New York: Yeshiva University, 1972.

———. *Modern Medicine and Jewish Law*. New York: Yeshiva University, 1972.

Roth, Cecil. *The Haggadah: A New Edition*. With drawings by Donia Nachshon. London: Soncino Press, 1934.

———. "Some Revolutionary Purims." *Hebrew Union College Annual* 10 (1935), 451–482.

———. "Supplement to 'Some Revolutionary Purims,' *HUCA* X (1935), pp. 451–482." *Hebrew Union College Annual* 12–13 (1937–38), 697–699.

Rothkoff, Aaron. "Sick, Visiting the." *Encyclopaedia Judaica* 14, 1496–1498.

Routtenberg, Lilly S., and Seldin, Ruth R. *The Jewish Wedding Book*. New York: Schocken Books, 1968.

Rubenstein, Shmuel. *Kashruth*. Published by the author.

———. *Miqweh Anthology*. Published by the author. Bronx, N.Y., 1967–68.

Sassoon, Salomon D. *A Critical Study of Electrical Stunning and the Jewish Method of Slaughter (Shechita)*. Letchworth, England: Letchworth Printers, 1955.

Schauss, Hayyim. *The Jewish Festivals*. Cincinnati: Union of American Hebrew Congregations, 1938.

Schechter, Solomon. *Studies in Judaism. Second Series*. Philadelphia: Jewish Publication Society, 1908.

Schwartz, Herbert. "To Open the Ears of the Deaf." *Conservative Judaism* 28:2 (Winter 1974), 59–63.

Schwarz, Jacob D., comp. *Responsa of the Central Conference of American Rabbis*. New York: Union of American Hebrew Congregations, 1954.

Segal, Jack. "Weddings During the Three Weeks." *Proceedings of the Rabbinical Assembly* 32 (1968), 224–228.

Shiloh, Isaac S. "Marriage and Divorce." *Israel Law Review*, October 1970, 492.

Silberman, Lou H. "Farewell to Confirmation." *CCAR Journal* 13:6 (June 1966), 31–34.

Silverman, Morris. *Passover Haggadah*. Hartford, Conn.: Prayerbook Press, 1959; Bridgeport, Conn., c. 1972.

Sisson, Septimus. *The Anatomy of the Domestic Animals*. Revised by James D. Grossman. 4th ed. Philadelphia: Saunders, 1968.

Smith, W. Robertson. *The Religion of the Semites*. 1889. Reprint. New York: Meridian Books, 1956.

Steinberg, Milton. *Basic Judaism*. New York: Harcourt, Brace, 1947.

"Sun, Blessing of the." *Encyclopaedia Judaica* 15, 518.

Tigay, Jeffrey. "Triennial Confusion." *Conservative Judaism* 24:1 (Fall 1974), 81–84.

Union of Orthodox Jewish Congregations of America, Rabbinical Council of America. *Kashruth: Handbook for Home and School*. New York, 1972.

Universal Jewish Encyclopedia. 10 vols. Ed. by Isaac Landman, New York: Universal Jewish Encyclopedia, 1939–43.

Vainstein, Yaacov. *The Cycle of the Jewish Year: A Study of the Festivals and of Selections from the Liturgy.* 2d ed. Jerusalem: Department for Torah Education and Culture in the Diaspora, World Zionist Organization, 1971.

Waxman, Meyer. *Handbook of Judaism.* New York: Bloch, 1947. 2d ed. Chicago: L. M. Stein, 1953.

———. *Judaism: Religion and Ethics.* New York: T. Yoseloff, 1958.

———, ed. *Tradition and Change.* New York: Burning Bush Press, 1958.

Williams, John Whitridge. *Williams' Obstetrics.* 14th ed. by Louis M. Hellman, Jack A. Pritchard with Ralph M. Wynn. New York: Appleton-Century-Crofts, 1971.

Witmer, Helen L., et al. *Independent Adoption.* New York: Russell Sage Foundation, 1963.

Wolf, Arnold Jacob. "Ten Theses on Confirmation." *CCAR Journal* 13:6 (June 1966), 11.

Yellen, Hiram S. "Bloodless Circumcision of the Newborn." *American Journal of Obstetrics and Gynecology* 30 (July 1935), 146 f.

Zimmels, Hirsch Jacob. *Ashkenazim and Sephardim.* New York and London: Oxford University Press, 1958.

———. *Magicians, Theologians, and Doctors.* London: E. Goldston, 1952.

Zlotnick, Dov, ed. and trans. *Tractate Mourning.* New Haven: Yale University Press, 1966.

Zunz, Leopold. *Die synagogale Poesie des Mittelalters.* Berlin, 1855.

———. *Der Ritus des synagogalen Gottesdienstes.* Berlin, 1859.

Part II: Hebrew

Abudraham Hashalem. David ben Joseph ben David Abudraham. Jerusalem, 1963.

Ahi'ezer. 3 vols. Chaim Ozer Grodsensky. Vilna, 1922–39. Jerusalem and New York: 1945–46.

"'Al Happalah Mel'akhutit." Mosheh Yonah Halevi Zweig. *No'am* 7 (1963/64), 36–56.

'Arba'ah Turim. Jacob ben Asher. Warsaw, 1860–69.

'Arukh Hashulḥan. 8 vols. Yehiel Michel Halevi Epstein. New York: Pollak, Grossman, n.d.

Avnei Neizer, Yoreh De'ah. 2 vols. Abraham Bornstein. Tel Aviv, 1960/61, 1963/64.

Avnei Tsedeq. In *Sha'arei Tsedeq.* Menaḥem Mendel Panet. Brooklyn, N.Y.: Dejsher Yeshiva Maglei Zedek, 1970/71.

'Avodat Yisra'el. See *Seder 'Avodat Yisra'el.*

Avot Derabbi Natan. Solomon Schechter, ed. New York: Feldheim, 1967.

Bar Sheshet. Isaac ben Sheshet (Rivash). Jerusalem, 1974/75.

"Bedin Meqaddeish Be'eid Eḥad." Joshua Maimon. *No'am* 14 (1970/71), 185–192.

Be'eir Yitsḥaq. Isaac Elḥanan Spektor. Jerusalem, 1969 or 1970.

"Be'inyan Hardamah Bishe'at Hamilah." Ovadiah Yosef *No'am* 12 (1968/69), 1–10.

"Be'inyan Minnui Sofer We'eidim shel Geṭ 'al yad Haṭelefon." Yitsḥaq Liebes. *No'am* 5 (1961/62), 13–25.

"Be'inyan Piqquaḥ Nefesh shel 'Ubbar." Isser Yehuda Unterman. *No'am* 6 (1962/63), 1–11.

"Be'inyan Piryon Mel'akhuti." Benzion Firer. *No'am* 6 (1962/63), 295–99.

"Be'inyan Tenai Benissu'in." Menachem M. Kasher. *No'am* 12 (1966/67), 338–353.

"Be'inyan Zeman bein Hashemashot We'alot Hashaḥar." Leo Levi. *No'am* 5 (1961/62), 213–249.

Beirur Halakhah. In *Talmud Bavli im Halakhah Berurah.* Vol. 1. Abraham Isaac Kook. Jerusalem: Institute for Halacha B'Rura—Birur Halacha, 1970/71.

"Beirur Halakhah Be'issur Hishtamshut Bifriah Mel'akhutit." Samuel A. Yudelowitz. *No'am* 10 (1966/67), 57–103.

Beit Midrash Shem Wa'eiver. Naḥum Shemaryahu Schechter. Jerusalem, 1965.

Beit Mordekhai. Mordekhai Fogelman. Jerusalem: Mossad Harav Kook, 1970.

Beit Shmuel. Samuel ben Uri Shrage Phoebus. Dyhernfurth, 1688/89.

Beit Yitsḥaq, Even Ha'ezer. 2 vols. Isaac Judah Schmelkes. New York, 1960/61–1961/62.

Beit Yosef. Yosef Caro. In *'Arba'ah Turim.* Ed. Warsaw.

Benei Yisakhar. Zevi Elimelech Spiro. Lwow, 1860. New York, 1960/61.

Benei Yisra'el. Harabbanit Harashit Leyisra'el (Chief Rabbinate of Israel). Jerusalem, 1961/62.

Berit 'Olam. Jacob H. Bloom. New York, 1950.

"Bidevar Ṭevilat Geirim Wekhen Be'inyan Geir Shemipe'at Maḥalah Iy Efshar Lamulo." Tsvi Kahn. *Hamaor* 14 (1964), 9–11.

Binetivot Hatalmud. Simon Federbusch. Jerusalem: Mossad Harav Kook, 1956/57.

Da'at Kohen. Abraham Isaac Kook. Jerusalem: Mossad Harav Kook, 1942.

Darkhei Mosheh. Moses Isserles, In *'Arba'ah Turim.* Ed. Warsaw.

Darkhei Teshuvah 'al Yoreh De'ah. 7 parts in 4 vols. Zevi Hirsch Spira. New York: Talpiot, 1951–59.

Dat Wehalakhah. Mosheh Sternbuch. Jerusalem, 1970.

Derekh Erets Rabbah. In *Talmud Bavli.* Ed. Vilna.

"Dinei Milah." Jacob H. Bloom. With comment by S. A. Pardes. *Hapardes* 18 (1944), 37 f.

Dinei Mishpaḥah. Benzion Schereschewsky. Jerusalem: R. Mass, 1967.

Dinei Nissu'in Wegeirushin. Paltiel Dykan. Tel Aviv: Yavneh, 1956.

Divrei Ḥayyim. 2 vols. in 1. Ḥayyim Halberstam. Brooklyn, N.Y., 1944/45.

Divrei Malki'el. 6 vols. Malkiel Zevi Tenenbaum. Vilna, 1891.

Divrei Talmud. 2 vols. Abraham Elijah Kaplan. Jerusalem: Mossad Harav Kook. Vol. 1: 1958. Vol. 2: 1969.

Duda'ei Hasadeh. Eliezer Ḥayyim ben Abraham Deutsch. Seani, 1929.

'Eidut Leyisra'el. Oscar Z. Rand, ed. New York: Ezras Torah Fund, 1947/48.

'Eidut Leyisra'el. Jacob Werdiger. Bnei Brak: Hamakhon Leḥeiker Hatefilah Wehaminhagim, 1963.

Ein Tenai Benissu'in. Judah Lubetzky. Vilna, 1929/30.

'Ein Yitsḥaq. 2 vols. Isaac Elḥanan Spektor. Vilna. Vol. 1: 1889/90. Vol. 2: 1895/96.

Eishel Avraham. See *Peri Megadim.*

Encyclopedia Miqra'it. 7 vols. Jerusalem: Mossad Bialik, 1950–.

Encyclopedia Talmudit. 15 vols. Jerusalem: Mossad Harav Kook, 1947–.

'Ezrat Nashim. 3 vols. Meir Feuerwerger (Meir Meiri). Brussels and London, 1950–55.

Entṣiqlopeidyah Me'ir Netiv. Shelomo Zalman Ariel (Leibovich). Tel Aviv: Massada, 1960.

Geirim. In *Massekhtot Qeṭanot,* pp. 68–79. Michael Higger, ed. New York: Bloch, 1930. Jerusalem: Makor, 1970/71.

Gesher Haḥayyim. 3 vols. Jehiel Michael Tucatzinsky. Jerusalem, 1946/47.

Geṭ Mesudar. Eleazar Münz. Byelgora, 1932.

Ginzei Schechter. 3 vols. Louis Ginzberg. New York: Jewish Theological Seminary, 1928–29. Reprint. New York: Hermon, 1969.

Hafoqlor Hayehudi. Judah Bergmann. Jerusalem: R. Mass, 1953.

Hagahot Maharsham 'al Hashas. Shalom Mordecai Schwadron. Satu Maru, 1932.

Hagahot Maimuniyot. Meir Hakohen of Rothenburg. In Maimonides. *Mishneh Torah.* Ed. Vilna.

Ḥagei Yisra'el Umo'adaw. Nahum Wahrman. Jerusalem: Ahiasef, 1959.

"Hagelilah Limni'at Heirayon Keva'ayah Hilkhatit-Refu'it." Jacob Levy. *No'am* 11 (1967/68), 167–77.

Haggadah Shelemah. Menaḥem Mendel Kasher. Jerusalem: Machon Torah Shelemah, 1967.

Haggadah shel Pesaḥ. S. Knebel. New York, 1947/48.

Ḥagim Umo'adim. Yehudah Leib Maimon (Fishman). Jerusalem: Mossad Harav Kook, 1944, 1950.

Ḥakham Tsevi. Zevi Hirsch Ashkenazi. New York, 1944.

Hamanhig. Abraham ben Nathan of Lunel. Jerusalem: Lewin-Epstein, 1966/67.

Hamo'adim Behalakhah. Shelomoh Yosef Zevin. Tel Aviv, 1953/54.

"Happalat 'Ubbar Be'ishah Ḥolanit." Yehiel Ya'aqov Weinberg. *No'am* 9 (1965/66), 193–215.

Ḥagigah Datit. Menachem Elon. Tel Aviv: Hakibbutz Hadati, 1968.

Har Eivel Koleil Ḥesed Le'avraham Uma'amar Nishmat Ḥayyim. Abraham Ḥayyim ben Simon Oppenheim. Dyhernfurth, 1826/27.

Har Tsevi. 3 vols. Tsevi Pesaḥ Frank. Jerusalem, 1964–73.

"Hashaqah." *Encyclopedia Talmudit* 11 (1965), 189–225.

Hatalmud Weḥokmat Harefu'ah. Judah Leib Benjamin Katzenelson. Berlin, 1928.

Ḥatam Sofer. 6 parts in 4 vols. Moses Schreiber. Reprint. Jerusalem: Makor, 1969/70. Pt. 7 (1 vol.), Makhon Ḥatam Sofer, 1971/72.

Ḥavalim Bane'imim. Judah Loeb Graubart. Lodz, 1934.

Ḥawot Ya'ir. Yair Bacharach. Lemberg, 1896. Reprint. New York, n.d.

Ḥayyei Adam. Abraham Danzig. New York: Hebrew Publishing, n.d.

Ḥayyei 'Olam. Meir Lerner. Berlin, 1904/5.

"Hazra'ah Mel'akhutit." Shelomo Zalman Auerbach. *No'am* 1 (1957/58), 145–166.

"Hazra'ah Mel'akhutit." Obadiah Hedaya. *No'am* 1 (1957/58), 130–137.

"Hazra'ah Mel'akhutit." David M. Kreuzer. *No'am* 1 (1957/58), 111–128.
"Hazra'ah Mel'akhutit." Moses Aryeh Leib Schapiro. *No'am* 1 (1957/58), 138–142.
"He'arah Lenoam Sefer Shishi." Asher Feuchtwenger. *No'am* 7 (1963/64), 385 f.
Heikhal Yitsḥaq. 3 vols. Isaac Halevi Herzog. Jerusalem, 1959/60.
Ḥelqat Ya'aqov. 3 vols. Mordecai Jacob Breisch. Jerusalem and London, 1950–66.
Ḥemdat Hayamim. 4 vols. Nathan Benjamin Ghazzati or Benjamin Halevi of Safed. Livorno, 1762–64.
Ḥesed Le'avraham. See *Har Eivel*.
Ḥiddushei R. 'Akiba Eger. Akiba Eger. Berlin, 1857/58. Warsaw, 1891/92.
Ḥol Umo'ed. Michel Rabinowitz. Jerusalem: Histadrut Hatsioni, 1964/65.
Igrot Mosheh. 2 vols. Moses Feinstein. New York: Balshon, 1959.
Imrei Dawid. David Horowitz. Byelgora, 1933. Reprint. New York, 1966.
Imrei Yosher. 2 vols. Meir Arak. Vol. 1: Muncacz, 1912/13. Vol. 2: Crakow, 1920/21.
"Imuts Yeladim Lefi Hahalakhah." Mordecai Hakohen. *Torah Shebe'al Peh* 3 (1960/61), 65–84.
"'Iqrei Dinim Uminhagei Bet Kenesset." Y. E. Henkin. In *'Eidut Leyisra'el*, ed. Oscar Z. Rand, p. 111–208.
"Kashrut Hayelud." Abraham Neumark. *No'am* 1 (1957/58), 143–144.
Knesset Hagedolah Ḥeileq Yoreh De'ah. Ḥayyim Benveniste. Reprint. Jerusalem, 1969/70.
Kol Bo. New York: Shulsinger Bros., 1945/46.
Kol Bo 'al Aveilut. Leopold Greenwald. New York, 1947–51.
Leqeṭ Haqemaḥ Heḥadash. 3 vols. A. Katz. London, 1963/64.
Leqeṭ Yosher. Joseph ben Moses. Ed. J. Freimann. Berlin, 1903. Reprint. New York: Mekize Nirdamim, 1958/59.
Levush. 5 vols. Mordecai Jaffe. Berdichev, 1918–21. Israel, 1968.
Liquṭei Mehariḥ. 3 vols. Israel Hayyim Friedman. Jerusalem, 1969/70.
Madrikh Lehilkhot Niqqur. Israel Meir Levinger. Tel Aviv: Institute for Agricultural Research According to the Torah, 1964.
Maharam Schick. 2 vols. Moses Schick. Israel, 1971/72.
Maharil. See *Sefer Maharil*.
Maharshag. Simon Grünfeld. Vol. 1: Tel Aviv, 1974. Vol. 2: Jerusalem, 1961.
Maharsham. See *She'eilot Uteshuvot Maharsham*.
Maḥazeh Avraham. 2 vols. Abraham Menaḥem Halevi Steinberg. Vol. 1: Brody, 1927. Vol. 2: New York, 1963.

Maḥzor Vitry. Simḥah ben Samuel of Vitry. Simon Hurwitz, ed. Berlin, 1893.

Masoret Hashass. Isaiah ben Judah Loeb Berlin. Dyhernfuerth, 1800–1804.

Massekhet Soferim. Michael Higger, ed. New York, 1936/37.

Massekhtot Derekh Erets. 2 vols. Michael Higger, ed. New York: Debe Rabanan, 1935.

Maṭei Mosheh. Moses Mat. Frankfurt, 1719/20.

Megilat Ta'anit. Hans Lichtenstein. *Hebrew Union College Annual* 8–9 (1931–32), 257–371.

Mei Yehudah. 2 vols. Judah Altman. Balkany, 1934.

Me'ir Netiv. Mordecai Nathan. Venice, 1523.

Mekhilta Derabbi Yishma'el. Jacob Zallel Lauterbach, ed. Philadelphia: Jewish Publication Society, 1933–35.

Melamed Leho'il. David Hoffmann. Frankfurt a. M.: Hermon, 1925/26, 31/32. Reprint. New York: Frankel, 1954.

Melekhet Shelomoh. Solomon Adani. In *Mishnah*. Ed. Vilna.

"Meni'at Haheirayon Betokh Arba'im Yom Meihashash Shema Tishtagea'." *Hapardes* 31:1 (October 1956), 24–27, 31:4 (January 1957), 22–23.

Menorat Hama'or. Isaac Aboab. Jerusalem: Mossad Harav Kook, 1961.

Menuḥah Nekhonah. Eduard Biberfeld. Jerusalem, 1946.

"Middot Weshi'urei Torah Beḥayyei Yom Yom." Baruch Noeh. *Shanah Beshanah*, 1961/62.

Midrash Bereshit Rabba. 3 vols. Judah Theodor and Chanoch Albeck, eds. Jerusalem: Wahrmann Books, 1965.

Midrash Shir Hashirim. In *Midrash Rabbah*. Ed. Vilna.

Midrash Shmu'el. Samuel ben Isaac Uceda. Warsaw, 1868/69.

Midrash Tanḥuma. 2 vols. Salomon Buber, ed. Jerusalem, 1963/64.

Midrash Tanḥuma. Reprint. Tel Aviv. n.d.

Midrash Tehillim. Salomon Buber, ed. Vilna: Romm, 1890/91. Reprint. Jerusalem, 1965/66.

Midrash Wayiqra Rabbah. 5 vols. in 3. Mordecai Margulies, ed. Jerusalem: Wahrmann Books, 1972.

"Miminhagei Yisra'el." Yehuda Elzet [pseud. for Yehuda Leib Avida]. *Reshumot* (O.S.) 1 (1917–18), 335–377.

Minhagei Erets Yisra'el. Ya'aqov Gelis. Jerusalem: Mossad Harav Kook, 1968.

Minhagim. See *Sefer Haminhagim*.

Minḥat El'azar. 2 vols. Ḥayyim Eleazar Spira. Brooklyn, N.Y.: Yeshiva Minchas Eluzar, 1973/74.

Minḥat Yitsḥaq. 6 vols. Isaac Jacob Weiss. London and Jerusalem, 1955–71.
Mishnah. 12 vols. Ed. Vilna. Reprint. New York: Pardes, 1952/53.
Mishnah Berurah. 6 vols. Yisrael Meir Hakohen. New York, n.d.
Mishnat Avraham. Abraham A. Price. New York, 1944.
Mishneh Torah. 5 vols. Moses Maimonides. Ed. Vilna, 1899/1900. Reprint. New York, 1944/45.
Mishpaṭ Hamishpaḥah Wehayerushah Hayehudi Weshimusho Be'erets Yisra'el. Erwin Elchanan Scheftelowitz. Tel Aviv: S. Bursi, 1941.
Mishpeṭei Ishut. Abraham Akiba Rudner. Jerusalem, 1949.
Mishpeṭei 'Uzi'el. 3 vols. Ben-Zion Meir Ḥal Ouziel. Tel Aviv, 1935–40.
Mordekhai. Mordecai ben Hillel Ashkenazi. In *Talmud Bavli*. Ed. Vilna.
Moreh Nevukhim. Moses Maimonides. Reprint. Jerusalem, 1959/60.
Naḥalat Shiv'ah. Samuel ben David Moses Halevi of Mezhirech'ye. Amsterdam, 1667.
Naḥalat Tsevi. Gedalie Felder. New York, 1959.
Netiv Lageir. Baruch Yashar. Jerusalem, 1966.
Noda' Biyehudah. 2 vols. Ezekiel Landau. New York, 1965/66.
"'Of Ṭahor Nokhal Bemasoret." Israel Meir Levinger. *Sinai* 64 (1968/69), 258–281.
'Olat Re'iyah. 2 vols. Abraham Isaac Kook. Jerusalem: Mossad Harav Kook, 1963.
Orḥot Ḥayyim. Aaron ben Jacob ben David Hakohen of Lunel. Berlin, 1898–1902.
Or Zaru'a. Isaac ben Moses of Vienna. Zhitomir and Jerusalem, 1862–90.
Ot Ḥayyim Weshalom. Hayyim Eleazar Shapira. Jerusalem, 1964/65.
Otsar Hage'onim. 13 vols. Benjamin M. Lewin. Haifa, 1928–43.
Otsar Haposqim. 9 vols. Jerusalem: Otsar Haposqim Institute, 1962–65.
Otsar Hatefilot. See *Siddur Otsar Hatefilot*.
Otsar Kol Minhagei Yeshurun. Abraham Eliezer Hirschovitz. Lemberg, 1929/30. Reprint. Israel, 1969/70.
Or Haḥamah. Shelomo Zalman Segner. Munkacs, 1897.
Otsar Dinim Uminhagim. Judah David Eisenstein. New York: Hebrew Publishing, 1917.
Peirush Rashi. Solomon ben Isaac. In *Talmud Bavli*. Ed. Vilna.
Peirushei Ivra. Yosef Eliyahu Henkin. New York, n.d.
Peri Ḥadash. Hizkiah DeSilva. In *Shulḥan 'Arukh*. Ed. Vilna.
Peri Hasadeh. 4 vols. in 3. Eliezer Ḥayyim Deutsch. Paks, 1906–15.
Peri Megadim. Yosef ben Meir Teomim. In *Shulḥan Arukh*. Ed. Vilna. 2 pts.: *Eishel Avraham* and *Mishpetsot Zahav*.

Perishah. Joshua ben Alexander Hakohen Falk. In *Arba'ah Ṭurim*. Ed. Warsaw.
Pesaqim Ukhetavim. Israel ben Petaḥyah Isserlein. In *Terumat Hadeshen*. Reprint of Warsaw ed. Tel Aviv: N. Steiner, n.d.
Pesiqta Derav Kahana. Salomon Buber, ed. Lyck, 1868.
Pesiqta Rabbati. Meir Ish Shalom (Friedmann), ed. Vienna, 1880.
Pirqei de Rabbi Eli'ezer. Warsaw, 1851/52. Reprint. Jerusalem, 1969/70.
Pitḥei Teshuvah. Abraham Zevi Hirsch Eisenstadt. In *Shulḥan 'Arukh*. Ed. Vilna.
Porat Yosef. 2 vols. in 1. Joseph Zweig. Byelgora, 1933.
Qav Naqi. Avraham David ben Judah Leib Lawat. Warsaw, 1868.
Qitsur Shulḥan 'Arukh. Solomon Ganzfried. With ommentary *'Ir Dawid* by David Feldmann. Leipzig, New York, 1924.
Qitsur Shulḥan 'Arukh. 2 vols. in 1. Solomon Ganzfried. Ḥayyim Yeshayah Hakohen, ed. Jerusalem: Eshkol, 1954.
Qitsur Shulḥan 'Arukh. With *Hilkhot Erets Yisra'el* by Jehiel Michael Tucatzinsky. Foreword by J. L. Maimon. Jerusalem, 1949/50.
Qohelet Rabbah. In *Midrash Rabbah*. Ed. Vilna.
Quntres Birkat Haḥamah. Jehiel Michael Tucatzinsky. Jerusalem, 1896/97.
"Quntras Harefu'ah." Hanoch Zundel Grrosberg. *No'am* 10 (1966/67), 288–317.
Rabbenu Asher (Rosh). Asher ben Yeḥiel. In *Talmud Bavli*. Ed. Vilna.
Sedeh Ḥemed. 10 vols. Ḥayyim Ḥezekiah Medini. Warsaw-Piotrków, 1890/91, 1911/12. Reprint. Bnei Brak: Beth Hasofer, 1962/63–67.
Seder Avodat Yisra'el. Isaac Seligman Baer. Roedelheim, 1868. Tel Aviv, 1957.
Seder Eliyahu Rabbah Weseder Eliyahu Zuṭa (Tanna Devei Eliyahu). Meir Ish Shalom (Friedmann), ed. Jerusalem: Bamberger & Wahrmann, 1959/60.
Seder Mo'ed. See *Shishah Sidrei Mishnah*. Chanoch Albeck, ed.
Seder Niqqur Hama'asi Batemunot. Tsevi Yitsḥaq Hakohen Adler. Tel Aviv, 1964.
Seder Qiddushin Wenissu'in. Alfred H. Freimann. Jerusalem: Mossad Harav Kook, 1944.
Seder Rav 'Amram Ga'on. Ernst Daniel Goldschmidt, ed. Jerusalem: Mossad Harav Kook, 1971.
Sefer 'Eidut Leyisra'el. See *'Eidut Leyisra'el*.
Sefer Ha'agunot. Isaac Zeev Kahana. Jerusalem: Mossad Harav Kook, 1954.

Sefer Hamanhig. See *Hamanhig*.

Sefer Haminhagim. Isaac Tyrnau. Luneville: A. Priseck, 1805/06.

Sefer Hamitsvot. Moses Maimonides. Jerusalem: Epstein Brothers, 1952–53.

Sefer Hamo'adim. 9 vols. Isaac Loeb Baruch, ed. Tel Aviv: Dvir, 1961–63.

Sefer Haḥinukh. Aaron Halevi of Barcelona. Charles B. Chavel, ed. Jerusalem: Mossad Harav Kook, 1951/52.

Sefer Hasheṭarot. Judah ben Barzilai of Barcelona. S. Halberstam, ed. Berlin, 1898. Reprint. Jerusalem, 1966/67.

Sefer Hatashbeits. Simon ben Zemah Duran. Amsterdam, 1738, 1741. Tel Aviv: Gitler, 1963/64.

Sefer Hatoda'ah. Eliyahu Kitov [Pseud. for Abraham Mokotovsky]. Jerusalem and Tel Aviv: "A" Publishers and Ḥ. Gitler, 1966.

Sefer Maharil. Jacob ben Mosheh Halevi Moellin. Jerusalem, 1968/69.

Seridei Eish. Yeḥiel Ya'aqov Weinberg. Jerusalem: Mossad Harav Kook, 1961–69.

Sha'ar Halakhah. Mosheh Stern. *No'am* 7 (1963/64), 395–404. *No'am* 10 (1966/67), 321–330.

Sha'arei Efrayim. Ephraim Zalman Margolioth. New York, 1952.

Sha'arei Halakhah. 2 vols. Simon Efrati (Efrusi). Jerusalem, 1966/67.

Sha'arei Simḥah, 2 pts. Isaac Ibn Ghayyat. Furth, 1860–62.

Sha'arei Teshuvah. Hayyim Mordecai Margaliot. In *Shulḥan 'Arukh*. Ed. Vilna.

Sha'arei Tsion. Nathan Nata Hannover, ed. Amsterdam, 1720.

Shanah Beshanah 5727. Annual of Heikhal Shelomo. Jerusalem, 5727.

She'arim Metsuyanim Bahalakhah. 4 vols. Solomon Braun. Jerusalem and New York: Feldheim, 1968–72.

She'eilat Mosheh. Moses Samson Wasserman. Jerusalem: Mossad Harav Kook, 1946/47.

She'eilat Ya'avets. Jacob Israel ben Zevi Emden. Altona, 1739–59. Lemberg, 1884, New York, 1961.

She'eilot Uteshuvot. Menaḥem Azariah of (da) Fano. Jerusalem: Slomon, 1962/63.

She'eilot Uteshuvot. 4 vols. (7 pts.). Solomon ben Abraham Adret. Bnei Brak and Jerusalem, 1957/58–1964/65.

She'ilot Uteshuvot Maharsham. 6 vols. Shalom Mordecai Schwardron. Warsaw: 1902–46.

Sh'eilot Uteshuvot Rashdam. Samuel ben Moses de Medina. Lemberg, 1861/62.

She'iltot. Aḥai Gaon. Jerusalem: Mossad Harav Kook, 1975.
Sheiveṭ Sofer. Simḥa Bunim Sofer. Vienna, Budapest, 1908/9.
Shevut Ya'aqov. 2 vols. Jacob ben Joseph Reisher. Lemberg, 1860/61.
Shibbolei Haleqeṭ Hashalem. Salomon Buber, ed. Vilna, 1886.
Shishah Sidrei Mishnah. 6 vols. Chanoch Albeck, ed. Jerusalem: Mossad Bialik; Tel Aviv: Dvir, 1958. Vol 2: *Seder Mo'ed.*
Sho'eil Umeishiv. Yosef Shaul Nathansohn. Lemberg, 1873.
Shulḥan 'Arukh. 10 vols. Yosef Caro. Vilna, 1874/75.
Shulḥan 'Arukh. 4 vols. Shneur Zalman of Lyady. New York: Otsar Haḥasidim, 1970/71.
Siddur Minḥat Yerushalayim. I. Dvorkes and J. Dvorkes, eds. Jerusalem: Otsar Haposqim, 1972.
Siddur Otsar Hatefilot. 2 vols. New York: Otsar Hasefarim, 1966.
Siddur Rashi. Salomon Buber, ed. Berlin, 1911. Reprint. New York: Menorah, 1959.
Siddur Tefillah Tselota D'avraham. 2 vols. Abraham Landau. Tel Aviv, 1961–.
Sifrei Bemidbar [*Sifrei Devei Rav*]. H. S. Horovitz, ed. Jerusalem: Wahrmann Books, 1966.
Sifrut Hahistoriyah Hayisra'elit. 2 vols. Abraham Kahana. 1922–23. Reprint. Jerusalem, 1968/69.
Simlah Ḥadashah. Alexander Sender Shor of Zolkiew. Warsaw, 1864/65. Reprint. Israel, 1969/70.
Talmud Bavil. 20 vols. Vilna, 1865/66.
Talmud Yerushalmi. 7 vols. Vilna, 1921/22.
Tanya Rabbati. Jeḥiel ben Jekuthiel Anau, supposed author. Warsaw, 1872/73.
Tashbeits. See *Sefer Hatashbeits.*
Tenei Benissu'in Uvaget. Eliezer Berkovits. Jerusalem: Mossad Harav Kook, 1966.
Teshuvot Hage'onim. Abraham Elijah Harkavy, ed. Berlin, 1887. Reprint. Jerusalem, 1966.
Ṭohorat Hamayim. Nissen Telushkin. New York, 1946/47.
Toldot Ha'emunah Hayisra'elit. 4 vols. Yeḥezkel Kaufmann. Jerusalem: Mossad Bialik. Tel Aviv: Dvir, 1966/67.
Toldot Ḥag Simḥat Torah. Abraham Yaari. Jerusalem: Mossad Harav Kook, 1964.
Torat Hamishpaḥah. Mosheh Sternbuch. Jerusalem: Harry Fischel Institute, 1966.

Torat Hatefilah. Eliezer Levi. Tel Aviv: Abraham Zioni, 1967.
Torah Shelemah. 27 vols. to date. Menaḥem Mendel Kasher. New York: American Biblical Encyclopedia Society, 1949–.
Tosafot. In *Talmud Bavli.* Ed. Vilna.
Tosafot Yom Tov. Yom Tov Lipman Heller. In *Mishnah.* Ed. Vilna.
Tosefta Kifshutah. 8 vols. to date. Saul Lieberman. New York: Jewish Theological Seminary, 1955–73.
Tselota D'avraham. See *Siddur Tefilah Tselota D'avraham.*
Tsits Eli'ezer. 10 vols. Eliezer Yehudah Waldenberg. Jerusalem, 1945–70.
Tsofnat Pa'aneah. Joseph Rosen. Menaḥem M. Kasher, ed. Pt. I: Jerusalem, 1964.
Ya'aneh Va'eish. Eliyahu ben Amozegh. Livorno, 1885/86, 1905/06.
Yad Halevi. 2 vols. Seligman Baer Bamberger (Yitsḥaq Dov Halevi). Jerusalem. Vol. 1: 1964/65. Vol. 2: 1971/72.
Yad Me'ir. David Meir Frisch. Lemberg, 1881.
Yad Yitsḥaq. 3 vols. in 2. Abraham Isaac Glueck. 1902–8.
Yalquṭ Shim'oni. 2 vols. New York: Pardes, 1944.
Yehudah Ya'aleh (*Teshuvot Maharya*). Judah ben Israel Aszod. Vol. 1: Lemberg, 1873. Vol. 2: Pressburg, 1880.
Yesodei Yeshurun. 6 vols. Gedalia Felder. Vol. 1: Toronto. Vols. 2–6: New York, 1954–70.
Yesodot Hatefilah. Eliezer Levi. Jerusalem: Mossad Harav Kook, 1946–47. Reprint. Tel Aviv, 1967.
Yosef Omets. Joseph Juspa Nördlingen Hahn. Frankfurt a. M., 1927/28. Reprint. Jerusalem, 1964/65.
"Zeman ben Hashemashot." See "Be'inyan Zeman bein Hashemashot."
Zeqan Aharon. 2 vols. Aron Walkin. New York: Gilead, 1951–58.
Ziv Haminhagin. Judah Dov Singer. Givat Shmuel, 1965.
Zohar. 3 vols. Vilna, 1894.

Index